W9-CUZ-267

332.45
In8

132195

DATE DUE			

WITHDRAWN

International Money and Credit: The Policy Roles

Edited by
George M. von Furstenberg

INTERNATIONAL MONETARY FUND • 1983
WASHINGTON, D.C.

© 1984 The International Monetary Fund
First printing, January 1984
Second printing (softcover), January 1985

International Standard Book Numbers:
ISBN 0-939934-26-4 (hardcover)
ISBN 0-939934-27-2 (softcover)

Acknowledgments

Preparation and conduct of the Conference on International Money, Credit, and the SDR—which was held in the Executive Board Room of the International Monetary Fund in Washington on March 24-25, 1983—involved principally the following persons at the Fund:

Conference Host, Chairman, and Overall Direction
Mr. Wm. C. Hood
Economic Counsellor
and
Director of the Research Department

***

Chairpersons
Mr. William B. Dale
Deputy Managing Director

Mr. Alexandre Kafka
Executive Director
and
Dean of the Executive Board

Mr. J.J. Polak
Executive Director

Mr. Walter O. Habermeier
Counsellor and Treasurer

Mr. C. David Finch
Director
Exchange and Trade Relations Department

Mr. Rudolf R. Rhomberg
Deputy Director
Research Department

***

Organization, Content, and External Liaison
Mr. George M. von Furstenberg
Chief, Financial Studies Division
Research Department

Internal Liaison and Executive Board Arrangements
Mr. Alan Wright
Deputy Secretary, Secretary's Department

Editorial and Publication Arrangements
Messrs. A.W. Hooke and Paul Gleason
Editors, External Relations Department

Press Relations and Publicity
Mr. Charles S. Gardner
Deputy Director, External Relations Department

Biographical sketches of the presenters and discussants of conference papers, Chapters 1–8, are provided at the end of this volume. The summary of the conference findings, Chapter 9, was produced by Mr. George M. von Furstenberg on the basis of the panel discussion between presenters and Executive Directors which concluded this conference. Of the background papers, which were distributed in advance to conference participants (Chapters 10–13), Chapter 10 was written by Mr. Robert E. Cumby while he was in the Research Department of the Fund; Chapter 11 was prepared in the Research Department; and Chapters 12 and 13 in the Treasurer's Department, all in consultation with other departments.

Contents

Introduction

J. DE LAROSIÈRE

Managing Director

It is my pleasure to welcome all of you to the Fund and to this room where the Executive Board regularly takes the decisions that guide the Fund's efforts, decisions which it takes in a very pragmatic way, three times a week, without any political contention. The idea of this conference was actually conceived by the Executive Directors in this room during a Board discussion on "The Future of the SDR." In the course of that discussion, a suggestion was made by some Directors to canvas the thinking of economists from the more academic side of the profession. This conference is the direct result of that suggestion.

This is a time of great ferment in the international monetary system. Such periods should invite basic rethinking of the fundamental premises upon which the system is founded. I am not one of those who (sometimes with a considerable measure of cynicism) assert that we have no monetary system, but I am among those who feel that the system may be improved and that we should be seeking to formulate the improvements that are most needed in our times and to promote their adoption. The world is just beginning to emerge from a most unusual episode in its monetary experience. It has been a period of very great inflation and an extraordinary concentration of balance of payments surpluses. These developments have brought in their train unemployment, slow growth, and—in the developing countries particularly—a greatly increased burden of debt. Fundamental economic adjustments have been called for over an extended period.

In response to these requirements, basic changes in the financial system itself have occurred. The exchange rate system has been greatly modified. The banks have developed their role in international finance to a quite unprecedented prominence. The Fund, too, has changed. We have expanded our own lending; we have lengthened its terms somewhat; and we have modified the conditions under which it has been extended. Among other things, we are seeking to find a form of collaboration with the banking systems of the world that would keep the banks in the relationship that they have chosen to build up with their clients. At the same time, we are seeking to find suitable forms of cooperation with financial institutions

1

that will meet the needs of the system and can be adapted as those needs change. All of these developments will continue to evolve; and, it is to be hoped, the world will soon move into a period of greater growth and stability of economic and monetary values.

The recent period has not been conducive to the evolution of the SDR; it has not been thought suitable to add liquidity in this form to the system in a period of great inflation. Equally, in a period in which great adjustments were required, it has been contended that the Fund's assistance should be mainly in a form that actively encourages adjustment rather than—as some thought after 1973/74—merely in the form of financing. The international reserves of the world are now lower in nominal terms than they were a year ago, and in real terms they have been declining for a considerable period. I am not aware, however, that even in a system of widespread floating, there is a manifest decline in the need for—or, perhaps better put, in the demand for—international reserves in the world.

As we consider the future evolution of the system, how should we see the role of the SDR? Is it needed? How should the Fund use it and seek to have it used? Upon examination, these turn out to be very profound questions that reach to the great issues of the organization of the international monetary system and of the Fund and the character of the services provided by the Fund. So this conference is addressed to very basic matters. All of us at the Fund, Directors and staff, are interested in sharing the insights that you will provide on the matters which so deeply concern us. May I wish you every success in considering in particular the following subjects, which have been identified by Mr. Wm. C. Hood, Economic Counsellor and Director of the Research Department of the Fund, in convening this conference:

(1) The design and application of criteria for assessing the strengths and weaknesses of the present international financial system and of its potential for changes;

(2) The controllability and significance of international liquidity in the context of national monetary, price level, and exchange rate objectives;

(3) The choice of reserve currencies, international borrowing and lending, and their effects on economic welfare over time;

(4) Substitution between national moneys, seigniorage, and proposals for international money and central banking;

(5) The ability of international reserve assets, such as the SDR, and of aspects of management to improve the functioning of the system under current or foreseeable conditions;

(6) The record of international money and monetary arrangements in private markets, and existing impediments to wider use of basket-currency denominations;

(7) The use of SDRs to supplement or substitute for other reserve media or means of finance, and possible guidelines for and benefits from enhancing the role of the SDR;

(8) The scope and limits of fruitful international cooperation in the 1980s in monetary policy, exchange intervention, and reserve arrangements.

Thank you very much.

Functioning of the Current International Financial System: Strengths, Weaknesses, and Criteria for Evaluation

THOMAS D. WILLETT*

The organizers of this conference asked me to focus in this paper on three topics: (1) describing the key aspects of the functioning of our present multicurrency international monetary system; (2) providing a framework for assessing the system's performance; and (3) evaluating the system's strengths, weaknesses, and potential for change. This is a tall order, and I cannot possibly present a fully comprehensive treatment of these topics, since at a minimum this would require foreknowledge of the outcomes of the discussion of the various major issue areas highlighted in the following sessions of this conference. I shall settle for the more limited objective of presenting what I hope will be useful background analysis for the discussion of these specific issues and for the evaluation of the international monetary system as a whole.

In overview papers, there is always the major question of how to organize the discussion of numerous topics which interrelate in a complex manner. My plan of attack will be first to consider criteria and perspectives for assessing the performance of international monetary systems, and then to attempt to describe and evaluate the current international monetary system and possibilities for further reform against the background of postwar

---

*I am indebted to Mark Bremer, Benjamin Cohen, Jacob Dreyer, Randall Hinshaw, Alexander Swoboda, Edward Tower, and George von Furstenberg for helpful comments and to the Keck Institute for International Strategic Studies and the Lincoln Foundation for research support.

international monetary evolution. In the process, I shall attempt to focus on most of the main issues of controversy among experts and policymakers about the international monetary system and to consider many of the key reasons for differences of view. Thus, a major theme running through this paper will be an attempt to analyze in a systematic manner some of the major reasons why there has been (and, in my judgment, there will continue to be) so much controversy about international monetary issues.

Differences of view about such issues can be categorized under three main headings: (1) differences about the overall objectives of the international monetary system or the relative weights given to these objectives, (2) concern with distributional aspects of the operation of the system, and (3) differences in judgment about how various regimes would operate in terms of the first two categories. The first two of these categories are explicitly normative, while the third is positive. However, uncertainties about positive aspects of evaluation often lead to a subtle interaction of normative and positive analysis, even within this third category. There is also the possibility of direct overlaps between the categories, as there are, for example, in a normative value judgment that explicit distributional objectives, such as the transfer of real resources from industrial to developing countries, should be a major objective of international liquidity creation. Still, I believe that thinking of the sources of controversy in terms of these three categories will prove useful.

While I shall indicate my own views on numerous questions, I shall not attempt to weigh systematically the relative importance of the various major reasons for international monetary controversy. I find myself somewhere in between the judgments of Richard Cooper (1975) and Benjamin Cohen (1977) in their recent analyses of these questions.[1] Cohen argues (p. 49) that "The problem of distribution is undoubtedly the most fundamental source of controversy in world monetary affairs." Cooper's view (p. 64) is that "If [my] essay carries any principal message, it is that sources of disagreement do not generally derive from divergent interests, but rather from diverse perspectives and hence different conjectures about the consequences of one regime as compared with another. In short, disagreement arises mainly from ignorance about true effects, so that we must use reasoned conjecture rather than solid fact to guide our choices." Like Cooper, I am very much struck by the considerable extent to which there are vast differences in the positive analysis invoked to support alternative positions in the international monetary area. While ultimately such differences involve the interpretation of past or future facts, I have also been very impressed by the extent to which the conceptual frameworks adopted by dif-

---

[1] I should add that my delineation of issues in this paper draws heavily in places on the treatments of international monetary controversy by these two authors.

ferent analysts and the ways they phrase their questions influence their ultimate empirical judgments.

In discussing international monetary issues today, we find two radically different perspectives often being adopted. One views our current international monetary arrangements as being fundamentally unsound and requiring basic reform. The second views the framework of our international monetary system as sound and focuses on how we may reduce current international monetary problems by policy changes or evolutionary institutional innovations within the context of our current framework. Of course, not all views fall neatly into one or the other of these categories, and one person's fundamental reform may seem quite marginal to another expert. It is also important to distinguish clearly between evaluation of the structure of the international monetary system itself and evaluation of the general performance of economic policies and the world economy under any particular system. There is general agreement that the global economic performance of the past decade has been dismal. The relevant questions from the standpoint of international monetary reform, however, are the extent to which the structure of the international monetary system has contributed to this poor economic performance and what changes in that structure can be expected to improve future economic performance. The judgments of supporters and critics of the current system obviously differ greatly on these issues.

Even those (such as myself) who believe that the basic framework of our current system is relatively sound will typically see numerous areas in which improvements are needed. Obviously, the current third world international debt problems present an enormous challenge to international financial management and cooperation. Likewise, no one would argue that recent records of inflation, unemployment, and exchange rate volatility have been satisfactory. Nor are our provisions for international economic policy coordination and safeguards against beggar-thy-neighbor policies as strong as many of us would like. Still, one may see the best practical hope for reducing such problems as lying with an evolutionary process within the framework of the current system.

Others hold the view that the current system is fundamentally unsound, indeed, that it is best termed a nonsystem.[2] Critiques from this perspective frequently argue that exchange rate volatility and uncontrolled interna-

---

[2]I shall use the terms international monetary or international financial system, regime, and order interchangeably to refer to the international monetary arrangements which exist at any particular point in time or to proposals for major changes in these arrangements. While granting the point that such arrangements may at times be neither systematic nor orderly, I shall not emphasize semantic distinctions about the minimal levels of structure necessary to call a set of arrangements a system, although there has been considerable controversy over whether our current arrangements should be called a system or a nonsystem. For further discussion and references on this set of issues, see Cooper (1975) and Willett (1977).

tional liquidity creation have been the major causes of world-wide stagflation, that the Jamaica international monetary reforms were fundamentally incomplete, and that we are far from the degree of internationally centralized control of the international monetary system that is needed.

One of the most important (although by no means the only substantive) reasons for such differing views stems from the extent to which one adopts a historical political economy approach, which stresses the difficulties of reaching political agreement and tends frequently to judge current institutional arrangements in terms of whether they are stronger or weaker than those they preceded, or what might be called an optimal policy approach, which tends to ignore problems of collective decision making and policy implementation and focuses on deviations between real-world arrangements and theoretical ideals.[3] As the following brief historical review indicates, it is quite possible to conclude that the current international monetary system is a substantial improvement over its predecessors, yet still falls far short of the ideal.

We may highlight the major differences among alternative international monetary systems in terms of their relationships with respect to (1) exchange rate regimes and the balance of payments adjustment process, (2) mechanisms for international liquidity creation and balance of payments financing, and (3) the structure of decision-making authority. The Bretton Woods negotiators sought (successfully, I believe) to create a system which avoided the major difficulties of its predecessors—the gold standard and the nationalist system of independent economic policy that prevailed during the interwar period.[4]

While it can be argued that, in practice, the rules of the game were seldom followed all that closely, the gold standard generally worked quite well in terms of the international criteria of fostering international exchange and facilitating relatively harmonious potential relationships among countries. Its fatal flaw was the substantial loss of domestic macroeconomic control which it implied. The interwar system went much too far to the other extreme of nationalist economic policymaking designed to gain short-term advantages, and predictable disasters duly ensued.

Bretton Woods was based on the twin economic principles that exchange rates and balance of payments policies were matters of international as well as national concern and that countries should not be required to subject their economies to major inflations or deflations in order to balance pay-

---

[3]For discussion of these alternative approaches to international economic policy issues, see Tollison and Willett (1976) and Willett (1981). A number of writers have recently emphasized the need to blend economic and political considerations in international monetary analysis. See, for example, Aliber (1980), Cohen (1977), Cooper (1975), and Strange (1976).

[4]For more detailed discussion of the historical development of the international monetary system, see Willett (1977) and the many references cited therein.

ments. It also established a formal apparatus for collective interpretation and decision making through the International Monetary Fund. These principles and the international cooperation which they helped foster have served us well and continue as the basis for our current international monetary system.

For many years, the Bretton Woods system operated quite satisfactorily. It was certainly instrumental in avoiding a repeat of the 1930s. Over time, however, a number of serious deficiencies in the system became increasingly apparent and were, in turn, exacerbated by structural changes in the world economy.

Political biases against prompt adjustment of par values, combined with increasing use of activist macroeconomic policies in the pursuit of full employment and the growth of international capital mobility made the exchange rate system increasingly crisis-prone. At the same time, the slower-than-expected rate of gold production, the political infeasibility of using the provisions for universal par value adjustments to increase the value of gold, and the expanding role of the dollar as a reserve currency combined to create the Triffin dilemma: to meet the growing needs of international liquidity, further expansion of official dollar holdings were needed, but, given the level of gold backing of the dollar, this would be likely to undermine confidence and lead to an international monetary crisis.[5] With the development of a full-fledged dollar standard ruled out on political grounds, the needed remedies for these difficulties in the Bretton Woods structure involved both the creation of a new international source of reserve holdings (the special drawing right (SDR)) and substantial improvements in the operation of the adjustment process. The failure to make major progress in the latter area combined with the substantially increased strains on the system created by overheating of the U.S. economy, induced by the financing of the Viet Nam War, led to an uncontrolled explosion of international liquidity and the breakdown of the system.

I believe that the widespread adoption of flexible exchange rates has made major contributions to ameliorating all three of the problems of the Bretton Woods system—adjustment, liquidity, and confidence. Greater exchange rate flexibility has improved the operation of the adjustment process, both by offering many countries the easier use of an effective means of adjustment and by reducing the political biases against adjustment which existed under the par value system. It has improved the international liquidity problem by offering countries greater flexibility in accumulating reserves and in shielding themselves from undesired reserve accumulations.

[5]See Triffin (1960). For recent analyses and references to the subsequent discussion of this issue, see Cumby (1983); Part I of "The Evolving Role of the SDR in the International Monetary System," which is Chapter 11 in this volume; and Willett (1977).

The confidence problem has been lessened by substantially reducing the availability of one-way speculative options.

Flexible rates do not provide the complete solution to all international monetary problems, however. Even with ideal private speculation, not all countries would want to float freely because of optimum-currency-area considerations.[6] Furthermore, the evidence that private speculation has always been strongly stabilizing is far from strong, and there may be macroeconomic externality arguments for official intervention by independent floaters even where private speculation is efficient in an ex ante sense.[7] Thus, a zero intervention rule for exchange rate surveillance is not a viable option. Therefore, in addition to questions of domestic macroeconomic policy coordination, issues of international liquidity management and international surveillance of the adjustment process remain.

Views on the nature and seriousness of these issues vary tremendously. Apart from direct distributional considerations, I believe that most of the controversy over the adequacy of our current international monetary arrangements has stemmed from two major sources: differences in view about (1) the best exchange rate and macroeconomic policy strategies, and (2) about the degree of effective international control over international liquidity and adjustment matters.

Section I will discuss in more detail a number of the major economic and political objectives frequently advocated for the international monetary system. This discussion will form the basis for indicating the types of criteria used for evaluating international monetary questions. The discussions of different criteria for evaluation are illustrated with applications to particular international monetary issues.

I. OBJECTIVES FOR THE INTERNATIONAL MONETARY SYSTEM AND FRAMEWORK FOR ANALYSIS

The performance of the international monetary system must be judged in terms of how well it meets the objectives delineated for the system. From an economic perspective, these objectives parallel those of domestic monetary systems to help facilitate the process of specialization and exchange and the full utilization of resources. The need for an international monetary system arises from the existence of sovereign states whose domains do not exhaust the potential benefits from specialization and exchange.

From a positive perspective, the economic objectives of the international monetary system are usually expounded as the promotion of microeco-

---

[6]For discussion and references, see Tower and Willett (1976).

[7]The analysis of this issue is still in its infancy. See Willett (1978 b) and the references cited therein.

nomic efficiency in the allocation of resources (including the usefulness of money) and the macroeconomic objectives of achieving a satisfactory combination of low inflation and unemployment and high rates of economic growth.[8] Viewed from an alternative perspective, international monetary systems have also been frequently evaluated in terms of their ability to handle particular problems which may arise from the operation of the system, particularly the problems of international liquidity, confidence, and adjustment. International monetary relations also have important political components. These include concerns with distributional effects and constraints on national sovereignty and more general political objectives, such as the enhancement of national power and prestige.

The emphasis on a political economy perspective also has implications crucial for the positive analysis of the behavior of governments in the operation of the international monetary system. This, in turn, has important implications for the practical relevance of various normative proposals. For example, there is a tremendous difference in the agenda for policy coordination and international monetary reform implied by an optimal economic policy framework which ignores collective decision making and implementation problems and one implied by a public choice approach which emphasizes such difficulties.

This section begins with discussion of the traditional economic criteria for evaluating the performance of the international monetary system: promoting microeconomic and macroeconomic efficiency and minimizing international liquidity, confidence, and adjustment problems. It then moves on to the analysis of distributional issues, national sovereignty, and other political considerations.

Microeconomic Efficiency

Our standard microeconomic criteria for judging microeconomic efficiency is the extent to which marginal social costs and benefits are equalized. Our theory suggests that with well-informed decision makers, competitive markets will tend to approximate this outcome in the absence of such conditions as externalities and public goods. In the international sphere, our analysis indicates a presumption in favor of free trade and investment in the absence of persuasive arguments that specific market failures exist.[9] It furthermore shows that on economic efficiency grounds, the first-best solution to most market failures associated with arguments for international restrictions involve domestic, rather than international, policy measures. For example, the first-best policy measure for stimulating an infant indus-

---

[8]For more detailed discussions, see, for example, Cooper (1975) and Tower and Willett (1976).

[9]See, for example, Corden (1982).

try is generally a direct subsidy rather than tariff protection. Where exchange rates are at equilibrium levels, it seems not unreasonable to use the extent of international trade and payments restrictions as a crude index of the magnitude of deviations from global microeconomic efficiency in international exchange. (It is, of course, possible for international restrictions to raise the economic welfare of one country at the expense of others.) However, where exchange rates deviate from equilibrium levels, there is a distortion in the price signals given to private economic actors which will tend to generate differences between private and social costs and benefits. In such circumstances, selective measures which tend to compensate partially for overvaluations or undervaluations of currencies may lead to increases, rather than decreases, in economic efficiency. Furthermore, even in the absence of disequilibrium exchange rates, economists' views on the economic welfare effects of free international capital flows have been much more mixed than their views on the welfare effects of free international trade flows. The principal designers of the Bretton Woods system, John Maynard Keynes and Harry Dexter White, were both skeptical of the benefits of free international capital flows under many circumstances, and such views are still shared by a number of economists.[10] For example, it has been argued that interest rate differentials often are not a good reflection of differences in the marginal productivity of capital and, hence, that taxes or controls to dampen international capital flows may carry relatively low efficiency costs.

While it is clear that stable equilibrium exchange rates are conducive to efficiency and that exchange rate fluctuations due to destabilizing speculation are harmful, there has been relatively little analysis of the effects of exchange rate volatility that reflects changes in underlying economic developments and expectations about future developments. Using the criterion of efficient information processing that is frequently adopted in modern financial theory and the rational expectations literature, it is clear that such exchange rate movements, even if highly volatile, promote economic efficiency given underlying circumstances. This approach suggests that the focus of those concerned with improving economic performance should be on reducing this volatility of underlying economic conditions. Skepticism about the implications of this efficient-market view has focused both on the extent to which exchange rate movements have been dominated by efficient speculation and on whether there are not important externalities and

---

[10]Such a distinction between the case for free international trade and the case for free international capital flows was made by the major negotiators at Bretton Woods. See, for example, Willett (1977, and the references cited therein). For recent discussions and references on views about the freedom of international capital flows, see Cooper (1975) and Dornbusch (1982).

rigidities in the goods and labor markets which would impose efficiency costs in other sectors of the economy. So far, relatively little progress has been made toward reconciling these opposing points of view.

While it is now generally accepted that we cannot safely assume that unchanged nominal exchange rates are a good guide to equilibrium exchange rates or that large, rapid movements in rates are necessarily the result of destabilizing speculation rather than reasonable shifts in expectations about economic fundamentals, wide divergencies of opinion exist about how closely the movements of flexible exchange rates have approximated equilibrium rates. In my judgment, the considerable amount of technical research on these issues has served primarily to suggest that one should be cautious about making statements that a particular exchange rate clearly is, or is not, close to an equilibrium level.[11] As will be discussed further below, different views about the predominant causes of the exchange rate fluctuations are probably the major cause of differences in judgments about how well flexible rates have worked.

Nor have we made considerable progress to date in evaluating the welfare costs of different patterns of deviations from equilibrium exchange rates. For example, what are the comparative efficiency costs of small, but persistent and growing, one-sided deviations from equilibrium, as might occur under a sticky adjustable peg, versus frequent large deviations which are of limited duration and which tend to average out.[12] Many have argued that there have been frequent large deviations under flexible exchange rates because of imperfections in private speculation or exchange rate overshooting owing to short-term variations in monetary policy.

We likewise still have not solved the decades-old controversy about whether pegged or flexible exchange rates are likely to stimulate more trade restrictions. My own view is that without the flexibility of exchange rates which we enjoyed (or suffered) over the past decade, we would have faced a higher level of restrictions. However, flexible rates certainly did not lead to as much liberalization as many advocates had hoped, and there have been cases in which it can be argued that exchange rate fluctuations have stimulated restrictions. Perhaps the strongest conclusion we can draw at this point is that whether the shift from the adjustable peg system to more widespread floating has led ceteris paribus to a marginal increase or decrease in the efficiency of international exchange, the effects do not appear to have been extremely large, especially in comparison with the

[11]For discussion of, and references to, the extensive literature on exchange market efficiency and exchange rate modeling, see Dornbusch (1980); Dreyer, Haberler, and Willett (1982, Parts II and III); Levich (1979); Mussa (1980); and Willett (1980 a). This question will be discussed further in Section II.

[12]For further discussion and extensive references to the literature on these issues, see Pigott, Sweeney, and Willett (1982) and Thursby and Willett (1982).

beggar-thy-neighbor independent nationalistic economic policies of the 1930s.[13] The evidence also seems consistent with the view that the choice of exchange rate regime is not one of the most important determinants of international restrictions.

Macroeconomic Goals

Traditionally, the macroeconomic aspects of the operation of the international monetary system have been considered in terms of the constraints which balance of payments adjustment requirements have placed on domestic macroeconomic policies. One of the major objectives of the Bretton Woods negotiators was to construct a system in which countries would not be forced to accept major inflations or recessions in order to convert disequilibrium nominal exchange rates into equilibrium ones. In such cases of fundamental disequilibrium, internal considerations were to have primacy over external ones, subject of course to the avoidance of beggar-thy-neighbor policies.

This desire to keep the requirements for international monetary balance from seriously impinging on domestic macroeconomic objectives typically has been shared both by Keynesians and monetarists. It is not a universally held view, however. A number of writers have been quite suspicious of the types of macroeconomic policies which may be stimulated by democratic politics and have sought to have the international monetary system impose discipline over domestic financial policies. Although most often associated with advocates of the return to some form of gold standard, such arguments are also frequently made for an international or regional return to pegged exchange rates per se. While it is not clear that flexible exchange rates will necessarily impose less discipline and stimulate greater inflationary pressures than typical forms of pegged-rate systems, the objectives of most of those who have engaged in the debate over discipline clearly fall into two diametrically opposed camps—those who seek to increase, and those who seek to constrain, the freedom of domestic macroeconomic decision makers.[14] There is a similar opposition between those who view accommodation of divergent national priorities as a major objective and those who advocate instead a forced harmonization of policies. The arguments in both of these areas involve economic and political aspects which cannot be

[13]For discussion and references to the evidence on this point, see Thursby and Willett (1982) and Willett (1982 a).

[14]My own view is that a rather strong case can be made for some constitutional constraints on the freedom of domestic monetary and fiscal authorities but that return to a gold standard is not an efficient approach to this problem. For further discussion and references on these issues, see Willett (1983); Willett and Mullen (1982); and United States, Commission on the Role of Gold in the Domestic and International Monetary Systems (1982).

adequately resolved here. Suffice it to say that these different schools of thought will hold quite different views about the desirability of the degree of macroeconomic permissiveness of the international monetary system.

In recent years, the traditional view of balance of payments considerations as a constraint on domestic macroeconomic policies has at least partially given way to analysis from the standpoint of open economy macroeconomics. This perspective emphasizes the short-term and medium-term effects of exchange rate and balance of payments developments on inflation-unemployment relationships and on the state of activity in the economy. The adoption of flexible exchange rates has been perhaps the major force behind this shift in perspective, although analysis along these lines was quite prevalent well before the 1970s. Ideally, from the perspective of a single country, an international monetary system which serves as an automatic stabilizer for domestic economic fluctuations, while limiting the importation of disturbances from abroad, would be preferred. From a global perspective, it would be preferable to have a system which does not itself generate disturbances and which, on average, yields a net stabilizing influence from uncontrolled disturbances while preserving countries' freedom to engage in domestic policy actions to counter the effects of disturbances, whether of domestic or foreign origin.

The different aspects of these criteria may, of course, conflict in particular situations. Depending on the particular patterns of disturbances and the structure of the economies in question, either pegged or flexible exchange rates may provide the best-short run macroeconomic environment for a particular country or aggregation of countries.[15] In two-country Keynesian models, it has been shown that depending on the particular disturbance in question, both countries could enjoy more stable output with pegged exchange rates or with flexible rates, or there might be conflicts of short-run interest so that one country would be better off with a pegged rate and the other with a flexible rate. The analysis becomes even more complicated when inflation-unemployment relationships are taken into account. In general, exchange rate movements which worsen inflation in the short run will stimulate output (once the initial perverse J-curve effects on the trade balance are reversed) and vice versa, but there has been relatively little analysis of possible effects on differences in medium-term inflation-unemployment trade-offs, and the short-term and medium-term effects may be quite different. For example, maintaining a pegged rate in a booming economy may have the favorable effect of reducing inflation in the short run, but at the expense of contributing to an artificial ratcheting-up of real wages which will worsen future inflation-unemployment relationships.

[15]For recent analysis and references to the literature on this subject, see Bryant (1980), Henderson (1982), and Tower and Willett (1976).

The choice of international monetary regimes may also have important influences on the effects of macroeconomic policy instruments. In traditional IS-LM, open-economy theoretical models, a shift from pegged to flexible exchange rates will strengthen the effects of monetary policy on aggregate spending, while the strength of fiscal policy will be increased or decreased, depending whether international capital mobility is low or high.[16] Similarly, with respect to international policy coordination, under pegged exchange rates expansionary monetary or fiscal policy at home generally will have an expansionary effect abroad (although the magnitude of these effects is often a matter of some dispute), while under flexible rates, expansionary monetary policy will have a contractionary effect abroad. Fiscal policy will still influence foreign economies in the same direction as at home, but the magnitude of transmission will be influenced by whether the degree of capital mobility leads to an appreciation or depreciation of the exchange rate.

The international monetary regime can also have an important influence on the way in which spending changes break down between price and output effects in the short run. For example, with exchange rate flexibility, the effects of exchange rate movements on the prices of traded goods will speed up the aggregate price responses to changes in monetary policy, steepening the short-run inflation-unemployment trade-off. While this has often been taken as an argument that flexible rates will be more inflationary than pegged rates, it should also be recognized that disinflationary effects are also speeded up. This acceleration may make it more feasible politically to follow anti-inflationary policies through to completion and may reduce the possible inflationary bias owing to differences between short-run and long-run inflation-unemployment trade-offs which is emphasized in the literature on political business cycles.[17]

All of these considerations are further complicated when the important distinction is made between the effects of anticipated and unanticipated policy changes. As has been emphasized by the rational expectations revolution, in the absence of institutional rigidities such as long-term contracts, monetary expansions which are fully anticipated should affect only prices and not real magnitudes. In such circumstances, exchange rates would adjust along with domestic prices, completely insulating national economies from each other's monetary policies. In other words, under the assumptions necessary for the domestic-policy-ineffectiveness theorems of the rational expectations literature to hold, international monetary interactions cease to be a matter of concern. While most economists would prob-

---

[16]For a discussion of the original analysis of these issues by J. Marcus Fleming and Robert A. Mundell and more recent contributions, see Dornbusch (1980 b) and Willett (1976).

[17]On these issues, see Dornbusch and Krugman (1976) and Willett and Mullen (1982).

ably argue that the assumptions of the policy-ineffectiveness theorems are not sufficiently close to reality to make this approach a sound guide to policy, the emphasis they place on the role of expectations captures an important element of truth which cannot safely be ignored.

These considerations complicate further the tasks of identifying the types of disturbances to which economies are being subjected and the effects of alternative policy responses. For example, we cannot safely predict whether rising interest rates will lead a currency to appreciate or depreciate; it may do either, depending whether the increase in interest rates was due primarily to an increase in inflationary expectations or a tightening of monetary policy. Given the wide diversity of expectations which may be quite plausible in particular circumstances, it is often difficult to evaluate developments accurately ex post, much less contemporaneously, as would be required for discretionary policy responses. Increased recognition of such difficulties in short-run discretionary policy implementation has led to a rather widespread reduction in the scope for policy activism that is viewed as feasible, but the implications of this development for the choice of international monetary regimes are not entirely clear.

It has sometimes been argued that while optimal policy strategies for particular situations may be quite complicated, as long as the aggregate world economy is relatively stable, then there is an argument for pegged exchange rates on the risk-reducing, portfolio-diversification principle that the typical country will gain more in stability by being able to disperse abroad, at least partially, the effects of its local disturbances than it will lose by importing net disturbances from abroad. Given the high degree of aggregate instability in the world economy in recent years, there must be some question about the current applicability of this argument. Perhaps more importantly, the same types of argument which explain why flexible exchange rates have not provided as much economic insulation and policy independence as was widely anticipated also imply that domestic disturbances may be spread out over the world economy, rather than being entirely bottled up, even under flexible exchange rates. Indeed, with very high international capital mobility, the spreading out of the effects of a domestic boom or slump in aggregate demand via the Keynesian trade balance mechanism can be greater under flexible than under pegged exchange rates (see, for example, Modigliani and Askari (1973)). As has been pointed out many times, to the extent that private speculation is stabilizing and trends in equilibrium exchange rates are not prevalent, the differences between pegged and flexible exchange rates may be minimal.[18] Substantial differences in inflation trends among countries, however, make the main-

---

[18] See Tower and Willett (1976) and Enders and Lapan (1979).

tenance of pegged rates difficult, while destabilizing or insufficiently stabilizing speculation makes pegged rates or substantial official intervention more desirable. In a world of both substantial differences in inflation trends and poorly behaved speculation, managed flexibility of some form (which could include some type of crawling-peg regime) would seem to be the only feasible type of policy, as long as the trends cannot be substantially altered.

Flexible exchange rates have frequently been blamed for contributing substantially to world inflation through the generation of vicious circles of inflation and depreciation. My own research suggests that while exchange rate depreciation can, at times, contribute to domestic inflation and the difficulties of macroeconomic management, the charges that flexible rates have been a major cause of world-wide inflation are greatly overstated. Often depreciation is just a reflection of domestic inflationary pressures and, at times, as noted above, flexible rates can contribute to, rather than have negative effects upon, domestic macroeconomic stability.[19]

The major source of policy disagreement in such an environment involves the issue of whether changes in the international monetary regime can be used to force changes in underlying policy trends and lower the transition costs of re-establishing financial stability because, as has been emphasized by the recent literature on expectations, the more widely believed are announcements of disinflationary policies, the lower will be the transitional unemployment costs that these policies generate. This is a particular formulation of the discipline and policy harmonization arguments considered above. Whether exchange rate pegging should lead or follow domestic macroeconomic policy harmonization has, of course, been an important topic of debate surrounding the various efforts at European monetary integration.[20] While Europe's experience must make one skeptical of the strength of exchange rate pegging strategies for inducing desired changes in domestic macroeconomic policies, it is certainly possible, at times, for such regime commitments to help promote stability. The credibility of such commitments becomes perhaps the most crucial issue here. Unfortunately, over the past two decades, few governments have been able to avoid suffering serious erosion of the credibility of their macroeconomic policy pronouncements.

While the Fund's seal of approval on international stabilization policy has also suffered some decline in credibility over this period, it has lost much less than the policy announcements of most national governments. Thus, as a practical matter, the credibility of the International Monetary

---

[19]For discussion and references on the vicious circle debate, see Willett and Wolf (1983). See also Goldstein (1980).

[20]See, for example, the discussion of this issue in Halm (1970) and Katz (1979).

Fund (and ad hoc groups of official lenders) may enable it to have a major influence in helping to promote the restoration of global financial stability.

As the previous discussion illustrates, it is difficult to draw strong conclusions about the contributions of alternative international monetary regimes to macroeconomic stability. Those who have drawn strong conclusions on the subject have typically focused on only a particular subset of relevant considerations. As a practical matter, at the present time, perhaps the strongest conclusion which we can reasonably draw is the negative one that to the extent feasible, the international monetary system should avoid the creation or magnification of instabilities and should not force major sustained inflationary or deflationary pressures on individual countries.

Minimizing International Liquidity, Confidence, and Adjustment Problems

Indeed, we are used to analyzing the international monetary system from a negative perspective, in particular from the standpoint of avoiding or minimizing the instabilities generated by the three problems of international adjustment, liquidity, and confidence (see, for example, Machlup (1962)). It has become standard to analyze alternative international monetary systems in terms of how they deal with these problems. The efforts to reform the Bretton Woods system during the 1960s were heavily influenced by this perspective.[21] The interrelationships among these problems are, of course, important. With a system of instantaneous adjustment, international liquidity problems could not arise and confidence problems would be unlikely to arise. On the other hand, the slower and more uncertain is the adjustment process, the greater is the need for international liquidity and the greater are the prospects for confidence problems resulting from concerns about the prospects for individual national currencies and the relationships among multiple reserve assets. Likewise, the nature and rate of international liquidity creation may substantially influence both the speed of balance of payments adjustment and its distribution between surplus and deficit countries.

A textbook automatic gold standard solves all three of these international monetary problems but at the expense of forcing domestic macroeconomic policies to adjust to the balance of payments and the growth of the global gold supply.[22] Bretton Woods sought to reduce the strength of

---

[21]For discussion and references, see Cumby (1983), Dam (1982), Solomon (1982), and Willett (1977 and 1980 a).

[22]With a full-fledged gold standard, gold is the source of international liquidity to which the world economy adjusts; and since adjustment to gold flows is automatic, there are no problems of confidence or the distribution of adjustment responsibilities. Of course, real-world gold standards have included substantial elements of discretion, and confidence and adjustment issues have not been entirely absent.

the balance of payments constraint over domestic policies by providing for the adjustment of par values. It did not provide a strong system for determining adjustment responsibilities, however, with the consequence that the exchange rate system became much more sticky than was originally envisioned, and par value adjustments generally occurred only after a series of cumulating crises.

The failure of the Bretton Woods agreement's provisions for the growth of international liquidity over time has been widely discussed in terms of the Triffin dilemma. While expansion of dollar holdings initially met the needs for expanding international liquidity, the continuation of this process brought into question the sustainability of the convertibility of the dollar into gold at $35 an ounce. Termination of the dollar deficits would have produced a shortage of international liquidity, while continuation was viewed as leading inevitably to a crisis of confidence. The proposed solution was the creation of a new centrally managed international reserve asset, and international negotiations culminated in the creation of the special drawing right.

However, as some had warned, the principal deficiency of the Bretton Woods system was less its lack of adequate provisions for international liquidity than its lack of adequate provisions for balance of payments adjustments. It was rather ironic that the Bretton Woods system broke down during the first period of SDR allocation. The breakdown was primarily caused by the large U.S. balance of payments deficit, generated by the way in which the Viet Nam War was financed, and was precipitated by massive private capital outflows. While my research suggests that the resulting international liquidity explosion was not responsible for as high a proportion of the subsequent acceleration of world-wide inflation as global monetarist explanations imply, this was certainly the type of massive generation and magnification of instability which a well-functioning international monetary system should avoid. (See Willett (1980 a) and Laney and Willett (1982).)

Our post-Bretton Woods international monetary system as ratified at Jamaica has also been charged with failing to solve liquidity, confidence, and adjustment problems. While perhaps most analysts grant that the widespread adoption of flexible exchange rates has substantially improved the operation of the international adjustment process, some question this and further argue that flexible rates have generated continuing crises because of their instability and have, themselves, been a further major cause of world inflation through the generation of vicious circles of depreciation and inflation. And even a number of those who have been relatively sanguine about the adjustment effects of flexible rates have argued that the Jamaica reforms have left essentially untouched the international liquidity and confidence problems that plagued the Bretton Woods system. It is certainly true that managed floating does not present the complete solution to these three problems that either freely floating rates or an automatic gold standard would provide. Such critiques have frequently tended to overlook, however, the extent to which the adoption of widespread flexibility reduces the problems of international liquidity, confidence, and conflicts over balance of payments adjustment as they existed under Bretton Woods or as they would have existed under the Committee of Twenty blueprint for return to dollar convertibility and a "new look" par value system. Flexible exchange rates did not lead to the avoidance of a second international liquidity explosion in the late 1970s, associated primarily with foreign intervention to limit the fall of the dollar, but countries had a great deal more freedom to decide upon their mix of responses to the weakness of the dollar between official intervention and exchange rate changes, taking into account the effects of both on domestic economic objectives. Likewise, flexible exchange rates did not eliminate concern about reserve switching but, by reducing the one-way speculative option frequently generated under the Bretton Woods adjustable peg, tended to reduce the incentives for frequent switching.

In such an analysis, it is important to make clear one's standard of comparison. In my judgment, our current system has made substantial improvements over Bretton Woods in handling the problems of international adjustment, liquidity, and confidence; but these problems are certainly not completely solved.[23] Strategies for further improvements in handling these problems will be discussed in Section III.

National Sovereignty and Distributional Concerns

The previous discussions have focused primarily on various aspects of economic efficiency. The international monetary system is composed, how-

---

[23] I have presented my reasons for this judgment in more detail in Willett (1977 and 1980 a). See also the discussions in Mundell and Polak (1977) and Dreyer, Haberler, and Willett (1982).

There are three main arguments to the effect that exchange rate flexibility has not improved the adjustment process. One, associated with the global monetarists, is that exchange rate changes cannot have real effects and, hence, cannot induce adjustment. While this may be true for very small, open economies (as emphasized in the theory of optimum currency areas), there is considerable evidence that exchange rate changes can have real effects on medium-sized and large countries (see Willett (1982)).

The second argument is that flexible exchange rates have often been pushed to disequilibrium levels. The third argument is that safeguards against beggar-thy-neighbor adjustment policies have been loosened. The evidence on speculation and equilibrium exchange rates is discussed in Section II. Concerning the third argument, my judgment is that while it would be desirable to further strengthen international surveillance of exchange rates and the adjustment process, it should also be recognized that the adoption of flexible exchange rates has not caused a net increase in beggar-thy-neighbor problems. An additional consideration is that although managed flexibility has not always prevented countries from postponing necessary adjustment, it would be difficult to argue that maintenance of the Bretton Woods regime would have reduced this problem.

ever, not only of private economic actors but also of sovereign nation-states whose governments are often more concerned with the distributional effects of the system's operation on their particular countries than with seeking global economic efficiency and who view international monetary relations as just one aspect of their overall strategies of international diplomacy. From a purely economic perspective, the operation of the international monetary system is a mixed-motive game. All gain from the efficient operation of the international monetary system and avoidance of severe breakdowns in international monetary cooperation. But within this context, there are often substantial conflicts of interest over who adjusts their policies with respect to whom; whether the emphasis should be on balance of payments adjustment or macroeconomic stabilization; and how to distribute the costs of joint undertakings, such as the transfer of resources to the developing countries.

Governments will typically wish to retain a good deal of at least nominal freedom of action, even if this leads to persistent aggregate inefficiencies, as long as their magnitude is not overwhelming. The disasters of the 1930s led to substantive modifications in the domains of effective national sovereignty in international monetary affairs claimed by major countries, so that blatant beggar-thy-neighbor policies are today much less of a problem. However, the willingness of most countries to cede substantial decision-making power to international bodies and to engage in positive discretionary acts of international monetary cooperation is still rather limited. As a result, there is a strong presumption that international monetary cooperation will be less than optimal from the standpoint of global economic efficiency.

The uncertainties about the issues of positive economic analysis discussed above further increase the difficulties of implementing strategies to achieve global economic efficiency. The more complicated and uncertain the technical issues, the less likely it is that a set of well-defined rules will prove effective in promoting efficiency. As a consequence, greater reliance is likely to be placed on case-by-case discretionary decision making. I have argued elsewhere that while a number of objective indicators can be useful presumptive criteria in the analysis of international balance of payments and exchange rate surveillance, none is likely to work well enough to form the basis of binding rules. (See Willett (1977, Chapter 4) and (1978 b).) As a result, a good deal of discretionary case-by-case analysis is needed.

By ceding strong authority to international decision makers, countries would forgo an uncertain—and potentially quite substantial—amount of national sovereignty. Without going so far as to claim that governments engage only in worst-case analysis, my experience is that they tend to display a considerable degree of risk aversion in such situations and thus are willing to bear a considerable degree of expected efficiency loss in order to preserve options for greater national influence.

This must be accepted as a basic fact of international life in any realistic efforts to improve the international monetary system. It also implies that we should not necessarily be greatly concerned about every economic analysis which concludes that the system or patterns of policy actions are operating with less than ideal efficiency, or that some future contingency is possible that current mechanisms and procedures cannot handle well. This does not mean, however, that considerable effort should not be made to attempt to promote more effective international cooperation. Analysts should continue to emphasize the prospective gains which could be made, or losses which could be avoided, on average, through greater willingness of countries to engage in collective actions.

We may also hope that good experiences with current mechanisms will foster greater trust in international decision making. This could help induce countries to support a gradual strengthening of the scope for international authority over time.[24] This process can work both ways, however. Furthermore, to the degree that international monetary affairs become increasingly politicized, it may become more difficult to strengthen our international monetary organizations. Attempts to lock oneself into an environment which requires major increases in the degree of cooperative behavior to maintain stability frequently prove counterproductive.

Recognition of the political realities of countries concerned with national sovereignty and distributional considerations and of the difficulties of collective decision making has important implications for the design of effective international agreements and collective decision-making structures. One is that since the degree of international cooperation is likely to be quite limited, it is important to focus international negotiations on the most important issues which have a reasonable chance of resolution. Of course, reasonable people may differ on the ranking of issues at any particular point in time, but it is still important that this perspective be adopted. Concern with distributional aspects also calls for focusing on limiting the liabilities of the agreeing parties and for seeking a tolerable degree of balance in the distributional effects of proposals.

The difficulties of providing compensation for losers (whether in relative or absolute terms) is one of the most severe impediments to reaching agreement on potential welfare-improving policies. One crude, but useful method which is already widely employed in international negotiations is the linking of issues with different perceived distributional effects. Contrary to the frequent interpretation of such linkages in the international relations literature as examples of power politics, such linkages may often offer a cooperative method of securing better balance in distributional effects and consequently

---

[24]For a useful discussion of the role of trust and risk aversion in international monetary issues, see Cooper (1975).

may play a very constructive role in international negotiations (see Tollison and Willett (1979)). Such issues need to receive a good deal more attention.

Another implication of such distributional concerns is that often countries will be willing to cooperate much more fully on a bilateral or small-group basis than on a global level. This means that while the International Monetary Fund should play a crucial role in the management of the international monetary system, making it the exclusive focus of international monetary cooperation would involve a substantial reduction in overall international cooperation. While the current overlapping pattern of cooperative discussions and actions—including bilateral discussions, regional groupings, economic summits, the Group of Ten, the Organization for Economic Cooperation and Development (OECD), the Group of 77, and the Fund—is extremely untidy and clearly in part elitist, it is nevertheless necessary.

Some Additional Political Considerations and Their Implications

Up to this point, the discussion in this section has focused primarily on the distribution of economic effects at national levels. The political aspects of international monetary relations go considerably beyond this, however, and include both domestic distributional considerations and noneconomic objectives. One of the basic insights of public choice theory is that rational governments seeking re-election may pursue objectives which deviate systematically from aggregate economic efficiency. Even if government decision makers are well informed about the aggregate economic effects of various policies, a substantial portion of the electorate may not be, and well-organized interest groups may carry far greater influence in the political process than is implied by the mere number of voters they represent. Even governments with a great deal of insulation from immediate domestic political pressures may seek to use international monetary issues to obtain diplomatic objectives and to give considerable weight to symbolic considerations and the appearance of political balance rather than simply to deal with questions of global economic efficiency and international economic distribution effects. Typically, the rationale for such emphasis will be to obtain greater domestic political support by attempting to shift the blame for economic difficulties to others and to rally nationalistic support for attacks on various types of perceived foreign imperialism.

It is probably true, as Benjamin Cohen argues (1977, p. 231), that Americans tend to pay too little attention to such matters, as do economists in general. It is not surprising that economists typically feel quite frustrated in having to deal with such matters, for not only do they in general make international cooperation and the implementation of economically efficient policies more difficult but often these politically motivated statements and analyses are based on questionable economic reasoning or greatly exaggerated implicit estimates of the magnitude of various effects. Yet economists interested in improving the operation of the international monetary system must pay serious attention to such considerations because they often have major influences on countries' positions and the prospects for substantive international cooperation.

I suggest that economists should take a two-pronged strategy in dealing with such political considerations. We need to continue to analyze the economic content of such positions and highlight where they are based on questionable or exaggerated economics. Examples include the tendency of national political statements to imply that their national economies are being dominated by adverse international economic developments to a far greater extent than is suggested by most careful empirical research and to exaggerate the amounts of seigniorage which the United States has gained from the international reserve position of the dollar. The latter discussions frequently overlook the fact that the United States pays competitive rates of interest on most foreign official dollar holdings. While the special role of the dollar probably does reduce the interest cost of financing U.S. deficits, the magnitude of this effect is quite small in relation to the amount of attention it has received. (See, for example, Cooper (1975, pp. 67-71).)

Second, we need to recognize that such political considerations play a legitimate role in international monetary relations and need to be taken into account in proposals for particular policy strategies and institutional reforms. One may quite consistently engage in persuasive attempts to reduce over time the degree of nationalistic political activism in international monetary discussions, while at the same time recognizing that viable policy proposals must, at present at least, give considerable weight to such considerations. At one level, this analysis suggests that we must learn to live with a good deal of political posturing in international forums and should attempt to make provisions for these widely-felt needs in ways which have minimal influences on actual international cooperation and substantive economic policies. In other words, we need to learn not to be offended by a great deal of public political posturing and to try to minimize the impediments which these create for substantive cooperative action. Examples of successful applications of this approach include the semantic brilliance of the first two amendments of the Articles of Agreement of the International Monetary Fund. While both amendments were of substantive importance in creating the SDR and legalizing and strengthening our current system based on flexible exchange rates, they contained sufficient compromise on wording and details to permit all major negotiating parties to claim at least symbolic victories.[25]

[25]For discussion and references, see Solomon (1982) and Willett (1977).

Not all such aspects of political objectives can be handled so easily, however. Some may require much more fundamental compromises. While adopting a political economy perspective will not be sufficient to avoid all political conflicts through diplomatic skill, it has extremely important implications for analysis of how the international monetary system works and for formulation of realistic strategies for international monetary reform in areas of more fundamental conflict as well. A few of these implications will be briefly discussed below.

While economists quite appropriately focus on opportunity costs in their analysis of economic efficiency, political officials typically believe, with some justification, that their constituents, based on rationally limited information, will focus more on positive acts which governments take than on actions which they fail to take and will place much heavier weight on how satisfactory current developments are than how they might have been if alternative policies had been adopted. Thus, models of government decision making which emphasize satisfying behavior, with a strong bias toward preservation of the status quo, have a great deal of explanatory power. One implication of such behavior in the international monetary area is the prediction that many national governments will behave in a manner more "Keynesian" than "monetarist" with respect to international reserve developments—that is, will view reserve positions more as a constraint than as a variable in the government's utility function (see Sweeney and Willett (1977) and Willett (1980 a)).

The first application is important, since it implies that control of international reserve aggregates may have only very limited usefulness as a strategy for controlling the macroeconomic behavior of the world economy. Both the short-run and long-run effects of a given change in aggregate international reserves will depend importantly on its distribution among countries and developments in their own overall financial positions. Thus, we cannot expect to have nearly as close a relationship between international reserve aggregates and global macroeconomic developments as there is between national money supplies and national spending (see Willett (1980 a)).

A second implication is the need to pay attention to who initiates adjustment actions, in addition to what the ultimate economic effects will be. This emphasis yields important implications for the breakdown of Bretton Woods and the case for flexible exchange rates. Under fixed exchange rates, there is a strong (although, of course, not perfect) correspondence between who takes adjustment actions and how the costs of adjustment are distributed. It is not surprising that deficit countries typically prefer adjustment to mutual payments imbalances to come from macroeconomic expansion in surplus countries, while surplus countries prefer restraint in the deficit countries.

With exchange rate adjustments, the distribution of economic effects is much less closely related to who initiates the adjustments. However, under the Bretton Woods system, national officials typically felt that political blame and international status were closely related to who initiated adjustment. Devaluations were widely viewed as a blow to national prestige and an admission of policy failure, and even revaluations carried political costs in terms of opposition of export interests and perceptions that revaluation meant giving in to the deficit countries (see Marris (1970)). As a consequence, a strong bias toward inaction developed with respect to exchange rate adjustments as well as macroeconomic policy adjustments. In my judgment, these fundamental political considerations tend to be underemphasized considerably by advocates of the view that under the "new look" par value system envisioned in the Committee of Twenty blueprint for international monetary reform, adjustments would be made much more promptly and effectively than under the old adjustable peg system. (This is not to deny that some learning behavior can be expected to take place. The adjustable pegs within the European Monetary System have certainly been used a good deal more flexibly than under the Bretton Woods system.) Still, apart from their strictly economic merits (and limitations), flexible exchange rates have played an extremely useful role in helping to reduce the politicization of exchange rate adjustments.

The Search for Symmetry

The search for symmetry is a fundamental political aspect of the debate over international monetary reform. Quite apart from whatever economic advantages the special role of the dollar has given the United States, the desire to scale down the role of the dollar is an understandable concern of countries that care about status and political appearances. Yet in an asymmetrical world, the search for complete symmetry runs into severe practical difficulties, even apart from questions of power relationships whereby countries occupy privileged positions they are reluctant to give up. From the beginning, some critics, such as John Williamson, were skeptical of the attempt at universality embodied in Bretton Woods. The evolution of the special role of the dollar was consistent with his predictions, as is the increased recognition, embodied in the Jamaica reforms, that size, openness, and other factors as enumerated in the theory of optimum currency areas (see, for example, Tower and Willett (1976)) imply that different exchange rate regimes will be preferable for different countries.

The Bretton Woods system had formal symmetry, since any country was free to choose either option for its exchange rate obligations, maintaining fixed price convertibility with gold or with a currency pegged to gold. But, in practice, the United States was the only country to select the former option, and the dollar clearly took on a special role over time. Likewise, the current system of permissive exchange rate flexibility provides formal symmetry, but the dollar still plays a special, if somewhat reduced, role. While a strong economic case can be made for various forms of dollar standard and the distribution of economic benefits from these systems would be considerably more balanced than critics of dollar imperialism typically imply, in political terms it is easy to understand why many would find such a system objectionable.[26] Many of the charges leveled against such a system are overstated. For instance, the seigniorage gains to the dollar are quite small; and a flexible rate dollar standard would not give U.S. policy the dominance in the determination of the monetary policies of other countries that would result from a fixed rate dollar standard under which the U.S. faced no effective balance of payments constraint (the type of system which critics frequently seem to have in mind).

Furthermore, while the adoption of a passive exchange rate and balance of payments policy by the United States Government would relieve it of the political cost of initiating adjustments, it would also subject it to greater political pressures from domestic mercantilist forces who might argue that overvaluation of the dollar was causing unemployment and undermining the U.S. industrial base. Still, the political imagery of anything looking like a dollar standard carries negative connotations. In this context, the creation of the SDR has been of considerable symbolic, if not yet substantive, advantage by creating the impression of a more symmetrically based international monetary system.

The SDR also gives us a better basis for developing a more symmetrical and centralized international monetary system. Progress in this direction has been rather limited, however, largely because of other fundamental political considerations. Some have interpreted the failure of international monetary negotiations to reach agreement on reforms along the lines of the Committee of Twenty's Outline of Reform to the parochial efforts of the United States to preserve its privileged position and its consequent insistence on greater tightness in the rules for adjustment than in the rules for convertibility.

I believe that there is an element of truth in this view, but that it was not one of the fundamental causes of the failure of the Committee of Twenty's blueprint to gain official acceptance. Essentially, we never came close enough to agreement on effective reform of a par value system for the particular concerns of the United States to have blocked the process. While there is considerable reason to doubt whether this approach would have proved workable, even with strong international control, it is clear that

---

[26]For discussion and references to this literature, see Willett (1977, Chapter 3).

implementation of the Committee of Twenty's convertibility, par value approach would have required a high degree of international control over the adjustment policies and reserve management behavior of member countries. Thus, the political objective of creating an international monetary system that was more symmetrical in appearance came into direct conflict with another major political goal—preserving a considerable degree of national sovereignty over adjustment and reserve management policies.

A benign interpretation of the primary emphasis of the U.S. position (which, I believe, contains a great deal of truth) was the need for consistency (or symmetry) between the degree of tightness of centralized control of the adjustment process and the provisions for convertibility. U.S. officials indicated a willingness to go along with a system which was either consistently loose or consistently tight; but they argued—correctly, I believe—that a system with much tighter rules for convertibility than for international supervision of the adjustment process would soon break down. Faced with this dilemma and the mounting evidence that flexible rates were much more workable than many had anticipated, most countries indicated a strong revealed preference for preserving a high degree of national sovereignty. Thus, we adopted a loose system based on exchange rate flexibility for the dollar and resisted the political attractions of a more structural and symmetrical-looking tight system based on some form of convertibility of the dollar into reserve assets (including the possibility of indirect conversions through the Fund rather than direct conversion of dollar holdings by national governments) and substantial international control over national adjustment and reserve management questions.

It is possible that had a substantial proportion of countries given priority to creating a tighter, more symmetrical system, the negotiations would still have failed because of disagreements over technical considerations (such as the disagreements over the merits of the specific U.S. reserve indicator proposals) or disagreements with the United States over what constituted a balanced and consistent relationship between convertibility and adjustment provisions. As it happened, however, the negotiations never really came close to achieving this degree of finality. The failure to negotiate a highly symmetrical centralized system along the lines of the Committee of Twenty's blueprint reflected widespread unwillingness to cede the necessary degree of authority to international rules and/or discretionary decision making and not just an unwillingness of the United States to give up international monetary privileges.[27]

This outcome assures that there will be continuing complaints about dollar dominance and lack of symmetry in the current international monetary

[27]For further discussion of the details of the Committee of Twenty's negotiations, see Solomon (1982), Willett (1977), and Williamson (1977) and (1982).

system, but the frequency of such complaints cannot be taken as strong evidence of widespread support for substantial increases in the degree of centralized authority over the operation of the international monetary system. Attitudes may, of course, change over time, but I am convinced that for some time to come the most productive approaches to improving the operation of the international monetary system will be those which focus on specific innovations within the current loose framework, rather than those which emphasize a massive restructuring and more centralized control of the system.

II. IMPROVING INTERNATIONAL MONETARY ANALYSIS

Because of the diversity of objectives, the importance of political constraints, and the inconclusiveness of a great deal of the positive analysis discussed above, it should not be surprising that there is so much disagreement over international monetary issues. What seems less justified is the strength with which opposing views are often put forward. In my judgment, this has often been the result of seriously incomplete or defective analysis.

A distressingly high proportion of the conclusions drawn in international monetary writings and political discussions is based on erroneous analysis. While increased exposure of such misstatements and overstatements will not, by itself, yield correct answers, it is an important step toward improving the quality of international monetary debate and facilitating progress toward finding such answers. Furthermore, greater recognition of the complexity of many of these issues may make a small contribution to promoting international monetary harmony by helping to mute the vehemence of some disputes. This section offers several illustrations of fallacies put forward or overstatements made in international monetary discussions.

As was indicated in Section I, views about equilibrium exchange rates are crucial to the analysis of alternative exchange rate systems in terms of both microeconomic and macroeconomic efficiency. While there is little disagreement that major exchange rates have displayed a great deal of volatility at times since the adoption of floating, supporters of flexible rates have tended to interpret these fluctuations as primarily reflecting reasonable responses to volatile underlying economic and financial conditions, while critics have tended to view them as major independent sources of instability stimulated by frequent episodes of destabilizing or insufficiently stabilizing private speculation. Differences in belief about the relative explanatory power of these two hypotheses is perhaps the major source of disagreement among those who advocate a generalized return to pegged rates, heavy managed floating, or relatively free floating. (Of course, even in a system of relatively free floating among major currencies, smaller countries may want a considerably higher degree of exchange rate management on optimum-currency-area grounds.)

How can we narrow this range of dispute? There has been no dearth of statements that this or that currency has become clearly overvalued or undervalued. Frequently, however, such statements are based explicitly or implicitly on some simple criterion such as purchasing-power-parity calculations or relative rates of monetary growth. Recent research has clearly indicated that while such considerations are certainly relevant to exchange rate determination, they are not sound guides to either short-run or long-run equilibrium exchange rates. Modern analysis shows that expectations and real shocks also have important effects on equilibrium exchange rates. Given uncertainties about plausible ranges of expectations and structural relationships, the width of the zone of plausible estimates of equilibrium rates is typically quite wide. With such a wide gray area and the substantial differences in a priori beliefs about the correct hypothesis, it is not surprising that there is such a range of opinion. It is important to keep in mind, however, that evidence which is found to be not inconsistent with a particular hypothesis is quite different from evidence which strongly supports one hypothesis and appears to be inconsistent with another.

Despite the correctness of the view that the purpose of central banks is not to make money, tests of the profitability of official intervention and the existence of unexploited profit opportunities for speculation can give us useful information on whether official intervention and private speculation have been stabilizing or not.[28] Such testing has cast considerable doubt on the extreme hypothesis that the major foreign exchange markets have been systematically dominated by major bandwagon effects. It has also cast doubt on the alternative extreme hypothesis that exchange rates are always at their equilibrium levels and that official attempts to influence exchange rates through sterilized intervention have no effects, even in the short run. The use of filter rules and autocorrelation analysis to study systematically the time patterns of exchange rate movements since generalized floating generally does not suggest the predictable reversibility of the large swings in exchange rates that would be consistent with views that massive destabilizing bandwagon effects have been a dominant cause of exchange rate volatility. On the other hand, neither does such testing find as strong support for the efficient markets hypothesis in the major foreign exchange markets as has been found for the U.S. stock market. Coupled with judgmental assessments of the thinness of the foreign exchange markets at times and the findings of frequent losses on official interventions by central banks, this suggests the possibility that excessive leaning against the wind by cen-

[28]For discussion and references on testing for unexploited profit opportunities in the foreign exchange markets, see Sweeney (1982 a) and (1982 b) and Willett (1982 a). On the profitability (or lack thereof) of official intervention, see Argy (1982) and Taylor (1982).

ral banks combined with private speculation which is unable to dominate the market (as it does in efficient markets models) may be a major cause of the inefficiencies (unexploited profit opportunities) suggested by recent testing. At this point, such a conclusion is itself quite speculative, however. At present, we are left with rather wide sway for differing interpretations of the role for official exchange market intervention.

In addition to the tendency to overgeneralize from specific pieces of empirical evidence, there is a similar tendency with respect to the results of particular theoretical exercises. Both the microeconomic and macroeconomic effects of exchange rate changes often depend crucially on the causes of the changes (see Willett (1982 a)). It is easy to construct scenarios in which a particular disturbance or pattern of disturbances, combined with particular assumptions about the structure of the economy, can make either fixed or flexible rates more inflationary or less conducive to the stability of output. Analyses which draw strong conclusions about alternative exchange rate systems on these grounds have typically relied on a quite limited number of scenarios (often only one) without attempting to investigate the full range of likely possibilities and their relative probabilities.

Another common set of fallacies involves the failure to consider how relationships may change as the system moves from pegged to flexible exchange rates. One example was the tendency to charge that the exchange rate flexibility embodied in the Jamaica reforms dealt only with adjustment problems and made no contribution to reducing the liquidity and confidence problems. While reasonable people can certainly differ over whether the Jamaica reforms made sufficient progress in these latter areas, it cannot be argued that the removal of adjustably pegged prices among reserve assets does not reduce the confidence problem. (Remember that Gresham's Law was developed to explain behavior toward moneys with pegged, not flexible, rates of exchange.) Likewise, while flexible exchange rates certainly do not offer complete monetary independence, they clearly do offer countries at least somewhat greater protection against the effects of liquidity creation in the rest of the world.

Another example is some of the early versions of the so-called locomotive proposals for internationally coordinated economic expansion by the major industrial countries. These failed to consider the extent to which flexible exchange rates might dampen international transmission and how monetary and fiscal policy combinations might have substantially different short-run effects under flexible rates than under pegged rates (see Willett (1978 a)). In none of these examples just considered can we safely assume that the adoption of flexible rates completely solves the policy issue at hand, but it is important to recognize how analysis developed in a pegged-rate context may need to change under flexible rates.

A somewhat similar difficulty results from the tendency to reverse ends-means relationships over time. To the Bretton Woods negotiators, the par value exchange rate system was clearly seen as a means of achieving broader ends; but, over time, in the minds of many officials and international monetary specialists, it became such a symbol of international monetary cooperation that the system was widely viewed as almost an end in itself, with many people (fortunately incorrectly) believing that the termination of the par value system would lead to a major breakdown in international financial cooperation. Some have likewise tended to view convertibility of reserve assets as a basic international monetary objective rather than as one particular method of regulating international monetary relationships.

Promotion of the SDR sometimes seems to be viewed in a similar vein. While this seems a perfectly legitimate end in itself in political terms, it is sometimes combined with a failure to distinguish between marginal and inframarginal effects to imply that there is a prospect of more substantial economic effects than thorough analysis suggests are likely to occur. For example, expansion of the role of the SDR is sometimes advocated as a means of gaining greater control of international liquidity creation. The major sources of uncontrolled international liquidity creation result from exchange market intervention decisions and offical borrowing from the private international financial markets. Better centralized control over these activities requires international surveillance and influence over these national activities, which would be little influenced if the proportion of SDRs in official international liquidity rose from 5 to 10, or even to 50, percent. The establishment of a strict ratio between SDRs and total reserve holdings would, of course, be quite another matter, but the previous analysis suggests that adoption of such a constraint over national reserve management is quite unlikely to be politically acceptable to most countries, at least in the near term. There are also important technical questions about whether this would be the most effective type of approach, even if such increased centralization of authority did prove feasible.

A similar tendency to exaggerate substantially the benefits of international actions has sometimes occurred with proposals to regulate the Euro-currency markets and to create a Fund substitution account to convert official foreign exchange holdings into SDRs. Advocates of international regulation of the Eurocurrency markets sometimes talk as if measures such as harmonization of reserve requirements would substantially increase the degree of international financial independence. A good case can be made that an international agreement on reserve requirements for Eurobanks would be desirable, but it would do relatively little to reduce international capital mobility, which is the major source of loss of domestic financial autonomy.

Likewise, I believe that a good case can be made for a Fund substitution account (see Willett (1980 a)), but it would likely make only a modest, rather than a major, contribution to increasing international financial stability. Despite the attention it has received, the magnitude of official reserve switching has been relatively small compared with private currency switching and has tended to respond to the same types of incentives. The elimination of exchange market effects of official reserve switching would likely only modestly reduce exchange rate instability, which, in my judgment, is influenced primarily by private responses to expectations about underlying economic and financial conditions.

One last difficulty I would like to mention is the frequency with which the establishment of a theoretical interdependence leads analysts to accord it major policy significance without considering empirical magnitudes and the feasibility of policy responses. For example, while it is true that extremely high elasticities of currency substitution would make flexible exchange rates between these currencies, as well as interest rates in the countries concerned, unstable, it does not follow that the detection of statistically significant (but relatively low) degrees of substitution implies such instability (see Laney, Radcliffe, and Willett (1982)). The degree of optimal discretionary international policy coordination under the assumptions of perfect information and no collective decision-making costs vastly exceeds the degree that is practically feasible.

While abstract theoretical modeling obviously can be extremely valuable, its translation into effective policy advice requires a good deal of judgment and common sense. On the one hand, there is danger that unrealistic attempts to strive for theoretical maxima may be counterproductive; pursuit of the best may sometimes be the enemy of the good. On the other hand, we must guard against becoming so overwhelmed by the practical difficulties of decision making that we become excessively complacent and view any status quo short of disaster as being optimal from a practical perspective. Avoiding these extremes is the essence of good applied policy analysis.

While the complexity of international monetary issues assures that our knowledge will always be a great deal less than is desired, there is still tremendous scope for improving the technical quality of international monetary discussions and our knowledge of key aspects of how the international monetary system is working. While a good deal of progress has been made, we still have a long way to go in better integrating policy-level discussions and technical research. There is enormous scope for mutually beneficial interactions, especially in guiding empirical work toward our most pressing policy concerns and in increasing the capability and willingness of high-level officials to make use of such research (see Willett (1982 b)).

III. EVALUATING THE CURRENT SYSTEM: A SUMMING UP

The preceding sections have discussed a number of important elements which I believe must be taken into account in evaluating international monetary issues and have illustrated their application to a wide range of international monetary considerations. This section seeks to pull the major strands of this analysis together in a summary evaluation of the current international monetary system and the prospects for strengthening it.

A major theme of the preceding analysis is that there is such a vast range of both normative and positive reasons for differing evaluations of international monetary questions that controversy will always be with us and therefore that its presence per se cannot be taken as a strong indication that the system is not working fairly well.

It is clear that the operation of any real-world international monetary system will fall far short of the ideals perceived by any particular theorist. The system will always be in need of improvement from any one particular perspective, but the directions of change suggested by different legitimate perspectives will often conflict. The limited willingness of national governments to cede power to centralized authority reflects not only shortsighted concerns about maintaining traditional degrees of national sovereignty but also genuine concerns about what the outcomes of centralized decisions should be, even if purely national concerns were put aside. It is inevitable that any international monetary system will reflect compromises among different objectives, perceptions, and degrees of willingness to engage in cooperative action to gain long-term advantages by forgoing some short-term advantages.

In my judgment, the evidence to date is broadly consistent with my initial view (Willett (1977)) that our new international monetary system, ratified by the Jamaica agreements, represents a substantial improvement over its predecessors. It has kept much of the best of the institutional structure and spirit of international obligations and cooperation of the Bretton Woods system and provides a more flexible exchange rate mechanism.

A worrisome aspect of the current system is that there is not strong enough centralized international control over the operation of the international monetary system to offer absolute assurance that we will avoid severe beggar-thy-neighbor problems, excessive international liquidity creation, and short-term financial crises. But it is often forgotten what a relatively modest degree of effective international control was available under Bretton Woods. In the absence of a willingness to cede substantially greater power to international authority, the Jamaica agreements represent a sound response which reduces somewhat the amount of international control needed to keep the system working tolerably well. The adoption of greater exchange rate flexibility has made substantial contributions to reducing important aspects of the international liquidity, confidence, and adjustment problems. Except for very small, open economies, exchange rate changes are an effective (although certainly not a painless) instrument of balance of payments adjustment, and greater exchange rate flexibility has helped to reduce the problem of deciding how mutual adjustment responsibilities should be shared. Likewise, flexible rates have reduced (although, of course, they have not eliminated) the incentives for reserve switching compared with those existing under the adjustable peg and have given countries greater scope to protect themselves from excessive international liquidity creation. It is more difficult to judge its effects on microeconomic and macroeconomic efficiency, but I do not believe that charges that flexible rates have had a disastrous effect on international trade and investment and have been a major cause of global stagflation are supported by the available evidence. While the macroeconomic performance of most countries has been quite unsatisfactory, I believe that this has been due much more to basic domestic political and economic causes than to the operation of the international monetary system and that flexible exchange rates probably give individual countries a greater opportunity to take the lead in restoring domestic stability. While the substantial appreciation of the dollar which has accompanied the recent U.S. anti-inflation efforts has had painful effects abroad (as the efforts have had painful effects at home), it has helped to speed the decline of inflation in the United States, which, in turn, has made it more feasible to carry these efforts through to a successful conclusion.

To date, international cooperation under our current loose system has been sufficient to avoid the major disasters many of the critics of the Jamaica agreements foresaw. But we certainly have no reason for complacency. Even apart from questions of the ability to head off the possibilities of financial collapse and economic warfare, management of the system today is particularly complicated. The substantial increase in underlying instabilities, both in macroeconomic conditions and international economic relations (such as those brought about by the oil shocks), has made the design of optimal economic policies much more difficult. The growth of official borrowing from private international financial markets has greatly reduced the "special privilege" of the United States of financing balance of payments deficits by increasing liabilities rather than reducing assets and has played a major beneficial role in the recycling of the oil surpluses. It has substantially weakened, however, the already weak relationship between international reserve aggregates and the behavior of the world economy. Similarly, while the move toward diversification of reserve holdings across a wide range of currencies is beneficial from the standpoint of efficient risk reduction, it also further increases the complexities of operating the system. Simple rules for the management of international reserve aggregates are unlikely to be effective.

At the same time, the substantial increase in the number of individual countries and groups of countries which have a major influence on international monetary developments has substantially increased the difficulties of formal collective decision making. While the move away from hegemony is desirable based on global political criteria, it does substantially increase the scope for "blocking coalitions" which can frustrate attempts at positive international agreements. The increased complexities of operating the current system make the formulation of clear-cut rules to deal with issues of exchange rate and balance of payments adjustment and international liquidity management increasingly difficult. Apart from an understanding of the realities of national political considerations, what is primarily needed to strengthen the efficiency of the operation of the system is either a highly structured set of limitations on national behavior which would make international rules more workable or greater discretionatory central control over countries' balance of payments financing and adjustment and reserve management policies.

The prospects for such radical revision in the scope of authority given to international rules and/or discretionatory decision making are not bright, at least for the near future. However, for the reasons indicated in this paper, with some increase in the financial resources available for crisis management and to deal with the developing countries' debt problem and with good luck, I believe that the current level of international control is likely to prove adequate, even if far less than optimal. Over the past decade of generalized floating, global macroeconomic performance has certainly been dismal, but I think that the contribution of deficiencies in the operation of the international monetary system per se have been small rather than large. Thus, I believe that the best prospects for improved global economic stability rest with better management of national economic policies, including paying better attention to, and coordination of, the international consequences of these policies.

Perhaps the greatest advantage of the current system is that while optimal policymaking is probably more difficult than it was under the Bretton Woods system, the current system has shown substantial shock-absorbing capabilities which have substantially limited the international damage generated by poor national policies and the inconsistencies among national objectives. Thus, I see the most productive strategy for improving the operation of the international monetary system as one involving continuing efforts to increase gradually over time the influence of the International Monetary Fund in the surveillance of countries' balance of payments adjustment and financing policies. Because of the important influence of Fund attitudes and policies on the willingness of private lenders to provide credit, the Fund already has much greater leverage than is implied by its formal authority; but such control is far from perfect, and efforts to increase this leverage further deserve high priority.[29]

Likewise, on account of its expertise and role as an honest broker, the Fund may be able to play a highly beneficial role in the discussion of exchange rate and macroeconomic policy coordination issues among the major industrial countries. While the quality of technical analysis which is used as a basis for national official discussions of such questions has risen substantially over the past decade, it is still often distressingly low. Better technical analysis will certainly not eliminate all disputes and will often suggest that it is difficult to know what the best policy is. But even an understanding of such difficulties can make a substantial positive contribution to efforts to achieve international cooperation when the alternative is, as it frequently has been, disagreements among disputants who are strongly convinced that they are clearly right and their opponents are clearly wrong. From the standpoint of improving the technical quality of official international monetary analysis, it seems particularly regrettable that the Fund does not appear to be playing a substantial role in the review of official intervention policies of the major industrial countries, an activity deemed important at the Versailles economic summit.

Given the limitations on the willingness of most countries to give up substantially increased amounts of national sovereignty, I believe that our basic strategy should be to focus on attempting to secure marginal improvements in the structure and operation of the current system and to keep our fingers crossed that conflicts of national objectives and/or international financial crises do not produce greater strains than the system can handle. In practice, the likelihood of ad hoc coordination among the major industrial countries makes their capacity to handle substantial international financial crises much greater than is implied by the formal structure of current arrangements. Still, there is a strong case for substantially increasing the emergency borrowing and lending powers of the Fund, both to reduce further the likelihood of emergency cooperation among the major financial powers breaking down and to allow a greater proportion of such crisis management to take place through formal international channels.

With respect to international liquidity and reserve management issues,

[29]For a recent evaluation of the relationship between official and private financing of balance of payments deficits, see Cohen (1981).

I see a strong case for a sustained modest rate of SDR creation, as much (or more) for political as for economic reasons. Even with managed floating, there is a secular increase in the demand for owned international reserves over time. I see no compelling reason why the issuance of SDRs should not be the main method of meeting this increased demand. I also believe, however, that there should be a substantial tilt in official international liquidity creation away from owned reserves and unconditional borrowing provisions and toward conditional loans. The requirement that the Fund's conditional loans be based on sound stabilization programs should play an important role in helping to restore greater global economic stability. Assuming that major crises are avoided, this may be the most important positive role which international monetary institutions can play in improving the operation of the world economy. It should be remembered, however, that the effectiveness of the Fund's lending and its "seal of approval" in reducing the cost of restoring greater stability rests crucially on the continued credibility of such policies.

Given the apparent widespread preferences for autonomy in national reserve management, I see little prospect of the SDR becoming the principal reserve asset in the system; nor would this have major economic effects unless we moved to a system with very strong central control. On political grounds, however, it is probably useful to maintain this stated objective. Furthermore, some of the actions which should be taken on their own merits, such as facilitation of greater private market use of the SDR and the creation of a Fund substitution facility, are likely to contribute to a gradual shift toward increasing use of the SDR.

I continue to believe that creation of a Fund substitution facility would be desirable, although I would expect the effects to be marginal rather than major. International interest in such a facility seems to wax and wane with the ups and downs of the dollar. I likewise believe that national governments and the Fund should support, rather than discourage, the growth of private SDR use. There is a good microeconomic case for the use of composite currency units, and the new five-currency SDR basket may make the unit an attractive candidate for many private transactions. International financial innovation seems likely to continue, and one is likely to see both greater use of composite units and greater diversification across currencies in the future.

Paradoxically, greater diversification marginally reduces, rather than increases, exchange rate instability over time. While it is clear that going from one to two currencies (or reserve assets) contributes to a confidence or stability problem, it is not clear that going from two to three currencies, from three to four currencies, and so on will further increase the potential instability. With more diversified portfolios, the changing prospects of individual assets might lead to less, rather than more, asset switching. Since it is extremely unlikely agreement will be reached on a single-reserve-asset system, we have to learn to live in a multi-asset system. While conceptually it would be desirable to have improved mechanisms for minimizing the exchange rate consequences of autonomous shifts in both private and official asset preferences, it is not clear how important such autonomous currency switching has been compared with shifts generated by changing expectations. Likewise, there has been little analysis of how well such shifts could be identified in the time available to governments for deciding on accommodating policy actions. These issues, along with questions about the effectiveness of alternative strategies of national official intervention and macroeconomic policy coordination, should be major topics of further international policy research and analysis.

In summary, I believe that the current system should be evaluated quite favorably in light of historical comparisons and political realities. In the absence of the most extreme combinations of severe shocks and bad luck, the current formal and informal structure of the system should remain basically sound. Thus, while I view the prospects for radical reform of the system as being extremely remote because of basic political considerations, I do not see this as a major cause for alarm. Our basic strategy, in my judgment, should be to improve the operation of the current system. Within this content, there is considerable scope for improvement. While hopes of creating a more stable international environment must rest in large part on the future course of national economic policies, there is also considerable room for strengthening our international monetary institutions and the influences they have over time. The political prospects of such improvements are difficult to evaluate, but continuing efforts along these lines should certainly be made.

BIBLIOGRAPHY

Aliber, Robert Z., "Issues in U.S. International Monetary Policies," in *International Economic Policy Research: Papers and Proceedings of a Colloquium Held in Washington, D.C., October 3, 4, 1980*, Washington: National Science Foundation, 1980, pp. I-59-75. (Hereinafter this book will be referred to as *International Economic Policy Research*.)

Argy, Victor E., *Exchange-Rate Management in Theory and Practice*, Studies in International Finance, No. 50 (Princeton, New Jersey: International Finance Section, Princeton University, 1982).

Bryant, Ralph C., *Money and Monetary Policy in Independent Nations* (Washington: Brookings Institution, 1980).

Cohen, Benjamin J., *Organizing the World's Money: The Political Economy of International Monetary Relations* (New York: Basic Books, 1977).

_____, in collaboration with Fabio Basagni, *Banks and the Balance of Payments: Private Lending in the International Adjustment Process* (Montclair, New Jersey: Allanheld, Osmun and Company, 1981).

Cooper, Richard N., "Prolegomena to the Choice of an International Monetary System," in *World Politics and International Economics*, ed. by C. Fred Bergsten and Lawrence B. Krause (Washington: Brookings Institution, 1975), pp. 63-97.

Corden, W. Max, "The Normative Theory of International Trade," University of Stockholm, Institute for International Economic Studies, Seminar Paper No. 230 (November 1982), forthcoming as Chapter 2 in R. W. Jones and P. B. Kenen, eds., *Handbook of International Economics*, Vol. 1 (Amsterdam: North-Holland Publishing Company, to be published in 1984).

Cumby, Robert E., "Special Drawing Rights and Plans for Reform of the International Monetary System: A Survey," Chapter 10 in this volume.

Dam, Kenneth W., *The Rules of the Game: Reform and Evolution of the International Monetary System* (Chicago: University of Chicago Press, 1982).

Dornbusch, Rudiger (1980 a), "Exchange Rate Economics: Where Do We Stand?" *Brookings Papers on Economic Activity: 1* (1980), pp. 143-85.

_____ (1980 b), *Open Economy Macroeconomics* (New York: Basic Books, 1980).

_____, *Flexible Exchange Rates and Interdependence*, National Bureau of Economic Research, Working Paper No. 135 (Cambridge, Massachusetts, November 1982).

_____, and Paul Krugman (1976), "Flexible Exchange Rates in the Short Run," *Brookings Papers on Economic Activity: 3* (1976), pp. 537-84.

Dreyer, Jacob S., Gottfried Haberler, and Thomas D. Willett, eds., *The International Monetary System: A Time of Turbulence* (Washington: American Enterprise Institute for Public Policy Research, 1982). (Hereinafter this book is referred to as *The International Monetary System*.)

Enders, Walter, and Harvey E. Lapan, "Stability, Random Disturbance and the Exchange Rate Regime," *Southern Economic Journal*, Vol. 46 (July 1979), pp. 49-70.

Goldstein, Morris, *Have Flexible Exchange Rates Handicapped Macroeconomic Policy?* Special Papers in International Economics, No. 14 (Princeton, New Jersey: International Finance Section, Princeton University, 1980).

Halm, George N., ed., *Approaches to Greater Flexibility of Exchange Rates: The Bürgenstock Papers* (Princeton, New Jersey: Princeton University Press, 1970).

Henderson, Dale, "The Role of Intervention Policy in Open Economy Financial Policy: A Macroeconomic Perspective," in *Political Economy of International and Domestic Monetary Relations*, ed. by Raymond E. Lombra and Willard E. Witte (Ames, Iowa: Iowa State University Press, 1982), pp. 261-89.

Katz, Samuel I., ed., *U.S.-European Monetary Relations* (Washington: American Enterprise Institute for Public Policy Research, 1979).

Laney, Leroy O., and Thomas D. Willett, "The International Liquidity Explosion and Worldwide Inflation: The Evidence from Sterilization Coefficient Estimates," *Journal of International Money and Finance*, Vol. 1 (August 1982), pp. 141-52.

Laney, Leroy, Chris Radcliffe, and Thomas D. Willett, *International Currency Substitution by Americans Is Not High: A Comment on Miles,* Claremont Working Papers, No 27 (Claremont, California: Claremont Graduate School, 1982). This paper will be published in a forthcoming issue of the *Southern Economic Journal.*

Levich, Richard, "The Efficiency of Markets for Foreign Exchange," in Rudiger Dornbusch and Jacob A. Frenkel, eds., *International Economic Policy: Theory and Evidence* (Baltimore: Johns Hopkins University Press, 1979), pp. 246-67.

Lombra, Raymond E., and Willard Witte, eds., *Political Economy of International and Domestic Monetary Relations* (Ames, Iowa: Iowa State University Press, 1982). (Hereinafter this book is referred to as *Political Economy of Monetary Relations.*)

Machlup, Fritz, *Plans for Reform of the International Monetary System*, Special Papers in International Economics, No. 3 (Princeton, New Jersey: International Finance Section, Princeton University, 1962).

Marris, Stephen N., "Decision-Making on Exchange Rates," in *Approaches to Greater Flexibility of Exchange Rates: The Bürgenstock Papers*, ed. by George N. Halm (Princeton, New Jersey: Princeton University Press, 1970), pp. 77-88.

Modigliani, Franco, and Hossein Askari, "The International Transfer of Capital and the Propagation of Domestic Disturbances Under Alternative Payment Systems," Banca Nazionale del Lavoro, *Quarterly Review*, Vol. 26 (December 1973), pp. 295-310.

Mussa, Michael, "Public Policy Issues in International Finance," in *International Economic Policy Research*, pp. I-76-104.

Mundell, Robert A., and Jacques J. Polak, eds., *The New International Monetary System* (New York: Columbia University Press, 1977).

Pigott, Charles, Richard J. Sweeney, and Thomas D. Willett, *The Costs of Disequilibrium Under Pegged and Flexible Exchange Rates,* Claremont Working Papers, No. 46 (Claremont, California: Claremont Graduate School, 1982).

Solomon, Robert, *The International Monetary System, 1945-1981* (New York: Harper and Row, 1982).

Strange, Susan, *International Monetary Relations* (London: Oxford University Press, 1976).

Sweeney, Richard J. (1982 a), "Intervention Strategy Implications of Purchasing Power Parity and Tests of Spot Exchange-Market Efficiency," in *The International Monetary System,* pp. 65-109.

_____(1982 b), "Speculation: Stabilizing or Destabilizing," Claremont Working Papers, No. 59 (Claremont, California: Claremont Graduate School, 1982).

_____, and Thomas D. Willett, "Eurodollars, Petrodollars, and Problems of World Liquidity and Inflation," in *Stabilizing of the Domestic and International Economy*, ed. by Karl Brunner and Allan H. Meltzer, Carnegie-Rochester Conference Series on Public Policy, Vol. 5 (Amsterdam: North-Holland Publishing Company, 1977), pp. 277-310.

Taylor, Dean, "Official Intervention in the Foreign Exchange Market, or, Bet Against the Central Bank," *Journal of Political Economy*, Vol. 90 (April 1982), pp. 356-68.

Thursby, Marie, and Thomas D. Willett, *The Effects of Flexible Exchange Rates on International Trade and Investment: A Survey of Historical Views and Recent Evidence,* Claremont Working Papers, No. 62 (Claremont, California: Claremont Graduate School, 1982).

Tollison, Robert D., and Thomas D. Willett, "Institutional Mechanisms for Dealing With International Externalities; A Public Choice Perspective," in *The Law of the Sea*, ed. by Ryan C. Amacher and Richard J. Sweeney (Washington: American Enterprise Institute for Public Policy Research, 1976), pp. 77-101.

_____"An Economic Theory of Mutually Advantageous Issue Linkages in International Negotiations," *International Organization*, Vol. 33 (Autumn 1979), pp. 425-50.

Tower, Edward, and Thomas D. Willett, *The Theory of Optimum Currency Areas and Exchange-Rate Flexibility*, Special Papers in International Economics, No. 11 (Princeton, New Jersey: International Finance Section, Princeton University, May 1976).

Triffin, Robert, *Gold and the Dollar Crisis: The Future of Convertibility* (New Haven, Connecticut: Yale University Press, 1960).

United States, Commission on the Role of Gold in the Domestic and International Monetary Systems, *Report to the U.S. Congress,* Vols. I and II (Washington: Government Printing Office, 1982).

Willett, Thomas D., "The Eurocurrency Market, Exchange-Rate Systems, and National Financial Policies," in *Eurocurrencies and the International Monetary System*, ed. by Carl H. Stem, John H. Makin, and Dennis E. Logue (Washington: American Enterprise Institute for Public Policy Research, 1976), pp. 193-221.

_____, *Floating Exchange Rates and International Monetary Reform* (Washington: American Enterprise Institute for Public Policy Research, 1977).

_____(1978 a), "It's Too Simple To Blame the Countries with a Surplus," *Euromoney* (February 1978), pp. 89-96.

_____(1978 b), "Alternative Approaches to International Surveillance of Exchange-Rate Policies," in *Managed Exchange-Rate Flexibility: The Recent Experience* (Boston: Federal Reserve Bank of Boston, October 1978), pp. 148-72.

_____(1980 a), *International Liquidity Issues* (Washington: American Enterprise Institute for Public Policy Research, 1980).

_____(1980 b), "Policy Research Issues in a Floating Rate World: An Assessment of Policy-Relevant Research on the Effects of International Monetary Institutions and Behavior on Macroeconomic Performance," in *International Economic Policy Research,* pp. I-24-45.

_____"The Causes and Effects of Exchange Rate Volatility," in *The International Monetary System*, pp. 24-64.

_____*A New Monetary Constitution*, Claremont Working Papers, No. 71 (Claremont, California: Claremont Graduate School, 1981). This paper will be included in

Alvin Rabushka and W. Craig Stubblebine, eds., *Constraining Federal Taxing and Spending* (Palo Alto, California: Hoover Institution Press, forthcoming in 1983).

_____, and John Mullen, "The Effects of Alternative International Monetary Systems on Macroeconomic Discipline and Inflationary Biases," in *Political Economy of Monetary Relations*, pp. 143-59.

Willett, Thomas D., and Matthias Wolf, *The Vicious Circle Debate: Some Conceptual Distinctions*, Claremont Working Paper, No. 81 (Claremont, California: Claremont Graduate School, 1983). This paper will be published in a forthcoming issue of *Kyklos*.

Williamson, John H., *The Failure of World Monetary Reform, 1971-74* (New York: New York University Press, 1977).

_____"The Failure of World Monetary Reform: A Reassessment," in *The International Monetary System Under Flexible Exchange Rates: Global, Regional, and National*, ed. by Richard N. Cooper, Peter B. Kenen, Jorge Braga de Macedo, and Jacques van Ypersele (Cambridge, Massachusetts: Ballinger, 1982), pp. 297-307.

Comments

Rudiger Dornbusch

Professor Willett's paper is ambitious and far-reaching, covering a range of topics from market efficiency to the political science of "dollar imperialism." Yet I find myself disappointed and baffled by his central contention that our ten years of experience with flexible rates has been, by and large, satisfactory and that our present international financial arrangements are superior to the Bretton Woods system. Specifically, he argues on page 9 that "the widespread adoption of flexible exchange rates has made major contributions to ameliorating all three of the problems of the Bretton Woods system—adjustment, liquidity, and confidence." On page 37, he adds that "the current system has shown substantial shock-absorbing capabilities which have substantially limited the international damage generated by poor national policies and the inconsistencies among national objectives." Later, Professor Willett expresses the conviction that "our basic strategy should be to focus on attempting to secure marginal improvements in the structure and operation of the current system and to keep our fingers crossed that conflicts of national objectives and/or international financial crises do not produce greater strains than the system can handle."

These judgments are certainly at odds with the preoccupations of the day. A recent issue (March 1983) of *Finance & Development*, for example, contains articles entitled "Protectionism," "Toward a More Orderly Exchange Rate System," and "External Debt—The Continuing Problem."

Concern about protectionism today runs deeper than at any time since the 1930s. Disequilibrium exchange rates are perceived to be as pervasive, if not more so, than they were in the 1960s. Macroeconomic performance is exceptionally poor. Finally, confidence in the system is low, and competitive depreciation and debt default, themes from the 1930s, are becoming topical again. How much responsibility for all this rests with the exchange rate regime, and, more broadly, the international financial system is not clear. But it surely cannot be argued either that the Bretton Woods system deserves no credit for the unrivalled progress and stability of the 1960s or that the present system bears no responsibility for the lack of economic progress and stability today. After all, the international system is not altogether irrelevant. Perhaps it is the system that makes possible, or even encourages, the poor national policies that Willett would blame for our troubles.

45

Adjustment

A well-functioning international monetary system would promote the efficient allocation of resources—in particular, full employment, free trade, and efficient international lending—under conditions of price stability. It is quite apparent that our existing system is far from reaching these goals, both absolutely and quite likely also by comparison with the 1960s. Consider, for example, the issue of adjustment. Chart 1 shows the Japanese current account as a fraction of gross domestic product. It is clear that current account imbalances are as large, and probably also as persistent, as they were in the 1960s. But of course, it will rightly be objected that there is no reason why current accounts should, in any short period, tend to average to zero. The adjustment issue must then concern the question whether changes in relative prices operate sufficiently fast to maintain not current account balance but rather full employment. Do relative prices respond—in the face of shifting comparative advantage, supply shocks, and shifting trends in fiscal policies—so as to maintain high employment? In this respect, the system works poorly.

CHART 1. JAPAN: CURRENT ACCOUNT SURPLUSES EXPRESSED AS PERCENTAGES OF GROSS DOMESTIC PRODUCT, 1960–82

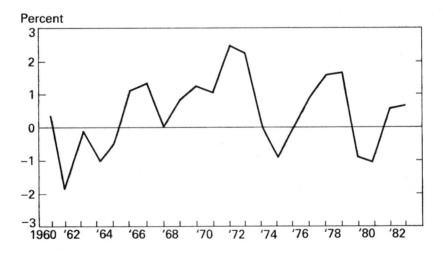

It is now well understood that the exchange rate is dominated by events in asset markets, rather than by the need to ensure full employment. While wages and prices are sluggish, the exchange rate shares the flexibility of asset prices and interest rates. It links asset and goods markets, and that very linkage is the source of macroeconomic instability. To give just one example, the prospect of large U.S. full-employment budget deficits implies high long-term real interest rates. The rise in long-term real interest rates, to an extent not matched abroad, leads to currency overvaluation and slower recovery than there would be under a less flexible rate system. The exchange rate, in our present system—which includes, of course, the instability of policies—thus may be moving too far and responding to the wrong signals. There is an insufficient discrepancy between nominal and real exchange rates to promote simultaneous achievement of price level autonomy and full employment.

Chart 2 compares bilateral relative prices in manufacturing, bringing out the extraordinary variation in relative price levels which accounts for a

CHART 2. RELATIVE PRICES IN MANUFACTURING, 1973-82
(1975 = 100)

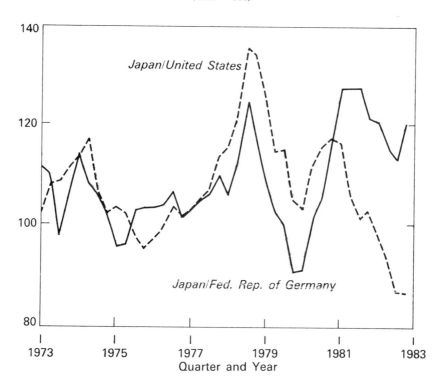

good part of today's protectionist sentiment. The source of the real exchange rate movement is, in large part, the unsynchronized use of monetary and fiscal policies. There will be currency appreciation in the country that pursues a mix of relatively tight money and relatively expansionary long-run fiscal policy. Those who question the flexible exchange rate system today as an effective system for international adjustment do not worry very much whether current accounts respond to variations in real exchange rates. They worry instead about the source of real exchange rate movements. To the extent that capital flows are not primarily guided by employment and external balances, they may well be perverse. Unrelated to the productivity of capital, international lending among industrial countries is directed toward areas where tight money policies lower the return on real capital but raise the return on paper assets. There is nothing efficient or desirable about such patterns of capital flows, even if they are the result of the unhampered functioning of the world capital market. As is well known, in a world of second best, partial moves to freely functioning markets may be very costly.

The adjustment question, in our present international financial system, arises equally with respect to developing country borrowing. With the benefit of hindsight, there is no question that overlending, to use Kindleberger's expression, has taken place, just as it did in the 1920s. Then the need for reconstruction served as the justification, while today recycling does. But, of course, when borrowing has no counterpart in incremental productive capital formation, serious problems lie ahead.

In these cases and in many others, the international capital flowed far too freely and served to perpetuate and aggravate serious disequilibria. Free capital flows have favored the financing of payments imbalances and the maintenance of disequilibrium exchange rates—and disequilibrium standards of living. Of course, we are now living with the consequences, which are that there is no financing, only adjustment. It is difficult to identify precisely when adjustment should have taken over from financing. But there is little doubt that in 1980–81, the International Monetary Fund should have, loudly and unequivocally, called for real depreciation and adjustment in countries like Chile, Brazil, and Argentina. Needless to say, that would have been very unpopular. Still, the Fund is in a favorable position by virtue of the expertise of its staff and relative permanence—at least compared with elected governments—to advocate long-run, system-wide stability. Excessive sensitivity to political pressures has led the Fund to shy away from these responsibilities, but the severity of today's world economic problems affords the Fund an opportunity to reflect on its role and exercise stronger leadership.

Transmission of Business Cycle

The system of flexible exchange rates supposedly gives countries autonomy in conducting their monetary policies. But that autonomy turns out to be sharply limited. It is limited because the absence of wage-price flexibility means that nominal exchange rate movements change both the price level and competitiveness. When a large (center) country chooses to tighten money and, in response, experiences exchange appreciation, it immediately enjoys disinflation through reduced import prices. But it also exports spillover effects abroad. Abroad, inflation increases and competitiveness improves. If inflation is a chief objective of policy abroad, the response there must be to match the center country's tight money, keeping exchange rates relatively fixed but inducing synchronized movements in world aggregate demand.

The current world recession is the outcome of these interdependence effects. U.S. monetary tightness was matched by a tightening of money abroad. Judged by the U.S. reduction in inflation, the policy has been splendidly successful. But, of course, part of that success is only transitory, to the extent that it depresses the real prices of commodities and entails a loss of external competitiveness. Once the overvaluation of the dollar and the undervaluation of commodities is undone, inflation will resume and may threaten the recovery here and abroad. The experience of the last three years seems to indicate that flexible rates are a particularly poor system for periods of transition. The exchange rate is too flexible a price, and exchange rate movements induce synchronized policies in the world, thus aggravating the business cycle.

Economists have become accustomed to thinking about the choice between fixed and flexible exchange rates and assuming that countries will pursue autonomously their national monetary and fiscal policies. In that perspective, flexible rates used to be thought of as providing more insulation from external shocks and more independence for domestic monetary policy. It is now clear that this is altogether wrong. There is no such thing as independence so long as governments have inflation, real wage, and employment objectives. Given traditional monetary and fiscal policies, fixed rates have little advantage over flexible rates, and vice versa. Improvements in world macroeconomic performance can, though, be brought about by using the system more effectively. A policy mix should be formulated, taking into consideration the exchange rate system and the extent of wage-price flexibility, to bring about improved performance. In my judgment, that means choosing a flexible exchange rate system, a relatively exogenous monetary policy, and an aggressive incomes policy. Such a mix would avoid, to the greatest extent possible, sharp movements in interest rates and exchange rates and would minimize both the domestic costs of adjustment and the export of instability abroad.

Reserve Assets and Fund Lending

Even though the world economy is under flexible exchange rates, reserve use has been extensive. Chart 3 shows, for example, cumulative foreign exchange market intervention by the Federal Republic of Germany starting in the second quarter of 1973. In the context of reserve assets, two areas of discussion appear immediately: the role of the dollar and of substitution facilities, on the one hand, and the creation and allocation of new reserve assets and credit, on the other.

CHART 3. FEDERAL REPUBLIC OF GERMANY: CUMULATIVE FOREIGN EXCHANGE MARKET INTERVENTION, SECOND QUARTER 1973–FOURTH QUARTER 1982
(In billions of deutsche mark; second quarter 1973 = 0)

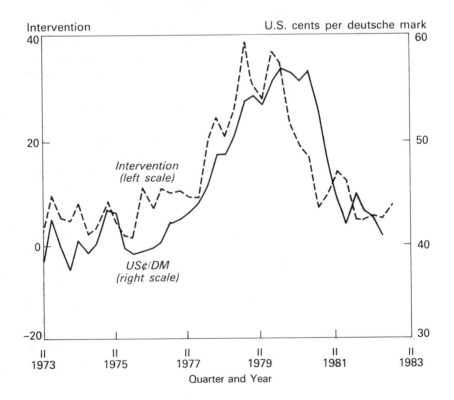

The dollar has been strong, and accordingly there have been no calls for a substitution facility recently. But, of course, when and if the current dollar overvaluation is undone, that issue will arise once again. I believe it is important to distinguish sharply between the inframarginal and the marginal dollar. The problem is to manage the marginal dollar, not the inframarginal one. Just as sterilized intervention is appropriate in the case of private portfolio shifts between currencies, so it is in the context of official portfolio shifts. All this presupposes, naturally, that one accepts the proposition that central banks, just like any individual speculator, should be allowed to make waves in world financial markets. The point of drawing the distinction between marginal and inframarginal portfolio dollars is to indicate that an effective substitution facility is really an intervention account. To make the system effective, an agency such as the Fund would have to be in a position to reshuffle the currency composition of international debt—for example, buying dollar treasury bills and selling yen or deutsche mark treasury bills. Freezing a lot of dollars in some account would not be an effective way of operating a substitution facility.

The international debt crisis has made it clear that the Fund needs ample resources to cope with system-wide payments imbalances that defy correction in the short term and thus threaten the world capital market. Increased Fund lending under conditionality can help ensure there will be no outright debt default. But there is continuing concern that conditionality may be excessive or misdirected. One cheerfully applauds the notion that budget deficits should be corrected in deficit countries and that their imports should be cut to provide foreign exchange to pay interest on their debts. Still, insufficient attention is being paid to the adjustments of external balances through real depreciation, maintaining employment. Moreover, there is even less attention being paid to the system-wide implications of the current debt crises. Clearly, world expansion and liberalized market access are alternatives to deeper recessions in the adjusting countries. The current international financial system, by placing the burden of adjustment on deficit countries, aggravates the employment costs of world disturbances. This must be viewed as a highly undesirable feature, especially when it is remembered that all these problems were, in large measure, caused by the macroeconomic policies of the center countries.

János Fekete

Professor Willett's paper provides an excellent basis for discussion of the topics to be explored by the introductory panel. Its actively polemic approach, its in-depth examination of the pros and cons of different exchange rates regimes, and, not least, its pointing out of the deficiencies of economic theory and analysis in adequately explaining many current problems, should all stimulate further thinking.

Within the necessarily limited space allowed for a discussant's paper, it is, of course, impossible to discuss extensively the wide range of issues analyzed by the author, especially when views are considerably divergent. Instead, I will try in what follows to focus on the evaluation of the current financial regime and to draw some conclusions for the future.

A major theme of Professor Willett's paper is the examination of the reasons for controversies over international monetary questions. The author arrives at the conclusion (p. 35) that "there is such a vast range of both normative and positive reasons for differing evaluations of international monetary questions that controversy will always be with us and ... its presence per se cannot be taken as a strong indication that the system is not working fairly well." I would certainly agree with that in a broad philosophical sense, but I fear that applying this proposition to the real world of international monetary problems may lead one toward the acceptance of the system existing at any given time.

Departing from the positive criteria of *economic efficiency*, the author concludes it is difficult to draw strong conclusions about the contributions of alternative exchange rate regimes toward both microeconomic and macroeconomic stability. In evaluating the performance of different exchange rate regimes using these criteria, the author proceeds to discuss each criterion in the context of diverse monetary problems and episodes. The latter are used to support arguments for and against a given exchange rate regime. The following phrase (p. 32) is quite characteristic of the author's approach: "It is easy to construct scenarios in which a particular disturbance or pattern of disturbances, combined with particular assumptions about the structure of the economy, can make either fixed or flexible exchange rates more inflationary or less conducive to the stability of output."

It should not be forgotten, however, that the international monetary system is not a collection of constructed scenarios and assumptions but is a framework in which real countries, with different real problems and levels of development, coexist. Thus, we should draw a clear distinction between scientific discussion either not, or only indirectly, influenced by divergent national interests, and discussions between government representatives. It is the latter which are relevant to the soundness or unsoundness of the system. It is quite natural that in a community of creditors and debtors, for instance, there constantly are "apples of discord." As the balance of payments positions of countries change, their views on different issues may change too.

From the standpoint of economic efficiency, the regime of flexible exchange rates is, in my view, a source of serious difficulties, on both microeconomic and macroeconomic levels, that cannot easily be sidestepped. The exaggerated and unpredictable volatility of exchange rates, which are dominated by forces independent of the basic performance of the economy, leads to misdirection of trade and misallocation of resources, as well as to caution in international operations and pressures for protectionism. No less devastating are the effects of exchange rates misaligned over an extensive period. Difficulties in formulating an exact definition of a misaligned exchange rate should not serve as pretexts for minimizing the importance of the problem; on the contrary, they present a challenge to economic theory and analysis and should spur further research.

Using the *negative criterion* of avoidance or minimization of the instabilities generated by the problems of international adjustment, liquidity, and confidence, *the author gives the present system high marks*—at least compared with the Bretton Woods system—though he concedes that these problems are not completely solved. The developments of the seventies do not seem to support this favorable judgment. There exists no effective mechanism either to assure balance of payments adjustment or to prevent the development and persistence of severe, chronic imbalances. Previous hopes that were attached to the floating regime in this regard have quickly faded.

Also, the explosion of uncontrolled liquidity composed mostly of short-term funds in the Euromarkets not only has introduced further instability into the system by facilitating quick, massive moves from one currency into another, but also has made it relatively easy for many debtor countries to finance their balance of payments deficits, and thus to delay taking the steps necessary to achieve structural adjustment. An aggravating factor has been that countries with active balances of payments over an extended period have usually been countries with low absorptive capacities, while those which had a strong propensity to import—the majority of the developing countries—were not able to export enough to pay for all of their imports, not least because of the low absorptive capacities of the others. The result was a self-destructive international distribution of income and labor.

The recycling of these funds carried out primarily by the commercial banking system was, in itself, a positive phenomenon but it has only postponed the problem, which emerged recently as the present debt crisis. The assertion that the system has proved to have a great shock-absorbing capacity is questionable: the market, which took care of recycling in the past has now reached its limits.

I fully share the opinion of the author that (p. 21) "it is important to make clear one's standard of comparison." The proof of the pudding is, after all, in the eating. When we compare the present system—or, more exactly, nonsystem—of floating to Bretton Woods, we hardly can ignore the striking differences in their respective performances. While the volume of world trade grew at an average rate of 8.5 percent a year during 1962-72, the average annual increase was 5.9 percent during 1972-76, 4.6 percent during 1976-1980 and since 1980 has decreased—for the first time since World War II—at an average annual rate of approximately 2 percent. Prospects for improvements in 1983 are slim. The same comparisons of performance can be made for world economic growth, employment, price stability, and so on. All of them will be unfavorable for the present system.

It is perfectly clear that it is not possible to draw far-reaching conclusions based on this empirical evidence alone. But while the international monetary system is far from the sole component influencing the functioning of the world economy, it is certainly a major one, especially when, as at present, world interdependence is growing.

Nevertheless, the breakdown of the Bretton Woods system provided clear evidence of its serious inherent problems. The conclusion we should draw from this evidence, however, is not that a system of fixed exchange rates with a key currency linked to gold is not sustainable or effective but rather that *the national currency of one country*—even one as large as the United States—cannot, in a world characterized by new power relations, play the role of key currency any longer. Whenever national interests are in conflict with international obligations, one cannot expect a central bank to give priority to the international commitments of the country against its national interest. The author's analysis of the reasons for the breakdown of Bretton Woods provides support for this argument: it was, indeed, the overheating of the U.S. economy, induced by the way the Viet Nam War was financed, that ultimately led to the breakdown of the system. This is one more example of the curious phenomenon of the same analysis leading to quite different conclusions.

Concerning the political considerations, much emphasis is put, throughout the paper, on the difficulties in bringing about international monetary cooperation that are primarily caused by the reluctance of governments to cede authority to international bodies, thus reducing their freedom in the field of domestic economic policy. The proposition is advanced that an increase of international monetary cooperation would, therefore, be less than optimal from the standpoint of economic efficiency. Later, when evaluating the current system, the author states (p. 36) that: "To date, international cooperation under our current loose system has been sufficient to avoid the major disasters many of the critics of the Jamaica agreements foresaw." Thus, a *substantial* increase in international cooperation and control is, in the author's view, neither feasible nor necessary.

Part of a counterargument to this reasoning is given by the author's own words (p. 34): "we must guard against becoming so overwhelmed by the practical difficulties of decision making that we become excessively complacent and view any status quo short of disaster as being optimal from a practical perspective." This warning also applies in my opinion, to collective decision making.

The reluctance of governments to increase international cooperation is, indeed, one of the main reasons why the present system of monetary disorder has prevailed for so long. Floating, we should remember, was initially introduced as a temporary emergency regime. It has led, together with diverging nationalistic domestic policies—the other side of the same coin— to the present situation. The world economy today is bogged down in a major financial and economic crisis.

In face of this situation, our tasks should be divided into two parts so that they can be carried out as effectively as possible. *In the present and the short term*, the most urgent problems—among them the debt crisis— should be solved within the framework of the existing system, with increased involvement of the international organizations. In this respect, I agree with most of the recommendations of the author. The political support and consensus for such actions seem to exist. *In the medium and long terms*, however, it is clear that superficial, ex post treatment will not be enough to prevent such a situation from reoccurring.

While I sincerely share the author's wishes of good luck to the international monetary system, I am afraid that "to keep our fingers crossed that conflicts of national objectives and/or international financial crises do not produce greater strains than the system can handle" (p. 38) is not the best strategy in the current situation, and is not enough.

A substantial reform aimed at restoring order in international finance in order to help to get the world economy back on the path of sustained growth, price stability, and full employment should become the order of the day. This reform should make the international monetary system universal— with the institutional participation of the socialist countries, which account for about 30 percent of world industrial production—and should ensure a better distribution of resources among rich and poor countries. (The distribution issue is referred to by the author; however, I believe it deserves more attention than he gives it.)

In any new financial system worthy of the name, a strengthened International Monetary Fund should certainly be a pivotal institution. The special drawing right should become the internationally managed key currency and linked to gold, thus exempt from the problems of a national paper currency. Gold should serve as a numéraire as well as backing for the international currency, with the exact relationship to be defined by the Fund.

I fully share the view that (p. 37) "the best prospects for improved global economic stability rest with better management of national economic policies." But domestic policies will not change without international coordination and some form of control. It is to be hoped that the present crisis will help countries to realize that such control does not necessarily lead to less, but rather to more, freedom for national governments to solve their own countries' problems. Indeed, such freedom must be achieved by concerted actions necessary to solve the common problems of an interdependent world. The seeming antagonism between national freedom and international cooperation and control reminds me of the Marxist thesis, "freedom is recognized necessity."

Alexander K. Swoboda

We would all agree that the world economy has performed much less well in the late 1970s and early 1980s than it did in the 1950s and, especially, the 1960s. Yet we cannot seem to agree on whether the current international monetary system is an advance over the preceding one—that is, on whether floating rates are serving us badly or well. The problem is that the outcomes we observe can be attributed to a variety of causes. The coincidence of the changeover from the Bretton Woods system to the present one with high inflation, low growth, massive payments imbalances, financial instability, and rising debt problems provides few clues as to causation. This, of course, is the essence of the difficulty in evaluating the functioning of any monetary arrangement: we do not know what part of the behavior of economic variables is to be attributed to the monetary regime in existence. Nor do we know how these variables would have behaved under another regime.

Any evaluation will, in these circumstances, be a matter of judgment. That judgment will be, implicitly or explicitly, based on some criteria. A major portion of Professor Willett's paper is devoted to a listing and survey of possible criteria for evaluating the performance of the international monetary system. The list is a standard one: an international monetary system is to be judged by whether it promotes economic efficiency; allows for macroeconomic stability; solves system issues such as the triad of adjustment, liquidity, and confidence problems, and by how it deals with distributional concerns and political considerations.

The answer, not surprisingly, is it all depends on circumstances. This we know from standard open-economy models as well as from the optimum currency area literature. That literature, which Willett surveys at some length, finds that there is not much to choose between fixed and flexible exchange rates in models that display homogeneity. On the other hand, when there are short-run rigidities, everything depends on the origin and nature of shocks as well as on the information at the disposal of the public and the authorities. The same type of conclusion emerges with respect to the welfare effects of alternative exchange rate regimes from the explicit utility-maximizing models of the overlapping-generation variety: with complete markets and symmetry of information, and without rigidities, both fixed and flexible exchange rates can lead to efficient outcomes, though allocations may differ, depending on the specific regime (monetary rule) postulated. Here again, as Helpman and Razin (1982) have shown, some sand must be thrown into the machine (e.g., incomplete contingent markets) for the systems' welfare implications to differ. The upshot is that no strong conclusions as to whether fixed or flexible rates are to be preferred can be drawn on purely analytical grounds. The resulting agnosticism is well represented in Willett's paper. To quote but one typical example (p. 19): "As the previous discussion illustrates, it is difficult to draw strong conclusions about the contributions of alternative international monetary regimes to macroeconomic stability."

Yet Willett does come to definite conclusions about our present international monetary system. It has, in his view, served us well: the adoption of more flexible exchange rates has contributed significantly to providing a solution to the adjustment, confidence, and international liquidity problems. The system, to be sure, is not perfect. But no massive reform efforts are required, although marginal improvements should be sought. The first question I wish to ask is what the basis for Willett's judgment is. I will then touch briefly on rules versus discretion, credibility, and the degree of cooperation required under alternative systems.

An international monetary system (IMS) can, according to Willett, be characterized by three features or, if you prefer, by the way it discharges three functions: the prevailing exchange rate regime and the adjustment process it entails; the mechanism for international liquidity creation and balance of payments financing; and the structure of international decision-making authority. An IMS is, of course, much more than this, and one might have wished for a fuller description of the present system. Be that as it may, Willett's discussion concentrates mainly on the first of these features, the exchange rate regime.

On the exchange rate regime, the discussion reflects what may be termed the conventional wisdom of the strengths and weaknesses of the Bretton Woods system and of the successor regime. In Willett's view, Bretton Woods broke down because of a bias against the use of both macroeconomic policy and exchange rate changes as instruments for the pursuit of external balance which, coupled with increasing capital mobility, made the exchange rate system increasingly crisis-prone. Inadequate growth of gold production and increasing use of the dollar as a reserve asset created the Triffin dilemma. And the refusal to adopt an outright dollar standard or tighter criteria for adjustment, coupled with unduly expansionary policy in the United States, meant that the breakdown was inevitable. Given countries' unwillingness to cede national macroeconomic autonomy to international decision making, the current system is the only possible one and, on the whole, a satisfactory one. To quote Willett (page 36):

> The adoption of greater exchange rate flexibility has made substantial contributions to reducing important aspects of the international liquidity, confidence, and adjustment problems. Except for very small, open economies, exchange rate changes are an effective (although certainly not a painless) instrument of balance of payments adjustment, and greater exchange rate flexibility has helped to reduce the problem of deciding how mutual adjustment responsibilities should be shared. Likewise, flexible rates have reduced (although, of course, they have not eliminated) the incentives for reserve switching compared with those existing under the adjustable peg and have given countries greater scope to protect themselves from excessive international liquidity creation.

One can take issue both with the conventional interpretation of the breakdown of Bretton Woods and with Willett's sanguine view of the strengths of the current system.

I would question the view that excessive rigidity of exchange rates or lack of convergence of inflation rates was the most important or basic reason for the breakdown of Bretton Woods. I would rather emphasize failure to accept the *logic* of the fixed-exchange-rate system and lack of agreement as to the mechanism governing the supply of international reserves and its implications for the macroeconomic evolution of the world economy.[1] That is, the main problem was not that individual exchange rates were getting increasingly out of line; if anything, the system forced national inflation rates into line with existing nominal exchange rates. It was the inflation rates that became unacceptable to a number of countries—inflation rates that were, themselves, broadly governed by the rate of expansion of international reserves. That rate of expansion, in turn, was broadly and jointly determined by the rate of U.S. monetary expansion and the rest of the world's rate of domestic credit expansion as a consequence of existing reserve-holding arrangements.[2] The crucial question, therefore, was to secure an appropriate (acceptable) stance of U.S. monetary policy and constraints on dollar accumulation by the rest of the world. A cosmopolitan

---

[1] For a summary of this view and some supporting empirical evidence, see Genberg and Swoboda (1982 a).

[2] It is important to note that, according to that view, the world rate of monetary expansion is, in the long run, largely determined by U.S. monetary policy, but the rate of growth of international reserves is *not*. The latter rate of growth is endogenous and is jointly determined by the U.S. rate of monetary expansion and the rest of the world's rate of domestic credit expansion, among other factors.

stance of the nth country and the link of its currency to gold (however loose) at an appropriate price were two means of achieving such agreement. Failure to find a jointly acceptable control mechanism for the supply of international reserves under the fixed-exchange-rate Bretton Woods system spelled its demise.

Note that these two contrasting views of the breakdown of the Bretton Woods system are not incompatible. It is, indeed, true that capital mobility exacerbates the problems created by macroeconomic policies that go counter to the requirements of external balance. And such policies make maintenance of fixed rates well-nigh impossible. Note also that the statement that a fixed rate system can work (and may be preferable in terms of transparence of commitments, simplicity of required rules, short-run stability of relative prices and of some asset prices, etc.) is not equivalent to proposing adaption of, or return to, such a system. The conditions for fixed rates to work properly may not be met and, in that case, a floating rate system may well be preferable and more viable. The shift of emphasis in explaining the breakdown of Bretton Woods, however, is important in evaluating both the prospects for, and the requirements of, a properly working system of fixed rates. The conventional view emphasizes the need for frequent adjustments of exchange rates at the expense of explicit provisions for the composition and growth of international liquidity. The opposing view emphasizes liquidity creation mechanisms and, if anything, would argue that nominal exchange rates remain fixed, save in extreme circumstances. The two views also have different implications for the nature and required degree of international cooperation, a point to which I return briefly below.

Turning to Willett's case for the present system, I find it not entirely convincing for two main reasons. The first is that Willett's case for the present system is essentially a case against the preceding one. Little evidence is provided to document the claimed contributions of the present system to solving the adjustment, liquidity, and confidence problems. Such evidence is indeed difficult to provide, as I stated earlier. This does not entirely justify the standard practice of judging the virtues of one system by the defects of another.

What, then, are the virtues of the present system? In Willett's view, they are mainly that "greater exchange rate flexibility has improved the operation of the adjustment process, both by offering many countries the easier use of an effective means of adjustment and by reducing the political biases against adjustment which existed under the par value system" (page 9; compare this with the statement quoted before). One may question the contribution of exchange rate flexibility to adjustment on both analytical and factual grounds. On analytical grounds, adjustment is a matter of bringing absorption into line with income, given a sustainable inward or outward transfer of capital. The contribution of exchange rate changes to easing that process depends essentially, as the optimum currency area debate makes clear, on money illusion or rigidities, the existence of which cannot be relied upon systematically. Moreover, it is possible to show that the correlations one observes between nominal and real exchange rate variations, and between the latter and output and the balance of trade do not necessarily imply a systematically exploitable trade-off between nominal exchange rates and the variables that should adjust.[3] Finally, and perhaps unfairly, payments imbalances in recent years have reached proportions that cast doubt on the adequacy of adjustment under managed flexibility.

I find the case for the present system, as it is made by Willett—and by most of us, for that matter—not entirely satisfactory for a second reason. The current system's main virtue seems to be that it is the only workable system given existing political constraints. Flexible exchange rates resolve policy conflicts in the marketplace and thus require less cooperation to work than a fixed rate system. This is, indeed, a positive feature of flexible rates, but one should be careful not to elevate feasibility to virtue. This is recognized by Willett (though he does not always heed his own warning) in the following passage (page 34): "we must guard against becoming so overwhelmed by the practical difficulties of decision making that we become excessively complacent and view any status quo short of disaster as being optimal from a practical perspective."

That floating rates require less explicit policy cooperation than fixed rates to be viable seems an eminently reasonable proposition. It is well to remember, however, that severe constraints must be placed on national economic policies for a system of floating rates to work properly—that is, in stable fashion—rather than simply remaining viable. The first step in achieving a properly working international monetary system is to recognize both political and economic realities. Here, Willett's list of common analytical fallacies is indeed a useful and perceptive one. To his list, I would add a number of points.

First, as already mentioned, exchange rate flexibility is no substitute for basic macroeconomic adjustment. Failure to undertake adjustment will lead to the breakdown of a fixed-exchange-rate system; it will lead to unstable exchange rates under floating. In other words, adjustment is required whatever IMS prevails. Second, the nth country problem arises under managed floating as well as under fixed rates. Under the latter regime, the nth country's monetary policy need not be aimed at external balance; what the country does with its monetary policy will tend to deter-

---

[3]See Saidi and Swoboda (1983) for a model that demonstrates the point and provides some empirical evidence.

mine the world price level (and possibly economic activity in the short run); this is why it is important that its policy be compatible with the requirements of the rest of the world. Under managed floating, a similar problem arises: the nth country should refrain from having an exchange rate target lest inconsistencies arise. This is why it is both legitimate for the United States not to intervene in foreign exchange markets and for the rest of the world to ascertain its stake in, and concern for, the course of macroeconomic policy in the reserve-issuing country.

Third, floating exchange rates do not automatically make for macroeconomic independence among countries. A growing analytical and empirical literature has emphasized the channels of transmission of business cycles across countries and hinted at the existence of a world business cycle, independent of the exchange rate regime.[4] This literature lends support to two notions. The first is that the degree of coordination of policies that is required for the smooth functioning of a system of floating rates may be as high as, or higher than, that required for a system of fixed exchange rates. The second is that the main contribution of floating rates to policy independence is allowing differences in trend inflation rates across countries. This raises the question of why countries should want different inflation rates. Fiscal considerations are one reason, differences in political or social systems another.

This leaves open the requirements for a stable floating rate system and the constraints they entail for national macroeconomic policy. In a previous paper, Hans Genberg and I (see Genberg and Swoboda (1982 b)) have argued that these requirements may be as difficult to meet as those for a stable fixed rate system. Our conjecture is that stability of a floating rate system requires some form of effective precommitment of national economic policies. In other words, some precommitted rule should govern the future path of monetary (and fiscal) policy. The rule need not be a fixed-growth rule but may involve feedback relationships to output, inflation, or the exchange rate itself.

The argument for precommitment is based on two considerations. First, the asset-market view of exchange rate determination emphasizes that current exchange rates depend on expectations of future events, including future policy. The benefit of a rule would be to simplify the forecasting problem of economic agents, since the path of future monetary policy would be subjected to less arbitrary variation. Commitment to the rule must, of course, be credible. The second consideration takes the work of Kydland and Prescott (1977) and of Barro and Gordon (1981) as its point of departure. We advance three conjectures in this context. First, the pursuit of a

---

[4]See Dornbusch (1983) and Swoboda (1983) for examples.

time-consistent discretionary policy will tend to lead to excessive inflation in each floating country. Second, to the extent that the optimal policy turns out to be time-inconsistent, the volatility of exchange rates may be increased as a result of the unpredictability of future policy. Third, since floating rates are not entirely insulating, "misbehavior" on the part of other countries will have undesirable consequences for the domestic economy. Such misbehavior may involve the pursuit of optimal discretionary policy; it may also involve exploitation by one country of the knowledge that another is following a previously announced rule for its policy. The resulting game-type behavior may further exacerbate instability. In other words, it is necessary that all major countries pursue precommitted policy rules for the system as a whole to function properly.

The thrust of the argument above is that credible precommitment of macroeconomic policies may well be essential to the proper functioning of any international monetary system. One major issue in evaluating the strengths of alternative systems then becomes the requirement for credible precommitment of policies as well as the likelihood that credibility can be achieved. In this respect, "in-between" systems such as "stable but adjustable" pegs may well be more difficult to operate in a stabilizing manner than either pure floating or fixed rate systems. Be that as it may, the moral to be drawn from this discussion is that arguments to the effect that precommitments are not politically feasible do not constitute a case for an international monetary system based on flexible rather than on fixed exchange rates. Credibility of commitments to some form of policy rule is as crucial to the functioning of one system as it is to the functioning of the other.

REFERENCES

Barro, Robert J., and David B. Gordon, *A Positive Theory of Monetary Growth in a Natural-Rate Model*, National Bureau of Economic Research, Working Paper No. 807 (November 1981).

Dornbusch, Rudiger, "Flexible Exchange Rates and Interdependence," International Monetary Fund, *Staff Papers*, Vol. 30 (March 1983), pp. 3-30.

Genberg, Hans, and Alexander K. Swoboda (1982 a), "Gold and the Dollar: Asymmetries in the World Money Stock Determination, 1959-1971," Chapter 15 in *The International Monetary System under Flexible Exchange Rates*, ed. by Richard N. Cooper and others (Cambridge, Massachusetts: Ballinger, 1982), pp. 235-57.

_____(1982 b), "Fixed Exchange Rates, Flexible Exchange Rates, or the Middle of the Road: A Reexamination of the Arguments in View of Recent Experience," paper presented at the Wingspread Conference on The Evolving International Financial System (Racine, Wisconsin, 1982).

Helpman, Elhanan, and Assaf Razin, "Comparison of Exchange Rate Reserves in the Presence of Imperfect Capital Markets," *International Economic Review*, Vol. 23 (June 1982), pp. 365–88.

Kydland, Finn E., and Edward C. Prescott, "Rules Rather than Discretion: The Inconsistency of Optimal Plans," *Journal of Political Economy*, Vol. 85 (June 1977), pp. 473–91.

Saidi, Nasser, and Alexander K. Swoboda, "Nominal and Real Exchange Rates: Issues and Some Evidence," Chapter 1 in Emil Claassen and Pascal Salin, eds., *Recent Issues in the Theory of Flexible Exchange Rates* (Amsterdam: North-Holland, 1983), pp. 3–27.

Swoboda, Alexander K., "Exchange Rate Regimes and U.S.-European Policy Interdependence," International Monetary Fund, *Staff Papers*, Vol. 30 (March 1983), pp. 75–102.

2

International Liquidity and Monetary Control

JACOB A. FRENKEL*

This paper deals with the relations among international liquidity, the exchange rate regime, and the effectiveness of monetary policy. A typical argument for the choice of a flexible exchange rate regime is that such a regime provides countries with an added degree of freedom in the pursuit of macroeconomic policies. It is claimed that the added degree of freedom (or the added policy instrument) stems from the elimination of the legal commitment to peg the exchange rate, and, therefore, that the adoption of a flexible rate regime reduces the need for international reserves. In practice, however, one of the striking features of the international monetary system since the early 1970s has been the continued use of international reserves even though, legally, countries could have adopted flexible exchange rate regimes. In spite of the change in the legal framework associated with the breakdown of the Bretton Woods agreement and formalized by the Second Amendment to the Articles of Agreement of the International Monetary Fund, countries have continued to use international reserves and have continued to intervene in the markets for foreign exchange. As a matter of fact, an observer of the pattern of countries' holdings and uses of international reserves would be hard pressed to detect a drastic change in those patterns corresponding to the drastic legal change. The change in economic behavior has been much less pronounced

*I am indebted to Craig S. Hakkio, Lauren Feinstone, and Helen Roberts for helpful comments and assistance and to the National Science Foundation for financial support (Grant No. SES 78-11480-A01). This research is part of the National Bureau of Economic Research's research program in International Studies and Economic Fluctuations. Any opinions expressed are my own and not necessarily those of the National Bureau of Economic Research.

than might have been expected on the basis of theory concerning the benefits from the additional degree of freedom provided by the flexible exchange rate regime.

Section I reports the results of an empirical study of the demand for international reserves during 1963-79. The main findings are that (i) a country's holdings of international reserves can be characterized with reasonable accuracy as a stable function of a limited number of economic variables, and (ii) the move to greater flexibility of exchange rates has not fundamentally changed the general patterns of reserve holdings. It therefore follows that, in contrast to earlier predictions, the questions concerning the provision of international reserves and the discussions concerning the role of the International Monetary Fund in this context are as relevant now as they were during the Bretton Woods era.

Section II extends the scope of the discussion to the more general issue of the constraints that the openness of the economy imposes on the effectiveness and proper conduct of monetary policy, as well as the dependence of these constraints on the exchange rate regime. Section III discusses the question of whether the monetary authorities possess the capacity to sterilize the monetary implications of the balance of payments and the monetary implications of interventions in the foreign exchange market. This question is relevant when one is attempting to determine the extent to which monetary control can be regained in view of the international constraints. In this context, a distinction is drawn between sterilized and nonsterilized interventions.

The discussion in Sections II and III deals with the influence that external constraints exert on the effectiveness of monetary control. Section IV turns the question on its head by examining ways in which monetary policy can influence the external constraint. Issues that are discussed in this context include the role that monetary policy should play in affecting exchange rates, as well as the role that exchange rates should play in guiding monetary policy. Here it is argued that policymakers can use information provided by the foreign exchange market in order to improve the conduct of monetary policy. Thus, it is argued, while the openness of the economy imposes severe constraints on the effectiveness of monetary controls, it also provides a potentially useful source of information.

Section V concludes the paper with a brief discussion of the role of the International Monetary Fund as well as some proposals for institutional reform.

I. INTERNATIONAL RESERVES

This section analyzes the determinants and the patterns of reserve holdings under alternative exchange rate regimes. It contains an empirical analysis of the demand for international reserves in which cross-sectional estimates of the demand for reserves by developed and developing countries, as well as estimates of pooled time series and cross sections, are presented. In this context, the differences in behavior patterns of developed and developing countries are analyzed. The analysis then turns to the empirical question of timing—that is, of when the system moved from pegged to floating rates. The interest in this question stems from the belief that the timing of changes in economic behavior need not correspond to, or be associated with, the timing of changes in legal commitments. One of the conclusions that emerges from the analysis is that the change in economic behavior (as far as holdings of international reserves are concerned) has not been as extensive as might have been expected.

Determinants of Demand for International Reserves

Earlier studies of the demand for reserves considered the variability of international receipts and payments as an important argument in the demand function (see, for example, Kenen and Yudin (1965), Clower and Lipsey (1968), and Archibald and Richmond (1971)). In addition, other studies have suggested that the demand function also depends on the propensity to import (see, for example, Heller (1966), Kelly (1970), Clark (1970 a), Flanders (1971), Frenkel (1974 a, 1974 b, 1978), Hipple (1974), and Iyoha (1976)). These and other studies have recently been surveyed by Grubel (1971), Williamson (1973), Claassen (1974), Cohen (1975), and Cumby (1983); and the general issues of the role of, and needs for, international liquidity were discussed in International Monetary Fund (1970).

The choice of a variability measure as an argument in the demand function stems directly from the role of international reserves in serving as a buffer stock to accommodate fluctuations in external transactions. Consequently, it has generally been assumed that the demand for reserves is positively associated with the extent of these fluctuations.

The rationale for the use of the propensity to import as an argument is more involved. It stems from an application of the Keynesian model of the foreign trade multiplier. According to that model, an external disequilibrium that is induced by a decline in export earnings could be corrected by a decline in output proportional to the multiplier. The cost of output adjustment can be saved if the monetary authorities are able to run down their stock of international reserves, thereby enabling them to finance the external deficit. Since the foreign-trade multiplier (and thus the required dampening of output owing to the fall in exports) is inversely related to the marginal propensity to import, this approach argues that the cost of not having reserves, and hence the demand for reserves, is *inversely* related to the marginal propensity to import (see, for example, Heller (1966)). In the absence of data on the marginal propensity to import, earlier empirical studies have replaced it by the ratio of imports to income—that is, by the average propensity to import (typically referred to as the degree of "openness" of the economy). The coefficient of the average propensity to import frequently appears with the "wrong" (positive) sign when used to estimate the demand for reserves. Thus, Hipple (1974) and Iyoha (1976) argue that the average import propensity should not be used as a proxy for the cost of output adjustment but rather as a proxy for "openness," thus measuring the extent to which the economy is vulnerable to external disruptions. Accordingly, the positive coefficient on the average import propensity reflects the fact that the demand for reserves is a positive function of external vulnerability.

Using an adjustment mechanism which emphasizes the role of relative prices, the price level, and the demand for money, it has been shown (Frenkel 1974 a) that under certain assumptions, the demand for reserves is associated positively with the average propensity to import. This association has also been shown to be consistent with data for 1963-67 for both developed and developing countries (Frenkel 1974 b). A simplified derivation of the association between reserve holdings and the propensity to import is presented in Frenkel (1978), where it is shown that the relationship between these two variables is, in general, not clear-cut (although under some assumptions, this relationship is expected to be positive).

In what follows, cross-sectional estimates of the demand for international reserves are presented. In addition to the above-mentioned variables, a scaling variable is included as one of the determinants of that demand.[1]

Cross-Sectional Estimates of Demand for International Reserves

The empirical analysis includes data from 22 developed countries for 1963-79 and 32 developing countries for 1963-77. Appendices I and II con-

---

[1] An additional variable which, in principle, should have been included in the list of the determinants of reserve holdings is the opportunity cost of holding reserves. In practice, a large fraction of international reserves is held in the form of short-term, interest-bearing assets, and thus the opportunity cost is the difference between the alternative yield and the rate of return on reserves. Previous studies faced serious difficulties in estimating this cost. Clark (1970 a) decided to exclude this variable from his estimation. Heller (1966) assumed that the cost was the same for all countries (5 percent). Kenen and Yudin (1965) used per capita income as a proxy and found that it had the "wrong" sign and was not significant. Kelly (1970) used, in addition to per capita income, the value of foreign assets and liabilities as proxies but found that in all cases the latter had the "wrong" signs while in some cases the former had the "wrong" signs. Courchene and Youssef (1967) used the long-term interest rate as a proxy and found that in five out of nine cases, its coefficient was not significantly negative. All these attempts taken together provided the rationale for not including this variable in the estimating equations. For an incorporation of the rate of interest into a stochastic framework, see Frenkel and Jovanovic (1981).

tain, respectively, the lists of countries and definitions of variables used in the analysis. The classification of countries as developed and developing is based on that developed by the International Monetary Fund. The choice of countries and the period of analysis were determined by the availability of continuous series of data.[2] As indicated above, the demand function was assumed to depend on three variables: (1) a measure of variability of international receipts and payments denoted by σ, the value of which was estimated for each year by computing the standard deviation over the previous 14 years of the trend-adjusted annual changes of the level of reserves;[3] (2) a scaling variable measuring the size of international transactions represented by the level of gross national product (GNP), Y (in the few cases where GNP was not available, it was replaced by gross domestic product (GDP)), and (3) the average propensity to import, $m = IM/Y$, where IM denotes imports.

The functional form of the demand function is assumed to be

$$\ln R_t = \alpha_0 + \alpha_1 \ln \sigma_t + \alpha_2 \ln Y_t + \alpha_3 \ln m_t + u_t \tag{1}$$

where u_t denotes an error term. Finally, and in contrast to most of the earlier empirical formulations, the demand for reserves is specified in *real* terms. Thus, as indicated in Appendix II, R_t denotes the real value of international reserves.

Tables 1 and 2 present for each year the cross-sectional, ordinary-least-squares estimates of the demand for reserves by developed and developing countries. In all cases, the coefficients have the expected positive sign; and in most cases, these coefficients are statistically significant at the 95 percent confidence level.

In summary, it should be noted that the overall fit of the regressions reported in Tables 1 and 2 (as measured by the coefficients of determination R^2) is very satisfactory. This point is noteworthy, since these results pertain to cross-sectional estimates. Of special interest is the good fit of the cross-sectional regressions for the last few years reported in Tables 1 and 2.[4] During the latter years of the sample period, the international

---

[2]From the list of countries for which data were available, two countries—Canada and the United States—were excluded from the analysis. Canada was excluded since it had a flexible exchange rate system during most of the period for which the variability measure was calculated. Since the discussion focuses on the behavior of countries as demanders of reserves, the exclusion of the United States as the main reserve supplier seems justified.

[3]As is indicated in Appendix II, in order to obtain a variability measure that is free of scale, the standard deviation of the trend-adjusted changes in reserves was divided by the value of imports.

[4]It is also noteworthy that in most cases the income elasticity of reserve holdings is about unity and is estimated with great precision. This suggests that a country's size is an important determinant of its reserve holdings. The unitary elasticity suggests that the dependence of the reserves/income ratio on the measures of variability and openness is similar to the dependence of reserve holdings on these measures.

TABLE 1. DEVELOPED COUNTRIES ($N = 22$): CROSS-SECTIONAL EQUATIONS FOR INTERNATIONAL RESERVES ESTIMATED USING ORDINARY LEAST SQUARES, 1963-79 [1]

Year	Constant	$\ln \sigma$	$\ln Y$	$\ln m$	R^2	Standard Error
1963	4.081 (0.678)	0.625 (0.198)	1.063 (0.086)	1.398 (0.295)	0.90	0.434
1964	4.240 (0.775)	0.607 (0.236)	1.012 (0.091)	1.348 (0.293)	0.88	0.477
1965	4.476 (0.876)	0.492 (0.270)	1.061 (0.103)	1.373 (0.333)	0.86	0.530
1966	4.415 (0.925)	0.592 (0.284)	1.100 (0.107)	1.634 (0.349)	0.86	0.542
1967	4.201 (0.918)	0.659 (0.282)	1.147 (0.109)	1.755 (0.350)	0.86	0.557
1968	4.184 (1.151)	0.580 (0.325)	1.151 (0.125)	1.602 (0.365)	0.85	0.588
1969	4.277 (0.970)	0.519 (0.270)	0.995 (0.109)	1.266 (0.319)	0.84	0.553
1970	3.985 (0.838)	0.574 (0.249)	1.016 (0.105)	1.196 (0.324)	0.85	0.536
1971	4.378 (0.785)	0.356 (0.243)	1.017 (0.105)	0.779 (0.340)	0.86	0.540
1972	3.572 (0.629)	0.742 (0.220)	0.943 (0.079)	1.014 (0.325)	0.90	0.425
1973	3.862 (0.675)	0.716 (0.275)	0.972 (0.093)	1.272 (0.446)	0.88	0.472
1974	3.083 (0.788)	0.872 (0.325)	1.061 (0.099)	1.581 (0.481)	0.88	0.526
1975	3.311 (0.941)	0.704 (0.349)	1.190 (0.135)	1.750 (0.601)	0.85	0.603
1976	3.260 (0.915)	0.816 (0.338)	1.139 (0.122)	1.923 (0.564)	0.85	0.582
1977	3.225 (0.608)	0.825 (0.216)	1.275 (0.082)	2.222 (0.340)	0.93	0.411
1978	4.382 (0.751)	0.306 (0.257)	1.113 (0.101)	1.256 (0.377)	0.88	0.552
1979	3.681 (0.670)	0.564 (0.222)	1.136 (0.085)	1.585 (0.298)	0.91	0.486

[1]Figures in parentheses are standard errors.

TABLE 2. DEVELOPING COUNTRIES ($N = 32$): CROSS-SECTIONAL EQUATIONS FOR INTERNATIONAL RESERVES ESTIMATED USING ORDINARY LEAST SQUARES, 1963-77 [1]

Year	Constant	$\ln \sigma$	$\ln Y$	$\ln m$	R^2	Standard Error
1963	5.724 (0.663)	0.297 (0.174)	1.244 (0.108)	1.895 (0.294)	0.84	0.523
1964	5.641 (0.705)	0.241 (0.190)	1.196 (0.116)	1.732 (0.299)	0.80	0.553
1965	5.529 (0.635)	0.189 (0.179)	1.125 (0.116)	1.412 (0.293)	0.79	0.539
1966	4.866 (0.710)	0.380 (0.201)	1.114 (0.139)	1.509 (0.359)	0.73	0.627
1967	4.108 (0.830)	0.586 (0.223)	1.253 (0.174)	1.697 (0.431)	0.70	0.753
1968	4.518 (0.737)	0.425 (0.193)	1.215 (0.147)	1.526 (0.352)	0.74	0.684
1969	4.531 (0.748)	0.297 (0.204)	1.206 (0.135)	1.244 (0.317)	0.77	0.655
1970	4.212 (0.796)	0.293 (0.222)	1.207 (0.141)	1.077 (0.327)	0.76	0.719
1971	4.810 (0.826)	0.240 (0.235)	1.237 (0.134)	1.312 (0.312)	0.77	0.684
1972	4.981 (0.713)	0.269 (0.203)	1.232 (0.109)	1.330 (0.249)	0.83	0.592
1973	3.747 (0.614)	0.549 (0.187)	1.191 (0.093)	1.148 (0.214)	0.86	0.537
1974	2.872 (0.774)	0.703 (0.257)	1.103 (0.118)	0.995 (0.280)	0.78	0.700
1975	3.328 (0.665)	0.603 (0.205)	1.070 (0.125)	1.142 (0.281)	0.75	0.737
1976	3.623 (0.753)	0.462 (0.224)	1.158 (0.134)	1.007 (0.293)	0.74	0.807
1977	3.383 (0.803)	0.569 (0.255)	1.141 (0.133)	1.072 (0.296)	0.76	0.759

[1]Figures in parentheses are standard errors.

monetary system moved towards a greater flexibility of exchange rates. This move was expected to result in different as well as less stable estimates of the parameters of demand for reserves. Since, as will be shown below, the cross-sectional estimates seem to have remained stable (at least during 1963-72 and 1973-79), more efficient estimates may be obtained by pooling the time series with cross sections.

Pooled Time Series and Cross Sections—Pegged Versus Floating Exchange Rates

In order to examine the effect of the move to a flexible exchange rate regime, the sample was divided into the pegged exchange rate period (1963–72) and the flexible exchange rate period (1973–79). A formal justification for this division will be provided later on in this paper.

To the extent that the coefficients of the cross-sectional equations remained stable within 1963–72 and 1973–79, one may obtain more efficient estimates by pooling the time series with the cross sections. Table 3 contains the ordinary-least-squares estimates of the pooled regressions for both periods. In all cases, the coefficients are positive and significant at the 95 percent confidence level.

I turn now to a comparison of the regression coefficients of developed and developing countries during the two periods. The first method used for this comparison was the dummy variables method outlined by Gujarti (1970). According to this method, each and every coefficient was allowed to differ between developed and developing countries by including dummy variables pertaining to developed country data. The estimated coefficients of the dummy variables (not reported here) reveal that for the first period, the coefficients of the constant term and of income are significantly lower for developed countries, while the developed country coefficient of the vari-

TABLE 3. DEVELOPED AND DEVELOPING COUNTRIES: POOLED TIME-SERIES AND CROSS-SECTIONAL EQUATIONS FOR INTERNATIONAL RESERVES ESTIMATED USING ORDINARY LEAST SQUARES [1]

Period	Group	Constant	$\ln \sigma$	$\ln Y$	$\ln m$	R^2	Standard Error
1963–72	Developed countries	4.108 (0.249)	0.594 (0.074)	1.059 (0.039)	1.353 (0.100)	0.85	0.504
	Developing countries	4.848 (0.225)	0.317 (0.062)	1.191 (0.040)	1.428 (0.099)	0.76	0.623
1973–77	Developed countries	3.381 (0.361)	0.750 (0.137)	1.106 (0.049)	1.619 (0.219)	0.85	0.543
	Developing countries	3.346 (0.310)	0.575 (0.096)	1.114 (0.518)	1.020 (0.117)	0.77	0.694
1973–79	Developed countries	3.615 (0.290)	0.636 (0.105)	1.105 (0.038)	1.520 (0.160)	0.86	0.532

[1]Figures in parentheses are standard errors.

ability measure is higher. For the latter period, however, the behavior of the two groups with respect to international reserves is much more similar.

The dummy variables method focuses on comparisons between individual coefficients. The second method that was employed in the comparison between developed and developing countries was that of the Chow test, the results of which lead to the conclusion that the difference between the international reserve-holding behavior of developed and developing countries diminished significantly during the second period. It is of interest to explore in greater detail the patterns of the move to the floating rate regime that are implied by the characteristics of reserve holdings.

International Reserves and Change in Regime

The analysis in the previous sections made a distinction between 1963-72 and 1973-79. The presumption was that the evolution of the international monetary system from pegged exchange rates to floating exchange rates might have resulted in a structural change in the demand for international reserves. The present section formally examines the timing and extent of the structural change following the method proposed by Quandt (1958, 1960).[5]

Consider a situation in which a structural change occurred in year t^* within the period $1, \ldots, T$ and assume that the demand for reserves corresponding to the two regimes (before and after t^*) can be characterized by two distinct regression equations such as equations (2) and (3)

$$y_{it} = x_{it}' \beta_1 + u_{1it}, \qquad t \leq t^* \tag{2}$$

$$y_{it} = x_{it}' \beta_2 + u_{2it}, \qquad t > t^* \tag{3}$$

where u_{1it} and u_{2it} denote the error terms that are assumed to be distributed as $N(0, \sigma_1^2)$ and $N(0, \sigma_2^2)$; and β_1 and β_2 denote the vectors of the regression coefficients corresponding to the two regimes; and $i = 1, \ldots, N$ denotes the countries (for the developed countries, $N = 22$; and for the developing countries, $N = 32$). The analysis of the timing of the structural change amounts to searching for the value of t^*. Quandt's method of estimating t^* involves the following: first, a maximization of the likelihood function (4) conditional on t^*

---

[5]For this and other methods of analyzing switching regressions, see Goldfeld and Quandt (1976, Chapters 1 and 4). The same procedure was used in Frenkel (1978). The application in the present paper uses an extended data base and, more importantly, employs a specification of the demand for reserves in which reserves are measured in real terms and the variability measure is free of scale.

$$L(y|t^*) = \left(\frac{1}{2\pi}\right)^{NT/2} \sigma_1^{-Nt^*} \sigma_2^{-N(T-t^*)}$$

$$\exp\left\{-\frac{1}{2\sigma_1^2} \sum_{t=1}^{t^*} \sum_{i=1}^{N} (y_{it} - x_{it}'\beta_1)^2\right.$$

$$\left. -\frac{1}{2\sigma_2^2} \sum_{t=t^*+1}^{T} \sum_{i=1}^{N} (y_{it} - x_{it}'\beta_2)^2\right\} \tag{4}$$

where N denotes the number of countries and T denotes the number of years, and second, determination of the breakpoint t^* as the value which yields the highest maximum likelihood $L(y|t^*)$. The application of this procedure to determining the breakpoint in the demand for reserves yields 1972 as the estimate for t^* for developing countries. For the developed countries, the breakpoint is less clear, and the choice of the relevant breakpoint as lying between 1972 and 1973 is somewhat arbitrary.

Based on these results, 1972 is used as the estimate of the breakpoint for both developed and developing countries, implying that from the viewpoint of reserve holdings, 1972 marks the end of the first subperiod. The validity of this assumption was tested by applying the likelihood-ratio test to the null hypothesis that no switch took place between 1972 and 1973. The likelihood-ratio statistic is

$$\phi = \hat\sigma_1^{N\hat{t}^*}\hat\sigma_2^{N(T-\hat{t}^*)}/\hat\sigma^{NT}$$

where $\hat\sigma^{NT}$ denotes the estimated standard deviation of the residuals from the single regression estimated over the entire period 1963-79 for developed countries and over 1963-77 for developing countries.

According to the null hypothesis, $-2\ln\phi$ is distributed χ^2 with degrees of freedom corresponding to the number of constraints. The null hypothesis was rejected for both groups of countries at the 99 percent confidence level.[6] The practical implications are that, for the purpose of estimation, data from 1963-72 should not be pooled with those from the subsequent period and that the structural change occurred by the end of 1972.

In addition to the above test, one may also use a Chow test to test for equality of regression coefficients between the two periods. The resulting values of

[6]It should be noted that the application of this method to the problem at hand is not without conceptual difficulties, since it requires differentiating the likelihood function with respect to t^*. It should also be noted that the analysis assumes that the structural change has taken place at a given point in time. An alternative approach would allow for a gradual evolution and would estimate regression equations with variable coefficients. For references and discussion of the properties of the distribution of $-2\ln\phi$, see Goldfeld and Quandt (1976, Chapter 1).

the F-statistics relevant for testing the null hypothesis were well above the critical values at the 99 percent confidence level for both groups of countries. Thus, the Chow test also leads to rejection of the null hypothesis. The overall inference is that the system had changed by the end of 1972. It is this conclusion which provides the rationale for the pattern of the intertemporal pooling that is employed in Table 3. As may be seen from that table, the main changes in the estimated coefficients occurred in the constant term and in the coefficient of σ. For both groups of countries, the constant term declined with the move to greater flexibility of exchange rates, indicating that for given characteristics of the other economic variables, the holding of reserves (in real terms) declined during the second period. Likewise, both groups of countries revealed higher sensitivity to the variability measure during the second period. In general, it is relevant to note that the results concerning the patterns of reserve holdings are consistent with the findings of Suss (1976) and Heller and Khan (1978). Finally, it is important to emphasize that the above discussion associated the structural change with the change in the exchange rate regime; it could, of course, reflect other (not necessarily unrelated) phenomena which occurred in the early 1970s, like the oil crisis and the commodity price boom.

Country-Specific and Time-Specific Factors

The estimates of the demand for international reserves in Table 3 combined cross-section and time-series data using ordinary-least-squares (OLS) estimation. Implementing this estimation method requires that the residuals in equation (1) be uncorrelated among countries at a point in time as well as over time. This assumption, however, may not be fully justified in view of earlier findings (e.g., Frenkel (1974 b, 1978)) that there are countries whose reserve holdings exhibit persistent positive residuals (Switzerland and Austria) or persistent negative residuals (the United Kingdom and New Zealand). This phenomenon suggests that there might be some country-specific and possibly also some time-specific factors which determine the demand for international reserves. These country-specific factors may be the result of historical, political, and social influences that are not captured by the conventional set of arguments in the reserve function. Although it may not be possible to explain these factors, it is important to take account of their influence on the error structure. Incorporation of these factors in the estimation procedure should increase the efficiency of the estimated parameters, and the improved estimates should be useful in assessing the "adequacy" of international liquidity and its distribution among countries.

In what follows, the possibility that the residuals from the estimated demand for reserves contain country-specific factors and time-specific factors is allowed for by applying the error-components model (see Balestra and Nerlove (1966)).[7]

In order to emphasize the possibility of country-specific factors, equation (1) is written below as equation (5) without suppressing the country index i.

$$\ln R_{it} = \beta_0 + \beta_1 \ln \sigma_{it} + \beta_2 \ln Y_{it} + \beta_3 \ln m_{it} + u_{it} \tag{5}$$

where, as before, R_{it} denotes the real value of reserves held by country i at time t; σ_{it} denotes the variability measure for country i at period t; Y_{it} designates the scale variable; and the openness of the economy is measured by the average propensity to import, which is denoted by m_{it}. The subsequent analysis focuses on the 22 developed countries.

The error term u_{it} is assumed to be composed of three independent parts: (1) u_i, the country-specific factor, which is assumed to be invariant with respect to time; (2) λ_t, the time-specific factor, which is assumed to be common to all countries in the cross section; and (3) ϵ_{it}, a serially uncorrelated, identically distributed random variable. Formally, the error-components model can be specified as

$$u_{it} = \mu_i + \lambda_t + \epsilon_{it} \qquad (i = 1, 2, \ldots, N; t = 1, 2, \ldots, T) \tag{6}$$

where μ_i, λ_t, and ϵ_{it} denote independent normal variables, each with zero mean, such that

$$E(\mu_i \mu_{i'}) = \begin{cases} \sigma_\mu^2, i = i' \\ 0, i \neq i' \end{cases}$$

$$E(\lambda_t \lambda_{t'}) = \begin{cases} \sigma_\lambda^2, t = t' \\ 0, t \neq t' \end{cases}$$

$$E(\epsilon_{it} \epsilon_{i't'}) = \begin{cases} \sigma_\epsilon^2, i = i' \text{ and } t = t' \\ 0 \text{ otherwise} \end{cases}$$

The specification of the errors implies that u_{it} is homoskedastic and that its variance is the sum of the variances of three components

$$\sigma_u^2 = \sigma_\mu^2 + \sigma_\lambda^2 + \sigma_\epsilon^2 \tag{7}$$

The assumption that the errors are correlated requires the application of a generalized-least-squares (GLS) estimation method. Table 4 reports the GLS estimates of equation (5) for pegged and flexible exchange rate regimes. A comparison of the parameter estimates in Table 4 with the cor-

---

[7]The subsequent discussion builds on Frenkel and Hakkio (1980).

TABLE 4. DEVELOPED COUNTRIES ($N = 22$): POOLED TIME-SERIES AND CROSS-SECTION EQUATIONS FOR INTERNATIONAL RESERVES USING GENERALIZED LEAST SQUARES, 1963-72 AND 1973-79 [1]

Period	Constant	ln σ	ln Y	ln m	σ_μ^2	σ_λ^2	σ_ϵ^2
1963-72	4.196	0.315	0.953	0.582	0.215	0.016	0.063
	(0.412)	(0.083)	(0.078)	(0.187)			
1973-79	3.748	0.432	1.031	0.925	0.196	0.018	0.086
	(0.461)	(0.119)	(0.078)	(0.218)			

[1] Figures in parentheses are standard errors.

responding estimates in Table 3 reveals the extent of the differences. In comparison with the OLS estimation method, the GLS estimation method yields lower estimates of the coefficients of the measures of variability and openness. The GLS estimates also reveal that the variance of the error σ_u^2 is mainly due to the variance of the country-specific factors σ_μ^2 which underlie the cross-sectional regressions. In contrast, the variance of the time-specific component σ_λ^2, which underlies the variations in the time series, plays a relatively minor role.

Forecasts

The previous results demonstrated that, as a *statistical* matter, the system underwent a structural change by the end of 1972, and that allowance for country-specific factors alters the numerical value of the estimates of the various parameters. The relevant question is, what is the operational relevance of these findings? Do they imply that the move to the second regime rendered the estimates based on data from the first regime obsolete? This question is of some practical importance, since quite frequently a relatively long period of time elapses before sufficient new data are accumulated and before additional research efforts yield new estimates. Likewise, does the fact that GLS estimates differ from the corresponding OLS estimates imply that the latter are useless? To shed some light on this question, the accuracy of forecasts of reserve holdings during the second regime based on parameter estimates from the first regime (1963-72) are examined.

First, the series of forecasts based on the GLS estimates of Table 4 are computed. Since the time-invariant, cross-sectional component of the errors plays a major role in accounting for the overall residual variance, one should be able to exploit this information in forecasting reserve holdings. For that purpose, the country-specific factor $\hat{\mu}_i$ is first estimated as

$$\hat{\mu}_i = \left(\sum_{t=1}^{T} \ln R_{it} - \hat{\beta}_{GLS} \sum_{t=1}^{T} x_{it} \right) \Big/ T \tag{8}$$

where $\hat{\beta}_{GLS}$ denotes the vector of the GLS parameter estimates of equation (5) and x_{it} denotes the vector of the right-hand-side variables of equation (5). Since the expected values of λ_t and of ϵ_{it} are zero, it is assumed that

$$\sum_{t=1}^{T} \lambda_t = \sum_{t=1}^{T} \epsilon_{it} = 0 \qquad \text{(for all } i\text{)}$$

and thus $\hat{\mu}_i$, which was estimated from data corresponding to 1963–72, is treated as an *estimate* of the expected residual for the ith country for the second period.[8] The forecast of reserve holdings for country i for the second period is therefore

$$\hat{\beta}_{GLS} x_{it}^* + \hat{\mu}_i$$

where the superscript (*) indicates that the right-hand-side vector is based on data for 1973–79. This forecast utilizes the fact that the expected residuals u_{it}^* from the GLS regressions for 1973–79 are correlated with the residuals from the GLS regression for 1963–72. In contrast, for the OLS regressions, the corresponding best forecast is $\hat{\beta}_{OLS} x_{it}^*$.

Table 5 contains the results of an evaluation of various forecasts of reserve holdings for the flexible exchange rate regime on the basis of the information from the period of the pegged rate regime. These forecasts were derived from the parameter estimates of the OLS and the GLS regressions for 1963–72, as reported in Tables 3 and 4. As may be seen, the correlation coefficients between the series of predictions and actual outcomes are quite high—ranging from 0.84 for the developing countries' OLS estimates and 0.96 for the developed countries' GLS estimates. Generally, the forecasts based on GLS estimates are superior to those based on OLS estimates. For example, comparing the quality of forecasts for developed countries, the root-mean-square error and the mean error are 0.66 and -0.40, respectively, for the OLS forecast, while the corresponding errors for the GLS forecast are only 0.46 and -0.23, respectively.[9]

An additional procedure for evaluation of the quality of various forecasts follows Theil (1961). Consider a series of predictions $P_1, \ldots, P_n$ and

---

[8]Setting $\Sigma \lambda_t = 0$ does not imply, of course, that the time-specific factor is ignored, since it is implicit in the estimates of $\hat{\mu}_i$ and $\hat{\beta}_{GLS}$.

[9]The high degree of accuracy of the forecasts based on the parameter estimates from 1963–72 is especially remarkable in view of the significant changes in the roles played by gross and net measures of reserves and in view of the different practices concerning the valuations of gold. On the role of gold and on estimates of the demand for non-gold reserves, see von Furstenberg (1982).

TABLE 5. DEVELOPED AND DEVELOPING COUNTRIES: PREDICTIONS OF RESERVE HOLDINGS USING PARAMETER ESTIMATES FOR 1963–72 [1]

Developed Country Predictions for 1973–79 Based on:	Developing Country Predictions for 1973–77 Based on:	Correlation Coefficient	Root-Mean-Square Error	Mean Error	Theil's Inequality Coefficient	Fraction of Error Owing to:		
						Bias	Different variation	Different covariation
Ordinary least squares, 1963–72		0.93	0.66	−0.40	0.04	0.37	0.05	0.58
	Ordinary least squares, 1963–72	0.84	0.77	−0.10	0.06	0.02	0.04	0.95
Generalized least squares, 1963–72		0.96	0.46	−0.23	0.03	0.26	0.03	0.71

[1] The predictions are based on the parameter estimates reported in Tables 3 and 4.

a series of the corresponding actual outcomes $A_1, \ldots, A_n$. Theil's inequality coefficient, which is bounded by zero and 1, is

$$U = \frac{\sqrt{\dfrac{1}{n}\Sigma(P_i - A_i)^2}}{\sqrt{\dfrac{1}{n}\Sigma P_i^2} + \sqrt{\dfrac{1}{n}\Sigma A_i^2}} \tag{9}$$

according to which $U = 0$ in the case of perfect forecasting ($P_i = A_i$ for all i), and $U = 1$ in the case of extremely poor forecasting. The variance of the forecast errors (the square root of which is the numerator of U) can be decomposed as

$$\frac{1}{n}\Sigma(P_i - A_i)^2 = (\bar{P} - \bar{A})^2 + (s_p - s_A)^2 + 2(1 - r)s_P s_A$$

where $\bar{P}$ and $\bar{A}$ denote the means and s_P and s_A the standard deviations of the series of predictions and actual outcomes, respectively, and where r denotes their correlation coefficient. Denoting the denominator of U by D, Theil defines

$$U_M \equiv (\bar{P} - \bar{A})/D \qquad U_S \equiv (s_p - s_A)/D$$

and

$$U_C \equiv \sqrt{2(1 - r)s_P s_A}\,/D$$

and thus

$$U_M^2 + U_S^2 + U_C^2 = U^2 \tag{10}$$

where the three terms on the left-hand side of equation (10) are referred to as the partial coefficients of inequality owing to unequal central tendency, to unequal variation, and to imperfect covariation, respectively. Normalizing these terms by U^2 yields

$$U^M + U^S + U^C = 1 \tag{11}$$

where $U^M \equiv U_M^2/U^2$; $U^S \equiv U_S^2/U^2$; and $U^C \equiv U_C^2/U^2$.

In equation (11), U^M, U^S, and U^C denote the proportions of the inequality owing to the above-mentioned three different sources that are termed by Theil the bias, the variance, and the covariance proportions, respectively. It is clear that in the absence of perfect forecasting, a desirable distribution of the inequality over the three sources is

$$U^M = 0; \qquad U^S = 0; \qquad \text{and} \quad U^C = 1$$

since small values of U^M and U^S indicate that systematic errors do not play a major role in forecast errors.

As may be seen in Table 5, Theil's inequality coefficients are very low, ranging from 0.03 to 0.06. Furthermore, the forecast errors possess the "desirable" properties that most of the errors are not systematic, as indicated by the fact that their largest fraction is due to different covariation. Also, in this respect, it seems that the quality of the GLS forecasts for developed countries is better than that of the corresponding OLS forecasts, in that the fraction of the forecast error due to bias and to different variation is lower for GLS forecasts than OLS forecasts. Based on the relative magnitudes of the fractions of the errors owing to the various sources, it seems that the quality of the forecasts is somewhat better for developing countries than for developed countries. Consistent with the previous results, it seems that the behavior of developed countries with respect to reserve holdings underwent a more drastic structural change than that of developing countries. In fact, on the basis of the relatively good forecasts, it seems clear that the structural change, while statistically significant, was not of sufficient magnitude to make the old estimates completely obsolete.

The relative stability of the patterns of reserve holdings suggests the following interpretation: during the pegged rate regime the rate was adjustable rather than fixed, and during the so-called floating rate regime the rate has been managed rather than free. Economic behavior seems to have been more stable than legal arrangements. Central banks have revealed that their choice is neither of the extreme exchange rate systems, but rather the intermediate system of managed floating. Since managing the float requires international reserves, one would expect to find a relatively stable demand for reserves, which might not differ greatly from the demand estimated for the adjustable peg regime.

Dynamics of Adjustment

The analysis up to this point has assumed that countries were "on" their long-run demand functions. The following discussion draws a distinction between short-run and long-run demand functions and examines the speed of adjustment of reserves to their long-run desired values. While cross-sectional studies have identified the key variables which determine the holdings of international reserves, some work on the dynamics of adjustment has found that the speed at which actual reserves adjust toward target reserves is very slow and is often not significantly different from zero (see, for example, Clark (1970 b) and Iyoha (1976)).[10] If correct, these findings cast

[10]For a study reporting a relatively *high* speed of adjustment, see Edwards (1980).

some doubt on the usefulness of the cross-sectional studies for analyzing the adequacy of international reserves, since evidence of a stable long-run demand function is of little value if it cannot be used to show that discrepancies between actual and desired stocks are eliminated over time.

In Bilson and Frenkel (1979 a and 1979 b), however, it was shown that the earlier estimates of the speeds of adjustment were biased downward and that, in fact, the speeds of adjustment were reasonably high for both developed and developing countries. Here, this framework is extended so as to allow the dynamic adjustment of international reserves to reflect both the central bank's excess demand for reserves *and* the public's excess demand for money. Changes in the stock of international reserves reflect considerations emphasized in the literature on the demand for reserves as well as considerations emphasized in the literature on the monetary approach to the balance of payments. Equation (12) describes one general form of the reserve-adjustment equation

$$\Delta \ln R_{it} = \alpha(\ln R_{it}^* - \ln R_{it-1}) + \beta(\ln M_{it}^* - \ln M_{it-1}) + u_{it} \qquad (12)$$

where R_{it}^* and M_{it}^* denote, respectively, the desired levels of reserves and money for country i at period t, and where α and β denote the speeds of adjustment of reserves to disequilibrium in holdings of reserves and money, respectively.[11]

In order to estimate these speeds of adjustment, it is necessary to obtain an estimate of the desired level of reserves and money as well as to specify the properties of the error term u_{it}. The previous findings revealed that country-specific factors play important roles in governing countries' holdings of international reserves. Time-specific factors, on the other hand, have played only an insignificant role. Accordingly, it is assumed here that the properties of the error term can be characterized by equation (6), with λ_t—the time-specific factor—suppressed to zero.

Under the assumption that, *on average*, the holdings of international reserves and of real money balances equal their target levels, these target levels can be estimated from equations (13)-(14).

$$\ln R_{i.} = \beta_0 + \beta_1 \ln \sigma_{i.} + \beta_2 \ln Y_{i.} + \beta_3 \ln m_{i.} + \mu_i \qquad (13)$$

$$\ln \left(\frac{M}{P}\right)_{i.} = \gamma_0 + \gamma_1 \ln Y_{i.} - \gamma_2 i_{i.} + \epsilon_i \qquad (14)$$

where $R_{i.}$ denotes the average level of reserves for country i (where an average over time for country i is denoted by "$i.$"). Equation (14) is a conventional equation in which the demand for money is expressed as a function of

---

[11]This formulation draws on the author's joint work (in progress) with John F.O. Bilson. For a recent attempt to integrate monetary and reserve considerations, see Levi (1983).

income Y and the rate of interest i. In equation (14), M denotes the monetary base and i the short-term nominal rate of interest. The choice of the monetary aggregate was made for two reasons. First, most countries do not pay interest on the monetary base, whereas financial practices for broader monetary aggregates differ widely across countries. Second, the monetary base may be considered the more appropriate aggregate for balance of payments analysis.

The first stage of the estimation procedure involves estimating equations (13) and (14) from the sample averages of the time-series and cross-sectional data base. The resulting estimates for the sample of 22 developed countries over the two subperiods are reported in Table 6. The estimates of the parameters of the average demand for reserves are very similar to those reported in Table 3; and the estimates of the demand for money reveal a unit income elasticity and a negative interest elasticity. During the second period, the interest elasticity declined (in absolute value), and its magnitude did not differ significantly from zero.

In the second stage of the estimation procedure, the estimated parameters of Table 6 are used to construct estimates of the target levels of reserves and money for country i at period t. These magnitudes are estimated as

$$\ln R_{it}^* = \hat{\beta}_0 + \hat{\beta}_1 \ln \sigma_{it} + \hat{\beta}_2 \ln Y_{it} + \hat{\beta}_3 \ln m_{it} + \hat{\mu}_i \tag{15}$$

$$\ln M_{it}^* = \hat{\gamma}_0 + \hat{\gamma}_1 \ln Y_{it} - \hat{\gamma}_2 i_{it} + \ln P_{it} + \hat{\epsilon}_i \tag{16}$$

where the coefficients $\hat{\beta}_i$ ($i = 0, \ldots, 3$) and $\hat{\gamma}_i$ ($i = 0, \ldots, 2$) are the estimates of the corresponding coefficients in equations (13) and (14), as reported in Table 6, and where the estimated values of the country-specific factors μ_i and ϵ_i are defined as

$$\hat{\mu}_i = \ln R_{i.} - \hat{\beta}_0 - \hat{\beta}_1 \ln \sigma_{i.} - \hat{\beta}_2 \ln Y_{i.} - \hat{\beta}_3 \ln m_{i.} \tag{17}$$

$$\hat{\epsilon}_i = \ln \left(\frac{M}{P} \right)_{i.} - \hat{\gamma}_0 - \hat{\gamma}_1 \ln Y_{i.} - \hat{\gamma}_2 i_{i.} \tag{18}$$

Equations (17) and (18) define the country-specific factors μ_i and ϵ_i as the systematic deviations of ith country's holdings of reserves and cash balances from the average holdings of the group of countries. In contrast to previous studies, the definitions of the target levels of reserves and cash balances in equations (15) and (16) *include* the country-specific factors. The conventional approach to the analysis of the dynamics of adjustment has been to append the equilibrium specifications of the demands for reserves and for cash balances with a lagged dependent variable. The obvious problem with this approach arises from the existence of a country-specific factor. If this factor is not accounted for in the specification of the

TABLE 6. DEVELOPED COUNTRIES ($N = 22$): "AVERAGE" DEMAND FOR RESERVES AND REAL BALANCES ESTIMATED USING ORDINARY LEAST SQUARES [1]

Period	Dependent Variable	Constant	$\ln \sigma_i$	$\ln Y_i$	$\ln m_i$	$\ln i_i$	R^2	Standard Error
1963–72	$\ln R_i$	3.959 (0.790)	0.661 (0.240)	1.066 (0.090)	1.424 (0.300)		0.89	0.458
	$\ln \left(\dfrac{M}{P}\right)_i$	−1.105 (0.420)		1.027 (0.060)		−0.186 (0.060)	0.93	0.393
1973–79	$\ln R_i$	3.478 (0.699)	0.730 (0.263)	1.138 (0.088)	1.737 (0.395)		0.91	0.449
	$\ln \left(\dfrac{M}{P}\right)_i$	−2.199 (0.743)		1.001 (0.096)		−0.010 (0.053)	0.87	0.570

[1]Figures in parentheses are standard errors.

target levels of reserves and cash balances, the coefficients of the lagged dependent variables will be biased toward unity, so that the estimated speed of adjustment will be biased downward. As should be evident, the two-stage procedure outlined here is not subject to this bias.

Using equations (15) and (16) to construct the target levels of reserves and cash balances, the estimates of the speeds of adjustment in equation (12) are reported in Table 7. The results support the specification in the adjustment equation (12). They also demonstrate that the actual changes in reserves are influenced by *both* the central bank's excess demand for reserves and the private sector's excess demand for money. The speeds of adjustment are higher than those typically obtained by estimates of the coefficients on lagged dependent variables.

Finally, and somewhat surprisingly, the estimated speeds of adjustments are higher during the flexible exchange rate regime than during the pegged-rate regime. As may be seen in Table 6, the adjustment coefficient of an excess demand for international reserves rose from 0.370 to 0.488, while the adjusted coefficient to an excess demand for money rose from 0.298 to 0.357.

Summary

The preceding parts of this section contain an analysis of the role of international reserves under pegged exchange rates and under managed floating. Evidence was presented on the stability of the demand for reserves during 1963–72 and 1973–79. It was shown that developed countries' demand for reserves differs from that of developing countries and that the system underwent a structural change by the end of 1972. In view of the drastic changes in the international monetary system, the structural change (in particular, with reference to the behavior of developed countries) has not been as extensive as one might have expected. This finding led to the observation that economic behavior seems to be more stable than legal arrange-

TABLE 7. DEVELOPED COUNTRIES ($N = 22$): DYNAMICS OF ADJUSTMENT OF INTERNATIONAL RESERVES [1]

Period	Dependent Variable	$\ln R_{it}^{*} - \ln R_{it-1}$	$\ln M_{it}^{*} - \ln M_{it-1}$	R^2	Standard Error
1963–72	$\Delta \ln R_{it}$	0.370 (0.076)	0.298 (0.101)	0.13	0.24
1973–79	$\Delta \ln R_{it}$	0.488 (0.083)	0.357 (0.174)	0.25	0.25

[1]Figures in parentheses are standard errors.

ments. The evidence indicates that countries have continued to hold and use international reserves and that they have chosen to manage their exchange rates rather than to let them float freely. This suggests that the move to a floating-rate regime has not reduced significantly the need for international reserves; nor has it removed the need to establish clearly the means of and mechanisms for providing such reserves.[12] The section concluded with an analysis of the dynamics of adjustment to disequilibrium reserve holdings. It was shown that changes in the holdings of international reserves reflect both the central bank's excess demand for reserves and the private sector's excess demand for money. The estimated speeds of adjustment were shown to be larger than those reported in earlier studies.

While much of the discussion in this section evolved around the details of econometric specifications and estimation procedures, the central implications should not be lost. The stability of the demand for international reserves and the adjustment mechanism that is triggered once reserve holdings differ from the desired level suggest that governments have chosen to include an international reserves target on the list of targets which guides and constrains the conduct of macroeconomic policies. The evidence suggests that the move to greater flexibility of exchange rates has not removed this constraint in any material way. The next section deals with the more general questions of the constraints that the openness of the economy imposes on the effectiveness of policies and the impact of the exchange rate regime on the effectiveness of these constraints.

II. INTERNATIONAL CONSTRAINTS ON MONETARY CONTROL

The discussion in the previous section ended with the conclusion that the evidence on the stability of demand for international reserves across exchange rate regimes indicates that attempts to attain desired reserve holdings have influenced and constrained the conduct of monetary policy. This section addresses the broader issue of the nature of the international constraints on monetary policy.[13]

Generally, macroeconomic policies for open economies differ in funda-

---

[12]For analyses of the effects of the move to floating exchange rates on the demand for and the optimal provision of international reserves, see Grubel (1976), Makin (1974), and Williamson (1976).

[13]The subsequent analysis draws on Frenkel (1983). The author's assignment for this conference has been to deal with monetary control; therefore, the subsequent discussion focuses on the role of monetary policy. This focus should not be interpreted as implying that fiscal policy considerations are of lesser importance. For an analysis of the constraints on fiscal policies, see Frenkel and Mussa (1981).

mental ways from the corresponding policies for closed economies. The openness of the economy imposes constraints on the effectiveness and proper conduct of macroeconomic policies in general and of monetary control in particular. These constraints stem from the interdependence between the economy and the rest of the world. The open economy and the rest of the world have three key linkages: (1) through international trade in goods and services, (2) through international mobility of capital and (3) through international exchanges of national money. (See Frenkel and Mussa (1981) for a detailed analysis of the implications of these linkages for macroeconomic policies.)

International trade links prices in different national economies. While the evidence on purchasing power parities reveals that this link is not rigid, it is evident that a country cannot choose its long-run inflation rate trend independent of the long-run courses of monetary policy and the exchange rate. This relation thus imposes a severe constraint on monetary policy.

International mobility of capital links interest rates on financial assets. In addition, by permitting countries to finance current account imbalances, it provides a channel through which macroeconomic disturbances are transmitted internationally. The international mobility of capital limits the power of monetary policy. Under a fixed exchange rate regime, a monetary expansion in excess of money demand is likely to have only limited success in sustaining the change in the nominal money stock. Any temporary reduction in the domestic rate of interest will induce capital outflows and a loss of foreign exchange reserves, and any attempts to sterilize the monetary consequences of the loss of international reserves are unlikely to be viable in the long run (more on this in Section III). Under a flexible exchange rate regime, the monetary authorities regain control over the nominal money stock, but the international mobility of capital still imposes a severe limitation on the ability of monetary policy to affect significantly the evolution of output and employment. A monetary expansion is likely to induce a rapid change in the exchange rate, which leads to prompt adjustment of prices and wages.

The implications of capital mobility for the efficiency of policies are illustrated in Figure 1 (adapted from Frenkel and Rodriguez (1975)), which describes the effects of open market operations under fixed exchange rates. Consider a portfolio which is composed of real cash balances M/P (where P denotes the price level) and common stocks K, and let the price of a security in terms of goods be denoted by p_k. It is assumed that the economy is small and fully integrated in world capital markets. Since the foreign rate of interest is assumed to be given, p_k is also assumed to be fixed for the small, open economy. The price level P for the small, open economy is assumed to equal SP^*, where S denotes the exchange rate and P^* denotes the given foreign

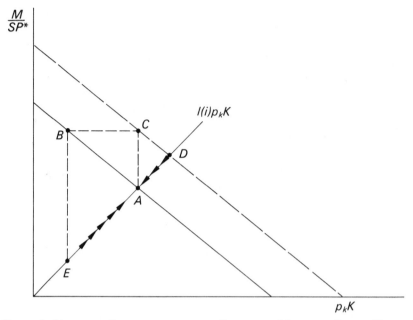

FIGURE 1. PORTFOLIO EQUILIBRIUM AND THE EFFECTS OF MONETARY POLICY UNDER FIXED AND FLEXIBLE EXCHANGE RATE REGIMES

price. Thus, under fixed exchange rates, the price level is given. The value of wealth W is thus

$$W = \frac{M}{SP^*} + p_k K \tag{19}$$

Suppose that the desired money/securities ratio depends negatively on the rate of interest, as in equation (20)

$$\frac{M}{SP^*} = \ell(i) p_k K \tag{20}$$

Portfolio equilibrium is described by point A in Figure 1. The negatively sloped schedule describes the wealth constraint; and the positively sloped schedule describes the desired composition of assets, given the rate of interest. An open market purchase moves the economy from point A to point B, at which the money supply has risen and the private sector's holdings of securities have fallen. Since at point B the composition of the portfolio has been disturbed and since asset holders have access to world asset markets at the given rate of interest, they will restore portfolio equilibrium instantaneously by exchanging the increased stock of cash for foreign securities, thereby returning to point A. Thus, because world capital markets are integrated and because open market operations are conducted in assets traded internationally at a given price, the private sector can nullify the actions of the monetary authority. In fact, in this case, open market operations amount to an exchange, of foreign exchange reserves for securities, between the monetary authorities and foreign asset holders; and the entire process of adjustment is effected through the capital account of the balance of payments. The leverage of monetary policy can be somewhat enhanced if it operates in financial assets that are isolated from world capital markets, since, in the short run, the links between rates of return on such assets and world rates of interest are not as tight.

The same figure can be used for the analysis of a once-and-for-all rise in the quantity of money that is brought about through an unanticipated transfer of cash balances which moves the economy from point A to point C. This policy raises the value of assets and raises the relative share of money in wealth. Portfolio composition equilibrium is restored by an immediate exchange of part of the increased money stock for equities, as individuals move to point D. This exchange is effected through the capital account of the balance of payments. Since at point D, the value of assets exceeds the equilibrium value at point A, individuals will wish to run down their holdings of both equities and real cash balances by increasing expenditures relative to income. This part of the process will be gradual. The transition toward long-run equilibrium follows the path from D to A and is characterized by a deficit in the current account, a surplus in the capital account, and a deficit in the monetary account of the balance of payments.

Under flexible exchange rates, adjustments of real balances occur through changes in the exchange rate. Using the same diagram, the effects of monetary policies are very different. An open market operation which brings the economy from point A to point B in Figure 1 cannot be nullified through the capital account, since under flexible exchange rates, money ceases to be an internationally traded commodity. Portfolio equilibrium is restored by an immediate rise in the exchange rate (i.e., a depreciation of the currency) which moves individuals from point B to point E. As may be seen, the percentage rise in the exchange rate exceeds the percentage rise in the money stock; this is the overshooting phenomenon. Since at point E, the value of assets falls short of the long-run equilibrium value, individuals will wish to accumulate both equities and real balances by reducing expenditures relative to income. This part of the process is gradual; and the transition from E to A is characterized by a surplus in the current account, a deficit in the capital account, and an appreciation of the currency.[14]

---

[14]While these are the general characteristics of the adjustment process, the details of the precise path are somewhat more complicated, since the expected transitional changes in the exchange rates will alter transitorily the rate of interest. Along the path between E and D, the domestic currency appreciates and, if this appreciation is expected, the domestic rate of

In contrast, when the rise in the quantity of money is brought about through a transfer which moves the economy from point A to point C, the new equilibrium will be restored instantaneously through an equiproportionate depreciation of the currency which restores equilibrium at A.

The previous analysis of open market operations assumed implicitly that the returns on government holdings of securities are rebated to the private sector (in a lump-sum fashion) but that the private sector does not capitalize the expected future flow of transfers. As a result, the open market operations did not change the wealth position of individuals who moved from point A to point B along the given wealth constraint. Under the alternative assumption that asset holders anticipate and capitalize the flow of transfers and treat them like any other marketable asset, they effectively conceive of the equities that are held by the government as their own. In that case, the open market purchase only raises the supply of real cash balances and moves the economy from point A to point C. The effects of this policy are identical to the effects of the pure monetary expansion brought about through the governmental transfer.

The analysis of these two extreme cases implies that when international capital markets are highly integrated, the effectiveness of the constraints on monetary policy under fixed and flexible exchange rate regimes depends on the degree to which the private sector capitalizes future streams of taxes and transfers, as well as on the marketability of claims to such streams.[15] When such claims are not fully perceived by individuals or by the capital market, the effects of open market operations are nullified rapidly under fixed exchange rates, while the adjustment is gradual under flexible exchange rates. In constrast, when individuals and capital markets do fully perceive these claims, the adjustment to open market operations is only gradual when the exchange rate is fixed and is rapid when the exchange rate is flexible. These cases illustrate that the ranking of alternative exchange rate regimes according to their speeds of adjustments to monetary policies is not unambiguous, since it depends on the mechanism of monetary policies and on the public's perception of such policies.

The international exchange of national money and the requirement of monetary equilibrium also impose a severe limitation on the effectiveness of monetary policy. As stated before, under a fixed exchange rate regime, the

---

interest is below the world rate owing to interest arbitrage. Therefore, during the transition period, the desired ratio of money to equities will exceed the one described in Figure 1. The new equilibrium is reached at point A when the exchange rate reaches its new level and when the domestic and the foreign rates of interest are equalized.

[15]The importance of the degree of capitalization and marketability of claims to future income streams was analyzed in the context of a closed economy by Metzler (1951) and Mundell (1960).

authorities lose control over the nominal money stock; while under a flexible rate regime, the requirement of monetary equilibrium ensures that in the long run, changes in the nominal money stock lead to a proportionate change in all nominal prices and wages. Because of the rapid change in the exchange rate, the constraint on monetary policy that is implied by the homogeneity postulate is likely to be manifested much more promptly in an open economy with flexible exchange rates than in a closed economy.

An additional constraint on the conduct of monetary policy follows from the dynamic linkage between current exchange rates and expectations of future exchange rates (see Mussa (1976, 1979)). This dynamic linkage implies that the effect of monetary policy on the exchange rate and, consequently, on other economic variables depends on expectations concerning future policies. These expectations, in turn, are influenced by past policies and the current course of policy; and it is likely that the mere recognition of this dynamic linkage will influence the conduct of policy. The government, which is aware that the effectiveness of any particular policy measure depends on the measure's influence on the public's expectations of future policies, may become more constrained in employing the instrument of monetary policy.

In summary, the openness of the economy imposes constraints on monetary policy. These constraints are reflected in a reduced ability to influence the *instruments* of monetary policy (like the nominal money supply under fixed exchange rates), in a reduced ability to influence the *targets* of monetary policy (like the level of real output), or in an increased prudence in using monetary policy because of the potentially undesirable effects on expectations.

This discussion suggests that while the exchange rate regime affects the nature of the constraints on policy, the constraints themselves stem from the openness of the economy. Furthermore, the choice of the exchange rate regime does not relax the fundamental constraints, even though it influences the manifestation of these constraints. With this perspective, one may rationalize the findings (reported in Section I) that economic behavior with respect to reserve holdings has been more stable than might have been expected in view of the major changes in legal arrangements. Policymakers seem to have recognized that although a move to clean floating could have reduced the need for reserves, it would also have imposed significant costs associated with prompt translation of monetary changes into exchange rate changes as well as with large changes in real exchange rates. In view of these costs, policymakers have chosen not to enjoy fully the "degree of freedom" provided by clean floating.

The constraints on the conduct of monetary policy depend on the exchange rate regime. Therefore, the question of the country's *choice* of the optimal set of constraints on monetary policy can be answered in terms of the analysis of the choice of the optimal exchange rate regime. Such analysis reveals that the optimal exchange rate regime depends on the nature and the origin of shocks that affect the economy. Generally, the greater is the variance of real shocks which affect the supply of goods, the more desirable increased fixity of exchange rates becomes. The rationale for this proposition is that the balance of payments serves as a shock absorber which mitigates the effect of real shocks on consumption. As the importance of this factor diminishes, the greater is the degree of international capital mobility. On the other hand, as the desirability of exchange rate flexibility increases, the greater are the variances of shocks with respect to the excess supply of money, to foreign prices, and to deviations from purchasing power parities (see Frenkel and Aizenman (1982)).

III. EXCHANGE MARKET INTERVENTION

The analysis of the international constraints on monetary policy is closely related to the analysis of whether the authorities can sterilize the monetary implications of the balance of payments and of interventions in the foreign exchange market. The need for occasional interventions in the foreign exchange market provides some of the rationale for the continued stable holdings of international reserves which were discussed in Section I. In this context, however, the difficulties in analyzing that question start with definitions, since exchange market intervention means different things to different people (see Wallich (1982 a and 1982 b)). Some, especially in the United States, interpret foreign exchange intervention to mean *sterilized* intervention—that is, intervention which is not allowed to affect the monetary base and thus amounts to an exchange of domestic bonds for foreign bonds. Others, especially in Europe, interpret foreign intervention to mean *nonsterilized* intervention. Thus, according to Europeans an intervention alters the course of monetary policy, while according to Americans it does not.

The distinction between the two concepts of intervention is fundamental; and the exchange rate effects of the two forms of intervention may be very different, depending on the relative degree of substitution among assets. In principle, sterilized intervention may affect the exchange rate by means of portfolio-balance effects (see Allen and Kenen (1980), Branson (1979), and Henderson (1977)) and by signaling to the public the government's intentions concerning future policies, thereby changing expectations (see Mussa (1981)). To the extent that sterilized intervention is effective in managing exchange rates, the constraint on the conduct of monetary policy will not be severe, since the undesirable exchange rate effects of monetary policy may be offset by policies which alter appropriately the composition of assets. In practice, however, the evidence suggests that nonsterilized intervention which alters the monetary base has a strong effect on the exchange rate, while an equivalent sterilized intervention has very little effect (see Obstfeld (1983)). These findings are relevant to both the theory of exchange rate determination and the practice of exchange rate and monetary policies. As far as the theory is concerned, these findings cast doubt on the usefulness of the portfolio-balance model; in practice, they demonstrate that distinguishing between the two forms of intervention is critical if the authorities mean to intervene effectively. Thus, it may be inappropriate to assume that the open-economy constraints on monetary policy can be easily overcome by sterilization policies.

The preceding discussion defined interventions in terms of transactions involving specific pairs of assets. In evaluating these transactions, it might be useful to explore the broader spectrum of possible policies. Figure 2 summarizes the various patterns of domestic and foreign monetary policies and foreign exchange interventions. These policies are divided into three groups as follows:

I: Domestic nonsterilized foreign exchange intervention
I^*: Foreign nonsterilized foreign exchange intervention

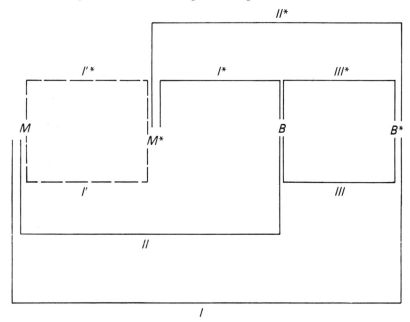

FIGURE 2. PATTERNS OF DOMESTIC AND FOREIGN MONETARY POLICIES AND FOREIGN EXCHANGE INTERVENTIONS

II: Domestic monetary policy
II^*: Foreign monetary policy
III: Domestic sterilized foreign exchange intervention
III^*: Foreign sterilized foreign exchange intervention

This classification is based on the types of assets that are being exchanged. Thus, when the authorities exchange domestic money M for domestic bonds B, the transaction is referred to as domestic monetary policy (as in II); while when the authorities exchange domestic bonds B for foreign bonds B^*, the transaction is referred to as domestic sterilized foreign exchange intervention (as in III). Some have characterized pure foreign exchange intervention as an exchange of domestic money M for foreign money M^* rather than an exchange of domestic money for foreign bonds; to complete the spectrum, these two types of exchange are indicated in Figure 2 by I' and I'^*, respectively.

This general classification highlights two principles. First, it shows that the differences between the various policies depend on the different characteristics of the various assets being exchanged. These different characteristics are at the foundation of the portfolio-balance model. Second, it shows that domestic and foreign variables enter symmetrically into the picture. Thus, for example, a given exchange between M and B^* can be effected through the policies of the home country or through a combination of policies of the foreign country. This symmetry suggests that there is room (and possibly a role) for international coordination of exchange rate policies. It also illustrates the "$(n-1)$ problem" of the international monetary system: in a world of n currencies, there are $(n-1)$ exchange rates, and only $(n-1)$ monetary authorities need to intervene in order to attain a set of exchange rates. To ensure consistency, the international monetary system needs to specify the allocation of the remaining degree of freedom (see Mundell (1968)).

By and large, the evidence on the effectiveness of sterilized intervention has been based on a comparison of patterns I and III within a single-country framework. It is possible that some of the findings emerging from the single-country studies may be modified once the foreign country's behavior is taken into account. But, until one is presented with such evidence, it is reasonable to conclude that it is very difficult to conduct effectively independent monetary and exchange rate policies.

IV. GUIDELINES FOR MONETARY POLICY

The analysis in Section II emphasized the constraints imposed on monetary control in an open economy. Under fixed exchange rates, these constraints may be somewhat eased on account of sterilization policies; but the evidence casts some doubt on the effectiveness of such attempts. As was also indicated, under flexible exchange rates, rapid changes in exchange rates also impose a constraint on the effectiveness of monetary policy, in that they speed up the translation of monetary changes into changes in prices and wages. Furthermore, the recent volatility of exchange rates and the accompanying large divergences from purchasing power parities have been costly and have fostered the perception that exchange rate changes reduce the leverage of monetary policy. Attempts to alleviate some of these constraints have given rise to various proposals concerning rules for intervention in the foreign exchange market. Some of these proposals are variants of a purchasing-power-parity (PPP) rule, according to which the authorities are expected to intervene so as to ensure that the path of the exchange rate conforms to the path of the relative price levels. These proposals, if effective, amount to guidelines for the conduct of monetary policy.

There are at least four difficulties with a PPP rule. First, there are intrinsic differences between the characteristics of exchange rates and the prices of national outputs. These differences, which result from the much stronger dependence of exchange rates (and other asset prices) on expectations, suggest that exchange rates' greater movement than the price level does not constitute sufficient evidence that exchange rate volatility has been excessive.

Second, the prices of national outputs do not adjust fully to shocks in the short run. Thus, intervention in the foreign exchange market to ensure purchasing power parity would be a mistake. When commodity prices are slow to adjust to current and expected economic conditions, it may be desirable to allow for "excessive" adjustment in some other prices.

Third, there are continuous changes in real economic conditions that require adjustment in the equilibrium relative prices of different national outputs. Under these circumstances, what seem to be divergences from purchasing power parities may really be reflections of equilibrating changes.

Fourth, if there is short-run stickiness of domestic goods prices in terms of national money, then rapid exchange rate adjustments, which can change the relative prices of different national outputs, are a desirable response to changing real economic conditions. An intervention rule which links changes in exchange rates rigidly to changes in domestic and foreign prices in accord with purchasing power parity ignores the occasional need for equilibrating changes in relative prices. While it might be tempting to "solve" the problem of divergences from PPP by adopting a rigid PPP rule, this would be a policy mistake.

What should be the exchange rate's role in the design of monetary policy? Generally, given that monetary and exchange rate policies should not be viewed as two independent instruments, consideration of the external value of the currency should play a relatively minor role in the design of monetary policy. The major consideration guiding the monetary authorities should be the achievement of price stability.

While this prescription may seem a revival of the "benign neglect" attitude, the opposite is the case. In the past, one of the major arguments for the benign neglect attitude in the United States was that the U.S. economy was relatively closed and the foreign trade sector was relatively unimportant. The typical statistic used to justify this position was the low share of imports in GNP. This argument was inappropriate in the past and is even less appropriate now. The United States has always had an open economy. The relevant measure of openness to international trade in goods and services is not the share of actual trade in GNP but rather the share of tradable commodities (i.e., of potential trade) in GNP, which is far larger than the share of actual trade. Furthermore, as was stated in Section I, one of the main linkages of the United States to the world economy operates through world capital markets with which the United States is clearly well integrated. The same principle applies to measures of the openness of most countries.

The prescription is based on the notions that the economy *is* open; that the external value of the currency *is* important; that the restoration of price stability is an important policy goal; and that policy which views the exchange rate as an independent target or, even worse, as an independent instrument, is likely to result in unstable prices. Furthermore, if monetary policy succeeds in achieving price stability, it might be useful to allow for fluctuations of the exchange rate which provide some insulation from misguided foreign monetary policies.

Even when monetary policy is not guided by exchange rate targets, it might attempt to offset disturbances arising from shifts in the demand for money. Such shifts in demand may be especially pronounced under a regime of flexible exchange rates. A policy which accommodates such demand shifts by means of offsetting supply shifts would reduce the need for costly adjustments of exchange rates and national price levels. The difficulty with implementing this policy is in identifying when a shift in money demand has occurred. As is obvious, the nominal rate of interest is not a reliable indicator of money market conditions. The more relevant indicators are the components of the nominal rate of interest—the real rate of interest and the expected rate of inflation—but these components are unobservable.

Here the exchange rate may be a useful indicator of monetary policy, especially when frequent changes in inflationary expectations make nominal interest rates an unreliable indicator of fluctuations in money demand. In order to determine the way in which exchange rates may serve as a useful indicator of the conduct of policy, it is useful to start with an examination of the empirical record concerning the links between interest rates and exchange rates.

Interest Rates and Exchange Rates

One of the striking characteristics of the relation between the exchange rate and the interest differential has been its dramatic reversal since the latter part of 1979. The empirical record is illustrated in Chart 1, which shows the relation between the value of the dollar, in terms of a trade-weighted basket of foreign currencies, and the corresponding interest differential. As may be seen, there were generally two phases to the link between the value of the dollar and the interest differential. First, from 1973 through mid-1979, a higher interest rate in the United States (relative to foreign rates) was associated with a depreciation of the dollar; and second, since about mid-1979, a higher interest differential has been associated with an appreciation of the dollar in terms of foreign exchange.

CHART 1. FOREIGN EXCHANGE VALUE OF THE U.S. DOLLAR AND INTEREST RATE DIFFERENTIAL, JANUARY 1976–JULY 1981 [1]

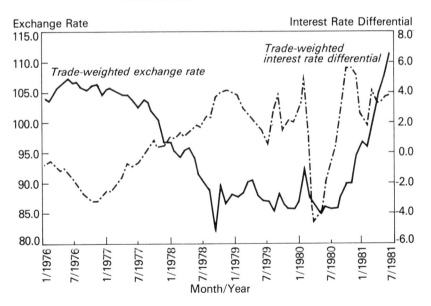

[1]The exchange rate is a trade-weighted average of the foreign currency value of the dollar. The interest differential is the 3-month U.S. commercial paper rate minus a trade-weighted foreign rate. The weights are from *Federal Reserve Bulletin*, Vol. 60 (August 1978), page 700.

The same inference can be drawn from a comparison of the correlation coefficients between innovations (news) in the interest differentials and in the various exchange rates. As shown in Table 8, the correlation coefficients have changed sign since the latter part of 1979. This general pattern is independent of whether the various interest rate innovations are correlated with exchange rate levels or with rates of change of exchange rates. Nor does it depend on whether one uses the various measures of exchange rates or the innovations (news) in these measures.

The reversal of the relation between U.S. interest rates and the external value of the dollar which has taken place since mid-1979 indicates that recently the prime cause of fluctuations in U.S. interest rates has not been variations in inflationary expectations but rather variations in the *real* rate of interest. This distinction between the real rate of interest and inflationary expectations is the key factor in interpreting the empirical record.

The relation between the exchange rate, the real interest rate, and the expected rate of inflation (relative to the corresponding foreign rates) can be derived from the following basic parity conditions. Equation (21) describes the interest-parity condition that is implied by interest arbitrage

$$s_t = E_t s_{t+1} + i_t^* - i_t \tag{21}$$

where s_t denotes the logarithm of the exchange rate in period t; E_t denotes the expectation operator (based on information available at period t), and thus $E_t s_{t+1}$ denotes the expected logarithm of the exchange rate for period $t+1$ based on the information available at period t; and i_t and i_t^* denote the rates of interest on domestic and foreign securities that are identical in all respects except for the currency of denomination.

The second parity condition is the Irving Fisher condition which expresses the nominal rate of interest i as the sum of the real rate r and the expected inflation. Equations (22) and (23) describe this condition for the domestic and the foreign rates of interest

$$i_t = r_t + E_t(p_{t+1} - p_t) \tag{22}$$

$$i_t^* = r_t^* + E_t(p_{t+1}^* - p_t^*) \tag{23}$$

where p_t denotes the logarithm of the price level in period t and where asterisks are used to denote variables pertaining to the foreign country.

Using equation (21), the interest parity for period $t-1$ is

$$s_{t-1} = E_{t-1} s_t + i_{t-1}^* - i_{t-1} \tag{24}$$

Subtracting equation (24) from equation (21) and using equations (22) and (23) yields

$$s_t = s_{t-1} + [(p_t - p_{t-1}) - (p_t^* - p_{t-1}^*)] + [(r_t^* - r_{t-1}^*) - (r_t - r_{t-1})]$$

$$+ E_t[s_{t+1} - (p_{t+1} - p_{t+1}^*)] - E_{t-1}[s_t - (p_t - p_t^*)] \tag{25}$$

TABLE 8. CORRELATIONS BETWEEN INNOVATIONS IN INTEREST RATE DIFFERENTIALS AND EXCHANGE RATES USING MONTHLY DATA: JUNE 1973–JULY 1979 AND AUGUST 1979–JANUARY 1982 [1]

Exchange Rates	Innovations in 1-Month Interest Rate Differentials		Innovations in 12-Month Interest Rate Differentials	
	June 1973–July 1979	August 1979–January 1982	June 1973–July 1979	August 1979–January 1982
ln S Dollar/pound	0.06	−0.21	0.08	−0.22
Dollar/franc	0.14	−0.11	0.13	−0.16
Dollar/deutsche mark	0.07	−0.09	0.07	−0.14
Innovations in ln S Dollar/pound	0.27	−0.65	0.37	−0.68
Dollar/franc	0.30	−0.48	0.29	−0.70
Dollar/deutsche mark	0.25	−0.30	0.24	−0.45
Δ ln S Dollar/pound	0.29	−0.56	0.37	−0.59
Dollar/franc	0.28	−0.46	0.26	−0.69
Dollar/deutsche mark	0.25	−0.31	0.24	−0.48
Innovations in Δ ln S Dollar/pound	0.23	−0.65	0.34	−0.68
Dollar/franc	0.31	−0.47	0.25	−0.69
Dollar/deutsche mark	0.24	−0.29	0.24	−0.44

[1] Interest rates used are the 1-month and 12-month Euromarket rates. The expected interest rate differentials used in generating the innovations in the interest rate differential were computed from regressions of the interest rate differential on a constant, two-lagged values of the differential, and the logarithm of the lagged forward exchange rate. The expected logarithm of the exchange rate used in generating the innovations in exchange rates was computed from a regression of the logarithm of the exchange rate on constant, lagged values of the logarithms of the spot and the forward exchange rates and lagged interest rate differentials. The expected change in the logarithm of the exchange rate was computed from a regression of the percentage change in the exchange rate on lagged values of the percentage change of the exchange rate, lagged values of the forward premium, and lagged values of the interest rate differential.

In deriving equation (25), it was assumed that the expected value of a variable for period t, based on the information available in period t, equals the actual value of that variable—that is, $E_t p_t = p_t$.

Equation (25) demonstrates the relation between the exchange rate and the components of the nominal rate of interest. The first bracketed term in equation (25) suggests that a rise in the domestic rate of *inflation* relative to foreign inflation is associated with a *depreciation* of the domestic currency (a rise in s_t). The second bracketed term in equation (25) suggests that a rise in the domestic *real* rate of interest relative to the foreign rate is associated with an *appreciation* of the domestic currency (a fall in s_t). The additional terms on the right-hand side of equation (25) describe differences in expectations concerning real exchange rates.[16] The different relations between the exchange rate, on the one hand, and the two components of the nominal interest rate, on the other, form the basis for the policy prescription specified below.

Policy Prescription

The recommended policy prescription is based on the supposition that data from the foreign exchange market can be used in combination with data on interest rates to provide the monetary authorities with useful information on money market conditions. Such information can contribute to the improved conduct of monetary policy in spite of the difficulties which stem from the constraints imposed by the openness of the economy. Accordingly, the *combination* of a high nominal interest rate differential and a depreciation of the currency, which seems to have prevailed in the United States during most of the 1970s, may have indicated a rise in inflationary expectations, which should obviously not have been fueled by an increase in the money supply. On the other hand, the *combination* of a high nominal interest rate differential and an *appreciation* of the currency that seems to have prevailed since the latter part of 1979 may have indicated a rise in the demand for money, which *should* have been accommodated by an expansionary monetary policy (this argument draws on Frenkel and Mussa (1980, 1981) and Frenkel (1981)).

This prescription, which is based on the relation between exchange rates and interest rates, can also shed light on the recent controversy concerning the proper conduct of U.S. monetary policy in view of the high rates of interest that have prevailed since 1980. The relatively tight monetary policy

---

[16]The distinction between the roles of real and nominal rates of interest has been emphasized by Frankel (1979). The framework underlying equation (25) is based on Isard (1983). See also the discussion in Edwards (1983). The interpretation of the empirical record in terms of the three bracketed terms in equation (25) should be viewed as only suggestive, since in practice these terms represent endogenous variables that need to be explained, along with the exchange rate, in terms of the exogenous variables.

which accompanied the high nominal rate of interest in the U.S. was explained by the fact that the high nominal rate of interest was primarily due to high inflationary expectations. As a counterargument, it was stated that the prime reason for the high nominal rate of interest was the high real interest rate rather than inflationary expectations. Obviously, the two alternative prescriptions call for fundamentally different monetary policies. To combat inflationary expectations, monetary policy had to be tight; but to combat high real rates of interest, a case could be made for a more relaxed monetary policy.

Here again, the relation between the exchange rate and the rate of interest can provide the monetary authorities with information that can be helpful in solving the "signal extraction" problem. By and large, since the latter part of 1979, the high nominal rate of interest in the United States has been accompanied by an appreciation of the dollar. This suggests that from late 1979 to the present (end of 1982), the important factor underlying the evolution of the U.S. nominal interest rate has been the evolution of the real rate of interest rather than inflationary expectations. Under such circumstances, U.S. monetary policy could have been more relaxed and could have paid even more attention to the underlying reasons for the high real interest rates.

Several factors have contributed to the rise in real interest rates. First, there have been large current and prospective budget deficits in the United States and in the rest of the world associated with large borrowing needs for government finance. Second, especially in the United States, the disinflation policies and monetary tightness created a liquidity shortage and induced upward pressures on real rates of interest. Third, stagflation lowered the hedging quality of bonds. (With a weak economy and high inflation, the real interest rate on bonds declines. For bonds to be more attractive to bondholders, they must bear a higher real yield.) Fourth, high real interest rates reflected a rise in the risk premium, which could be attributable to several factors: (a) the projected rise in future budget deficits may have created uncertainty about how these deficits would be financed; (b) the volatility of monetary policy since late 1979 may have induced a rise in the risk premium; and (c) the fragility of the world financial system, the sequence of banking crises, the increased perception of sovereign risk, increased sensitivity to large exposures, and the increased reluctance to extend additional credit may all have contributed to the rise in the risk premium and in real interest rates. This rise in risk has been reflected in the increased yield spread between high-quality and low-quality bonds. Fifth, it has been argued that changes in the laws dealing with the treatment of depreciation and with bankruptcies have also contributed to the rise in real interest rates.

This perspective suggests that monetary policy can use the information provided by the foreign exchange market to identify the source of variations in nominal rates of interest. Thus, the external sector, while imposing severe constraints on monetary policy, is also providing the monetary authorities with useful information.

V. ROLE OF THE FUND AND INSTITUTIONAL REFORM

The unprecedented heights of real rates of interest in the United States and in the rest of the world, coupled with world recession and with the debt explosion of developing countries, have resulted in severe difficulties in world credit markets and have served to focus attention on the provision of international liquidity and credit, as well as on the role of the lender of last resort.

The responsibility of the lender of last resort is to step in and lend (possibly at penalty rates) so as to ensure that credit markets do not dry up. How is this responsibility related to the International Monetary Fund? Generally, the role of the lender of last resort for domestic banks must be assumed by each central bank, keeping in mind, of course, that its purposes are to protect depositors and to prevent panic without necessarily protecting stockholders. With respect to the role and size of the Fund, it is relevant to note that the Fund's lending operations are secondary to its main responsibility of maintaining the smooth operation of the international payments mechanism. The instruments which the Fund has at its disposal are the various conditionality measures it uses as criteria for lending. The application of the Fund's conditionality measures may signal potential lenders that the risk of lending to the countries in question has been reduced and, thereby, may open up credit lines. Of course, this operation may not be as smooth in the short run, when the Fund itself may need to step in and prevent the drying up of credit lines to countries which are seriously illiquid. For such cases, there is indeed a serious argument for an increase in the Fund's financial resources and possibly even for the institution of some collaborative arrangements between the Fund and major commercial banks concerning the proper provision of credits. If such resources are not provided, countries may be tempted to regain monetary control by imposing protectionist measures.

Indeed, world recession and rising unemployment have led to the dangerous growth of protectionism and inward-looking policies. These policies have been reflected in the imposition of barriers to the free international flow of goods and capital as well as in attempts to manipulate exchange rates. Countries introduced these measures in attempts to diminish the constraints that the openness of the economy imposes on the effectiveness of their policies.

In principle, the legal framework necessary for the prevention of such measures is partially in place. The principles and procedures for Fund surveillance of exchange rate policies should contribute to diminishing the number of incidents of exchange rate manipulation which are aimed at preventing effective balance of payments adjustment. Likewise, the rules of the General Agreement on Tariffs and Trade (GATT) are intended to reduce the number of policy-induced trade barriers. Consequently, it is extremely important that such international institutions be strengthened.

There is, however, a need for an important institutional reform that would provide a key addition to the GATT and to Fund surveillance. The GATT deals with interventions that affect the trade account of the balance of payments, and Fund surveillance deals with interventions that affect exchange rates. Under a clean float, however, any policy that affects the current account of the balance of payments must also be fully reflected in the capital account, and vice versa. It follows that capital market interventions may have protectionist trade effects as severe as those resulting from the imposition of more conventional trade barriers.[17] A third agreement is therefore required to deal directly with interventions that affect the capital account of the balance of payments. Without a capital account analog to the GATT—which may be called the General Agreement on Capital Flows (GACF)—or without a proper extension of the principles of surveillance to the broader range of monetary policies and capital market interventions, efforts to reduce protectionism may be rendered futile by countries' attempts to regain monetary control by imposing barriers to the free flow of capital.

[17]While the protectionist impacts of capital account interventions may be as severe as those arising from conventional trade barriers, there are important differences between the two forms of protection. Capital account intervention tends to result in a closer synchronization of expenditures and income and, consequently, in smaller current account imbalances. Trade intervention may also affect the size of the current account, but its pronounced effects may be reflected in the commodity composition of trade.

APPENDICES

I. List of Countries [1]

Developed Countries	Developing Countries	
United Kingdom	Argentina	Jamaica
Austria	Brazil	Israel
Belgium	Chile	Jordan
Denmark	Colombia	Egypt
France	Costa Rica	Burma
Germany, Fed. Rep.	Dominican Republic	Sri Lanka
Italy	Ecuador	China
Netherlands	El Salvador	India
Norway	Guatemala	Korea
Sweden	Honduras	Malaysia
Switzerland	Mexico	Pakistan
Japan	Nicaragua	Philippines
Finland	Panama	Thailand
Greece	Paraguay	Ghana
Iceland	Peru	Sudan
Ireland	Venezuela	Tunisia
Portugal		
Spain		
Turkey		
Australia		
New Zealand		
South Africa		

[1]Classification of countries is based on that developed by the International Monetary Fund.

II. Definitions and Variables

All data sources are from *International Financial Statistics (IFS)* tapes obtained from the International Monetary Fund (the December 1979 version for the developed countries, and the May 1979 version for the developing countries), except as indicated. Data for the developed countries have been updated using the August 1980 issue of *IFS*.

R: *International reserves* are measured in real end-of-period millions of U.S. dollars using the U.S. GNP deflator P. Reserves are defined as the sum of gold (valued at the former U.S. dollar equivalent of SDR 35 per ounce), SDRs, foreign exchange, and reserve positions in the Fund. When reserves are reported in local currency, they are converted to U.S. dollars using the end-of-period exchange rate.

IM: *Imports* are measured c.i.f. in billions of U.S. dollars. When reported in local currency, they are converted to U.S. dollars using the average exchange rate for the period.

Y: *Real income*. GNP and GDP are reported in local currency units. These figures are converted to real billions of U.S. dollars using the average exchange rate for the period and the U.S. GNP deflator, P.

m: The *average propensity to import* is defined as the ratio of imports to GNP. When the latter data are unavailable, GDP is used instead.

σ: *Variability measure*. To calculate the value of σ_T^2 for the year T for a given country, the following regression is first run with reserves in nominal terms:

$$R_t = \alpha + \beta_{T-1} t + u \quad \text{over} \quad t = T - 15, \ldots, T - 1$$

(except for 1963, for which (owing to lack of data) $\bar{\sigma}_T^2$ is based on the previous 14 observations). Then, using the estimated trend $\hat{\beta}_{T-1}$, $\bar{\sigma}_T^2$ is defined as

$$\bar{\sigma}_T^2 = \sum_{t=T-14}^{T-1} (R_t - R_{t-1} - \hat{\beta}_{T-1})^2 / 14$$

Thus, $\bar{\sigma}_T^2$ is defined as the variance of the trend-adjusted changes in the stock of international reserves. A plot of the time series of reserves reveals that the assumption of a linear trend seems more appropriate than that of an exponential trend. In order to obtain a measure of variability that is free of scale, the variability measure for period T that is used is the ratio of the standard error of the trend-adjusted changes in reserves to the value of imports. Thus, $\sigma_T = \bar{\sigma}_T / IM_T$.

P: Prices are measured by the U.S. GNP deflator from the *IFS* annual issue dated May 1976. They are updated using the August 1980 issue of *IFS*.

REFERENCES

Allen, Polly R., and Peter B. Kenen, *Asset Markets, Exchange Rates and Economic Integration* (Cambridge, England: Cambridge University Press, 1980).

Archibald, G.C., and J. Richmond, "On the Theory of Foreign Exchange Reserve Requirements," *Review of Economic Studies*, Vol. 38 (April 1971), pp. 245-63.

Balestra, Pietro, and Marc Nerlove, "Pooling Cross Section and Time Series Data in the Estimation of a Dynamic Model: The Demand for Natural Gas," *Econometrica*, Vol. 34 (1966), pp. 585-612.

Bilson, John F.O., and Jacob A. Frenkel (1979 a), *Dynamic Adjustment and the Demand for International Reserves*, National Bureau of Economic Research, Working Papers, No. 407 (November 1979).

―――― (1979 b), "International Reserves: Adjustment Dynamics," *Economics Letters*, Vol. 4 (June 1979), pp. 267-70.

Branson, William H., "Assets Markets and Relative Prices in Exchange Rate Determination," *Sozialwissenschaftliche Annalen* (No. 1, 1979), pp. 69-89.

Claassen, Emil M., "The Optimizing Approach to the Demand for International Reserves," *Weltwirtschaftliches Archiv* (No. 3, 1974), pp. 353-98.

Clark, Peter B. (1970 a), "Demand for International Reserves: A Cross-Country Analysis," *Canadian Journal of Economics*, Vol. 3 (November 1970), pp. 577-94.

_____ (1970 b), "Optimum International Reserves and the Speed of Adjustment," *Journal of Political Economy*, Vol. 78 (April 1970), pp. 356-76.

Clower, Robert, and Richard Lipsey, "The Present State of International Liquidity Theory," *American Economic Review: Papers and Proceedings of the Eightieth Annual Meeting of the American Economic Association*, Vol. 57 (May 1968), pp. 586-95.

Cohen, Benjamin J., "International Reserves and Liquidity: A Survey," in *International Trade and Finance*, ed. by Peter B. Kenen (Cambridge, England: Cambridge University Press, 1975), pp. 411-51.

Courchene, Thomas J., and G.M. Youseff, "The Demand for International Reserves," *Journal of Political Economy*, Vol. 75 (August 1967), pp. 404-13.

Cumby, Robert E., "Special Drawing Rights and Plans for Reform of the International Monetary System: A Survey," Chapter 10 in this volume (1983).

Edwards, Sebastian, "A Note on the Dynamic Adjustment of the Demand for International Reserves by LDC's," *Economics Letters*, Vol. 5 (1980), pp. 71-74.

_____, "Comments on 'An Accounting Framework and Some Issues for Modelling How Exchange Rates Respond to the News'," in *Exchange Rates and International Macroeconomics*, ed. by Jacob A. Frenkel (Chicago: University of Chicago Press, forthcoming in 1983).

Flanders, M. June, *The Demand for International Reserves*, Studies in International Finance, No. 27 (Princeton, New Jersey: International Finance Section, Princeton University, 1971), pp. 1-50.

Frenkel, Jacob A. (1974 a) "Openness and the Demand for International Reserves," in *National Monetary Policies and the International Financial System*, ed. by Robert Z. Aliber (Chicago: University of Chicago Press, 1974), pp. 289-98.

_____ (1974 b) "The Demand for International Reserves by Developed and Less-Developed Countries," *Economica*, Vol. 41 (February 1974), pp. 14-24.

_____, "International Reserves: Pegged Exchange Rates and Managed Float," in *Economic Policies in Open Economies*, ed. by Karl Brunner and Allan H. Meltzer, Carnegie-Rochester Conference Series on Public Policy, Vol. 9 (Amsterdam: North-Holland, July 1978), pp. 111-40.

_____, "Flexible Exchange Rates, Prices and the Role of 'News': Lessons from the 1970's," *Journal of Political Economy*, Vol. 89 (August 1981), pp. 665-705.

_____, "Monetary Policy: Domestic Targets and International Constraints," *American Economic Review: Papers and Proceedings of the Ninety-Fifth Annual Meeting of the American Economic Association*, Vol. 73 (May 1983), pp. 48-53.

_____, and Joshua Aizenman, "Aspects of the Optimal Management of Exchange Rates," *Journal of International Economics*, Vol. 13 (November 1982), pp. 231-56.

Frenkel, Jacob A., and Craig S. Hakkio, "Country-Specific and Time-Specific Factors in the Demand for International Reserves," *Economics Letters*, Vol. 5 (1980), pp. 75-80.

Frenkel, Jacob A., and Boyan Jovanovic, "Optimal International Reserves: A Stochastic Framework," *Economic Journal*, Vol. 91 (June 1981), pp. 507-14.

Frenkel, Jacob A., and Michael L. Mussa, "The Efficiency of Foreign Exchange Markets and Measures of Turbulence," *American Economic Review: Papers and Proceedings of the Ninety-Second Annual Meeting of the American Economic Association*, Vol. 70 (May 1980), pp. 374-81.

———, "Monetary and Fiscal Policies in an Open Economy," *American Economic Review: Papers and Proceedings of the Ninety-Third Annual Meeting of the American Economic Association*, Vol. 71 (May 1981), pp. 253-58.

Frenkel, Jacob A., and Carlos A. Rodriguez, "Portfolio Equilibrium and the Balance of Payments: A Monetary Approach," *American Economic Review*, Vol. 65 (September 1975), pp. 674-88.

Goldfeld, Stephen M., and Richard E. Quandt, eds., *Studies in Nonlinear Estimation* (Cambridge, Massachusetts: Ballinger, 1976).

Grubel, Herbert G., "The Demand for International Reserves: A Critical Review of the Literature," *Journal of Economic Literature*, Vol. 9 (December 1971), pp. 1148-66.

———, "The Optimum Supply of International Reserves in a World of Managed Floating," Paper presented at the Conference on The New International Monetary System, Washington, November 11-12, 1976. This paper is reproduced in Robert A. Mundell and Jacques J. Polak, eds., *The New International Monetary System* (New York: Columbia University Press, 1977), pp. 133-61.

Gujarti, Damodar, "The Use of Dummy Variables in Testing for Equality Between Sets of Coefficients in Linear Regressions: A Generalization," *American Statistician*, Vol. 24 (December 1970), pp. 18-22.

Heller, H. Robert, "Optimal International Reserves," *Economic Journal*, Vol. 76 (June 1966), pp. 296-311.

———, and Mohsin S. Khan, "The Demand for International Reserves Under Fixed and Floating Exchange Rates," International Monetary Fund, *Staff Papers*, Vol. 25 (December 1978), pp. 623-49.

Hipple, F. Steb, *The Disturbances Approach to the Demand for International Reserves*, Studies in International Finance, No. 35 (Princeton, New Jersey: International Finance Section, Princeton University, May 1974).

International Monetary Fund, *International Reserves: Needs and Availability* (Washington, 1970).

Isard, Peter, "An Accounting Framework and Some Issues for Modelling How Exchange Rates Respond to the News," in *Exchange Rates and International Macroeconomics*, ed. by Jacob A. Frenkel (Chicago: University of Chicago Press, forthcoming in 1983).

Iyoha, Milton A., "Demand for International Reserves in Less Developed Countries: A Distributed Lag Specification," *Review of Economics and Statistics*, Vol. 58 (August 1976), pp. 351-55.

Kelly, Michael G., "The Demand for International Reserves," *American Economic Review*, Vol. 60 (September 1970), pp. 655–67.

Kenen, Peter B., and Elinor B. Yudin, "The Demand for International Reserves," *Review of Economics and Statistics*, Vol. 47 (August 1965), pp. 242–50.

Levi, Victor, "Demand for International Reserves and Exchange-Rate Intervention Policy in an Adjustable-Peg Economy," *Journal of Monetary Economics*, Vol. 11 (January 1983), pp. 89–101.

Makin, John H., "Exchange Rate Flexibility and the Demand for International Reserves," *Weltwirtschaftliches Archiv* (No. 2, 1974), pp. 229–43.

Metzler, Lloyd A., "Wealth, Savings and the Rate of Interest," *Journal of Political Economy*, Vol. 59 (April 1951), pp. 93–116.

Mundell, Robert A., "The Public Debt, Corporate Income Taxes and the Rate of Interest," *Journal of Political Economy*, Vol. 68 (December 1960), pp. 622–26.

———, *International Economics* (New York: Macmillan, 1968).

Mussa, Michael L., "The Exchange Rate, the Balance of Payments and Monetary and Fiscal Policy Under a Regime of Controlled Floating," *Scandinavian Journal of Economics*, Vol. 78 (May 1976), pp. 229–48. This article is reprinted in Jacob A. Frenkel and Harry G. Johnson, eds., *The Economics of Exchange Rates: Selected Studies* (Reading, Massachusetts: Addison-Wesley, 1978).

———, "Empirical Regularities in the Behavior of Exchange Rates and Theories of the Foreign Exchange Market," in *Policies for Employment, Prices, and Exchange Rates*, ed. by Karl Brunner and Allan H. Meltzer, Carnegie-Rochester Conference Series on Public Policy, Vol. 11 (Amsterdam: North-Holland, 1979), pp. 9–57.

———, "The Role of Official Intervention," Group of Thirty, Occasional Papers, No. 6 (New York, 1981).

Obstfeld, Maurice, "Exchange Rates, Inflation and the Sterilization Problem: Germany, 1975–1981," *European Economic Review*, Vol. 16 (forthcoming in 1983).

Quandt, Richard E., "The Estimation of the Parameters of a Linear Regression System Obeying Two Separate Regimes," *Journal of the American Statistical Association*, Vol. 53 (December 1958), pp. 873–80.

———, "Tests of the Hypothesis that a Linear Regression System Obeys Two Separate Regimes," *Journal of the American Statistical Association*, Vol. 55 (June 1960), pp. 324–30.

Suss, Esther C., "A Note on Reserve Use Under Alternative Exchange Rate Regimes," International Monetary Fund, *Staff Papers*, Vol. 23 (July 1976), pp. 387–94.

Theil, Henri, *Economic Forecasts and Policy* (Amsterdam: North-Holland, 2nd ed., 1961).

von Furstenberg, George M., "New Estimates of the Demand for Non-Gold Reserves Under Floating," *Journal of International Money and Finance*, Vol. 1 (April 1982), pp. 81–95.

Wallich, Henry C. (1982 a), "Intervention Differences Hinge on Definition," *Journal of Commerce*, Vol. 353 (August 12, 1982), p. 4A.

＿＿＿ (1982 b), "Intervention's Psychological Impact Mulled," *Journal of Commerce*, Vol. 353 (August 13, 1982), p. 4A.

Williamson, John, "International Liquidity: A Survey," *Economic Journal*, Vol. 83 (September 1973), pp. 685-746.

＿＿＿, "Generalized Floating and the Reserve Needs of Developing Countries," in *The International Monetary System and the Developing Nations*, ed. by Danny M. Leipziger (Washington: Agency for International Development, 1976), pp. 75-86.

Comments

Ryutaro Komiya

The first half of Professor Frenkel's paper presents the results of an empirical study of the demand for international reserves and concludes that countries' behavior with regard to reserves did not change much on account of the changes in the legal framework of the exchange rate regime, and that the move to greater flexibility of exchange rates has not reduced significantly the need for international reserves. This result is quite interesting but not surprising, and it could be misleading in a way, especially when one is considering policy issues concerning major developed countries.

In terms of the number of countries, a large majority of Fund members either still peg their currencies or have adopted heavily managed floating systems and thus are not making much use of the greater flexibility allowed. But four or five major countries or currency areas—the United States, the European Community, Japan, the United Kingdom, and Canada have, by and large, adopted freely and widely fluctuating exchange rates. This adoption of floating rates by these four or five has changed the world monetary and financial scenes greatly.

Besides these four or five, only a few countries have adopted freely—or nearly freely—fluctuating exchange rate systems. This is because the floating system is workable only when certain conditions are met. The country must have well-developed financial and foreign exchange markets, and both trade and capital movements must be largely liberalized. Also, perhaps the country must have a certain size, in order to avoid monopolistic selling or buying of its currency, and also for optimum-currency-area reasons. Presumably, these conditions are not met in a large majority of countries.

In Japan, the behavior of the foreign exchange authorities in regard to reserves and the meaning of reserves have both changed greatly during the last ten years. I think this is, more or less, true of other countries that have adopted the freely floating system. Frenkel's equations (1) and (12) may be appropriate as descriptions of the pattern of reserve behavior of a majority of Fund members in Frenkel's sample, which still peg their currencies or have adopted heavily managed floating systems by severely restricting capital flows, but not of the four or five major countries over the past ten years. The exchange rate systems of the latter countries or currency areas nowadays are very close to an entirely freely floating system.

110

The amount of Japan's official reserves at present is approximately US$24 billion, which puts them among the five or six largest in the world. Yet official reserves are very small relative to the volume of trade, equivalent to only about two months of Japan's imports. In the spring of 1980, reserves went down to a record low level of about 1.5 months of imports. In the early 1960s, Japan had reserves amounting to 3 to 4 months' imports, but then it was not yet an Article VIII member of the Fund and severely restricted import and other foreign exchange payments.

Moreover, nowadays Japanese private banks have heavy short-term debts vis-à-vis nonresidents. Their *net* external indebtedness increased enormously after 1979, and is now more than US$40 billion. The international liquidity position of the Japanese Government, central bank, and private banks combined, including official reserves and short-term lending and borrowing, is a negative value of about US$17 billion at present.

In Japan, even as late as 1975, when the net short-term external indebtedness of the private banks exceeded the official reserves for the first time since such statistics began to be published in 1964, the foreign exchange authorities considered such a situation alarming and thought it should be corrected by increasing the official reserves, by reducing borrowing, or both. But today, with a very low level of official reserves relative to imports and with huge net short-term borrowing, few Japanese, including the officials in charge, worry about Japan's liquidity problem.

Why do few Japanese worry about Japan's very thin reserve position? Because Japan has adopted the floating system and is now well accustomed to it. Under the floating system, private capital flows have increased very substantially in volume as well as in variety. These increased flows have resulted primarily from the liberalization of capital movements made possible by the shift to the floating system. Under the system, capital flows respond, generally speaking, not to changes in interest rates but to movements of exchange rates. Basically, in recent years, when people think that the yen has depreciated sufficiently, capital flows into Japan; and when people think the yen has appreciated enough, capital flows out of Japan. Thus, international liquidity is made available whenever needed, mainly through these private capital flows responding to movements in the exchange rate. Therefore, there is no need to keep a large amount of official reserves.

The fact that Japanese banks have heavy short-term debts vis-à-vis nonresidents is a reflection of the fact that Japan is increasingly playing the roles of a banking center and of a major capital exporter. Japanese banks are raising funds by means of short-term borrowing or accepting deposits and are actively lending on long and medium terms.

Thus, the main reason why Japan's international reserves are now very small relative to trade volume and short-term liabilities is that large reserves are not necessary under the floating system. Another reason is that it is sometimes not easy for the Japanese authorities to increase reserves, even when they think it is necessary or desirable to do so. As I mentioned earlier, in 1975, the international liquidity position of the Japanese Government and banking sector combined turned negative for the first time. This was primarily the result of selling intervention conducted in the autumn of 1975: the Japanese authorities sold about US$2.7 billion to keep the yen-dollar rate from depreciating beyond 300 yen. When the yen began to appreciate gradually in early 1976, the Japanese authorities bought about US$1.5 billion through market intervention; this was a much smaller amount than had been involved in the selling intervention just a few months earlier. I suppose that the buying intervention was conducted, at least partly, because Japan's total liquidity position had recently turned negative for the first time. Yet the buying intervention by the Japanese authorities at the beginning of 1976 was strongly criticized by the U.S. and some European Governments as an attempt to keep the yen undervalued to promote exports during a worldwide depression. Thereafter, the Japanese Government was much more reserved and cautious in conducting buying intervention, until the yen rose very sharply beginning in the autumn of 1977.

Similarly, in 1979–82, the Japanese Government often conducted selling intervention on a large scale in an attempt to keep the yen exchange rate from depreciating further. A very large amount of reserves was sold to the market, but Japan did not have much success in stopping further depreciation of the yen. This was done partly to avoid criticisms from foreign countries that Japan was intentionally keeping the yen undervalued. These events show that the reserve behavior pattern represented by Frenkel's model is not applicable to Japan in recent years.

Now, I turn to the effectiveness of exchange market intervention, which is discussed in Section III of Frenkel's paper.

In the first years of the floating system, market participants more or less believed in the ability of the foreign exchange authorities to determine the market rate and to forecast the future rate correctly, so that intervention was often effective. This is the effect of intervention achieved by affecting expectations. But, as time went on, and especially after the autumn of 1977, market participants became disillusioned about the authorities' abilities to stabilize the exchange rates. Nowadays, the effectiveness of intervention in keeping the exchange rate at a particular level or within a particular range depends on what Frenkel calls portfolio-balance effects.

However, the portfolio-balance effect appears to have been very small in recent years, at least in Japan, compared, first, with the volume of foreign exchange transactions arising from exports and imports and, second, with the balances of foreign-currency-denominated assets and liabilities held by the public.

In Japan, exchange controls have been very substantially liberalized and, under present conditions, leads and lags in the settlement of exports and imports can easily take place on a large scale in various forms and do, in fact, take place every day, depending upon movements of exchange rates and the state of market participants' expectations, although I will not go into the details of this process here. Since in Japan the size of the official reserves is now approximately equal to two months' imports, as stated earlier, only one month's leads and lags in export and import payments could either wipe out the reserves or double them in a few weeks. Either could happen if the authorities intervened strongly against the market forces in an effort to keep the exchange rate at a level incompatible with expectations dominant among market participants.

Moreover, for Japan, the volumes of both capital inflows and outflows have increased enormously since 1977–78. Both Japanese and foreign investors have been increasingly diversifying their portfolios. Also, both Japanese and foreign corporations have been diversifying their sources of funds. As a result, the balance of foreign-currency-denominated financial assets held by residents (excluding direct investment) plus the balance of yen-denominated liabilities owed by nonresidents is now perhaps of the order of 5 to 7 times official reserves. On the other hand, the balance of yen-denominated financial assets held by nonresidents plus the balance of foreign-currency-denominated liabilities owed by residents is, again, perhaps of the order of 6 to 8 times reserves. Compared with these investment and debt balances, the amount of funds which could reasonably be mobilized for intervention without jeopardizing domestic price stability, whether sterilized or nonsterilized and whether by Japan alone or jointly with other countries, is miniscule.

An unknown, but fairly large, proportion of these assets and liabilities is held without forward cover or without being hedged in other ways. When people expect an imminent sharp appreciation or depreciation of the yen, but the foreign exchange authorities intervene strongly against market forces trying to keep the exchange rate from appreciating or depreciating, people will sell these assets, cover assets or obligations by means of forward exchange dealings, and hedge by borrowing funds in one currency and changing them into another. This will result in a scramble for either dollars or yen that cannot be effectively counteracted by official intervention.

In view of the large fluctuations in exchange rates in recent years, the so-called target-zone approach has been proposed from time to time. However, such an approach will encounter the same difficulties as the old adjustable-peg system once the market rate hits the ceiling or the floor of the target zone. Such proposals seem to ignore the fact that the volume of potential payment flows arising from trade-related leads and lags and from shifts and hedging between assets and liabilities in different currencies has increased enormously since the last years of the Bretton Woods regime. Thus, exchange rate intervention can no longer be effective. The only possible way to stabilize the exchange rate is to stabilize the expectations of market participants.

Finally, on the problem of monetary control and constraints on monetary policy under fixed and floating rate systems, I think that under fixed rates it is difficult for a country to control the national nominal money stock, as Frenkel states, and inflation tends to spread from one country to another. A similar situation arises if the foreign exchange authorities intervene strongly against market forces under the floating system. Monetary control in each country is generally much easier under the floating system.

Under the floating system, depreciation of a country's currency pushes up domestic prices, as Frenkel points out, but I think such an effect would be relatively small, so long as the domestic money supply was controlled reasonably well.

Recent high interest rates in the United States are thought to cause appreciation of the U.S. dollar, and it has been asserted that European countries and Japan are forced to raise their domestic interest rates in order to avoid sharp depreciation of their currencies. In this way, it is said, either inflation or high interest rates spread from one country to another even under the floating system. As a matter of fact, from March to November 1982, the Bank of Japan tried to raise short-term interest rates in an attempt to check further depreciation of the yen without much success, in spite of stagnant domestic business conditions.

I do not think such a policy of monetary tightening in a depression for the purpose of avoiding depreciation is a well-advised one. First, I am still skeptical about the linkage between interest rates and the exchange rate. The linkage is, at best, a weak one, and it depends on the state of expectations, as Frenkel demonstrates very clearly.

Second, for most countries, so long as the money supply is reasonably well controlled, depreciation of its effective exchange rate resulting from volatile exchange rate movements will be within a range of, say, 15 to 30 percent, rather than a range of 40 to 60 percent, within a year. Capital movements under the floating system will not always be stabilizing in the narrow range and in the short run, but will be stabilizing within a certain wider range and over the medium-to-long term. Thus, the inflationary effect of volatile fluctuations in the exchange rate upon the gross national product (GNP) deflator will, normally, not be too large: probably 2 to 3 percent at most for a major country, unless a vicious wage-price spiral has already been started within the country by its own inflationary monetary policies.

In this regard, I fully agree with Frenkel (p. 96) that "consideration of the external value of the currency should play a relatively minor role in the design of monetary policy" and that "the major consideration guiding the monetary authorities should be the achievement of price stability."

In conclusion, I would like to suggest that in today's turbulent world, where unexpected events occur often, countries cannot have the following three things at the same time: (1) independent, uncoordinated monetary policies; (2) liberalization of both trade and capital movements to take full advantage of the benefits provided by worldwide markets in goods and services, as well as in capital funds; and (3) fixed or stable exchange rates.

Each country must give up one of the three. Even though we have experienced wide fluctuations of exchange rates among major currencies in the last few years, I still think that giving up fixed exchange rates is the best choice, at least for major countries, because such a choice makes individual countries' macroeconomic stabilization policies much easier to carry out than either of the other choices do.

Douglas D. Purvis

Jacob Frenkel's paper is rich in terms of breadth and depth of topics covered. Indeed, it is what I would call a "linear combination" paper—that is, it is a linear combination of several shorter papers. In commenting on such a paper, one could either look at the individual pieces that are combined, or at the links that do the combining. I will do a little of both.

There is a good deal of useful analysis and discussion in Frenkel's paper. There is certainly no shortage of material for a discussant to draw on. The topic Frenkel was assigned is broad enough to ensure it would be hard for any paper to touch all the bases and still have substance. But it seems to me that some institutional and policy aspects of international liquidity and monetary control are omitted here, as I shall note below. Nevertheless, I shall focus my comments primarily on what has been written, not on what has *not*. While Frenkel does make a number of useful and interesting points, I should point out that the nature of my task is to concentrate on the major points of disagreement.

Demand for Reserves

The first section of the paper presents some empirical results on the demand for reserves. The purpose is to verify and explain the puzzling phenomenon of holding and use of reserves not substantially decreasing internationally since the move to flexible exchange rates in the early 1970s. Frankly, I do not feel much better informed about this after reading Frenkel's empirical results.

Frenkel does identify a structural shift in 1972—primarily a substantial fall in the constant term and an increased sensitivity to the variability measure. As he emphasizes, the overall behavior of reserve holdings was not, however, substantially changed. This is further evidence that the continued use of reserves is greater than would have been predicted prior to the move to flexible exchange rates. But the regression analysis is not particularly revealing as to why.

The cross-section estimates do not appear to me to be nearly as good as Frenkel would have us believe. The scale variable—the income term— consistently enters with a coefficient near one and a very large t-statistic. So we have the result that large countries hold more reserves than do small countries, which was true both before and after the move to flexible exchange rates. If, however, we try to explain the reserve-to-income ratio— probably a more useful way of running the regression—we will not do as well.[1] For many purposes, Frenkel's specification is appropriate, but for the current issue of identifying and explaining structural change in the pattern of reserve holdings, the specification seems to me to be inappropriate. It overstates the "goodness of fit" and it understates the changes that occur. Scaling reserves by income would result in a poorer fit, but the results might be more informative in evaluating the impact of the change in exchange rate regime.

The constant term does most of the remaining work; and in cross-section data, it is tempting to interpret this as a measure of the unexplained part of reserve holdings. It would have been useful to know more about the data, especially sample means, so that his results could be more accurately interpreted. Only in the pooled data do the more interesting variables—the import propensity and the partial variability measure—play a more important role.

The rest of the empirical section further documents the continued importance of reserve use, suggesting that "the move to a floating-rate regime has not reduced significantly the need for international reserves; nor has it removed the need to establish clearly the means of and mechanisms for providing such reserves (p. 86)." This provides the link to the analytical and policy discussions that constitute the remainder of the paper.

---

[1] In the current form, using *levels* of reserves, the data could be ordered by income, and the Durbin-Watson statistic used to test the specification.

Stabilization Policies

The next sections focus on the interaction between domestic stabilization policies and the international environment. The general conclusion (p. 87) is one I am in complete agreement with: "The openness of the economy imposes constraints on the effectiveness and proper conduct of macroeconomic policies in general and of monetary control in particular." However, there are a number of specific issues I wish to take issue with.[2]

Frenkel proceeds, in line with the current fashion, to relegate fiscal policy to a subordinate role. (This could, of course, be justified in terms of the specific topic he was assigned. However, I feel that ultimately one cannot fully discuss monetary control without consideration of both the domestic monetary-fiscal mix and the international coordination of fiscal policies.) There seem to be three sources of this fashion.

First, the well-known Mundell-Fleming (M-F) results indicate that fiscal policy is ineffective under flexible exchange rates. Hence, it seems natural that a move to flexible exchange rates would be accompanied by a de-emphasizing of fiscal policy. However, as shown in the Appendix, the M-F results are not robust, and there is a theoretical basis for the view that fiscal policy is effective. Further, I daresay that careful empirical work drawing on the experience of the last decade will confirm that view.

Second, the lack of credibility of "fine tuning" and the pre-eminence of "monetary growth rules" over the past decade have also contributed to the decline of interest in fiscal policy. But fine tuning is not the issue—some gross tuning may have been in order in the current recession. Further, the monetary growth rules have typically emerged as part of a concerted effort to control inflation. Recent work (Sargent and Wallace (1982), Bruce and Purvis (1983 b)) argues that for such policies to be effective, they must eventually be accompanied by fiscal contraction.

Third, recent record government budget deficits, though widely misunderstood owing to inflation distortions in their measurement (see, for example, Buiter (1983)), have severely handicapped the flexibility of fiscal policy. While such deficits did pose a real constraint on the effective use of fiscal policy—the real price we pay for past fiscal excesses—they did not preclude it. Nevertheless, the concern about deficits is real, and the possibility of "revenue grabs" by national governments in response to such concerns should be added to the concerns about rising protectionism discussed in the first session this morning; such grabs are a major cause for worry about the future performance of the world economic system.

Frenkel concludes that international capital mobility severely hinders

---

[2]The Appendix outlines a simple model which illustrates the results used below.

the effectiveness of monetary policy under flexible exchange rates and will lead to (p. 91) "increased prudence in using monetary policy." I see little in the evidence to support either of these propositions. I will, however, restrict my comments to the former.

It is true that in the long run, the homogeneity postulate ensures money neutrality. Further, in the open economy, some prices (especially those directly linked to exchange rates) are likely to adjust more quickly than conventional closed-economy macro models would have us believe for prices in general. But if other prices (domestic goods prices, for example) still adjust slowly, then this fact of rapid exchange rate adjustment will, rather than leading to money neutrality, give rise to *systematic* short-run nonneutralities that make monetary policy effective. Monetary expansion will, at given domestic prices, give rise to a sharp (real and nominal) depreciation, thus stimulating domestic demand. (Indeed, as long as domestic interest rates fall, the exchange rate will rise more than proportionately on impact—the now-famous Dornbusch overshooting result.)

This relative price change and the ensuing relative demand shift then create the "signal" for domestic producers to start raising their prices. *The short-run effectiveness of monetary policy is the vehicle by which prices respond and eventually restore neutrality.* Capital mobility in this framework speeds the process up by increasing the short-run effectiveness of monetary policy. (In the long run, of course, monetary policy can only influence the underlying inflation rate, an option that is not available under fixed exchange rates.)

I do believe that this part of Jacob Frenkel's paper understates the case for effective use of monetary and fiscal policies under flexible exchange rates. In particular, I think that the general de-emphasizing of fiscal policy in this paper and in the literature is misplaced, a point I shall return to below.

Policy Interdependence

We are left, then, with the following puzzle: if, indeed, flexible exchange rates do provide room for policy independence, why have we not observed any? National inflation rates and business cycles remain closely correlated after ten years of floating rates. I believe the explanation lies in the international repercussions of domestic policy.

In particular, it has long been known—again from the M-F model—that under flexible exchange rates, monetary policy is a beggar-thy-neighbor policy. In the Keynesian models of the 1960s (see the Appendix), monetary expansion leads to currency depreciation, thus shifting demand away from trading partners.

What seems to be not so well understood is that in an inflationary environment, monetary contraction is also a beggar-thy-neighbor policy. The rise in the domestic real interest rate elicits a real appreciation. For trading partners, failure to respond to this means a depreciation and, hence, increased domestic inflation. Just as expansionary monetary policy in a Keynesian world leads to the "export of unemployment," contractionary monetary policy in an inflationary world leads to the "export of inflation." Of course, the increase in foreign inflation is only temporary, but nevertheless, the short-run inflation-unemployment trade-off is worsened.

Faced with this possibility following the U.S. monetary contraction in the early 1980s, a number of countries raised their own real interest rates in order to defend their currencies. As a result, we experienced a substantial and concerted worldwide monetary contraction. This concert had no conductor, but instead each member of the orchestra tried to stay in tune with her neighbor with little or no regard for the musical outcome. The result was harmonious in only a very limited sense, and was certainly not melodic. The result was the severe worldwide recession we are now starting to recover from.[3]

At the risk of straining the metaphor, I quote Mark Twain, who said of Wagner that "his music is much better than it sounds." I have always taken this as a statement about either the conductor or the "conductibility" of his scores. That seems to be a central question when we evaluate the current international monetary system: is it the system which is not "conductible," or is it just that the system has been poorly conducted to date.

Until some arrangement can be made according to which national policies can be better coordinated, the system of flexible exchange rates will leave the international economy subject to influence by national government policies of dominant countries such as the United States. Any potential for independent policy action and insulation will be wasted on account of the implicit interdependence of stabilization policies.

One solution is a stronger role for the International Monetary Fund in coordinating monetary policies. A second is an increased role for national fiscal policy. In the face of a U.S. real interest rate hike, expansionary fiscal policy could be effective, since it would "protect the currency" and thus honor the commitment to disinflation while not reinforcing the U.S. contraction on an international scale. Fiscal policies need not be beggar-thy-neighbor policies in their international repercussions.[4]

---

[3] As Professor Komiya has pointed out, the one major country that did not play along was Japan, which accepted a significant depreciation. Of course, Japan is now being castigated for running such a large current account surplus.

[4] To add to Frenkel's menu for institutional reform, I add the potential need for coordination of national fiscal policies—perhaps by the Organization for Economic Cooperation and Development (OECD).

Specific Comments

While Frenkel's simple discussion of adjustment to monetary disturbances is quite useful, I was disappointed to see it draw so heavily on the tradition that (p. 89) "under flexible exchange rates, money ceases to be an internationally traded commodity." This puts all the onus on gradual adjustment of portfolios via the current account.

This view is extreme. International private holdings of money are prominent, and trade in money does not require central bank intervention. If different holders of money react differently to a given shock, at least part of the response will be an instantaneous portfolio reaction. (The strong view taken by Frenkel rules out, for example, forward cover as a possibility, since the currency-denomination mix of the portfolio is given at a point of time.)

Further, the view ignores the "n-1" problem—in response to a monetary shock in country A, the central bank of country B may intervene to provide the needed country A currency, since the original change in country A's money supply will have repercussions on country B. (A related point is that foreign financial intermediaries may increase or decrease their supply of country A's assets, again providing a role for asset swaps.) This issue of conventions and rules governing the currency of intervention and the international provisions of domestic money warrants more attention in the Frenkel paper.

Let me turn to two parts of Frenkel's paper with which I am in strong agreement. First is his skepticism about the constructive role for sterilized intervention—the seemingly clear message of the past ten years (if not longer) is that there is virtually no scope for independent control of the money supply and the exchange rate. A second is his skepticism about the constructive role for purchasing-power-parity (PPP) exchange rate rules. Here I would emphasize in particular the need to allow room for changes in the real exchange rate.

Two other minor points of agreement are (1) his emphasis that the United States should be thought of, and should think of itself as, an open economy, and (2) his emphasis, and useful summary of the evidence on, the change in the interest rate-exchange rate nexus in 1979 reflecting the increased role of real interest rate movements.

But I find unsatisfactory his later discussion of the source of these real interest rate movements. Let me now turn, in closing, to that discussion and the related prescriptions for policy. His discussion of the post-1979 increase in U.S. real interest rates and real appreciation of the dollar as something for monetary policy to respond to, rather than something caused by monetary policy, strikes me as bizarre. Perhaps the message here is not that the Federal Reserve System should have been more expansionary in response to these shocks, but that it should not have been so contractionary in the first place.

Nevertheless, his policy prescription of using interest rate *and* exchange rate observations to guide monetary policy strikes me as useful, if a bit oversold. Here I would emphasize the problem of identifying real exchange rate movements—anticipated and nonanticipated, permanent or transitory— and then deciding the optimal mix of nominal exchange rate changes and domestic price level changes to facilitate the change in the real exchange rate. Such problems, combined with the above-mentioned problems of sorting out the current effects of past monetary policy, leave me less optimistic about the information content of exchange rates and interest rates for monetary policy.

I believe that this section of Frenkel's paper, in contrast to the earlier sections, overstates the role for constructive policy.

APPENDIX

A Taxonomy of Macro Models Under Flexible Exchange Rates

This appendix lays out a highly simplified open-economy macro model and several specific variants. Except for interest rates i, all variables are expressed in logarithms. Except where noted, all parameters (Greek symbols) are positive.

Demand for domestic output (1)

$$y^d = \gamma + \alpha (e - p)$$

Demand for money (2)

$$m - \beta e - (1 - \beta)p = \phi y - \lambda i$$

Uncovered interest arbitrage and regressive expectations (3)

$$i = i^F + \theta(\bar{e} - e)$$

Supply of domestic output (4)

$$y^S = \sigma(p - e)$$

where p denotes the price of domestic goods, e the exchange rate (also the domestic price of imported goods), and a bar over a variable its long-run value.

Mundell-Fleming Model

The M-F model fixes domestic prices ($p = p_0$), assumes static expectations ($\theta = 0$), abstracts from aggregate supply ($y = y^d$), and ignores the role of import prices in the consumer price index ($\beta = 0$). This means, in terms of equation (2), that there is a unique relationship between m and y, establishing the well-known result that monetary policy is effective ($dy/dm = 1/\phi$) and fiscal policy is not ($dy/d\gamma = 0$). The latter result reflects an appreciation ($de/d\gamma = -1/\alpha$) sufficient to ensure that net exports fall by an amount equal to the increase in γ.

In the context of this Keynesian fixed-price, static-expectations model, the assumption that $\beta = 0$ is crucial. If the appreciation did increase real liquidity, then there would be some room for output expansion ($dy/d\gamma = \beta/(\beta + \phi\alpha)$). This was recognized by Mundell, but has often been neglected in the ensuing literature.

Sachs-Purvis Model

A number of recent studies focusing on flexible domestic wages—either via wage indexation (Sachs) or market clearing (Purvis)—have stressed that equilibrium output will depend on the relative price of the home good—equation (4). (See the discussion and further references in Bruce and Purvis (1983 a)).

In this model, which might be thought of as a long-run model ($y^d = y^S = y$, $\bar{e} = e$, and $\bar{p} = p$), monetary policy is impotent ($dy/dm = 0$) while fiscal policy is effective ($dy/d\gamma = \sigma/(\sigma + \alpha)$). The former result just reflects the homogeneity of the system and the classical result of monetary neutrality. The latter result reflects the fact that the increased demand for home goods raises their relative price (a real appreciation) and increases equilibrium output.

(Setting β equal to zero in this model requires that p fall in response to a fiscal-induced output expansion.)

Dornbusch Model

A link between the short-run Mundell-Fleming model and the long-run Sachs-Purvis model is provided by the framework introduced by Dornbusch (1976). He focuses on the dynamics of exchange rate and output adjustment when prices adjust slowly in response to an output gap. Long-run results are just like those derived using the Sachs-Purvis model. For impact or short-run results, the key difference from the Mundell-Fleming model is the role of exchange rate expectations, which are rational in the sense that the model solution for $\bar{e}$ is used in equation (3). (Rationality also imposes a particular value for θ, a point we abstract from.)

It is easiest to see this model where $\beta = 0$, so that real balances, now given by $m - p$, are fixed. However, in contrast to the Mundell-Fleming model, it is possible for output to change in response to fiscal policy, since domestic interest rates can deviate temporarily from i^F owing to exchange rate expectations. Fiscal policy will alter the long-run exchange rate $\bar{e}$ and, hence, will lead to expectations of exchange rate movements.

If fiscal policy is effective in raising output—which occurs if $1 - \alpha\phi > 0$—then the interest rate rises, and e falls by more than $\bar{e}$; i.e., the exchange rate overshoots. (This is the same as the condition for e to overshoot in response to monetary policy!) If $1 - \alpha\phi < 0$, then y, i, and e all fall, with the latter falling less than $\bar{e}$. Thus if $1 - \phi\alpha < 0$, the effects of fiscal policy on output will be perverse; the direct effects of a rise in γ will be outweighed on impact by the real appreciation it engenders. (This result is closely related to the "Dutch Disease" phenomenon—see Buiter and Purvis (1983).)

A similar, though more complicated, set of results holds where $\beta \neq 0$. Overshooting and ambiguous interest rate and output effects are all possible, but the relationship between them is more complicated.

REFERENCES

Bruce, Neil, and Douglas D. Purvis (1983 a), "The Structure and Influence of Goods and Factor Markets in Open Economy Macroeconomic Models," Chapter 16 in *Handbook of International Economics*, ed. by Peter B. Kenen and Ronald W. Jones (Amsterdam: North-Holland, forthcoming in 1983).

_____ (1983 b), "Some Unpleasant Keynesian Arithmetic: Long-Run Constraints for Fiscal Policy," in *Budget Deficits: How Big and How Bad* (Ontario Economic Council, forthcoming in 1983).

Buiter, Willem H., "Measurement of the Public Sector Deficit and Its Implications for Policy Evaluation and Design," International Monetary Fund, *Staff Papers*, Vol. 30 (June 1983), pp. 306-49.

_____ , and Douglas D. Purvis, "Oil, Disinflation, and Export Competitiveness," in *Macroeconomic Interdependence and Flexible Exchange Rates*, ed. by J. Bhandari and J. B. Putnam (Cambridge, Massachusetts: MIT Press, 1983).

Dornbusch, Rudiger, "Expectations and Exchange-Rate Dynamics," *Journal of Political Economy*, Vol. 84 (December 1976), pp. 1161-76.

Fleming, J. Marcus, "Domestic Financial Policies Under Fixed and Under Floating Exchange Rates," International Monetary Fund, *Staff Papers*, Vol. 9 (November 1962), pp. 369-80.

Mundell, Robert A., *International Economics* (New York: Macmillan, 1968).

Sargent, T. J., and Neil Wallace, "Some Unpleasant Monetarist Arithmetic" (unpublished, Federal Reserve Bank of Minneapolis, 1982).

Rainer Masera

(1) Professor Frenkel's paper on international liquidity and monetary control continues his well-established tradition of professionally competent and sophisticated conference papers. They always pose a very difficult task to any discussant, who, after all, is supposed to take a critical approach by drawing attention to weak or questionable points. This is especially true on the present occasion, in part because the exceedingly long paper—which covers at least three not unrelated, but certainly different, topics—did not reach me early enough to allow me fully to capture and master all the important arguments developed by Frenkel, and I apologize in advance if my remarks do not do justice to the paper.

(2) Let me start by saying that I agree with each of the three main conclusions reached by Frenkel. The first part of the paper is devoted to an

analysis of the demand for international reserves during 1963-79. A lengthy econometric analysis of the pattern of reserve holdings, which draws heavily on the author's earlier work, purportedly indicates relative stability throughout the period, although a structural change can be detected in 1972. The conclusion drawn is thus that (p. 81) "during the pegged rate regime the rate was adjustable rather than fixed, and during the so-called floating rate regime the rate has been managed rather than free. Economic behavior seems to have been more stable than legal arrangements. Central banks have revealed that their choice is neither of the extreme exchange rate systems, but rather the intermediate system of managed floating." A few pages later (p. 86) Frenkel states that "the evidence indicates that countries have continued to hold and use international reserves and that they have chosen to manage their exchange rates rather than to let them float freely." Who would want to quarrel with this kind of observation? Some would, indeed, argue that spending thirty pages in order to establish that heavily managed floating has been a crucial characteristic of the last decade is somewhat unnecessary.

The well-known figures published by the International Monetary Fund (IMF) and the Bank for International Settlements on actual interventions over this period are, for instance, quite sufficient in themselves to establish the point. However trivial the main conclusions may be deemed to be, one can argue that there is considerable interest in the finding of relative stability in demand for real reserve holdings from 1963 onward. On this finding, I do have, however, some reservations, to which I shall return.

(3) Let me continue by stressing my agreement with the main conclusions reached in the second part of the paper, which deals specifically with the issue of international constraints on monetary policy.

The well-known distinction is drawn here between sterilized and nonsterilized intervention. We are reminded that sterilized intervention can only affect the exchange rate when portfolio-balance effects are present and/or, temporarily, when such intervention affects market expectations by signaling a change in policies.

The intrinsic symmetry between domestic and foreign variables in the foreign exchange intervention process is also recognized and it is pointed out that "this symmetry suggests that there is room (and possibly a role) for international coordination of exchange rate policies." All in all, it is thus "reasonable to conclude that it is very difficult to conduct effectively independent monetary and exchange rate policies" (p. 94). Here again, who would seriously challenge this not entirely novel conclusion? Even those who, like myself, are convinced of the basic validity of the portfolio-balance model can only concur with this view.

(4) A paper on international liquidity and monetary control—even if it were not presented at a conference sponsored by the Fund—could hardly

avoid some reference to the world's most important international financial institution. It is thus no surprise that the third part of Frenkel's paper is devoted to the role of the Fund. I would venture to say that this is the weakest part of the paper.

I cannot but concur with the view that "there is indeed a serious argument for an increase in the Fund's financial resources and possibly even for the institution of some collaborative arrangements between the Fund and major commercial banks concerning the proper provision of credits. If such resources are not provided, countries may be tempted to regain monetary control by imposing protectionist measures" (p. 102).

But again, who—except possibly some persons on Capitol Hill—would take exception to these arguments? Indeed, the agreement reached on the Eighth General Review of Quotas, the enlargement of the General Arrangements to Borrow, and the moral (or immoral?) suasion of monetary authorities on commercial banks to ensure that they do not cut credit to developing countries all show that major steps in these directions have already been taken. Care has, however, been taken—rightly, I believe, and contrary to what Frenkel seems to imply and advocate—not to convey the impression that the Fund would act directly as a lender of last resort, thereby weakening its conditionality.

Frenkel ends his paper by suggesting that, however important these efforts may be, they should be supplemented by a major institutional reform involving a key addition to General Agreement on Tariffs and Trade (GATT) and Fund surveillance (p. 103):

> The GATT deals with interventions that affect the trade account of the balance of payments, and Fund surveillance deals with interventions that affect exchange rates. Under a clean float, however, any policy that affects the current account of the balance of payments must also be fully reflected in the capital account, and vice versa. It follows that capital market interventions may have protectionist trade effects as severe as those resulting from the imposition of more conventional trade barriers. A third agreement is therefore required to deal directly with interventions that affect the capital account of the balance of payments.

Two considerations must be mentioned here. First, having just established that nothing like a system of clean floating obtains in the real world, it is not entirely appropriate to draw the inference that there is a need to ensure a free flow of capital to reduce protectionism from the well-known identity of the current and capital accounts under perfect floating.

Second, the issue of capital mobility, which I believe to be a very important one, must be treated with great care, and would have merited greater attention in a paper primarily concerned with international liquidity and domestic monetary control.

The literature on the desirability of completely free capital movements in a context of free trade of goods and services does not lead to uniform conclusions. Indeed, if I remember rightly, just about the only thing on which

Keynes and White agreed at Bretton Woods was that short-term capital flows had to be strictly controlled. More recently, Tobin has, for instance, argued that a tax should be imposed on all foreign exchange transactions, with a view to reducing excessive capital mobility.

I cite these instances not because I agree with them but simply to note that the question of capital mobility is a complex one, particularly when one allows for the fact that ex ante financial policies among major financial centers have often not been coordinated.

I would thus stress the need for more effective Fund surveillance policies, which should be devoted to analysis of overall fiscal, monetary, and exchange rate policies.

(5) Now that I have indicated my full agreement with Frenkel's main conclusions, let me come to some dissenting views.

The first point I want to make concerns the analysis of the stability of the demand for international reserves. Some critical remarks of a technical nature can be addressed to the econometric analysis per se.[1] More generally, the approach taken in the study is simplistic, in that it does not attempt to take into account the impact of two major changes which occurred in the

---

[1]It appears possible to question the validity of his inference from the econometric results of both a single structural break and a minor change in behavior after the break on the following grounds:

(i) As Frenkel admits, Quandt's procedure for searching for the timing of the structural change is weak, since time is not continuously varying in the case under examination. In addition to determining a single breakpoint t^* (1972 or 1973), further insights should have been gained from an analysis of the likelihood function at different dates over the whole sample period in order to ascertain whether it had a smooth evolution or whether there were signs of additional peaks implying other possible changes.

(ii) In the "judgmental" evaluation of forecasts for 1973–79 generated from the sample estimates for the previous ten years, Frenkel uses extrapolations of both the ordinary-least-squares and generalized-least-squares estimates. To start with, he considers in the latter case only an error-component model, which takes care of $random$ country and time-specific effects, but he does not consider similar effects which could be discerned from the coefficients of the regressions; furthermore, his predictions for the country-specific factors ($\hat{\mu}_i$) should not be based on expression (8). Instead, they should be based on an expression weighted by a ratio depending upon the relative variances of this country-specific factor and the other error term ϵ_{it} (see, for instance, Taub (1979) and Judge and others (1980, pp. 334 and 343)).

(iii) The evaluation of the forecasts is, anyhow, not entirely appropriate. Frenkel uses an inequality measure U and a decomposition of this measure into three terms, two of which, U^M and U^S, should equal zero and the third, U^C, should equal one for the forecast errors to possess the "desirable" property of not being systematic. It is well known, however, as shown by Granger and Newbold (1973), that the inequality coefficient, as well as the decomposition considered by Frenkel (except for the bias component U^M), can produce misleading results, do not in general have clear-cut interpretations and should be replaced with another measure and another decomposition (see also Granger and Newbold (1977), pp. 281–82 and 287–88). Furthermore, with reported bias components of 37 percent or 26 percent, it is difficult to claim, as Frenkel does, that (p. 81) "most of the errors are not systematic."

(iv) Finally, the analysis of residuals of the many regressions is not presented. Since these regressions are based on cross-sectional data, a minimum requirement would have been proper testing for possible heteroskedasticity. In the case of pooling of time-series and cross-section data, serial correlation should obviously have been investigated as well.

period under consideration. Gold, which was an active reserve asset to start with, gradually lost this role, becoming more of a pledge against borrowing after 1973. This is a more fundamental issue than that of gold *valuation*, which, by the way, is not considered by Frenkel.

In this respect, I find it very naive to lump together gold and foreign exchange reserves without addressing the question of the opportunity cost of reserves.

Additionally, what is altogether missing in Frenkel's paper is the fact that after 1973 international reserves underwent a profound change. They used to be "net" foreign assets and represented the foreign component of the overall monetary base. After 1973, many countries resorted to the practice of liability financing in international markets: a growing difference arose between gross and net reserves, with the former no longer representing a direct counterpart of the stock of domestic high-powered money.

Before 1973, international reserves could be regarded as the international monetary base of the world's financial system. Later, they gradually lost this character, as a credit system developed in close connection with the expansion of the Eurocurrency markets. In this system, the effective regulators became the rate of interest and the spread between borrowing and lending rates.

Indeed, when, largely as a result of inadequate recognition of sovereign risks, spreads were very small, the opportunity cost of acquiring gross reserves became negligible, as was shown by the simultaneous occurrence of large rises in many countries' reserves and compensatory borrowings.

It was only in this way that countries could maintain their "gross" reserve holdings. Time does not allow me to expand further on these considerations, except to come back briefly to the question of the monetary regulator of the international financial system. Frenkel draws attention in his paper to the height of real interest rates in the United States since 1980 without, however, stressing the crucial impact on the world economy via the change brought about in the burden of international debt, largely denominated in dollars.

Taking a broader perspective, one can argue that a major constraint on the conduct of domestic monetary policies in all countries is the level of U.S. real interest rates. It is not only a question of fluctuations in real domestic dollar rates but also of the changes in the relationship between U.S. domestic inflation and world inflation as measured by the dollar prices of internationally traded goods.

In the fifties and the sixties, U.S. real rates (deflated by U.S. domestic inflation) were positive (1–2 percent); they were much higher in world terms (4–5 percent) because world trade inflation was significantly less than inflation in the United States. In the seventies, not only did U.S. real rates become negative but they turned out to be strongly negative in world terms: in other words, one could argue that during the last decade, the posture of U.S. monetary policy may have contributed, via the Eurodollar market, to "excessive" credit creation, since real interest rates were far too low for international equilibrium. In the years 1981–82, the picture changed again dramatically: U.S. domestic real rates may have been in the region of 6 percent, but they averaged well over 20 percent when deflated by the dollar prices of internationally traded goods (see Table 1 for estimates of average real short-term interest rates for the periods discussed above).

TABLE 1. ESTIMATES OF AVERAGE REAL SHORT-TERM INTEREST
RATES: 1952–69, 1970–80, AND 1981–82

Periods	U.S. federal funds rate minus U.S. consumer price inflation rate	Eurodollar interest rate minus percentage change in world import unit value measured in U.S. dollars
1952–69	+1.3	+4.5
1970–80	−0.1	−5.5
1981–82	+6	+21

A dilemma thus arises between the appropriate level of real interest rates for domestic and international equilibrium, given the workings of the Eurodollar and the primary role of the dollar. It is this dilemma which, I believe, should be the focus of a paper addressing the question of the controllability of national and international liquidity and assessing the efficacy of possible control mechanisms in meeting domestic and external objectives for economic growth and price stability.

REFERENCES

Granger, C. W. J., and P. Newbold, "Some Comments on the Evaluation of Economic Forecasts," *Applied Economics*, Vol. 5 (March 1973), pp. 35–47.

――――, *Applied Economic Forecasting* (New York: Academic Press, 1977).

Judge, G. C., and others, *The Theory and Practice of Econometrics* (New York: John Wiley, 1980).

Taub, A. J., "Prediction in the Context of the Variance-Components Model," *Journal of Econometrics*, Vol. 10 (1979), pp. 103–107.

3

International Balance of Payments Financing and Adjustment

WILLEM H. BUITER and JONATHAN EATON

With the decline in the role of gold in the international economy, the primary method that countries have used to finance payments imbalances has been borrowing and lending denominated in terms of *national* currencies. In the last century, sterling was the primary reserve currency, while in this century it has been the U.S. dollar. Recently the currencies of a number of additional countries have emerged as international stores of value. These currencies have also served as the primary currencies of denomination of international loans. The introduction of special drawing rights (SDRs) constitutes an attempt to replace national moneys with an international money for use as an international reserve. Its adoption thus far has been only partial, however, and its value remains tied to that of national currencies. In the absence of a credible commitment to a commodity exchange standard, such as the gold exchange standard, the value of assets and liabilities denominated in national currencies has been subject to the political control of the governments and central banks issuing those currencies. The use of these currencies to finance payments imbalances will depend upon the expectations held by international transactors about the strength of these institutions' commitment to maintain the real values of their currencies.

Nevertheless, a currency's introduction into use as an international store of value changes the context in which the issuers of currencies act. First, the process whereby national currencies are distributed throughout the world economy requires an adjustment via payments imbalances that may have severe economic consequences for reserve issuers and holders alike. Second, the presence of large currency balances held outside the country of issue and of loans abroad denominated in local currency has serious implications for the effect of central bank policy on national welfare. As a consequence, one might anticipate that being thrust into the role of a reserve issuer or international lender may significantly change the issuing country's monetary policy.

It is widely recognized that the use of a currency as an international reserve and currency of denomination of international assets and liabilities requires trust in the issuer's willingness and ability to maintain the real value of its currency. Triffin's (1961) discussion of the dollar problem emphasized that the U.S. dollar's widespread use as a reserve currency could, by itself, undermine belief in its long-run stability. The incentives facing a reserve issuer to undermine the value of its currency by inflation have been discussed by Mundell (1971) and Calvo (1978).

The use of national moneys as international reserves raises a number of questions: (i) What characteristics of a country make it likely to emerge as a reserve issuer? (ii) How does becoming a reserve issuer affect the inflation rate that is optimal from a national perspective? (iii) If, in fact, the rate of return on a currency is likely to fall if it is adopted as an international reserve, why are other countries' central banks willing to hold this currency as a reserve if they perceive this effect? and (iv) What are the costs and benefits of becoming a reserve issuer and a reserve holder?

The purpose of this paper is to develop a model of the interaction of national monetary policy and international reserves to answer these questions. The issue is considered from the perspective of both reserve issuers and reserve holders.

To understand how the use of national moneys as international reserves affects the conduct of monetary policy, one needs to specify the objectives of the government and the technology and preferences of the private sector. To generate a demand for currency at the national level, the exact consumption-loan model of Samuelson (1958) is adopted. While this framework is very simple and highly stylized, it does generate a demand for money based directly on an underlying technology and individual preferences. Precise welfare comparisons across regimes are therefore possible.[1]

It is assumed that the government of each country must meet an exogenous level of government spending each period. This expenditure may be financed via a nondistortionary tax imposed on the current younger generation or by monetary issue. The government's objective is to maximize a weighted average of the lifetime utilities of all generations of its citizens.

Section I presents a closed-economy version of the model. The tax rate and inflation rate that obtain in each period reflect the government's weighting of the younger and older generations currently alive. The greater

---

[1]Recently, Townsend (1980) has shown that the exact consumption-loan specification can be generated by a much larger class of transactions technologies than that suggested by the Samuelson model and subsequent literature.

the weight placed on the older generation, the lower the inflation rate, and conversely. Only when equal weight is placed on the representative member of each generation alive does the steady-state rate of return on money balances equal the growth rate, achieving the golden rule. Otherwise, the lifetime utility of the representative citizen in the steady state is below the maximum possible level. When, in fact, this is due to a rate of return on currency below the growth rate (when the government places greater weight on the utility of the younger generation), the outcome is not Pareto efficient. The problem arises because the government in any given period cannot credibly commit itself or its successor in the next period to avoid inflating the currency at a faster rate, thereby reducing the rate of return on savings to the current younger generation. It constitutes an example of the problem of the time inconsistency of optimal policy discussed by Kydland and Prescott (1977).

Section II introduces foreign reserves into the model. It incorporates both domestic holdings by the government of foreign currency and foreign holdings of domestic currency. It is assumed that reserve holders take current and future returns on foreign currencies as given, anticipating them correctly, and that reserve issuers take current and future holdings by foreigners of their currency as given, anticipating these correctly as well. It is shown that holding a foreign currency as a reserve does not affect the steady-state inflation rate of the reserve-holding country. The demand for reserves depends not only upon the government's weighting of the two generations currently alive but upon its weighting of future generations. When the government assigns future generations weights that decline geometrically into the future, then foreign reserves are demanded perfectly elastically at the rate of return on domestic currency. When the government acts only in the interests of generations currently alive, the demand for reserves is also infinitely elastic, but at a rate of return that is higher than that on domestic currency.

The rate of inflation in the reserve issuer is, however, affected by changes in foreign holdings of domestic reserves. The effect of an increase in foreign holdings on impact is ambiguous, but in the new steady state, in which more reserves are held abroad, the rate of inflation in the issuing country is necessarily higher.

Section III considers global equilibrium in a world in which there are two types of countries, one characterized by a low inflation rate under financial autarky and another by a high inflation rate under financial autarky. Two cases are distinguished, one in which gross international lending is always denominated in the currency of the lender, in which case reserves are constrained to be nonnegative, and the opposite case in which borrowing is always denominated in the currency of the borrower. The two cases generate quite different equilibria. The model developed in this paper does not predict which type of equilibrium will emerge, or whether it will be an intermediate one instead. This paper suggests, however, that a theory of default combined with an assumption of current account convertibility may be incorporated into the model to endogenize this decision.[2]

It is shown that when loans are denominated in the currency of the borrower, countries with low rates of inflation under financial autarky become borrowers, while countries with high inflation rates become lenders. Becoming a borrower in its own currency raises a country's steady-state inflation rate but has no effect on the steady-state inflation rate of the lender. Moving from financial autarky to trade in reserves thus raises the average world inflation rate. The effect during the transition from one steady state to the other may be quite different, however, with the reserve issuer experiencing a *lower* inflation rate along the way. The opposite results with respect to inflation arise when loans are denominated in the lender's currency. In this case, the high-inflation countries lend to low-inflation ones in the former group's currencies. These loans then provide an incentive for lenders to lower their inflation rates but have no effect on inflation in the second group. The average world inflation rate is consequently lower in the long run.

The model allows one to compute the welfare effects of trade in reserves. It is found that in the steady state, the utility of the representative generation is higher in lender countries but can be lower in borrower countries. The effects on generations alive during the transition may be quite different, however. The results thus suggest a justification for attempts by some governments to prevent their currencies from becoming reserve currencies.

Section IV discusses some possible extensions of our analysis that should be especially worthwhile. Each of the issues raised here can potentially be analyzed in the framework that has been developed, but they lie beyond the scope of a single paper. Section V provides a summary of the major results.

I. CLOSED-ECONOMY MODEL

The points made below are illustrated using a very simple model. This paper's point of departure is the Samuelson (1958) exact consumption-loan model. Individuals live two periods, earning income only in the first period and saving a fraction of that income in order to consume in the second period. Individuals who enter the labor force in period t earn, before tax,

---

[2]More generally, as Kareken and Wallace (1981) have pointed out, the multicountry model of the type this paper is dealing with is characterized by multiple equilibria. The paper restricts its attention to equilibria in which gross and net reserve positions are equal, and in which there is either a nonnegativity constraint or nonpositivity constraint on reserve positions. These restrictions identify a unique steady-state equilibrium.

an exogenously given amount y_t in the first period of their lives, a fraction τ_t of which is taxed by the government. Domestic government debt, which is assumed to be monetary, is the only asset available to individuals as a store of value. Output is nonstorable.

It is assumed that the utility function of a representative individual entering the labor force in period t is given by

$$U_t = \ln C_t^y + \beta \ln C_{t+1}^0 \qquad 0 \le \beta \tag{1}$$

where C_t^y denotes consumption in the first period of life, t, when the individual is young, and C_{t+1}^0 consumption when the individual is old, in period $t + 1$. While the Bernoulli assumption is special, it provides a number of restrictions that simplify the analysis substantially. The implications of relaxing some of these assumptions will be discussed later on.

Let P_t denote the price level in period t, and let m_t^d denote the real savings, and hence the real money holdings, at the end of period t of an individual born in period t. In period t, then, the individual chooses C_t^y and m_t^d to maximize U_t subject to the budget constraints

$$y_t(1 - \tau_t) - C_t^y - m_t^d \ge 0 \tag{2}$$

$$C_{t+1}^0 \le \pi_{t+1} m_t^d \tag{2'}$$

Here we define the inverse of one plus the inflation rate from period t to period $t+1$ as

$$\pi_{t+1} \equiv \frac{P_t}{P_{t+1}}$$

which equals one plus the rate of return on real money balances.

First-order conditions for a maximum imply

$$C_t^y = \frac{1}{1 + \beta}(1 - \tau_t)y_t \tag{3}$$

$$m_t^d = \frac{\beta}{1 + \beta}(1 - \tau_t)y_t \tag{3'}$$

$$C_t^0 = \pi_{t+1}\frac{\beta}{1 + \beta}(1 - \tau_t)y_t \tag{3''}$$

The government is required to meet a real expenditure path G_t. It collects, in period t, a real amount, $\tau_t y_t L_t$, in tax revenue where L_t equals the number of young individuals in period t. The deficit is financed by monetary issue. The government budget constraint is therefore

$$G_t - \tau_t y_t L_t = \frac{M_t^d - M_{t-1}^d}{P_t} \tag{4}$$

where M_t^d denotes the nominal money supply at the end of period t.

Using the definition

$$m_t^d \equiv \frac{M_t^d}{P_t L_t}$$

and dividing equation (4) by L_t yields, in per worker terms,

$$g_t - \tau_t y_t = m_t^d - m_{t-1}^d \pi_t (1 + n_t)^{-1} \tag{4'}$$

where n_t denotes the growth in the labor force from period $t - 1$ to period t and g_t denotes government spending per worker. The government's objective in each period t is to choose a tax rate τ_t to maximize a weighted sum of the utilities of all generations subject to equation (4) or (4'). Thus, in each period t, the government's objective function W_t is given by

$$W_t \equiv \sum_{i=-\infty}^{\infty} w_{t+i} U_{t+i} \tag{5}$$

In choosing τ_t in period t, the government takes all past τ_i as given and assumes that it or its successor will behave equivalently in the future. Governments are therefore assumed to behave in a *time-consistent* fashion and to anticipate this behavior correctly. Solving the government budget constraint (4') incorporating optimal private savings behavior characterized by equation (3') yields, as an expression for the rate of return on currency in period t,

$$\pi_t = \frac{\left[\left(\frac{\beta + \tau_t}{1 + \beta}\right) y_t - g_t\right](1 + n_t)}{M_{t-1}^d} \tag{6}$$

Substituting equations (6) and (3) into equation (1) yields, as an expression for the utility of a representative member of the generation born in period t,

$$U_t = k + (1 + \beta) \ln y_t + (1 + \beta) \ln (1 - \tau_t) + \beta \ln \pi_{t+1} \tag{1'}$$

$$k \equiv \beta \ln \beta - (1 + \beta) \ln (1 + \beta)$$

where π_t is as defined in (6). Substituting equations (1') and (6) into the government's objective function (5) and maximizing with respect to τ_t yields, from the first-order condition for a maximum,

$$\tau_t = \frac{\beta(1 - \delta_t)y_t + \delta_t(1 + \beta)g_t}{(\beta + \delta_t) y_t}; \qquad \delta_t \equiv \frac{w_t}{w_{t-1}} \tag{7}$$

which, from equation (6), implies

$$\pi_t = \frac{\beta(y_t - g_t)(1 + n_t)}{(\beta + \delta_t) m_{t-1}^d} \tag{8}$$

Note from expression (7) that when $\delta_t = 1$ (generations born at t and at $t + 1$ enter the government's objective function with equal weight), then

$$\tau_t = g_t / y_t \tag{7'}$$

—that is, all government spending is tax financed. When $\delta_t > 1$, so that greater weight is attached to the utility of the younger generation, then $\tau_t < g_t / y_t$, so that some government spending is financed by monetary issue. Conversely, when $\delta_t < 1$, so that greater weight is attached to the older generation, $\tau_t > g_t / y_t$—that is, taxes exceed expenditure—so that debt is retired. If the government's objective function is a Benthamite one, so that the weight of each living generation is proportional to the number of its members, then $\delta_t = (1 + n_t)$, in which case, if population growth is positive, there is an ongoing deficit.

From expression (8), observe that the inflation rate in period t is higher: (i) the greater government spending is relative to income, (ii) the higher real money balances are at the end of the previous period, and (iii) the lower the population growth rate is.

From equation (3),

$$m_{t-1}^d = \frac{\beta}{1 + \beta} (1 - \tau_{t-1}) y_{t-1} \tag{9}$$

which, if optimal tax policy was pursued in period $t - 1$ and $\delta_t = \delta_{t-1} = \delta$, implies, from equation (8), that

$$\pi_t = \frac{(1 + n_t)}{\delta} \left(\frac{y_t - g_t}{y_{t-1} - g_{t-1}} \right) \tag{10}$$

When the two living generations receive equal weight ($\delta = 1$) *and* income less government spending is equal across periods, then the rate of return on money balances equals the population growth rate: the economy is following the golden rule. If $\delta > 1$ or if income less government spending is decreasing, then the rate of return on money balances is less than the population growth rate, and conversely. In the case of the Benthamite utility function and constant population growth, the rate of return on money is zero.

II. OPEN-ECONOMY MODEL WITH RESERVES

Consider now a situation in which the government of the country being considered (i) has available to it a foreign money which can be held as a reserve currency or (ii) finds that some of its money is held abroad as a reserve currency. Denote foreign holdings of domestic money denominated in domestic currency in period t as M_t^f and domestic holdings of foreign currency denominated in foreign currency in period t as M_t^{*d}. Let P_t^* denote the price level in terms of foreign currency in period t and E_t the domestic currency price of one unit of foreign currency. It is assumed that purchasing power parity obtains, so that

$$E_t = P_t / P_t^*$$ (11)

Allowing for these government holdings of assets modifies the government budget constraint, equation (4), so that it becomes

$$G_t - \tau_t Y_t L_t = \frac{M_t^d - M_{t-1}^d}{P_t} + \frac{M_t^f - M_{t-1}^f}{P_t} - \frac{E_t(M_t^{*d} - M_{t-1}^{*d})}{P_t}$$ (12)

It is assumed that no international transfers take place.

Defining real domestic currency holdings abroad per *domestic* worker as

$$m_t^f \equiv \frac{M_t^f}{P_t L_t}$$ (13)

and real foreign currency holdings by the domestic government per foreign worker (where L_t^* denotes the number of foreign workers in period t) as

$$m_t^{*d} \equiv \frac{M_t^{*d}}{P_t^* L_t^*}$$ (14)

the real rate of return on foreign currency as

$$\pi_t^* \equiv \frac{P_{t-1}^*}{P_t^*}$$ (15)

and the ratio of foreign workers to domestic workers in period t as

$$\lambda_t \equiv \frac{L_t^*}{L_t}$$ (16)

the government budget constraint may be written

$$g_t - \tau_t y_t = m_t^d - m_{t-1}^d \pi_t (1 + n_t)^{-1} + m_t^f - m_{t-1}^f \pi_t (1 + n_t)^{-1}$$
$$- \lambda_t [m_t^{*d} - m_{t-1}^{*d} \pi_t^* (1 + n_t^*)^{-1}]$$ (17)

where n_t^* denotes the growth in the number of foreign workers between period $t - 1$ and period t.

Behavior of a Reserve Holder

Consider first the situation of a country whose currency is *not* held abroad but which contemplates holding a foreign currency as a reserve. It is assumed that this country treats the rate of return on the reserve currency, π_t^*, as exogenous to its own behavior for all i. One reason is that this country may be one of a large number of small countries that hold this reserve currency, and its contribution to total demand is negligible. It is assumed that this country anticipates perfectly the actual rate of return on foreign currency.

Setting $m_i^f = 0$ for all i in equation (17), this country chooses in each period t a tax rate τ_t and an amount of reserves $\lambda_t m_t^{*d}$ to maximize its objective function W_t, which, it is assumed, continues to be given by equation (5), with $\delta_t = w_t / w_{t-1} = \delta$.

Defining

$$\hat{g}_t = g_t + \lambda_t [m_t^{*d} - \pi_t^* (1 + n_t)^{-1} m_{t-1}^{*d}] \tag{18}$$

the optimal tax rate τ_t is given by

$$\tau_t = \frac{\delta(1 + \beta)\hat{g}_t + \beta(1 - \delta)y_t}{(\delta + \beta)y_t} \tag{19}$$

The rate of inflation is consequently

$$\pi_t = \frac{(1 + n_t)}{\delta} \left(\frac{y_t - \hat{g}_t}{y_{t-1} - \hat{g}_{t-1}} \right) \tag{20}$$

Substituting these expressions into W_t yields

$$W_t = \sum_{i=-\infty}^{\infty} k_i + \ln(y_i - \hat{g}_i) + \beta \ln(y_{i+1} - \hat{g}_{i+1}) \tag{21}$$

where

$$k_i \equiv -(1 + \beta) n (\delta + \beta) + \ln \delta + \ln \beta + \ln(1 + n_{i+1})$$

Differentiating this expression with respect to m_t^{*d} yields, as a first-order condition for a maximum,

$$\frac{-\lambda_t(w_t + \beta w_{t-1})}{\tilde{y}_t - \lambda_t(m_t^{*d} - m_{t-1}^{*d} x_t)} + \frac{\lambda_{t+1}(w_{t+1} + \beta w_t)x_{t+1}}{\tilde{y}_{t+1} - \lambda_{t+1}(m_{t+1}^{*d} - m_t^{*d} x_{t+1})}$$

$$+ \sum_{i=t+1}^{\infty} \frac{dW_t}{dm_i^{*d}} \cdot \frac{dm_i^{*d}}{dm_t^{*d}} = 0 \tag{22}$$

where

$$x_t \equiv \pi_t^* (1 + n_t)^{-1}$$

$$\tilde{y}_t \equiv y_t - g_t$$

Note that since m_t^{*d} depends upon m_{t-1}^{*d}, in general *future* values of m^{*d} will be affected by the *current* reserve holding decision. The best choice from the current perspective must incorporate the effect of that choice on the country's own future policy response.

This paper will now focus on two special cases

Case 1. $w_i = w_{t-1} \rho^i;$ $i = t, ..., \infty$ $\rho < 1$

In this case, one may write

$$W_t(m_{t-1}^{*d}) = (w_{t-1} \beta k_{t-1} + w_t k_t) \ln(y_t - g_t) + \rho W_{t+1}(m_t^{*d}) \quad (23)$$

If optimal policy is pursued in each period $i > t$, then

$$\frac{dW_i}{dm_i^{*d}} = 0 \quad i \geq t+1$$

and expression (23) reduces to

$$-\frac{(w_t + \beta w_{t-1})}{\tilde{y}_t - \lambda_t(m_t^{*d} - m_{t-1}^{*d} x_t)} + \frac{(w_{t+1} + \beta w_t) x_{t+1}}{\tilde{y}_{t+1} - \lambda_{t+1}(m_{t+1}^{*d} - m_t^{*d} x_{t+1})} = 0$$
$$(23')$$

In the steady state,

$$\lambda_t = \lambda_{t+1} = \lambda, \quad \tilde{y}_{t+1} = \tilde{y}_t = y, \quad x_{t+1} = x,$$

$$m_{t-1}^{*d} = m_t^{*d} = m_{t+1}^{*d} = m^{*d}$$

Therefore expression (23') can be obtained only if

$$x = \rho^{-1}$$

When x exceeds ρ^{-1}, the demand for foreign reserves is infinite in the steady state, while if x is less than ρ^{-1}, demand equals negative infinity. From Section I, the autarkic inflation rate is $(1 + n)/\delta$. Consequently, since $\delta = \rho$ in this case, the demand for foreign reserves in the steady state is bounded only when the rate of return on foreign reserves equals the return on domestic money. In other words, the demand for reserves is infinitely elastic at the domestic inflation rate.

Case 2. $w_i = 0$ $i \neq t-1, t$

In this case, the current government only takes into account the welfare of generations currently alive. It assumes that future governments will act equivalently. The current government and future governments thus pursue different objectives. In particular, the current government must incorporate the effect of its current policies on the future government's treatment of the current younger generation.

To solve for optimal reserve demand, it is assumed that at each period t, foreign reserves are held according to the formula

$$m_t^{*d} = a_t + b_t m_{t-1}^{*d} \quad (24)$$

where a_t and b_t denote parameters to be determined. Substituting expression (24) into the objective function for m_{t+1}^{*d} yields

$$W_t = (w_{t-1}\beta k_{t-1} + w_t k_t) + (\beta + \delta)\ln[\tilde{y}_t - \lambda_t(m_t^{*d} - m_{t-1}^{*d} x_t)]$$
$$+ \delta\beta \ln[\tilde{y}_{t+1} - \lambda_{t+1}(a_{t+1} + b_{t+1}m_t^{*d} - x_{t+1}m_t^{*d})]$$

Differentiating this expression with respect to m_t^{*d} yields, as a first-order condition for a maximum,

$$\frac{dW_t}{dm_t^{*d}} = \frac{-\lambda_t(\beta + \delta)}{\tilde{y}_t - \lambda_t(m_t^{*d} - m_{t-1}^{*d}x_t)}$$
$$+ \frac{\delta\beta\lambda_{t+1}(x_{t+1} - b_{t+1})}{\tilde{y}_{t+1} - \lambda_{t+1}(a_{t+1} + b_{t+1}m_t^{*d} - x_{t+1}m_t^{*d})} = 0 \quad (25)$$

Solving equation (25) for m_t^{*d}, one obtains

$$m_t^{*d} = \frac{\lambda_{t+1}\delta\beta(x_{t+1} - b_{t+1})\tilde{y}_t - \lambda_t(\beta + \delta)(\tilde{y}_{t+1} - \lambda_{t+1}a_{t+1})}{\lambda_{t+1}\lambda_t(b_{t+1} - x_{t+1})(\beta + \delta + \delta\beta)}$$
$$+ \frac{\delta\beta x_t}{\beta + \delta + \delta\beta}m_{t-1}^{*d} \quad (26)$$

Since an equivalent problem will be solved in period $t + 1$, one may set

$$b_{t+1} = \frac{\delta\beta x_{t+1}}{\beta + \delta + \delta\beta} \quad (27)$$

Substituting this expression into equation (26), it is found that

$$a_t = \frac{\lambda_t(\beta + \delta + \delta\beta)\tilde{y}_{t+1} - \lambda_{t+1}\delta\beta x_{t+1}\tilde{y}_t}{\lambda_{t+1}\lambda_t(\beta + \delta + \delta\beta)} + a_{t+1} \quad (28)$$

The steady state requires that

$$\tilde{y}_{t+1} = \tilde{y}_t = \tilde{y}, \; x_{t+1} = x_t = x, \; \lambda_{t+1} = \lambda_t = \lambda$$

and that

$$m_{t+1}^{*d} = m_t^{*d} = m^*$$

Inspection of equation (26) shows that the steady state is only compatible with a finite demand for reserves if

$$x = \frac{\beta + \delta + \delta\beta}{\delta\beta} \quad (29)$$

or

$$\pi^* = \frac{(1 + n)(\beta + \delta + \delta\beta)}{\delta\beta} \quad (30)$$

If the rate of return on foreign reserves exceeds this level, demand will grow to infinity, and conversely. Thus, in the long run, the demand for foreign reserves is perfectly elastic at the rate of return $(1 + n)(\beta + \delta + \beta\delta)/\delta\beta$. This rate of return will exceed the return on domestic money, which remains $(1 + n)/\delta$. Therefore, a country in which the government maximizes the welfare of only generations currently alive will not hold reserves unless the return on them strictly exceeds the rate of return on domestic currency. The reason is that the unborn generation, or the younger generation in period $t+1$, will share the return from an investment in reserves in period t with the younger generation in period t. The myopic government weighs only the second gain in making its decision. Consequently, a higher rate of return is required for an investment in reserves to appear worthwhile.

Behavior of a Reserve Issuer

Consider now the behavior of a country which holds no foreign currencies but finds that foreign countries hold its currency as a reserve. It is assumed that this country takes foreign holdings of its own currency, m_i^f, as given in each period i. That is, when the government makes its taxation decision, other countries have made their past and contemporaneous reserve holding decisions. Because it raises a complicated, but very interesting, set of issues that lie beyond its scope, this paper ignores the possibility of a reputation effect whereby reserve holders' expectations of future inflation are determined by past performance. Rather, reserve holders form expectations of future inflation by calculating the optimal behavior of the reserve issuer each period.

Setting $m_i^{*d} = 0$ for all i in equation (17), the expression for inflation, given τ_t, becomes

$$\pi_t = \frac{(1 + n_t)\left[(\beta + \tau_t)y_t - (1 + \beta)g_t + (1 + \beta)m_t^f\right]}{\beta(1 - \tau_{t-1})y_{t-1} + (1 + \beta)m_{t-1}^f} \tag{31}$$

Since equations (3) and (3'') continue to define consumption in each period, the utility of an individual entering the labor force in period t is

$$U_t = k_t' + (1 + \beta)\ln(1 - \tau_t) - \beta\ln\left[\beta(1 - \tau_t)y_t + (1 + \beta)m_t^f\right]$$
$$+ \beta\ln\left[(\beta + \tau_{t+1})y_{t+1} - (1 + \beta)g_{t+1} + (1 + \beta)m_{t+1}^f\right] \tag{32}$$

$$k_t' \equiv \ln\beta - (1 + \beta)n(1 + \beta) + \ln(1 + n_t)$$

Continuing to assume a government objective function of the form of equation (5), the first-order condition for an optimal tax rate τ_t is given by

$$\frac{dW_t}{d\tau_t} = w_{t-1}\frac{\beta y_t}{\Delta_{1t}} - w_t\frac{(1+\beta)}{(1-\tau_t)} + w_t\frac{\beta^2 y_t}{\Delta_{2t}} = 0 \tag{33}$$

$$\Delta_{1t} \equiv (\beta + \tau_t)y_t - (1+\beta)g_t + (1+\beta)m_t^f$$

$$\Delta_{2t} \equiv \beta(1-\tau_t)y_t + (1+\beta)m_t^f$$

Note that the solution to equation (33) involves only contemporaneous variables. The effect of an increase in contemporaneous money holdings, m_t^f, is given by

$$\frac{d\tau_t}{dm_t^f} = -\frac{\dfrac{d^2 W_t}{d\tau_t\,dm_t^f}}{\dfrac{d^2 W}{d\tau_t^2}} = -\frac{(1+\beta)\beta y_t(w_{t-1}\Delta_{2t}^2 + \beta w_t\Delta_{1t}^2)}{\beta y_t(w_{t-1}\Delta_{2t}^2 - \beta^2 w_t\Delta_{1t}^2) + \dfrac{w_t(1+\beta)\Delta_{1t}^2\Delta_{2t}^2}{(1-\tau_t)^2}} \tag{34}$$

which is a negative number: the domestic tax rate falls as foreign holdings of the domestic currency rise.

Consider now the effect of an increase in foreign holdings of domestic currency on the rate of return on currency. Given current holdings, m_t^f, an increase in the previous period's holdings, m_{t-1}^f, lowers π_t. This result is evident from inspection of expression (31). The effect of an increase in m_t^f, given m_{t-1}^f, is

$$\frac{d\pi_t}{dm_t^f} = \frac{(1+n_t)y_t\dfrac{d\tau_t}{dm_t^f} + (1+\beta)}{\Delta_{2t-1}} \tag{35}$$

which, incorporating expression (34), has the same sign as

$$(\beta+2)(\beta-1)\beta(1-\tau_t)^2 y_t^2 + 2(1+\beta)^2\beta(1-\tau_\tau)y_t m_t^f$$
$$+ (1+\beta)^3(m_t^f)^2 \tag{36}$$

This expression is negative if m_t^f is small and β exceeds 1. For large values of m_t^f, it is positive. Therefore, an increase in foreign reserve holdings has an ambiguous effect on the inflation rate for that period.

Consider an increase in foreign reserve holdings in period t from a level of zero to some positive permanent level $\bar{m}^f$. The effect on π_t on impact is given by the sign of expression (36). The effect on π_i, $i > t$, assuming constant values of y_t and g_t, is given by

$$\frac{d\pi}{dm^f} = \frac{(1+n_t)(1+\beta)\{[\beta y + g + (1+\beta)m^f]\dfrac{d\tau}{dm^f} - \tau\}}{\Delta_2^2} \tag{37}$$

which is necessarily negative. This result establishes the following proposition:

Proposition 1: A permanent increase in foreign holdings of domestic currency lowers the rate of return on the currency (i.e., raises the inflation rate) in the steady state.

All new foreign holders of the domestic currency will earn the new steady-state rate of return on that currency, since increased holdings in period t raise π_{t+1} to the new steady-state level. During period t in which new reserves are acquired, however, the rate of return will never fall by as much as the steady-state change and may even rise. A permanent increase in reserves held abroad will consequently increase the *permanent* inflation rate, though it may initially lower the inflation rate.

III. MULTICOUNTRY EQUILIBRIUM

Consider a world in which there are two types of countries, type I and type II. Each type of country can be characterized by a steady-state inflation rate that would obtain under reserve autarky ($\pi_j^A, j = I, II$) and a rate $\bar{\pi}_j$ at which the long-run demand for foreign reserves is infinitely elastic. It is assumed that $\pi_I^A < \pi_{II}^A$—that is, type I countries have higher inflation under autarky; and that $\bar{\pi}_I < \pi_{II}^A$—that is, type I countries demand reserves at a rate of return below the autarky rate of return on type II currency.[3] This section considers how the introduction of internationally held currencies will change the steady state of the world economy. It focuses first on two extreme cases, one in which reserves cannot be held in negative amounts and one in which reserves cannot be held in positive amounts. The first case corresponds to one in which loans are denominated in the borrower's currency, and the second to one in which they are denominated in the lender's currency. While the model does not preclude a priori the possibility of two-way transfers of reserves, attention will focus only on steady states in which net and gross reserve positions are identical.

Nonnegative Reserves

The following proposition can now be established:

Proposition 2: In a steady state in which foreign reserves are held at a positive, finite level, (i) type II (low-inflation) currency will be held by type I (high-inflation) countries as a reserve, and (ii) the rate of return on type II currency will fall to $\bar{\pi}_I$.

---

[3]Recall from the first subsection of Section II that when the weights on the utilities of each generation in the government's objective function in period t are of the form $w_{t+\tau} = \rho^\tau w_t$ for all t and i, then $\bar{\pi}_j = \pi_j^A$; while if $w_i = 0, i \neq t, t-1$, then $\bar{\pi}_j > \pi_j^A$.

If the weights attached to future generations by each government decline geometrically—so that $\pi_j^A = \bar{\pi}_j, j = I, II$—then the inflation rate in type I countries does not change, while the inflation rate in type II countries will rise to π_I^A. Thus, while under autarky $\pi_I^A = (1 + n)/\delta^I$, $\pi_{II}^A = (1 + n)/\delta^{II}$ (from equation 10), when reserve holdings are allowed, $\pi_I^R = \pi_{II}^R = (1 + n)/\delta^I$; introducing reserves has raised inflation everywhere to the level in the high-inflation countries. The superscript R denotes steady-state rates of return when international lending takes place. The reason is that type I countries find type II currencies attractive at their autarky inflation rates. An excess demand for these currencies will exist until the inflation rate is driven up to the level in type II countries. As type I countries accumulate reserves, the increased reserves provide an incentive for type II countries to inflate at a higher rate, imposing an inflation tax on type I countries. Since the welfare of foreign holders of its currency, as opposed to domestic holders, does not enter the reserve issuers' objective functions, they are less constrained to maintain low inflation rates.

The case in which $\bar{\pi}_j > \pi_j^A$ for $j = I$ or $j = II$ is slightly more complicated. If, say, $\pi_I^A < \bar{\pi}_I < \pi_{II}^A$, then, again, type II countries will issue reserves to type I countries. In the new steady state, $\pi_{II}^R = \bar{\pi}_I$. Again, becoming reserve currency issuers has raised inflation rates in type II countries, but not as high as the autarky inflation rate in type I countries. Type II countries will again experience strictly higher inflation rates in the new steady state.

These results suggest how introducing liabilities denominated in the borrower's currency can create more inflation in the world economy. The welfare implications of introducing international reserves can be analyzed in terms of this model. This paper will not attempt a thorough discussion but will make the following points:

(1) In a steady state with finite reserves, type I (high-inflation, reserve-holding) countries have as an additional source of government revenue an amount $\lambda \hat{m}^{*d}[\bar{\pi}_I(1 + n)^{-1} - 1]$ per worker where $\hat{m}^{*d}$ denotes steady-state reserve holdings. When $w_i = \rho^{t+i}w_t$ for all $i > 0$, this amount equals $\lambda m^*(1 - \delta^I)/\delta^I$ and when $w_i = 0$ ($i \neq t-1, t$), i_t equals $\lambda m^*(\beta + \delta^I)/\beta\delta^I$. Taxes are lower and the rate of return on currency has not changed: the representative individual in type I countries is better off in the *steady state*. (Here δ^I denotes type I countries' value of δ.)

(2) In a steady state with finite reserves, type II (low-inflation, reserve-issuing) countries transfer an amount $m^f[1 - \pi^*(1 + n)^{-1}]$ to type I countries each period. The representative individual in type II countries can be worse off in the steady state because the rate of return on his savings has declined.

(3) The older generation in the period in which reserves are *acquired* in the reserve-holding countries suffers from the transition. The rate of return

on their money holdings is lower than under autarky. (This result may be seen by setting $m_{t-1}^{*d} = 0$ in equation (18) and observing the effect of increasing m_t^{*d} on π_t in equation (20).)

(4) The younger generation in the period in which reserves are *issued* by the reserve currency country benefits from lower taxes in that period but experiences a lower return on savings in the subsequent period. The net effect on welfare is therefore ambiguous.

(5) The effect of the transition on the older generation in the reserve-issuing country is ambiguous, depending whether π_t rises or falls as a consequence of issuing reserves.

Thus, the long-run effect of a move from reserve autarky to trade in currencies raises steady-state welfare in the reserve-holding countries but can lower steady-state welfare in the issuing countries. The effects during the transition, however, may go in the opposite direction.

One remaining question is how much currency of a typical type II country will be held abroad at the point where the rate of return on that country's currency equals $\bar{\pi}_I$. If all type II countries are identical in all respects except relative population size, each type II country will have the same *per worker* money stock held abroad as a reserve currency in reserve equilibrium. The contribution of each type II country to total international reserves will therefore be proportional to that country's population.

Nonpositive Reserves

The following proposition can also be established:

Proposition 3: In any steady state in which international borrowing takes the form of issuing *foreign*-currency-denominated liabilities at a finite, positive level, (i) type II (low-inflation) countries will borrow from type I (high-inflation) countries, and (ii) the rate of return on type I currency will rise to $\bar{\pi}_{II}$.

Consider first the case in which $\bar{\pi}_j = \pi_j^A, j = I, II$. If type II countries can issue liabilities denominated in type I currency, they will do so until π_I rises to π_{II}^A. Thus, when positive, rather than negative, reserve holdings are precluded, international financial integration reduces, rather than increases, inflation. The reason is that when countries *lend* in their own currency, rather than borrow by issuing reserves denominated in their own currency, their governments have an incentive to reduce, rather than to increase, their inflation rates.

The welfare effects of international financial integration when borrowing is *foreign*-currency-denominated, both on impact and in the steady state, can be analyzed as well. The effects are substantially similar, so this issue will not be discussed here.

Relaxing the Nonnegativity Constraints

If no constraint is imposed on the sign of reserve issue, our model admits an infinite number of solutions. While borrowing in both domestic- and foreign-currency-denominated assets occurs in international financial markets, the possibility of outright default may place an upper bound on the extent to which foreign-currency-denominated borrowing occurs. Default on such liabilities can occur without affecting the value of domestic agents' savings. As long as currency is internationally mobile, default on domestic currency held abroad could only occur if domestic households were defaulted upon as well. This ramification is likely to limit the incentive of a national government to default on its domestic currency or to destroy its value through inflation.

Introducing a Nominal Interest Rate on Borrowing

It has been assumed that money pays a zero nominal rate of return. Introducing a nonzero nominal interest rate would not affect the results, except that the inflation rate would equal the nominal rate minus the real rate of return derived here—that is, the inflation rate would adjust to reinstate the real returns derived here. Whatever nominal return a reserve issue offers its creditors ex ante, it determines the real rate of return ex post through its inflation policy.

IV. POSSIBLE EXTENSIONS

This paper has developed a model for analyzing the effects of introducing reserve currencies on inflation and welfare in the world economy. In order to obtain concrete results, the analysis has been kept very simple. The paper will conclude with a discussion of some issues, which the authors believe are of considerable interest, that could be analyzed in terms of the framework developed here.

Non-Bernoulli Preferences

The assumption of the model that utility is logarithmic in consumption levels leads to savings behavior and private currency demand that is independent of the rate of return on the currency. The analysis is enormously simplified by this assumption. Alternative specifications would lead to much more complicated responses to alternative policies. In particular, the effect of expectations of future policy on the current private demand for currency would have to be incorporated into the model. Introducing non-Bernoulli preferences would consequently introduce a much richer set of dynamics as well as an additional source of potential time inconsistency of optimal policy.

Distortionary Taxation

The model assumes that the government has access to proportional income taxes as a means of raising government revenue. Since income is exogenous in our model, such taxes are nondistortionary. If taxes do, in fact, impose an excess burden, then an additional role for seigniorage arises, as an alternative distortionary source of revenue. Differences in autarky inflation rates may then reflect different financing needs among countries as well as different valuations of generations by governments. The role of seigniorage as a form of optimal taxation in an open economy has been analyzed in a small, open economy context by Calvo (1978) and Eaton (1982), but the role of reserves in redistributing tax burdens internationally has yet to be studied.

Default Risk

The model does not introduce formally the possibility of outright default on foreign debt. The issue of default has by now been investigated extensively. See, for example Eaton and Gersovitz (1981 a, 1981 b), Sachs and Cohen (1982), or Kletzer (1982). One topic of potential interest would be to integrate analytic models of default into this paper's framework. As suggested earlier, one important issue that such research might shed light on is the currency of denomination of international debt.

Productive Capital

No role for productive capital exists in the model. The effects of international capital market integration on the allocation of capital has been analyzed in a nonmonetary overlapping generations model by Buiter (1981). It would be of considerable interest to investigate how the monetary phenomena considered here would interact with the international allocation of capital in the steady state. In particular, it would be interesting to determine to what extent the trading of monetary assets can substitute for trade in physical capital.

Uncertainty

The model assumes perfect certainty. Introducing uncertainty about future values of exogenous variables would provide insight into a number of issues. For example, the effects of uncertainty on the rates of return of alternative currencies could be examined. Optimal reserve portfolios could then be characterized, which would presumably include more than one reserve held simultaneously. The role of government policy in redistributing risk between generations domestically and the role of reserves in reallocating risk internationally could be examined. Lapan and Enders (1980), Aizenman (1981), and Eaton (1982) have considered the implications of alternative exchange rate regimes for the international allocation of risk. The implications of their analysis for reserve positions in a multicountry context have yet to be drawn out.

Strategic Behavior

In the model, governments make decisions taking other countries' inflation rates and reserve positions as given. While this assumption can be justified in a competitive context in which the numbers of countries of different types are large, it is less appropriate in a world where some countries are unique in their relevant characteristics. One possibility is that strategic competition among potential reserve issuers will arise. The country which is most successful at establishing a reputation as providing a high and stable return on currency might then emerge as the sole reserve issuer.

V. CONCLUSIONS

The major conclusions of our analysis can be summarized in the following points:

(1) Under financial autarky, inflation rates in different countries can be explained by their monetary authorities' attitudes toward the welfare of the younger and older generations. The problem of time consistency may yield an inflation rate that is not optimal.

(2) A government's demand for a foreign currency as a reserve in the long run may be infinitely elastic at a rate of return that is equal to or higher than the rate of return on that country's currency. Holding a foreign currency as a reserve does not affect the steady-state inflation rate of the reserve holder.

(3) The steady-state inflation rate of a country increases when foreign demand for that country's currency as a reserve rises to a higher permanent level.

(4) Trade in assets denominated in the borrower's currency raises the average steady-state world inflation rate, while trade in assets denominated in the lender's currency has the opposite effect.

(5) Trade in assets raises steady-state lifetime welfare in reserve-holding countries but can lower it in reserve-issuing countries, although the effect on the welfare of generations alive during the transition from autarky to the

new steady state may be reversed. Governments may therefore be justified in acting to prevent their currencies' use as international reserves.

REFERENCES

Aizenman, Joshua, "The Use of the Balance of Payments as a Shock Absorber in Fixed and Managed Float System," *Journal of International Economics*, Vol. 11 (November 1981), pp. 479-86.

Buiter, Willem H., "Time Preference and International Lending and Borrowing in an Overlapping-Generations Model," *Journal of Political Economy*, Vol. 89 (August 1981), pp. 769-97.

Calvo, Guillermo A., "Optimal Seigniorage from Money Creation: An Analysis in Terms of the Optimum Balance of Payments Deficit Problem," *Journal of Monetary Economics*, Vol. 4 (August 1978), pp. 503-18.

Eaton, Jonathan, *Optimal and Time Consistent Exchange Rate Management in an Overlapping Generations Economy*, Economic Growth Center Discussion Paper No. 413, Yale University (July 1982).

_____, and Mark Gersovitz (1981 a), "Debt with Potential Repudiation: Theoretical and Empirical Analysis," *Review of Economic Studies*, Vol. 48 (April 1981), pp. 289-309.

_____ (1981 b), *Poor Country Borrowing in Private Financial Markets and the Repudiation Issue*, Studies in International Finance, No. 47 (Princeton, New Jersey: International Finance Section, Princeton University, June 1981).

Kareken, John, and Neil Wallace, "On the Indeterminacy of Equilibrium Exchange Rates," *Quarterly Journal of Economics*, Vol. 96 (May 1981), pp. 207-22.

Kletzer, Ken, "A Model of International Lending with Default Risk" (unpublished, University of California, Davis, November 1982).

Kydland, Finn E., and Edward C. Prescott, "Rules Rather than Discretion: The Inconsistency of Optimal Plans," *Journal of Political Economy*, Vol. 85 (June 1977), pp. 473-91.

Lapan, Harvey E., and Walter Enders, "Random Disturbances and the Choice of Exchange Regimes in an Intergenerational Model," *Journal of International Economics*, Vol. 10 (May 1980), pp. 263-83.

Mundell, Robert A., *Monetary Theory: Inflation, Interest and Growth in the World Economy* (Pacific Palisades, California: Goodyear Publishing, 1971).

Sachs, Jeffrey, and David Cohen, *LDC Borrowing with Default Risk*, National Bureau of Economic Research, Working Paper No. 925 (July 1982).

Samuelson, Paul A., "An Exact Consumption Loan Model of Interest with or without the Social Contrivance of Money," *Journal of Political Economy*, Vol. 66 (December 1958), pp. 467-82.

Townsend, Robert M., "Models of Money with Spatially Separated Agents," in *Models of Monetary Economics*, ed. by John H. Kareken and Neil Wallace (Minneapolis, Minnesota: Federal Reserve Bank of Minneapolis, 1980), pp. 265-303.

Triffin, Robert, *Gold and the Dollar Crisis: The Future of Convertibility* (New Haven, Connecticut: Yale University Press, 1961).

Comments

Ricardo H. Arriazu

Since I am not an expert in overlapping-generations models, I found the reading of the paper by Professors Buiter and Eaton to be instructive, fascinating, and arduous.

As stated by the authors, the purpose of the paper was to develop a model of the interaction of national monetary policy and international reserves to answer questions such as: what characteristics of a country make it likely to emerge as a reserve issuer?, how does becoming a reserve issuer affect the inflation rate that is optimal from a national perspective?, and the other two questions raised by the authors on page 130 of their paper. All of these questions are relevant to the subject under discussion—international balance of payments financing and adjustment.

The main contribution of the paper is the treatment of balance of payments financing and adjustment as part of a simultaneous optimizing process by individuals and government alike, thus bringing it more into line with developments in other areas of economic analysis.

Naturally, in their quest for rigor and precision, the authors were forced to use simplifying assumptions that substantially limit the applicability of the model. However, the model has repeatedly proved to be much more powerful for the analysis of day-to-day problems than it appeared to be on first reading. Even the assumption of a government optimizing an objective function that takes into account the welfare of present and future generations—which might seem theoretical to an analyst observing how, in practice, economic policies in general are frequently the result of political pressures exerted by different sectors of society—can be reconciled with these developments assigning greater weights either to the welfare of the generations alive—to the detriment of future generations—or to the older generation—to the detriment of the younger generation. Case 2 in Section II is an extreme example of an objective function based exclusively upon the welfare of the generations currently alive, but which takes into account future governments' reactions to present policies.

Turning now to the theoretical aspects of the paper, I will concentrate my comments on the structure of the model and on its principal conclusions, trying to separate those aspects that would remain valid in more general models from those derived exclusively from the particular set of assumptions used in the paper.

In Section I, the authors develop an overlapping-generations model for a closed economy. The Bernoulli assumption in the utility function guarantees that unless the younger generation is characterized by collective suicidal tendencies, a positive demand for assets as stores of value will always exist. Combined with the assumption that establishes domestic money as the sole asset available as store of value and the assumption that goods cannot be stored from one period to another, the Bernoulli assumption assures a positive global demand for money (even though, in a particular period, the nominal flow demand for money can be negative). As a consequence, real per capita money holdings are a function of disposable income $(1 - \tau_t) y_t$ and of preferences as between present and future consumption (β); the size of money holdings is independent of the rate of return on them. The government is, therefore, assured that the tax base to which it applies inflationary taxes (if the optimization process so requires) is stable, independent of the level of such taxes.

Under these circumstances, the main conclusions derived from the application of the model to closed economies are logical: if all generations enter the government's objective function with equal weight $(\delta = 1)$, the optimum policy should be to finance all government expenditures with ordinary taxes $(\tau_t \cdot y_t = g_t)$ and not to use the inflation tax as a means of financing real government expenditures $(\pi_t = 1)$; similarly, if the government attaches greater weight to the utility of the older generation $(\delta > 1)$, the optimal policy mix would be to run a budget deficit and to use some inflationary tax $(\pi_t < 1)$ and the opposite when $\delta < 1$. The only conclusion that seems to go against common-sense economics is (ii) on page 135, which asserts that inflation rates in period t will be higher, the higher real money balances are at the end of the previous period, which goes against the basic economic principle that for a given total amount of taxes required, the tax rate will be lower, the larger the tax base. As a matter of fact, this contradiction seems to be the result of direct mathematical reasoning—which is repeated several times in the paper—that is basically correct but is not adequately expressed in terms of traditional economic reasoning. The above-mentioned conclusion is derived from equation (8) by taking the partial derivative of π_t with respect to m_{t-1}^d, which obviously has a negative sign (higher inflation), since it is equivalent to saying that given a certain real budget deficit, the lower the per capita flow demand for real money balances, the higher will be the inflation rate. The alternative question would be: given constant per capita real money balances $(m_{t-1}^d = m_t^d)$—or a fixed per capita flow demand for real balances—and a predetermined fiscal deficit, what would be the effects of higher m_{t-1}^d upon π_t? From equation (4'), it is clear that the inflation rate will be lower, the higher the level of m_{t-1}^d.

As the authors themselves recognize, the analysis would be greatly enhanced if the Bernoulli assumption were modified, in particular if the widespread effects of inflation upon real government expenditures, real taxes, and—especially—real money demand were taken into account. In its present form, high inflation is a possibility under certain conditions, but hyperinflation cannot be generated.

In Section II, the authors develop the model for open economies under two different situations: (1) one in which the government is allowed to hold foreign money as reserves, and (2) another in which some of the domestic money is held abroad as a reserve currency. Unfortunately, the authors have omitted from the analysis a third situation which, in my opinion, raises the most interesting theoretical questions and is extremely relevant to the analysis of recent developments in the world economy—one in which individuals are allowed to hold international liquid assets. I will return to this subject later in my comment.

The model assumes strict purchasing power parity, given by $E_t = P_t/P_t^*$ which implies that differences in inflation rates should materialize, in price-taker countries, through changes in exchange rates. As a matter of fact, the exchange rate system behind the model seems to be a special case of floating, in which, once the authorities fix their reserve targets (which may be different from zero) and their domestic credit policies (fiscal deficits), the equilibrium exchange rate is automatically determined by market forces. The definition of domestic currency holdings abroad per *domestic worker* and that of domestic holdings of foreign money per *foreign worker* could have been reversed, and perhaps they should have been.

Although it is not clearly indicated in the paper, the counterpart of reserve movements must be trade flows, in order to satisfy the budget constraints. Loans, as the counterpart of reserve accumulation, even though they are made very frequently in a world of interest-bearing financial assets, do not make sense in a model where the sole financial assets are non-interest-bearing monetary assets (whose rate of return, including return of principal, is given by π). The only meaningful interpretation of loans in this model would be instances where the issuer of a currency convinces other countries to "lend" it real resources in exchange for currency. While the case of loans denominated in borrowers' currencies is similar to the case of reserve accumulation, the paper also allows for the denomination of loans in lenders' currencies, which raises a completely different set of very interesting questions.

The conditions under which a government will hold reserves, derived under two sets of assumptions related to the weighting of the different generations in the government's objective function, are both mathematically and logically correct. In Case 1, where the government weights of generations are given by: $w_i = w_{t-1} \, \rho^i; \, i = t, \, \ldots \, \infty, \, \rho < 1$ it is clear that the government will accumulate reserves if, and only if, the sacrifice required of the generations presently alive is at least compensated in the future by higher utilities accruing to future generations. This requires that $\pi_t^* \geq \pi_t$; and if π_t^* is strictly larger than π_t, the demand for reserves will be infinite in the steady state.

It seems to me, however, that the above-mentioned condition is necessary, but not sufficient, for reserve accumulation to occur. In addition, it is necessary that $\pi_t^* > 1$, since otherwise the country that accumulates reserves would be permanently paying an inflationary tax to the issuer, creating not a mere transfer among living individuals within the country but a permanent transfer abroad (reflected in permanent increases in M_t^{*d} in order to maintain m_t^{*d} constant).

In the case of $\rho > 1$ (greater weights assigned to future generations), the conditions for this accumulation of reserves only require that $\pi_t^* > 1$, since $\pi_t < 1$ in the steady state.

Similarly, Case 2 requires not only that $\pi_t^* > 1$ but that π_t^* considerably exceed the domestic rate of return under autarky, since the welfare losses of the first period should be more than compensated for by the return on foreign assets, allowing for the increase in utility in the second period and for the maintenance of a certain level of reserves for the future in order to avoid retaliatory policies by future governments upon individuals presently alive.

The impact of reserve accumulations upon π_t and τ_t is not specifically examined in the paper, but in the conclusions it is stated that holding foreign reserves does not affect the steady-state inflation rate of the domestic currency. This conclusion is derived directly from equation (20). As a matter of fact, the paper establishes that the distribution of the tax burden between ordinary taxes and inflationary taxes is dependent only upon the rate of population growth and the weights assigned by the government to each generation. This is a very important theoretical finding, and, in the case of reserve accumulation, it implies that future returns on that investment will be reflected exclusively in lower tax rates. It should be noticed, however, that when $\pi_t^* > \pi_t$, if the resulting reserve accumulation were finite rather than infinite (a case excluded from the paper but one that could take place as a consequence—for example—of institutional restrictions), the inflation rate in the accumulating country would—after the initial increase of the transition period—be permanently reduced and the discrepancies in inflation rates would be reflected in the exchange rate.

Examining the case from the point of view of the reserve issuer poses more difficult questions. The paper treats the foreign accumulation of domestic currency as exogenously given, and it does not require the accumulating country to also maximize some form of objective function, thus allowing for hoarding even when the net rate of return in the reserve currency is negative ($\pi_t < 1$). Similarly, the paper does not clarify whether the reserve issuer is a price taker or not. This lack of specification reduces the general validity of some of the conclusions reached in Section II. The accumulation of domestic currencies by foreigners implies an initial transfer of real resources to the issuing country—in exchange for its currency—and, as a consequence, a lower tax rate and inflation rate for the issuer. In subsequent periods, however, the impact of the reserve accumulation on these variables depends upon the policies of the hoarding countries, the policies of the issuer countries, the rate of return on domestic currency, etc.

In the case when $\pi_t > 1$, the real rate of return will be positive, and if the hoarding countries follow a policy of maintaining the real value of their reserves, then there will be a permanent transfer of real resources from the issuer to the holder (similar to what takes place when real rates of interest are positive), and all taxes should rise in the issuing countries. However, since π_t implies that the issuing country does not use the inflationary tax as a means of financing, the rate of return will, ceteris paribus, remain positive, but smaller than before, a result which goes against the main conclusion of the paper. Similarly, if $\pi_t < 1$, the issuing country receives an inflationary tax from the rest of the world (in the form of a transfer of real resources required to maintain the real value of reserves), and therefore all existing taxes will be reduced.

A case can be made, however, against this reasoning. It is used by the authors on page 143, when they say that "as type I countries accumulate reserves, the increased reserves provide an incentive for type II countries to inflate at a higher rate, imposing an inflation tax on type I countries." While this is true and, likewise, that a country can maximize its welfare by imposing an inflationary tax on other countries willing to hold its currency, there is nothing in the model that allows this policy to be considered Pareto optimal, since, while it was inflating, the issuer would also be imposing an inflationary tax domestically, as well as reducing ordinary taxes. The negative effects upon the older generation do not permit one to consider the inflationary policy optimal. Of course, the government could use the inflation tax collected from abroad to subsidize the older generation, and, in this case, the new situation would be superior to the initial one, creating incentives to inflate; but this conclusion is not derived from the model, and if the underlying assumption were to be introduced indirectly into the model, an assumption about the effects of higher inflation rates on holders' willingness to maintain the same real stock of reserves should also be included. These opposing forces of the desire to inflate, on the one hand, and the desire to avoid "runs out of reserve currencies," on the other, have traditionally played an important role in the international economy. Proposition 1, therefore, is valid only under very specific assumptions which cannot be derived from the model but which are quite plausible in real life and, as such, deserve special attention.

Section III examines the conditions for multicountry equilibrium and the dynamics of the adjustment process in the transition from reserve autarky to partial currency integration. Proposition 2 is based upon the principal conclusions derived in the previous sections and is valid under the conditions of infinite elasticity of demand on the part of reserve holders and the simultaneous compensation of the losses experienced by the older generations in the inflating countries. If both of these conditions do not hold, multicountry equilibrium is not guaranteed, and some form of uncertainty or of institutional restrictions will be required to avoid a permanent transfer of real resources from the hoarder to the issuing country (as shown by the experience of high-inflation countries, whose private sectors permanently increase the real value of their international liquid asset hoardings at a rate in excess of the rate of return on their initial stocks). Borrowings by countries that are not reserve centers, denominated in the reserve-issuers' currencies, are of extreme importance in evaluating the effects of the emergence of markets, such as the Eurocurrency and offshore markets. This has been adequately differentiated in the paper and should be considered an important contribution to the subject.

As was stated earlier, the paper does not consider the case where individuals are allowed to acquire international liquid assets. I imagine that this is partly due to the fact that the question of substitution between national moneys and its macroeconomic effects will be taken up in the next chapter of this volume. However, since the problem touches so directly on the subject of balance of payments financing and adjustment, I think the subject deserves some attention here also.

It seems clear that there are many reasons why an individual may hold foreign currencies, and the overlapping-generations model provides another possible explanation for these hoardings. In some sense, parts of the reasoning are similar to the reasons for a government's willingness to hold reserves, but, in addition, individuals may choose to hold foreign assets as stores of value and as means of avoiding payment of the inflation tax to their own governments. In the extreme case, if the rate of return were the only element influencing individuals' decisions, then each one of them would have to decide to which government he would pay an inflationary tax, if any. The model as it stands allows for the selection of only one currency as a store of value. The multicountry model would determine that one currency would dominate all others (the one offering the highest rate of return), and countries would be forced to follow extremely prudent fiscal policies if they wanted to avoid transfers of real resources abroad.

We know, however, that while some form of currency dominance exists, no country—except by its own choice—has been deprived of the opportunity to issue its own currency and to have it earn some degree of acceptance. The proportion of total liquid asset holdings denominated in domestic currency has varied immensely from country to country (a relatively small fraction in high-inflation countries like Argentina, and almost unity in stable countries like Switzerland and the Federal Republic of Germany), but not even in high-inflation countries has this proportion approached zero. When the proportion does approach zero, hyperinflation is likely to ensue, followed by stabilization measures, which would prove the principal conclusion of the previous paragraph. The reasons why total currency dominance has not materialized is a subject that deserves special attention, but it lies beyond the scope of this chapter.

On the other hand, these private holdings of international liquid assets introduce great distortions in international transactions accounting and, therefore, in the definition of balance of payments disequilibria and the working of the adjustment process; consequently, such private holdings deserve a few general comments. In the absence of private holdings of international liquid assets or private external debts, the current account of the balance of payments will be identical to the difference between domestic expenditures—including net interest payments abroad—and gross national product (GNP), and, as such, should also equal the aggregate of changes in net financial wealth (Δ NFW) of each individual sector in the economy (including the government). In these circumstances, the balance of payments would measure, in the accounts of the monetary authorities, the financing of the current account disequilibrium. Adjustment, in the strict sense of the word, would, therefore, imply the elimination of the current account disequilibrium either by means of traditional fiscal policy or exchange rate policy—through its effects upon relative prices (if strict purchasing power parity did not hold) and, primarily, through its impact upon inflation taxes.

When net foreign exchange positions of the private sector are included, the national current account remains equal to the discrepancy between domestic expenditures—which now also include interest paid and interest received by the private sector—and GNP and also equal to the aggregate of Δ NFW—which now also includes the effects of net interest payments upon each individual's net financial wealth.

This "national" current account differs from the "official" current account, since by convention the official accounts traditionally include interest payments sent abroad by the private sector but do not include—perhaps owing to lack of information—interest receipts on the private sector's holdings of foreign assets. In addition, the official balance of payments reflects the impact upon the monetary authorities' net external position of the above-mentioned current account *plus* the portfolio changes of the private sector and other official sectors (as transactors). In the national balance of payments, portfolio changes among sectors within the country cancel out. There are, therefore, two definitions of the current account and two definitions of the balance of payments, each relevant for certain purposes. In making economic policy, the government should take account of these two concepts, keeping in mind that different combinations of results in these accounts will definitely call for different policy mixes. For example, if the national balance of payments and current account are in surplus and the official current account and balance of payments are in deficit, is the exchange rate the appropriate policy instrument to solve this kind of disequilibrium? Has economic theory taken due account of the profound changes in the distribution of wealth among different sectors that take place, as by-products of exchange rate movements, when the economy operates with interest-bearing financial instruments?

Inflation is another source of distortion in balance of payments figures. As is true of all nominal accounting figures, the balance of payments does not necessarily reflect real flows, since it may be distorted by inflation, even though it continues to reflect financial flows. The identity between the expenditure-income gap in the real sector and the current account of the balance of payments does not hold nor does the relationship between the current account and the aggregate of changes in real net financial wealth. The nominal identities continue to exist, but they do not have any economic meaning (though they continue to have great financial meaning). Once again, to restore the identities in terms of real flows, it is necessary to construct inflation-adjusted current account and other balance of payments figures, for both the official and the national accounts.

Each of these definitions is important in its own way for the analysis of the balance of payments, the adjustment process, and financing needs. I think these subjects deserve ample attention from academicians, international organizations, and governments.

I will refrain from commenting further, since by doing so I might exceed the time allotted to me by the organizers, as well as step outside my role as a discussant. I would like, however, to conclude by emphasizing that Buiter and Eaton's paper makes an important contribution to the understanding of financing and adjustment, and by expressing the hope that in future works they will tackle some of the subjects I mentioned in the latter part of my comment.

Michael Bruno

The Age of Supply Shocks

One cannot assess the functioning of the international credit system and the adjustment problems of the last decade without considering the particular nature of the disturbances that have occurred in countries' balance of payments and the sources of both the growth and the rapidly changing conditions of foreign borrowing during this period. The story, of course, has to do with the oil and raw material price shocks and with the recycling of petrodollars, both of which have dramatically changed the nature of the adjustment problems and one's ways of thinking about them.

In the 1950s and 1960s, payments imbalances and the associated international financing problems could roughly be divided into two major categories, depending on the nature of the disturbance. One was the conventional short-term imbalance between a typical industrial country's imports and exports that was produced mainly by cyclical domestic and international demand-side fluctuations. Quite apart from the question of alternative policy prescriptions for adjustment of internal and external balance, it is clear that the availability of efficiently functioning international credit channels as a short-term buffer was of paramount importance for reasonably smooth functioning of the world trade and payment system. The International Monetary Fund's main function and ways of thinking in those days were geared to the efficient smoothing of demand-side or monetary disturbances within a short-term or medium-term horizon.

The other major category of imbalance was the so-called structural deficit problem typically associated with developing countries' longer-term investment financing. One way of looking at this imbalance was by analyzing the same ex ante import-export gap, except that here the emphasis was placed on "structural" elements—the inelastic demand for the typical country's primary exports and the consequent constraint imposed on production and growth by limited capacity to import raw materials and investment goods. This is also a context in which an intertemporal view of the resource gap was first formulated—namely, that the payments imbalance could, alternatively, be viewed as an efficient way of smoothing domestic savings and consumption over time and of enabling a country to invest more heavily in the early phases of development, so as to increase its capacity to produce import substitutes and exports and thus close the gap in the future. This aspect of international credit was handled by an entirely separate institutional setup, the most prominent element of which was the World Bank. The limited amounts of concessional aid provided and constraints and imperfections in the channels for nonconcessional long-term credit have certainly made this part of the credit market look very much like a supply-rationed market, with very few countries able to pursue the principles of unconstrained optimal foreign borrowing.

The years 1973–74 constituted a major watershed for almost every aspect of the system just described. The first major adjustment necessary had to do with understanding the nature of macroeconomic disturbances in domestic economies. It took some time for analysts to realize that the sharp contraction and unemployment in industrial countries was not a pure demand-insufficiency problem which would quickly take care of itself if only Organization of Petroleum Exporting Countries (OPEC) members recycled their oil proceeds quickly enough into the commodity markets of the industrial countries. At least part of the contraction in the industrial countries had to do with aggregate supply shifts owing to a rise in input prices. These caused a direct profit and productivity squeeze which, in many cases, was aggravated by the failure of real wages to adjust downward. The profit squeeze, in turn, depressed investment and long-term growth. This had two important implications. One is that a supply shock cannot be tackled using only conventional demand-management tools. The other is that the short-term and long-term aspects of the adjustment problem become intertwined. We shall come back to the implications for the payment imbalances of countries later on. For the moment, suffice it to say that the conventional view of short-term, demand-dominated disturbances had to give way to a view encompassing a more complex combination of supply and demand factors. Moreover, the conceptual, as well as institutional, distinction between short-term disturbances and long-term structural imbalances has become rather blurred.

Next, consider the capital-flow aspect of recycling. One of the major worries at the time of the first OPEC price shock—that the international financial system would be unable to recycle petrodollars adequately—turned out to be ill-founded. The ease with which the international financial system intermediated between the unprecedented surpluses and deficits in balances of payments was truly remarkable. But this was not the only surprise. One might have thought, ex ante, that the OPEC surplus would be matched by a large deficit of the major oil importing industrial countries. As it turned out, and as is well known (see Table 1), after OPEC I (the first major petroleum price increase by its members, which occurred in late 1973 and early 1974) the industrial countries by and large kept their payments in balance, while the middle-income countries incurred a deficit more or less equal to the OPEC surplus. This massive flow of funds through the international financial system was accompanied, at least until 1978, by a considerable fall in real interest rates to zero and negative levels. The composition of long-term financing of middle-income countries—that

TABLE 1.[1] INDUSTRIAL AND DEVELOPING COUNTRIES: SUMMARY OF PAYMENTS BALANCES ON CURRENT ACCOUNT, 1973–82[2]

(In billions of U.S. dollars)

Country Group	1973	1974	1975	1976	1977	1978	1979	1980	1981	1982[3]
Industrial countries	17.7	−13.9	17.8	−2.2	−4.9	30.5	−10.2	−43.7	−3.7	11.0
Seven larger countries	12.7	−4.9	22.1	7.5	7.6	33.9	2.7	−17.5	13.0	23.5
Other industrial countries	5.0	−8.9	−4.3	−9.7	−12.6	−3.5	−12.9	−26.2	−16.7	−12.5
Developing countries										
Oil exporting countries	6.7	68.3	35.4	40.3	30.8	2.9	69.8	116.4	68.6	25.0
Non-oil developing countries[4]	−11.6	−37.0	−46.5	−32.0	−28.3	−39.2	−58.9	−86.2	−99.0	−97.0
Total [5]	12.8	17.4	6.7	6.1	−2.4	−5.8	0.7	−13.7	−34.1	−61.0

[1]This is a shortened version of Table 6 in International Monetary Fund, *Annual Report, 1982* (Washington, 1982), p. 18.
[2]On goods, services, and private transfers. For a classification of countries in groups shown here, see Tables 1 and 2 in International Monetary Fund, *Annual Report, 1982* (Washington, 1982), pp. 6, 12.
[3]Fund staff projections. Figures are rounded to the nearest $0.5 billion.
[4]Excludes data for China prior to 1977.
[5]Reflects errors, omissions, and asymmetries in reported balance of payments statistics on current account, plus balance of listed groups with other countries.

is, how it was divided between public concessional aid and commercial credit—changed dramatically. For the first time, there was a sizable group of developing countries for whom the choice of development strategy could follow an almost textbook description of optimal foreign borrowing in a virtually unlimited foreign credit market. Developing countries' relative growth performance during 1974–78 was, indeed, impressive (see Table 2), while that of the industrial countries was miserable. The theoretical reasons and practical implications of this major, albeit short-lived, development will be further discussed later on. Also, we shall return to the catch in this apparent debtors' blessing. Rollover credits which have to be renewed at six-month intervals and variable interest rates are a very different type of

TABLE 2. SELECTED INDUSTRIAL AND DEVELOPING COUNTRIES:
ANNUAL AVERAGE RATE OF CHANGE OF SELECTED VARIABLES, [1]
BY COUNTRY GROUP: 1960–73 AND 1973–80 [2]

Line number	Variable	19 OECD countries [3]		10 MICs [4]		19 MICs [5]	
		1960–73	1973–80	1960–73	1973–80	1960–73	1973–80
1.	Gross domestic product (GDP)	4.7 (1.8)	2.6 (2.2)	6.7 (4.9)	6.0 (3.8)	6.6 (3.6)	6.3 (3.4)
2.	Employment	1.2	0.7	4.0	2.9	—	—
3.	GDP per employed person	3.6	2.0	2.7	3.0	—	—
4.	Gross investment	6.4	0.4	8.9	6.6	9.7	8.1
5.	Public consumption	4.8	2.3	9.9	6.6	8.4	7.7
6.	Import/export prices	−0.5	1.5	−0.5	−0.5	0.2	0.5
7.	Consumer prices	4.7 (1.8)	10.8 (2.9)	6.3 (3.8)	18.5 (9.0)	7.2 (4.8)	19.5 (9.4)
8.	Current account deficit/GDP	1.5 (1.5)	0.9 (2.0)	3.9 (4.6)	8.0 (4.6)	0.3 (3.0)	3.6 (3.2)

Sources: Line 1: For the OECD, a Divisia index based on OECD accounts is used.
Lines 4–6, 8: Organization for Economic Cooperation and Development, *National Income Accounts*, and World Bank, *World Debt Tables*.
Line 7: International Monetary Fund, *International Financial Statistics*.

[1] Figures in parentheses are mean standard deviations.
[2] On line 8, 1965–73 is the first period for all countries, and 1973–79 is the second period for some middle-income countries.
[3] Comprising all Organization for Economic Cooperation and Development (OECD) countries except Greece, Iceland, Luxembourg, Portugal, and Turkey.
[4] The 10 middle-income countries are Kenya, Mauritius, Korea, the Philippines, Singapore, Yugoslavia, Syria, Zambia, Egypt, and Israel.
[5] The 19 middle-income countries include the 10 specified in footnote 4 plus Ivory Coast, Morocco, Malaysia, Pakistan, Thailand, Greece, Turkey, Brazil, and Colombia.

investment financing from the long-term credits debtors had been accustomed to in the era preceding OPEC I.

OPEC II (which occurred in 1979) brought the next set of surprises. The second-round OPEC surplus, this time shorter-lived, did not produce deficits only in the middle-income countries. The industrial countries incurred larger deficits (see Table 1), and many of the middle-income countries now had to pay both higher oil prices and higher real interest rates. When oil prices started coming down, some of the oil producers (Mexico, Nigeria) joined the ranks of developing countries experiencing serious liquidity problems. The period of high real interest rates (with shortening maturities and higher spreads over the London interbank offered rate (Libor)) in which we still find ourselves has been termed the OPEC III supply-price shock, and in many ways it has affected the system like an input-price shock. The world is now waiting for a revival of economic activity in the United States and other industrial countries which, it is to be hoped, will also ease the tension in international financial markets.

Some Theoretical Considerations

The major developments in the area of payment imbalances and world capital markets can be rationalized within the theory of adjustment to input supply shocks in a national and international setting.[1] A relevant framework of analysis is one that views the current account as the difference between national savings and investment under capital mobility and intertemporal borrowing.[2] Countries borrow abroad to smooth their consumption path and to finance investments aimed at increasing future production. They would thus borrow optimally up to the point at which the marginal product of capital goods in the production of tradable goods equals the marginal cost of foreign borrowing.[3]

The opening up of a hitherto restricted capital market, when potentially profitable investment opportunities are available, and a fall in real interest rates induces a borrowing country to borrow more heavily for both investment and consumption (private and public) purposes. A raw-material-

[1] For a sample of rather closely related papers see Sachs (1981), Svensson (1981), van Wijnbergen (1981), and Bruno (1982). The discussion here is mainly based on the last of these.

[2] The intertemporal aspect can be dealt with more profoundly in an overlapping-generations model, such as the one employed by Buiter and Eaton (see Chapter 3 in this volume), but the specific set of simplifying assumptions required (no production, no physical investments, and no bonds) make it of only limited use for the problems discussed here.

[3] When there are nontradable goods in the system, the relative price of tradables in terms of nontradables must increase over time at a rate which equals the difference between the domestic real rate and the marginal cost of foreign borrowing. This provides a rule for changes in the real exchange rate over time and for the growth of exports and import substitutes.

price shock reduces the wealth of net importers (most industrial countries and many middle-income developing countries) and increases the wealth of the net exporters (OPEC) of such goods, with corresponding effects on the consumption and savings of the respective groups of countries. An added effect comes from the differential response of real wages to the input-price shock, with countries having more flexible wages harmed less than countries with fixed wages (e.g., European countries) by a profit and investment squeeze. Finally, one can incorporate into the analysis the effect of more conventional Keynesian or monetarist demand-management policies on the output and current accounts of countries. The theory can account for the fact that Organization for Economic Cooperation and Development (OECD) countries' current accounts worsened only briefly in 1974 and then rapidly moved into surplus, mainly on account of the drop in their foreign investments, while the middle-income countries (MICs) expanded their output, investments, public consumption, and foreign borrowing, as is shown in Table 2.

The following cross-country regression was estimated for a group of 38 countries, 19 OECD countries and 19 MICs (see Table 2).

$$\Delta(D/V) = 3.55 - 2.02 \, \Delta(\dot{p}_n - \dot{p}_x)\gamma + 0.39 \, \Delta\dot{g} + 0.26 \, \Delta\dot{k}$$
$$\qquad\qquad (0.87) \quad (0.77) \qquad\qquad\qquad (0.17) \qquad\quad (0.14)$$
$$(\bar{R}^2 = 0.51)$$

The dependent variable is the average change in the ratio of the current account deficit to gross national product (GNP) $[\Delta(D/V)]$, at constant prices, from 1960–73 to 1973–80. The independent variables are the import share γ, the weighted terms-of-trade changes $\Delta(\dot{p}_n - \dot{p}_x)$, and the changes in real public consumption $(\Delta\dot{g})$ and real investment $(\Delta\dot{k})$ growth rates. (Numbers in parentheses below coefficients are standard deviations of coefficients.)

The terms-of-trade factor, which represents substitution between foreign and domestic goods (and possibly real-income effects), is highly significant. The other factors can be considered as representing shifts in aggregate savings and investment, respectively.

While any individual small or medium-sized country can be considered a price taker in the international loan market, real interest rates on world credit markets may, to a considerable extent, be endogenously determined by the supply of, and the demand for, loanable funds. One way of obtaining the determinants of the real interest rate by way of theoretical simplification is to aggregate individual countries' savings supply and investment demand into aggregate world savings and investment schedules, described as functions of the real interest rate R in Figure 1. An oil price shock will, at

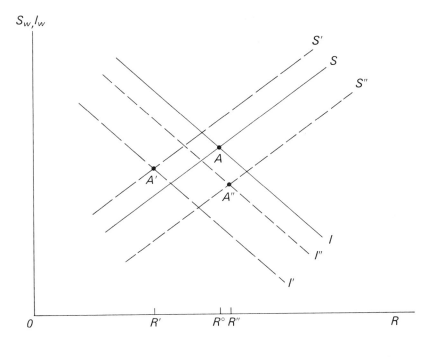

Figure 1

least in the short run (and if considered permanent), shift the investment schedule to the left. The savings schedule will shift to the right if the beneficiaries of rising oil prices (OPEC) have a marginal propensity to save out of the added wealth which exceeds that of the wealth losers. In this case, the resulting intersection of I' and S' at A' is at a lower real interest rate (R') than the one at A (R^0).

There are good reasons to suggest that at the time of OPEC II, the investment schedule shifted downward by less (I''), while the world savings schedule contracted (to S'') on account of higher consumption propensities of OPEC this time and sharper, Keynesian-type contractionary policies in OECD countries (though these were accompanied by rising government deficits), thus raising, rather than lowering, real interest rates (see movement from R^0 to R'' in Figure 1). One could also tell a complementary story about worldwide monetary contraction increasing nominal rates of interest as inflationary expectations were coming down.

The empirical link between supply shocks and real interest rate movements has recently been studied by Wilcox (1983).

Were Credit Conditions Too Easy?

In view of the recent financial crises, one could claim, in retrospect, that recycling in the mid-1970s may have proceeded too smoothly. Overly permissive standards of foreign lending may have been adopted by both private and public financial institutions. Such a view, however, can only be a partial-equilibrium view. It is most probably true that any particular private financial institution which eventually found itself overexposed could have avoided such exposure by more prudent lending policy. Yet, for the system as a whole, the underlying state of the world market and the aggregate flow of funds determine the outcome. The fact is that when the real oil price rises, an OPEC surplus must emerge, even if only temporarily. This surplus must be matched by a corresponding non-OPEC deficit. The aggregate financial terms at which the additional matching credit gets distributed around the world depend on the ex ante pressure of competing claims on this surplus.

The fact that most of this surplus was channeled at excessively low interest rates in the mid-1970s is related to the fact that the industrial countries by and large opted for, or accepted, a strategy entailing depressed investment, rigid real wages, slow growth, and a balanced current account while those middle-income countries with access to the new financial buyer's market enjoyed the "free lunch" while it lasted. In retrospect, maybe there was no free lunch. When a country borrows optimally for investment or public consumption at low interest rates which it hopes will last for successive biannual renewals of the loan, the domestic marginal product of such funds may very likely be substantially lower than the ex post cost of the renewed loan. The country gets locked into an investment program without being able to extricate itself once higher real interest rates are forced upon it. While real interest rates are most probably still too high now, relative to some reasonable long-run cost of world credit, they were harmfully low during much of the 1970s. As is true of the real price of oil, it is not the levels or long-run trends per se which are damaging, as much as the sharp fluctuations in the real cost of credit or other productive factors, since the response to an upward or downward shift is not symmetric, owing to rigidities, ratchet effects, and the like.

Policy Considerations

One major implication of the developments just described has to do with general coordination of industrial countries' macroeconomic policies in the medium run. The real cost of borrowing and the availability of credit are only part of a world adjustment problem. A smoother overall growth strategy will also avoid the sharp fluctuations in real factor prices, including that of capital. Another related implication for the conduct of individual borrowing countries may be the need to buffer sharp fluctuations in domestic interest rates by means of a suitable interest equalization tax or fund.

The private banking community probably knows best how to conduct its own affairs. The recent crises must have sharpened bankers' awareness of the need for greater care and more coordination on such questions as country rating and credit insurance schemes. Banking regulations will probably also be tightened in response to recent events.

The last issue has to do with the changing role of international institutions and, in particular, of the Fund and the World Bank. The experience of the last decade has shown that despite the emergence of new private international markets, the role of the Fund and Bank as financing institutions has remained critical. The special facilities created after OPEC I were of major importance in containing the crisis, especially for countries that had no access to the private market. The need for both short-term and long-term finance from a public source has not diminished and, if anything, is greater now, when the process of "privatization" of development finance has slowed down.

The growth of the world credit system has certainly enhanced the role of the international institutions as supervisory agencies. They must be involved in debt crises early on. The Fund's "seal of approval" provided by its lending to a particular country may be at least as important as a signaling device to other lenders as the actual finance that the Fund can come up with. On the other hand, this function necessarily is of less consequence if it is not bolstered by the Fund's ability to absorb some of the financial risk. Both the Fund and the World Bank thus require substantial additional funds from member governments if they are to fulfill their various functions efficiently. Finally, one should note that just as the events of the last decade have blurred the distinction between short-run and long-run adjustment problems (and, alas, the one between short-term and long-term finance), so the distinctions between the functions of the Fund and the World Bank have become less clear. The two institutions should be commended for the pragmatism they have shown in adjusting to this new circumstance.

REFERENCES

Bruno, Michael, "Petrodollars and the Differential Growth Performance of Industrial and Middle Income Countries in the 1970s" (unpublished, Hebrew University, December 1982).

Sachs, Jeffrey D., "The Current Account and Macroeconomic Adjustment in the 1970s," *Brookings Papers on Economic Activity:1* (1981), pp. 201–68.

Svensson, L.E.O., *Oil Prices and a Small Oil-Importing Economy's Welfare and Trade Balance: An Intertemporal Approach*, Institute for International Economic Studies, Seminar Paper No. 184 (Stockholm: University of Stockholm, October 1981).

van Wijnbergen, S., "Oil Price Shocks and the Current Account" (unpublished, World Bank, September 1981).

Wilcox, J.A., "Why Real Interest Rates Were so Low in the 1970s," *American Economic Review*, Vol. 73 (March 1983), pp. 44–53.

*Rimmer de Vries**

The topic of this session, "financing and adjustment," is high on everyone's agenda at this time of international debt troubles. International institutions, governments, and commercial banks are all grappling with the challenge to global stability and economic recovery. Basic to resolution of the present debt problems is the appropriate mix of financing and adjustment that will restore the creditworthiness of less developed countries (LDCs) and enable them to resume sound economic progress. The right mix of adjustment and financing should rest on the best possible appraisal of long-run debt capacity of the borrowers that is also compatible with sound expansion of international lending.

While the goal is clear, the practical assessment of developing-country debt capacity is no easy task. It has proved elusive, for that matter, for industrial countries, not least the reserve centers. It is interesting to recall the debate, which began in the 1950s and dominated international financial conferences throughout the 1960s, on the nature, gravity, and solution of the chronic U.S. payments imbalance associated with the rapid increase in U.S. liabilities to foreigners. From the initial emergence of an excess of U.S. short-term liabilities over gold reserve assets until the suspension of convertibility in 1971, there was unending political, economic, and financial-market tension over the seigniorage advantage allegedly enjoyed by reserve centers and the intrinsic worth of their sovereign credit. The perceived "overhang" of foreign-held dollars undermined confidence and limited the policy options of both the United States and its creditors. The similar overhang of sterling liabilities was a major preoccupation of British policymakers for 30 years after World War II.

After the first oil shock, the focus of country creditworthiness concerns

*The views expressed herein are those of the author and not necessarily those of Morgan Guaranty Trust Company.

shifted, for the most part, to developing countries. In earlier postwar years, most LDC financing was provided from official sources. Private funds played no great role, and there was a body of conventional wisdom concerning debt capacity that guided the behavior of lenders and borrowers alike. Yet, as private markets rose to the recycling challenge of the 1970s, the older attitudes seemed outdated. New standards, however, did not take root. There was neither academic nor governmental agreement on what the fundamental yardsticks should be, and certainly none on their specific application. Instead, creditworthiness came increasingly to be identified with access to private international capital markets.

The second oil shock, however, bred an Organization of Petroleum Exporting Countries (OPEC) surplus even larger than the first and elicited a quite different policy response by the major industrial countries. Accelerating inflation and energy security concerns inspired severely restrictive monetary policies. Three years of recession followed, in which payments deficits were quickly reconcentrated among developing countries, including several OPEC members. Debt problems multiplied. Today, more than 35 developing and East European countries are in arrears on debt service, are in the process of rescheduling, or have recently rescheduled portions of their external debts. Before the end of this year, more countries are likely to be added to the list.

These problems naturally preoccupy us. Still, it is important that we plan ahead for a new era of stable and sound international finance. In thinking ahead, we should ask ourselves: What mistakes were made in the past that could have been avoided? and, What new standards of debt-servicing capacity and principles for lending will best foster world prosperity and stability? Beyond the present period of transition, private markets will continue to be the main providers of external finance to developing countries. It is unrealistic to suppose that private finance can be substantially replaced by some new Marshall Plan, although there is nonetheless a strategic role for official finance going beyond the critical initiatives so far undertaken. The emphasis of reform, therefore, must be to assure better functioning of private international markets: for borrowers, to appraise their debt capacity and development strategy with due regard for the uncertainties of their external environment; for lenders, to avoid inappropriate surges of lending to countries temporarily perceived as attractive credit opportunities; and, in all, to encourage extension of credit both on an informed basis and on terms tailored to a realistic appreciation of debt-servicing capabilities.

Looking Back: How and Why?

How did so many borrowers and lenders become so vulnerable to the economic and financial pressures of the past three years? Why did some LDCs borrow so much and incur such heavy debt-servicing obligations? Why did banks lend so much and on the terms that they did?

It is important to recognize that governments welcomed commercial recycling of the OPEC surplus to LDCs through the international banking system following the first oil shock. Politically, this was much easier than mobilizing massive official financing. Moreover, sustained growth in LDC gross national product (GNP) and import demand was a helpful offset to domestic demand weakness in the industrial countries.

To spur economic growth, monetary policies of the major industrial countries encouraged borrowing. Incentives for borrowing were greatly increased by accelerating inflation. This was especially the case during the mid-1970s, when real rates of interest were very low or negative. Many LDCs, especially oil exporters, at times found their export prices advancing even more rapidly than the general level of prices in industrial countries; for them, real interest rates were substantially negative. Borrowing seemed virtually costless. At the same time, economic growth in the industrial countries underwrote expansion of world trade and LDC export markets. Thus, even though external debt levels and debt-servicing obligations of LDCs mounted rapidly in absolute terms, their climb was considerably less pronounced relative to GNP and exports. Since 1979, by contrast, real interest rates have turned strongly positive; commodity producers have suffered drastic deterioration in their terms of trade; industrial-country protectionism has escalated; and demand for LDC exports has waned. Debt levels that seemed rational, even comfortable, in an era of expansion proved precarious in a period of pronounced and prolonged economic contraction.

Lenders did not always know fully the uses to which the proceeds of their loans were put. Even aside from general-purpose balance of payments loans, some loans for specific projects and investment programs were made without thorough appraisal of the projects and programs. Moreover, projects with prospective payout horizons stretching over several decades were too often financed by five- or seven-year loans that would inevitably require rollover or refinancing. Furthermore, with new loan commitments drawn down quickly, and with money being fungible, borrowers had ample scope for reshuffling loan proceeds to uses other than the ones initially intended. Lenders who merely monitored project progress had too narrow a view of the uses, abuses, and risks of their credits.

It is often asserted that much foreign lending in the 1970s served simply to finance unsustainable consumption. Some financing of consumption was inevitable after the two oil price shocks: it was widely considered desirable to recycle OPEC surpluses for a while, rather than to attempt to adjust too quickly. Abrupt adjustment would have unduly depressed overall economic activity and seriously disrupted development programs. However, at various times and in various countries, adjustment clearly lagged, which meant that some LDCs borrowed to maintain consumption for too long. At times, the ready availability of finance clearly delayed needed adjustment.

While some LDC borrowing no doubt financed consumption, it should be stressed that borrowing also sustained investment. For major groups of LDCs, in fact, investment rates, expressed as shares of investment in GNP, increased following the first oil shock and were generally maintained at these higher levels through 1980. Increased net foreign capital inflows do not appear to have discouraged domestic savings, which edged up through most of the 1970s.

This, of course, says nothing about the productivity of the investment that was financed out of domestic savings and foreign borrowing. The rate of real GNP growth slowed in many major LDC borrowers after the first oil shock, despite increases in the share of GNP devoted to investment. Overall returns on investment probably decreased over the past decade, slowing the growth in debt-servicing capacity at a time when external debt and servicing requirements were growing rapidly.

The long-run productivity in LDCs of external finance, which should be a basic consideration of creditworthiness, is not easy to assess. There is considerable anecdotal evidence of unproductive or low-return investment in LDCs, both oil exporters and oil importers. Undesirable as this is, waste will never be wholly avoided in a development process and is hardly unknown, of course, in advanced industrial countries. The apparent overall deterioration of investment yield may be partly explained by the fact that sharply higher energy prices rendered some of the existing capital stock uneconomic: some of the incremental investment was devoted to related structural adjustments. Moreover, the measured efficiency of investment was bound to be affected adversely during a prolonged period of sluggish or negative world economic growth.

Although many lenders and borrowers made serious attempts to analyze developing countries' debt-carrying capacity, their judgments were unduly influenced in practice by the borrowers' perceived access to additional credit, especially from banks. Creditworthiness and debt-servicing capacity increasingly were identified with access to credit markets. Current account deficits and the related growth of external debt-servicing obligations were said to be sustainable as long as they were financeable. Thus, borrowers' access to credit sometimes became an overriding consideration in loan decisions. To oversimplify, lenders got caught up in circular reasoning: a country was judged to be creditworthy if it could borrow enough, and a country could borrow enough as long as it was viewed as creditworthy.

The preoccupation with credit access, and underemphasis on long-term considerations, was exacerbated by the intensely competitive market pressures that prevailed during much of the 1970s and early 1980s. More and more banks entered into a lending field thought to offer attractive returns with reasonable risk. Expansion, or at least maintenance, of market share became a key objective of increased lending. Inevitably, loan-rate spreads were driven down to levels that were insufficient in relation to the risks that have surfaced in the 1980s.

More balanced, in-depth analysis of debt-servicing capabilities might have lessened the present difficulties in LDC financing. Yet the art of appraising debt-service capacity is fraught with pitfalls, ambiguities, and fashions. A recent issue (December 1982) of International Monetary Fund *Staff Papers* contains an excellent survey of the literature on the subject by Donogh C. McDonald. As the author observes, the volume of literature has grown about as rapidly as LDC external debt. The literature has been useful in highlighting the general principles of debt capacity. But no one has come up with any simple formula for determining the optimal level of external indebtedness for a country, despite numerous, often elaborate, attempts.

Even when borrowing plans and lending decisions were based on a balanced and comprehensive appraisal of debt-servicing capacity, borrowers and lenders alike tended to use this debt capacity to the fullest, where debt could be serviced without difficulty only under a continuation of relatively favorable circumstances. In retrospect, the possibilities of adverse circumstances, whether internal or external to the borrowing country, were not adequately taken into account. To be sure, it was realized that commodity prices might not hold firm forever, that markets could weaken, that inflation might wane, and that the days of cheap money could end. Few analysts, however, foresaw the potential degree or simultaneity of the adverse forces that have arisen in the 1980s. Sensitivity exercises were limited to "moderate" changes in assumptions within the spectrum of "reputable" opinion. Consequently, the risks of current account deterioration were underestimated. Other financing risks also were inadequately perceived; for example, the strain on official liquidity occasioned by the massive private capital flight that political uncertainties can provoke. Even when the financial outlook was uncertain, lenders have too often presumed that borrowers were willing and able to make requisite performance adjustments, or that some third party would come to the rescue.

There has been excessive reliance on short-term borrowing. This increased countries' vulnerability to debt-servicing problems while giving lenders a false sense of security. The short-term debts of many major LDC borrowers grew faster than their total external debts, particularly toward the end of the 1970s and in the early 1980s: more than one third of LDCs' total external debt at the end of 1982 matures in 1983, as does roughly half of their debt to banks.

Borrowers frequently resorted to short-term credit because loan spreads were narrower than on medium- or long-term credit. Moreover, fewer questions were raised because lenders regarded short-term credit as less risky. Banks believed that short-term credit gave them the flexibility to withdraw if conditions deteriorated and risks increased. However, what seemed to make sense for an individual lender provided little protection once many lenders attempted to withdraw simultaneously as borrowers' performance deteriorated.

Closely connected with the dangers of excessive short-term borrowing has been the lack of timely and comprehensive information on the scale and growth of short-term debt. Individual lenders often were unaware of the extent of short-term lending by others to the same borrower, at least at the time such borrowing was taking place. Thus, decisions have been made on the basis of inadequate information regarding a major portion of a borrower's debt obligations. It should be emphasized that, by its nature, short-term debt falls due in short order, and that in consequence, the timely availability of information on short-term positions is vital if such information is to be at all useful. Timeliness has not been the hallmark of official information gathering and dissemination in this field. Nor have borrowers been consistently forthcoming and comprehensively informed as to their own short-term positions.

Indeed, there are several aspects of short-term debt which neither borrowers nor lenders fully appreciated. One relates to liabilities sourced from the interbank markets of the major industrial countries. Overseas banking offices of banks based in some of the major LDC borrowing countries borrow predominantly short-term interbank funds, in part for on-lending at short- or medium-term to their parent or other entities in the home country. The home country recognizes—at least, it should recognize—such funds as part of overall external debt. It should also recognize their fundamentally short-term character: when an LDC experiences a liquidity squeeze and encounters debt-servicing difficulties, such as Brazil did recently, these overseas banking offices may be faced with a runoff of their liabilities. This runoff can become a significant drain on the foreign exchange resources of the parent bank, and ultimately those of the latter's central bank. Failure of an LDC borrower to take responsibility for meeting the foreign exchange liabilities of these overseas banking offices seriously endangers that country's ability to roll over other maturing credits, thereby further worsening the country's liquidity and debt-servicing difficulty. Very little information is readily available on the overall magnitude of short-term liabilities of these overseas offices of LDC-based banks, yet they represent a potential drain on LDC foreign exchange resources.

There are other ways in which conventional compilations of external debt figures, comprising obligations to nonresidents, fail to represent comprehensively the full potential claims on foreign exchange resources. There may be substantial additional foreign-currency liabilities, actual or contingent, to residents of a country. This is obviously the case for advanced countries that maintain free currency convertibility. Among developing countries, resident foreign currency claims have complicated debt crises in at least two recent cases. Yugoslavia has foreign currency obligations to nationals who remitted earnings from working abroad. Mexico permitted resident peso depositors to open dollar accounts in local banks. Transfer of such short-term funds to U.S. banks was one contributor to the major flight of capital from Mexico last year as confidence deteriorated and the debt crisis came to a head.

Not only are external debt data deficient, both in themselves and as measures of foreign-currency liabilities, but so also are published figures of international reserves. Experience has shown that reserve assets, as reported by the International Monetary Fund (IMF), may include assets that are very illiquid: assets, for example, that are encumbered or pledged, or that consist of trade receivables that are past due or unmarketable.

Finally, it has to be accepted that LDC debt problems would not have reached such troubling dimensions had the major industrial powers and official institutions played a more assertive role in the initial period following the second oil shock. Of course, the Fund and the World Bank are limited by the wishes of their member governments. But passivity was an unfortunate response. The success of recycling after the first oil shock induced a certain complacency. The major borrowing countries were thought to have graduated from the ranks of poorer countries dependent on official financing. They were neither willing to accept, nor did official creditors actively pursue, outside policy guidance. Indeed, while ample private funds were forthcoming, it seemed appropriate to confine limited official resources to the poorest countries lacking access to private credit markets. There was no perceived urgency to call forth major expansion of Fund or World Bank resources and lending facilities. Yet if the Fund and Bank were not going to provide credit to the graduate borrowers, a closer working relationship with the commercial banks, who were assuming the financing burden, should have been developed well before the present debt difficulties.

Looking to the Future: Avoiding Excesses

As noted earlier, past efforts to develop measures of debt capacity and guides to appropriate levels of external debt and international lending have been inconclusive. Nevertheless, the search must not be abandoned. Not the least of our present difficulties is the absence of fundamental standards that are independent of the shifting values of the market: the collective judgment of the market is not always conducive to long-term financial stability.

The problem has much in common with that of appraising appropriate exchange rate behavior—specifically, whether exchange rate determination ought to be left solely to market forces or should be guided by official intervention and policy initiatives. While it is difficult to identify correct exchange rate relationships with conviction, few would deny that market forces have led to instances of currency overshooting and undershooting which have been costly in terms of economic performance. Similarly, excessive foreign borrowing or lending can have adverse consequences for borrowers and lenders alike. Although the immediate policy focus remains the need to secure bank lending to LDCs at a level consistent with official programs and financing, thought should also be given to ways that excessive borrowing or lending can be avoided once LDC creditworthiness and market access are restored.

An obvious priority is provision of more complete and timely information on international debts and assets. The primary responsibility for identifying, collecting, and disseminating relevant statistics rests with the Fund, the World Bank, the Bank for International Settlements (BIS), and central banks. Progress has been made since the early 1970s, but important gaps remain. For most countries, there are no available data on external debt owed by private nonbank entities that is not publicly guaranteed. Trade debt typically is underreported. Fairly comprehensive data are available on debt to banks, but only with a lag of approximately six months. This is too long, given the speed with which short-term debt can run up. Bank debt figures should be published on a monthly rather than a quarterly basis, and with much less delay between data collection and publication.

Besides closing these information gaps, there is need to reconcile discrepancies in external debt data. At present, information must be compiled from a variety of national and international sources that follow inconsistent accounting treatments. For some countries, there remain sizable disparities in the resulting estimates of external indebtedness. A comprehensive official source of international debt statistics is urgently needed. The Fund and the World Bank could assist borrowing countries in establishing comprehensive reporting systems, in providing technical assistance where needed, and in monitoring debtor reporting on a continuous basis, functioning also as an outside auditor. Full use should be made of data on claims reported by creditors—including international institutions, governments, their agencies, and commercial banks—as well as information furnished by debtors. Any discrepancies should be reconciled.

Similar considerations apply to information on external assets. The principal need is for more detailed and timely information on the individual components in order to render sound judgments on the overall quality and liquidity of reserve assets.

A second priority is development of early-warning signals and thresholds that will flag countries at risk of payments arrearages or debt reschedulings. There are several indicators and related thresholds that we have found to be useful, especially the first three of the five listed in Table 1.

Exports of goods and services (plus net private transfers if positive) are the denominator for the first four ratios. Exports are more relevant and reliable than GNP as a numéraire for debt-servicing capacity, especially in developing countries prone to inappropriate exchange rate policies. All five indicators include short-term debt. This overlap is deliberate, in recognition of the importance of short-term debt as a source of vulnerability to liquidity problems. In the past, there was a tendency to ignore such debt, not only because of inadequate data but also because it was assumed that most short-term debt was related to trade financing whose rollover was normally automatic. In fact, many countries' short-term debts exceed any reasonable relationship to their trade financing, and there may be nothing automatic about rollover.

TABLE 1. EARLY WARNING INDICATORS AND THRESHOLDS

	Thresholds	
Indicators	First signal	Second signal
Total external debt as a percentage of exports[1]	160+	200+
External debt maturing within one year as a percentage of exports[2]	50+	70+
External debt service as a percentage of exports[3]	65+	80+
Gross foreign borrowing as a percentage of exports[4]	65+	80+
Liquid foreign exchange reserve assets as a percentage of imports and maturing debt[5]	7−	4−

[1]Total debt includes public- and private-sector, long- and short-term obligations.

[2]Debt maturing within one year includes debt with an original maturity of one year or less, plus amortization of longer-term debt.

[3]Debt service includes interest on total debt and amortization on longer-term debt (the traditional measure of debt service) plus debt with an original maturity of one year or less.

[4]Gross foreign borrowing is measured by the current account deficit (after official transfers) plus all debt maturing within the year, adjusted for changes in reserve assets and net private direct investment. This could be further refined to reflect capital flight and changes in other external assets, such as export credit extended to trading partners.

[5]The denominator of the traditional reserve cover ratio is expanded to include imports of goods and services plus all maturing debt (amortization of longer-term debt and original maturity short-term debt).

The threshold levels were selected from study of the experience of countries that relied on bank credit for a significant portion of their gross foreign borrowing after the first oil shock. Using these ratios, thresholds in the first set generally were exceeded at least two or three years before the onset of debt-servicing problems. Those in the second set were often exceeded one year prior to, or in the year of, problems.

These ratios, assessed both as levels and rates of change, indicate the onset of liquidity problems at least as well as any others we have examined. We are aware of their shortcomings. The thresholds do not capture all countries that experience debt-servicing problems—so called Type I errors. Some countries, at least for the time being, have exceeded the thresholds without running into liquidity problems—Type II errors. It should be stressed that these thresholds, developed on the basis of past experience, need periodic review as the international economic and financial environment changes. Debt ratios that were appropriate in the past may be untenable in a noninflationary environment of high real interest rates, deteriorating export markets, and slower growth of international lending. It is also desirable to allow for some margin of safety, given the speed with which external debt has risen in the past few years. Both factors suggest that lower trigger points than those indicated may be warranted.

Apart from establishing general yardsticks, special attention should be given to the level and use of short-term credit. While it is natural for a country to finance part of its foreign trade by borrowing short term, some countries have accumulated short-term debts that exceed their total annual imports.

What is an appropriate level of short-term debt? One approach relies on the usual practice of extending trade financing for up to 90–120 days. Thus, a country could reasonably incur short-term liabilities connected with its imports, while at the same time borrowing to extend similar terms to its customers. Allowance should be made, however, for that portion of trade, most often in capital goods, for which medium-term financing is provided. Allowance also needs to be made for seasonal swings in payments patterns. All in all, it would be reasonable for a country's short-term debt to average at most one quarter of its total trade. Furthermore, strong guidelines are needed to avoid the abuse of short-term foreign currency deposit schemes, swap facilities, and borrowings in the interbank market for long-term balance of payments financing.

Once useful early warning signals are developed and refined, how might they be applied? The Fund could play a valuable role in counseling countries on appropriate levels and structure of external indebtedness as part of the annual surveillance exercise, in which specific threshold levels tailored to the country could be identified. As the Managing Director has indicated, steps need to be taken to reinforce surveillance of external borrowings and indebtedness of member countries, including issuance of more explicit warnings where external financing problems seem likely to emerge.

As a borrowing country approaches or exceeds the thresholds for the early-warning indicators, with the implied increase in the probability of debt-servicing problems, the country's leeway for policy errors and its ability to absorb shocks without running into liquidity problems diminish. Depending on the particular ratios that approach their thresholds, a borrowing country would need to take appropriate steps to slow the growth of its debt, improve the structure of its debt, and, when necessary, rebuild its liquid assets. Remedial action may be desirable when the set of first thresholds is passed. The need for policy correction would increase as the ratios approached or exceeded the secondary thresholds. Guidelines on short-term borrowing, in particular, should be discussed with the borrower and be incorporated in the performance criteria for Fund stabilization programs.

What about the World Bank? So far, the Fund has been at the center of attention, particularly in short-term liquidity matters. However, the World Bank, with its orientation toward long-term development assistance, also has an important role to play. The Bank recently announced several changes in its lending policies, including accelerated disbursement of funds, designed to help countries currently experiencing debt-servicing problems. However, the Bank continues to focus increasingly on the poorest countries, while seeking to "graduate" those middle-income countries with access to international capital markets. Actual experience has shown that these latter countries are able to obtain only very limited amounts of truly long-term funds for economic development in these markets. Many of the World Bank's LDC clients now find themselves heavily loaded up with medium- and short-term obligations to commercial banks. And, as a result of recent events, it may be many years before some LDCs regain even limited access to international bond markets.

The principle of graduation, which has been strongly endorsed by the U.S. Government, should be re-examined and broadened. There are a number of countries approaching graduation (e.g., Argentina, Brazil, Chile, Mexico, Portugal, and Yugoslavia) that are nonetheless in difficulty. Current conditions clearly necessitate delay in implementing the graduation process. If the World Bank is to provide significant assistance to medium- and high-income countries, it must have adequate sources. A speedup by member governments of the planned $40 billion increase in the Bank's capital would certainly help.

Beyond providing long-term financing, the Bank's expertise in measuring and assessing the longer-term aspects of debt capacity could be exploited more fully. The short-term liquidity aspects of creditworthiness have been at the center of attention in recent years. Not enough emphasis has been placed on longer-term considerations. There is a need to get a better fix on the productivity of investment. More work needs to be done in analyzing the longer-term impact of investment on exports and imports. The impact of changes in policies and institutional arrangements on domestic savings behavior should be studied further. The benefits of an increased role for foreign private direct investment ought to be re-examined. In bringing its expertise to bear on these key questions of resource mobilization and allocation, the World Bank can usefully supplement Fund consultations on macroeconomic policies and external debt management.

Further, while it is preferable to contain the buildup of external debt from the borrowing countries' side, these efforts need to be supplemented by some steps designed to avoid large, erratic surges of bank lending and increased concentrations of credit exposure. Direct credit controls are not the answer. They would hinder efficient resource allocation and be at odds with the liberalization of international trade and capital flows that has occurred in the post-World War II era. The setting of formal lending limits would inevitably be highly politicized, given the differences in size and other characteristics of countries. Limits, by themselves, would neither prevent the making of bad loans to individual countries nor protect against systematic risks affecting all borrowers, such as the present world recession. Direct controls also could take away vitally needed flexibility to deal with temporary disturbances affecting trade and capital flows.

A more constructive approach is for banks, on their own, to strengthen prudential rules or guidelines. Planned growth of lending to individual countries could be slowed as the country approaches or exceeds the kind of thresholds discussed earlier. The extent of the lending slowdown would vary with the strength of the warning signals and the degree of existing portfolio concentration.

However, if some banks adopt this suggested approach while others choose to ignore the warning signals and take the opportunity to expand their market shares, surges in overall lending will not be avoided. Such surges will enable borrowing countries to delay needed adjustment, which will result in increased credit risk for all lenders, including those that showed restraint. This possibility reinforces the need for the international institutions to tackle the problem of excessive debt accumulation by working closely with individual borrowers.

In conclusion, the close working relation that has emerged in the past year among the Fund, major LDC borrowers, and the international banking community must be maintained after the present emergency situation has passed. With the banks providing the vast bulk of financing to developing countries, but the policy leverage to impose adjustment programs residing with the Fund, it is logical that the banks and the Fund should work closely together to assure a proper blend of financing and adjustment. As indicated earlier, such a closer relationship among the various participants should have been established following the second oil shock. This cooperation and more comprehensive and timely information on external assets and liabilities, stronger Fund surveillance, and stepped-up World Bank assistance to major LDC borrowers are the most promising ways of assuring that private capital markets allocate international investment prudently and efficiently.

REFERENCE

McDonald, Donogh C., "Debt Capacity and Developing Country Borrowing: A Survey of the Literature," International Monetary Fund, *Staff Papers*, Vol. 29 (December 1982), pp. 603–46.

The SDR and the IMF: Toward a World Central Bank?

STANLEY FISCHER*

After throwing its reserves and its influence over private banks into battle in a succession of financial crises in the nineteenth century, the Bank of England emerged as central banker to the English, and thus the world, monetary system. The Bank functioned as a central bank in a limited sense: it acted as lender of last resort, but did not take actions, beyond the prevention of financial collapse, to smooth the trade cycle. Nor did it pay explicit attention to financial developments in the rest of the world except to the extent that they affected London.

In the 1982–83 world economic crisis, the International Monetary Fund (IMF) has contributed to the smooth running of the international financial system, using its limited resources and its influence over government and private institutions in the battle to prevent financial collapse and to promote adjustment. It has thus begun to carry out the first task of a central bank, which is preventing a financial crisis from becoming a financial collapse. In doing so, it has acted like a traditional central bank in being more concerned with the provision of liquidity than with the problems of reconstruction finance. Beyond this, the Fund has, in the First Amendment to the Articles of Agreement, which defines the special drawing right (SDR), taken upon itself the second task fulfilled by a modern central bank, that of using its portfolio in an attempt to stabilize the trade cycle. Except in the current crisis, it has not carried out this function.

It is natural and tempting to speculate whether the Fund is a fledgling

*I am indebted to Rudiger Dornbusch, George von Furstenberg, and John Williamson for helpful discussions; to Michael Parkin and Don Roper for valuable comments; and to the National Science Foundation for research support.

179

world central bank, moving through crises and constitutional change toward the wider purposes that Keynes (1943, p. 76) saw for the International Clearing Union. I shall, of course, succumb to the temptation. However, the main aim of this paper is to discuss the benefits and weaknesses of alternative structures of the world monetary system and the role of the central bank. I examine several models of the world monetary system.[1] The first is that of a single world fiat money, with the monetary unit called the WM; the second is the WM exchange standard; and the third allows for flexible parities against the WM. Finally, I start from the current Fund and ask what it would take for the international organization to become a world central bank.

I. A SINGLE WORLD MONEY

Suppose there is a single world money, the WM, and a world central bank, the WCB. The world money stock consists of high-powered money—reserves and currency—issued by the WCB and of bank deposits, denominated in WM in all countries. The WM is the world medium of exchange, used in exchanges within each country and between residents of different countries. It is also the unit of account and the standard of contracts. In brief, the WCB plays the role of the Federal Reserve System (Fed) in the U.S. monetary system, and the WM has the role of the dollar.

There are no national currencies. All governments have agreed to use the WM, and only the WM, in transactions with their own residents and with other governments. The governments retain their spending and taxing powers, along with the power to intervene in trade.

Control of the Monetary and Financial Systems

The WCB acts as a central clearinghouse for the world monetary system. Governments or national central banks maintain accounts at the WCB. Payments are cleared first within each country through private and central bank clearing systems, and then internationally through government accounts at the WCB. (Alternatively, suppose private banks could maintain reserve and clearing accounts at the WCB. Since the existence of a world money would encourage the further integration of world capital markets, it would be desirable to allow banks to hold WCB accounts.)

Accounts held at the WCB can earn interest. The rate of interest paid is determined by an extended inflation tax analysis, which takes into

---

[1] An interesting examination of closely related issues is contained in von Furstenberg (1982).

account the practical difficulty of paying interest on currency. But an optimal tax analysis is unlikely to suggest that no interest be paid on reserves. There is an array of alternative taxes on banks—based, for instance, on profits or turnover—that are not obviously dominated by an implicit tax on reserve holdings.[2]

All the classic issues of monetary policy arise in considering the basis for regulating the stock of high-powered money. Three elements are essential. First, there must be a mechanism to ensure that the WCB does not become an engine of world inflation.[3] It must therefore be difficult for the WCB to deviate from a low growth rate of the stock of high-powered money. Second, there must be a mechanism to handle secular changes in the velocity of circulation of high-powered money arising from continued invention of money substitutes. The growth rate of the stock of high-powered money has accordingly to be subject to regular revision. Third, so long as the financial system is built on the multiple expansion of credit, financial panic and collapse are possible. The WCB, which controls the supply of base money, is the agency responsible for preventing collapse. The WCB therefore has the authority to act as lender of last resort,[4] and consequently to violate rules that strictly limit the growth rate of the base. (In the hypothetical situation described, it should not be difficult to combine these three requirements in the constitution of the WCB.)

There are two alternative approaches to the control of the financial system. One develops a set of regulations designed to distinguish banks from other financial institutions; imposes reserve requirements on the banks; and perhaps tries to control the interest rates they pay, attempting thereby to control the stock of money. Such attempts lead to financial evolution that requires continuing changes in the regulations. An evolving system of this type can be operated successfully, so long as the central bank retains flexibility in its definition of money.

The second approach recognizes the difficulty of permanently defining a usable concept of money and instead leaves financial institutions free to operate in the assets they choose, with the portfolios they prefer. Financial institutions are regulated by the rules governing corporations in the countries in which they operate. (Alternatively, they might be regulated by the

---

[2]For an exploration of some of these issues, see Romer (1982).

[3]I assume that the optimal rate of inflation for tax purposes is low. See Fischer (1983) for calculations suggesting this to be the case: Barro (1972) provides alternative estimates of low optimal inflation taxes.

[4]Rudiger Dornbusch has pointed out that the WCB is uniquely placed to act as lender of last resort only in the event of a run on the banks for currency. This the central bank alone can provide. But if a financial panic is caused by a justified fear that borrowers will default on loans—as is currently felt in the world monetary system—national treasuries may be the best guarantors that the real resources promised by the borrowers will be provided to the lenders.

WCB or national banking authorities, or both, to try to ensure the adequacy of the institutions' capital and to prevent fraud.)

This second type of system, with minimal control over competition among financial institutions, depends in the final analysis on its control over the stock of high-powered money to control the world price level. The demand for high-powered money in such a system is largely a demand for currency. In the absence of alternative currencies, if rates of inflation remain low and the banking system remains secure, there are unlikely to be large shifts in currency demand. There is also a demand for high-powered money to hold as reserves. Stability of the demand for this component of the monetary base depends on the WCB's known willingness to act as lender of last resort, and could be enhanced by deposit insurance—which would, in addition, stabilize the demand for currency.

The demand for high-powered money thus provides the basis for price level control in the world economy. One factor making for better price level control than in existing economies is the absence of currency substitution. But the empirical evidence does not suggest that currency substitution has been a major cause of price level instability (much of the evidence is summarized in Spinelli (1983)), and there is accordingly little basis for believing that price level stability would be significantly enhanced by the use of a single world currency, except to the extent that the WCB was a superior discretionary monetary authority. Nor would any of the standard dilemmas of stabilization policy be absent.

By definition, the single world money system includes no competing government moneys. There remains the question of private hand-to-hand currency issue, which would emerge if the world inflation rate became high. These currencies cannot be viable unless they promise convertibility into the dominant WM, but can pay a rate of return indexed to a price level or commodity (perhaps gold) price. Such issues can be thought of as a form of bank deposit. Because the WM, by assumption, enjoys worldwide acceptability, private currencies are likely to come into existence only if the inflation rate—the cost of holding WM currency—is high, and therefore above the optimal rate. For this reason it is not desirable to outlaw private currency issue, for the possibility of issue provides a check on the behavior of the WCB.

Open Market Operations

The mechanics of monetary policy in our hypothetical situation are not different from those of monetary policy in existing economies. The money stock and credit conditions can be changed through open market operations.

The nationality of the securities in which open market operations are conducted is of little significance, because the debts of all countries are denominated in WM. The debts of the countries with major capital markets would be close-to-perfect substitutes, for there are no exchange risks and no major differences in liquidity. If countries nonetheless want the WCB to be active in their national markets, perhaps to encourage the development of such markets, the WCB may agree to conduct its open market operations in specified security baskets along the lines of the SDR.

Seigniorage and the Fiscal System

All the world's seigniorage accrues in the first instance to the WCB. If market rates of interest are paid on reserves, the annual flow of seigniorage, as a fraction of the world gross national product (GNP), is determined by

$$\frac{\dot{c}}{y} = \frac{\dot{c}}{c}\frac{c}{y} = [\eta_y g_y + \pi]\frac{c}{y} \tag{1}$$

where c denotes the nominal stock of currency, y denotes world GNP, η_y denotes the income elasticity of demand for currency, g_y denotes the growth rate of real income, and π denotes the inflation rate.[5]

In the developed world, currency-to-GNP ratios are in the range of 0.03 to 0.13. Ratios are higher in the developing countries. A world ratio of about 0.08 gives appropriate orders of magnitude. Assuming an income elasticity of demand of unity, a growth rate of world real GNP of 4 percent, and zero inflation, seigniorage would be about 0.3 percent of world GNP, $(0.04 \times 0.08 = 0.0032 = 0.32$ percent) or about \$35 billion–\$40 billion per annum. Seigniorage would double at a 5 percent inflation rate.[6]

Returning to our hypothetical situation, the WCB is able to generate significant income from the issue of currency. Of course, this source of income has been taken away from national governments. Further, if the WCB succeeds in enforcing a low rate of world inflation, it will reduce the total amount of seigniorage earned world-wide. Table 1 presents estimates of average seigniorage obtained by governments over 1960–78. Seigniorage was typically more than 1 percent of GNP over this period. Indeed, some governments in some years earned more than 5 percent of GNP from seigniorage.[7]

[5]It is assumed in equation (1) that the world nominal interest rate is constant. Equation (1) is derived by assuming the demand function for currency takes the form $c/p = L(y)$, where y denotes real income. Differentiation with respect to time then gives an expression for $\dot{c}/c$ which leads to the right-hand side of equation (1).

[6]The assumption here is that the currency-to-income ratio would drop by 12.5 percent, from 0.08 to 0.07, if the inflation rate (cost of holding currency) rose from 0 to 5 percent per annum. At a currency-to-income ratio of 0.07, the amount of seigniorage is $(0.09 \times 0.07) = 0.0063 = 0.63$ percent of income.

[7]For estimates of rates of seigniorage for a variety of countries, see Fischer (1982).

TABLE 1. SEIGNIORAGE RATES FOR SELECTED COUNTRY GROUPS, 1960-78

Country Group	Percentage of GNP
Industrial countries	1.05
Other Europe	2.1
Oil exporting countries	2.1
Other Western Hemisphere	2.2
Other Middle East	3.8
Other Asia	1.4
Other Africa	1.3

Source: Fischer (1982), Tables 1 and 2, pp. 302 and 303.

Given high rates of seigniorage earned by many governments, the loss of this revenue would be a major impediment to the creation of a WCB. The basis for the allocation of seigniorage gains would thus be crucial to the successful creation of a WCB. A method that would likely succeed would award the seigniorage gains on a basis inversely related to real GNP, on the grounds that low-income countries typically have less efficient tax systems and therefore optimally rely more on the inflation tax and seigniorage for revenue than developed countries do.

In our hypothetical situation, the loss of the inflation tax as an independent instrument of national policy is the main fiscal consequence of the creation of the WCB. Aside from the loss of routine seigniorage, the national government also loses use of inflation as a tax of last resort. In Keynes's well-known description, "A government can live by this means when it can live by no other" (Keynes (1923, p. 37)).

The loss of an emergency source of revenue would be another significant impediment to creation of a WCB. And here there would be less room for the WCB to compensate, since it might otherwise find itself offering to finance, at concessionary rates, any wars that countries desired. In emergencies where a government would formerly have used the inflation tax, it could now use explicit taxation, perhaps a capital levy. One form of wealth holding that can easily be taxed is bank deposits; such taxation partly substitutes for the inflation tax.

International Capital Movements

The use of a single world money would enhance world capital mobility by removing exchange risk in international lending.[8] It would also remove

[8]Michael Parkin points out that even holders of, and transactors in, a single currency face exchange risk in a multicurrency world, for exchange rate movements affect the relative prices of goods they buy. Further, they have always to consider the option of holding foreign exchange.

one major reason for government intervention in international capital markets, since capital flows would no longer affect the exchange rate. For both these reasons, capital markets should become more efficient.

Countries wanting to prevent wealth transfers abroad would still want to control capital movements. Monitoring of transactions by domestic residents would probably become more difficult if all transactions were in the same currency, and thus control of capital movements would probably be more difficult, too.

Capital controls are, however, not incompatible with a world money. Countries could tax the import and export of financial capital and maintain an interest rate different from the world rate. They could even maintain the essence, if not the form, of exchange controls by forbidding residents to take more than a specified amount of currency with them when leaving the country and by forbidding the holding of assets abroad.

Benefits and Disadvantages

The use of a world money would ensure truly fixed exchange rates. Some of the issues in appraising the desirability of such a system are set out in the optimal currency area analysis (see, for example, Mundell (1961) and McKinnon (1963)). This analysis suggests that relatively closed economies should maintain flexible exchange rates with the rest of the world, as should areas between which factors do not flow freely. In each case, the argument rests on a presumption of wage and price stickiness within each country or region.

The growth of world trade in the past two decades has left few tightly closed economies in existence. International labor and capital mobility have also increased. These are grounds for believing that larger, rather than smaller, currency areas than existed in the 1960s would now be optimal. But if optimal currency areas are now larger, it is surprising that there is now more flexibility of exchange rates than there was in the sixties. Even the European Monetary System (EMS), which can be viewed as an attempt to set up an optimum currency area, is smaller than the fixed exchange rate area of the 1960s.

The increased flexibility of exchange rates, despite an apparent increase in the size of optimal currency areas and the rapid growth in the volume of world trade in the seventies, appear to support the views that flexible exchange rates are essential to adjustment and that the optimal currency area analysis is simply wrong in assuming there are national economies that should maintain fixed exchange rates with other countries.

The weakness in the optimal currency area analysis arises from its treating factor (particularly capital) mobility as exogenous. The developments of the seventies suggest that the extent of trade and factor mobility is not independent of exchange rate arrangements. In particular, adjustment to the oil shocks, which themselves induced a substantial increase in trade and capital mobility, probably would not have been as smooth under fixed rates as it was under flexible rates. In the United States in particular, the fall in the real wage that followed each oil shock would have been more difficult to obtain if domestic prices had not risen and the dollar had not depreciated, allowing the real wage to decrease while the nominal wage continued to increase at its trend rate. If domestic adjustment had been more difficult, governments would have intervened to reduce trade imbalances and capital mobility, thereby reducing trade and factor mobility.

But this is not the final word on the desirability of fixed exchange rates. Although there have been episodes in which the flexibility of exchange rates helped adjustment, real exchange rates did fluctuate excessively during the seventies. Real exchange rates have moved by as much as 20–30 percent in a year, and some of these movements were subsequently reversed. Conceivably, each rate adjustment might have been justified on the basis of what could reasonably have been known at the time. Nonetheless, accumulating evidence (for example, Shiller (1981)) on the behavior of stock and bond prices suggests that these asset prices fluctuate excessively, providing indirect support for the view that exchange rates do likewise.

The second reason that the behavior of exchange rates during the seventies does not constitute decisive evidence concerning the desirability of a world money is that the responses of wages and prices are affected by the nature of the monetary system. In a system in which monetary policy validates the stickiness of nominal wage trends, exchange rate flexibility helps countries achieve real adjustment. If the exchange rate is not free to adjust, then wages are more likely to do so.

Eventual movement to a world money might well be desirable. But such a change, even if it had the enthusiastic support of governments, would have to come slowly. Wage and price stickiness are facts of life that could be changed only slowly.[9]

Enthusiastic support of governments for a world money is in any case unlikely, for several reasons. The move to a world money would deprive governments of the ability to run independent monetary policies and of

---

[9]For formal evidence on the stickiness of prices, see Rotemberg (1982). For informal evidence on the stickiness of prices and the slow adjustment of price and wage behavior to monetary regime changes, consider the responses in the United States to the change in monetary policy in 1979. The fact that prices stabilize rapidly after hyperinflation reinforces the point: it typically takes the destruction of the monetary system to change wage and price stickiness as facts of life.

seigniorage. It would make control of capital movements more difficult. The benefits that governments would obtain from adoption of a world monetary system would be a right to be heard in the setting of world monetary policy; a share in world seigniorage; and a possibly welcome, though unwelcomed, external constraint on the rate of inflation. The EMS, for instance, provides such an external constraint on monetary policy.

Governments would also be pleased if exchange rate fluctuations no longer were a source of distress. But the use of a single money would not end financial or trade policy difficulties. Countries that needed to adjust would have one weapon taken away from them and would therefore be more likely to turn to others, such as import restrictions or tariffs. (Such restrictions were common in the nineteenth century.) Commercial policy would likely develop as an alternate means of adjustment.

In sum, a single world money is unlikely to evolve in the foreseeable future, because under such a system governments would have to give up seigniorage and countercyclical monetary policy in exchange for a smoother-running international financial and monetary system—a reward difficult to share in a way that would make all governments better off.

II. WM EXCHANGE STANDARD

The WM exchange standard requires much less change in the monetary system than does a world money. In the WM exchange standard, each country maintains fixed exchange rates against all other currencies. One of two basic sets of institutional arrangements is in force. Under the first, the WM is held only by central banks or governments. Foreign exchange markets deal only in national currencies. But each country is obliged to clear all balances against other countries through WM accounts at the WCB. In this scheme, the WM operates purely as an international reserve asset. The obligation to maintain convertibility at fixed exchange rates forces countries to adjust their monetary policies on the basis of their WM reserves.

Under the second set of arrangements, the WM may be held privately as well as by the public sector. WCB liabilities, the WM, can circulate as currency and be used as reserves by both governments and private financial institutions. Individuals and institutions can hold the WM and buy and sell it freely in the open market. It is this second set of arrangements that will be discussed in this section. The analogy drawn is with the gold exchange standard.

The WM is a fiat asset, whose value derives purely from its acceptability in exchange. That acceptability results, in the first instance, from government agreement to accept the WM in exchanges and willingness at all times to pay WM to demanders. National currencies remain in existence, with exchange rates fixed, permanently, against the WM.

The quantity of WM is controlled by the WCB, subject to the same three requirements—low growth (to keep the inflation rate low), flexibility in changing the growth rate as the financial system evolves, and the WCB's standing ready to act as lender of last resort—that were specified earlier for the case where the WM is the only world money.

With each country maintaining convertibility and reasonably stable reserve ratios (perhaps, though not necessarily, required reserve ratios), the potential exists for active WCB monetary policy to influence the price level and the level of economic activity. Open market operations affect the supply of WM and, indirectly, aggregate demand. Such operations are carried out by purchase or sale of government securities in national financial markets. The WCB wants to balance its operations across currencies, perhaps using a prespecified basket of securities in its trades for WM.

To maintain convertibility of its currency into WM, each country holds reserves of WM and can engage in its own open market operations in the domestic markets. (The basis for reserve creation and distribution by the WCB would, of course, be one of the prime points of negotiation in setting up the WCB.) All individuals and institutions can hold the WM and buy and sell it freely in the open market.

The essential difficulty with the WM exchange standard is maintenance of parities. Under the gold standard, the mystique of gold induced countries to be religious about maintaining parities. The WM has no such mystique and suffers also from the knowledge, gained during the seventies, that a flexible rate system is workable.

The constitution of the WCB gives it the power to intervene in national markets to attempt to maintain parities. For instance, the WCB can sell securities in any national market where monetary growth is excessive. But the WCB also must have the right to require governments to buy back WCB excess holdings of national currencies if such intervention is not merely to result in the WCB becoming the ultimate holder of each government's excess money creation. The WCB must, in addition, charge interest to the governments whose currencies it holds in excess amount.[10] In effect, each government gives the WCB the right to undo national monetary policies.

---

[10]If the fixed parity system were effective, exchange guarantees would not be needed. But since a WM exchange standard would, in the end, become one with adjustable parities, there would also have to be some agreement on whether the WCB or national governments would bear exchange risk. Forcing the exchange risk onto national governments would provide a greater incentive for them to avoid policies leading to parity changes and would make it less likely they would enter such a system.

Such requirements suggest that the WM exchange standard is neither credible nor workable as a fixed-parity system. So long as governments have the ability to issue their own currency, they will do so, on occasion to excess. The WCB can exercise surveillance; it can complain and cajole; but it cannot ultimately maintain fixity of exchange rates unless it is given powers that are equivalent to those it would need to maintain a single world money. The gold exchange standard was not, after all, a fixed-rate system, for governments left gold or changed the parity when circumstances demanded.[11]

III. FLEXIBLE-RATE WM SYSTEM

Once we recognize that the WM exchange standard cannot be a fixed-rate system, we return to the familiar discussions of the adjustable peg versus floating rates. The adjustable peg is not viable when capital moves as rapidly as it does in existing capital markets. Similarly, crawling pegs are unlikely to be maintainable against rapid capital flows. If parities are not immutably fixed by the abolition of other government moneys, any WM system will ultimately become a floating-rate system.

The key question in such a system is the extent of use of the WM as a portfolio asset, medium of exchange, and unit of account.[12] For purposes of the analysis, I assume that the WM has been, or shows promise of being, sufficiently well managed to be used in some private transactions; that private institutions and individuals hold and issue WM balances; and that WM-denominated securities exist.[13]

Open Market Operations Under Flexible Parities

Suppose the WCB decides that the world economy is expanding at an undesirable rate, and that credit and monetary conditions have to be tightened. It can sell bonds issued by national governments, or perhaps WM-denominated bonds, from its portfolio, demanding payment in WM. The world supply of WM will consequently be reduced.

The Appendix contains a formal analysis of the effects of an open market sale.[14] The sale of securities has two immediate effects. First, by increasing the world supply of securities, it increases world interest rates. Second, because the relative supply of WM is reduced, the WM appre-

---

[11]Indeed, the single world money system poses the same difficulty, for countries might, in extreme circumstances, choose to leave the system and issue their own currencies.

[12]Vaubel (1978) discusses in depth many of the issues raised in this section.

[13]It is the assumption of private holding and use of the WM that primarily distinguishes the model of this section from the current international monetary system.

[14]Girton and Roper (1981) examine related issues, focusing on portfolio substitutability.

ciates against other currencies. The world money supply, measured in those other currencies, is not necessarily reduced. The question thus arises whether the open market sale puts any contractionary pressure on the real economy.

Real effects of an open market operation in a closed one-money economy arise from two possible sources.[15] First, there are the various nonneutralities associated with changes in asset proportions held in private portfolios, and—if there is a change in the growth rate of the money stock—the nonneutralities associated with changes in the inflation rate. These can be referred to as the equilibrium effects of open market operations. The second source is price inflexibilities, which turn changes in the nominal stock of money into real changes. These effects are transitory, are associated with the slow adjustment of prices and wages, and can be referred to as the disequilibrium effects of open market operations.

The equilibrium effects of an open market sale of WM arise because the world stock of debt has been increased and the world stock of money reduced. The interest rate thus rises. Exchange rates between the WM and national currencies change to an extent that depends on the degree of substitution in use in transactions between the currencies. The less good substitutes the currencies are, the more the exchange rate moves. The WM will appreciate relative to other currencies. But the overall equilibrium effects of the change in the interest and exchange rate associated with the open market sale are likely to be small if all markets adjust smoothly to a new equilibrium.

Now we come to the key question of what the real, disequilibrium effects of the open market sale are. Assume that wages are predetermined (in some numéraire—either WM or domestic currency) in the current period. Now we compare two situations. First, assume that wage rates are fixed in units of WM. And second, suppose the unit of contract is the domestic currency. The model in the Appendix implies that the contractionary effects of the open market sale are larger when the WM is the unit in which the wage is fixed. For, in this case, the open market sale, causing the WM to appreciate, raises the wage relative to the domestic price level and is therefore more contractionary than when the wage is specified in domestic currency units. More generally, the effectiveness of the open market sale in reducing the level of output will depend positively on the proportion of sticky prices or wages that are set in terms of the world, rather than the domestic, numéraire.

Thus, the ability of the WCB to affect real activity is not primarily a function of the size of its portfolio. Rather, the key determinant of the

---

[15]Parkin (1979) presents an earlier examination of these issues.

effectiveness of open market operations between WM and securities is the extent to which the WM is the unit of contract or account—the unit in which prices are denominated.

WCB As Central Bank Under Flexible Parities

The WCB's power as world central banker in fulfilling the first task of central banking, broadly defined as ensuring the stable operation of the financial system and more narrowly defined as preventing financial collapse, depends on the size of its portfolio and its ability to mobilize resources from governments and private institutions to help those in need. Assuming the WCB has the authority to act as lender of last resort by expanding the stock of WM, its power as central banker will also depend on the extent to which the WM is held in portfolios, which is, in turn, affected by the extent of WM use in transactions.

The WCB's power to stabilize the trade cycle is determined by much the same factors, as well as by the extent to which contract prices are fixed in WM. This means that the WCB's economic power depends, to a large extent, on the use of the WM as money in private transactions.

The WCB can seek to increase the use of the WM in private transactions by making it easy to use and ensuring the stability of its value. Its acceptance would be increased if the WCB issued WM currency, and did not keep the asset purely as a reserve asset of countries and financial institutions. It could also permit the private issue of WM.

All this is to say that the more the WM becomes like a single world money, the more power the WCB will have. But the more power the WCB has, the less power the national central banks and governments will have. The discussion of the difficulty of setting up a single world money thus is relevant to consideration of whether the WM could become widely used alongside other currencies.

IV. THE IMF AND THE SDR

Is the IMF a WCB in its cocoon, and the SDR an incipient WM? Not at this stage. Although the Fund has indeed begun to intervene to prevent financial collapse, it is not, and has not in the current crisis been, the ultimate source of liquidity for the financial system. That role has been played by the Fed. The Fund has played a valuable part in the execution and certification of policy, but the size of its portfolio and the lengthy process of negotiation that must precede an increase in the stock of SDRs preclude the Fund's serving as the lender of last resort.

The SDR remains far from being a world money. It is used as a unit of account by some organizations; official SDRs serve as a store of value to governments that hold them; and there are some privately issued SDR-denominated bonds and bank liabilites. But the SDR is not used as a medium of exchange. Rather, it is more like a treasury bill with desirable yield characteristics. Further, there is no link between official holdings of the SDRs and private transactions in SDRs. Changes in the stock of official SDRs are changes in the quantities of credit and reserves available to holders but are not directly changes in the stock of money.[16]

The power of the Fund to stabilize the trade cycle would be enhanced by wider use of the SDR, by increases in the SDR's role as a reserve asset, and particularly by the breakdown of the barrier between official and private SDR use. One step toward breaking down the barrier would be the addition of private institutions—many of them—to the list of prescribed holders.

At present, the SDR derives its yield characteristics from those of the currencies in terms of which it is defined. Its transition to a fiat money would occur when the SDR was being held for use in transactions as well as in portfolios. In order for this to occur, the SDR would have to be used more as a unit of contract or account.

As the system adapted to its use, the link between the SDR and the basket of currencies could be broken, and it could stand on its own. At that stage, the Fund would begin to be able to exercise the powers of a WCB operating in a sytem with flexible parities.

Should the IMF Become a WCB?

A world central bank becomes more effective only as national central banks lose power—in particular, the power to stabilize the national economy and the power to collect seigniorage. This fact of life ensures that the development of a world central bank will be slow at best.

But is such a development, in any case, desirable? There is obviously an elegance in the creation of a world fiat money, and in elimination of the familiar $(n - 1)$ problem of systems based on national currencies, which, stated briefly, is that if all parities are fixed against one currency, that currency cannot be devalued, and its producer may have excessive freedom to create world liquidity.

But serious assessment of the benefits of a WCB turns on two issues. First, there are the issues connected with optimum currency areas, which have already been discussed. And second, even if the world were the opti-

---

[16]There may, however, be an indirect effect of increased reserve allocations on the money stock, if countries ease up on monetary control when their reserve situations improve.

mum currency area, it would be necessary to predict how well a WCB would behave compared with the Fed.

At this stage, differences in the degree of wage and price flexibility among monetary areas suggest that the world is not now the optimum currency area. Thus, any WCB has to allow for flexible exchange rates, leaving national moneys to coexist with the WM (or SDR), at the same time as the WM (or SDR) is gaining circulation. An evolutionary or gradualist process could result in the SDR being widely used as a money and thus give the Fund the ability to moderate the trade cycle.

The second issue—the likely behavior of a WCB, compared with the Fed—is even more speculative. Part of the attraction of the gold standard was that its operation was supposed to be automatic (although subsequent research has destroyed that belief).[17] A WCB can operate a fiat money system automatically—for example, by increasing the stock of WM at a steady rate. There is little evidence to support the belief that such automaticity would make for good policy or would lead to performance better than that of the Fed.

But once the WCB is taken off automatic pilot, it may follow paths that look desirable in the short run but that ultimately produce worse results than would be obtained by resolutely following a preordained plan.[18] All national central banks and policy authorities face the same problem, and some have obviously done better than others. A WCB is likely to avoid sudden changes of policy—because of the need for agreement among the national representatives. But it is also clear that there will be substantial conflicts among national representatives in deciding on optimal world monetary policy.

Such difficulties are suggested by the inability of leaders of the industrial countries to agree on desirable U.S. monetary policy under the current system. Perhaps monetary policy decisions could be handled with less conflict if they were treated as technical matters and left to the technicians of the WCB. But they are not technical matters: the choice of monetary policy affects interests within a country and among countries differentially; monetary policy questions, therefore, are intensely political issues. Similar difficulties would extend to decisions on the allocation of seigniorage among the members, precisely because the sums at issue would be large.

The Board of Directors (or Governors) of a WCB would thus be handling issues on which national interests diverge far more than they do on

---

[17]See, for instance, Bloomfield (1959), Cooper (1982), and Dornbusch (1982).

[18]This issue is examined in the literature on dynamic inconsistency of optimal policy. See, for example, Barro and Gordon (1981).

the allocation of Fund quotas or on the decision to intervene to prevent financial collapse. The divergence of interests would likely restrict policy-making. Provided the Board was not totally immobilized, the resultant policy might come close to being optimal—monetary policy intervention would take place only when it was "clearly" needed. At other times, the Board, by its inactivity, would avoid creating disturbances.

In sum, the argument is that the time is not yet ripe for a WCB. Nor is any rapid development toward a WCB likely. But such movement is more likely, the more the SDR is used in private transactions, particularly as a unit of contract. The IMF can foster its development as a WCB by encouraging the use of the SDR in private contracts. As the Fund makes the SDR more attractive to use and hold, it will provide greater assurance that the international governing body of a WCB would run a steady and stabilizing world monetary policy.

APPENDIX

The Medium of Exchange, Unit of Contract, and the Effectiveness of Monetary Policy

This Appendix presents two stripped-down models that illustrate the role of assumptions about the medium of exchange and the unit of contract in determining the effects of open market operations between the world money and bonds.

In both models, this paper examines a single economy whose residents may hold both the world money (WM) and domestic money (M). There is a third asset, bonds, which are denominated in domestic currency. Thus

$$W = WM \frac{e}{p} + \frac{M}{p} + \frac{B}{p} \tag{2}$$

where W denotes wealth, e the exchange rate between the world money and domestic money, p the price level measured in domestic money, and B the stock of bonds.

Money-demand equations are

$$WM \frac{e}{p} = f(r, y)W \tag{3}$$

$$\frac{M}{p} = g(r, y)W \tag{4}$$

where r denotes the interest rate on bonds. Expectations are static, in that no changes in the price level or exchange rate are expected.

A rise in the interest rate reduces the demands for both moneys. The effects of an increase in income on asset demands depend on which money is the medium of transactions. If the world money is the medium of transactions, then $f_2 > 0$. If the domestic money is the medium of transactions, then $g_2 > 0$. For analytic clarity, it is assumed that when $f_2 > 0$, $g_2 = 0$, and vice versa—that is, changes in the level of income have no effect on the demand for the money which, at the margin, is not the medium of transactions.

The demand function for bonds is implied by equations (3), (4), and the budget constraint (2).

Given the supplies of assets and the level of output, the demand functions (3) and (4) determine the interest rate r and the exchange rate. Figure 1 shows a negatively sloped WM schedule derived from the demand function for world money. An increase in the interest rate reduces the demand for WM; a reduction in e that reduces net supply is therefore necessary to restore equilibrium.

The domestic monetary equilibrium curve MM is positively sloped. An increase in the interest rate reduces demand; an increase in e that increases wealth (measured in domestic currency) is therefore necessary to maintain equilibrium.

An open market sale of WM for bonds reduces the stock of world money without, in the first instance, changing wealth. There is an excess demand for WM, and the WM curve accordingly moves to WM'. The interest rate r increases, and the exchange rate e rises, indicating that the WM has appreciated relative to domestic money.

Effects of an Increase in Income on the Asset Markets

An increase in income will have different effects on the asset markets, depending on which money is the medium of exchange.

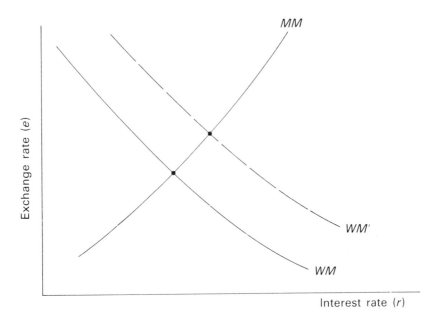

FIGURE 1. ASSET MARKET EQUILIBRIUM

Suppose that income rises. If world money is the medium of transactions ($f_2 > 0$, $g_2 = 0$), the WM curve shifts out to the right, because the increased demand requires a higher interest rate to keep demand for WM equal to supply. Both e and r rise: the world money appreciates in this case.

If the domestic money is the medium of transactions ($g_2 > 0$, $f_2 = 0$), an increase in income shifts the MM curve out to the right. The interest rate rises, and e falls: the world money depreciates in this case.

To understand these results, note that when income rises, there is, in both cases, a reduction in the demand for bonds. The interest rate accordingly rises. In addition, there is a relative shift in demand between the two money assets. If foreign money is the medium of transactions, demand shifts toward WM and causes it to appreciate relative to domestic money. If domestic money is the medium of transactions, demand shifts toward the domestic money, causing it to appreciate relative to the world money; e therefore falls.

Model 1

The aggregate demand function is

$$y^d = D(r, W), \qquad D_1 < 0, \qquad D_2 > 0 \tag{5}$$

In Figure 2, the aggregate demand function is shown by the downward-sloping schedule, AD. The schedule is drawn for a given interest rate.

In Model 1, it is assumed that the domestic money is the unit of contract and that the wage rate is accordingly fixed in terms of domestic money. The aggregate supply function is

$$y^s = \phi(p/w) \tag{6}$$

where w denotes the fixed (in the short run) nominal wage. The aggregate supply curve, AS, is shown in Figure 2.

The aggregate supply curve of course shifts over time as the wage adjusts to market conditions. But we concentrate here only on short-run impact effects of monetary changes.

Now suppose there is an open market sale of world money. The interest rate rises, as shown in Figure 1; and, at a constant wealth level, the aggregate demand curve shifts to AD', as shown in Figure 2. The price level and level of output both fall. There are now further repercussions in the asset markets, with those effects in turn feeding back to the goods markets. Despite some ambiguities caused by wealth effects, under reasonable restrictions the final result of the open market sale of world money is to reduce both the price and output levels.

The effects of the open market sale tend to be larger when the world money is the medium of exchange.[19] The new equilibrium exchange rate depends on which asset is the medium of exchange.

Model 2

This model has the same aggregate demand function, equation (5), but assumes the world money is the unit of contract. Thus,

[19]This statement assumes that there is no change in wealth as a result of the open market sale.

$$y^s = \phi(p/ew) \tag{6'}$$

where w is now fixed in terms of world money. The aggregate supply function, AS', is shown in Figure 3. The exchange rate e is assumed constant in drawing AS'.

Now suppose there is an open market sale of world money. In the asset markets, e and r rise. In Figure 3, the AD curve shifts to AD', as in Figure 2. But, in addition, the higher exchange rate raises the wage measured in domestic currency. The AS curve shifts to AS'. The level of output certainly falls, but the price level will either fall less than it does in Figure 2 or (perhaps) rise. There are, once again, feedbacks from the changed price and output levels to the asset markets and back to the goods markets. Under reasonable circumstances, though, the level of output is reduced by the open market sale and the real exchange rate increased.

Now, it makes a difference which asset is the medium of exchange. If it is the world money, then the reduction in income will reduce the demand for world money, partially *offsetting* the effects of the initial open market sale. We can, accordingly, say that the open market sale of the world money will be less effective in reducing real output if the world money is the medium of exchange, given that it is the unit of account.

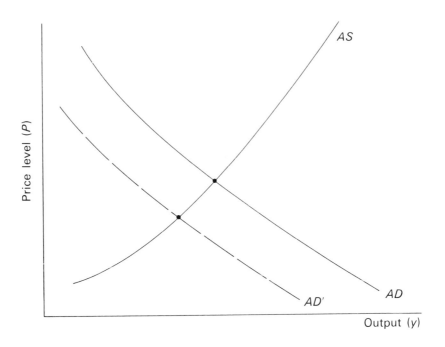

FIGURE 2. SHORT-RUN GOODS MARKET EQUILIBRIUM FOR MODEL 1

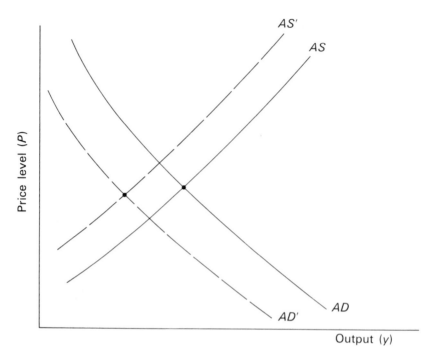

FIGURE 3. SHORT-RUN GOODS MARKET EQUILIBRIUM FOR MODEL 2

Conclusions and Extensions

(i) Even if the world money is neither medium of exchange nor unit of account, an open market sale of world currency for domestic bonds will under reasonable restrictions reduce domestic price and output levels.

(ii) Use of the world money as medium of transactions will enhance the effects of an open market sale if the world money is not also the unit of contract.

(iii) If the world money is the unit of contract, an open market sale of world money will have a smaller contractionary effect on output when the world money is the medium of transactions than when the domestic money is the medium of exchange.

REFERENCES

Barro, Robert J., "Inflationary Finance and the Welfare Cost of Inflation," *Journal of Political Economy*, Vol. 80 (September–October 1972), pp. 978–1001.

_____, and David B. Gordon, *A Positive Theory of Monetary Policy in a Natural-Rate Model*, National Bureau of Economic Research, Working Paper No. 807 (1981).

Bloomfield, Arthur I., *Monetary Policy Under the International Gold Standard: 1880-1914* (New York: Federal Reserve Bank of New York, 1959).

Cooper, Richard N., "The Gold Standard: Historical Facts and Future Prospects," *Brookings Papers on Economic Activity: 1* (1982), pp. 1-45.

Dornbusch, Rudiger, "Comment," *Brookings Papers on Economic Activity: 1* (1982), pp. 46-51.

Fischer, Stanley, "Seigniorage and the Case for a National Money," *Journal of Political Economy*, Vol. 90 (April 1982), pp. 295-313.

_____, "Seigniorage and Fixed Exchange Rate: An Optimal Inflation Tax Analysis," in *Developing Countries in the World Financial Markets*, ed. by P. Aspe, R. Dornbusch, and M. Obstfeld (Chicago: University of Chicago Press, 1983).

Girton, Lance, and Don Roper, "Theory and Implications of Currency Substitution," *Journal of Money, Credit and Banking*, Vol. 13 (Feb. 1981), pp. 12-30.

Keynes, John Maynard, *A Tract on Monetary Reform* (first edition, 1923) (London: Macmillan, 1971).

_____, "Proposals for an International Clearing Union," reprinted from British Government Publication, Cmd. 6437 (London: H.M. Stationery Office, 1943), in *World Monetary Reform, Plans and Issues*, ed. by Herbert G. Grubel (Stanford, California: Stanford University Press, 1963), pp. 55-79.

McKinnon, Ronald I., "Optimum Currency Areas," *American Economic Review*, Vol. 53 (September 1963), pp. 717-25.

Mundell, Robert A., "A Theory of Optimum Currency Areas," *American Economic Review* (September 1961), pp. 657-64.

Parkin, Michael, "Price and Output Determination in an Economy with Two Media of Exchange and a Separate Unit of Account," *Zeitschrift für Wirtschafts- und Sozialwissenschaften* (1979), pp. 95-111.

Romer, David, "Bank Regulation, the Inflation Tax, and Interest Taxation" (unpublished, Massachusetts Institute of Technology, Department of Economics, 1982).

Rotemberg, Julio J., "Sticky Prices in the United States," *Journal of Political Economy*, Vol. 90 (December 1982), pp. 1187-1211.

Shiller, Robert J., "Do Stock Prices Move Too Much to Be Justified by Subsequent Changes in Dividends?" *American Economic Review*, Vol. 71 (June 1981), pp. 421-36.

Spinelli, Franco, "On the Case for International Monetary Cooperation (unpublished, International Monetary Fund, May 12, 1983).

Vaubel, Roland, *Strategies for Currency Unification; The Economics of Currency Competition and the Case for a European Parallel Currency* (Tübingen: J. C. B. Mohr, 1978).

von Furstenberg, George M., "Internationally Managed Money," *American Economic Review, Papers and Proceedings of the Eighty-Fifth Annual Meeting of the American Economic Association*, Vol. 63 (May 1983), pp. 54-58.

Comments

Michael Parkin

Stanley Fischer has provided a clear-headed analysis of the special drawing right and the International Monetary Fund and the question of whether this instrument and institution constitute embryonic forms of, respectively, world money (WM) and a world central bank (WCB). His answer to this question is that they probably do not. The central purpose of his paper is not, however, to speculate on this matter but to offer a normative analysis (with some occasional positive offshoots) of alternative world monetary systems. Three alternatives are considered: a single world money system; a world money exchange standard with adjustable parities; and a system of flexible exchange rates against a world money. The main analytical content of the paper is the presentation of a model of a two-money world with a flexible exchange rate (a model which in some respects parallels that of Parkin (1979)).

I will begin my discussion of Fischer's paper by examining his analysis of a single world money system. Such a system is one which, in broad terms, both Fischer and I generally approve of but which each of us believes to be politically impractical under present circumstances. Although I am in broad agreement with Fischer's conclusions on such a system, there are some details of the way in which he makes his case with which I disagree and on which I shall focus.

First, several references are made, by way of analogy, to the similarities between a single world fiat money system and a gold standard. Fischer understands, of course, that there is a crucial difference between a commodity and a fiat money standard. He does not, however, allow that understanding to shine through as brightly as I should like. The key distinction is, of course, that a gold standard provides an automatic method for regulating the value of money, while a fiat money standard does not provide for such automatic regulation. Regulation of the value of money resides in the subsidiary arrangements made for controlling the supply of the fiat money. The failure to emphasize this important distinction manifests itself most clearly in the lack of any serious analysis of the objectives of, and the constraints faced by, a WCB possessing the power to issue WM. Indeed, Fischer treats the task of achieving low and steady WM growth, along with the flexibility required to fulfill the lender-of-last-resort function, as "technically straightforward." He does not, unfortunately, set out the solution to this technically straightforward problem, either in terms of prescriptions for the behavior of the WCB or in terms of an analysis of the way in which the WCB would behave when pursuing its own objectives (subject, of course, to constraints).

Indeed, Fischer goes on to show (implicitly) that the incentives for a WCB to generate considerable inflation are extremely strong. It is his analysis of seigniorage that implies this conclusion. It is a conclusion which is not, however, stressed sufficiently by Fischer. In his analysis of seigniorage, he assumes the demand function for WM to be of the Cagan (1956) semilogarithmic form. It is a function which, at a zero rate of inflation, would have a ratio of world high-powered money to world income of 0.08 and a semielasticity with respect to the inflation rate of -2.5. On these assumptions (which I find reasonable), Fischer shows that at a zero rate of inflation, approximately 40 billion dollars per annum of seigniorage would be realized. At a 5 percent inflation rate (on the same assumptions), seigniorage would double. On my calculations, again using the same assumptions, seigniorage would be maximized at an inflation rate of 40 percent per annum. While it is true that there are plenty of offsetting considerations preventing a central bank from moving to the seigniorage-maximizing rate of inflation, the temptation to move in that direction must surely be very strong. Too little attention is paid to the task of effectively constraining the WCB to hold it closer to the optimum, rather than the seigniorage-maximizing, rate of inflation. Fischer does suggest that it would not be appropriate to outlaw the issue of private money, and clearly this would help place a competitive constraint upon the WCB. That constraint would probably not, however, be binding until inflation was well in excess of the optimum.

Let me now turn to an appraisal of Fischer's analysis of the implications of a single-world money for world capital markets. His prediction concerning this is that national debt instruments would become perfect substitutes for each other, so that a single rate of interest would prevail throughout the single-money world. The broad conclusion that world capital markets would become more perfect is clearly correct. There does, however, appear to be ample evidence available which indicates that they would not become as perfect as Fischer suggests. In the world as it currently operates, many governments issue debts denominated in U.S. dollars. Such debts bear no exchange risk—only default risk. There is solid evidence that the capital market believes that Canada is at present 1 percent more likely to default than is the United States, that Australia is 2 percent more likely, and that Mexico is of the order of 8 percent more likely (see Wirick (1983)). These observations suggest that while improved capital mobility would almost certainly result from a single WM, interest rates would not equalize and countries would be free to pursue policies perceived as likely to raise the probability of default, but with appropriate interest adjustments compensating investors for that perceived change in risk. In other words, countries would remain free to pursue their own fiscal policies and their own financing arrangements. They would, as now, have to face the market consequences of their actions.

It is in his discussion of the disadvantages of a single WM system that Fischer gives me the most difficulty. Such a system is not a viable possibility for the foreseeable future for political reasons. It does not, however, suffer from two of the defects which Fischer suggests it does—or, at least, these defects are less serious than he suggests.

One disadvantage identified is the loss of the inflation tax for use in emergency situations. It is suggested that its place could be taken by a capital levy on other assets. I have two problems with this line of reasoning. First, it is not an unambiguous disadvantage to deny governments the capacity to use a particular form of taxation in an emergency situation. Governments are subject to moral hazard just like private individuals are, and that being so, the fewer sources of revenue a government can use in emergencies, the fewer emergencies there may be! My real quarrel, however, is with the idea that capital levies might be used in the event of such emergencies when a single world money system has deprived governments of the use of the inflation tax. This approach suffers from a serious time-inconsistency problem of the type analyzed by Kydland and Prescott (1977).

The alleged disadvantages of a single world money arising from optimum-currency-area considerations are the ones that strike me as the weakest part of Fischer's analysis. He correctly points out that the old optimum-currency-area debate was one based on the notion of some exogenously given degree of wage and price stickiness. He points out, again correctly, that there is no reason to suppose that the degree of wage and price stickiness is independent of the monetary arrangements in place. He does, however, conclude that the world displays too much wage and price stickiness to be able confidently to entertain a single WM in present circumstances. He also offers the opinion that the degree of wage and price stickiness is not likely to be very responsive to a change in a world monetary system which introduced a single WM. My major problem with all this is not the conjectures. They strike me as reasonable ones. It is the lack of any systematic evidence on the matter, and the lack of any suggestions as to how we might go about generating such systematic evidence. We do, after all, have a very large amount of variability in the monetary arrangements in place in a variety of countries. We also observe varying degrees of wage and price flexibility. Some cross-section (cross-country) investigation of the association (or lack thereof) between the degree of wage and price flexibility and the degree of exogeneity of the money supply process could be a way of addressing this issue and of moving it on from the level of guessing (with a suitable injection of prejudice) to a higher, more scientific plane. Theoretical models of the type suggested by John Taylor (1979 and 1980) would appear to be useful vehicles for pursuing such an investigation.

Fischer moves on from his discussion of a single WM to that of a WM exchange system. He dismisses such an arrangement rather swiftly, and I fully agree with his analysis of this and with his conclusion that destabilizing speculation would make such a system nonviable.

It is in his discussion of a flexible exchange rate world money system that Fischer makes the most analytical progress. He presents (in the Appendix to his paper) a neat model of the determination of output and prices in a single closed economy that has two moneys and a bond. Either world or national money may be used as the transactions medium. Two further variants of the model are analyzed, one in which world money is used as the unit of contract, and one in which national money serves that purpose. The conclusion that arises from the analysis is that the money used as the unit of contract dominates the determination of output, regardless of the importance of that money unit as a transactions medium. The main conclusions of the model can be derived more directly and intuitively with a stripped-down version of what is contained in the paper. Since the central purpose of the analysis is to determine the effects of open-market operations which are wealth-preserving, it is possible to treat wealth as a constant (and normalize it to unity). Further, since our task is to investigate the effects of monetary policy on output, prices, and the exchange rate, we may adopt a "horizontal IS curve" formulation. That is, we may assume that the rate of interest is given. Making these assumptions (and focusing only on a zero-inflation equilibrium), Fischer's aggregate demand function simply determines the rate of interest. We are thus left with three equations—equilibrium in the world money market; equilibrium in the national money market; and the aggregate supply function to determine output, prices, and the exchange rate.

The model may be set out succinctly as follows: First, equilibrium in the world money market is given by

$$WMe/P = (f(y))^a; \qquad f'(y) > 0 \tag{1}$$

This is Fischer's equation (3) with wealth set equal to unity and with the interest rate ignored (since it is being treated as a constant in the present analysis). If the parameter a is equal to one, then world money serves as the transactions medium. If a is equal to zero, world money does not serve as the transactions medium, and (by choice of units) we are normalizing the real world money stock at unity. Equilibrium in the national money market is given by

$$M/P = (f(y))^{(1-a)} \tag{2}$$

This corresponds to Fischer's equation (4)—again, with wealth normalized at unity and ignoring the interest rate. In addition, I have supposed that the demand for transactions balances is the same, regardless of whether world or national money serves the transactions function. Notice that if a is equal to unity with world money serving as the transactions unit, then real national balances are normalized at unity. If a is equal to zero, then it is national, rather than world, money that serves as the transactions unit. Aggregate supply is given by

$$y = \phi(P/we^b); \phi'(\ ) > 0 \tag{3}$$

With b equal to zero, national money is the unit of contract and wages are fixed at w in national money units. In that case, equation (3) corresponds to Fischer's equation (6). If b is equal to one, then wages are fixed in world money and their national money equivalent has to be obtained by converting that fixed world money wage into national money. This would correspond with Fischer's equation (6').

The solution to the price level, the exchange rate, and output may be obtained straightforwardly by solving equations (1), (2), and (3) to give

$$P = M/(f(y))^{(1-a)} \tag{4}$$

$$e = (f(y))^{(2a-1)}M/WM \tag{5}$$

$$y = \phi\{[1/(f(y))^{(1-a+b(2a-1))}]M^{(1-b)}WM^b/w\} \tag{6}$$

There are four possible extreme cases corresponding to which of the two moneys serves the purpose of the transactions medium and the unit of contract. If world money serves both of these purposes, then a and b are each equal to unity. If national money serves both of these purposes, then a and b are each equal to zero. If world money is the transactions medium but national money is the unit of contract, then a is equal to one and b is equal to zero. If world money is the unit of contract and national money is the transactions medium, then a is equal to zero and b is equal to one.

As is apparent from inspecting the solutions above, the determinations of the price level and of the exchange rate depend mainly on which of the two moneys serves as the transactions medium. That is, if world money is the transactions medium, then

$$P = M \tag{4'}$$

while if national money is the transactions medium, then the price level will be

$$P = M/f(y) \tag{4''}$$

Thus, the price level will be proportional to the national money stock. It will also, however, when the national money is the transactions medium, be influenced by the level of output, the determination of which will be discussed later on.

The exchange rate is determined by the ratio of the two moneys. The higher is the stock of national money relative to that of world money, the higher is the exchange rate (the cheaper is national money). The way in which output affects the exchange rate depends upon which of the two moneys is the transactions unit. If national money is the transactions unit, the exchange rate is given by

$$e = f(y)M/WM \tag{5'}$$

That is, a higher income level is associated with a lower exchange rate (a more valuable national money) because the higher income raises the demand for national money. If world money is the transactions medium, then the exchange rate is given by

$$e = (1/f(y))M/WM \tag{5'}$$

That is, a higher level of income is associated with the higher value of e, since a high level of income is associated with a higher demand for WM which makes WM relatively more valuable.

It is the solutions for output that are the most interesting. Evidently, the way in which output is determined depends both on which of the two moneys serves as the transactions medium and which as the unit of contract. If world money serves as both transactions medium and contract unit, then output is given by

$$y = \phi[WM/wf(y)] \tag{6'}$$

If national money serves both purposes, then output is given by

$$y = \phi[M/wf(y)] \tag{6''}$$

If national money serves as the unit of contract but world money serves as the transactions medium, then

$$y = \phi(M/w) \tag{6'''}$$

and if world money serves as the unit of contract but national money serves as the transactions medium, then

$$y = \phi(WM/w). \tag{6''''}$$

Understanding of these output results is enhanced by considering the aggregate supply function. When national money serves as the unit of contract, the only way in which output can change is by way of a change in the price level (since, in that case, the exchange rate is irrelevant). Where world money serves as the unit of contract, however, output will vary as the ratio of the price level to the exchange rate changes (P/e) varies. From the equilibrium condition for the national money market, we know that the price level depends only on the national money stock (and also on income when national money serves as the transactions unit). Thus, when national money is the unit of contract, only changes in national money can produce changes in output. The magnitude of the change in output will, however, be influenced by whether or not national money serves as the transactions medium. When it does not, the effect on output will be larger than when it does. This (perhaps seemingly paradoxical) result can be explained as follows. When national money is not the transactions medium, a rise in national money simply produces a proportional rise in the price level and a corresponding change in the real wage, with an appropriate induced-output response. Conversely, when national money serves as the transactions medium, a rise in national money which stimulates a rise in output will produce, among other things, a rise in demand for national money. This will lower the amount by which the price level will rise for any given rise in national money and thereby reduce the size of the change in real wages.

When world money serves as the unit of contract, the ratio of the price level to the exchange rate between the two moneys provides the source of variation in output. That ratio is determined purely by the equilibrium condition in the world money market. That is, from equation (1), the ratio of the price level to the exchange rate depends only on world money (and, when world money is the transactions unit, the level of income). Thus, changes in world money change the ratio of the price level to the exchange rate. Therefore, world money, and not national money, influences the level of output. Again, the size of the response of output to a change in world money depends upon whether or not world money is used also as the transactions unit. When world money serves as the transactions unit, the effect of a change in world money on output will be smaller than when national money serves that purpose.

Although these special cases are interesting, they are really just that—special cases. It is possible to visualize a world in which both moneys serve as the unit of transactions and in which some agents write their contracts in one of those moneys and other agents write theirs in the other money. In that case, equations (4), (5), and (6) provide the general solution, with the parameter a measuring the extent to which world money serves as the transactions medium and the parameter b measuring the extent to which world money serves as the unit of contract.

These analytical results are all straightforward enough. The relevance of this model (and of Fischer's more general one) is, however, far from clear. What these models do not determine is how people choose the units in which to write their contracts and the moneys in which to conduct their transactions. How these choices are influenced, both by the predictable trend inflation rate (measured in terms of either money), or by the variability and unpredictability of inflation (again, measured in either money) is a matter urgently requiring analysis. Further, whether or not there is any interaction between the moneys that are used as transactions media and those used for writing contracts needs to be analyzed. Before a money will be used as a unit of contract, must it be well established as a transactions medium? Or, put another way, is it possible to establish a unit of contract that has no transactions role? Understanding how an economy with more than one money operates and understanding what determines the choice of transactions units and units of contract is an urgent matter, not simply for the completion of theoretical models of the type discussed here. It is an urgent matter for understanding how the world we live in operates. For that world is very unlike the single-money world of conventional macroeconomics and monetary theory and much more like the world abstractly presented here.

As a matter of fact, it is by making progress with these questions that we shall better be able to speculate upon the larger question addressed by Fischer—namely, whether or not the International Monetary Fund and the special drawing right constitute embryonic forms of, respectively, a WCB and a WM. I have no disagreements with his bottom line on this matter. That bottom line is that (1) monetary policy, in the present state of the world, is simply too political to be hived off into an essentially technocratic international organization, and (2) the realization that a great concentration of power would result from centralized access to the printing press makes the existing diversified holders of the power to print money extremely reluctant to relinquish it.

REFERENCES

Cagan, Phillip, "The Monetary Dynamics of Hyperinflation," in *Studies in the Quantity Theory of Money*, ed. by Milton Friedman (Chicago: University of Chicago Press, 1956), pp. 25-117.

Kydland, Finn E., and Edward C. Prescott, "Rules Rather Than Discretion: The Inconsistency of Optimal Plans," *Journal of Political Economy*, Vol. 85 (June 1977), pp. 473-91.

Parkin, Michael, "Price and Output Determination in an Economy with Two Media of Exchange and a Separate Unit of Account," *Zeitschrift für Wirtschafts- und Sozialwissenschaften* (1979), pp. 95-111.

Taylor, John B., "Staggered Wage Setting in a Macro Model," *American Economic Review, Papers and Proceedings of the Ninety-First Annual Meeting of the American Economic Association*, Vol. 69 (May 1979), pp. 108-13.

____, "Aggregate Dynamics and Staggered Contracts," *Journal of Political Economy*, Vol. 88 (February 1980), pp. 1-23.

Wirick, Ronald G., "Fiscal Policy 'Crowding Out' of Private Investment in an Open Economy: The Case of Canada" (unpublished, 1983).

Don Roper

Stanley Fischer's paper is a careful, well-balanced analysis of alternate structures of the world monetary system and the role of a central monetary authority. The structure to which he gives most attention is one with a single world money and a world central bank. In the Appendix to his paper, he gives two analytical characteristics which must be fulfilled in order for one money, say the special drawing right (SDR), to be the "single world money." One characteristic is that any stickiness in wages must be in terms of the world money or SDR. The other characteristic is that transactions balances be held in (or backed by) SDRs. His major conclusion is that any rapid movement of the SDR toward a single world money is unlikely, primarily because national monetary authorities will be reluctant to forgo the seigniorage and control over monetary policy that the International Monetary Fund (IMF) would acquire.

I would like to address my comments to two aspects of his paper. My first and primary concern is with the characterization of the roles that a world money would play. Or, stated another way, how might we depict the alternative directions in which the SDR might evolve? The last part of this comment concerns the question of whether national monetary authorities might relinquish the seigniorage or control that the Fund would acquire if the SDR assumed a more important role.

Our usual characterization of the roles of money is over a century old. The typical textbook statement is that money is the unit of account, medium of exchange, and a store of value. Since many things are stores of value, the crucial distinction in this venerable trilogy is between the unit of account and the medium of exchange. Scholars of over a century ago, upon examining today's world, would be quick to point out that although central bank balances at the Fund might be contracted in SDRs (the unit of account), a currency like the dollar might be used as a vehicle for transferring the SDR balances.

Since deposit moneys (as opposed to moneys like hand-to-hand currencies or gold coins) have emerged as the dominant form of money, the unit-of-account—medium-of-exchange distinction does not provide the same level of discrimination that it once did. I will develop this point by first considering a relatively new money, U.S. money market funds (MMFs), and then apply the results of this inquiry to the SDR.

As is well known, the owner of a MMF account in the United States does not own dollars—he or she owns a fraction of the MMF's portfolio. The unit of account is a basket of money market instruments such as treasury bills, commercial paper, and certificates of deposit. But checks on these accounts are written in dollars, which would appear to be the medium of exchange. Just as contracts might have been written in gold and executed in silver a century ago, the units in which MMF balances are contracted are quite separate from the dollars used to transfer such balances.

Although this century-old distinction makes clear that the unit in which contracts are written is separable from the medium in which the exchange is executed, it suggests a qualitative distinction between the unit of account and the medium of exchange which is unwarranted in the realm of deposit moneys. A check written on a MMF is, itself, a contract and, as a contract, it must be expressed in some unit. When "spending" MMF money or any other deposit money, a short-term contract (like a check) is necessary because of the lapse of time between the agreement between parties and the time the recipient's balance is credited. If funds were transferred electronically, such that this time lapse (and float) were eliminated, a person with balances contracted in currency A could transfer balances (at the spot exchange rate) to a person with balances contracted in currency B without having to go through any medium of execution. But without electronic funds transfers, an additional contract expressed in a particular unit is required to transfer deposit balances. Since there are two kinds of contracts—contracts between money issuers and money holders and a contract used to transfer balances—it is inappropriate to refer to "the" unit of account. There is a unit in which the transfer contract is written, and there are one or more units in which deposit moneys are denominated.[1] It is unnecessary for deposits to be denominated in the same unit used in the transfer contract.

---

[1] From a legal standpoint, MMF liabilities are not considered "deposits," because their liabilities are not contracted in (spot) dollars. The phrase "deposit money" is used in the text to mean transferable accounts contracted in units which can, at least technically, differ from the transactions unit.

The reason for emphasizing that the medium of exchange, among deposit moneys, is itself a contract is that it helps us identify the different roles that SDRs might someday perform and to see clearly, I think, the particular roles of money that Stanley Fischer has modeled.[2] Consider, for example, the units in which wages and prices are quoted or, for Fischer's model in particular, the units in which wages are sticky. If all money were like MMF money, the units in which wages would most likely be sticky (if there were no escalator clauses) would be the units in which the transfer contract was written, not the units in which the contract between money issuer and money holder was written. I believe Fischer's model shows, therefore, that the ability of a world central bank to conduct monetary policy would depend crucially on whether the unit for transferring private deposit balances was the world money unit.

This brings us to the question of what determines the transactions unit. From a historical viewpoint, the choice of transactions unit appears to have been heavily influenced by the unit in which hand-to-hand currency is measured. This is due to the fact that the unit in which the ownership of hand-to-hand currency is measured cannot differ from the unit employed in a transaction involving the currency. For all non-deposit moneys, such as hand-to-hand currency or commodity money, the transactions unit and the unit of denomination are one and the same, and this unit is appropriately called "the" unit of account. Since the transactions unit and the unit of denomination cannot be separated for non-deposit moneys, the transactions unit for deposit moneys has historically been chosen to conform to the unit in which non-deposit money is measured. But the example of MMF money shows that the unit in which a deposit money is *denominated* can be selected independently from the units in which non-deposit moneys have been measured.

The transactions unit is not necessarily determined by the units in which hand-to-hand currency is measured. Some of the conference background papers by the Fund's staff and the paper by David Lomax (Chapter 6 in this volume) discuss the development of a private clearing system which uses the European Currency Unit (ECU) as the transactions unit. Some smaller private efforts at an SDR clearing system have also been made. The selection of the ECU and the SDR as the transactions units in such clearing systems is obviously being accomplished without the prior use of the ECU or the SDR

---

[2]Michael Parkin (1979) has developed a similar model of the distinction between the unit of account (or units in which prices are set) and the medium of exchange. The distinction used here between the transactions unit and the unit of denomination is a further breakdown of the medium (in Parkin's model) in which trade takes place. This breakdown becomes feasible only when one distinguishes between deposit and non-deposit moneys. The papers by Fischer and Parkin, like most literature in the theory of multiple moneys, employ models which abstract from the distinction between these two forms of money.

as a hand-to-hand currency. I see a clearing arrangement in SDRs as an alternative to SDR currency since either would facilitate the SDR becoming a unit in which prices are quoted and other contracts are written. Although currency units have historically dominated the choice of transactions unit and, thereby, dominated the unit in which prices have been quoted, a private SDR clearing system would facilitate other private uses of the SDR without having to go through a currency phase.

Consider what a world might look like with an SDR clearing system which exploited the potential of deposit moneys—that is to say, the feasibility of separating the transactions unit from the unit in which balances are denominated. Money issuers (like MMFs) in country A and money issuers in country B which had balances in a SDR clearing system could allow transfers to be written in SDRs. A merchant banking in A would not have to go through an exchange market to make a purchase from a merchant banking in B. There would still be a "balance of payments," in the sense of an increase or decrease in money issuers' SDR balances at the clearinghouse, but there would not necessarily be any market for exchanging moneys between parties holding accounts with money issuers who, outside official channels, allow balances to be transferred in SDRs. Just as U.S. residents currently quote prices and write checks in dollars on MMF accounts denominated in other units, international parties could quote prices and make transfers in SDRs while holding deposit balances denominated in, say, national currency units like pounds and lire. Although a market may always be necessary to exchange hand-to-hand currencies issued by national central banks, it would be possible to make international transfers between MMF-type deposits without generating any corresponding activity in the exchange market.[3]

The second matter I would like to briefly address in the remainder of my comment concerns whether the Fund might acquire greater influence over world monetary policy or a larger share of world seigniorage. It is important first to notice that the development of a SDR clearing mechanism would probably not require a redistribution of seigniorage comparable to the redistribution that would be required for the Fund to issue SDRs as hand-to-hand currency. The policy issue does not, of course, concern SDR currency but rather SDR clearing arrangements, as discussed, for example, by Warren Coats (1982).

If the Fund made a major effort to support an SDR clearing arrange-

---

[3]The elimination of the need to go through an exchange market might result in substantial resource saving. Such a saving is suggested by the apparent difference between the small charge levied by MMFs for writing and receiving checks and the relatively large charge levied by commercial banks for trips through the exchange market. The magnitude of the inefficiencies which might be reduced is emphasized by Benjamin Klein and Michael Melvin (1982).

ment, this would enhance the use of the SDR as a transactions unit, which should lead to a more widespread use of the SDR as a unit of account for debt contracts and eventually as a unit for invoicing traded goods. This would, as Fischer's model indicates, give the Fund more control over world monetary policy. Would national central banks give up this control easily?

When we look at the historical development of central banks, such as the Federal Reserve System or the Bank of England, it is clear that their acquisition of control and seigniorage was achieved through various quid pro quos. Agreements were worked out which allowed for the enhanced role of such institutions. One obvious role which the Fund could play to "earn its keep" in the international community is as lender of last resort. This role would, of course, require greater resources than the Fund presently commands. The Fund could offer to play such a role in return for the necessary resources.

REFERENCES

Coats, Warren L., Jr., "The SDR as a Means of Payment," International Monetary Fund, *Staff Papers*, Vol. 29 (September 1982), pp. 422–36.

Klein, Benjamin, and Michael Melvin, "Competing International Monies and International Monetary Arrangements," in *The International Monetary System: Choices for the Future*, ed. by Michael Connolly (New York: Praeger, 1982), pp. 199–228.

Parkin, Michael, "Price and Output Determination in an Economy with Two Media of Exchange and a Separate Unit of Account," *Zeitschrift für Wirtschafts- und Sozialwissenschaften* (1979), pp. 95–111.

5

Is There an Important Role for an International Reserve Asset Such as the SDR?

W. M. CORDEN*

The question set for this paper raises issues that are central to this conference. The aims will be to highlight basic principles and underlying assumptions of various arguments and to focus on realities. But it must never be forgotten that today's dreams may become tomorrow's realities, so I shall also examine carefully the implications of various "dreams." I propose to avoid technicalities. Furthermore, in view of Chapter 11 in this volume, which is entitled "The Evolving Role of the SDR in the International Monetary System," it is not necessary to give any systematic account of past developments or of various proposals for changes.

Right from the beginning, one distinction must be stressed. This is between the concept of the special drawing right (SDR) as an internationally created reserve asset and its denomination as a currency basket. It was originally denominated in terms of a fixed quantity of gold valued at the official U.S. dollar price of gold. An internationally created asset could be denominated in various ways, for example, in terms of dollars or even commodities other than gold. Although much attention has been given recently to the matter of denomination, this is not the central issue. The use of a particular denomination—currently, a weighted-value average of a basket of five currencies—in the private market does not mean that there has been any international creation of a reserve asset. In general, I shall be concerned here with the reserve asset question, not the denomination

*I am indebted to George von Furstenberg and Herbert Grubel for valuable comments on an earlier draft.

question. As Machlup (1981) has pointed out, it is unfortunate that the same term is used both for the new kind of asset and for its denomination.

It seems best not to start with the "dreams" but with the current situation. The current situation is that the SDR does not have a very significant role in the international monetary system, making up only a small part of world reserves. This is so in spite of the intention expressed in the Articles of Agreement of the International Monetary Fund (IMF), since 1978, to make "the special drawing right the principal reserve asset in the international monetary system." At the time of writing, it does not appear that governments propose to move in the direction of fulfilling this intention. Thus, there is certainly a dramatic gap between realities and proclaimed intentions.

This "realities-intentions gap" could be interpreted in two ways. The first is that the supposed intention is simply a relic of circumstances that gave rise to the SDR and of theories that have gone out of fashion. Perhaps, in due course, the relic will be buried. The second is that the proclaimed intention lays the groundwork for a possible change in realities; it reflects a desire for change, though the kinds of change that would be appropriate in the new economic environment that has existed since the early seventies have not yet been envisaged. It could then be among the purposes of a conference such as this to sort out the issues, with a view to changing realities.

In either event, it would be necessary to examine aspects of the current system, including its inadequacies, if any, and to ask to what extent the large-scale creation of an international reserve asset could overcome these inadequacies either within, broadly, the current system (discussed in Section I) or possibly as part of a complete change in the system (discussed in Section II). In Section III, I shall look back at past discussions and circumstances and relate them to the present. Section IV summarizes the practical implications.

I. SDRs WITHIN CURRENT SYSTEM

Current System—Chaotic "Nonsystem" with a Logic

Broadly, we have a decentralized international market system—one characterized by a kind of laissez-faire and under which governments and their central banks are major players, with their actions subject to few, if any, effective rules. The system has generated liquidity and reserves endogenously. Reserves can be earned in the international market, either by the net sale of goods and services—that is, through a current account surplus—or by the sale of bonds. When reserves are built up through a sale of bonds, there is an exchange of medium-term or long-term assets for short-term assets.

It would be wrong to say that reserves are determined by demand; rather, the level of reserves is the outcome of a demand-and-supply equilibrium. If increased reserves are to be earned through current account surpluses, there must be a corresponding willingness on the part of others to incur current account deficits (i.e., a willingness to sell financial assets for goods and services). Equilibrium is attained essentially through interest rate variations. If there is an excess demand for financial assets relative to goods, so that the algebraic sum of desired current account surpluses is positive, the interest rate will fall; this will increase real investment and perhaps reduce savings, thereby reducing desired surpluses and raising deficits until equilibrium is attained. If increased reserves are to be earned through medium-term and long-term borrowing, long-term rates will rise and short-term rates will fall until the private capital market chooses to supply what the central banks are demanding. At the same time, the changing structure of interest rates may lead the central banks to adjust their demands. Furthermore, the existence of the market provides liquidity—the potential availability of funds when needed—and thus reduces the need for owned reserves, whether private or public.

To the surprise of some, this market brought about the recycling of the oil surpluses. In fact, its emergence was completely unplanned and occurred at the very same time that lengthy official discussions were proceeding about the problems of reserve adequacy and the reconstruction of the whole system. Only a few economists noted the significance of the private capital market in generating reserves and in achieving an equilibrium between short-term and long-term assets for different countries and different financial institutions.

The prevailing exchange rate arrangement can also be described as a laissez-faire system under which governments, through their central banks, are important actors, intervening in the market as little or as much as they choose; perhaps fixing their exchange rates in a particular way—whether to another currency, to a trade-weighted basket, or even to the particular basket called the SDR; and fixing them for any period they choose. It is well known that the interventions in the markets of major countries that practice managed floating seem to have the general characteristic of "leaning against the wind;" but the degree of "leaning" is optional and is different at different times. Also to be noted is the establishment of a regional par value system—a kind of "mini-Bretton Woods"—in the form of the European Monetary System.

The world system that has emerged is unplanned and apparently chaotic. It has been described as a nonsystem. In the view of some, it is desperately in need of "control" (especially control of the Eurocurrency market). But the point I wish to stress is that it nevertheless has some internal logic, essentially the logic of the market.[1] There are the same tendencies to equilibrium in the system as in any market, and it may well be efficient for the same reasons that—subject to qualifications—markets are generally or widely regarded as efficient ways of organizing economic relationships. The fact that a market is unplanned and uncontrolled does not mean that it is inadequate. Nor does the fact that public bodies, such as central banks, operate in it make it less of a market.

The standard market paradigm thus seems the best starting point for analysis. Given certain assumptions, markets lead to efficient solutions. Even though efficient, they are not necessarily "optimal" solutions, because they may lead to income and wealth distribution outcomes that are, by some criteria, inequitable or undesirable. Thus, ideally, an efficient market may need to be supplemented by redistributive arrangements; or, alternatively, intervention in the market may be justified if it has desirable redistributive consequences. In addition, the assumptions required for market efficiency may not be fulfilled. The various qualifications—externalities, public goods, information deficiencies, market power of major actors making them price makers rather than price takers, and introduction of oligopolistic effects—are well known.

It is also well known and important to note that the existence of market failure in itself does not justify just any kind of intervention. Intervention should be directed specifically at dealing with the relevant market failure. Furthermore, the operators of the intervention themselves become actors in the system, and their efficiency and motivations must be considered, so that the possibility of political or bureaucratic failure must be set against market failure.

I do not propose to pursue this approach to studying the international monetary system in a formal way, although it would be well worth doing, but I shall use it as a general framework. If one could assume that the system was efficient, there would be no need for an international reserve asset or any other kind of internationally coordinated action. The next step is to consider possible inadequacies of the system—that is, qualifications to the assumption—and in each case to ask whether the inadequacy might justify the establishment, or expansion in the supply, of an international reserve asset such as the SDR. I shall consider three possible inadequacies—namely

---

[1]The line of argument to follow, which runs through this paper, is developed more fully in Corden (1983). Essentially it is a development of the ideas of McKinnon (1969) and Kindleberger (1981); and it is clear that Grubel (1982), in reassessing the impact of Triffin (1960), has been thinking along similar lines. See also Haberler (1977) and Polak (1981). The stress on the endogeneity of reserves can be found in recent issues of the *Annual Report* of the Fund.

(1) the instability of exchange rates, (2) the tendency for the system to give rise to inflation or recession, and (3) the inadequacies of the international capital market.

Instability of Exchange Rates—Multicurrency System and Substitution Account

A principal source of dissatisfaction with the current international monetary system is the instability of exchange rates, especially the large medium-term swings in nominal and real rates. A particular problem has arisen with the swings in the yen/dollar rate; whenever the yen depreciates in real terms, pressures for protectionism increase in the United States.

In general, the objection to severely fluctuating exchange rates is not so much that they may have adverse effects on trade and capital movements—for which there is, in fact, no clear evidence—but that they have unwelcome and politically awkward effects on the distribution of domestic incomes, as between different sectors. Real appreciations adversely affect profits and possibly employment in countries' export and import-competing industries. Real depreciations tend to lower real wages. If there is real wage resistance, nominal depreciations can give rise to "vicious circles." The rise in domestic prices resulting from depreciation generates nominal wage increases designed to restore real wages. To prevent these wage increases from causing unemployment, monetary expansion then follows, eliminating the initial benefits of the depreciation and thus leading to further depreciation and further price and wage rises.

The main causes of major exchange rate fluctuations appear to be divergences in monetary and fiscal policies, either in their impact on overall demand or in the policy mix leading to real interest rate divergences. When Japan follows a tight overall aggregate demand policy and the United States an expansionary one, the yen tends to appreciate. On the other hand, when policy mixes diverge (for any given overall demand outcome)—for example, tight money and easy fiscal policy in the United States and the opposite in Japan—the exchange rate is again influenced; in this example, the yen depreciates. These episodes are well known.

Countries follow policies designed primarily to suit domestic considerations, and their governments respond to political pressures and ideologies that differ between countries. Policies are also liable to change drastically as governments change. Exchange rate outcomes are essentially by-products of these domestically motivated policies, and the problem is that governments are unlikely to subordinate their domestic motives to the objective of exchange rate stability. Furthermore, expectational effects may intensify or moderate the exchange rate outcomes. If expectations are correct, they anticipate changes that would otherwise take place, and they may smooth out fluctuations. It is widely believed, at least by advocates of exchange market intervention, that markets have a tendency to overreact to "news" and, in general, to expect more changes than underlying conditions justify. Nominal exchange rate fluctuations seem to lead to fluctuations in real rates, although the latter may be somewhat smaller in amplitude. The main sources of difficulty—especially because of their effects on the distribution of income between different domestic sectors—are the changes in real rates.

How does this problem relate to the question posed for this paper? The obvious solution is to deal with the underlying causes—unstable domestic macroeconomic policies and little coordination when changes are made in these policies. It is beyond the scope of this paper to discuss the practical implications of this simpleminded prescription. Here, I shall discuss only the implications for the reserve asset question.

First, the problem would disappear—almost by definition—if countries committed themselves (and adhered to their commitments) to a fixed exchange rate system. The implications of such a system for the reserve asset question will be discussed in Section II. Of course, while the exchange rate problem would disappear, if the underlying causes were not dealt with, the problem would manifest itself in other ways, essentially as balance of payments problems of individual countries. For the moment, I continue to assume that the world stays with its laissez-faire exchange rate system.

The second implication for the reserve asset question has to do with the development of a multicurrency system. The familiar argument is that a multicurrency system increases exchange rate instability. If central banks held only one asset—ideally the SDR—instability would be reduced. This is the argument for the substitution account (ideally with compulsory substitution), with regard to existing foreign exchange assets, and for imposing rules on the acquisition of new assets, essentially designed to limit the scope for substitution between assets in response to fluctuations in expectations. The implication is that speculation by official holders is destabilizing.

There seem to be two reasons why one should be skeptical about the usefulness of a substitution account as a solution to the exchange stability problem.

First, not only would *official* holders have to be confined to one asset but something would also have to be done about private holders. Presumably their speculation would also be destabilizing. A severe restriction on market forces would have to be imposed. Japanese residents will always hold yen, and American residents dollars; far-reaching exchange controls would be needed to discourage the holding of each other's currencies, or bonds denominated in each other's currencies, when it appeared profitable. And, as one well remembers from the days when the postwar international capital market was in its infancy and exchange controls were very tight in Europe, there is always scope for leads and lags in payments.

Second, there is very little evidence that the gradual move from a dollar system to a multicurrency system has been a significant cause of exchange rate instability. Rather the instability of the dollar, caused by macroeconomic policy changes in the United States, and possibly other countries, has stimulated that move. The concern about the development of the multicurrency system was at its peak around 1978, when there was a dollar depreciation, the causes of which were macroeconomic policy divergences. It is also worth noting that the move has been mainly from dollars to deutsche mark, and not to yen; nevertheless, as mentioned earlier, there have been severe fluctuations in the yen/dollar rate—a major cause of international economic tensions.

The implications of a substitution account are discussed in several other chapters. Essentially the Fund (or the special account) would go into the business of exchanging dollars for a particular currency basket. If it retained the dollars, it would clearly be incurring a risk. Use of the account would be a way of locking the world outside the United States (in this argument, the Fund is considered part of that world) into dollars. For the Fund, the deal might not be good business. If it were, then, presumably, private agents would go into this business of buying dollars and selling SDR baskets. But the central issue, on which negotiations broke down, is who would cover the possible losses and presumably gain the possible profits? In other words, for whom would the Fund act as agent? Would it be the United States, or would it be the world community? If this question were resolved, the issue would remain as to whether the whole exercise was worthwhile from the point of view of exchange rate variability; skepticism seems justified in this respect.

Inflation and Recession—Is the System to Blame?

The current international monetary nonsystem has developed more or less concurrently with the new era of inflation and recession that began in 1973. Therefore one must hesitate to suggest that such a system can possibly be efficient or optimal when its evolution has coincided with such a marked deterioration in the world economy. Is there an inadequacy in the system that is responsible for our current macroeconomic troubles? Are these troubles caused by exchange rate variability, by excessive or inadequate reserves, or perhaps by the growth of the international capital market? And, if so, could they be remedied by creation of more SDRs? In general, it seems to me that the answers must all be negative.

The world inflation originated during the operation of the Bretton Woods system and was exported from the United States and voluntarily imported by other countries through the mechanism of fixed rates. Countries could have insulated themselves by appreciating their currencies sufficiently relative to the dollar, but they chose not to do so. The variations in inflation rates that inevitably resulted made exchange rate flexibility inevitable. This is an oversimplified story, but it would be difficult to tell a story in which flexible exchange rates were the prime movers. Current unemployment can be attributed to the combination of real wage resistance and low productivity growth (resulting, perhaps, from low investment) and, in the last few years, relative monetary tightness in the major industrial countries.

Flexible exchange rates allow countries freedom in choosing their money supply policies. Insofar as nominal demand policies can affect real macroeconomic outcomes—as they usually can in the short run—flexible rates introduce a significant element of national independence. Of course, links through trade and the capital market impose real constraints on nations: the terms of trade and real interest rates may be given from outside. Alternatively, a unilateral nominal demand expansion, leading inevitably to devaluation, may worsen the terms of trade. But, subject to constraints that depend on the policies of other countries, some national policy independence with regard to inflation and unemployment does remain. For some countries, this freedom may make their problems worse, for others better. With regard to making it worse, it can certainly be argued convincingly that the inflationary explosions in 1973 and 1974 in some countries, such as the United Kingdom and Italy, were made possible by the removal of the balance of payments constraint of fixed rates. On the other hand, a degree of insulation became possible for the Federal Republic of Germany.

It could be argued that instabilities imported from abroad through terms of trade variations and through real exchange rate instability—the latter, in turn, caused or intensified by the international capital market—increase both inflation and unemployment. The mechanism is through asymmetric wage effects: increases in demand for the outputs of one industry increase wages and prices there, while decreases in demand for the outputs of other industries fail to lower wages but do raise unemployment. Yet it seems evident to me that this is not where the principal causes of inflation and unemployment since 1973 are to be found.

Is it possible that within the current laissez-faire exchange rate system, there are either excessive reserves—hence generating inflation—or too few reserves—hence causing unemployment? As stressed earlier, the reserve supply is essentially endogenous—the outcome of a demand-and-supply equilibrium—so the question is whether the process by which the system generates or destroys reserves is deflationary or inflationary. My answer is that *in the flexible-rate system*, the process is *not* necessarily deflationary or inflationary. I shall consider here the case where there is initially a perceived shortage of reserves, although the analysis could be applied symmetrically to the case where countries feel they have excessive reserves.

First, one can look at a small country that wishes to increase its reserves. It can do so either by borrowing—that is, by incurring longer-term liabilities to acquire short-term assets—or by running a current account surplus. Presumably the need for deflation only arises in the second case. Aggregate demand (absorption) has to be reduced to generate the external surplus. In that sense, a deflationary policy is certainly required. But the interesting question is what happens to the demand for domestic output. At the initial exchange rate, demand for home-produced goods will fall, this being a by-product of the objective of reducing demand for imports. If nominal wages are rigid or sluggish downward, then unemployment will result. This is the fixed-rate story. But under the current system, the country is free to depreciate its exchange rate, an action that would switch demand from imports to home-produced goods. The combination of reduction in absorption and depreciation can keep constant the demand for home-produced goods, yielding the desired current account surplus without a net reduction in domestic employment.

Similarly, a country that finds its reserve supply excessive, and therefore wishes to run a current account deficit for some time in order to transform some of its financial assets into goods, can do so without domestic inflation. It needs to appreciate its exchange rate while raising real absorption. Domestic deflation in the first case and inflation in the second would still result if the country failed to make use of its exchange rate instrument, but that would be its choice and not a requirement of the system.

What would happen if all countries wished to increase their reserves? To what extent does the argument just developed for the small country still apply? Again, one can distinguish between the generation of reserves through financial asset transformation and the purchase of reserves through current account surpluses. The capital market can generate extra reserves by the private sector (principally the large international banks) exchanging assets with the world public sector (the central banks). This happens when central banks borrow to replenish their reserves. Insofar as this process raises medium-term and long-term interest rates, and hence reduces investment, it would be deflationary and would need to be offset within each country by appropriate monetary or fiscal expansion.

But let us now consider the example where all countries wish to run current account surpluses in order to increase reserves. Of course, they cannot achieve their objectives. The question is whether the effort of trying to achieve the inconsistent objectives need be deflationary. In a fixed-exchange-rate regime, it would be. But with flexible rates in a two-country world, we can imagine that both Country A and Country B buy each other's currency, aiming to depreciate their own currencies. This is a situation of .competitive depreciation. Neither will achieve its exchange rate objective or its current account objective, but each will accumulate the currency of the other and thus will, incidentally, have succeeded in increasing its gross reserves.

There is no reason in this example why either country should actually reduce its absorption of goods and services, unless it actually does achieve a depreciation of its currency. It seems reasonable to assume that the exchange rate is targeted on the (unattainable) current account target, while for each country expenditure (absorption) policy is targeted on attaining the desired level of demand for domestic goods and services. The same argument applies when there is a world excess of reserves, in which event there might be attempts at competitive appreciation but there need not be inflation.

The conclusion thus is that under the flexible-exchange-rate system, there is not an inevitable relationship between reserve adequacy and world deflation or inflation. The story is different, of course, in a fixed-rate system, and this I shall discuss later.

Here one might note a feature of the current system that may have led to money supply instability in major industrial countries other than the United States. The essential cause is the failure to allow exchange rates to float freely because of governments' desires to avoid severe real exchange rate changes that would have effects on the domestic distribution of income between sectors. Thus, policies of leaning-against-the-wind intervention are being followed. When the motive of intervention to moderate appreciation is to protect profits and employment in export and import-competing industries, the policy can be called "exchange rate protection."

The implications for the world money supply of such intervention policies have recently been noted by McKinnon (1982). When the dollar is expected to depreciate, for whatever reason, capital seeks to move out of the United States, and part of the effect is absorbed by depreciation of the dollar and part by monetary expansion in countries such as Japan and the Federal Republic of Germany. These countries do not succeed in sterilizing the domestic monetary effects, so their money supplies go up and inflation accelerates. At the same time, there is automatic sterilization in the United States. Thus, the world money supply rises unduly when the dollar depreciates (but *because* it does not depreciate enough) and similarly falls unduly when the dollar appreciates.

If one regards this outcome as undesirable and accepts both leaning-against-the-wind policies and nonsterilization (or inadequate sterilization) as inevitable, it is necessary to look at the causes of the expectational shifts that have fueled the actual and incipient capital movements. Are the changes in expectations rational or not? Furthermore, are the resultant capital movements encouraged or made possible by the multicurrency system? In fact, one comes back to the same issues that were discussed earlier. In general, it seems to me that instabilities in policies of major countries—caused by understandable and perhaps inevitable political factors—must be blamed for instabilities in expectations about exchange rates. And, with regard to the multicurrency system, the scope for speculation, whether rational or otherwise, would hardly alter if all official reserves were held in one currency, since the opportunities and motivations for private-sector speculation would still exist.

Is the International Capital Market Adequate?

The international capital market is the generator of official reserves and of liquidity, and the question is whether SDRs should supplement or replace it in some way. Presumably, there would be no need for SDRs if the capital market were entirely adequate. I shall explore three possible inadequacies and then go on to consider whether SDRs could do better.

To begin with, it must be noted that the international capital market is certainly perfect in the usually accepted sense of that term, or, at least, it must be one of the more perfect markets existing anywhere in the world. It absorbs and makes use of a vast amount of information and has given rise to a great information industry of its own. There is free entry. Its pricing is extremely flexible, as is reflected in the numerous and continuously changing margins for different borrowers and the term structure of interest rates. It has been remarkably neutral politically. Although there are some very large borrowers, lenders, and—above all—intermediaries, the market is in no sense monopolized. Let us now consider three possible inadequacies—namely, (1) unwise lending and borrowing, (2) inadequate insurance, and (3) failure to redistribute world income.

Unwise Lending and Borrowing

In the discussion of unwise lending and borrowing, I shall first look backward and then forward.

With hindsight, we can see that some of the market participants have not shown foresight. We, and they, can now see that they may have been foolish or ignorant. Or perhaps they were only running some calculated risks. With respect to banks, good profits were made for many years by running risks. With respect to sovereign borrowers, political rewards were reaped by spending generously out of borrowed funds, or by postponing needed adjustments. Similarly, some private companies may have run undue risks or made misjudgments. But now there is trouble. Could these problems have been prevented or reduced by official controls of some kind, possibly by supervision from the Fund?

This raises three questions. First, does the private sector tend to take excessive risks—excessive from a social point of view, bearing in mind that lending governments may have to rescue banks and possibly sovereign borrowers when the risks do not pay? It is worth noting that there are other occasions—for example, new industrial developments—when the private sector is often accused of not being willing to take enough risks. Nevertheless, it would surely be widely agreed both that the international banks have relied on the lender-of-last-resort role of central banks and that such reliance *is* likely to be an incentive to undue risk taking. The second question is whether an official controller, whether the Fund or a central bank, would have better foresight or knowledge than the market participants. It is not obvious why this should be so. Presumably, any superior information could be readily fed to the market. Staff with proven analytic ability and good judgment can be as easily employed by private banks and consulting agencies as by public bodies. On the other hand, the Fund benefits from economies of scale in this respect. The third question is whether official intervention would have been motivated in a favorable or unfavorable direction by political and strategic considerations. Presumably, the introduction of any noneconomic motivations would increase the possibility of losses or of forgone profits overall, other things being equal. Here it has to be noted that governments of major lending countries strongly supported bank lending to some of the countries that subsequently turned out to have big debt problems.

In spite of this last factor, I suspect that if funds had been channeled through the Fund or through the central banks of major lending countries, they would have been more cautiously applied; and, in total, the flow of funds to developing countries would have been far less, with more going to governments and corporations in developed countries. In spite of current difficulties, it is not clear that this would have been a better outcome. From the point of view of world efficiency, quite apart from international income distribution considerations, the public bodies might have erred in the opposite direction from the private banks by being overcautious.

So much for looking backward. Now, what about the future? In view of current problems, the question must arise whether the role of the capital market in providing funds to many sovereign borrowers may be coming to an end. Although some lending may have been excessive in the past, we could be moving into a period of unwise or undesirably limited international lending, at least to developing countries. Because of a tendency to overreact, lending may be too limited not only from a world efficiency point of view but also from the point of view of the potential private lenders. This implies, of course, that the private market may not be efficient and raises the related issue of whether supplementary public lending would compensate to the right extent or would overreact by providing funds too readily, at least to those sovereign borrowers viewed with favor by the political masters of the public agencies.

Returning to the problem created by the lending of the recent past, the issue arises of arrangments for rescue, whether of sovereign borrowers or of international banks. This is essentially an insurance issue, to which I come next.

Inadequate Insurance

Although there is a private insurance market, one cannot insure against major liquidity crises or bankruptcy in this market. Domestic depositors in banks are usually protected, and the banks themselves have some degree of insurance through the lender-of-last resort commitments (insofar as these exist) of central banks. Because of the "moral hazard" problem, the insurer must exercise some degree of supervision, and this provides the logic for central bank supervision of private banks. If the latter are not willing to be supervised—as evidenced by their escaping the net, say, through an offshore market—they cannot expect to be insured. Those that do not insure often regret it afterward, but they may be taking a calculated risk.

Here, I want to focus specifically on the insurance problems of sovereign borrowers. It is not really possible for a nation to insure in the normal way against unexpected exogenous developments, such as deterioration in the terms of trade, or against the consequences of mistakes in policies. The problem is that the country may not be able to borrow in the international capital market because of unexpected circumstances that preclude such borrowing or because of prohibitive interest rates. A country may then be faced with major problems of reducing real expenditures. It is at this point that the Fund and international reserve assets come in.

The insurance is not just against unexpected developments affecting the particular country concerned but also against an unexpected tightening of conditions in the international capital market for whatever reason, or even against a breakdown in the market owing to a loss of confidence, possibly caused by defaults. This is the eventuality that, at least in its more moderate form, appears to be in prospect now. Governments insure against such situations by accumulating owned reserves. To that extent, the international capital market does provide the required service. But, in addition, governments provide mutual insurance for each other at no immediate cost by setting up swap arrangements and by creating international reserve assets.

Fund quotas can be regarded as part of a sovereign insurance system. Governments provide a line of credit, in effect, to the World Insurance Company (the IMF); and it, in turn, is prepared to come to the rescue of its customers. An insurance company, of course, must exercise some supervision to ensure that the customer tries to avoid getting into trouble, and if and when he does, that he puts his house in order and avoids mistakes in the future. There is a sovereign moral hazard problem that provides the logic for conditionality and for one of the principal activities of the Fund, surveillance.

Failure to Redistribute World Income

The private market discriminates against bad risks, in the worst cases by refusing to lend to them at all and more generally by charging higher interest rates. The bad risks tend to include the poorest nations, yet there is no inevitable relationship between a particular sovereign risk and the per capita gross national product of that country. Although this tendency of the market is not explicit discrimination against poor countries, neither is it discrimination *in favor* of the poor. It does not help those whose poverty has pushed them out of the world market. For them, there is obviously no element of aid.

Coming back to first principles, the distinction between efficiency and optimality was stressed earlier. Efficiency considerations ignore income-distribution effects. It is legitimate to concentrate on efficiency if independent income distribution policies to implement a "world social welfare function" (something that can only be implicit) are being pursued. In practice, we know they are not, so there is at least a logical basis for taking world-income-distribution considerations into account when making various international arrangements, such as those under discussion here. This is the argument for a link. On the other hand, some prefer to maintain a clear separation between the efficiency objective and the income-distribution objective and thus prefer international monetary arrangements to be directed at achieving (or moving closer to) world efficiency, while leaving redistribution objectives to other parts of the system, such as bilateral aid and the activities of the World Bank Group.

Capital Market Inadequacies and the SDR

I now consider the implications of these three possible capital market inadequacies for proposals to expand the role of the SDR.

First, something must be said about the fundamental characteristic of the SDR, as it exists now. A country that uses its SDRs is making use of a line of credit at a concessional rate of interest. The SDR interest rate is based on the short-term market rates of the five countries whose currencies make up the basket. For some borrowers, these interest rates are close to the rates at which they can actually borrow, so that there is little element of concession and hence little motive for using SDRs. On the other hand, for others, these five rates are well below the rates at which they can actually borrow, or at which they can always be certain they could borrow.

The certainty that this line of credit is always available is, in itself, a quality that the general availability of the private capital market does not provide. The certainty depends on the extent to which holders can be sure that the Fund will always designate some country to accept SDRs and that this country will always adhere to the obligations it incurred when it became a participant in the SDR scheme.

It has to be remembered that while the user of the SDR—that is, the borrower—is getting an implicit subsidy, the assigned recipient, the lender, may be paying an implicit tax. The extent to which there is such a tax is indicated by the extent to which countries are reluctant to hold SDRs, so that assignment (by designation of participants) is necessary. If the SDR interest rate were truly an appropriately weighted market rate for riskless bonds (and if there were no limitations on the use of SDRs by net acquirers), there should be no reluctance to accept SDRs, and hence no implicit tax on lenders, because the Fund, after all, has assumed the risks. The only risk then for holders of SDRs would be that the Fund might not fulfill its obligations.

Would SDRs Reduce Unwise Lending?

If large issues of SDRs had been made in 1974 and every year thereafter, many sovereign borrowers would not have needed to go to the world capital market. The low absorbers of the Organization of Petroleum Exporting Countries (OPEC), Japan, the Federal Republic of Germany, and some others would have accumulated SDRs instead of dollars. Some countries that had both current account deficits and had earlier accumulated dollar reserves could have been obliged to accept SDRs and so would have reduced their dollar holdings, which would then have ended up in the private sector. For some borrowers, the total amounts they would have borrowed might not have changed, but they would have paid a lower interest rate, so that there would essentially be just an income transfer. In addition, some developing countries would have become large international borrowers for the first time through using their SDRs. With an increased demand for funds, the free market rate of interest would have risen and other borrowers who continued to use the market (in addition to SDRs) would have been crowded out to some extent.

The question is whether possibilities of unwise lending or borrowing would have been less. On the SDRs themselves, interest rates would have been less than in the capital market; to that extent, the strain would have been reduced. But the possibility would have remained that a country that was using its SDRs and thus committing itself to regular interest payments would not have been able to make them; the possibility of default would have remained. But this time the intermediary would not have been a private bank but rather the Fund. The Fund would have borne the risks, and its members would have covered any losses in proportion to their quotas. This might have been regarded as desirable, since there is a virtue in risk spreading. Furthermore, it could be argued that because of the greater potential power of the Fund, especially in a regime where it disposes of SDRs on a large scale, the risk that countries might default to the Fund is much less than the risk that they might default on debts to private lenders or individual governments. Thus, SDRs would reduce world risks—presumably leading to a world efficiency gain—and would allow the spread between interest rates paid by borrowers and received by lenders (depositors in Eurocurrency markets) to narrow.

On the other hand, the uniform interest rate on SDRs has to be contrasted with the varying margins that the private market charges. This seems to me an important consideration that weighs against SDRs. It is clearly efficient for interest rates to include margins for risk; in this important respect, then, the SDR is inefficient. The private market imposes margins and, in the limiting case, can actually refuse to lend to a really risky potential borrower. Thus, a strong incentive is provided for countries to maintain their creditworthiness by managing their economies sensibly and, above all, by not defaulting. By contrast, irrespective of the recipient's creditworthiness, SDRs are automatically issued to all participants. The probability of a participant defaulting on the interest payments cannot be taken into account when issuing SDRs. If the participant does default, he is no longer entitled to his share of SDRs.

Looking back, then, greater issues of SDRs would have led to a partial replacement of private lending by SDRs, with the consequences just discussed. Looking forward, the same analysis applies. If SDRs were issued on a large scale, to a considerable extent they would replace private lending, changing its pattern, presumably in the direction of those countries—primarily developing countries—that would be able to borrow little or nothing in the private market. In addition, there might be some net rise in total international lending, induced by a higher market interest rate than would otherwise prevail. As discussed earlier, whether this effect would be desirable depends on the extent to which the private market may be inefficiently *over*reacting to recent events by *under*lending to developing countries.

Quotas Compared with SDRs as Insurance Mechanism— Conditionality Issue

Issues of SDRs are a form of insurance, as is any arrangement for mutual increases in owned reserves. The logic is the same as that for Fund quotas, which has already been discussed. Swap facilities under the General Arrangements to Borrow fall into the same category. If it is desired to increase the level of sovereign insurance, is this done better by an increase in quotas or an increase in SDRs?

This raises the question of how SDRs compare with quotas. One aspect has received much attention, but seems to me relatively minor. This is the matter of denomination of a reserve asset. When the market continually adjusts spot exchange rates of the major currencies to take into account expected exchange rate changes (and, insofar as intervention regulates spot rates, when the market adjusts interest rates), it seems to matter relatively little to a borrower in which currency cocktail, consisting of one or more of the major currencies, his loan is denominated. It matters only when the expectations of the particular borrower differ from those of the market. Presumably, he is better off choosing his own cocktail rather than being forced to accept a prepackaged one like the SDR. Of course, even if there is no difference in expectations, after the event, the choice of currencies will turn out to have mattered, since expectations usually turn out to have been wrong.

The key distinction between quotas and SDRs is that beyond the first credit tranche, the former involve conditionality and the latter do not. This refers to SDRs as at present issued. If they were issued not directly to participants but rather to the Fund itself, which could then use them for lender-of-last-resort lending subject to conditionality, the distinction would disappear. As discussed earlier, insurance always involves the problem of moral hazard, and this requires the insurance company to exercise some supervision. Hence a scheme with conditionality seems more appropriate than one without.

Here it might be noted that reserve positions in the Fund also represent reserve assets that are available unconditionally. I refer here only to reserve positions that represent the net creation of new reserve assets and not to positions that result purely from the deposit with the Fund of other reserve assets. Such reserve positions differ from SDRs and from tranche positions in two crucial aspects: first, they are not "created" in a systematic universal fashion, since they come into existence only as a by-product of the extension of credit by the Fund to its members; and second, they are acquired at a cost in terms of potential resource used, since the reserve position of Country A is built up only when Country B acquires Country A's national currency through Fund drawings with the intention of spending it.

There remains the somewhat complex question of the extent to which the creation of unconditional reserve assets internationally *actually* reduces the conditionality of international borrowing.[2] It might be argued that drawing too sharp a distinction between conditionality and the lack of it is not really justified. Provided the *marginal* borrowing of a country is conditional—whether through Fund conditionality or through conditionality, explicit or implicit, imposed by the private market—a country's total policies will, in effect, be subject to conditions imposed by lenders. These conditions will thus apply also to those policies or activities apparently sustained by the unconditional part of its borrowing.

The position at present is that a country that only borrows up to the point where it uses its SDRs and then proceeds to its first credit tranche is borrowing unconditionally. The availability of such opportunities for unconditional borrowing might be justified from the world point of view on the grounds that the maximum amounts involved are small in relation to the size of the relevant economy. The situation changes once the country borrows, in addition, on the private market. In this event, there are always implicit conditions affecting margins above the London interbank offered rate (LIBOR) and the availability of credit; and if no explicit conditions are being applied, one can assume that the implicit conditions concerning economic management, political stability, and so on, are fulfilled. Furthermore, if the country is borrowing from the Fund in the higher credit tranches, conditionality also applies. It follows that any country that is either borrowing on the private capital market or borrowing beyond its first tranche from the Fund, or both, is subject to conditionality.

An increased issue of SDRs is likely to reduce countries' borrowing from the Fund or the private market, or both. But it could be argued that, as long as countries continue to borrow to some extent either beyond the first credit tranche or on the private market, the degree of conditionality will not really be altered. Only if countries are issued sufficient SDRs to allow them to avoid such conditional borrowing (or to allow them to move to lower credit tranches) will there be a weakening of conditionality. In practice, it seems inevitable that a universal issue of SDRs of an amount significantly above present levels *would* put many countries in this position—weakening condi-

---

[2] I am indebted to George von Furstenberg for drawing my attention to this issue and suggesting the general line of approach.

tionality and possibly making all their borrowing unconditional. This could be true, in particular, of all those countries that have low credit ratings on the private market and possibly are making little use of the market now.

If one accepts the case for associating conditionality with the international creation of official liquidity to supplement the private market on the grounds of the "insurance argument," it seems to follow that one must have reservations about a large-scale issue of unconditional SDRs. The case is stronger for increasing quotas or issuing SDRs direct to the Fund to strengthen its resources for conditional lending.

At this point, something must again be said about the relationship of the preceding discussion to the current situation. It has been a theme of this paper that the private capital market has been available to generate both owned reserves and liquidity, so that the official "insurance" arrangements need only be regarded as supplementary. Furthermore, it will be stressed later that a flaw in much of the discussion of international monetary reform until the mid-seventies was a failure to appreciate the crucial role of the capital market. But I have noted above the possibility or prospect that the role of the capital market in providing funds to many sovereign borrowers may be coming to an end, and that the private market may be overreacting in this respect. The review of the past in Section III, below, suggests that discussions of supposedly long-term international monetary issues have frequently been overinfluenced by current conditions or preoccupations. One should beware of this now. Nevertheless, the possibility that a decline or change in the private market will justify a considerable expansion of the resources of the Fund must be taken into account. At the same time, since private lending is essentially conditional, whether implicit or explicit (and where it is not, it must be regarded as unwise lending), it seems reasonable that if some private lending needs to be replaced, it should be replaced primarily by *conditional* public lending.

SDRs as Aid

A general issue of SDRs subsidizes borrowers and possibly taxes lenders. The subsidy benefit goes not only to those who would have been borrowers in the private market in any event but also to those who are able to borrow for the first time. Because the latter consist mainly or wholly of the poorest developing countries and the former also consist more of developing than developed countries (although this varies year by year, and a generalization is difficult), this particular international redistribution of income would probably tend to favor the poor over the rich—the latter including, notably, the OPEC low absorbers, the Federal Republic of Germany, and Japan. On the other hand, it has to be remembered that a rich nation is not prohibited from using its SDRs.

The SDR system provides the opportunity to introduce much more explicit discrimination into the system, thus raising the "link" issue. But a possibility of discrimination also exists in determining the size of Fund quotas (or the size of drawing rights relative to quotas), so that there is not necessarily a distinction between these two devices in this respect. It is understandable that developing countries prefer to receive unconditional liquidity—even though the interest rate on SDRs is much closer to market rates than it was once—rather than conditional liquidity. If aid is to be given in this form rather than through the usual channels, my own preference would be for conditionality, but this raises issues that go well beyond the scope of this paper.

Conclusion—SDRs Within the Present System

Suppose we stay within the present laissez-faire system. There will be a need for some officially owned reserves and certainly for liquidity. In this system, the international capital market has, until now, generated both as required. The problem of reserve adequacy or excess has not arisen. Because exchange rates can move, a country can choose its own monetary policies, and its reserve situation—which in any case is endogenous—need not determine domestic inflation or recession. There are, of course, many external constraints on countries—real interest rates and terms of trade, principally—so that exchange rate flexibility does not give them independence in a real sense. Within the constraints, it only frees them to influence those real effects (e.g., short-term unemployment) that depend on domestic money supply policies.

There is an argument in favor of a substitution account designed to reduce exchange rate fluctuations, but I find this argument tenuous. The only connection between SDRs and the domestic macroeconomic disequilibria that have dominated countries since 1973 is through exchange rate variability; only if a substitution of SDRs for a multicurrency system actually succeeded in reducing exchange rate variability—itself a doubtful assumption—might SDRs also have some favorable effect—although hardly an overwhelming one—on domestic macroeconomic situations.

It is doubtful that there is a really significant role for the SDR to play within the framework of the current system. This does not, of course, exclude a modest role. Possibly some weight should be given to the risk-spreading role of a large financial intermediary owned by all the world's governments that would have the ability to reduce, rather than merely shifting, world risks, and consequently to narrow interest rate margins. Unless the world capital market breaks down (that is, if international, as distinct from national, lending and borrowing cease or become very difficult), there will be no need to use SDR allocations to influence aggregate world reserve levels. But it may be justified to create some SDRs to compensate for a possible tendency of the international capital market to overreact to recent events and *under*lend to developing countries. If this is the motive, it would be logical to limit the SDR issue purely to developing countries.

The issue of SDRs or any kind of international reserve asset can be regarded as a desirable mutual insurance system, but here an association with conditionality seems to be appropriate, so that an increase in quotas, or of Fund resources possibly denominated in SDRs and available for conditional lending, is preferable to an increase in unconditional SDRs. This would also be a way of preparing for the possibility of reduced lending to sovereign borrowers by the international capital market. Finally, the issue of SDRs can have some effect, even if small, on international income distribution and the question is whether this could be better done through SDR allocations than through two alternatives—namely, differential quota arrangements associated with conditionality or explicit aid, bilateral or multilateral.

II. A FIXED-EXCHANGE-RATE WORLD

It seems unlikely that the major industrial nations will return to a system of fixed exchange rates, with or without occasional exchange rate adjustments. Now that they have tasted monetary policy freedom, it is improbable that they would give it up. This is so, even though much lip service is paid to the virtues of fixed rates and though it is clear that no one really likes fluctuating exchange rates. What national decision makers like is the monetary policy freedom that inevitably leads to fluctuating rates. Similarly, it seems unlikely that they will accept constraints on their use of the international capital market, including constraints on their choice of reserve assets. Nevertheless, one can, perhaps, envisage two different scenarios.

According to the first scenario, the world economy gradually calms down and stabilizes, essentially because of greater stability in macroeconomic policies and more successful ad hoc policy coordination between different countries aimed at avoiding the large medium-term exchange rate variations that the world has seen since 1973. But this would be the outcome not of formal international constraints or rules but of improved domestic policies. An agreement to fix nominal exchange rate relationships for as long as possible, without firm commitment—rather like an extended European Monetary System—might then be the result of such an essentially evolutionary process. The question is what implications this would have for the SDR.

It would mean that the choice of one currency basket over another would matter little to central banks. When there is reasonable certainty about future exchange rate relationships—a special case of which is certainty that rates will stay fixed to each other—there is less need to choose portfolios carefully, provided interest rates are flexible and capital markets (including forward markets) free. This means that countries would be more willing to subscribe voluntarily to a substitution account if there were some international pressure to do so. On the other hand, it also means that they might just as well hold dollars, or whatever was the favored reserve currency in that far-ahead halcyon era. In other words, the SDR might become more acceptable because it would matter less. These developments might lead to increased use of Fund-issued SDRs, or of private baskets denominated in SDRs, because world stability had been restored and not because such stability resulted from, or depended on, the SDR. We have no argument in favor of the SDR here; only an expectation of its innocuousness.

The second scenario—which seems rather less probable—is that exchange rate conditions get more and more unstable; elements of the international financial system "collapse"; and inflation and/or unemployment get worse. In other words, there is a crisis, whether slow or sudden. This may then lead to so much dissatisfaction—with blame being attached to the international monetary system—that policymakers will be psychologically ready to try a drastic change. One can imagine a great international conference designed to sort out all these problems. Possibly it would be preceded by major changes of governments, with the new governments all promising to come up with solutions. One can then conceive of a decision to establish a fixed-exchange-rate system with centralized determination of reserves and with the Fund turning into some kind of international central bank. The Fund might be instructed, or constitutionally committed, to follow a conservative monetary policy. The Keynes Plan or the various plans inspired by Triffin might then come into their own.

In current conditions, one finds this latter scenario hard to imagine. After all, if the major economies become more and more unstable, and especially if inflation and unemployment worsen, this is likely to occur mainly because governments have found it difficult to constrain their own citizens—that is, to impose constraints on sectional interests and to make compatible their excessive competing demands. Would it then be possible for the international community—in effect, a collective of major governments—to impose constraints on its constituent parts? But it is in such a situation that the SDR might come into its own, not because of its particular denomination but because of its status as the sole official international reserve asset, the regulation of which would ensure that world reserves were neither inadequate nor excessive. It is, of course, with fixed exchange rates that reserve levels determine, or at least influence, world inflation.

This is the Keynes-Triffin vision. As it has been spelled out so often, I hardly need go into it in detail here. Countries would still have some flexibility, since they would be able to borrow and lend in the world capital market. Presumably, the official sector would be prohibited from operating in the market directly, but budget deficits could be financed by sales of bonds at home; and, through the linking of capital markets, such deficits would, in effect, be financed on the world market. There would have to be compulsory substitution of existing reserve assets and a prohibition on central banks' dealing in gold. Although the dollar might still be the intervention currency, there would have to be a firm limit on the amount of dollars that could be held by central banks. Finally, and perhaps most importantly, the United States would have to be treated like any other country. It would have to settle its deficits in SDRs. To use the once-popular jargon, there would have to be "symmetry" through "asset settlement."

It is possible to imagine a fixed-rate system in which the SDR is neither the sole nor a major reserve asset. The world could return to a more or less fixed-rate system on a dollar standard. We know that such a system can work. On the other hand, it would give the United States the privilege of determining (or greatly influencing) the world inflation rate. Therefore, it is hardly conceivable that the imaginary international conference would agree to so asymmetrical an arrangement, although its outcome might be just as good as, or even better than, the outcome if crucial money supply decisions were made through some international mechanism. It follows that a decision to move to a fixed-rate system would inevitably involve a major role for an international reserve asset.

The outside possibility of such a system being established suggests that there is a case for keeping SDRs going currently (quite apart from their use within the present system). They may not have a very significant current role, and possibly little future role, but it seems useful to have a device in operation that can be utilized and expanded should a real or perceived need for SDRs arise.

Finally, one cannot leave this discussion of a world-wide fixed-exchange-rate system and a world central bank without noting the underlying issue. This concerns the desirable degree of centralization of monetary decision making. At the one extreme is the present decentralized system, with the market, combined with ad hoc arrangements, coordinating the consequences of national governmental and private decisions. At the other extreme is internationally centralized decision making. The issue is not whether governments should intervene—they inevitably do so through their monetary and fiscal policies—but whether there should be a substantial element of "world government," with international voting or political bargaining within a centralized framework replacing the market and ad hoc bargaining.

This issue does not arise when various modest proposals for the SDR within the present system are discussed—for example, whether SDRs should be increased to a small extent, supplementing existing reserve assets, or whether there should be a voluntary substitution account. In that event, the Fund would become just another actor in the market. It arises only in connection with the ambitious Keynes-Triffin world central bank proposals that are only meaningful if exchange rates are fixed.

Let us put aside for the moment the question of which system of organization would be preferable from a world point of view. The prior question is whether there is the slightest chance that decentralized market forces can be prevented from operating. We know that even in socialist countries, it is difficult—in spite of all the authority of the state—to hold market forces down. It seems obvious that this must be so in the international community, where there is no effective state authority. The proposal really is to make the world—or perhaps the major industrial countries, combined with any other countries that choose to join—an area of monetary integration.

There are cases where sovereign nations have effectively been part of monetary unions; but in those cases the leadership—that is, the monetary decisions—has come from a major nation, to which others have voluntarily attached themselves and from which they have been free to detach themselves. Usually the minor partner has been an ex-colony or economic dependency of some kind. It is a different matter for genuinely sovereign nations, several of large economic size, to engage in monetary integration without prior or simultaneous political integration. These difficulties have been discussed in connection with proposals for European monetary integration. It has not been possible to bring about monetary integration in the European Community; it is unlikely to be possible for a much larger grouping.

Logically, one must distinguish the possible or probable from the desirable. Perhaps attainment of the Keynes-Triffin vision may not be very probable, but would it be desirable? The present system certainly leads to considerable disharmony and friction. Policies of particular governments with respect to their monetary, exchange rate, and fiscal policies may have adverse effects on other countries or, at least, on sectors of other countries; an example is the recent tight money policy of the United States. The policies may also be unwise from the point of view of the interests of their own citizens. But would a world central bank do better? Would it produce steadier monetary growth? Presumably, it would have to estimate changes in the world demand for international money (SDRs) assuming zero or steady inflation, but this might present some difficulty if national moneys were still used domestically and, perhaps, if the private sector were still using national moneys in international trade and the capital market.

Governments are frequently faced with dilemmas. They have to balance increased unemployment in the short run against increased inflation later. Political judgments must be made to strike the balance, bearing in mind the need to maintain public support for policies, to avoid social tensions, and to maximize the present value of the expected real-income effects, perhaps weighted by income-distribution considerations. It seems to me that decisions like these are best made within the nation-state. Of course, the theory of optimum currency areas teaches us that a state can be too small, or its size at least nonoptimal, to conduct an independent monetary policy. At the moment, one can conceive of Western Europe making up an optimal currency area, but it seems to me highly unlikely that this could be said about a larger grouping that would include, in addition, North America and Japan, let alone the whole nonsocialist world.

III. A REVIEW OF THE PAST

The SDR does seem to be a relic of the visions of the recent past. If it did not exist already, we might now create it, but certainly with far less ambitious intentions than have prevailed at various times. In any event, given that the SDR exists, there is good reason for keeping it, at the minimum, in hibernation. Let me now review this past in a little more detail. Are any of the arguments for the SDR that were used in the past relevant now? What has changed? What were the crucial assumptions?[3]

The Triffin Problem—Inadequate Reserves?

The Triffin (1960) argument, which was so widely accepted in the sixties and early seventies, rested completely on the assumption of fixed exchange rates, fixed not just relative to the dollar but also relative to gold. It was argued, or usually implied, that dollars were being held not as a store of value that could buy U.S. goods and services but for their convertibility into gold. With the gold stock rising very slowly, the growth of world reserves depended on the U.S. deficit. This deficit, if it continued, would steadily lower the ratio of U.S. gold holdings to U.S. international liabilities.

Eventually, confidence in the convertibility of dollars into gold would be lost. Then, the dreaded moment might arrive when the system would

---

[3]In preparing this section, I have benefited particularly from reading Whitman (1974), Solomon (1977), Williamson (1977), and Willett (1980). It has also been instructive to reread various classic writings, notably Triffin (1960) and Machlup (1968).

"break down"—that is, the dollar would have to be devalued relative to gold and possibly relative to other currencies. It also seemed to be implied at first that the U.S. deficit was a current account deficit; later, account was taken of long-term capital outflows, which yielded a "basic deficit." The implication was usually that this deficit was, in some sense, exogenous and could not be run indefinitely, even if the confidence problem did not come to a head.

Thus, the dollar deficit would have to come to an end, and reserves would cease to grow, apart from small increments resulting from new gold production. It would, therefore, become necessary to supplement world reserves with a new internationally created asset, the supply of which would grow in accordance with the requirements of world trade. This was the basic logic of the SDR. It would not be necessary to stop countries acquiring dollars or to encourage them to substitute dollars for SDRs—that idea came later— because either the supply of new dollars would come to an end in any event (because the U.S. deficit "could not go on") or countries would not want to hold dollars—or extra dollars—any more (because of the confidence problem). The implication was that the dollar exchange standard would atrophy. Gradually, the SDR would replace gold and the dollar as the principal reserve assets held outside the United States.

Later, there were some in the United States who saw the SDR as a way of saving the dollar from the confidence problem. SDRs issued to the United States would provide as good a backing for the dollar as gold. The implication was that the gold exchange standard could be turned, at least partially, into an SDR exchange standard.

Even while continuing to accept the fixed exchange rate and fixed price of gold assumptions, it seems to me that there were two flaws in this approach.

First, the potential convertibility of dollars into gold was, arguably, not the central feature of the system at all. Formally it was—as a relic of a system of the past—but, in practice, dollars were being held for their own sake, as a source of liquidity that could potentially be turned into goods and services and that earned a reasonable positive real rate of interest. This became clear even before the formal ending of convertibility, when the dollar was already de facto inconvertible (or, at least, its convertibility was already much in doubt); yet countries were accumulating dollars on a vast scale. To some extent this accumulation was by accident, a by-product of a reluctance by various countries to appreciate their exchange rates because of an "exchange rate protection" motive to help their export industries. It may also be admitted that the U.S. Government put pressure on other governments not to convert dollars into gold. But if other countries did want to move out of dollars into gold or other currencies, while the U.S. Treasury (and U.S. private companies) wished to continue short-term borrowing from foreigners, directly or indirectly, the U.S. authorities could have increased the inducement by raising short-term interest rates. But the interest rate was not a variable in the popular "Triffin-type" models.

The second flaw was that the approach ignored the role of the private capital market in generating reserves. This was noted by Depres, Kindleberger, and Salant (1966). The point was developed further by Kindleberger (see various papers reprinted in Kindleberger (1981) and McKinnon (1969)). Reserves were generated not just through current accounts but by countries borrowing long from the United States and lending short. In fact, strictly, they did not borrow from and lend to "the United States," but to a considerable extent from and to banks that were mainly, but not wholly, American and operated in dollars. The vital role of the world capital market is clearly seen now. At the time, the market was only emerging, and understanding of its significance was limited. It has to be stressed that the market can generate reserves—and, by providing ready liquidity, can also reduce the need for owned reserves—even in a fixed-exchange-rate system.

The Triffin model really reflected "current account thinking." This was understandable, because the world capital market, or the access of the world to the U.S. capital market, had only got underway in the sixties, mainly owing to the gradual reduction of exchange controls and the growth of multinationals. Formal models still focused on the current account, treating long-term capital movements as exogenous and short-term capital movements (operating partly through leads and lags) as destabilizing, irrational nuisances.

The Triffin Problem with Flexible Rates

What difference does removal of the fixed-exchange-rate assumption make to the whole argument? At the time, exchange rate flexibility—other than in the form of agreed and infrequent changes in par values—was ruled out, because of memories of the competitive devaluations of the thirties. No doubt these were more a consequence than a cause of the Great Depression and the prolongation of unemployment; but just as exchange rate flexibility has to take more blame in popular thinking than it deserves in the seventies and now, so this was true of the thirties. The "breakdown of the system," rarely specified in detail, was visualized as a return to the exchange rate "disorder" of the thirties.

It was sometimes suggested that *if* exchange rates were flexible, there would be no need for official reserves. This is only correct if one is referring to a *pure* floating system. The move to flexible rates has not made the earlier discussion of reserve need and adequacy irrelevant, since we have not moved to a pure floating system. Our laissez-faire, managed-floating-exchange-rate system still generates a need for official reserves, as well as for liquidity available to central banks in the form of ready access to borrowing from the world capital market. Thus, in this respect, the earlier discussions are not outdated. Furthermore, if there *were* a pure floating system (with no official intervention at all), there would still be a need for nations to run current account imbalances and to import or export short-term capital in order to smooth out real spending in response to various shocks. This would be done wholly by the private sector or by elements of the public sector borrowing and lending abroad, thus bypassing the central bank. There would be a greater need for liquidity, and possibly also for owned reserves, on the part of the private sector.

In another respect, the earlier discussions do seem outdated. With flexible rates, a reserve inadequacy—if there is one because the capital market does not function fully—need no longer lead to world deflation. As explained earlier, the inevitable link between reserve situations and the pressure of demand for domestic resources is broken. Countries may still choose to intervene in foreign exchange markets and fail to sterilize the domestic monetary effects, but international commitments do not compel them to do so.

Here it must be noted that the discussions about a new monetary system usually assumed firmly fixed rates, although they allowed for rare and reluctant discrete exchange rate adjustments. In practice, under the Bretton Woods system, it was up to countries to alter par values, an opportunity that France made use of several times and Britain twice. Thus, reserve inadequacy for a few countries could be dealt with by depreciation associated with appropriate domestic disabsorption. But a worldwide inadequacy would imply widespread devaluations—that is, competitive devaluations. In fact, for the non-U.S. world it could be resolved by an appreciation of the U.S. dollar relative to all other currencies, something that in practice could only be brought about piecemeal. This would mean also, incidentally, an appreciation of the price of gold in terms of all non-U.S. currencies.

The Breakdown—Excessive Reserves?

The system finally broke down in February 1973. The non-U.S. world had accumulated dollars on a vast scale over a few years, the result of U.S. monetary expansion combined with the reluctance of other countries to appreciate their currencies relative to the dollar. This reluctance reflected partly a natural lag in understanding the significance of the new situation and partly the exchange rate protection motive. It is not unreasonable to say—contrary to General de Gaulle—that the dollar accumulations of countries outside the United States were essentially voluntary. Nonetheless, in due course, there had to be appreciations by countries like the Federal Republic of Germany if they were to insulate themselves, at least partially, from the inflation that had originated in the United States. But many countries failed to revalue, or to do so sufficiently, so that the inflation was indeed exported all round the world, subsequently feeding on itself within each country through the inflationary expectations that were generated and largely accommodated by monetary expansion. Furthermore, the inflationary response to reserve accumulations reflected, in some cases, deliberate expansionary policies designed to stimulate growth—policies that were no longer inhibited by balance of payments constraints. At the same time, in 1971, the United States had a strong exchange-rate-protection motive to devalue the dollar relative to other major currencies, especially the yen.

It should be added here that gold convertibility of the dollar ceased in 1971. Thus, the formal gold exchange standard broke down at that point. But this was not, in my view, the crucial development. The key events were, rather, the devaluation of the dollar relative to other currencies and the general move toward flexibility.

The new situation of dollar accumulation and flexible rates created a complete transmutation of attitudes about the SDR. It did not seem sensible to add to world reserves, so that the new instrument, born in 1967, was not allowed to grow in its crucial infancy stage. The need was now seen to *limit* reserves. But this is a much more difficult task than creating a new reserve asset and thus (possibly) increasing total reserves. Instead of allowing the use of the dollar to atrophy, or at least allowing it to become progressively less important over time, it appeared to become necessary to impose restrictions to limit its use. This led to proposals that appear, in retrospect, somewhat unrealistic. It is much easier to add a new asset to the world's portfolio than to force sovereign governments to give up an existing asset.

The more important implication of the new flexible exchange rate regime was, as discussed earlier, that it broke the inevitable nexus between reserve levels and the domestic pressure of demand. It could not be said that countries had to inflate because they had lots of reserves. In fact, it was more the other way round: the countries with low inflation tended to accumulate the reserves. But this nexus was not broken in the international monetary reform discussions that were in progress at the very time the new laissez-faire era was beginning, because the view prevailed that it was desirable—and likely—that the world would return to a more regulated, possibly a new par value, system.

The Dollar Obsession

At about the same time a concern—even an obsession—developed, not about the total of reserves but about the "monopoly of the dollar," the asymmetry of the system. The objection was both that the United States obtained seigniorage and that, apparently, it had a freedom of monetary policy that other countries did not have. Motivating the various schemes for replacing dollars with SDRs or, alternatively, raising the price of gold and forcing the United States into "asset settlement" (i.e., automatically converting dollars held by non-U.S. central banks into gold or SDRs) were the great dollar accumulation of 1970-72 and the anti-Americanism pervading Europe in the late sixties. There are three aspects to this question.

First, there was the view that the United States was able to export inflation and, implicitly, other countries were forced to import it. As I have stressed, this was a result of the fixed-exchange-rate system, or of the reluctance of other countries to alter par values. With flexible rates, there is no need to import inflation, and yet the dollar can continue to be the main reserve asset.

Second, there was the argument that the use of the dollar as a reserve asset generated seigniorage for the United States. It would clearly be better if this went either to the world community in general or to developing countries. The implication was that either zero interest was paid on dollar balances or that the interest rate was below market rates. It came to be recognized that banks were competitive, and operations in the Eurodollar market were not limited to U.S. banks. Furthermore, interest was paid on U.S. Treasury bills. Thus, seigniorage would either be low or competed away completely. Nevertheless, there would be some modest seigniorage going to the United States because of the increased need for U.S. base money, and one might guess that the U.S. financial community would benefit somewhat from the world use of the dollar.

This relates to the third aspect. The special role of the dollar is not arbitrary. It is not arbitrary that once sterling was the principal world currency and reserve asset; then, there was a gradual shift to the dollar—so that there was a period when there was a multicurrency system; and now there is some modest shift to the deutsche mark and, to a lesser extent, to yen and Swiss francs. A greater shift to yen would certainly seem logical. Central banks are free to compete for the privilege of producing the base for a reserve asset. If a country is a major trader, if it has a well-functioning capital market which depends, above all, on the absence of inhibiting regulations, combined possibly with some appropriate supervision, and if it has political stability and the assurance of this lasting for a long time, it can get its currency used as a reserve asset. There are economies of scale in this, as in other businesses, so it is not surprising that the tendency is toward oligopoly and, at times, even monopoly. But there is free entry.

It is well known that countries like the Federal Republic of Germany, Japan, and Switzerland have not desired this supposed privilege. It is curious that the United States has been keen for the dollar to remain a (or the) reserve asset—even though this may lead to more fluctuations in the dollar than otherwise—while other governments have not wanted their currencies to move into this field—even though they are forgoing some modest amounts of seigniorage and profits. A natural conservatism all around may be reflected in these national preferences.

Multicurrency System and Substitution Problem

The concern about the special privilege of the dollar seems now to have died down. To a considerable extent, it was, as I have said, a result of the great dollar accumulation of 1970-72. Subsequently there has been some switch from dollars to deutsche mark, yen, and other currencies. Presumably, this should have been welcomed by those who regretted the special privileges of the dollar. But it was not. A new concern came to the fore.

When the dollar was devalued sharply relative to other major currencies in 1977 and 1978, the expectation of further devaluation intensified switching from dollars to other currencies. It is also possible that switching itself contributed to the devaluation, although the prime causes of the dollar devaluation clearly lay in domestic macroeconomic policies. These events gave rise to fears of an avalanche of dollars falling on the foreign exchange market or, at least, that a sufficient amount of dollars would be sold to create great instability. Thus, there was once more a transmutation of motive for SDRs. In any case, the recent dollar appreciation seems to have laid to rest for the moment the fears of an unstable multicurrency system. Now—until the dollar is devalued again—everyone seems to be happy holding dollars, even though the dollar no longer has the overwhelmingly predominant role in official foreign exchange reserves that it had less than ten years ago.

Role of Gold

I have said little about gold so far. Central to the Triffin approach was the objection to a rise in the price of gold. Although the U.S. authorities were not always, or possibly ever, sympathetic to the idea of a new reserve asset, they were in agreement that the price of gold should not be raised. The reasons—adverse wealth and income distribution effects, combined with the waste of real resources resulting from stimulating gold production—seem very plausible. So the SDR was originally conceived of as "paper gold." A period ensued when gold appeared to have been phased out of the system, with the central banks of the Group of Ten agreeing neither to buy nor to sell it. Combined with the accumulation of dollars, this meant that the principal competition for the SDR seemed to come from foreign exchange, not gold;

hence, the SDR interest rate was raised, and the SDR is now equivalent to a basket of five risk-free, interest-bearing currencies.

With regard to gold, as Grubel (1982) has noted, market forces have gradually reasserted themselves. The price of gold rose in the free market, and the attempt to isolate the official sector from this market has only partially succeeded. It is now usual to value officially held gold at the market, rather than the official, price; and official gold has formally entered the system through the arrangements of the European Monetary System. The real test will come when a major gold holder, such as France, badly needs to use its reserves. Will it then treat gold just like foreign exchange reserves, spending it as needed?

Gold seems, thus, to be creeping back into the system. Even though gold holders receive no interest, the expected rate of return is positive because of expected capital appreciation that, in turn, varies sharply with the degree of uncertainty in the world. The variability of this expected rate of return reduces, but does not eliminate, the attraction of gold as a reserve asset. The positive relationship between uncertainty in the world and the expected rate of return on gold rests on historical and sociopsychological factors. Hence, it is hard to believe that the SDR can ever substitute for gold; insofar as it can substitute for anything, it can do so only for foreign exchange.

IV. CONCLUSION

At the beginning of this paper, I noted the "realities-intentions gap" about the SDR and speculated whether the SDR was just a relic or whether the proclaimed intention to make the SDR "the principal reserve asset in the international monetary system" laid the groundwork for possible changes.

The greater part of the paper has been devoted to an analysis of the current international monetary nonsystem and to a detailed discussion of possible problems or limitations of this system and of the extent to which SDRs could deal with these problems. I then speculated whether a new fixed-rate system with centrally controlled reserves might be established and considered the implications of such a system. Finally, I proceeded to a review of the evolution of thinking about the SDR and how this has been related to actual events. The reasons for the creation of the SDR have changed over time. At first, there was a concern about inadequate reserves, then about excessive reserves, next about the special role of the dollar, and finally about the multicurrency system. Perhaps we have now moved into a fifth stage where the concern is not about inadequate reserves for the world as a whole, but specifically for developing countries.

Let me conclude by summarizing the practical implications that seem to come out of this discussion.

First, there is always the outside possibility that at some stage the international community will decide to construct a new fixed-exchange-rate system with centralized determination of reserves. This might be the response to a major international crisis, though it is an outcome that seems unlikely. In that case, an international reserve asset such as the SDR would come into its own. It would then be useful if the SDR, and the various arrangements associated with it, already existed. Thus, even though the SDR might have little significant role or prospects within the present system, it might be a good idea to keep it going at a modest level should the situation change.

Second, it seems improbable that a voluntary substitution account would make much difference to the instability of exchange rates. The basic causes for instability can be found in the macroeconomic policies of the major countries. There are difficulties about a substitution account (discussed in other chapters), but from the point of view of the system, voluntary substitution might conceivably do a little good by modifying short-term shifts between currencies; it is unlikely to do any harm—other than to those who would ultimately bear any losses the account might incur.

Third, the SDR can be an instrument of international income redistribution, especially for those countries that at present are not able to use the international capital market at all, or only to a very small extent. The number of these countries has increased lately. A case can, of course, be made for such redistribution. But if really large sums are to be involved, the donors—in fact, the potential acquirers of SDRs—would surely look for some degree of conditionality.

Fourth, it is possible that the effect of recent difficulties in the international capital market will be an undue reluctance by the private capital market to lend to developing countries. By "undue," I mean that lending would be too low from a world efficiency point of view, bearing in mind prospective risks. This can provide a qualified argument for an increase in SDRs within the present system. The issue might be limited to developing countries; possibly it ought to be associated with conditionality (through the issue being made to the Fund, which could then supplement or replace the lending of private banks, as appropriate); and it would certainly not represent a move toward "making the special drawing right the principal reserve asset of the international monetary system."

Fifth, and most important, the principal justification for the international creation of reserve assets is as a mutual insurance arrangement among nations. But this raises the issue of moral hazard, which calls for supervision by the World Insurance Company. It is here that one can see the key role of the Fund. The annual consultations can be regarded as a form of supervision before claims on the company are made, while conditionality is supervision associated with the controlled payment of claims. Perhaps the analogy can be pushed too far, but it does draw attention to the crucial role of conditionality.

SDRs are at present *unconditional* drawing rights, and I have suggested that—insofar as a significant expansion of international liquidity is justified on insurance grounds (and I believe that it is)—this would then be better done through increases in quotas or the expansion of the direct resources of the Fund. This could, alternatively, be achieved by issuing SDRs initially to the Fund rather than directly to members. Hence, to that extent, there appears to be a clear potential role for an expansion of SDRs within the present system. But it has to be added that much the same objective could be achieved through the normal expansion of quotas or by the Fund borrowing on the capital market, in the latter case with members of the Fund collectively guaranteeing the loans.

REFERENCES

Corden, W. M., "The Logic of the International Monetary Non-System," in *Reflections on a Troubled World Economy*, ed. by F. Machlup and others (London: Macmillan (for the Trade Policy Research Center), 1983).

Depres, Emile, Charles P. Kindleberger, and Walter S. Salant, "The Dollar and World Liquidity—A Minority View," *Economist*, Vol. 218 (February 5, 1966), pp. 526-29.

Grubel, Herbert G., "Gold and the Dollar Crisis: Twenty Years Later," Ch. 12 in *The International Monetary System Under Flexible Exchange Rates: Global, Regional, and National*, ed. by Richard N. Cooper, Peter B. Kenen, Jorge Braga de Macedo, and Jacques van Ypersele (Cambridge, Massachusetts: Ballinger, 1982), pp. 185-202.

Haberler, Gottfried, "How Important Is Control over Reserves?" in *The New International Monetary System*, ed. by Robert A. Mundell and Jacques J. Polak (New York: Columbia University Press, 1977), pp. 109-32.

Kindleberger, Charles P., *International Money: A Collection of Essays* (London: Allen & Unwin, 1981), pp. 1-328.

Machlup, Fritz, *Remaking the International Monetary System: The Rio Agreement and Beyond* (Baltimore: Johns Hopkins Press, and New York: Committee for Economic Development, 1968).

_____, *The World Monetary Order*, Zahid Husain Memorial Lecture Series, No. 5 (Karachi: State Bank of Pakistan, 1981), pp. 1-26.

McKinnon, Ronald I., *Private and Official International Money: The Case for the Dollar*, Essays in International Finance, No. 74 (Princeton, New Jersey: International Finance Section, Princeton University, 1969).

_____, "Currency Substitution and Instability in the World Dollar Market," *American Economic Review*, Vol. 72 (June 1982), pp. 320-33.

Polak, Jacques J., *Coordination of National Economic Policies*, Group of Thirty, Occasional Paper No. 7 (New York, 1981).

Solomon, Robert, *The International Monetary System, 1945–1976* (New York: Harper and Row, 1977).

Triffin, Robert, *Gold and the Dollar Crisis: The Future of Convertibility* (New Haven, Connecticut: Yale University Press, 1960).

Whitman, Marina v.N., "The Current and Future Role of the Dollar: How Much Symmetry?" *Brookings Papers on Economic Activity: 3* (1974), pp. 539–91.

Willett, Thomas D., *International Liquidity Issues* (Washington: American Enterprise Institute for Public Policy Research, 1980).

Williamson, John H., *The Failure of World Monetary Reform, 1971–1974* (New York: New York University Press, 1977).

Comments

Sven Grassman

Corden's paper is a lucid and forceful analysis on the well-known theme of international monetary reserves. It contains an instructive summary of a four-decade-long tradition of academic theorizing. With today's staggering economic and social problems, the subject acquires some of the serious concern and sense of urgency that surrounded the Keynesian origination of the Bretton Woods system during World War II. While some passages take new looks at the old, intriguing issues, I feel that Corden's paper basically tries to show that the whole traditional strand is somewhat futile, that the issue, as usually formulated, is a kind of blind alley and not very helpful in rescuing us from today's predicaments.

The conflict between the professional legacy and the pressing need to eliminate policy stalemates is illustrated by the author's struggle to find a role for the SDR under varying conditions. Corden shows how different, actually even contrary, arguments have been used to motivate SDR allocations.

One might have wished to see in the paper more suggestions of a new, constructive approach beside the elegant critique and burial of the old issues. In my comment, I will resist the temptation to talk about the old issues (although I would take much nostalgic pleasure in this). Instead, I will try to set out what, in my view, must be the new orientation of our analysis.

Today, the analysis of international monetary phenomena must not be preoccupied with reserves and the practical offsetting of national net surpluses and deficits. These issues are important, but they are largely symptoms and reflections of the basic forces that govern international relations and economic performance. As in marital relations, the exchange of golden rings may be important, but more important is the analysis of income, housing, sex, and psychology. My metaphor is brutal, but not altogether unfair to the hundreds of subtle articles we have seen in the glamorous literature on international reserves.

In Corden's paper, I sense an impatience with old issues and an urge to concentrate on conditionality, market relations, and other mechanisms that could affect internal macro behavior. But I would like to go much further and propose a more radical shift of perspective. Let me try to indicate some of the old and new issues as I see them (see Table 1).

248

TABLE 1. REDEFINITION OF INTERNATIONAL MONETARY ISSUES IN A SLUMPING
WORLD ECONOMY

New Focus	Old Focus
Exchange Rate Theory	
Gross financial assets	Net real flows
Scope	
Overall financial structure	Official reserves
Policy Issues	
Internal macro policy	International side effects
Output, prices, and interest rates	Budget and current account balances
National Targets	
Price stability and exports seem now to be main concern.	Not consumption and imports (which is presupposition in reserve approach)
Roots of Disorder	
National conflicts—business/labor, private/public, and over internal wealth— determine output, inflation, and exchange rates.	Not residual imbalances between countries *Exception*: oil
Political Forces	
Household and union interests must have stronger influence on policy in each country (and obviously on international institutions).	Banks, businesses, and men (!) essentially rule the world today.

The current account balance, and thus the real net transfer of resources, is at the center of traditional analysis. But the underlying assumptions of high employment with present consumption and imports as major positive arguments in national welfare functions are not fulfilled. Low capacity utilization and export surpluses seem to be the revealed preference rather than full employment and high consumption. In terms of a political trade-off, unemployment has, in many countries, become less forbidding than inflation.

In this context, lack of reserves is hardly the constraining factor. In foreign exchange markets, current account developments get swamped by financial effects of macro policy—as they should, if we think that assets determine exchange rates, and if payments are not limited to current transactions—as was largely the case before the 1970s.

Conditionality is one particular aspect where the reserve issue is not only a matter of financial settlement but where terms and prices may feed back to behavior. However, in a world of massive excess savings and deep mercantilist undercurrents in the dominant industrial world, the need to discipline deficit countries does seem less important than the need to reward lower savings and to increase strong countries' willingness to incur external and internal financial deficits.

Attitudes to current account and budget deficits can only marginally be affected by changes in reserve arrangements. Conflicts and tensions are of such an open and fundamentally political character within nations that they seem to result in either overall stagnation or expansion, depending on the balance between industry and labor, conservative forces and more progressive ones. By their nature, changes in reserves and lending conditions cannot do much to alter the outcome of the intense political struggle that now goes on within major countries and that for years has upset macro policies.

Whatever could be done to improve financial setoffs, recycling, and reserve arrangements must be done, of course. But I tend to agree that private capital markets have delivered and solved their task, limited as it has been, quite well in the last decade. Improvements are welcome but will not greatly affect the major political struggle that upsets our economies.

This is not said in a sense of resignation. Maybe political behavior is even more susceptible to argument and change (when the consequences of faulty policy measures become clear to us) than complicated technical circumstance that is often perceived as necessity. It is even possible to discuss deeper political change disguised as changes in technical arrangements.

Maybe Lord Keynes' sense of urgency, his clear insights into our true economic dilemmas, and the very fact that he and others discussed international monetary relations in a very serious atmosphere was more important than their vision and specific actions on the technical arrangements.

Much has changed in 40 years. But with new methods, fresh perspectives—some of which I have hinted at in the table—and the same sincerity, I trust that reason can prevail and that some progress can be made in reforming the system.

There is, however, *one* technicality that requires our immediate attention, which is cleaning up international statistics, on which all policy and reform decisions are based!

Government policies are founded on attitudes toward abstract concepts, statistical signals concerning deficits, etc. that are defined by we economists. While endeavors to combat world depression by issuing new SDRs and improving international finance are commendable, I would propose a single operational measure that would carry much more weight and could be implemented quickly: to take away the imaginary global deficit on current account, which is now close to 100 billion U.S. dollars per year. This bias exaggerates statistically the already deep trauma of current account deficits that has largely motivated stagnation and that has brought about the marked shift in political concern from wages to profits, from public to private, and—allegedly—from consumption to exports. This transformation, which has haunted the industrial world since the mid-1970s, was also brought about by (unjustified) fears of export market share losses, incorrect and inflated foreign debt figures, and other biased concepts.

Getting a correct picture of the levels of current account deficits seems more important than a one-shot increase in reserves, the size of which must be limited and the effects of which leave economists divided.

As long as the Earth has a deficit—presumably to the Moon—a deficit much greater than the one that has, at least officially, driven the industrial world to stagnation and forced unprecedented political change, we should not feel comfortable professionally spending our time in academia on the cosmetics of reserve creation.

Payments statistics are so bad as to make most of our deliberations meaningless, however theoretically fascinating they may be. In Sweden, it took six years to correct statistically a cumulative deficit for the 1970s that was inflated by 400 percent, while the economy was unnecessarily dragged down into stagnation and forced to undergo political change in the process. For a closed system such as the Earth, or the close-to-closed system of the Organization for Economic Cooperation and Development (OECD), it should be easier to correct a statistical absurdity like the one we are facing. I hope this will not take us another six years.

I am not talking of a technical subtlety but of problems which are perceived to be some of the most serious and pressing of our time. Not to take action because there are difficulties involved in allocating the error to individual countries is sheer evasion. Whatever allocation is chosen, the deficits that haunt many countries will fall to a fraction of their present, imaginary levels—or disappear.

This week France devalued its currency, and it may take measures that will force new masses of people onto the unemployment rolls. But maybe France's deficit is quite manageable—maybe it is really a surplus. The Federal Republic of Germany revalued—maybe its surplus is several times as big as we think. We cannot know, because exchange movements are completely swamped by enormous capital flows (which are, in turn, largely triggered by official statistics). Nor can we draw any strong conclusions from differential inflation rates, since these are strongly affected by exchange rate policies in individual countries.

With Thomas Mann I would say that this game is undignified. As economists, we should refuse to play along. A conference like this could probably start a change for the better overnight. Yes, the SDR should be given a more important role, but basic statistical reform, which in my view is both easier to carry out and much more consequential, must first be achieved. Let us get the score right before buying new instruments.

Herbert G. Grubel

I am in general agreement with most of the points made in Professor Corden's paper, except for the most central one made in the conclusion of Section I. There, he describes how, in the present system of flexible exchange rates and a globally integrated capital market, private international liquidity has been provided in adequate amounts. From this he concludes that "The problem of reserve adequacy or excess has not arisen" and that "it is doubtful that there is really a significant role for the SDR to play within the framework of the current system" (page 232).

Corden's conclusions are based on the correct analysis that, in terms of what I would like to call static efficiency, a globally collective approach to liquidity creation through the International Monetary Fund has no distinct advantages and is beset by a number of technical and political problems which give the private solution an edge. My criticism of this analysis and conclusion is essentially that it is incomplete. It has neglected dynamic criteria of efficiency, which swing the balance to the advantage of the collective approach, if its operation is properly protected from the influence of political interest groups.

In the following, I develop my analysis by first drawing a parallel between the nature of domestic and international liquidity. Then I review the case for and against the use of central banks for the creation of domestic liquidity. In the next section, I make the case for SDRs on the same dynamic arguments used as a rationale for central banks. Recently, the "New Monetary Economics" (see Hall (1982 a, p. 1552)) has challenged this rationale, and we may interpret Corden's analysis as being in this tradition.

It will be obvious from the following analysis that it is designed to provide general and broad ideas about the future of special drawing rights (SDRs) and the Fund. It provides a compass setting for policies, rather than a road map. As such, it concentrates on the basic issue of whether the SDR system improves world welfare through increased efficiency in the operation of national economies in an economically interdependent world.

Similarity of Domestic and International Liquidity

Modern theory emphasizes the usefulness of money in carrying out purchases that have a stochastic time profile that is different from that of income. An analogous lack of synchronization in foreign exchange receipts and payments characterizes the international financial relations of all countries and gives international liquidity its utility.

This simple analogy is flawed, of course, because exchange rate changes and speculators can always equalize the demand for, and supply of, foreign exchange, so that in principle there is no need for a central authority to hold international money and arbitrage differences in the timing of income and expenditures. On this fact rests the case for freely floating exchange rates. In the following, I will disregard this case and simply assume that the efficiency of international exchange is enhanced by appropriate exchange rate stabilization efforts of national governments.[1] Otherwise there is no need at all for analyzing questions of international liquidity. The assumption also allows me to concentrate on the question of whether the money for intervention should be provided by free market processes or by an institution created collectively by international agreement among nation-states.

The Merit of Central Banks

It may be useful to set the stage for the following analysis by posing a question that is rarely found in the literature: What is so peculiar about money that its supply cannot be left to the private market? I find this not only a legitimate question but also an important one in our time, when economists have been rediscovering the merit of market solutions generally, even in the presence of externalities, because government programs seem inevitably to produce so-called nonmarket failures of their own.[2] In my answer to this question, I distinguish static, dynamic, knowledge, and political criteria of efficiency.

Static Efficiency

The great resource cost of commodity money makes it inevitable that even under complete laissez-faire, fiduciary money will take its place. However, there are significant externalities costs in the use of private coins and bank notes. The use of private currency forces transactors into generating expensive information about the creditworthiness of issuers. The information problem is complicated by the ease with which currency can be counterfeited.[3]

---

[1] In Grubel (1977) and (1982), I have developed price-theoretic models to argue that managed exchange rates are optimal.

[2] Prominent exponents of this view are Stigler (1971), Peltzman (1976), and Wolf (1979).

[3] Friedman (1960, page 8) notes that "the features of money that justify government intervention [are] the resource cost of a pure commodity currency and hence its tendency to become partly fiduciary; the peculiar difficulty of enforcing contracts involving promises to pay that serve as a medium of exchange and of preventing fraud in respect to them."

A central bank, as the monopoly issuer of legal-tender currency, internalizes these externalities in the service of society. In addition, it reaps the benefits of economies of scale in the production and surveillance of the currency. The excess profits earned by the central bank monopoly accrue to society as a whole, since the central bank is required to transfer them to general government use.

The case for the collective approach to the issue of currency on static efficiency grounds is almost unassailable in principle. The magnitude of the gains, however, is likely to be quite small in today's world, where the services of currency represent a tiny fraction of total income and where modern technology might well produce very efficient methods for dealing with the information externalities. A strong case for or against central banks must rest on the potentially much larger dynamic efficiency criteria.

Dynamic Efficiency

Business cycles and random shocks to stability are an unalterable fact of economic life. While cycles have a certain beneficial cathartic effect, most economists believe that public welfare is greater, the smaller are the frequency and magnitude of business cycle fluctuations and the more readily economies adjust to other disturbances.[4] There is strong historic evidence that free banking tends to contribute to cyclical instability. The reason is that bankers' behavior produces procyclical variations in the money supply, since their expectations are formed by much the same forces that make the rest of the economy alternate between unsustainable overspending and underspending. Historic evidence also suggests that sometimes, private banking systems have been unable to deal effectively with exogenous shocks, such as massive increases in gold supplies or harvest failures. To strengthen this conclusion, it is worth quoting Milton Friedman (1960, p. 8) on this subject: "Something like a moderately stable monetary framework seems an essential prerequisite for the effective operation of a private market economy. It is dubious that the market can by itself provide such a framework. Hence, the function of providing one is an essential governmental function on a par with the provision of a stable legal framework."

This dynamic case for the collective-money-supply solution is widely accepted in principle. Until recently, few economists other than F. v. Hayek (1976) appear to have doubted its quantitative importance. At any rate, the modern literature on money and banking is dominated by concern with the technique by which central banks can carry out their stabilization function. The basic rationale for these policies is rarely questioned.

---

[4]It is not clear whether a smaller variance leads to higher or lower average growth rates. However, it is certain that the instability of growth rates itself gives rise to a reduction in welfare.

Knowledge

Economists who believe in the social usefulness of central banks as dynamic stabilizing agents are divided into two groups. The first envisages the central bank making countercyclical policy, raising interest rates during booms and lowering them during recessions. The second is skeptical of the ability of central banks to make successful countercyclical policy because of the lags between changes in interest rates and because their effect on real variables is variable and unpredictable. Moreover, nominal interest rates often are a misleading guide for stabilization policies.

The disagreement over the efficacy of monetary policy in economic stabilization is at the heart of the continuing controversy between Keynesians and monetarists. The monetarist case has been articulated and documented by Friedman and his disciples. Their interpretation of history has led them to advocate that central banks be required to adhere to constant-money-supply-growth rules.

Political Criteria

The modern theory of regulation argues that it leads naturally to non-market failures, the social cost of which exceeds that of unregulated markets. This outcome stems from the power of interest groups which politicize the regulatory process and turn it to their advantage rather than that of society as a whole. In addition, there tends to be overregulation because its cost is diffuse and unlikely to injure the interests of the administrators using their considerable discretionary power.[5]

The dangers of a politicized central bank have, of course, been recognized for a long time. They provide the other justification for the Friedman recommendation that the Federal Reserve System be required by law to follow a monetary growth rule. Most recently, it has been argued that the money supply should be governed by rules enshrined in the constitution to prevent them from becoming politicized by simple-majority voting.[6]

The Case for Private Money

The merit of the case for a central bank just made on dynamic grounds is disputed by the New Monetary Economics school, even if money-supply rules in the constitution prevent destabilizing policies and politicization of the supply process. Under these conditions, there would still exist the costs

---

[5]See Stigler (1971) and Peltzman (1976).

[6]Milton and Rose Friedman (1979) have proposed such a constitutional provision for the United States. I have done so (see Grubel (1982)) for Canada.

of distortion accompanying all regulation.[7] This cost is perceived to be greater than the cost of instability under private money-supply systems.

I think it is interesting here to note Friedman's view on the overall merit of private and collective-money-supply systems. In most of his publications, he appears to accept implicitly that there is a case for central banks. In some publications, he appears to reject this view. In preparation of this comment, I wrote to him to request clarification of his position. In his response, he said "there is ample reason for misinterpretation of my position because I have always, rightly or wrongly, felt it desirable to discuss reform on different levels and not simply to deal with the ideal reform . . . I have always been in favor of abolishing the Federal Reserve System in the United States."[8] In the same letter, he describes his current view as follows:

> In the present situation I have been increasingly moving in the direction of believing that under present circumstances perhaps the least bad (which is the same as the best) solution would be to have a government issue fiduciary money in the form of high powered money strictly limited in quantity. That is to say for the United States simply to fix the level of currency plus Federal Reserve deposits at what it is now; convert the Federal Reserve deposits into currency; abolish the Federal Reserve System; abolish the Comptroller of the Currency, the Federal Deposit Insurance Corporation, and so on, and just let the system go from that point on. A constant supply of high powered money would probably be reasonably consistent with fairly stable prices given the likelihood of continued technological improvements permitting the ratio of total money to high-powered money to rise over time.

The Case for Collective International Liquidity

The merit of institutions and agreements for the collective creation of international money, such as SDRs, can now be examined in the light of the preceding analysis of domestic issues. In doing so, I consider the pure case where countries hold only SDRs as reserves but use small inventories of key currencies for actual market intervention. Shortages or surpluses of such currencies are settled through SDR exchanges with the Fund.

Let us first consider *static efficiency*. It seems that, as is the case with most collective approaches, the exploitation of scale economies and the benefits of standardization give a slight edge to the collective solution and SDRs, while the dynamic innovation characteristics favor private suppliers. In the end, there is not enough difference to influence the choice decisively.

The problem of distributing the seigniorage which accrues to a monopoly issuer of money has been solved ingeniously by the method used to create

---

[7]"The money stock itself is a creature of inefficient regulation. Standard microeconomic principles dictate the deregulation of transactions and intermediation for exactly the same reasons they call for free-market policies in other markets like air travel" (Hall (1982 a, p. 1555)). In his review article, Hall (1982 a) mentions, as contributors to what is also called the Neo-Chicagoan View, Hall (1982 b), Greenfield and Yeager (1982), Fama (1980 and 1982), Bilson (1981), and Black (1970).

[8]From a personal letter dated January 25, 1983.

SDRs and to charge and credit interest on them. Under the present method, seigniorage accrues to holders of reserves in proportion to their contribution to its existence. It is, therefore, distributionally neutral and approaches the market solution.[9]

In terms of *dynamic efficiency*, the SDR system promises to offer the same kinds of external benefits as does the system of collectively managed domestic money supplies. Thus, SDRs could be created countercyclically and to deal with random disturbances. Above-normal increases in international reserves during global demand deficiencies would permit deficit countries to maintain demand and exchange rates at higher levels than they could in the absence of these reserve increases. As a result, global aggregate demand would either be maintained or would shrink less. Analogously, below-normal increases in reserves during global booms would limit excess demand. The principles of Keynesian countercyclical money-supply management and policies to deal with a wide variety of exogenous shocks are applicable directly to international reserve management. The welfare benefits from such policies are obvious.

However, the importance of the *knowledge* and *political problems* associated with collective solutions suggests that the actively countercyclical and shock-absorbing creation of reserves may give rise to serious nonmarket failures. For instance, the recent inability to reach agreement on a substitution account and on significant increases in SDR supplies may be interpreted as the result of the politicization of the process. Powerful interest groups, perceiving a threat to the rents they have obtained from existing arrangements, have effectively prevented policies that many neutral observers would view as enhancing global welfare.

By the same reasoning, of course, there exists also the threat that interest-group coalitions will develop which, at other times, will force the excess or procyclical creation of SDRs. The link proposal would encourage the formation of such coalitions. For this main reason it appears that the link would be detrimental to global welfare in the longer run.

To deal with the problems of politicization of the international money supply system, it seems important, therefore, to have SDRs created by rules similar to those recommended by monetarists for central banks. Countercyclical variations in interest rates under such a regime would serve to dampen the magnitude of cyclical fluctuations. Growth-rate rules for SDRs would produce additional benefits if, in fact, there were unknown lags from their creation to their effectiveness. On the other hand, such rules would reduce the ability of the system to respond to random disturbances.

---

[9]I think that this proposition is now accepted as valid by most analysts (see Grubel (1977) for a rigorous analysis), even though politicians often ignore it in their rhetoric about the inequities of the world.

It is clear that a collective approach to international liquidity creation guided by rules would be considered likely to lead to inefficiencies by Hayek and the New Monetary Economics school, and most likely also by Friedman. Corden did not address the issues raised in this comment directly, but I think that his analysis may be interpreted as favoring the conclusions, if not the detailed reasoning, of these proponents of a private solution to the problem of international liquidity creation in the context of the international monetary system.

Summary and Conclusions

Politicians and policymakers have been said to turn to economists for the same reason that drunks turn to lampposts, for support rather than illumination. The preceding analysis was designed to provide illumination. Unfortunately, it showed that determining the merit of collective solutions to liquidity creation involves very difficult conceptual and measurement problems, which economists have only begun to address. As a scholar, I cannot honestly interpret existing knowledge as lending strong support for either case.

However, in conclusion, I would like to give free reign to all of the psychological and historic influences that shape judgment, in contrast with scientifically rigorous knowledge. In doing so, I will provide a lamppost for some politicians and policymakers at this conference. In a nutshell, my judgment is that money and international liquidity are different from potatoes and air travel in essential ways that are relevant to the present problem. For this reason, I believe there is an important role for an international reserve asset, such as the SDR, to play in providing greater global stability.

The main specific policy conclusion based on the preceding analysis, mixed with personal judgment, is that SDR growth rates should be depoliticized as much as possible by the employment of growth rules. Any loss of benefits owing to countercyclical variation in SDR growth rates caused by the adoption of growth rules would be minor relative to the gains from reducing political influence on the SDR creation process, especially if unknown lags resulted in countercyclical policies achieving limited success. While the original setting and periodic review of rules are political in themselves, the use of qualified-majority voting can reduce the likelihood that the system will be abused by narrow interest groups and their coalitions.

In fact, of course, the Fund has already enacted the rule that increases in SDRs must be approved by members having a qualified majority of 85 percent of total votes. In addition, the distribution of approved increases in SDRs normally occurs in equal amounts over a period of years, a provision which is almost equivalent to a growth rule. My analysis suggests that these provisions are efficient and serve to protect the system from political abuse and the destabilization of the global economy. National politicians concerned about these potential costs of SDR creation can take comfort from the existence of these safeguards and support an increased role for SDRs in the international monetary system with much less concern than would be warranted otherwise.

REFERENCES

Bilson, John F. O., "A Proposal for Monetary Reform" (unpublished, Hoover Institution, March 1981).

Black, Fischer, "Banking and Interest Rates in a World Without Money: The Effects of Uncontrolled Banking," *Journal of Bank Research*, Vol. 32 (Autumn 1970), pp. 8-28.

Fama, Eugene, "Banking in the Theory of Finance," *Journal of Monetary Economics*, Vol. 6 (January 1980), pp. 39-57.

_____, "Fiduciary Currency and Commodity Standards" (unpublished, University of Chicago, January 1982).

Friedman, Milton, *A Program for Monetary Stability* (New York: Fordham University Press, 1960).

_____, and Rose Friedman, *Free to Choose* (New York: Harcourt Brace, 1979).

Greenfield, Robert L., and Leland B. Yeager, "A Laissez Faire Approach to Monetary Stability" (unpublished, University of Virginia, 1982).

Grubel, Herbert G. (1977 a), "How Important is Control Over International Reserves?" in *The New International Monetary System*, ed. by Robert A. Mundell and Jacques J. Polak (New York: Columbia University Press, 1977), pp. 133-61.

_____ (1977 b), *The International Monetary System* (Harmondsworth, England: Penguin Books, third ed., 1977).

_____, "Reflections on a Canadian Bill of Economic Rights," *Canadian Public Policy*, Vol. 8 (Winter 1982), pp. 57-68.

Hall, Robert E. (1982 a), "Friedman and Schwartz' Monetary Trends—Three Views: A Neo-Chicagoan View," *Journal of Economic Literature*, Vol. 20 (December 1982), pp. 1552-56.

_____ (1982 b), "Explorations in the Gold Standard and Related Policies for Stabilizing the Dollar," in *Inflation*, ed. by Robert E. Hall (Chicago: University of Chicago Press, 1982), pp. 127-86.

Hayek, Friedrich von, *Denationalization of Money*, Hobart Paper Special No. 70 (London: Institute of Economic Affairs, 1976).

Peltzman, Sam, "Toward a More General Theory of Regulation," *Journal of Law and Economics*, Vol. 19 (August 1976), pp. 211-40.

Stigler, George J., "The Theory of Economic Regulation," *Bell Journal of Economics and Management Science*, Vol. 2 (Spring 1971), pp. 3-21.

Wolf, J. C., "A Theory of Non-Market Failures," *Journal of Law and Economics*, Vol. 22 (April 1979), pp. 107-39.

6

International Moneys and Monetary Arrangements in Private Markets

DAVID F. LOMAX

I. INTRODUCTION

This paper first outlines the main features of national markets as they relate to the use of money and financial instruments. In most countries, a national money is used within the national boundaries for the whole range of commercial and financial transactions. This introduction indicates many of the features of the financial markets which emerge in these circumstances and lead to the development of the national currency. By implication, other moneys will only thrive in use by the residents of such countries if there are weaknesses in the national money that frustrate the usual development of the relationship between the national money and the national economy. This paper will illustrate general points with examples drawn from the United Kingdom institutional context.

A central feature of a national system is the close relationship between financial transactions of all types and of all sizes. There is a continuum of financial transactions between spending 20 pence to buy a newspaper and spending several hundreds of millions of pounds to invest in a steel mill. There is a link between the movements of millions of small accounts in the building societies and banks and the placing of hundreds of millions of pounds in the money markets. Different institutions, specializing in different areas of the capital markets, provide an integrated and overlapping coverage of all areas of the market, from overnight to twenty-year or irredeemable maturities, and from nominal interest bonds and index-linked paper to equities. The capital, goods, and manpower markets use the same currency as a matter of course. Activity in the goods markets, such as physical investment, is influenced directly by activity in the financial markets, through changes in interest rates and in expectations about inflation.

In this context the old-fashioned definition of money—as a means of exchange, a unit of account, and a store of value—comes into its own. A good money may satisfy all three criteria in a national environment. It may fail to do so for a variety of reasons, for instance if its use is taxed (explicitly or implicitly) excessively, if it suffers unduly from inflation, or if its use is hedged around too much with controls.

Bolstering the natural pervasive relationship between money and economic life, the use of the currency and the strength of the financial markets are basic interests, political and social, of any government. In a recent discussion of these issues Congdon (1981, pp. 2–21) argues that the acceptability of money is essentially derived from the support given to it by the state and its organizations. Successful money cannot develop in a marketplace without government support. There are many features of money which the market needs desperately and which only government support can provide. Governments provide crucial support for the use of money by establishing a legal framework, taking specific measures to relieve holders of certain risks, intervening in the money markets at many maturities to enhance liquidity and reduce risk, and being closely involved in virtually every financial market. Activity takes place under comprehensive legislation intended to block fraud and to protect the interests of investors, savers, and money users.

The main criteria which make a financial market attractive to users are its scale, the variety of choice it can accommodate, and its liquidity. The range of preferences or risks which people would wish to accommodate are several. They include pure risk, such as insurance; the achievement of income from instruments yielding pure nominal interest; protection against price risk, through hedging financial assets against each other or obtaining financial assets whose prices should serve as hedges against prices of other assets or goods; preservation of real values, such as through inflation-proof assets like index-linked securities or real estate; the achievement of capital gains and appreciation, on a profit-maximizing basis, through skillful investment in equities or at the appropriate phases of interest cycles; the achievement of time preference by maturity transformation, and the conversion of savings today into income or assets at a later date.

The institutions taking part in the financial markets, directly or indirectly, include government, financial organizations of all types, nonfinancial companies, and the personal sector. These are the most powerful groups in the land in financial terms. The various institutions in the financial markets have the function of bridging different dimensions of the choices and preferences of different sectors. Thus, the transition of small finance into large capital masses is achieved by the banks, the building societies, the pension funds, and the life insurance companies, all of which operate at the retail level and convert the deposits and savings of the bulk of the population into sums of money of significance at the macro level. The more developed the country, the higher the income level, and the more that the modern financial institutions are accepted by the mass of the population, the greater will be the complexity and variety of the financial structure.

The concept of development in capital markets relates to the presence of a sufficiently wide range of instruments so that the preferences of most or all investors, for profit incentive or hedging, are satisfied by the instruments available. A developed capital market should be more complete in this sense, so that transactors may satisfy their needs most accurately within it. A market would fail in this respect if it were limited in capacity, if it were inadequately regulated, if it were not given support for liquidity purposes, if the range of instruments were few, and if activities in it were controlled so as to limit unduly the purposes for which it could be used.

Transitions between different types of investment, such as property, equities, fixed-interest, and index-linked, are made by the long-term investment funds on the asset side and by the corporate sector and government on the other. Changing perceptions of the risk and return on different types of investment are indicated by interrelated changes in the desires of these various organizations to use the different instruments. Maturity transformation takes place on a very substantial scale in the banks and the building societies, both of which take relatively short-term deposits and convert them into long-term assets. The holding of pure liquidity against risk is undertaken by most financial and commercial organizations, including the insurance companies, which have to cover pure risk.

The structure of these financial markets is linked to the conceptual theory of the real economy and its practical functioning, such as for example in the structure of the British Stock Exchange and its relationship to capital raising, the financial position of industry, and production and investment. Likewise, the building societies are integrally linked to the housing market, which is a matter of prime concern to the majority of people and also to the government.

The functioning of the vast majority of these markets and institutions is of deep concern to the government and is supported legally, politically, and administratively by the government in various ways. There is comprehensive legislation surrounding the functioning of most types of financial institutions, such as banks, building societies, pension funds, insurance companies, and the Stock Exchange. The government takes a detailed, almost paternal, interest in the functioning of the short-term money markets, operating through the discount houses. The health of the organizations associated with the housing market is of major political importance to the government, and active steps are taken to influence the level of interest rates and the supply of funds. The scale and liquidity of the long-term capital markets are also of prime importance to the government, in view of its need for economical financing. General political and consumer interests, allied with antimonopoly considerations, lead to public policies to ensure competition and the safety of deposits and savings. These steps include a deposit insurance scheme, regulation of the Stock Exchange, acts relating to trusteeships and investment management, and close supervision of the banks.

The strength of the financial markets in a national economy is enhanced by the fact that each market is used by a variety of organizations, each of which uses that market for a particular part of its own business. The fact that different types of organizations impinge upon the same markets for different reasons at different times and with different objectives in mind gives the variety of interests, and hence the market features, which provide liquidity and breadth. The government is deeply concerned with the interest rate, the exchange rate, and the inflation rate of its own currency and, therefore, has an all-pervasive interest in the development of these markets. It is also sometimes interested in blocking financial innovations or alternative markets.

The above illustrative detail from the United Kingdom does, it is to be hoped, provide sufficient evidence to bring home the point that there is a deep connection between the financial markets in a country and its social, economic, and political fabric. The vast majority of participants in the markets and the people who help build up the organic structure of the markets are committed mainly to their national currency. Most individuals and organizations would expect the bulk of their financial transactions to be in their country's own currency. There is an inevitable bias toward the combined efforts of the institutions of a national economy which leads to fully developed financial markets in national currencies, and not in composite currencies.

International Portfolio Diversification

However, many countries apply exchange controls, which mean that organizations with international interests and risks may be unable to satisfy their needs. The inadequacy of certain markets may encourage the use of other instruments, such as foreign moneys.

Deficiencies in national markets may be remedied, to a greater or lesser extent, by the use of international moneys. One of the most powerful factors increasing the potential use of international money is the development of multinational industry and commerce over the past 30 years. Indications of this are the proportion of the balance sheets of banks held either outside their own currency or outside their area of domestic jurisdiction, and the proportion of the profits of major companies stemming from investment abroad.

There are two main reasons why national interests may lead to the use of international moneys even when there are well-developed national financial markets. The first is that investors need to diversify their portfolios. Even if national markets are well developed, a portfolio investor may hope to obtain a greater return for the same risk, or the same return for less risk, by diversifying. If there are not enough adequate instruments in national markets, then diversification abroad may be a rational way of achieving these objectives. This may be justifiable even if all the contractual liabilities of the investment organization, such as a pension fund, are denominated in the national currency, such as the pound sterling. This applies particularly if the liabilities are effectively determined in real terms. If the investment manager is convinced that he may be able to obtain a greater return from investing abroad, then that in itself is justification for doing so. A benefit could occur from diversification even if the investment manager only expected to achieve the same average return from investments abroad. This is because he would benefit from the balance between diversity, return, and risk. This phenomenon has been shown relatively clearly in the British experience. Even when there was exchange control, many long-term investment institutions invested abroad, either by buying from the investment currency pool or by borrowing currency abroad. With the abolition of exchange control in October 1979, a very substantial outflow of U.K. portfolio investment took place.

The second reason for the use of international moneys is that national companies have multinational interests. One may draw a distinction between a multinational and an international business. A company may have units in many different countries, each of which would normally be concerned solely with its own domestic market. In that case, the company would have a multinational financing structure, with each of its units being associated with financing in the national currency. In the international phase, when a company is more concerned with a variety of international markets and trading relationships, then it may find it helpful to operate in the Eurocurrency markets more generally, hedging the risks as appropriate. It would thus have outgrown the national markets of its subsidiaries, and its requirements for liquidity and scale could be satisfied only by the major Euromarkets.

Competition Between National Moneys and Currency Cocktails

If one considers the use of international moneys in the light of these points, an international money such as a currency cocktail is most unlikely to achieve the organic development of a national currency. Some institutions of importance in the total market structure, such as building societies, could never be developed in the context of a currency cocktail. Because of the risks and opportunities faced by many participants, cocktails are meaningless for them. Substantial size transformation, the accumulation of small financial units to make large masses of capital, is unlikely to take place in currency cocktails. One is unlikely to see the use of cocktails for risk transformation, with investors having the choice of switching between equities, nominal interest stock, property, and index-linked stock, as can be done flexibly within a national market. One is also unlikely to see in a currency cocktail the same maturity transformation, such as the accumulation of short-term and possibly small deposits and their translation into longer-term assets. Even a limited maturity transformation is riskier. In a national market, the diversity of financial organizations builds up the scale, liquidity, and variety of the market. In national currencies, the strength of the markets is related to the efforts of governments to preserve their quality. No government is likely to wish to enhance the use of an international cocktail in preference to its own currency. Most international currency cocktails will be used in international markets, where the degree of supervision is considerably less than in national markets. In order to make the risks to participants acceptable, currency cocktails are likely to be used in relatively limited areas. They will be attractive for some of the largest and safest organizations. They have to depend on the general infrastructure of the Euromarkets, which is an offshoot of the infrastructures of financial markets in individual countries and of major financial organizations.

At times, investors may wish to use international markets and currencies other than their own. Even in this situation, currency cocktails are but one of the available choices. Investors may use the Eurocurrency markets or other national markets to which they have access. Considerations of liquidity, choice, and rate of return would bear heavily in deciding which international or other national currency to use. A currency cocktail would compete with the Japanese stock market, the Swiss franc bond market, the deutsche mark bond market, Wall Street, the Eurodollar market, and what have you. These markets would almost inevitably have more attractive features regarding scale, choice, and liquidity.

Those who would seek to obtain a substantial market niche for a currency cocktail face an uphill struggle. A theme that emerges at this stage, which is strengthened and developed later in this paper, is that successful national financial markets do not develop accidentally. They all have strong government support. If one wishes to see a currency cocktail established, then it has to be given very substantial governmental or institutional support so as to overcome its handicaps.

II. USE OF NON-DOMESTIC MONEYS

There are many examples of countries which, for a variety of reasons, do not wish to establish full financial independence and thus use the money of other countries, either alone or in conjunction with their own currency. Two examples of monetary unions are those between the Republic of Ireland and the United Kingdom and between Belgium and Luxembourg. The Anglo-Irish monetary union has existed historically, and it was not broken when the Republic of Ireland achieved independence in 1921. The Irish Government decided, however, on March 13, 1979 that it should be severed. The Irish pound then joined the European Monetary System, including its exchange rate mechanism, in contrast to the British pound. On severing the monetary union, the initial expectation in the Republic of Ireland was that the Irish pound would appreciate against sterling. This happened initially for a few days only, but since then the Irish pound has moved to a substantial discount against sterling.

One of the reasons for the Irish decision to break the monetary union was their realization that through it they were forced to accept the monetary conditions of the United Kingdom, which was inevitably the dominant partner. This meant importing inflation in line with the British rate, which had been very high during the 1970s. Subsequently, given the impact of Mrs. Thatcher's policies and the status of the pound sterling as a petrocurrency, the Irish pound would have had to appreciate dramatically with sterling had there been a monetary union, which would have been against the Republic's economic and trading interests.

The long-standing economic integration between the Republic of Ireland and the United Kingdom and the general presumption that that monetary union was there to stay led to some financial integration between the two countries. Certain banks which operated in Ireland, both in Ulster and in the Republic, did so through the same corporate structure, with no excessive concern to match assets and liabilities in each of the currencies. In some cases, there was a certain ambiguity as to the currency in which assets and liabilities were denominated. During the period of the monetary union, the pound sterling circulated freely in the Republic of Ireland alongside the local currency.

Similar geographic factors encouraged the monetary union between Belgium and Luxembourg. Both the Belgian franc and the Luxembourg franc circulate in Luxembourg. The maintenance of this union has aroused increasing criticism in Luxembourg, given the different economic structures of the two countries and the weakness of the Belgian franc. Luxembourg has a different economy from Belgium and does not share the latter's structural weaknesses. As an expression of this political discontent, after the 8.5 percent depreciation of the Belgian and Luxembourg francs decided on February 21, 1982 at the request of the Belgian Government, the Deputies of the Luxembourg Parliament approved on March 11, 1982 a motion that

The Chamber of Deputies invites the Government
—to examine all possible alternatives to the monetary union with Belgium
—to examine more particularly the linking of the Luxembourg franc to the European ECU

Some commentators regard this as an expression more of frustration and irritation, than of intention. Thus, a monetary union which appears sensible and even inevitable, faces strains as the relative fortunes and perceptions of the countries change with changing circumstances. But this and the Irish evidence may indicate that once a degree of financial and economic integration has been achieved, it may be difficult and costly for the smaller partner to go it alone.

An example of a monetary union which is substantially more complete, yet still leaves the circulation of different national currencies side by side, is that of England and Scotland. Certain Scottish banks are permitted to issue notes, providing they hold a 100 percent backing of Bank of England money. There is the circulation side by side of English currency and notes issued by three Scottish banks. There is no independent monetary creation in this process, since the Scottish notes issued have to be backed 100 percent by English notes.

There are many examples of countries in which other currencies are fully acceptable. To quote a few, the United States dollar is used alongside the local dollar in Bahamas, Bermuda, Panama, and Liberia. The pound sterling is used alongside the local pound in the Falkland Islands and Gibraltar. The South African rand is used alongside the local currency in Swaziland.

This process is taken a stage further when a foreign currency is used exclusively in a country and there is no domestic monetary creation. Thus, the Swiss franc serves also Liechtenstein, the French franc Monaco, the Italian lira San Marino, and the Australian dollar Kiribati. In all these cases, overriding factors of politics and/or geography are clearly decisive in leading to these currency arrangements.

On a more informal basis, the deutsche mark is reportedly used to a notable extent in the German Democratic Republic, and the United States dollar and other hard currencies unofficially through Eastern Europe.

There are also examples of countries joining together or being joined together to develop one currency to serve them all. One example is the East Caribbean dollar, which is used in Anguilla, Antigua, St. Kitts, St. Lucia, Nevis, St. Vincent, and other islands. A more conspicuous and more highly developed example is the Communauté Financière Africaine (CFA) franc zone, which will be examined at greater length in the next section.

III. CFA FRANC ZONE

In two articles, from which much of the following is taken, Liddell (1979, pp. 105-11; 1982, pp. 41-43) describes the outline of the CFA franc system, which covers many of France's ex-colonies in North and Middle Africa. The system is based on two central banks and two zones—the West African monetary area comprising Benin, Ivory Coast, Upper Volta, Niger, Senegal, and Togo, and the Central African area comprising Cameroon, the Central African Republic, Congo, Gabon, and Chad. The monetary zones are formed by treaties between their respective members and between each zone and France.

Each zone has its own central bank, with headquarters respectively in Dakar and Yaoundé. The Boards of Directors are made up of representatives of each member country and of France. The Ministerial Council for each zone consists of ministers of the government of each country, including the finance minister. The member countries' reserves are pooled with the two respective central banks, which, in turn, are obliged to hold 65 percent of their reserves in the French Treasury. Thirty-five percent may be employed in other assets at the discretion of the central banks. The central banks manage the International Monetary Fund positions of their members. The French franc reserves are fully convertible, and there is an unlimited guarantee by France of the money issued by the central banks.

Member countries harmonize their policies with respect to credit and interest rates. Credit is controlled by the central banks through the application of ceilings on government borrowing and on bank credit expansion. The limit for each government is set at 20 percent of its revenues for the previous fiscal year. There are limits for each bank, covering short-term and medium-term discount facilities, and limits for any institution, corporation, firm, or individual over a certain threshold. These limits are agreed with the National Monetary Committee for each country, whose members are the national directors of its central bank, the governor of the central bank, and private citizens appointed by the government.

This system would probably not have been established had there not been the colonial links between France and the various member countries. The system has stood the test of time well. The backing of France has enhanced the creditworthiness of member countries (notably the Ivory Coast in recent years). The nature of the agreements between the member countries indicates how strong such treaties need to be if one currency is to be used throughout several separate sovereign countries. The nature of the treaties creating the CFA franc zone indicates how far the European countries may have to go if they ever wish to make the European Currency Unit (ECU) a common currency in Europe.

The success of the CFA franc zone has benefited from the relatively *dirigiste* tradition of France in monetary matters and from the fact that all the members pursue policies not only with similar objectives but also with similar structures. The treaty members, France included, are evidently in a position to exert sufficient influence on each other to ensure that compatible and acceptable policies are pursued.

The economic benefits to the member countries, received in exchange for some loss of sovereignty, include a stable credible currency, good technical advice, a saving on reserves, and a better credit rating, all of which imply a readier and cheaper access to external capital.

The author has been unable to discover any external use of the CFA franc outside the two zones. The total CFA franc money and quasi-money supply is relatively small in world terms, at about 39 billion French francs at the end of 1981, which is 2.6 percent of the similar figure for France at the same date.

IV. CURRENCY UNITS

In the European context, there have been many units of account, some of which have been used purely officially and some in the private markets as well. The best published description of this is in Kredietbank material (Kredietbank (1980)), to which I am indebted for much of the following.

A first distinction in the European context is between official and private units of account. Several units of account have been created in both the private and the official markets.

A second distinction relates to the valuation principal. There have been both parity units of account and basket units of account. In the period of fixed exchange rates, the units of account were of the parity type; in the present period of floating exchange rates, basket units are more common.

For a parity unit of account, the key issues are the currency (or currencies) of repayment, the exchange rate at which repayment will be made, and the party (lender or borrower) who has any choice in such matters. Parity units differ in relation to the currencies in the unit and the means of determining the three key issues.

Basket units of account are a weighted sum of the component currencies.

Official EEC Units

The original official European Unit of Account (Eua) was based on the accounting unit of the now defunct European Payments Union and was defined as being the equivalent of 0.88867088 grams of fine gold, the same gold content as the U.S. dollar.

After the collapse of the fixed exchange rate system in 1971, when some currencies floated while others observed central rates, ad hoc units of account were floated for certain areas of Community policy.

The situation at one time was so confused that the value of one Eua converted into a national currency differed according to the area of application, such as exchange rate policy, agriculture, European Coal and Steel Community (ECSC), the budget, and so on. A first step toward a solution was taken in April 1975 by switching from the parity principle to the basket principle for the valuation of the Eua.

The composition of this basket was based on the relative importance of the member countries in intra-Community trade and in the Community's gross national product (GNP) in the period 1969 to 1974. There was no provision for varying the composition of the basket. When the ECU was defined in 1978, it had the same composition, with the provision that this could be altered when necessary, as discussed later in this paper.

The basket Eua gradually replaced the parity Eua in different fields of application in the European Community.

The ECU came into operation on March 13, 1979, when the European Monetary System started operations, replacing the Eua fully by January 1, 1980. The ECU has become the linch pin of the European Community's exchange rate system.

Private Sector Units of Account

The two valuation principles, parity unit of account and basket of currencies, are also met in the units of account used in the private sector. Up to the present, units of account of the parity type have been most used. A European Unit of Account (EUA) has been used in the international capital market since 1961. In order to avoid confusion, the private sector unit is referred to as EUA, and the official version is referred to as Eua. In 1973, as a result of changes in the international monetary system, a major adjustment was made, so that bond issues in EUA were divided into "old" and "new" issues.

The "old" EUA was linked to 17 so-called reference currencies of the countries of the former European Payments Union. From 1961 to 1971, 41 international bond issues were floated according to the "old" EUA formula. As a result of the demonetization of gold, most currencies came to have no gold parity, while the status of others had become unclear. The only reference currency which still had a gold parity was the Swiss franc. Under the rules of the unit, the "old" EUA bonds became in effect Swiss franc bonds, but with a higher interest rate. This development was out of line with the specific objectives of the "old" EUA. Since the unit came to have advantages too one-sidedly in favor of investors—Swiss franc bonds, but with a higher interest rate—it was no longer attractive to borrowers. The promoters therefore devised an amended formula.

Since 1973, the "new" EUA has been linked to the currencies of the nine members of the European Economic Community (EEC) prior to the accession of Greece. The formula is admitted even by its promoters to be very complicated. Its essential principle is to limit the exchange risks for both borrower and lender by the manner in which it selects the exchange rate at repayment. To qualify as a reference currency, there has to be participation in an agreement to limit fluctuation margins, which is currently the European Monetary System (EMS). There are now thus eight reference currencies, since the United Kingdom, alone of the EEC member states, does not participate in the exchange rate mechanism of the EMS.

At the time of issue, the borrower may select a currency in which he wishes to be paid. The bondholder is entitled to choose a currency for payment of interest and redemption. The "new" EUA originally had gold as a common denominator, but since the inauguration of the EMS, this has become the ECU.

To elaborate the above explanation set out by Kredietbank, an example may be helpful. Kredietbank set out the value of the EUA in March 1980 as follows:

$$
\begin{aligned}
1 \text{ EUA} &= 1.1989019 & \text{ECUs} \\
&= 2.97579 & \text{deutsche mark} \\
&= 47.7031 & \text{Belgian francs} \\
&= 9.25955 & \text{Danish krone} \\
&= 7.00988 & \text{French francs} \\
&= 0.801098 & \text{Irish pound} \\
&= 1,388.06 & \text{Italian lire} \\
&= 47.7031 & \text{Luxembourg francs} \\
&= 3.28928 & \text{Dutch guilders} \\
&= 1 & \text{Pound sterling}
\end{aligned}
$$

[1]Sterling was not a reference currency, since it did not participate in the EMS.

Let us assume that by the maturity of a EUA loan or bond, the deutsche mark, Belgian franc, Luxembourg franc, and Danish krone have been devalued; the Irish pound is unchanged; and the other currencies have been revalued. These devaluations and revaluations are measured against the ECU, not against the central bilateral rates of the EMS. In that case, the EUA is unchanged as against the Irish pound, so for each EUA lent, the lender will receive the value of 0.801098 Irish pounds, plus interest.

As a second example, let us assume that against the ECU the first two currencies, plus the Luxembourg franc, have been devalued and the other five revalued. Let us further assume that the smallest devaluation is 2.3 percent for the Belgian franc and the smallest revaluation 2.5 percent for the Dutch guilder. Under the rule, the EUA moves with the smallest movement on the majority side. Thus, it goes with the guilder, despite the fact that the smallest revaluation was larger than the smallest devaluation. Thus, on repayment of principal, the lender would receive 3.28928 guilders for each EUA. The rules under other eventualities are extremely complicated. The details need not concern us here, and enquiries may be referred to Kredietbank.

In its time, the "new" EUA served its purpose well and attracted business from investors and borrowers who wished to operate in a multicurrency environment while controlling the exchange risk and allocating it fairly between borrower and lender. More recently, the "new" EUA has become moribund, since it has been overtaken by the ECU. The basket principle has more attractive features in controlling exchange risk, while the ECU benefits enormously from the backing given it by the EEC institutions.

Private-Sector European Currency Unit

A private-sector European Currency Unit has also been used. This unit of account, although bearing the same name, should not be confused with the European Commission's present ECU. It was defined vis-à-vis the currencies of the six original member countries, with fixed conversion rates for the entire term of the loan. The formula protected the international investor against exchange risk but left the borrower vulnerable. This rapidly became an expensive formula for borrowing after the Bretton Woods system broke down. Once this became obvious, this European Currency Unit was used only by borrowers who would otherwise have had difficulty in raising funds. Other borrowers, including the ECSC, which had initially promoted the formula, redeemed their bonds prematurely. This unit was used for bonds only in 1970, 1971, and 1972.

European Composite Unit (EURCO)

The EURCO is a currency basket composed of the nine European Community members before the accession of Greece. It consists of fixed amounts of each currency. The EURCO was used for the first time in 1973 for a bond issue by the Bank for International Settlements (BIS), and two further bond issues followed in 1974. The official ECU, closely allied to the EURCO in its composition, yet also in official use, has since been created, and it is unlikely that any new EURCO issues will be floated.

Non-European Units

The Arab Currency-Related Unit (ARCRU) was even less successful than other basket units, and only one private issue was made, for $12 million in 1974. It was hoped that the unit would appeal to Arab investors and serve as a means of recycling surplus oil revenues. The ARCRU was declared to be equivalent to the value of the United States dollar on June 28, 1974, and was based on the currencies of 12 Arab countries (Algeria, Bahrain, Egypt, Iraq, Kuwait, Lebanon, Socialist People's Libyan Arab Jamahiriya, Oman, Qatar, Saudi Arabia, Syria, and the United Arab Emirates). The two strongest and the two weakest currencies were eliminated from the group in making up the basket for an issue. The value of the resulting ARCRU was an unweighted average of the remaining currencies. The possible variation in the composition of the unit from one issue to another was a source of confusion for investors.

Other Units

Various banks have tried to obtain business prominence by inventing their own currency units, but these have not succeeded. Credit Lyonnais designed the International Financial Unit (IFU), which was declared to be equivalent to the U.S. dollar on April 1, 1974 and contained specific amounts of the currencies of the Group of Ten countries (United States, Federal Republic of Germany, France, United Kingdom, Italy, Netherlands, Belgium, Japan, Canada, and Sweden). A simpler unit, the B-Unit, was designed by Barclays Bank in 1974 and consisted of specific amounts of five currencies—the United States dollar, the deutsche mark, the French franc, the pound sterling, and the Swiss franc. Neither of these units, the IFU nor the B-Unit, has been used in issues.

Official European Currency Unit (ECU)

The international currency unit which is at present showing the greatest growth in market use is the ECU. I am indebted for much of the information on the ECU to the Istituto Bancario San Paolo di Torino (1982 a and b), which has provided by far the most comprehensive monitoring of ECU developments.

The ECU was created on the introduction of the EMS. It was defined as a basket of currencies whose composition (and currency amounts) was identical to that of the official European Unit of Account. The exchange rate mechanism of the EMS consists of obligatory exchange rate intervention commitments based on bilateral exchange rates and, in addition, a presumption of action when a currency moves against its ECU central rate to such an extent that it crosses the so-called divergence threshold.

There are provisions in the EMS agreement for the regular redefinition of the ECU, in case the weight of currencies in the basket should change too much. Over time, an appreciating currency has a larger weight in a basket, and a depreciating currency a smaller one. If any net appreciations and depreciations are cumulatively substantial, the change in weights may be significant, so that the basket fails to represent the balance it was intended to. Under a resolution of the European Council of December 5, 1978 on the establishment of the European Monetary System, the weights of the currencies in the ECU would be re-examined and, if necessary, revised within six months of the entry into force of the system and thereafter every five years or on request if the weight of any currency changed by 25 percent.

Council Regulation (EEC) No. 3180/78 of December 18, 1978 changed the name and definition of the unit of account used by the European Monetary Cooperation Fund (EMCF). With effect from January 1, 1979, the EMCF's operations were to be expressed in the ECU, which was defined as the sum of

0.828	deutsche mark
0.0885	pound sterling
1.15	French francs
109	Italian lire
0.286	Dutch guilder
3.66	Belgian francs
0.14	Luxembourg franc
0.217	Danish krone
0.00759	Irish pound

It was also resolved that the Council, acting unanimously on a proposal from the Commission after consulting the Monetary Committee and the Board of Governors of the European Monetary Cooperation Fund, should determine the conditions under which the components of the ECU may be changed.

On the accession of Greece to the EEC, it was agreed that the drachma would be included in the basket by December 31, 1985 at the latest. The drachma would be included earlier if, before that time, a revision of the basket had been undertaken in accordance with the procedures and under the conditions laid down in the Resolution (noted above) of the European Council of December 5, 1978 on the European Monetary System.

So far there have been no revisions of the ECU.

There are two "circuits" for the use of the ECU. The "official" circuit is among central banks and between them and the European Monetary Cooperation Fund. The private circuit in ECU-denominated assets is among EEC institutions, commercial banks, companies, individuals, and central banks. Both use the same definition of the ECU.

The ECU is the accounting measure for the institutions of the EEC, and for payments between EEC governments on community-related matters and for payments to and from the community's institutions.

The ECU's use as the accounting measure for EEC institutions provides the unit with a natural basis in real economic activity. It receives institutional support from organizations which find it convenient to use the ECU in financial markets.

The geographic region where the ECU is used coincides with a political entity, so that promotion of the ECU is a natural theme for those concerned with increasing the unity of the EEC and the strength of its institutions.

The Community is a zone of hoped-for currency stability. The objective, if not the achievement, of member governments is to move toward exchange rate stability. Because of member countries' political commitments to the Community, they have been willing to take some political, legal, and practical decisions to widen the potential uses of the ECU in financial markets.

ECU Deposits

Informed estimates put the volume of ECU deposits in the Euromarket at the end of 1982 at some ECU 3 billion. This is minimal in relation to the total scale of the market and, in particular, to the $1,500 billion scale of the Eurodollar market (gross size as of March 1982).

The interbank market is now of greater depth, and banks can obtain delivery of ECUs relatively freely, without having to build them up from the component currencies. The clearing system at present caters to the needs of over 200 central and commercial banks and their customers. A committee of banks has been formed to study the establishment of a more formal clearing system for ECUs. The member banks are Morgan Guaranty Trust, Crédit Lyonnais, Kredietbank, Istituto Bancario San Paolo di Torino, and Lloyds Bank. They have consulted with the BIS. The committee hopes to publish its views early in 1983. Although banks are able now to obtain delivery of ECUs, a formal clearing system would reduce the risk and would make the ECU more acceptable to a wider range of banks. The larger banks have no difficulty in building up the ECU from its component currencies. The computer technology is by now straightforward and in place. Some smaller banks may not have the same technology. They may also be more concerned with the risk of unavailability of some of the component currencies, should it not be possible to deal in ECUs themselves. Transactions in ECUs have become much cheaper than they were a few years ago.

There is now considerable market momentum behind the ECU, created by steady expansion of bond issues and bank syndications denominated in the unit. This has not so far resulted in a massive change in the scale of the market, but in various ways the quality of the market is improving. Increasing numbers of banks are taking the view that the ECU is to be taken seriously in the future, and so are devoting more resources to it.

A major change in quality in the market is that a very large proportion, up to 80-90 percent, of transactions in ECUs are done in that currency unit itself, without its being unbundled. This is an enormous convenience for banks, as it reduces the costs and complexity of transactions very considerably.

Many of the currencies in the ECU are not fully tradable or do not have full Euromarket structures, so that the ECU has to be unbundled through forward swaps, rather than through the deposit market. This provides less flexibility as regards ways of bundling and unbundling the basket. The ECU is traded for no more than a year. Market quotations are given on Reuters monitors, both for deposit rates and for spot and forward exchange rates.

Banks in the Federal Republic of Germany, Denmark, and Ireland have been inhibited by their national regulations regarding use of the forward markets and documentation of foreign exchange transactions, and have been less prominent in the ECU markets. The main momentum has come from banks in other EEC countries. A further development has been the willingness of certain banks to offer "nostro" accounts, or correspondent bank facilities, in ECUs. Kredietbank and Lloyds Bank have put themselves forward in this way. By offering what is in effect a private-sector clearing account, these banks are no doubt generating significant business, but at the same time they are taking on costs and risks. The need to cover their positions, in view of any mismatching that occurs near the end of the day, may involve them taking on both exchange rate and interest rate risks. If they decide to cover those, then their whole dealing position becomes more complicated.

The situation would be much easier if the BIS or some other central bank or governmental organization would take on the role of giving the clearing system residual support. So far, the BIS has not been willing to commit itself to this, and it remains to be seen whether its shareholders would agree to that.

Issues yet to be decided are where the clearing system should be domiciled (there is some support for both Brussels and Paris). The most effective way of achieving liquidity would be for a central bank or international organization to act as technical clearing agent and provider of liquidity if necessary, as recommended in the Resolution of the European Council of December 5, 1978 that set up the European Monetary System. However, the use of international organizations to support the ECU interbank market raises difficulties, because some European central banks are reportedly much less enthusiastic than others about an enhancement of the ECU's role. Without the backing of a central bank, the banks participating in these arrangements would need to take a more cautious approach, and the market would inevitably be less liquid.

Certificates of Deposit

The first certificates of deposit (CDs) denominated in ECUs were issued on February 23, 1981 by Lloyds Bank; these were short-term bonds in the form of one-month certificates. The same bank has continued issuing CDs since then. In February 1982, Crédit Lyonnais, in cooperation with Banque Internationale de Gestion et de Trésorerie, floated an ECU 15 million issue with a three-year maturity. In March 1982, certificates of deposit amounting to 10 million ECU, with a maturity of up to three months, were issued by Lavoro Bank International, the Luxembourg affiliate of Banca Nazionale del Lavoro. Both these CDs were issued to back loans, the first to Sanwa Bank and the second to the European Investment Bank.

Bonds

The status of ECU international bond quotations and yields as at 30 November 1982 is given in Table 1. This indicates that by then there had been some 18 ECU bonds, which had a total face value of ECU 710 million. By far the largest was the ECU 500 million for the Republic of Italy, of which ECU 450 million was issued in Italy itself and hence was not included in the above figure of ECU 710 million. The most frequent borrower has been the European Investment Bank, with four issues totaling ECU 185 million. Another Community borrower has been the Council of Europe for ECU 55 million. One borrower, Hydro Quebec, has no formal connection with the EEC. It has made two issues totalling ECU 90 million. Trading in ECU bonds functions well with a sizeable turnover.

A further impetus to the use of the ECU for bond issues was given on April 21, 1981 when Euro-Clear, the Brussels-based Eurobond clearing house founded by Morgan Guaranty Trust in 1968, accepted the ECU as a regular transaction currency for settlement of trades. Euro-Clear's participants may maintain ECU-denominated cash accounts and obtain clearance financing at Morgan Guaranty Trust Company, Brussels, for which Kredietbank, Brussels, is the ECU correspondent bank. Cedel, the Luxembourg clearing house founded in 1971 by 71 banks, has also accepted the ECU as a transaction currency (Lomax and Gutmann (1981, p. 149)).

As a means of tapping small investor interest, on October 2, 1982, Citicorp issued ECU 15 million of Eurobonds in small units of 1,000 ECU; the issue was ideal for small investors and sold out quickly.

Eurocredits

Many borrowers have taken ECU-denominated medium-term loans from the banks on a similar basis to normal Eurobank financing. The following list gives an indication of the organizations which have been using the ECU Eurocredit market:

In June 1980 and July 1981, Crédit Lyonnais granted Credit National a ten-year rollover bank credit amounting to ECU 20 million, and a five-year revolving credit amounting to ECU 200 million.

In January 1982, San Paolo-Lariano Bank, Luxembourg, granted an ECU 4 million loan of 5 years to Necchi SpA Pavia.

During the second quarter of 1982, an ECU 2 million loan of two-year maturity was granted to Parmalat by Paribas.

In the same period, Lloyds Bank International, Morgan Guaranty Trust, Kredietbank, and others granted an ECU 50 million loan of eight-year maturity to a telephone holding company controlled by the Istituto Per La Ricostruzione Industriale (IRI).

A syndication of banks coordinated by Istituto Bancario San Paolo di Torino granted an ECU 10 million loan of four-year maturity to Gruppo Industrie Elettro Meccaniche per Impianti all'Estero of Milan.

Banque Nationale de Paris S.A. and Morgan Guaranty Trust have made an ECU 100 million loan of seven-year maturity to Saint-Gobain.

Savings Banks

The Luxembourg State Savings Bank has been managing accounts in EUA for the European Commission since 1976. Since 1978, it has managed current accounts and term deposits in ECUs for the European Commission, the European Court of Auditors, the European Court of Justice, the European Parliament, and the European Investment Bank. An increasing number of accounts are being opened by private individuals.

The French Caisse des Dépôts et Consignations has managed term deposits in ECUs for the Commission since 1978. It has also managed the ECU accounts of the ECSC, on behalf of the Caisse Centrale de Coopération Economique, and ECU accounts for many French companies.

The Danish Faellesbanken has arranged loans in ECU for its Danish clients from banks in Luxembourg and Belgium since 1979. Loans have

TABLE 1. ECU BOND QUOTATIONS AND YIELDS, NOVEMBER 30, 1982

Amount Issued	Year of Issue/ Issue Price	Borrower/Coupon/ Maturity	Price	Yield to Maturity/ Yield to Average Life	Current Yield
Million ECUs		percent		$\longleftarrow$ percent $\longrightarrow$	
30	1982 99.75	Centrale Nucléaire Européenne Neutrons Rapides S.A. 13.875 2/15/1990	$104\frac{3}{8}$	12.88	13.29
15	1982 100.25	Citicorp Overseas Finance Corporation, N.V. 13.00 2/28/1989	$100\frac{1}{2}$	12.84	12.94
30	1982 100.75	Council of Europe 13.50 10/1/1992	$103\frac{1}{2}$	12.83	13.04
30				12.73	
25	1982 100.75	Council of Europe 14.25 3/30/1990	$107\frac{1}{2}$	12.58	13.26
50	1982 100.50	Crédit d'équipement aux PME 12.625 11/30/1990	$100\frac{1}{4}$	12.57	12.59
50	1982 99.50	Crédit Foncier 13.75 7/31/1989	$104\frac{5}{8}$	12.64	13.14
60	1982 100.75	European Investment Bank 12.875 10/26/1990	$102\frac{7}{8}$	12.27	12.52
40	1981 100.00	European Investment Bank 13.25 6/11/1989	106	11.84	12.50

40	1982 99.50	European Investment Bank 13.75 7/15/1989	107	12.11	12.85
45	1981 99.25	European Investment Bank 14.25 10/28/1989	106	12.87	13.44
50 50	1982 99.00	Gaz de France 13.00 9/30/1989	101	12.75 12.76	12.87
40	1982	Istituto Mobiliare Italiano	$100^{7/8}$	13.74 13.71	13.88
40	99.50	14.00 7/2/1989			
30	1981	Istituto Bancario San Paolo di Torino	$104^{3/4}$	13.54 13.32	14.08
30	100.00	14.75 12/3/1988			
50	1982 100.00	Italy, Republic of 14.00 2/22/1989	$102^{1/2}$	13.35	13.66
50	1982 100.00	Hydro Quebec 13.50 6/1/1989	$102^{3/8}$	12.89	13.19
40	1981 99.00	Hydro Quebec 14.25 9/16/1988	108	12.21	13.19
30	1982	Société de Développement Régional (France)	$104^{1/2}$	13.10 12.85	13.40
30	100.75	14.00 6/1/1992			
35	1981	Société Financière Pour Télécommunications et l'Electronique S.A. (Luxembourg)	101	12.63 12.64	12.87
33.6	100.00	13.00 4/21/1987			

Source: Association of International Bond Dealers, *Financial Times*, No. 28,952 (December 15, 1982), pp. 13–18.

terms of five to six years with interest rates on a six-month rollover basis. The loans tend to be small, with a minimum of ECU 20,000 per loan, and are ranged in packages of 10 to 20, giving totals of about ECU 500,000. The transactions in ECUs are based on an official fixing at the Danish central bank.

Since 1981, two Italian savings banks have granted short-term commercial credits in ECUs for 60 to 90 days, mainly to finance import/export operations.

Foreign Exchange

Figures of activity in foreign exchange markets are uncertain, since the details are not reported and published officially. Kredietbank reports an average turnover of some ECU 250 million a day, and about ECU 20 million of commercial orders. That makes the ECU the fifth most active currency in terms of turnover, behind the dollar, deutsche mark, Swiss franc, and Dutch guilder and ahead of the French franc. Lloyds Bank reports that the ECU is normally second to the dollar in Eurodeposit turnover, and the bank has one dealer working full time and another working part time in ECUs. (A list of banks claiming to work actively in ECUs—accepting ECU deposits, participating as comanagers in ECU bonds, or trading ECUs spot and/or forward against other currencies—is given in Table 2. This list should be treated with caution.)

Commercial Contracts

Commercial contracts have been denominated in ECUs. Some of the main Italian insurance companies have launched ECU-denominated life insurance policies. This became possible following the underwriting by Assicurazioni Generali and other companies of a ECU 42 million bond issue for Euratom. That gave the insurance companies ECU assets, against which they could create ECU liabilities.

The company Saint-Gobain has introduced the ECU in its intercompany billing since January 1980, using a single ECU transfer price for the business of the glass plate division between France, the Federal Republic of Germany, and Belgium. This has the benefit of splitting the exchange risk more evenly between the different plants.

Political Support

The development of the ECU has been supported by the EEC Commission and European governments. The EEC Commission and its affiliates

TABLE 2. RECENT DEVELOPMENTS IN PRIVATE USE OF THE ECU

Main Banks Working in ECUs

Here is a list of main banks working in ECUs. The list is not exhaustive and includes only banks accepting ECU deposits; participating as comanagers in ECU bonds; or trading ECUs, spot and/or forward, against other currencies.

Belgium
Kredietbank
Banque Bruxelles-Lambert
Société Générale de Banque
Morgan Guaranty Trust (Bruxelles)

Luxembourg
Caisse d'Epargne de l'Etat de Luxembourg
Banque Internationale à Luxembourg
Banque Générale du Luxembourg
Kredietbank S.A. Luxembourgeoise
Sanpaolo-Lariano Bank—Luxembourg

Netherlands
Amsterdam Rotterdam Bank
Algemene Bank Nederland

France
Société Générale
Crédit Lyonnais
Caisse des Dépôts et Consignations
Banque Nationale de Paris
Banque de l'Indochine et de Suez
Crédit Commercial de France

Federal Republic of Germany
Berliner Handels- und Frankfurter Bank
Dresdner Bank Aktiengesellschaft
Deutsche Bank AG

United Kingdom
Lloyds Bank Ltd.
Barclays Bank
Italian International Bank

Italy
Banca Commerciale Italiana
Banca Nazionale del Lavoro
Istituto Bancario San Paolo di Torino
Credito Italiano (London branch)

Ireland
Allied Irish Banks
Irish Intercontinental Bank Limited

Denmark
Copenhagen Handelsbank
Privatbanken Aktieselskab

Switerzland
Banque Keyser Ullmann

United States
Continental Illinois Limited
Salomon Brothers International
Chase Manhattan Limited
Kleinwort Bensen Limited
Chemical Bank

Japan
Bank of Tokyo International
Mitsubishi Bank (Europe)
Dai-Ichi Kangyo International

Source: Istituto Bancario San Paolo di Torino, *ECU Newsletter*, Vol. N-1 (February 1982).

wish to achieve monetary integration in Europe and to further the use of the ECU. The European Investment Bank's borrowing and lending in ECUs has given a substantial impetus to the use of the ECU by member governments and banks. Government support is necessary if a currency cocktail is to be used in financial markets.

A currency cocktail straddles both domestic and foreign currencies and so has no natural home within exchange control laws. This problem has been remedied by some governments' taking legal or administrative action. As from September 14, 1981, the ECU became a fully convertible currency in Italy. It is now quoted daily on the Rome and Milan stock exchanges. In Belgium and Luxembourg, as from March 1982, all operations in ECUs on behalf of residents, foreigners, and EEC institutions were authorized on the same terms and conditions that then governed operations in foreign currencies.

In France, a provision of May 21, 1982, which was issued by the Ministry of Economy and Finance, assimilates the ECU to foreign currencies under current exchange control regulations. Notwithstanding the general exchange control system, French banks are now allowed to provide nonresidents with the French franc equivalent of an ECU-denominated loan. The convertibility of the ECU is now recognized de jure in Italy, Belgium, Luxembourg, and France, and de facto in the Netherlands, the United Kingdom, Ireland, and Denmark. The only country in which serious difficulties still exist is Germany. The Federal Republic of Germany's 1948 Currency Law forbids "indexing" contracts and prohibits any "parallel currencies" from being used in the country.

Political support has come from member governments of the EEC, particularly those with weaker currencies, such as Italy, which have been willing to see their citizens and companies deal in ECUs to a greater extent than they would allow them to deal in other currencies. One means of allowing residents a controlled use of non-lira currencies is to permit them to use the ECU for certain purposes.

Incentives to Use the ECU

The ECU has established a niche for itself, given political, legal, and administrative support by EEC organizations and by many national governments. But it would not have done as well if it had lacked any of the existing economic incentives for its use. The ECU fulfills useful functions, and the following section will consider the economic rationale for its recent development.

There is no technical or financial difficulty in making use of cocktails such as the ECU. The banks are keen to develop such instruments when they become attractive in the marketplace. As far as bonds are concerned, at any one time only a few cocktails or currencies are acceptable in the market to both borrowers and lenders, and the banks are always seeking ways to produce a formula which is attractive enough to get an issue off the ground. In the banking markets, the technology is by now standard. The banks are keen to "show off" by developing new techniques. These may have substantial commercial value over and above the cash profit from the specific transactions, in terms of the boost they give the bank's public image and the other trade they may attract. The natural bias of the financial markets is to be responsive to profit opportunities provided by new financial vehicles.

The ECU has a natural strength, in that it is an excellent hedge for Europe. It naturally moves between the extremes of the main European currencies. If people wish to hold a currency as a proxy for "Europe," or to hedge against "Europe," then the ECU is an excellent vehicle. Many companies do have such needs.

People in weak-currency countries such as Denmark and Italy have a natural desire to borrow ECUs, because the exchange risk is less than if they borrowed genuinely hard currencies such as the guilder or the deutsche mark. Since the currencies available in a bond market tend to be the strongest, the ECU may thus be the least strong of the currency vehicles available for borrowing in the European context. As such, it is particularly welcome to residents of weak-currency countries, since the exchange risk is lessened. Similar considerations apply to Eurocredits, to which the main alternative would be dollar credits. In the latter case, the borrower would be taking an exchange risk which was more uncertain in relation to the movement of the European currencies against each other. There will be times when the ECU is, in investors' minds, less attractive than other currencies and ECU-denominated issues may not be acceptable. But so far this cocktail has proved adequately resilient, and issues have been well received. At current exchange rates, the deutsche mark and guilder together account for about 47.5 percent of the ECU.

The EEC has long-term objectives of political and economic integration. Even if there are many difficulties along the way, the sheer pressure of time and of economic integration will move member countries into closer relationships with each other. Substantial efforts are being made by governments within the EEC to make the EMS work and to keep currencies in relatively closer relationships with each other. Exchange rate stability is an objective of the majority of EEC member countries. Governments hope that the component currencies of the ECU will move together. The risks taken when the ECU is used in conjunction with European currencies should be controlled and reasonably foreseeable.

Not only is there in Europe political support for stability and integration but also countries suffer political costs if they face exchange rate weakness and currencies move against each other. There is a political incentive to adopt policies which will have the effect in due course of enhancing the credibility of the ECU.

The ECU gives a good spread between weak and strong currencies and between countries of differing real interest rates. The balance of exchange rate movements and interest costs should be acceptable and moderate in relation to the possible extremes that may occur if one were to use any individual EEC currency.

Despite these favorable developments, Rieke has pointed out (see Group of Thirty (1982)) some of the disadvantages facing the ECU. He has indicated legal difficulties which inhibit its use as a unit of account in certain countries. These stem from exchange controls, limitations in regard to banks' open foreign currency positions (e.g., the Federal Republic of Germany), monetary and credit controls, and national laws of contract or other legislation which effectively restricts its use. He considers it doubtful whether the ECU would provide a satisfactory means of reducing exchange rate risks or hedging costs in international trade, or even in intra-Community trade in current circumstances. At some point, ECU operations have to be broken down into the component currencies, whether for settlement, loans, deposits, or forward cover. Rieke recognizes that a number of European banks operate ECU accounts, but he argues that the procedure is laborious and costly and would tend to cause the banks' lending rates (deposit rates) to be higher (lower) than the weighted average of the interest cost (yield) on the individual currencies. He concludes (p. 54) that

> In order to achieve wider use of the ECU in banking transactions it would seem essential that the following legal conditions exist:
>
> (i) The ECU is fully convertible;
> (ii) Residents of each Community country are free to hold ECU-denominated bank accounts as well as ECU-denominated securities;
> (iii) The ECU must be capable of being used as a unit of account in commercial contracts.

However, banks operating in the market dispute that the procedure is laborious or the lending too costly, and would regard this as a pessimistic view.

Interest and Exchange Rates

There is at present no official fixing of the ECU in Brussels, but its value is computed officially each day, from the local currency prices of the dollar at 2:30 p.m. Many of the individual countries of Europe (such as Italy) have official fixings for their own exchange rates with the ECU.

Market rates are created, as with other currencies, on the basis of market exchange and interest rates as perceived by the quoting banks.

In order to make transactions in ECUs easier, most banks use an open ECU basket, rather than a closed one. This means that transactions take place in the ECU as it is defined at the moment. This definition may, of course, change during the life of a contract. The alternative system of using a closed basket means that each contract is based on the composition of the ECU in effect when the contract was first signed. Under this system, there could be several different ECU contracts in circulation at the same time. An open ECU basket is thus simpler for the participants. The banks are taking a certain very modest risk by using this procedure. This issue is, however, strictly academic so far, since the ECU basket has not been changed.

ECU interest and exchange rates must fundamentally be related to the rates on the unbundled individual currencies. Nevertheless, this comparison has a certain artificiality, in that a currency might not be available for certain transactions or might not be quoted freely in the Euromarkets. Thus, for example, in assessing a ten-year ECU Eurobond, one may have nothing to compare with the French franc, Italian lira, or Irish pound component, since those currencies may not be available for that maturity. There is no evidence that the interest rates on deposits, Eurocredits, or bonds are significantly above the weighted averages of the interest rates of the component currencies. The transaction cost element of putting an ECU bundle together is small, particularly for bonds.

V. BOND ISSUES IN ALL UNITS

Table 3 presents the issues of international and foreign bonds from 1973 to 1981. Total issues in all units of account over the nine years amounted to $2.6 billion, 1 percent of the total. Dollar issues accounted for 50 percent, Swiss franc issues for 18 percent, and deutsche mark issues for 16 percent. The item of units of account included all units, including the special drawing right (SDR) and the modern ECU, so the share of any individual unit of account was extremely small, a conclusion which is still valid if one adds in the official ECUs issued during 1982. Units of account issues tend to have less liquid secondary markets. They also pose more complicated funding problems for underwriters, who may need to borrow short term in order to carry their positions. When an institution is carrying a unit-of-account issue, it may have to take on exchange risks during the funding process, and the calculations regarding profitability and interest become more complicated. If one is carrying a dollar bond, one can borrow dollars and calculate relatively easily any running profit or loss, while there is no exchange risk. If one is carrying an SDR or ECU bond, one can avoid the exchange risk only by borrowing the individual currencies in the same proportion, which would be relatively complicated. If one finances the bond by borrowing, say, dollars, then one is taking on an exchange risk. The stronger interbank market in ECUs may make carrying positions easier than in other composite units.

Table 4 provides more detailed information regarding bond issues in individual units. This gives a total figure of $3,702.3 million from 1964 to

TABLE 3. CURRENCY DISTRIBUTION OF EXTERNAL BONDS, 1973-81
(In millions of U.S. dollars)

Year		U.S. Dollar	Swiss Franc	Deutsche Mark	Yen	Dutch Guilder	Canadian Dollar	OPEC Currencies[1]
1973	International bonds	2,408.4	—	997.6	—	191.8	—	—
	Foreign bonds	1,487.5	1,545.7	418.0	296.6	—	—	192.7
	Total	3,895.9	1,545.7	1,415.6	296.6	191.8	—	192.7
1974	International bonds	1,991.0	—	659.2	—	382.8	59.5	51.5
	Foreign bonds	3,576.7	986.1	—	—	4.1	20.2	623.3
	Total	5,567.7	986.1	659.2	—	386.9	79.7	674.8
1975	International bonds	3,381.5	—	2,917.6	10.1	651.4	566.4	147.3
	Foreign bonds	6,546.0	3,372.1	352.0	66.6	208.6	—	133.3
	Total	9,927.5	3,372.1	3,289.6	76.7	860.0	566.4	280.6
1976	International bonds	9,874.0	—	2,863.8	—	530.1	1,449.8	351.5
	Foreign bonds	11,015.6	5,322.4	1,073.0	226.1	674.2	—	—
	Total	20,889.6	5,322.4	3,936.8	226.1	1,204.3	1,449.8	351.5
1977	International bonds	11,592.8	—	5,173.3	111.3	362.7	653.7	304.9
	Foreign bonds	7,868.2	4,959.3	1,407.1	1,275.9	182.1	—	385.8
	Total	19,461.0	4,959.3	6,580.4	1,387.2	544.8	653.7	690.7

Year								
1978	International bonds	6,849.4	—	6,555.8	78.9	384.3	—	596.2
	Foreign bonds	6,358.6	7,411.7	1,431.1	4,387.9	351.5	—	164.5
	Total	13,208.0	7,411.7	7,986.9	4,466.7	735.8	—	760.7
1979	International bonds	10,214.5	—	4,769.9	115.1	307.5	467.9	383.7
	Foreign bonds	4,364.6	9,479.5	2,615.1	2,655.3	162.8	—	29.8
	Total	14,579.1	9,479.5	7,385.0	2,770.4	470.3	467.9	413.5
1980	International bonds	13,298.8	—	3,457.2	330.9	549.0	270.3	26.2
	Foreign bonds	2,736.4	7,469.9	4,951.5	1,542.6	325.3	—	144.3
	Total	16,035.2	7,469.9	8,408.7	1,843.5	874.3	270.3	170.5
1981	International bonds	21,251.8	—	1,377.3	407.9	415.8	686.8	387.4
	Foreign bonds	7,575.5	8,129.7	1,188.7	2,735.2	485.9	—	—
	Total	28,827.3	8,129.7	2,566.0	3,143.1	901.7	686.8	387.4
1973–81	International bonds	80,862.2	—	28,771.7	1,024.2	3,775.4	4,154.4	2,248.7
	Foreign bonds	51,529.1	48,676.4	13,436.5	13,186.1	2,394.5	20.2	1,673.7
	Total	132,391.3	48,676.4	42,208.2	14,210.3	6,169.9	4,174.6	3,922.4

TABLE 3. (concluded). CURRENCY DISTRIBUTION OF EXTERNAL BONDS, 1973–81
(In millions of U.S. dollars)

Year		Pound Sterling	French Franc	Units of Account[2]	BLEU[3] Currencies	Norwegian Kroner	Other	Total
1973	International bonds	29.8	161.8	164.6	124.4	—	37.9	4,116.3
	Foreign bonds	8.7	52.1	—	251.8	—	222.1	4,475.2
	Total	38.5	213.9	164.6	376.2	—	260.0	3,591.5
1974	International bonds	23.9	—	236.3	—	—	15.0	3,419.2
	Foreign bonds	—	—	—	131.8	—	21.8	5,364.0
	Total	23.9	—	236.3	131.8	—	36.8	8,783.2
1975	International bonds	—	326.0	600.7	38.6	44.8	31.4	8,715.8
	Foreign bonds	32.2	57.5	—	147.1	—	43.9	10,959.3
	Total	32.2	383.5	600.7	185.7	44.8	75.3	19,675.1
1976	International bonds	—	39.1	83.8	—	—	18.7	15,210.8
	Foreign bonds	—	76.4	—	27.1	—	45.5	18,460.3
	Total	—	115.5	83.8	27.1	—	64.2	33,671.1
1977	International bonds	220.9	—	33.5	—	—	171.7	18,624.8
	Foreign bonds	—	61.8	—	122.9	—	—	16,263.1
	Total	220.9	61.8	33.5	122.9	—	171.7	34,887.9

1978	International bonds	287.1	103.2	234.9	—	—	30.6	15,120.4
	Foreign bonds	—	252.7		354.6	—	29.0	20,741.5
	Total	287.1	355.9	234.9	354.6	—	59.6	35,861.9
1979	International bonds	291.3	373.5	412.4	—	—	17.1	17,352.9
	Foreign bonds	—	197.7		345.0	—	129.8	19,979.6
	Total	291.3	571.2	412.4	345.0	—	146.9	37,332.5
1980	International bonds	975.9	882.8	99.4	—	100.5	87.7	20,048.7
	Foreign bonds	177.9	262.5		262.6	—	80.7	17,953.7
	Total	1,153.8	1,145.3	99.4	262.6	100.5	168.4	38,002.4
1981	International bonds	538.7	533.1	747.7	—	52.6	87.5	26,486.6
	Foreign bonds	910.6	90.4		191.7	—	—	21,307.7
	Total	1,449.3	623.5	747.7	191.7	52.6	87.5	47,794.3
1973–81	International bonds	2,367.6	2,419.5	2,613.3	163.0	197.9	497.6	129,095.5
	Foreign bonds	1,129.4	1,051.1		1,834.6	—	572.8	135,504.4
	Total	3,497.0	3,470.6	2,613.3	1,997.6	197.9	1,070.4	264,599.9

Source: Organization for Economic Cooperation and Development, *Finance Market Trends*.
[1] Bahrain dinar, Kuwaiti dinar, Saudi Arabian riyal, Trinidad and Tobago dollar, U.A.E. dirham, and Venezuelan bolívar.
[2] ECU, EMU, EURCO, EUA, and SDR.
[3] Belgium-Luxembourg Economic Union.

September 1982 inclusive. (This table does not include bonds denominated in units but sold in national markets, such as the ECU 450 million of the ECU 500 million Italian bond issue which was sold to Italian residents.) Consistently the most successful unit has been the private sector European Unit of Account which in its "old" and "new" forms has been used for issues amounting to $1,525.7 million, or 41.2 percent of the total. Three minor units had a brief spell of relevance. The ARCRU, the EURCO, and the private European Currency Unit accounted in all for $329.7 million of issues, all during 1970-74. The SDR was used for $717.3 million of issues, during 1975-81. Recently the official European Currency Unit (ECU) has dominated the figures, accounting for $687.5 million of issues during 1981 and 1982, and 97 percent of total issues in individual units during the first three quarters of 1982. There were no SDR bond issues during 1982. The totals of official European Currency Units and SDR issues are similar— $687.5 million as against $717.3 million.

The potential for individual currencies or currency units in the bond markets varies according to expectations about interest and exchange rates. Borrowers may be unwilling to take on high-coupon borrowing for economic, commercial, or "political" reasons. One hears at times that it is more difficult for politicians to justify paying out of the exchequer a high interest payment than it is for them to worry about an exchange risk which either may be hidden in the national accounts or, if it surfaces, may affect their successor rather than themselves. Correspondingly, investors are concerned very much with the preservation of the value of assets and are, therefore, unwilling to invest in weak currencies. The international bond market is extremely innovative and competitive, and the various banks in this field are concerned continually to find the particular type of bond

TABLE 4. BOND ISSUES IN UNITS OF ACCOUNT, 1964-82
(*In millions of U.S. dollars*)

Currency of Issue	1964	1965	1966	1967	1968	1969	1970	1971	1972	1973
ARCRU	—	—	—	—	—	—	—	—	—	—
EURCO	—	—	—	—	—	—	—	—	—	64.8
Private European Currency Unit	—	—	—	—	—	—	60.0	95.0	30.0	—
Official European Currency Unit	—	—	—	—	—	—	—	—	—	—
"Old" European Unit of Account	10.0	—	75.6	19.0	57.0	60.0	54.0	166.5	—	—
"New" European Unit of Account	—	—	—	—	—	—	—	—	—	104.3
SDRs	—	—	—	—	—	—	—	—	—	—

TABLE 4. *(concluded).* BOND ISSUES IN UNITS OF ACCOUNT, 1964-82
(In millions of U.S. dollars)

Currency of Issue	1974	1975	1976	1977	1978	1979	1980	1981	1982 (Jan.- Sept.)	Total
ARCRU	12.0	—	—	—	—	—	—	—	—	12.0
EURCO	67.9	—	—	—	—	—	—	—	—	132.7
Private European Currency Unit	—	—	—	—	—	—	—	—	—	185.0
Official European Currency Unit	—	—	—	—	—	—	—	236.1	451.4	687.5
"Old" European Unit of Account	—	—	—	—	—	—	—	—	—	442.1
"New" European Unit of Account	171.4	387.6	102.7	33.5	202.8	305.8	79.8	125.5	12.3	1,525.7
SDRs	—	172.9	—	—	32.1	106.6	19.6	386.1	—	717.3

Source: Organization for Economic Cooperation and Development, *Financial Statistics.*

which appeals to customers and places them in a favorable competitive position.

These points are made not because this paper seeks to analyze in detail the mechanics of the bond markets, but to indicate that inevitably there will be certain times when particular forms of bonds are either particularly acceptable or not welcome in the bond market. Subject to that proviso, there is virtually no bias against the use of composite currency units, when both parties find that acceptable. The fee structure of SDR and ECU bonds is similar to that on other bonds. With a banking transaction in SDRs or ECUs, one can compare the interest rate with those on the unbundled individual currencies. This is not possible, however, in the case of bond issues, since markets do not exist in many of those currencies for the maturity or type of issue in question. It is not possible to make any meaningful comparison between the interest cost of a bond in a composite currency unit and that of bonds in its component currencies. Nevertheless, there is no evidence that terms on bonds of composite currency units are unreasonable in relation to those in national currencies. The market is a very competitive place, and abnormal gains are soon squeezed out. When there is an appetite on the part of investors for bonds in composite currency units, then terms are competitive.

VI. CORPORATE CURRENCY RISK MANAGEMENT

Corporate cash and exchange risk management is a major feature of the functions of treasurers of large corporations and has been examined in great detail in various publications. The attitude of the corporate sector to currency cocktails may be indicated by the amount and type of references to cocktails in these works. In general, the space devoted to currency cocktails is small compared with that devoted to other currencies and techniques, and the references are not particularly favorable.

Conceptually, there are three distinct ways in which companies frame their problems when hedging transactions or operating in the exchange and interest rate markets. First, they may need to hedge their transactions exposure, which relates to the exposure that impinges upon their profit and loss accounts. Thus, for example, a company may produce goods in a British factory, with costs based on the pound sterling, and may sell these to a buyer in the Federal Republic of Germany, invoiced in deutsche mark, and not receive payment for some months. In this case, the movement of the deutsche mark/pound sterling exchange rate in the intervening period will affect the company's profit on the transaction, and so the question arises whether the exposure should be run or hedged.

The second consideration relates to translation exposure, which is the hedging of balance sheet items. An example would be an American company which had a natural dollar base and had a factory in the United Kingdom. The value of that factory would be calculated in pound sterling terms and would move with the dollar/pound sterling exchange rate. As the exchange rate moved, the net worth of the company would be affected. The company could remove this balance sheet exposure by creating long-term sterling liabilities of a similar value.

Both the transaction and translation risks are what Donaldson (1980) calls financial risk, in that they may be controlled by actions in the financial markets. He distinguishes them from economic currency risk, which is the impact of currency movements on real profitability of underlying economic activity. An example of this, which may not be remedied by activity in the financial markets, would be the adverse impact on the profitability of a factory exporting from the United Kingdom stemming from the appreciation of the pound sterling during 1979–80.

A third approach by companies to treasury functions is to regard them as profit centers. Companies may expect their treasuries to take controlled risks, such as through taking uncovered positions in the foreign exchange market or through mismatching maturities in the deposit markets. By those means, they may generate income from their activity in the foreign exchange and financial markets.

The transactions required for hedging and for profit are extremely precise as to the currency, exchange rate, and interest rate and have to satisfy strict criteria regarding maturity and amount. The problem for a large trading company in controlling exchange risks is also complicated, both conceptually and in terms of being informed about and assessing the risk of an extremely large number of transactions.

Currency cocktails may well not coincide with the risks which a company is trying to hedge against, and the financial markets in cocktails are not well developed enough to provide the precision and liquidity which would be required if companies were to use them in a big way.

A company which wished to go for a profitability target, and thus to back its own judgment in selected areas, might find currency cocktails to be too blunt an instrument. Correspondingly, companies which wished to hedge only selectively, while leaving a large majority of their positions to run, might find that currency cocktails did not coincide with the precise risks which they wished to hedge, which would almost certainly relate to the risks as between particular individual currencies.

Currency cocktails and, in particular, the ECU are, however, helpful if they are used to minimize the risk of being caught in an extreme position, and where precision is not required. Thus, in the case of Saint-Gobain, the use of the ECU for transfer pricing within the company is a means of apportioning the exchange risk between the different plants and, because internal transfers are involved, the impact on the profit-and-loss account of the group as a whole is nil. When borrowers in Denmark or Italy borrow ECUs, they can rely on the fact that the movement of the ECU will be within the range of European currency movements and that they are therefore controlling the maximum risk which they would be subject to. The use of the ECU in that relatively long-term market is very sensible. The ECU may also be used well in hedging monetary compensatory amount (MCA) payments under the European Community's Common Agricultural Policy. But if a company had to hedge some tens of thousands of individual transactions, exporting to many other countries, with a variety of time periods of credit, then its risk problem is both complicated and precise, and no composite unit would be likely to coincide with its risk structure.

Whatever the use now made of currency cocktails, their markets cannot begin to compare with the markets in the main currencies, in relation to turnover, depth, and availability of assets and liabilities. It is precisely those features of the markets of the individual currencies which make them more attractive to companies when they are concerned with controlling exposure.

The study of corporate cash management and corporate exchange risk is well developed, and is a very important feature of the work of corporate treasurers. There have been many books and articles on this subject. Attitudes toward the use of currency cocktails for managing corporate exposure are influenced by the views of writers on corporate financial management. The views they express may be taken as an unbiased view of the potential role of international moneys and currency units. They are concerned to give unbiased advice to corporations and have no vested interest for or against the use of international moneys.

Kenyon (1981), in a book of 191 pages, makes only one reference to currency cocktails. He refers (p. 134) to:

> The case of a large financial institution in the United Kingdom or Italy, competing with rivals in Germany, Switzerland and France. Such an institution might well feel that its main competitive weapon is the size of its net worth relative to that of its competitors. It might therefore wish to measure its currency risk in terms of either a strong currency like the deutsche mark or in terms of a basket of currencies like the European Unit of Account or the SDR. Another case is that of the true multinational like Shell or Unilever, which had its financial ownership based in more than one country. It too might not be content to measure its currency position in just one currency.

The author then clearly identifies these as exceptional situations by going on: "It is enough to draw attention to these important exceptions, and to use the convenient expression 'reporting currency' to denote the currency in which the company wishes to measure its currency risk."

Donaldson (1980) makes no reference to currency cocktails at all. Kettell (1979), in a book of 275 pages, makes frequent references to cocktails. These are referred to descriptively in various parts, and on pages 198-202 he discusses currency cocktails at greater length. He points out that: "Currency cocktails are practical means of diffusing the effect of exchange rate fluctuations on international trade and investment." His conclusion is that: "There could certainly be benefits to importers and exporters in using currency cocktails to reduce exchange rate risks. This is particularly true for longer-term contracts or in the less universally used currencies where exchange cover is not easy to obtain. The evidence at present is, however, that the unavoidable complexities of currency 'baskets' and their unfamiliarity have deterred companies from adopting this type of technique."

Aliber (1978) makes only one reference to units of account or currency cocktails (p. 16) when he describes the special drawing right. He comments that: "Thus far this component of the total supply of international money has been small and not a disturbance to the exchange rate structure."

Jacque (1978) discusses units of account at reasonable length (pp. 220-34). He asserts (p. 220) that:

> In many respects, such artificial currency units of account are nothing more than contractual exchange risk-sharing devices. The idea is to substitute for a unit of account based on a single currency, a unit of account based on several currencies (artificial currency units of account). The foreign exchange risk is then apportioned between the borrowing and lending parties so that neither bears the full brunt of exposure to exchange gains or losses. Clearly the emphasis is on *sharing* exchange risks rather than on eliminating them.

In commenting on the EURCO (p. 228), he says:

> Even though the EURCO has pioneered the new and conceptually attractive concept of a currency basket, it has only been used for the denomination of three bond issues, two of

which were for the benefit of the European Investment Bank. The main weakness of the EURCO as a unit of account for denominating bonds is that approximately half its value is tied to European Economic Community currencies of doubtful prospective strength such as the pound sterling, the French franc, and the Italia lira.

In discussing the European Unit of Account (private version) he comments (p. 226): "...An investment in EUAs differs fundamentally from investment in a foreign currency; hence, its popularity as a vehicle for denominating long-term debentures on the international capital market." Concluding this passage (pp. 227-28) Jacque asks:

Does the denomination of long-term bonds in artificial currency units such as the SDR or the EUA reconcile the conflicting interests of borrowers and lenders? A superficial answer is a tentative 'no' if one considers the relatively minor share of bond issues that were denominated in artificial currency units as opposed to single currencies, such as the DM or the US dollar, during the 1971-1975 period. A more elaborate answer to this question must consider in some further detail the position of the lending and borrowing parties.

He continues: "Potential bond holders are generally interested in maximising interest payments while minimising exchange losses. This naive characterisation of investors' behaviour has to be qualified somewhat, depending upon the size and diversification of their portfolio as well as the degree of their risk aversion:" He adds that: "The currency diversification provided by artificial currency units based on the currency basket *concept* will be largely redundant for large institutional investors that have scientifically diversified their portfolio of assets." But for individual investors: "By limiting the risk of exchange losses, artificial currency units can restore individual investors' confidence in bonds whose primary attraction lies essentially in the fact that they are riskless return-yielding assets."

The following passage (pp. 228-29) sets out his views from the borrowers' point of view:

For borrowing institutions that are primarily domestic, such as utilities or municipalities, floating bond issues denominated in a foreign currency simply because of a lower nominal cost of the debt instrument is a hasty decision and may turn out to be a costly proposition if the currency of denomination happens to revalue (appreciate) vis-à-vis the operating currency of the borrower during the life of the loan. Under such circumstances, the borrower is well advised to denominate its bond issue in an artificial currency unit such as the SDR, the EUA, or the EURCO. The risk of capital losses are certainly not eliminated, but greatly reduced at a cost that is eminently reasonable (difference between the coupon rate on the artificial currency unit-denominated bond issue and the lowest nominal coupon rate available on the international capital market). Thus, the use of artificial currency units for denominating long-term debentures allows the borrower to maintain its access to this unique wholesale capital market without unduly exposing itself to potential exchange losses resulting from wild gyrations in the exchange rates of single currencies.

For corporations that are characterised by a wide geographical diversification of their assets and liabilities and that, as a result, generate income in several currencies, the added currency diversification, provided by debt instruments denominated in artificial currency units, appears to be eminently superfluous. Such borrowers are, therefore, advised to match, on a prospective basis, their debt instruments denominated in single currencies with income expressed in the same currencies.

Contractual devices for limiting exchange losses in international debt financing have been introduced on the international capital market in recent years. They essentially consist of denominating bonds in artificial units of account based upon the value of a *basket* of currencies.

Such contractual schemes that allow for the apportioning of exchange risk between lenders and borrowers include Special Drawing Rights (SDRs), European Units of Account (EUAs), European Composite Units (EURCOs), and Arab Currency-Related Units (ARCRUs).

Corporate borrowers whose economic activities are essentially domestic will consider the use of artificial currency units as a way of minimising exchange losses in long-term international financing. Multinational corporate borrowers whose assets and liabilities are widely diversified in a geographical sense will find the additional currency diversification provided by debt instruments denominated in artificial currency units largely redundant.

Heywood (1979) makes numerous references to units and currency cocktails. He points out (p. 50):

For most practical purposes worldwide, risk can be approximated by using seven currencies, possibly supplemented by the SDR. The usual seven chosen are dollars, deutsche marks, sterling, and the currencies of Netherlands, Norway, France and Japan; without too much loss of accuracy this list can be reduced further by dropping Netherlands, Norway and the sixteen-currency SDR.

He describes in Appendix B (pp. 137–45) various currency units. He points out (p. 137) that:

Ideally the treasurer should borrow in the currency in which he expects to receive income, and deposit the currency in which he expects to have outgoings. But this is not always possible to arrange, particularly where the currency of future cash flows is largely unknown, or is made up of many currencies. Here the use of 'currency baskets' or 'composite currencies' seeks to achieve a stable form of international money which can spread risk and give at least an approximate means of hedging.

He adds that: "These units command little more than a small specialised market as yet, but their importance is slowly growing."

As far as the private ECU was concerned, he comments (p. 142):

Several bond issues were made on an ECU basis in the years 1970–72 but it has been little used in more recent years. The fact that the investor in an ECU bond stands to make an exchange gain equal to the movement of the strongest of the six currencies and that this loss is borne by the borrower, coupled with the large exchange movements recently experienced, led to the abandonment of the ECU as a substantial borrowing medium. It simply was not possible to reconcile the interests of the investors with those of the borrowers.

He adds that the European Unit of Account: "is the only European based composite currency that has come into anything like a widespread use.... Its principal advantage is that it is consciously designed to be a very stable unit." He concludes (p. 144): "But, as clearly shown by the experience of the ECU, it is difficult to reconcile the conflicting interests of borrowers and investors: because of the very stability it offers borrowers, the ...

EUA ... is less attractive to the investor who, in today's times of changing exchange rates, increasingly seeks capital appreciation from revaluation."

As far as the official ECU is concerned, Heywood comments (p. 145): "Because of the increasing use of the ... ECU ... by the Community, it is likely that this composite will gradually come into commercial use in the same way as the SDR has already begun to do."

Aschheim and Park (1976) discuss in some detail the development of artificial currency units and link them with the concept of optimal currency areas. Their main conclusions are related to the role of such units in international monetary reform, rather than in relation to corporate funding and exchange risk control.

Ensor and Antl (1982), in a study of 265 pages, devote a short section to the use of the SDR in hedging procedures (pp. 205–209). In that section, Putnam argues (p. 205) that: "The new SDR may offer some interesting possibilities for managing residual forex and interest rate exposure and may be a useful vehicle for both borrowers and investors." He adds (p. 207) that "on an interest rate and foreign exchange basis, the behaviour of this arbitrary basket may provide a natural hedge for many corporations exposed to international financial risks." An advantage of using the SDR basket as against any other which a corporation might wish to create is that the SDR is also liquid.

> There are substantial transaction cost gains available. Perhaps more important is the opportunity to save the costs of constantly monitoring multi-currency positions.... There is a role for SDRs in managing residual foreign exchange and interest rate risk. Indeed, the attractiveness of the SDR as a residual risk management tool is that it automatically combines interest rate and foreign exchange management problems.

He adds: "SDR investments are likely to appeal to a wide variety of multi-currency portfolio holders in a world of divergent monetary policies. When interest rates across countries show wide differentials, the potential for major exchange rate movements is also heightened." The situation has been improved by the redefinition of the SDR (p. 209):

> With a multitude of currencies included, many with no capital markets of any size and no forward exchange markets, the SDR was doomed to illiquidity. But the new five-currency basket introduced in January 1981 has significant promise for liquidity. The overall liquidity of the SDR is limited by the smallest individual market of the five currencies, presently the French franc market.... The basic conditions that make interest rates and foreign exchange exposure management such a dangerous business are not likely to disappear in the near future.... In this context, such management tools as prepackaged currency cocktails, and specifically the SDR, may very well establish a small but important role.

Most of the commentators quoted above seem to be contributing a good deal of common sense to the debate on this subject. However, their work is relevant, whether or not it is sensible, because it contains the views which are being expressed to the corporate sector. The authors quoted above, in order to earn a living and to enhance their reputations, need to do the best they can to contribute good advice to the corporate sector, so the above may be taken as a relatively unbiased estimate of the judgments which the authors think the corporate sector should be making about the use of composite currency units.

The following is a broad summary of these comments. Most authors now feel obliged or wish to make a reasonable factual summary of the use of composite units in international financing. In many cases, the summaries are comprehensive. Second, most authors point out that these composite units tend to suit companies only with somewhat unusual circumstances, and do not coincide with the normal range of risks with which companies need to deal. Third, they point out the weakness of units which entail large exchange risks for borrowers or lenders. Fourth, they indicate the likelihood of official units such as the SDR and ECU acquiring a wider commercial use, provided that they satisfy other requirements, such as being relatively natural hedges and being reasonable means of apportioning exchange risks between the lender and borrower.

Survey of Corporate Opinion

In order to obtain a better perspective on what would be required to make currency units of greater interest to the corporate sector, I conducted a survey among 100 substantial companies. Seventy of these companies were British, and 30 non-British. Some were major multinational companies, and all were large companies. A questionnaire was sent to each corporate treasurer. The response was good, with 80 percent (56) of the U.K. companies replying, and 73 percent (22) of the non-British companies. Companies replying included such major names as Shell, Imperial Chemical Industries, Volvo, and Volkswagen, indicating the high quality of the respondents.

A full report is given in the Appendix. A brief summary of the results is as follows. Not surprisingly, only 10 of the respondents had used international money units, and 68 had not.

The reasons for not using such units divided between factors related to the quality of the market and structural weaknesses in the units themselves. There were 29 annotations that the units were too illiquid, had markets that were too small, or the company had not heard of them (2) or did not know how to obtain them. There were 60 annotations that the units did not coincide with the company's risk structure or had the wrong currency mix. (The annotations add up to more than 68 because multiple responses were allowed.)

There was no problem regarding the role of the financial institutions in informing companies of such units. Forty-five companies had had discussions with their banks about them, on 31 occasions at the bank's initiative.

Six companies had used the SDR, three the official ECU, and three the private sector European Unit of Account. In four cases the use of currency units amounted to up to 1 percent of a company's cash management, and in two cases to between 1 and 5 percent. The units were used for a range of transactions, including short-term (3), medium-term and long-term (2), and for hedging transaction exposure (3) and translation exposure (1). Of the suggestions for improvements in such units, most were related to the quality of the market. Forty-two wished a larger market, 7 finer terms, 20 greater liquidity, and 13 more regular quotation. Only four referred to a change of currency structure. In this case, comments were requested. Some companies indicated that their currency structures were unlikely to be satisfied by any unit. One company mentioned the development of the ECU as being interesting, while others referred to a need for a wide variety of units to choose from.

There was some optimism for the future, in that 15 companies thought that units could in the future compete, for their purposes, with the markets in the main currencies, although 34 thought that this was unlikely.

The flavor of the replies is given in the large number of comments which companies sent in, which are reported in full in the Appendix.

This survey indicates the small role played at present by currency units in companies' cash management. The financial marketplace clearly works, in that banks inform companies of the opportunities. The decisions rests with companies, which will decide the role of currency units in the context of other possibilities open to the companies. In many cases, the structure of a company's business makes it unlikely that any official unit could satisfy its needs. Nevertheless, there is hope for the future, in that an improvement in the quality of the market—as regards size, range, and liquidity—would make companies more willing to consider using such units.

VII. EUROMARKET DEVELOPMENT

One of the most spectacular developments in the postwar period has been the development of the Euromarkets. These comprise the banking market, which now amounts to some $2,015 billion, and the Eurobond and foreign bond markets. The amounts raised in the bond markets have been very substantial indeed in recent years, in some years rivaling the amount of new Eurocurrency finance raised.

This growth has taken place largely through organic market development, without governments or international organizations having taken positive steps to bring it about. This general situation is familiar, and there is no need to consider it in detail, but it is worthwhile mentioning in passing various reasons why the markets have developed so substantially, and to indicate how such factors are conspicuously lacking in the case of currency units. Their lack needs to be made up by positive government and institutional action if the use of currency units is to be expanded.

The great momentum for the growth of the Eurodollar market was the international dollar's strength, convertibility, and freedom from control, as well as its freedom from U.S. fiscal and regulatory requirements. Liquidity was guaranteed through the interrelationship between the Eurodollar market, the U.S. banks, and the U.S. domestic dollar. There was a natural business source in the activities of the multinational companies, many of them dollar based. Since the dollar was the most stable currency, it was a natural currency for citizens of other countries to wish to use.

The development of the Eurobond and foreign bond markets took place similarly, benefiting in many cases from the desire of investors to be free of regulatory and fiscal requirements. The investing currencies—mainly the dollar, the deutsche mark, and the Swiss franc—have been traditional bond currencies. The infrastructure of the market was built up by experienced investing houses and banks. The markets are usually integrated very closely with the national bond markets, and indeed all deutsche mark bonds are foreign bonds rather than Eurobonds. They are thus supported by close supervision and a strong institutional structure which it is very much in the interests of powerful banks and central banks to maintain.

The markets developed in recent years as governments began to encourage financial flows in the banking and capital markets, so as to help control the exchange rate or the money supply at times of fluctuating balances of payments. Faced with the financial pressures which followed the breakdown of the Bretton Woods system and the instability associated with the increases in and increased volatility of oil prices since 1973, countries have responded with a series of measures which have encouraged capital flows and, at the same time, created the conditions for greater future flows (see Lomax and Gutmann (1981, especially pp. 225-31 and 240-42)). Thus, Japan had a significant net long-term capital outflow up to 1974, which peaked in 1973. But during 1974-75, Japan ran large current account deficits and encouraged inward portfolio investment. However, by 1976, the current account was moving into increasing surplus, and capital exports were encouraged. In this last period, foreign borrowings in the Japanese bond market (the Samurai bond, or Japanese foreign bond, market) grew from $67 million in 1975 to $3,826 million in 1978 (see Lomax and Gutmann, pp. 76-101). In the course of this process, a new market was developed that facilitated the further expansion of capital flows in the future.

Without giving further examples, policy changes and new financial conditions led various countries to facilitate capital flows and develop new markets, without destroying the markets which existed to deal with other flows. There was the development of U.S. foreign bonds (Yankee bonds) and British foreign bonds (Bulldog bonds), as well as sharp fluctuations in the volume of deutsche mark, Swiss franc, and guilder foreign bonds according to the balance of payments situation and policy stance of the relevant authorities. By these processes, the international capital markets became more complete and more integrated.

The substantial development of the Japanese markets—including the international development of Japanese banks and finance houses, the increasing international use of the yen, the present pressures within Japan and abroad for further external use of the yen and for Japan to become an offshore center—is similar to the earlier development of markets in the Federal Republic of Germany. There is the inevitable pressure for a strong manufacturing country to become a financial center and for its currency to be used internationally. As the country exports successfully, foreign importers acquire debts in the currency in question and so wish to acquire assets to hedge their liabilities. The massive expansion of trade from manufacturing success leads to a desire for trade financing; and in order not to incur exchange risks, the exporter may wish to arrange the financing in his own currency. The Japanese institutions and banks have become larger because of the success of their country's economy, and their increasing size has encouraged them to look for foreign outlets for their capital and energy. Japanese organizations have begun to accumulate substantial savings, or have substantial financing requirements in the banking and bond markets to go with their strengths, and thus wish to hedge their risks by going into the international markets. Japanese companies are courted by international financial organizations. There is a natural desire among the Japanese to obtain for themselves a greater part of the value added by banking services in dealing with their own organizations, rather than allowing this to be earned by institutions abroad. Having achieved spectacular growth in manufacturing, the Japanese have begun to encounter market saturation, because of the slower growth of world trade and the spread of protectionism, and thus have been looking round for other means of generating employment and growth. Manufacturing takes a slightly lower priority in their view. The natural progression is to move toward a service economy, indeed, a financial service economy—a path that has been taken by many successful manufacturing nations—by internationalizing the currency.

The simple point is that these natural forces which have led to some very major changes in international markets in recent years have had little effect on currency units such as the ECU and the SDR. The lack of basic underlying day-to-day commercial contracts in composite currency units is a major weakness. Salaries are not paid in SDRs (although they are paid in ECUs); trade is not contracted significantly in SDRs; people do not naturally acquire assets or liabilities in SDRs and thus need to hedge them. The SDR does not have the depth or liquidity which was one of the key features of the dollar's development. It does not benefit from the cumulative forces, set out in the example above, which pushed the yen into prominence. It does not have a strong institutional structure backing it in financial markets, as Swiss franc and deutsche mark do in the bond markets. These factors mean it is highly unlikely that a composite currency unit will ever stand a chance of becoming as dominant as a major currency, particularly in the short-term markets. If such a unit is to acquire a niche, it will need strong official support to obtain that position.

VIII. THE SDR

This paper has refrained so far from examining in detail the role of the SDR. The two papers "Possible Further Improvements in the Existing SDR" and "Evolution of the SDR Outside the Fund" which are, respectively, Chapters 12 and 13 in this volume—cover this subject extensively. Nevertheless, a market view of the SDR is expected from the present author, and consequently this paper will highlight what appear to be key features of the SDR's present situation.

The SDR's image at present in the market place is one almost that of a declining asset. The volume of SDR deposits has been reduced very substantially from the peak of a few years ago, almost certainly by more than 50 percent. There were no bond issues denominated in SDRs in 1982. The reasons for this are complicated and inevitably uncertain, and this problem leads to speculation as to the best course of action in the future.

The SDR market was essentially created by one private sector depositor, Shell Brunei. It was presumed at the time that that organization wished to obtain a higher interest rate than it was possible to earn on dollars and, at the same time, was concerned about the strength of the dollar. The former 16-currency SDR provided investors with the opportunity to place funds in higher-yielding currencies. Whatever the merits of this analysis, the change in the SDR to a 5-currency basket largely coincided with the restoration of the fortunes of the dollar, which convinced investors that the dollar itself was a more attractive investment medium. Investors have done much better in dollars than in SDRs in recent years.

The SDR is nevertheless used still in the banking markets, although to a lesser extent than formerly. Trading in the SDR has to take place almost entirely through bundling the component currencies each time a transaction is undertaken. This is complicated, with an SDR commitment requiring up to 20 entries, compared with 2 for a deposit in a single currency. In order to cover the direct costs and the inconvenience involved, banks need to ensure that there is a certain minimum profit on each transaction. Margins on SDR transactions have fallen very substantially in recent years, but nevertheless are higher than transactions in single currencies. The concept of opportunity cost is relevant here. Any dealing operation contains scarce resources in the forms of space, time, trained dealers, and management skills. Many dealing rooms generate substantial profits through normal and relatively straightforward activity in the main currencies. Running a desk concerned with currency baskets requires segregating one dealer to engage in time-consuming transactions and to operate the minicomputer, yet the number of transactions he handles will be fewer than are handled by the dealers in national currencies. The larger the volume of dealing in a composite currency, the more likely it is that banks will be willing to use their scarce resources in this way, and the lower will be the transaction costs.

The main technical feature of the SDR of relevance to the market concerns the IMF fixing, at the middle rates at noon London time. The problem for the market is not that they are middle rates, but that traders may not find it possible to deal at those rates. Foreign exchange markets are very volatile and operate at fine margins. Even if banks try to cover themselves by trading at the same time, noon, they may find themselves using rates different from those fixed. This problem arises from the volatility of the market. Banks therefore try to steer new customers away from the Fund's fixing, but this may be impossible as regards substantial customers which have already used the Fund's system for many years.

The Certificate of Deposit (CD) market in SDRs continues to function, but there is virtually no secondary market, and new issues are few.

The situation of the SDR in the marketplace should give some cause for concern, and the question arises as to how it might be remedied. The evidence shows that if the customers are there, then the market will respond. There are customers for the ECU, but there are few customers for the SDR. Banks are willing to undertake the development effort required to use these baskets, even at a short-term loss, if the potential is there. The best way of remedying this situation is for others to judge, but if, for example, the Fund, the International Bank for Reconstruction and Development, central banks, and governments were to take and place in the private sector SDR market, then it would be revitalized. If they do not, then the market will not be able to pull itself up by its own bootstraps. This point is much more important than questions relating to the structure of the SDR itself.

The SDR has some advantages in that its component currencies are eminently tradable and that it may be built up either through the deposit market or through the swap market.

The fact that the SDR tended to be used rather less after its basket was reduced to five currencies led to speculation whether a larger number of currencies should be used. As indicated above, providing there were customers, any kind of SDR would be used. But that is not the whole answer to the question. There are two features which would inevitably limit the number of currencies which it would be wise to include in the SDR. The first is that investors would wish the SDR to be a reasonable standard of value and a hedge against currency movements. Including notoriously weak currencies in it would diminish its value considerably.

Second, since the SDR has largely to be traded by bundling and unbundling, it is vital that the currencies in it be fully tradable for the period for which one wishes to have an SDR market. For the 16-currency SDR, this was not always possible, and banks weathered that situation by taking a risk on the weak currencies which formed only a small part of the SDR and were not tradable. It would be preferable not to re-establish that situation, and banks would be unwilling to bear that risk if nontradable currencies formed a significant part of the SDR.

A question would arise regarding the Swiss franc, should Switzerland join the Fund, about which there has been press speculation. As a strong and well-used financial currency, the Swiss franc would be a candidate for inclusion in the SDR basket. Nevertheless, that would add yet one more low-inflation, low-interest-rate currency to the basket, and the question would arise of the appropriate weight to give European currencies in the whole basket.

At present, one or two banks are reported to be attempting to give correspondent bank facilities—"nostro" accounts—in SDRs, but these accounts are thought to be causing difficulty. Limited activity in the marketplace and the difficulty in engaging in transactions without unbundling the basket make this a relatively onerous and unrewarding venture.

A further possibility is that the ECU might be incorporated into the SDR, which then might comprise the dollar, the ECU, and the yen. This would have certain advantages. If one takes the view that the ECU and the move toward European monetary integration through the EMS are here to stay, then this would be a clear-cut and acceptable way in which the financial strength of the currencies of the United States, Europe, and Japan could be embodied in the SDR. Indeed, if one envisages that European monetary integration will be maintained, and ultimately will succeed, then this is the inevitable outcome, since the pound sterling, the French franc, and the deutsche mark would ultimately be subsumed into the

ECU. Using the ECU could be a less arbitrary and more acceptable way of incorporating European currencies into the SDR than the present system.

As far as the markets are concerned, there is no objection in principle. Providing the customers are there, the markets will trade in anything. More to the point, if the ECU is to be traded more and more as a currency unit in its own right, then trading in the ECU will be simpler than trading in an SDR of 5 currencies. While the SDR itself may still have to be traded in an unbundled form, one would reduce the number of components from five—the dollar, the pound sterling, the French franc, the deutsche mark, and the yen—to three—the dollar, the ECU, and the yen. That would make trading simpler.

If, however, the ECU were for some reason to be traded less in a bundled form and instead needed to be built from its component currencies, then increasing the number of component currencies in the SDR to include all the currencies in the ECU would be a retrograde step for the SDR. A move toward a dollar, ECU, and yen determination of the SDR would require as a precondition that the ECU be traded in its bundled form as a currency unit in its own right.

There is no hope of the SDR being widely used in the international financial markets unless it is given full institutional and political support. This would require that prominent organizations create financial assets and liabilities denominated in SDRs. Action by governments would be required, too. For example, legal action might be required to fit the SDR in with national legislation and administrative policies regarding exchange controls and the laws of contract.

The use of the SDR in the private markets would be enhanced if there were a central bank or central bank-type organization prepared to create liquidity and absorb timing and maturity differences.

There is no technical difficulty in using the SDR. The banks have the computer capability to bundle and unbundle it. This problem is even easier, given the present streamlined structure of that unit. Once the market became big enough, one would hope that SDRs could be traded without the banks having to worry continually about bundling and unbundling.

As for the commercial incentive to use the SDR in financial institutions, the fee-earning organizations, such as merchant banks, have a continuing need to move with the market and a continuing competitive requirement to innovate. They have a positive incentive to use new market instruments if the market so wishes. Commercial banks, which operate in the foreign exchange and deposit markets on the basis of very substantial turnover and relatively low profit margins, have no such compelling incentive to make use of any new instrument which is produced. The banks may well wish to develop their facilities in, say, the SDR to attract publicity and generate trade, and they will of course do so if enough customers want such facilities. But using the SDR regularly in their normal trading business would be much more attractive to commercial banks if the liquidity of the unit were enhanced. There is a certain critical mass in the use of any currency or unit in the marketplace, which, once it is reached, makes it worthwhile for the major commercial banks to operate in that unit. Even when units are not of that scale, it may nevertheless pay certain smaller organizations to specialize in these units and to obtain a large enough share of the business to make that specialization worthwhile.

Many of the features which make a currency or a currency unit acceptable are cumulative. Scale breeds liquidity, familiarity, and confidence; and these, in turn, give the unit greater attractiveness and, hence, greater scale. In this regard, the question of political commitment and institutional commitment is pre-eminent. Ultimately what makes national currencies useful within nations is the degree of political and legal commitment to them—the degree of administrative commitment by, for example, the central bank in ensuring that the markets in that currency operate smoothly. The national markets in any currency have not developed accidentally and are certainly not maintained accidentally, as is indicated by the enormous amount of trouble which most central banks take to understand what is going on in their markets and to deal with problems and smooth their operation. It is precisely that surveillance and positive supervision which makes the markets yet more attractive to borrowers and investors, because the risk in using those markets is thus lessened. It is clearly unrealistic to envisage the SDR market ever reaching the same depth and breadth as the markets for major currencies; but any use will certainly not develop accidentally, and positive commitment by institutions and governments is absolutely essential.

The SDR faces a difficulty in that because it encompasses so wide a range of currencies, it is not convenient for hedging between any of the three main currency areas. If one wishes to hedge either across the dollar and European currencies, the dollar and the yen, or the yen and the European currencies, then if one uses the SDR, one is nullifying some part of the hedge, because the SDR includes all three areas. One of the attractions of the ECU for borrowing by, say, Denmark is that the exchange risk is relatively closely defined, whereas the SDR would leave Denmark vulnerable to what might seem relatively random movements between European currencies and the dollar and the yen.

This paper examined earlier the reasons why companies and individuals use foreign currencies. The dollar was the central international currency in the postwar period. The deutsche mark and the Swiss franc are used very substantially as units of account in "turntabling" international capital flows, largely because of their presumed stability, given the low inflation and the balance of payments strength of the countries concerned.

There are three main reasons for these currencies to be used: their depth and liquidity, their lack of national exchange controls, and their stability. The SDR would satisfy the requirements regarding lack of controls. It should also provide relative stability, a feature particularly of interest to genuinely world-wide organizations, which can hold an asset or take on debt against their world-wide portfolio. It is, however, conspicuously lacking in the depth and liquidity which were two of the main reasons why the dollar became so ubiquitous in the postwar period.

IX. SUMMARY AND CONCLUSIONS

(1) The Introduction and Sections II and III of this paper describe at length and in detail the qualities of national financial markets, the reasons why such markets acquire those qualities, and the reasons why some countries choose to use international moneys or a common currency in their domestic environment. This information and analysis bring home the point that composite currency units like the SDR and the ECU can never hope to get as much support as, or to acquire all the attributes of, major national currencies. Those concerned with the use of composite currencies need to lower their sights in relation to what may be achieved by them and then ensure that everything within their power is done to achieve their more limited objectives.

(2) The factors which give national financial markets their breadth, depth, and liquidity are their integral relationship with the economic, social, and political fabric of their country, and the positive efforts made by the government to maintain the quality of the markets.

(3) No international currency unit can be expected to have a market with the same integral relationship with a national economy enjoyed by national financial markets, nor can it be expected to be given the same priority in the political objectives of governments as domestic markets.

(4) National economic agents may wish to use international moneys because of deficiencies in their own financial markets. Corporations may need to use other moneys in relation to their "multinational" business in other countries and to their "international" business. In those cases, composite currency units are competing with the range of other moneys, Euro-moneys, and other international moneys that is available to those economic agents.

(5) Geographical and political factors may lead countries not to create their own money but instead to use only the money of another country, use

the money of another country side by side with its own money, or use moneys jointly with other countries.

(6) Section IV shows that considerable ingenuity has been applied in the international marketplace in developing composite units of account in recent years. The market has fulfilled precisely the function which it should, selecting from among the many innovations offered to it those which have the attributes found to have the most consistent appeal to borrowers and to lenders. As far as parity units are concerned, the market requires that the exchange risk be apportioned fairly as between the borrower and the lender; and in this connection, the "new" EUA emerged as by far the most successful unit.

(7) Among basket units, the officially defined ECU and the SDR have emerged as the most successful. Basket units seem by their nature to have greater appeal than parity units. Both these units have been given substantial official support.

(8) The officially defined ECU has been supported by international organizations and governments that have taken action to supply liabilities and assets to the markets and to remove legal barriers to the use of this instrument. At present, clearing in ECUs is undertaken by banks. The clearing system would be enormously enhanced if, as banks hope, the BIS or other official organizations give the market clearing support.

(9) The official ECU is a natural hedge for "Europe." The vast majority of ECU transactions now take place in the unit as a whole, in which case there is no need to bundle or unbundle it.

(10) The market share of all currency units in international bond markets has not been more than about 1 percent. Nevertheless, the marketplace is receptive to new units, and terms of issues are comparable to those for bonds in national currencies (Section V).

(11) Great efforts are made by companies to manage exchange rate and interest risk. Most students of corporate risk management are aware of the potential of currency units, but these are relegated to a small role in their advice to companies. Companies are aware of the illiquidity and inconvenience of these units. As was indicated in the survey that was conducted among corporate treasurers, such units rarely coincide with the risks seen by companies (Section VI).

(12) In the postwar period, there has been a massive internationalization of the use of currencies, based on the tax and regulatory benefits from escaping "domestic" jurisdictions. The use of currencies internationally has often been strengthened by the infrastructure of, and the support received from, national institutions. These markets have provided breadth, depth, and liquidity, and they have served the interests of many market participants. A substantial infrastructure has been built up (Section VII).

(13) There is no technical difficulty in using the SDR. The computer technology is in place and is standard by now (Section VIII).

(14) The greater success of the SDR was associated with the 16-currency SDR. The move to a 5-currency SDR was associated with diminished use. It seems to informed observers that this was largely a coincidence. The 16-currency SDR was popular during a period of dollar weakness when the interest rate on the SDR was higher than that on the dollar. Since the dollar became stronger at the same time the SDR basket was changed, some observers may have erroneously concluded that the change in basket was responsible for the diminished attractiveness of the SDR.

(15) Nevertheless, the question arises whether the present basket is the most suitable. Critics say that it is too bland and does not provide an opportunity to invest in high-interest-rate currencies which may be respectably stable.

(16) But there are substantial risks in increasing the basket. Investors wish the SDR to be a reasonable hedge against currency movements and to be a good investment medium. The inclusion of notoriously weak currencies would make it unacceptable. Since the SDR now almost always has to be unbundled when it is used for transactions, the greater the number of currencies it includes, the greater the transactions costs and inconvenience to users will be. Since the currency unit has to be unbundled, its components must be currencies which are tradable for any period for which it is wished that the SDR itself be tradable. These constraints limit severely the number of currencies which it might be wise to include in the SDR. However, the Swiss franc could well be a strong candidate for inclusion, should that country join the Fund.

(17) An interesting question arises as to whether the ECU should be included in the SDR, in place of the pound sterling, the deutsche mark, and the French franc. The market would have no objection whatever, in principle. This substitution could be a useful means of representing the European currencies in a more acceptable way than the present system. But for this step to be justified, it would be essential that the ECU be traded almost entirely in a bundled form. In that case, the transactions costs of using the SDR would be reduced substantially, since it would then have three components rather than the present five. But if the ECU were traded by being made up from the individual currencies, then its inclusion in the SDR would be infeasible. It would be quite unrealistic to expect that the SDR should become a basket of 11 currencies, many of which would be untradable for the periods and purposes required.

(18) The SDR may suffer from the disadvantage of being too global, which means that it is not a natural hedge for any particular environment or jurisdiction. It has a more obvious role as a kind of "world hedge" and may

be attractive to organizations outside the main currency groups, or to persons and organizations with substantial net holdings of financial assets or net borrowings.

(19) The market in any currency is strengthened by cumulative factors. A certain minimum scale is required to bring banks into a market. The private SDR market would benefit enormously if powerful organizations were determined to use it, whether for borrowing or for placing. That would build up activity, which would enhance liquidity and, in turn, would make the market more attractive to other market participants.

(20) Liquidity would be enhanced if the SDR were backed by central banks or official organizations which were willing to back a private sector clearing system. The ECU is further advanced in this field than is the SDR. While banks are at present keen to establish a clearing system for ECU, the next crucial step in enhancing the liquidity of the market is the backing by official organizations (in that case, banks hope, the BIS) of the clearing system. Similar considerations will apply in the case of the SDR if its use increases. It would then be possible to make transactions in SDRs without having to bundle and unbundle the basket.

(21) While there may well be merit in various technical proposals for improving or enhancing the quality of the SDR, all the evidence indicates that that is not the crucial requirement as far as increased use is concerned. The market was developed initially when the technical stituation was weak, and it has since fallen away despite its technical features being improved. What the market needs are customers, high-quality names which will use the bond markets, the credit markets, and the money markets.

(22) International currency units such as the SDR would be unlikely to achieve more than a modest niche in the financial marketplace. Achieving even that requires very substantial support from international organizations and from national governments. In order for the SDR to achieve its objective in market terms, as much official support as possible needs to be given to the market as soon as possible.

APPENDIX

Questionnaire: Summary of Responses Received

Use of International Money Units in Corporate Cash Management

1. Has your company ever used international money units (e.g., SDRs, ECU, EUAs) for its cash management needs?	Yes	10
	No	68

2. If "No" to Question 1, why not?

(i) too illiquid .... $\boxed{7}$

(ii) does not coincide with our risk structure .... $\boxed{37}$

(iii) never heard of them .... $\boxed{2}$

(iv) do not know how to obtain them .... $\boxed{9}$

(v) wrong currency mix .... $\boxed{23}$

(vi) too small a market .... $\boxed{13}$

(vii) any other reason .... $\boxed{3}$

Comment:

—Complicates our currency management operation.

—Exact circumstances foreseen where they will be useful, but have not yet come to fruition.

—Not suitable for type of overseas trade adequately met by normal currency markets.

—Insufficient perceived advantages.

—No value in balancing our position.

—Do not know enough about them.

—Lack of familiarity and understanding, watching the market develop—particularly ECU.

—No need, we have always been able to sell pounds sterling or other freely convertible currencies.

—Irrelevant to our needs.

—Prefer to use currency in which we operate.

—Their advantages to this company with its current low gearing and seasonal cash needs are not apparent.

—Need not arisen.

—Too inflexible—multicurrency facilities can provide some benefits.

—Never seriously considered.

—Difficult to hedge.

—ECU market has only recently reached sizeable proportions, and SDR is weighted in favour of U.S. dollar.

—As we are relative newcomers to exposure management, we have not yet investigated stabilities of these units. Also at present have no borrowing requirements.

3. (i) Have discussions ever been held with your bank about using such units? Yes $\boxed{45}$ No $\boxed{32}$

(ii) If "Yes," was it at—their initiative? $\boxed{31}$ —your initiative? $\boxed{18}$

4. If you have ever used such units, please specify which:

SDR $\boxed{6}$ New official ECU $\boxed{3}$ Private sector EUA $\boxed{3}$

Other $\boxed{-}$

5. What proportion of your company's cash management turnover has been met by these units during the last year?

None $\boxed{55}$ * 1 percent $\boxed{4}$ ** 1-5 percent $\boxed{2}$ 5-10 percent $\boxed{—}$ More $\boxed{—}$

　　Comment: *One company wrote, "We did not get the contracts tendered for."
　　　　　　**Includes two replies which said less than 1 percent

6. What were the units used for?

　(i) short-term transactions $\boxed{3}$
　(ii) medium- and long-term transactions $\boxed{2}$
　(iii) assets $\boxed{—}$
　(iv) liabilities $\boxed{2}$
　(v) hedging transactions exposure $\boxed{3}$
　(vi) hedging translation exposure $\boxed{1}$

7. If you were to use such units, or use them more, what improvements would you require?

　(i) larger market $\boxed{42}$
　(ii) finer terms $\boxed{7}$

If you would require "change of structure," in what way would you like to see it done?

　(iii) more liquid $\boxed{20}$
　(iv) more regular quotation $\boxed{13}$
　(v) change of currency structure (if so, in what way?) $\boxed{4}$

　　—Greater liquidity which would come from a larger market.
　　—Development of ECU is particularly interesting.
　　—Various currency baskets to choose from, e.g., if we wanted one excluding, say, French franc we could choose that one.
　　—We are borrowing EUA's on the old formula (from 1968) which gives holders repayment in Belgian francs or Swiss francs.
　　—Viewed as impossible in content of currency mix of, say, 50 percent Irish pound—50 percent combination of pound sterling, Far East currencies, African currencies.
　　—Adjust currencies to match exchange risks more closely.
　　—More publicity and background on these instruments, "Public sector image" limiting.
　　—Weighting of currencies does not suit our requirements.

　(vi) other—please specify:

　　—An obvious lender of last resort with certainty of supporting resources.
　　—Banks seldom introduce these into discussions.
　　—Have thought of them for trans-Euro financing should we ever do it rather than specific country financing.
　　—No interest in using them.
　　—We prefer to match our own currency risks currency by currency rather than "broad brush" through a basket of currencies.

8. Are such units ever likely to be able to compete for your purposes with the markets in the main currencies?

Yes [15]
No [34]
Do not know [22]
Possibly [2]

Comment:
—Depends on mix.

9. Do you have any other comments to make?

—Designed for use by governments and financially illiterate?

—Our requirements in this respect are limited and are likely to remain so. Our knowledge of the market is therefore limited.

—These units are just not relevant to our business.

—We have some performance bonds denominated in SDRs due to government regulations.

—We regard the ECU development in business/commercial sector as being an important step. We are seriously considering such an issue as a way of improving our debt maturity and providing a degree of hedge at the same time.

—The Group's main borrowing requirements are in U.S. dollars, pounds sterling, Australian dollars, and South African rand. We have very limited requirement for European and other major currencies. It is unlikely that our preferred currency mix will change over two to three years. Hence lack of interest in international money units.

—Such units are only likely to be of use and interest to the very big corporations, e.g., Shell, Du Pont, who may have large money flows and businesses in a great many currencies. Even big corporations would not necessarily find them worth taking any interest in, certainly at the present level of availability.

—We see little, if any, advantage in investing in SDRs against choosing a specific basket of currencies to make up a particular portfolio, be it for hedging or currency exposure, or taking any form of speculative currency position. There is probably some appeal in the unit for companies which totally centralize their currency dealings and where the currency mix matches their own. Perhaps once the SDR becomes an accepted world-wide trading currency we might take a more active role, especially if it became appropriate to financing of our major projects in SDRs.

—Until, say, SDRs become so widespread that we would pay our workers in them, our costs will be in pounds sterling and hence we will want to deal in pounds sterling only. Thus for commercial use, I see little future but banks and governments may well see some advantage in them.

—(a) The reduction in the SDR basket from 16 to 5 currencies, on January 1, 1981, had the merit of simplifying the mechanics but may have eroded the attraction of SDR as a currency hedge.

(b) The SDR basket weightings were/are based on relative trade weightings. The disadvantage is that the attractions of the SDR as a financing instrument may be reduced thereby, since it does not include some important "financial" currencies, e.g., the Swiss franc.

—The weighting of the basket of currencies does not match our currency exposure.

—We are aware of the existence of International Money Units, but have not researched in any depth the market, as they do not seem appropriate at present for our funding needs.

—None of these units are particularly useful to us in managing our short-term asset/liability hedges. Our investment policy is generally aimed at particular countries/currencies. Because the banks have not tried to sell them to us, and because we have not been large currency borrowers over the last few years, we have not given serious consideration to this.

—Although the January 1981 reduction in the basket of currencies backing SDRs has obviously made them more commercially attractive, they are not suitable for our particular purposes, since our policy is to match assets and liabilities in the territories in which we operate. Nevertheless, I could envisage circumstances in which a commercial company whose trade pattern embraces the five currencies concerned and where its expenditures and receipts are mismatched, could in the future make use of SDRs, provided there was an effective market. Certainly in the future, if corporate liquidity were to come under pressure, then the SDR might, with some modification, help to ease the pressure.

—We have considered using the SDR as a target "store of wealth" for cash management purposes. In practice, we are more likely to use a target composite unit of our own construction that more clearly matches our own investment ambitions.

—We are unfortunate in having bonds in an EUA formula which allows lenders the option of repayment in Belgian francs or Swiss francs. Naturally they have chosen Swiss francs in recent years. Leaving aside this disadvantage on our present issue, which is small and matures in 1984, we find ECUs a difficult concept for borrowing. We prefer to borrow in specific currencies. This gives us greater flexibility and more obvious control, although some of the currency elements in the ECU cannot be borrowed in the Euromarket.

—For the purpose of spreading/reducing the risk associated with borrowing any one particular currency, other than a company's domestic currency, currency basket borrowings have some merit. However, if a company is totally risk averse, then it will be wishing to hedge closely its currency assets for which any particular basket (SDR, ECU, etc.) may be inappropriate. If the company is willing to take risk in this area, then by definition it will not be seeking to spread its risk by means of using these instruments.

—This Group is large enough to justify managing its exposures in separate currencies strictly relative to sales, etc. We deposit on a one-on-one basis with our banks roughly on a basis of business we have reciprocally. Many banks do not operate SDR accounts. If there were a highly developed interbank SDR market, then our policy could well change.

—If there were a liquid market we might use it (i) for borrowing medium-term and long-term, (ii) for short-term borrowing and transactionally to reduce exposure, and (iii) a forward market (of depth) would be essential.

—It seems unlikely that our currency/borrowing needs would ever correspond closely to the exact mix of an ECU, SDR, etc., and even if they did, at one time, the mix would probably change fairly quickly. We need to be able to change the mix to reflect changes in currency exposure, and hence a fixed "mix" is not likely to be of interest to us.

—It is easier to get the exact match of currencies you want in the currency markets than to be linked to an arbitrarily fixed percentage of currencies. Could be useful only from a psychological point of view when any kind of diversification is desired rather than a specific one.

—As a German supplier, we recently discussed with our main Italian customer an agreement on future contract prices being tied to ECU as a mutual hedge factor. We feel this is a useful device and are continuing discussions with our banks on this theme.

—As the Treasurer of a multinational company coordinating decentralized, largely autonomous, major subsidiary companies, my current interest in these units is limited to the pricing and financing of major export sales projects involving the sourcing of equipment and services from different countries and currencies. Given the normal operating timing uncertainties of such projects and inadequate forward exchange markets, I feel that these units would be the next best thing to fixed exchange rates in solving or reducing any currency denomination and exposure problems for such projects.

—On the whole, our exposures are relatively short term and do not coincide with makeup of units in currency terms. Our view at present is that the forward markets in the main currencies provide a more adequate, exact, and appropriate hedge mechanism.

—FASB-52 places premiums on having a specific currency to cover forex position.

—My company often has "long" exposure to currencies that are aligned to or fixed in a relationship to SDR. In these cases, SDR borrowings could "hedge" our exposure. Of course, the market would rapidly expand if a country started to call for tenders in SDRs!

—SDR's currency mix might be reasonably adequate for the purpose of hedging (by borrowing the SDR long term) the currency risk involved by the commercial activity of the producers of certain raw materials.

—We have so far found no practical value in the use of International Money Units, mainly because of the relationship of our particular foreign currency exposures, flexibility considerations with regard to specific hedging decisions, as well as for reasons of costs and conditions.

REFERENCES

Aliber, Robert Z., *Exchange Risk and Corporate International Finance* (London: Macmillan, 1978).

Aschheim, Joseph, and Y.S. Park, *Artificial Currency Units: The Formation of Functional Currency Areas*, Essays in International Finance, No. 114 (Princeton, New Jersey: International Finance Section, Princeton University, April 1976).

Commission of the European Communities, *European Economy* (Brussels), No. 12 (July 1982).

Congdon, Tim, "Is the Provision of a Sound Currency a Necessary Function of the State?" *National Westminster Bank Quarterly Review* (August 1981), pp. 2–21.

Coussement, André M., "Maturity at 17 for the EUA," *Euromoney* (June 1978), pp. 141–45.

Donaldson, J.A., *Corporate Currency Risk* (London: Financial Times Business Information Ltd., 1980).

Dufey, Gunter, and Ian H. Giddy, *The Evolution of Instruments and Techniques in International Financial Markets*, S.U.E.R.F. Series, 35A (Tilburg, Netherlands: Société Universitaire Européenne de Recherches Financières, 1981).

Group of Thirty, *The Functioning of the ECU*, ed. by Wolfgang Rieke (New York, 1982).

Heywood, John, *Foreign Exchange and the Corporate Treasurer* (London: Adam and Charles Black, 1979).

"International Money Management: Banks Warm Up to ECU," *Business Week* (October 18, 1982), p. 146.

Istituto Bancario San Paolo di Torino, *ECU Newsletter*, No. 1 (February 1982), and No. 2 (July 1982).

Jacque, Laurent L., *Management of Foreign Exchange Risk* (Lexington, Massachusetts: D.C. Heath and Lexington Books, 1979).

Kenyon, Alfred, *Currency Risk Management* (Chichester, United Kingdom: John Wiley and Sons, 1981).

Kettell, Brian, *The Finance of International Business* (London: Graham and Trotman Ltd., 1979).

Kredietbank, *Weekly Bulletin*, No. 11 (March 14, 1980).

Liddell, Andrew, "Financial Co-operation in Africa—French Style," *Banker*, Vol. 132 (January 1982), pp. 41–43.

_____, "Financial Co-operation in Africa—French Style," *Banker*, Vol. 129 (September 1979), pp. 105–11.

Lomax, David F., and P.T.G. Gutmann, *The Euromarkets and International Financial Policies* (London: Macmillan, 1981).

Prindle, Andreas R., *Foreign Exchange Risk* (London: John Wiley, 1976).

Putnam, Bluford H., "Using SDRs," Chapter 7 in *Management of Foreign Exchange Risk*, ed. by Boris Antl and Richard Ensor (London: Euromoney Publications Ltd., Second ed., 1982), pp. 205–209.

Walker, D.P., *An Economic Analysis of Foreign Exchange Risk*, Institute of Chartered Accountants, England and Wales, Research Committee Occasional Paper No. 14 (1978), pp. 6 and 30.

Comments

Marinus W. Keyzer

While in 1981 external bond issues and medium-term syndicated bank credits denominated in special drawing rights were of some importance within the overall context of international financial markets, during 1982 and well into 1983, new fund-raising activity in composite currency units has largely taken place in European currency units (ECUs), even when for other financial instruments (i.e., deposits) a market has continued to develop for SDR-denominated paper. On the whole, however, new financing in composite currency units has remained of relatively little importance.

To have a more than marginal impact upon private financial markets, it appears that composite reserve units will have to conform to either of two sets of criteria. First, it may be argued that a financial instrument composed of a basket of *national* currencies, as SDRs and some other composite reserve units are, will only be able to fulfill its role in international markets effectively if and when the economic and financial policies pursued in the countries issuing the currencies concerned have been sufficiently harmonized. The integration of capital markets, which is embodied in composite currency units used therein, is the logical end result of the unification of domestic policies: unless such harmonization has been accomplished, currency baskets will remain dependent on the vagaries of national policies, including the availability of currencies in the international marketplace.

Alternatively, it may be suggested that, rather than being developed out of national currencies with quite different strengths and prospects, a composite currency unit to be used in international financial markets should be more truly *international* in character. In this respect, one may be tempted to make a comparison with gold, whose role as an investment medium has become largely independent of national intervention, although particular characteristics of gold may make it unsuitable for use as a denominator for other international debt instruments.

If, under the auspices of the Fund, one would opt for an international investment medium composed of national currencies, it appears that several requirements would have to be met. First of all, harmonization of national economic and financial policies would have to be carried much further than it is now. The Fund would have to play an even more active

319

role in the adjustment policies countries are pursuing; the Fund should be concerned not only with the policies of deficit countries but also with those of surplus countries. Some of the recent relative success of ECUs as an investment medium may, indeed, be ascribed to the political and economic integration to which the member countries of the European Communities have committed themselves.

Another weakness of currency baskets as they are being applied at present is that their composition is subject to changes in accordance with criteria that may be quite ambiguous. Such changes, which are already creating potentially serious technical problems in managing composite currency units, emphasize the largely national character of the latter. In addition, such changes in composition will not necessarily conform to private market participants' views on the proper currency mix to be applied: this problem, already now affecting the popularity of these instruments to an extent that differs over time, may be further aggravated by such changes. In this respect, it may be argued that a basic dilemma faced by officially sponsored currency cocktails is that under conditions of changing currency preferences of private holders they are unable to reflect such shifts; but if they were altered to give them the ability to do so, this would reduce their utility as independent debt instruments significantly.

One problem confronting the SDR as a debt denominator in private financial markets, besides the lack of policy coordination between the countries issuing the constituent currencies, probably is not caused so much by the "blandness" of the instrument but by the ready availability of such currencies for international financial transactions: the SDR as an instrument just includes widely used national currencies, without drawing other moneys into the limelight. This, indeed, appears to be the major difference between the SDR and the relatively popular ECU, which offers borrowers the opportunity to borrow indirectly in currencies that are otherwise hardly available for international finance. As such, the ECU may be said to be more of an international currency denominator than the SDR; besides, an asymmetry in market perceptions has been created between borrowers and lenders, with the former being interested in the possibility of raising funds partly in relatively weak currencies, but the latter more interested in the strong currencies contained in the ECU. Such an asymmetry, which appears to be much less in evidence with the SDR, constitutes a basic catalyst for bringing about active two-way trade in both primary and secondary capital markets.

However defined, a composite currency unit like the SDR will have to win maximal acceptance by private market participants to be able to fulfill its functions properly. In this respect, the financial innovativeness that SDRs bring to financial markets will have to result in, and be accompanied by, a risk/reward ratio that makes the instrument appealing to investors and borrowers alike. The existence of vested interests in international finance, guarding existing lines of competing profitable business, may turn out to be quite an impeding factor here, one that needs to be overcome by pertinent policy actions. Once again, it may be instructive to make the comparison with the situation regarding ECUs: not only have the institutions of the European Communities taken an active role in furthering the use of this instrument but, in conjunction with such activities, Luxembourg banks, with the strong assistance of French banking institutions, have developed a free interbank market in ECUs, which has sharply increased the liquidity of this currency unit. While there has been some official and private support of SDRs, it appears that much more determined efforts are needed.

An important first step that might be taken by the Fund and/or World Bank is to borrow, and be seen borrowing, in international financial markets in SDRs. This would not only usefully supplement these institutions' funds available for lending but, at the same time, would meet international markets' need for prime quality paper and create necessary links to banks that play leading roles in managing major fund-raising operations in international markets. These financial institutions would be able to develop more fully interbank markets and other debt instruments denominated in SDRs, all of which is essential if the SDR is to secure wider acceptance in the marketplace. Such international official action might usefully be supported by measures at the national level aimed at increasing the attractiveness of the SDR as an investment medium, even though some of the basic characteristics of the SDR, as it exists today, may impede such efforts. Although the Euromarkets have largely developed owing to the absence of national restrictive action, market activity denominated in SDRs might be promoted by appropriate national policies. Active participation of governments in interbank SDR markets (including open market operations by central banks); active borrowing operations by governments or other public-sector agencies; preferential, or at least equal, treatment of SDRs within the framework of national regulations, etc. could be considered in this regard.

Such international and national official actions will not, however, be able to overcome the practical difficulties inherent in the present functioning of the SDR as a cocktail of national currencies. Among these is the problem, referred to earlier, that the composition of the SDR may not conform to the preferences of market participants; in addition, international investors are not necessarily interested in acquiring *similar* debt instruments denominated in national currencies, but their perceptions and expectations will most likely result in their acquiring *different* assets (differing as to kind, issuing entities, maturities, and other conditions). Clearly, SDRs cannot fulfill this particular diversification need, and this will remain an impeding factor to its further development. This will apply equally to the use of the SDR as a hedging instrument: the particular needs of corporations and other entities in this respect may be quite different from what markets for SDR instruments are able to offer at present.

On the basis of the above, it may thus be argued that the SDR, in its present form, presents major inconveniences to private financial markets owing to the composition of the instrument; the macroeconomic constraints under which it is supposed to operate; and, last but not least, the lack of official and private support the SDR continues to experience. These factors are clearly closely interlinked, and they suggest that a really viable SDR needs a more truly international character if it is to carve out a meaningful market share. Rather than reflecting the existence of national currencies, the SDR should be a factor linking countries together within the international financial system, just as gold was able to do under the gold and gold exchange standards.

A redefined SDR that would serve as a stronger international link than the instrument now in use and for which proponents are attempting to gain a larger market share clearly cannot be decreed into existence, but will have to reflect the needs of the marketplace. In view of the problems the world economy is currently facing and the need to solve them in a spirit of unity within the context of financial markets that continue to put a premium on innovativeness, one may argue that the general criteria for formulation of an "internationalized" SDR that would be more acceptable for private use are by no means impossible to define: a definition formulated in terms of global national income, a basket of commodities, or other parameters that are not directly linked to the existence of national currencies may serve this particular purpose.

Manfred J. M. Neumann

Dr. Lomax has provided us with a very useful, wide-ranging survey of the various experiments in composite currency arrangements that we have seen emerge from private initiatives in deposit markets, as well as loan and bond markets, since the early seventies. Though there has been a considerable variety of attempts by commercial banks to establish a standard composite unit, in most cases more or less closely resembling an official accounting unit, the cumulative evidence, as collected by Dr. Lomax and others, appears to be clear cut: standardized composite currency arrangements of all types have failed to gain a share in financial markets that is worth mentioning, while Eurocurrency markets, in contrast, are flourishing. Private business transacted in currency cocktails to date has been inconsequential, and those commercial bankers who think otherwise are merely indulging in wishful thinking. It is no coincidence that most of them are located in countries whose currencies are notoriously weak and are, consequently, of only local importance.

Many answers can and have been put forward to explain the failure of composite units. Let me summarize them as follows. First, there is no a priori reason to expect more than a very modest demand for standardized currency cocktails either from participants in international trade or from international investors, even in periods of greater-than-normal uncertainty about future exchange and inflation rates. Second, to surmount the barriers to entry and to meet the competition with national and international moneys, a standardized composite unit would have to be much more attractive and efficient than any of the commercial units we have seen so far.

With respect to the first point, it is useful to recall the trivial fact that composite currency units of the fixed-amount-basket type—like the European currency unit (ECU) or the special drawing right (SDR)—can be used to reduce exchange rate risk in a standard fashion but not to eliminate it. While there are well-defined conditions under which it would be optimal for a company, for instance, to invoice its international trade in a composite unit, in real economic life these conditions are the exception rather than the rule. The vast majority of exporters and importers observe that the country distribution of their trade differs considerably from the currency distribution available in standard baskets.

But even under more favorable conditions, a rational company would have a strong disincentive to start denominating its trade in any unit other than an already well-known and readily accessible medium of exchange.[1] The reason is that invoicing in a composite currency unit that has not reached the status of a world medium of exchange forces additional costs of information on customers, thus making the trade offer less competitive. For these reasons, companies in international trade avoid composite currency units. From daily experience, they know that well-developed forward markets are available which permit them to hedge any undesired portion of transactions or translation exposure in any convertible currency at comparatively low cost. This view is confirmed by the unfavorable eval-

---

[1] Consider an example from history. During the inflation of the 1920s, Sigmund Freud used the U.S. dollar as unit of contract, charging $25.00 for a session on his famous couch. The unit of transaction, on the other hand, was chosen differently, depending on the hour of the day. In the morning, when banks were open, Freud was prepared to accept the local currency. In the afternoon, in contrast, when banks were closed, one had to pay him in dollars. As Freud enjoyed a monopoly at the time he certainly could have chosen a composite currency unit as unit of contract, while a company in competition has no such choice.

uation that composite currency units received in the opinion survey Dr. Lomax conducted among the treasurers of a hundred large companies.

If there is some potential for permanent use of a standardized composite unit, it is to be expected from international investment activity. To international lenders and borrowers, a composite unit is certainly of principal interest as a means of minimizing exchange risk. But, again, one cannot overlook the fact that standardization is less important to large investors and borrowers than to small ones.

Large investors and borrowers are both able and accustomed to tailoring individual currency baskets to suit their circumstances, at relatively low transaction costs. Consequently a composite currency unit can be established in commerical markets on a permanent basis if, and only if, financial instruments denominated in it are created that are attractive enough to suit the smaller investor who may want to diversify internationally, at a reasonably reduced risk.

In "The Evolving Role of the SDR in the International Monetary System" (Chapter 11 in this volume), the staff of the Fund has put forward the contention that more stability than we have experienced during recent years—with respect to inflation, interest, and exchange rates—is a "'necessary condition" for a composite unit, like the SDR or the ECU, to make headway in international markets.[2] And my fellow discussant, Mr. Keyzer, has concluded that such units will only be able to play a role in the marketplace "if and when the economic and financial policies pursued in the countries issuing the currencies concerned have been sufficiently harmonized" (p. 319).

I disagree with these views. They tend to neglect the fact that the special productivity a standardized composite currency unit may provide is not constant but instead changes as frequently as international market conditions change and, hence, is affected by the degree of uncertainty about future exchange and inflation rates. The special productivity of a composite currency unit derives from its ability to save users information costs and to reduce their purchasing-power risk through diversification. The more closely, therefore, interest rates and inflation rates of the constituent currencies move together, and the more stable the respective exchange

---

[2]What the paper has in mind is that it would be most useful to include currencies in the basket on which purchasing power and exchange risk had been more or less equalized ex ante through policy harmonization around common goals. Currencies subject to high and volatile inflation should be excluded, since they are of little interest in international finance and since including them would destabilize the basket. For this reason, the study expresses the view that the more risk distributions differed among major currencies, the more difficult it would be for any basket of such currencies to compete with the U.S. dollar, provided the inflation risk attaching to the dollar remained comparatively small.

rates, the more the productivity of any composite unit diminishes and, consequently, the more potential demand diminishes.

For this reason, chances are that a standardized composite unit can be established in private markets only during periods when market participants are troubled by an exceptional uncertainty and when they believe that prospects for a return to more stable conditions are dim.

In opposition to this hypothesis it can, of course, be argued that the past ten years of floating have been rather turbulent. It is tempting, therefore, to conclude that the commercial failure of all composite units to date constitutes disconfirming evidence. But taking this view would, it seems to me, severely underestimate the considerable height of the barriers to entry—that is, the enormous costs of introduction—which the promoters of any new medium of exchange will have to face.

Consider, for example, a company which desires to launch not just a different brand, but a completely new product in the goods market. This company will not find it sufficient to produce and widely disseminate information about the properties and quality of the new product. Rather, it will seriously consider selling the product at an initial discount in order to make testing of the product attractive to prospective customers. Moreover, to maximize its chances of success, the company will make vigorous efforts to reach as many market participants as possible within a very short time. Stretching the introductory phase over many years is an invitation to failure.

To make a market for a new medium of exchange requires even more effort and resources than introducing a new good, for the well-known reason that the attractiveness of a new medium, unlike that of a new good, is highly dependent on the total number of users. The difficulties involved in an effective introduction of a new medium of exchange which is not legal tender can also be assessed by looking back into monetary history to the unfortunate experiences of hyperinflation. In the rare cases where new mediums entered into competition with the inflating legal tender, this entry consistently occurred after a very late stage of the inflation process had been reached. Examples are the local currencies which occurred during the German hyperinflation in the early 1920s and the commodity currency, consisting of cigarettes, which came into use in the late 1940s, just before the deutsche mark was created as the new legal tender.

On the basis of these considerations, it would seem that much more effort will be required than has been expended so far if a composite currency unit is to be established in private markets during more normal times, even if only as a standard unit of contract in international finance and investment. The cumulative experience of recent years has made it very clear that the international banking community finds the prospects of standardized composite currency units not bright enough to encourage banks to bear the relatively high costs of introduction and infancy. This does not mean, though, that commercial banks would not engage in serious promotion if they were adequately compensated for it by subsidies. The composite currency case, however, is not a public-goods case; there is, therefore, no justification for either direct or indirect subsidization.

Some of us may hold the view that the creation of attractive commercial SDRs is likely to promote the role of the official SDR as the principal reserve asset. But it seems to me that the reverse is true. The prospects for an evolution of commercial SDRs would be brighter if the official SDR were an attractive asset that was willingly held by Fund members rather than spent. The staff of the Fund, as well as others, have presented various proposals[3] for making SDRs more liquid and higher-yielding assets. Raising the profitability of SDRs to net holders will certainly be useful, though central bankers may not be particularly interested in profit maximization.

From the point of view of political economics, the much more fundamental question cannot be avoided: on what grounds can a case be made that national central bankers will ever be interested in giving up their monopoly power and pave the way for an efficient parallel currency? I do not see any.

A more successful approach to increasing the attractiveness of SDRs to central banks might, therefore, be the more modest one of encouraging their use as an instrument of domestic monetary policy. The idea is to mobilize SDR holdings by transforming them into money market paper. Whenever domestic policy goals required a reduction in base-money growth, a central bank could sell SDR bills instead of, or as a complement to, treasury bills. The bills could be sold to banks and nonbanks. They could have a maturity of three months, for instance, and they could carry an interest rate set at the discretion of the national central bank. This less ambitious scheme might attract national central banks for two reasons: first, central bankers prefer more instruments to fewer, and such an arrangement would provide them with an additional one; second, acceptance of the scheme would permit central bankers the claim to have taken another step in the promotion of international cooperation without requiring them to give away anything.

---

[3]The proposals presented by the Fund staff appear in Chapters 12 and 13 of this volume, which are entitled, respectively, "Possible Further Improvements in the Existing SDR" and "Evolution of the SDR Outside the Fund."

Use of the SDR to Supplement or Substitute for Other Means of Finance

PETER B. KENEN*

The international economy does not stand still, and as it changes the international monetary system changes with it. Most of us have said this frequently. We cite as examples the decline in the role of the U.S. dollar as an international currency that reflected the decline in the global dominance of the U.S. economy and the earlier decline in the role of sterling that reflected the decline in the dominance of the U.K. economy. Two errors, however, creep into our analyses.

On the one hand, we pay insufficient attention to differences in the timing and extent of changes. The decline in the role of the dollar, for instance, began later than the decline in the dominance of the U.S. economy and has been much smaller (Kenen (1982)). On the other hand, we tend to concentrate on discontinuous changes in the monetary system, even though they may merely dramatize or ratify processes that started earlier. The closing of the U.S. gold window on August 15, 1971, was a dramatic event, but it should be viewed as the last act in a long process that transformed the gold-dollar standard into a pure dollar standard. The Jamaica Agreement of 1976, which led to the Second Amendment of the Articles of Agreement of the Fund, was a landmark in the history of the monetary system, but it served

*I am grateful to Richard Cooper, George von Furstenberg, Jeffrey Goldstein, Mohsin Khan, Jacques Polak, Ellen Seiler, and John Williamson for comments on the first draft of this paper. I am particularly grateful to John Williamson for his answer to a student's question at a Princeton seminar. Asked why governments should want to hold the SDR in lieu of a tailor-made basket of currencies, he pointed out that the "optimality" of a basket depends on the costs of buying and selling it. If the SDR were easier to transfer, it could be bought and sold cheaply, and governments might find it more attractive than a tailor-made basket. His answer led me to think about making the SDR more usable as a means of payment and thus to develop one main theme of this paper.

327

mainly to ratify changes in exchange rate arrangements that started even earlier than 1973, when rates began to float.

It is very hard to locate precisely the dates of innovations in the monetary system, even with the benefit of hindsight. It may be impossible to know when we are living through one. Nevertheless, I am becoming convinced that we passed through one such date in the last two years—that there has been another major change in the monetary system. If I am right, moreover, this conference is well timed, because the latest change in the monetary system will force us to pay more attention to reserve supplies and thus more attention to the special drawing right (SDR) as a reserve asset.

In the first part of this paper, I give reasons for believing that there has been such a change and that the SDR may have a more important role to play. In the second and third parts, I warn against being excessively ambitious. There is no point in trying to make the SDR the "principal reserve asset in the international monetary system" as envisaged in the Second Amendment of the Articles of Agreement of the Fund and no good way to do so without drastic changes in the system as a whole. In the fourth part of the paper, I list the steps that must be taken to make the SDR a more important reserve asset. In the fifth, I look at ways of making it more usable. In the sixth, I look at ways of making it more prominent. In the final section, I look at ways of making the supply more flexible.

I. WHERE WE MAY BE GOING

The changes in the monetary system that took place in the 1970s reduced the importance of reserves and the attention paid to them. The demand for reserves was surprisingly stable, according to conventional econometric estimates. But that demand was satisfied rather differently than it was in the 1960s. Furthermore, governments that had to finance balance of payments deficits did not rely primarily on the use of reserves.

Demand for Reserves

Although I was one of the first to estimate a demand function for reserves, I am somewhat skeptical of the whole approach. I have no problem with the basic premise. Governments hold reserves to bridge gaps between demand and supply in the foreign exchange market; when the demand for foreign currency exceeds the supply, a government can use its reserves to keep its exchange rate from changing. If governments anticipate large gaps, they will hold large reserves, given the costs of closing the gaps by changing or switching expenditure and the opportunity cost of investing in reserves. On this same premise, however, it should be hard to estimate a demand function for reserves; actual holdings at any time can be expected to differ appreciably from optimal holdings.

This objection has been raised before, and efforts have been made to meet it.[1] But it seems to have more force in principle than in practice. There does appear to be a demand function for reserves, although there is debate about some of its finer properties. More to the point, the demand functions estimated recently resemble closely those that were estimated earlier. The time-series estimates of Heller and Khan (1978) show that demand functions shifted in 1972 or 1973. So do the cross-country estimates of Frenkel (1980). But the shifts were smaller than one might have predicted, knowing what has happened to exchange rate arrangements and to other aspects of the monetary system.[2]

Supply of Reserves

The important innovations took place on the supply side, and they are often deemed to cast doubt on the need to make the SDR a more important reserve asset.

In the 1960s, the United States was the main supplier of reserves. It ran balance of payments deficits for most of the decade, and other countries financed them by building up their dollar holdings. In other words, the United States engaged in "liability financing" many years before that term was coined, but did so in a special way: it issued debt denominated in domestic currency. The amounts seem small in retrospect—$2 billion or $3 billion a year—but looked large at the time, and there was widespread agreement on the need to end the process. That is why the SDR was put in place, and the first allocation would not have occurred in 1969 if the United States had not incurred a balance of payments surplus in 1968-69, owing to a capital inflow induced by a tightening of monetary policy, which caused a sharp decline in other countries' reserves (see Solomon (1982, Chapter VIII)).

No country can run a balance of payments deficit unless some other country runs a balance of payments surplus. It is therefore simplistic to say that the stock of reserves was "supply determined" in the 1960s.[3] The term is useful, however, as a way to summarize three features of the situation.

First, major exchange rates were pegged. Changes in exchange rates

---

[1] For more on this issue, see Black (to be published in 1984). The method used most frequently to deal with the issue is the estimation of a long-run demand function with a fixed speed-of-adjustment coefficient. But theory argues that the speed of adjustment is determined jointly with the optimal quantity of reserves, which means that the speed-of-adjustment coefficient should not be fixed. I know of only one empirical paper (Bilson and Frenkel (1979)) in which the speed of adjustment is endogenous.

[2] Research on the use of reserves supports this conclusion. Reserve use did not decline in the early 1970s, despite the change in the exchange rate regime. See Suss (1976) and Williamson (1976). On factors affecting the demand for reserves under the present exchange rate regime, see von Furstenberg (1982).

[3] Some said that the stock of reserves was "demand determined" in the 1960s, because the surplus countries wanted more reserves and thus followed policies that drove the United States into deficit; see, for example, Kindleberger (1965).

could take place from time to time, but they were exceptional in law and practice. Therefore, intervention was more or less mandatory. Second, the dollar was the main intervention currency and was by far the most important reserve currency. Therefore, intervention led to increases in dollar holdings, and most countries were willing to retain those holdings. Finally, the deficits of the United States were the main cause for intervention. Looking at matters from the standpoint of a single country, intervention was required because its currency was strong; looking at matters from a global standpoint, however, intervention was required because the dollar was weak.

It is likewise simplistic but quite useful to say that the stock of reserves was "demand determined" in the 1970s. Intervention was not mandatory, not even for countries that were pegging their exchange rates. The dollar continued to be the main intervention currency, but it was not the only major reserve currency. And the payments deficits of the United States were not the main cause for intervention. (There was, indeed, a sense in which its measured deficits reflected the desire or willingness of others to increase their dollar holdings. The U.S. authorities did not intervene on a large scale before 1978. Therefore, measured deficits could come into being only insofar as other governments and central banks acquired dollars willingly.) In brief, there was no single source of reserves, and more important, there was no clear way to decide whether there was a shortage or surfeit of reserves.

The "Nonsystem" as a System

None of this was changed by the Second Amendment of the Fund's Articles of Agreement. Even after it took effect, some said that we were living with a nonsystem rather than a system. There were too few rules, and they were too weak.[4] But others argued that we were building a new system and should take some pride in it. Its rules were not written down. They were set by markets. But they might be more effective for that very reason.[5]

How does a market-based system work? International financial markets set the terms on which governments must choose between financing and adjustment. Foreign exchange markets set the terms on which governments must choose between types of adjustment and also force them to make realistic use of their freedom to select their own exchange rate arrangements. Governments are made to behave like ordinary economic actors—large ones to be sure—in credit and currency markets alike.

Even those who had strong reservations about the sufficiency of these

---

[4] See, for example, de Vries (1976) and Williamson (1977).

[5] See Corden (1981) and his paper, "Is There an Important Role for an International Reserve Asset Such as the SDR?," which is Chapter 5 in this volume.

implicit rules and the consistency with which markets would apply them saw that there had been fundamental changes in the monetary system, in addition to the changes in exchange rate arrangements. The successful "recycling" of the surpluses of the oil exporting countries had demonstrated that liability financing was an option open to most governments—not only to reserve centers—and its availability could markedly reduce the need for reserves to finance balance of payments deficits. When reserves were needed, moreover, they could be created by borrowing, as well as by official intervention in the foreign exchange markets. There would thus be no need for organized reserve creation of the kind envisaged a decade ago, when the First Amendment of the Fund's Articles made way for the creation of SDRs.

Now that recycling has ended, however, we can see why so many countries were able to engage in liability financing—why recycling was successful. There were three special reasons:

(1) In the 1960s, many developing countries adopted "outward-looking" development strategies; they abandoned import substitution in favor of export promotion. One would expect this policy change to raise rates of return in export-oriented industries (and those related to them), and that is what seems to have happened. The countries that adopted outward-looking policies in the 1960s were, of course, the newly industrializing countries of the 1970s, and they were large borrowers when recycling started. This is, I believe, the explanation for the relationship that Sachs (1981) has discovered: capital formation continued at high rates in many developing countries by comparison with rates in developed countries, and the current account deficits of those countries were therefore associated with high levels of investment rather than "excessive" levels of consumption.

(2) Most of those same countries entered the 1970s with rather light debt-service burdens. There was some concern about those burdens in the 1960s. Yet Bacha and Díaz-Alejandro (1982) remind us that debt-service ratios were quite low by historical standards. Furthermore, it looked as though most countries could borrow large amounts without greatly increasing their debt-service burdens. At the start of each burst of borrowing, in 1974 and in 1979, nominal interest rates were low and real rates were even lower.

(3) The concentration of current account surpluses was unique, and so was its disposition. A handful of oil exporting countries were building up huge claims on the outside world, and they chose for various reasons to hold those claims in liquid forms. Thus, banks had large sums to lend just when they were wanted.

This set of circumstances would be hard to reproduce—and it did not last. In fact, it fell apart completely. A recession, increased resort to protection, and other events in the developed countries conspired to reduce rates of return in the developing countries. The policies that caused the recession, moreover, led to a sharp increase in debt-service burdens. Finally, the decline in the demand for oil induced by price increases and by the recession ended the concentration of current account surpluses.

In 1976-78, the years between the oil price increases, the developing countries built up their reserves. Total reserves (excluding gold) of the non-oil developing countries rose from SDR 28.4 billion at the end of 1975 to SDR 57.5 billion at the end of 1978. Broadly speaking, moreover, the buildup was deliberate: governments chose to borrow more than they needed to finance their countries' current account deficits. There is a fairly strong cross-country correlation between reserves and debts, and it easy to adduce good reasons for it. (See, for example, Eaton and Gersovitz (1981).) But events were soon to prove the truth of Robertson's remark that "owned reserves are no use unless you use them and borrowed reserves are no use if you *do* have to use them" (Robertson (1956, p. 111)). When the new market-based monetary system started to show signs of strain in 1981-82, the banks began to gobble up the reserves that they had furnished.

In the 1970s, the banks were part of the solution. In the 1980s, they are part of the problem. Governments must still choose between financing and adjustment on terms set by credit markets, but those terms have changed abruptly. Some governments continue to believe that market forces should determine their exchange rates, but there is growing discontent with the rates that markets choose. Changes in exchange rates are part of the solution, but they can be part of the problem as well.

Need for a Little Less Endogeneity

Looking back on the events of the last ten years, I arrive at one very general conclusion. We may have built too much endogeneity into the international monetary system. Movements in real exchange rates have been too large, because of the big medium-term swings in nominal exchange rates. Credit flows have been too large and now threaten to be too small. The supply of reserves may be too elastic—in both directions. It is, I believe, important to impart a bit more "viscosity" to the monetary system—to reduce the amplitude of exchange rate changes, to stabilize credit flows, and to keep reserve supplies from behaving perversely.

The need for a more stable stock of reserves has not attracted much attention. It may be less important than the need for more stable exchange rates or for more stable credit flows. It may attract attention too tardily, however, only after reserves have contracted sharply. We should therefore start work on the problem immediately, using to the fullest extent possible the powers and facilities of the Fund. It is the only agency that can create a reserve asset whose quantity and quality can be controlled precisely—an attribute that we may come to value highly in an increasingly uncertain world.

II. WHERE WE SHOULD BE GOING

The objective just set forth—to make the stock of reserves more stable by raising or reducing the supply of SDRs to offset in whole or part sharp fluctuations in supplies of other reserve assets—can be achieved without a change in existing law or practice. It is thoroughly consistent with the language of Article XVIII, Section 1(a):

> In all its decisions with respect to the allocation and cancellation of special drawing rights the Fund shall seek to meet the long-term global need, as and when it arises, to supplement existing reserve assets in such a manner as will promote the attainment of its purposes and will avoid economic stagnation and deflation as well as excess demand and inflation in the world.

If reserves begin to fall and the members of the Fund become concerned, the Managing Director can propose an SDR allocation, even in the midst of a "basic period" for which no allocation was voted initially (see Article XVIII, Section 3).[6]

The stabilization of reserves is, in fact, a modest aim compared with the avoidance of deflation and inflation, and very much more modest than the long-term objective "of making the special drawing right the principal reserve asset in the international monetary system," set forth in Article XXII.

Under present circumstances, however, stabilization is feasible only if there is a tendency for the supply of reserves to contract. The Fund can allocate additional SDRs. Stabilization is not feasible if there is a tendency for reserves to expand. The Fund can cancel existing SDRs, but there are too few to matter. That is why a large part of this paper will be concerned with ways of introducing SDRs into the system without necessarily increasing reserves and with ways of stimulating the demand for them by making the SDR more attractive. Before turning to these issues, however, let us look more closely at the long-term aim embodied in Article XXII.

Why the SDR Might Be Made the Principal Reserve Asset

Why would one want to make the SDR the principal reserve asset in the international monetary system? Two main reasons have been given:

The first has to do with economic stability. Unless the SDR becomes the principal reserve asset, it will be impossible to control the supply of reserves,

---

[6] Such an allocation should probably be voted in conjunction with the current round of increases in quotas. I return to this matter at the end of my paper.

and firm control is necessary in order to avoid the twin evils of deflation and inflation.

The second has to do with systemic stability. Unless the SDR becomes the principal reserve asset, it will be impossible to consolidate the stock of reserves, and consolidation is necessary in order to avoid the "inherent instability" of a multiple reserve asset system.

I am not greatly impressed by either of these arguments. A sharp contraction in the supply of reserves would be costly. That is why I stress the need for stabilization. I do not believe, however, that the world can avoid deflation and inflation merely by controlling the supply of international reserves. It is not sufficient or efficient for that purpose. Sudden shifts between reserve assets could be costly too, because they can exacerbate exchange rate instability. That is one of my reasons for favoring substitution, and I will return to this subject. I do not believe, however, that a multiple reserve asset system is a threat to systemic stability.

The Case for Control

There is by now abundant statistical evidence that reserves can "cause" inflation. But one must look behind this statistical relationship, especially in light of the finding by Khan (1979) for industrial countries that inflation "caused" reserves in the 1970s. In the years before the breakdown of the Bretton Woods system, most of the growth in reserves was due to the U.S. payments deficit, and much of it was monetized. In other words, reserve growth was part of the process by which U.S. monetary growth was transformed into global monetary growth. The evidence should not be read to say that reserve growth per se causes inflation.

I can make my point more strongly. Many say that money is the main cause of inflation, and some put the argument in global terms—most recently McKinnon (1982). But no one has been able to convince me that there is a close and stable relationship between money and reserves—for any single country or the world as a whole. When reserve creation takes place because of nonsterilized intervention, there will be an increase in the supply of money. When it is accomplished by bookkeeping alone, as is the case with an SDR allocation, it has no direct effect on the supply of money.

But what about the need for discipline? Is it not self-evident that governments are cowardly and irresponsible and will therefore produce inflations whenever they confront unpleasant choices? Is it not essential to constrain them externally by limiting the stock of reserves?

Governments do produce inflations. No one else can—for long. But external constraints cannot stop them. Governments violate those constraints whenever they get in the way. In fact, the case for imposing external constraints is based on quixotic logic. If governments are responsible enough to abide by external constraints, the constraints will be redundant. If governments are irresponsible enough to opt for inflation when they face hard choices, external constraints will not work. Governments will violate them—as they have before.[7]

Furthermore, reserve constraints are inefficient. They cannot have much influence on policies in countries that have floating exchange rates, and those are the countries that matter most for global stability. They can induce a country with a pegged exchange rate to deal quickly with a balance of payments deficit—but only if the country cannot borrow and must draw on its reserves. Even in these instances, moreover, they cannot control the quality of the adjustment process. They cannot force a country to choose sensible policies.

The Case for Consolidation

At the end of 1975, the U.S. dollar accounted for 79.4 percent of official foreign exchange holdings; at the end of 1981, it accounted for 70.6 percent. Its share in the reserves of industrial countries fell from 87.3 percent to 78.9 percent; its share in the reserves of developing countries fell faster and more sharply, from 70.8 percent to 61.7 percent.[8] The decline in the relative importance of the dollar as a reserve asset was matched by an increase in the relative (and absolute) importance of the deutsche mark, the Japanese yen, and the Swiss franc. The share of the deutsche mark in total foreign exchange reserves rose from 6.3 percent in 1975 to 12.5 percent in 1981. In brief, the world moved much closer to a multiple reserve asset system.

Many central banks and governments have engaged in reserve diversification. Their reasons are listed and discussed elsewhere (see Group of Thirty (1982)). The governments of the new reserve centers were at first

---

[7] Cooper (1982, p. 45) makes a similar point with reference to *all* monetary rules. He asks

...why one should think that experts are more clever at devising operational, nondiscretionary monetary regimes than they are at monetary management within a discretionary regime. If the desire for a nondiscretionary regime is really simply another way ... of assigning priority above all others to the objective of price stability in the management of monetary policy, that can be done directly by instructing the Federal Reserve unambiguously to take whatever action is necessary to ensure price stability. If collectively we are ambivalent about that priority, that is the principal source of the problem, not the nature of the regime.

Note that there would be something uniquely quixotic about an attempt to impose an SDR reserve constraint. If governments were determined to produce inflations, they would need merely to vote large allocations. They would control the reserve constraint.

[8] International Monetary Fund (1982, p. 65). These figures exclude European Currency Units (ECUs); those ECUs that were issued against dollars are treated as if they were dollars, and those issued against gold are omitted. When ECUs are treated as foreign exchange reserves, the share of the dollar in global foreign exchange holdings falls to 58.4 percent at the end of 1981, and its share in the holdings of industrial countries falls to 55.9 percent.

reluctant to accept more important roles for their currencies, but they have become increasingly comfortable with them (see the papers by Rieke and Leutwiler and Kästli in Roosa and others (1982)). There is no need to say much more about those matters here. It is important, however, to look at the consequences of these developments.

Two strong views obtain. Some say that a multiple reserve asset system is "inherently unstable" (see, e.g., Group of Thirty (1980)). Others have suggested, however, that it may contribute to stability by subjecting a larger number of important countries to more monetary discipline (see, e.g., Leutwiler and Kästli in Roosa and others (1982)).

The first of these two views is based on an invalid analogy. I have discussed it elsewhere (Kenen (1981, p. 408)):

> The bimetallic standard of the Nineteenth Century, based on gold and silver, was a multiple reserve-asset system, and it broke down eventually. The gold-exchange standards of the interwar and postwar periods, based on sterling and the dollar, were unstable too. But most analogies are imperfect, and so are these. The "inherent" instability of earlier reserve regimes derived from the authorities' attempts to peg the prices of the reserve assets despite changes in their relative scarcities. Those attempts invited self-aggravating speculation whenever it seemed possible that the authorities would exhaust their holdings of the scarce asset. Present arrangements may not invite this form of speculation, because the authorities do not try to peg the prices of the reserve assets. Exchange rates connecting the dollar, Deutschemark and other reserve currencies are managed, but management is very different from pegging in its implications for the stability of the reserve system. It does not invite self-aggravating speculation.

Flexible exchange rates cannot repeal Gresham's Law but can protect the reserve system from its worst effect—a "run" on the supply of one reserve asset that can exhaust official holdings and thus undermine the system.

What about the other view, that a multiple reserve asset system can impose an appropriate discipline on the reserve centers? The usual objections hold. The very feature that maintains stability in a multiple reserve asset system—exchange rate flexibility—also reduces the power of any external constraint to improve policy, and I have expressed other doubts about the efficiency of any such constraint (Kenen (1981)). But two additional objections apply to this particular version of the case for discipline.

Recent experience warns that we can suffer a surplus of discipline rather than a shortage. A shift of funds from one reserve currency to another, from the deutsche mark to the dollar, for example, can be produced by an excessively restrictive monetary policy on the part of the United States rather than an excessively lax policy on the part of the Federal Republic of Germany. The shift is then apt to foster a competitive tightening of monetary policies.

The argument, moreover, appears to be founded on an inconsistency. It tells us that governments cannot be trusted to make good policies—that they have to be disciplined by market forces. At the same time, it says that governments and central banks will manage their reserves in ways that will force others to improve their policies. If the government of country X cannot be trusted to keep its own house in order, why should it be trusted to manage its reserves in a manner that will force the governments of the United States, the Federal Republic of Germany, and Japan, to keep *their* houses in order?

Conceivably, a government or central bank will act prudently when managing its currency reserves even though it acts imprudently when managing its economy. To rely on this possibility, however, is to place great confidence indeed in the optimality of profitable speculation—and in the ability of governments and central banks to engage in profitable speculation. Some central banks have lost money (Group of Thirty (1982, p. 6)), and central banks as a group have tended to destabilize exchange rates when switching from one currency to another (Bergsten and Williamson (1983)). I do not have much confidence in their ability to optimize the policies of the reserve currency countries.

A More Modest Case for Consolidation

Nevertheless, there is a case for consolidation. It is based on the threat to exchange rate stability, not any threat to systemic stability, posed by the possibility of large switches between reserve assets.

I have already cited recent work by Bergsten and Williamson (1983), which covers seven currencies and examines separately behavior by developed and developing countries. Bergsten and Williamson are careful to point out that their methods are not perfect; an outright shift from one reserve asset to another is hard to segregate from a change in asset shares due to a change in total reserves, and they have used trend values of exchange rates to define "equilibrating" speculation. But theirs is the most careful study I have seen, and this is their conclusion:

> The results suggest rather strongly that reserve shifts were in general destabilizing. In only four [of fourteen] cases is there evidence of an overall stabilizing pattern, and one of those results is very weak. . . . For example, the largest shift (as measured) by the industrial countries into the dollar occurred in 1976:4, almost simultaneously with the dollar's peak, while the largest shifts out occurred during the weakness of 1978–79. . . . They moved into the DM when it first began to weaken in 1975:3 . . . but afterwards shifted out all through the period of DM weakness, only to shift back in as the DM strengthened in 1978. The shifts of the nonindustrial countries are less dramatically destabilizing, but the net effect was qualitatively similar.

No sensible observer would claim that these shifts by central banks and governments were the main reason for exchange rate fluctuations. Too many sensible people tend to disregard them, however, or belittle their importance in the past and the damage they can do in the future.

There is another reason for favoring consolidation, and it is more important for the main theme of this paper. It may be the fastest way to increase the quantity of SDRs in the reserve system and therefore to give the Fund significant symmetrical influence over the supply of reserves—the ability to cancel SDRs on a significant scale when and if it is appropriate to do so, as well as the ability to create them.

III. INTERDEPENDENCE OF INSTITUTIONAL ARRANGEMENTS

There are two ways in which the SDR could be made the principal reserve asset in the monetary system:

(1) By introducing a system of fractional reserve requirements based on the SDR.

(2) By moving in one step to a monetary system in which the SDR is the only reserve asset.

The first method could give the Fund partial control over the quantity of reserves—the power to keep reserves from rising, if not from falling. But it would be an awkward way to achieve control, and it would not insulate exchange rates from the effects of switches between other reserve assets, because it would not take them out of the system. The second method would require mandatory substitution—an exchange of newly issued SDRs for all other reserve assets. But that would not be enough. Mandatory substitution would have to be accompanied by mandatory asset settlement or by major changes in the functioning of currency and credit markets. I will give the reasons shortly.

Making the SDR the Primary Reserve Asset

A system of fractional reserve requirements was proposed by H. Johannes Witteveen when he was Managing Director of the Fund. Under his proposal, the SDR would become the principal reserve asset by becoming the "primary" reserve asset. National currencies would be treated as "secondary" reserve assets, and there would be "holding limits" on those secondary assets. They could not be larger than some multiple (or fraction) of a country's holdings of primary assets. By controlling the supply of primary assets, the Fund would limit its members' ability to hold secondary assets and could therefore control the growth of global reserve holdings.

There are fundamental difficulties with this plan. Here is what I said about it in another paper (Kenen (1977, p. 216)):

> Consider the plight of a country that has reached its holding limit. If it is unable to obtain additional SDRs, its holding limit is transformed into an absolute injunction against intervention to prevent appreciation of the country's currency. As such, it is exposed to all of my complaints about reserve-based rules to regulate intervention—and to the additional complaint that an injunction against intervention could be imposed by the compo-

sition as well as the level of a country's reserves, an accident of history that can have little bearing on the desirability of intervention.

There are, of course, two ways in which a country can acquire additional SDRs: it can buy them or can borrow them. No country, however, is entitled automatically to buy SDRs from another.... The Second Amendment does allow countries to deal more freely in SDRs than they could before; voluntary transfers, presumably including loans or sales subject to repurchase, can be agreed between two countries without specific IMF approval. But the removal of restrictions on transfers not mandated by "designation" is no guarantee that a country will find a voluntary seller or lender, and the likehood of finding a supplier is itself inversely related to the effectiveness of a holding limit.

It would, of course, be possible to give each member of the Fund the right to purchase SDRs from some other member when it came into possession of the other member's currency. But this solution would impose a form of mandatory asset settlement that would function in a strangely asymmetrical manner. The same problem arises in conjunction with the other way to make the SDR the principal reserve asset, and I will discuss it in that connection.[9]

Making the SDR the Only Reserve Asset

Suppose that the members of the Fund decide that the SDR should be the *only* reserve asset. They agree to exchange all other reserve assets for new SDRs and never again to hold those other reserve assets. Let us set aside the transitional problems and those that have to do with the final disposition of the other reserve assets. They will have a chance to plague us later. Let us focus on the problems that members of the Fund must solve after the exchange of assets has been completed.

Once the SDR becomes the only reserve asset, a government or central bank that acquires dollars by intervening in the foreign exchange market cannot hold those dollars as reserves. It has to exchange them for SDRs. Therefore, someone must stand ready to swap SDRs for dollars, and there are two candidates—the Fund and the United States. But both of them should be reluctant to take on that obligation.

If the Fund agreed to create SDRs whenever its members wanted to sell dollars, it would be seen as giving open-ended support to the currency and policies of a single member. The United States would continue to possess the "exorbitant privilege" of being a reserve currency country even though

---

[9] There are practical problems as well. Governments have many ways of hiding reserve assets; they can place them with commercial banks and nonmonetary institutions. It would be impossible for the Fund to monitor reserves comprehensively in order to make sure that members were obeying the fractional reserve requirement. Similar problems arise in connection with the proposal discussed below, under which the SDR would be the only reserve asset. It would be hard for the Fund to make sure that members were holding only SDRs (and even harder to make sure that the SDR was used in all official transactions that could affect reserves).

the dollar had ceased to be a reserve asset. In fact, it would possess a more potent privilege than ever before, because it could finance its "deficits" by running the Fund's printing press. (No matter that those "deficits" would be, as noted earlier, by-products of discretionary intervention on the part of other countries. They would say what they have always said—that U.S. policies forced them to intervene.)

If the United States agreed to sell SDRs for dollars, even at a market price that could change from day to day, it would be subject to a form of mandatory asset settlement, and that would be ironic. Mandatory settlement has no proper place in the present monetary system.

In the days of the Committee of Twenty, mandatory asset settlement was seen as a way of making the monetary system more symmetrical—of imposing a conventional reserve constraint on the United States. In present circumstances, mandatory settlement would make the monetary system *less* symmetrical. The vast majority of Fund members would continue to control their own reserve positions and be free to choose between financing and adjustment in the light of those positions. The United States and other key-currency countries would lose control of their positions and would thus be less free to choose between financing and adjustment. In fact, the key-currency countries might have to adjust precisely because other countries wanted to finance—to build up their reserves by purchasing dollars, deutsche mark, or Japanese yen and selling them for SDRs.

I have argued elsewhere (Kenen (1980)) that there is just one way out. If governments and central banks cannot hold national currencies as reserve assets, they cannot be allowed to use them. They must use the SDR instead. The SDR can become the only reserve asset in the international monetary system only when it has become the instrument of choice for *all* official operations that affect reserves—for intervention, borrowing, and so on. Otherwise, asymmetries will creep into the system.

The SDR cannot become the instrument of choice, however, until it is widely used in currency and credit markets. Central banks cannot begin to intervene in SDRs until the SDR is traded in the foreign exchange markets. Governments cannot begin to borrow SDRs until banks and other private institutions are capable of lending them.[10] The monetary system is a complicated organism. It can change by itself, rapidly at times. It can be

---

[10] It might indeed be necessary to alter commercial arrangements as well as financial arrangements. Many primary products, including oil, are sold for dollars, and some of the dollars find their way into the hands of central banks, more or less directly. There are several ways of preventing this from happening. Exports could be sold for dollars, but exporters could be required to go to the foreign exchange market to sell their dollars for SDR deposits at commercial banks. Exports could be sold for domestic currency, which means that importers would be required to go to the foreign exchange market to buy it. Exports could be sold directly for SDR deposits.

changed by governments, but it has to be changed carefully. It is hard to modify one of its main features without also modifying many other features.

IV. HOW TO MAKE THE SDR A MORE IMPORTANT RESERVE ASSET

If I am right about the interdependence of institutional arrangements and its implications for reform of the international monetary system, there is little point in dwelling longer on ways to make the SDR the principal reserve asset. It cannot be done without making many other institutional changes. If I am also right, however, in saying that the monetary system will work differently in the 1980s than it did in the 1970s, reserves will play a larger role in the years ahead, and more attention should be paid to the supply of reserves. Therefore, an attempt should be made to stabilize the stock or growth rate of reserves, and that can be done by altering the supply of SDRs to offset unanticipated increases and decreases in supplies of other reserve assets—especially to offset decreases brought about by abrupt withdrawals of borrowed reserves.

The supply of SDRs can, of course, be increased by resuming allocations. Experience suggests, however, that this method will add only slowly to the stock of SDRs. The major industrial countries must consent to any allocation, and they have little direct interest in increasing or stabilizing global reserves. They have their own credit facilities—the swaps, the European Monetary Cooperation Fund, and so on—and can still count on borrowing if that should be necessary. Furthermore, too many of their governments continue to believe that they must fortify their "credibility" and are thus prone to seize every opportunity, sensible or silly, to display their horror of inflation. Finally, other issues tend to "crowd out" allocations. If forced to choose between an increase of Fund quotas and an allocation of SDRs, I would have done just what the Managing Director did—devote most of my time and even more of my political capital to the increase of Fund quotas.

If time and capital are to be invested in the SDR, they should be used in these three ways:

—To make the SDR more attractive by making it more usable as a means of payment.

—To make the SDR more prominent by trying once again to induce voluntary substitution.

—To find ways in which the Fund can alter the supply of SDRs without having to allocate or cancel them formally.

These three objectives should be pursued simultaneously, but I attach particular importance to the first. Unless the SDR is made more attractive, it cannot be made more plentiful.

V. MAKING THE SDR MORE USABLE

In early discussions of the SDR, it was sometimes described as "paper gold" and did indeed resemble gold. Its value was defined in terms of gold; its interest rate was very low; and it was transferable between official institutions, not between official and private institutions.[11]

There were, of course, important differences between the SDR and gold, mainly with regard to transferability. No country could run down its holdings of SDRs unless it had a "balance of payments need" to use them, even if some other country wanted to accept them, and when a country used them for balance of payments purposes, it still had to "reconstitute" some of them eventually. No country was required to accept SDRs, even under "designation" by the Fund, if its holdings were already three times as large as its allocations.[12] Nevertheless, the two assets were more similar than different, because the SDR was deliberately designed to serve the same basic monetary function as gold—to make official settlements.

There have been many changes in the attributes of the SDR. Its value is defined today in terms of a basket of five currencies; its interest rate is based on short-term market rates in the five countries whose currencies go into the basket; and some of the restrictions on its use have been eliminated. (Voluntary transfers are permitted freely between official institutions, and the "reconstitution" requirement has been abolished.) The SDR has become a more attractive store of value and, to that extent, a more attractive reserve asset.

The changes in the attributes of the SDR, however, have not caught up with one fundamental change in the monetary system—the virtual elimination of official settlements. Governments continue to hold reserves for financing balance of payments deficits. When they use reserves, however,

[11] Gold was transferable between official and private institutions before March 1968 by way of the "gold pool" established in 1960. Once that arrangement was abandoned, however, and the free-market price of gold was allowed to rise, two gold stocks came into being—gold held officially and gold held privately—and they were strictly separated for several years. Note that the SDR as defined initially could have been used in much the way that gold was used in the nineteenth century—to maintain fixed exchange rates without active intervention. Suppose that the SDR had become the "pivot" for parities, and each government had posted prices for its currency in terms of the SDR—a buying price and selling price. Arbitrage in SDRs would have kept exchange rates within the margins corresponding to the posted prices. It would not have been necessary to permit private holdings of SDRs, only to issue transferable drafts on official holdings.

[12] For details and subsequent developments, see the background paper by the staff of the Fund, "The Evolving Role of the SDR in the International Monetary System," which is Chapter 11 in this volume.

they typically transfer them to private institutions rather than official institutions, through the foreign exchange market. Those official settlements that do take place today are mainly between governments and the Fund—and they are the ones that use the SDR most frequently.

To make the SDR much more attractive as a reserve asset, it must be made more usable as a means of payment. It must be made transferable to private institutions.

Transferability can be achieved by permitting private institutions to hold official SDRs, but this direct approach has three disadvantages: (1) it would require an amendment to the Articles of Agreement; (2) it would add hugely to the volume of transactions crossing the books of the Fund; and (3) it would complicate decision making in the Fund, because decisions affecting the supply of official SDRs would be seen to affect the liquidity of the private sector and thus to impinge directly on the powers and responsibilities of national central banks. I will soon show, however, that transferability can be achieved without permitting private holdings of official SDRs.

The Private Life of the SDR

Private use of the SDR has developed rapidly in the last two years, spurred by the simplification of the currency basket at the beginning of 1981. It is used as a unit of account in credit and bond markets, and a number of banks accept deposits denominated in it. Furthermore, official institutions have been involved importantly in these innovations. In fact, the bulk of borrowing in SDRs has been by governments and state-owned enterprises, and official institutions are said to hold some of the SDR deposits.[13] The SDR, however, is used in private markets *only* as a unit of account, not as a means of payment. Loan proceeds are transferred in national currencies (usually in dollars), and repayments are also made in currencies.

One could probably arrange to transfer an SDR deposit to pay for an SDR bond, even for one issued by an official institution. But this could be done only on an ad hoc basis, and it would be difficult, because the SDR in which the bond is denominated can differ in small but significant ways from the one in which the deposit is denominated. There are "open" and "closed" baskets and other definitions as well (see Coats (1982, p. 428)). Furthermore, an official institution that took in SDR deposits by borrowing or floating a bond issue could not add them to its balance with the Fund; it could not transform them into official SDRs.

---

[13] These developments are discussed by Sobol (1981) and in the background paper by the staff of the Fund, "Evolution of the SDR Outside the Fund," which is Chapter 13 in this volume.

The staff of the Fund has looked at ways of reducing the differences among private SDRs, with a view to broadening the private use of the SDR in international financial markets (see the background paper, "Possible Further Improvements in the Existing SDR," which is Chapter 12 in this volume). Coats (1982) develops one proposal in detail—the use of the Fund as a clearinghouse and of the official SDR as the instrument for making the private SDR an efficient means of payment. He is on the right track, but he does not emphasize sufficiently the most important advantages of his proposal, and his scheme is unnecessarily radical.

The Need for a Clearinghouse

If the official SDR were used to clear private payments, the small but tricky differences in private SDRs would begin to disappear. The official SDR would gradually become the standard SDR. This sort of standardization must take place if the SDR is to be used eventually in foreign exchange trading, and that has to happen before the SDR can be used for official intervention. Furthermore, use of the official SDR to clear private payments would link it directly to the private SDR, and this linkage must take place to make the official SDR a useful reserve asset—to catch up with the main change in the monetary system to which I referred earlier. Governments that borrow in SDRs should be able to add the proceeds to their SDR balances with the Fund, and they should also be able to use those balances to repay their debts. Governments that finance their balance of payments deficits by intervention in the foreign exchange market should be able to transfer SDRs to foreign exchange traders.

Under the plan proposed by Coats, members of the Fund would authorize their central banks to open SDR accounts for their own commercial banks. Such accounts could be used to clear transactions between banks in a single country. They could be used jointly with accounts at the Fund—official SDRs—to clear transactions between banks in different countries. Under this particular plan, however, governments would have to give up control over their own holdings of official SDRs. Whenever a French bank made an SDR payment to a British bank, official SDRs would be transferred automatically from the Bank of France to the Bank of England.

Under that same plan, moreover, it would be necessary to abolish immediately the "acceptance limit" on official holdings, along with the requirement of "balance of payments need," and the viability of "designation" may still depend on the survival of those two provisions. If the official SDR were freely transferable to private holders and thus fully usable for balance of payments purposes, there would be no need for "designation" and for the provisions that make it acceptable. But those provisions cannot be abolished in order to begin a process that renders them redundant only at the end.

These difficulties can be overcome, however, by inserting a clearinghouse between the central banks and the commercial banks. Transactions between commercial banks would take place on the books of the clearinghouse, even those involving banks in different countries, and there would be no need for transfers of official SDRs. But transfers of official SDRs would take place whenever central banks (or governments) had dealings with commercial banks—whenever official institutions wanted to "transform" private SDRs into official SDRs or to go the other way—by borrowing, repaying debt, or intervening in the foreign exchange market.

Table 1 traces the transactions involved in setting up a clearinghouse. If Lloyds Bank wanted to join it, it would use its (sterling) balance at the Bank of England to buy official SDRs and pay them over to the clearinghouse. In this example, its subscription is SDR 100 million. The accounts of the Bank of England show a 100 million reduction in official SDRs held by the Bank of England and in its (sterling) deposit obligation to Lloyds Bank. The accounts of Lloyds Bank show the same reduction in the bank's (sterling) balance at the Bank of England. It is offset by the bank's SDR deposit with the clearinghouse. The accounts of the clearinghouse show an SDR deposit with the Fund and an SDR deposit obligation to Lloyds Bank.[14]

Table 2 traces a transaction between two commercial banks and shows that it has no effect on the SDR holdings of any central bank. In this example, Lloyds Bank uses SDR 75 million to buy yen from the Bank of Tokyo, and the SDR transfer is made on the books of the clearinghouse. (I omit the balance sheet of the Bank of Tokyo, as I do not need it to make my point.) The accounts of Lloyds Bank show its additional holdings of yen and the reduction in its SDR balance at the clearinghouse. The accounts of

[14] In consequence of the transactions shown in Table 1, the Bank of England is a net user of official SDRs and loses interest income; the clearinghouse is a net holder and earns interest income. In this particular example, the clearinghouse holds official SDRs and must therefore be given quasi-official status so as to qualify as a holder under Article XVII, Section 3. But other arrangements are easy to devise. The clearinghouse could be private but have an official sponsor, such as the Bank for International Settlements. Its sponsor would hold the official SDRs transferred to the clearinghouse; the clearinghouse would hold SDR certificates issued by its sponsor and backed fully by those holdings. Subsequent transactions involving official SDRs, such as the one in Table 3 below, would be handled by issuing or canceling certificates. I owe this suggestion to Jacques Polak, although he made it in a somewhat different context. (Note that there is no need to allocate new SDRs to the clearinghouse when SDRs are allocated to official holders. At some point, however, the commercial banks might have to make supplementary subscriptions, which means that central banks would have to make additional transfers of official SDRs. To this limited extent, official holders would still give up control over their own SDR holdings.)

the clearinghouse show the SDR transfer from Lloyds Bank to the Bank of Tokyo.

Table 3 traces the effects of intervention by the Bank of England. In this example, it uses sterling to purchase SDR 50 million from Lloyds Bank. (Lloyds Bank could be replaced by a foreign bank without changing the story in any significant way.) The accounts of the three institutions change in much the same way that they did in Table 1, but the signs of the entries are reversed. The Bank of England acquires SDRs from the clearinghouse, and they are official SDRs. Lloyds Bank acquires sterling from the Bank of England. The books of the clearinghouse reflect the "transformation" of private SDRs into official SDRs.[15]

The transactions shown in Table 3 are similar to those that would take place on account of borrowing by the Fund itself. The Fund would be able to issue debt to private institutions and take payment in official SDRs. If someone holding an SDR deposit with Lloyds Bank lent SDR 50 million to the Fund, the books of the bank would show reductions of 50 million in its deposit liabilities and in its balance with the clearinghouse. The books of the clearinghouse would show what they do now—reductions of 50 million in its deposit obligations and in its balance with the Fund. The books of the Bank of England would not be affected. The General Resources Account of the Fund would show a 50 million increase in debt and a 50 million increase in holdings of SDRs (a claim on the Special Drawing Rights Department of the Fund). If the Fund were authorized to borrow in private markets, it could denominate the debt it issues in SDRs until a clearinghouse was established. However, it could not take payment of the proceeds in official SDRs. It would, instead, have to take payment in national currencies or in private SDRs.

Whenever a central bank or the Fund itself is involved in a transaction with a private institution, there is a change in the ownership of official SDRs. Transactions between private institutions, by contrast, affect the ownership of claims on the clearinghouse but do not affect the ownership of official SDRs.

---

[15] One reader of my first draft pointed out that the transactions in Tables 2 and 3, taken together, pose a problem for Lloyds Bank. It winds up with a debit balance in its account at the clearinghouse. Lloyds Bank would have to buy SDRs in the foreign exchange market or borrow them from other participating banks. The creation of a clearinghouse would probably give rise to an interbank market in SDR balances—the SDR counterpart of the federal funds market in the United States. (If all banks ran short of balances with the clearinghouse, because of large-scale official purchases, they would have to buy SDRs from their central banks to make supplementary subscriptions to the clearinghouse.) Note that intervention by the Bank of England has the usual effect on the money supply in the United Kingdom; the increase in the sterling balance held by Lloyds Bank constitutes an increase in the monetary base. If the effects of intervention are to be sterilized, it must be done deliberately. (Transactions between commercial banks, by contrast, do not affect the monetary base.)

TABLE 1. SETTING UP THE CLEARINGHOUSE

(In millions of SDRs and SDR equivalents of sterling)

Bank of England

Assets		Liabilities	
SDR balance with International Monetary Fund	-100	Sterling deposit obligation to Lloyds Bank	-100

Lloyds Bank

Assets		Liabilities
Sterling deposit with Bank of England	-100	
SDR deposit with clearinghouse	$+100$	

Clearinghouse

Assets		Liabilities	
SDR deposit with International Monetary Fund	$+100$	SDR deposit obligation to Lloyds Bank	$+100$

TABLE 2. AN INTERBANK TRANSACTION

(In millions of SDRs and SDR equivalents of yen)

Lloyds Bank

Assets		Liabilities
Yen deposit with Bank of Tokyo	$+75$	
SDR deposit with clearinghouse	-75	

Clearinghouse

Assets	Liabilities	
	SDR deposit obligation to Lloyds Bank	-75
	SDR deposit obligation to Bank of Tokyo	$+75$

TABLE 3. INTERVENTION BY BANK OF ENGLAND

(In millions of SDRs and SDR equivalents of sterling)

Bank of England

Assets		Liabilities	
SDR balance with International Monetary Fund	+50	Sterling deposit obligation to Lloyds Bank	+50

Lloyds Bank

Assets		Liabilities
Sterling deposit with Bank of England	+50	
SDR deposit with clearinghouse ..	−50	

Clearinghouse

Assets		Liabilities	
SDR deposit with International Monetary Fund	−50	SDR deposit obligation to Lloyds Bank	−50

Other Innovations

In the long run, of course, the need for "designation" should die away. It should perhaps be kept on the books of the Fund to guarantee the transferability of the official SDR, but the provisions that support it—the acceptance limit and the requirement of balance of payments need—stand in the way of transferability and should be repealed as quickly as possible. In the interim, additional steps might be taken to stimulate the demand for the SDR.

When the Fund's holdings of a member's currency fall below 75 percent of quota, the Fund should offer to sell SDRs to that member in exchange for its currency. The exchange would not affect the volume of reserves. The member would give up a claim on the General Resources Account, which is itself a reserve asset, for a claim on the Special Drawing Rights Department, which is another reserve asset. I have not been able to find any legal obstacle to an initiative of this sort—only the obvious practical obstacle that the General Resources Account cannot sell SDRs unless it has them. It has a large quantity now, however, and would be well-endowed with SDRs on a regular basis under a proposal made later in this paper.

An offer of this sort would be mildly attractive from the member's standpoint. The rate of remuneration paid on a reserve position is four fifths of the interest rate paid on the SDR. The offer could be made much more attractive by allowing the Fund to tack on a premium of, say, 1 percent (i.e., to sell SDRs at a discount). The Fund might go further. Whenever a member draws on the Fund, it should be encouraged to purchase SDRs rather than national currencies. Therefore, the Fund might impose an additional service charge of, say, $1/2$ of 1 percent on purchases of currencies and no such charge on purchases of SDRs. There may be legal obstacles to these innovations, but I have found no clear-cut prohibitions.[16]

Finally, the Fund might pay an interest rate premium on SDR holdings larger than some multiple of a member's allocation (and might charge a penalty on holdings smaller than a fraction of a member's allocation). In other words, it might replace the present uniform interest rate with a graduated schedule of rates, paving the way for repeal of the acceptance limit and increasing the attractiveness of an offer by the Fund to buy a member's currency in exchange for SDRs. This particular proposal cannot be implemented without amending the Articles of Agreement, which state that the same interest rate must be paid to all holders of SDRs and that the rate of charges must equal the rate of interest (Article XX, Sections 1–3). Therefore, the proposal should be introduced as part of a third amendment of the Articles of Agreement—the one that would repeal the acceptance limit and the requirement of balance of payments need and, what is more important, would make way for the larger innovations suggested in the next two sections of this paper.

VI. SUBSTITUTION ONCE AGAIN

If measures of the type proposed above succeed in increasing the demand for SDRs by official holders, it would not be hard to increase the supply. Substitution is an attractive approach. It does not add to the stock of reserves and is therefore immune to the main objection that governments might raise with regard to large allocations and other methods considered below.

[16] An increased use of SDRs in ordinary drawings can affect reserves. When Brazil draws SDRs and uses them to buy dollars from the United States, it increases the gross reserves of the United States. When Brazil draws dollars instead, it can increase the gross reserves of the United States to the same extent, but only if the Fund's holdings of dollars are not larger initially than 75 percent of the U.S. quota. At first, I thought of proposing that the Fund impose an additional service charge on repurchases made with SDRs (and no charge on repurchases made with currencies), to keep SDRs from coming back into the Fund. But my main aim is wide use of the SDR, including its use in transactions with the Fund, and a charge on repurchases made with SDRs would have the opposite effect. Furthermore, such a charge would remove an important incentive for members to accumulate SDRs. From this standpoint, it might be more sensible to place a service charge on repurchases made with currencies (i.e., to penalize currency sales to the Fund as well as currency purchases), in order to encourage the use of SDRs in *all* transactions with the Fund. Note, finally, that this entire proposal would be rendered obsolete if the Fund adopted the more ambitious plan proposed in the final section of this paper—if all transactions with the Fund were made in SDRs.

Some History

The first official discussion of substitution took place ten years ago in the Committee of Twenty, when substitution was suggested as a way to reduce the reserve currency role of the dollar and thus to facilitate the introduction of mandatory asset settlement (see International Monetary Fund (1974, pp. 162–82), and Williamson (1977, pp. 151–54)). That discussion ended inconclusively, when it became clear that mandatory settlement would not be introduced. The second discussion took place in 1979–80, when substitution was suggested as a way to divert the diversification of currency reserves and thus to prevent the emergence of a multiple reserve currency system (see Kenen (1981, pp. 407–12) and Solomon (1982, pp. 285–93)). That discussion also ended inconclusively, partly because governments could not reach agreement on the best way to maintain "financial balance" in the proposed substitution account and partly because the dollar began to strengthen, reducing the incentive for diversification.

Although the first discussion took place long ago and was based on views about the monetary system different from those held today, it is perhaps more relevant than the second. It was concerned with long-run reform of the system and dealt with substitution through the Fund, using the SDR. The second discussion was strongly influenced by short-run concerns—the effects of diversification on foreign exchange markets—and stressed the need for rapid action. In consequence, it dealt with substitution through a separate facility, managed by the Fund but segregated from it, and thus with use of an SDR-denominated claim but not the SDR itself. This ad hoc approach proved to be self-defeating (Kenen (1981, pp. 409–10)):

> The creation of a separate substitution account ... posed special problems, and the solution of those problems was greatly complicated by the need to attract participation on a voluntary basis and on a scale large enough to make the exercise worthwhile. The account would be able to issue claims denominated in SDR, but it could not issue the SDR defined in the Articles of Agreement. In consequence, those claims would not assume automatically the attributes of the SDR. The transferability (liquidity) of the SDR is guaranteed within limits.... The redemption of the SDR is guaranteed by the provisions of the Articles pertaining to the liquidation of the SDR Department.... The transferability of the new asset, its interest rate, and ways to guarantee its value in the event of liquidation—the problem of financial balance—had to be negotiated, and these issues were connected in complicated ways.
>
> Holders of claims on the account would be able to transfer them freely among themselves. But potential holders wanted to be sure that they would find buyers whenever necessary. It was therefore suggested that holders should have the right to cash in their claims.... Some said that this right should be unconditional, but others said that it should be circumscribed, to be exercised only as a last resort, and that penalties should be imposed to make the option costly.
>
> There were, of course, proposals for "designation" patterned on the plan for the SDR itself. But reliance on this mechanism, it was said, might discourage participation in the substitution account. Countries with strong currencies and large reserves, whose partici-

pation would be important for success, might be unwilling to make big deposits, because these would expose them to large-scale "designation" (i.e., the obligation to grant large amounts of credit to countries in balance-of-payments need). . . .

What rate of interest should the new claim pay? There had to be a sensible relationship between liquidity and yield, but two other relationships had to be considered—the relationship between the interest rate on the new claim and the rate paid on the SDR itself, and the relationship between the rate on the new claim and the rate that would be paid by the United States on the dollar holdings of the account.

The interest rate relationships were important for "financial balance" and the long-run solvency of the substitution account. Its solvency could be impaired if its income was smaller than its payments to depositors. This could happen if the interest rate paid by the United States was lower than the interest rate paid to the depositors. It could also happen, however, if the dollar depreciated against the SDR. Interest payments by the United States would be calculated in dollars, being payments on the dollars held by the account, but interest payments to depositors would be calculated in SDRs, being payments on the SDR-denominated claims held by the depositors. Therefore, a depreciation of the dollar would raise the interest payments made by the account relative to its receipts. What is more important, a depreciation of the dollar could impair the solvency of the account directly. The SDR value of its dollar holdings could fall below the value of its obligations to its depositors, and this possibility was particularly worrisome to governments that were concerned about the transferability of their claims on the account and that consequently wanted substitution to be reversible.[17]

If substitution were conducted through the Fund itself, using the SDR, some of these problems would be eliminated and others would be simplified. There would be no need to worry about transferability—which would be greatly enhanced by establishing a clearinghouse.[18] In consequence, there would be much less need to provide for reversibility and less need to worry about the problem of solvency. The account would not have to be self-balancing from year to year. In fact, there would be no separate

[17] For simulations showing the importance of interest rate relationships and their interaction with exchange rate fluctuations, see the simulations in Kenen (1981). When depositors received the SDR interest rate and the United States paid the treasury bill rate, there was a $20.8 billion shortfall in the account at the end of 15 years; when the United States paid the SDR interest rate, the shortfall was reduced to $13.1 billion. (The shortfall was not eliminated, because the dollar depreciated during the period under study, and the depreciation acted directly to reduce the SDR value of the dollar claims held by the account.)

[18] A study group established by the Group of Thirty looked to marketability as the long-run solution to the problem of transferability (see Group of Thirty (1980, pp. 12-15)). It made no mention, however, of the need for a clearinghouse to link official SDRs with private SDRs. The importance of that link was perhaps obscured because the study group based its own proposal on the one that was being discussed in official circles—the use of an SDR-denominated claim rather than the SDR itself.

account. Liquidation would take place only in conjunction with the liquidation of the Special Drawing Rights Department—for which provision is already made in the Articles of Agreement. There might still be hard bargaining about the interest rate payable on currency balances held by the Fund, but this issue would be simplified, because the rate payable to depositors would be the one payable on the SDR.

Nevertheless, three issues would remain: (1) Should substitution be mandatory or voluntary? (2) Should substitution take place once or twice, or should it be an open-ended option? (3) What should be done with the currencies deposited with the Fund in the course of substitution? These are the questions on which I will concentrate.[19]

Why Substitution Should Be Voluntary

A large increase in demand for the SDR might make it possible for governments to reach agreement on mandatory substitution. Each one would deposit a fraction of its currency reserves in a newly established account at the Fund and receive in exchange new SDRs.[20] They would not have to *hold* that fraction of reserves in SDRs; they would be free to add to their currency reserves. Mandatory substitution need not be accompanied by regulated reserve composition or used to tie total holdings of reserves to the supply of SDRs.

This approach, however, has one major defect. The amount of substitution could be governed by the views of the least-willing governments, as it would require an amendment of the Articles of Agreement of the Fund and, therefore, approval by three fifths of the members having 85 percent

[19] Questions can be raised about interest payments too, but they are less important in the present context than in earlier discussions, because the problem of solvency is less important. Members whose currencies were acquired by the Fund could pay interest in those currencies. Members holding SDRs issued in the process of substitution could earn interest in SDRs. In other words, interest payments could be transferred by supplementary substitution. (For this purpose, however, SDRs issued in the process of substitution would have to be excluded from cumulative allocations, regardless of their treatment in connection with the issues raised in the next note.)

[20] If the acceptance limit was not repealed before or concurrently with the introduction of mandatory substitution, members of the Fund would have to decide whether SDRs issued in the course of substitution should be treated as allocations and counted in actual holdings when calculating the acceptance limits (see Article XIX, Section 4). If included in cumulative allocations (and therefore the base on which acceptance limits are computed), they should be counted in actual holdings. If excluded from cumulative allocations, they should not be counted in actual holdings. A decision on this point would not be too difficult with mandatory substitution, because all members of the Fund would be affected uniformly, but would be quite difficult with voluntary substitution. A member of the Fund that swapped a large amount of currency reserves for SDRs would expose itself to large-scale "designation" if SDRs issued in the course of substitution were treated as allocations, even if they were counted in actual holdings as well.

of the votes. If a few large countries wanted to turn in only a small fraction of their currency reserves, they could hold the others back, and the exercise would not accomplish very much. It may therefore be best to plan for voluntary substitution, even though it might likewise require an amendment if it were conducted through the Fund itself. Some important governments would probably agree to put in place a framework for voluntary substitution if it did not bind them to participate fully.

When Substitution Should Take Place

There are many ways to deal with the problem of timing, but they are bounded by two possibilities. (1) Substitution could take place on a single day, in amounts negotiated in advance, or left to the participants' decisions on that day. (2) It could be an open-ended option, with regard to timing and amounts. As usual, the best course lies somewhere in between.

If substitution had to take place on a single day, the extent of substitution would be far too sensitive to short-term views about the outlook for exchange rates, the balance of payments prospects of the participants, and the progress made to date in improving the quality of the SDR as a reserve asset, especially in making it more usable in currency and credit markets. The outcome of the exercise might be disappointing, and an initial disappointment could make it very difficult for the Fund to organize a second round.

If substitution were open ended in timing and amount, the Fund would be in difficulty—the same sort of difficulty it would encounter if it were to serve as the residual buyer of dollars in an SDR-based reserve system.[21] It would be issuing SDRs whenever its members wanted to get rid of currency reserves and could be accused of giving unconditional balance of payments support to reserve currency countries. An open-ended approach could meet with one more objection. The United States and other reserve currency countries would have to reach agreement with the Fund concerning the currencies acquired by the Fund—one having to do with maintenance of value, currency use on the part of the Fund, and even amortization. I shall discuss some of these matters later. They are relevant here, however, because no government can be expected to sign an agreement with the Fund unless it knows how much of its country's currency might be acquired by the Fund.

I am thus led to conclude that the opportunity for substitution should be strictly limited in time and amount. Members of the Fund might agree, for example, to open up the option for a five-year period but to put a ceiling on its use by any member—a limit on the number of SDRs that a member can

---

[21] See Section III.

obtain by selling reserve currencies to the Fund. Such ceilings might be based on gross reserves at the start of the five-year period (or on quotas in the Fund) but would not have to be absolutely uniform. Members could request higher or lower ceilings. Each member should perhaps be asked to use the first 25 percent of the allotment corresponding to its ceiling at the very start of the five-year period, so as to get substitution under way (and to discourage applications for huge ceilings that would remain unused). A member could use the rest of its allotment and thus move to its ceiling at any time within the five-year period.

Rules for revising the initial agreement—extending the five-year period or altering the ceilings—could be included in the agreement itself or in the amendment of the Articles of Agreement that would be required to permit the Fund to issue SDRs in exchange for currencies.[22] No country, however, should be obliged to accept an increase or decrease in its ceiling during the first five-year period.

What Might Be Done with the Currencies

When substitution was discussed by the Committee of Twenty, much attention was paid to the disposition of the reserve currencies (International Monetary Fund (1974, p. 174)):

> There was strong support for the view that the currency balances surrendered to a Substitution Account should be eliminated gradually over time by amortization payments by the issuers of the currencies. Mention was made of amortization periods of from 10 to 30 years. . . . It was agreed that some flexibility to vary the rate of amortization in relation to the balance of payments situation of a reserve center would be appropriate, although there were differences as to the degree of flexibility to be permitted and the direction in which it should operate. The United States favored flexibility for reserve centers to speed up or slow down the rate of amortization in response to balance of payments developments. Some participants favored a facility to speed up payments, but no facility to slow down.

In the second discussion of substitution, less attention was paid to this possibility. The participants had come to understand that currency balances could remain indefinitely in a substitution account, and those who favored reversibility wanted them to stay there to guarantee the liquidity of the claims issued by the account. That is why the problem of financial bal-

---

[22] It might not be absolutely necessary to amend the Articles of Agreement. Members of the Fund could vote to allocate SDRs, agree to turn their allocations back to the General Resources Account, and then buy them back with reserve currencies. But this cumbersome procedure might have to be executed on a one-time basis, and it would work only if all members of the Fund agreed to participate in substitution to the full extent of their allocations. It might break down if any member asked itself the obvious question: Why give my SDRs back to the Fund merely to buy them back again with currency reserves? It might then decide to keep its SDRs and not participate in substitution.

ance became so important. If large numbers of dollars and other reserve currencies are to lie dormant for decades, there is bound to be concern about maintenance of value in terms of the SDR, even though no one expects to take the currencies out again. Provisions for limited use or amortization could therefore allay concerns about maintenance of value and make it easier to reach agreement on large-scale substitution.

Several possibilities come to mind, and they could be combined. The Fund might be allowed to use the currencies for purchases of SDR-denominated debt issued by the World Bank and other development institutions. This would forge the missing link between SDR creation and development assistance, and it would promote the use of the SDR as a unit of account in long-term capital transactions. The Fund itself might borrow currencies to finance drawings by its members, in much the same way that it has borrowed currencies from members during the last several years. In this instance, however, the Fund would not make repayments; it would be regarded as borrowing from itself rather than borrowing from the countries issuing the currencies.[23]

Finally, currency balances acquired by the Fund could be amortized indirectly by transferring them gradually to the General Resources Account, even if they were not needed currently to finance drawings on the Fund. Such transfers would reduce the reserve positions of the countries issuing the currencies—which is why the transfers would amortize the balances—and could take place in accordance with a schedule negotiated with those countries to reduce the balances at an agreed rate. The transfers would take place whenever the methods proposed above—lending to the World Bank and borrowing by the Fund itself—had not reduced the balances at the agreed rate, but they would not take place if the issuing country did not have a positive reserve position with which to amortize them.[24]

---

[23] In other words, this sort of borrowing should not affect the rights of the member issuing the currency (e.g., its right to appoint an Executive Director under Article XII, Section 3, and the number of votes it can cast under Article XII, Section 5). Such borrowing would, of course, reduce the member's obligation to pay interest to the Fund. Within the Fund itself, the Special Drawing Rights Department would obtain an SDR-denominated claim on the General Resources Account and would hold it indefinitely.

[24] An illustration will perhaps clarify matters. Suppose that dollars worth SDR 80 billion are deposited with the Fund in consequence of substitution, that the United States agrees to amortize them over 20 years (i.e., at SDR 4 billion a year), and that the Fund uses dollars worth SDR 1.5 billion during the second year to buy bonds from the World Bank. Dollars worth SDR 2.5 billion remain to be amortized by the end of the second year, and they would be transferred to the General Resources Account if, at the end of that year, the U.S. reserve position in the Fund was no smaller than SDR 2.5 billion. (If its reserve position was, say, SDR 1.0 billion, dollars worth only SDR 1.0 billion would be transferred. The rest of the dollars, equivalent to SDR 1.5 billion, would be added to third-year amortization or to the end of the 20-year schedule.)

VII. AN INTERNATIONAL MONETARY FUND BASED ALMOST FULLY ON THE SDR

If Keynes had won his great debate with White, the Fund would have functioned from the start as a fledgling central bank. It would have created credit instead of selling currencies when one of its members needed balance of payments support. The First Amendment of the Articles of Agreement, which introduced the SDR, took the first formal step required to transform the Fund into a central bank.

It is not time to take the next steps formally, because they would be big steps. But it may be possible to move informally in the right direction by allowing the Fund to make more extensive use of the SDR in transactions with its members and reducing in the process the need to increase quotas in order to enlarge the resources of the Fund.

A Short Look at the Long Run

The Fund has done much more, of course, than manage a pool of currencies. Keynes and White might be surprised by what has happened to it. Quoting Polak (1979, p. 5):

> The attempt to view transactions through which the Fund made resources available to members in payments difficulties as a mere exchange of one currency for another never took hold. Fund transactions (beyond the reserve tranche) are now generally regarded as the extension of balance of payments *credit*. This view is reflected, for example, in the adoption of the concept of "credit tranches" and the widespread use of the term "repayment" as both more general and more meaningful than "repurchase."

Polak goes on to point out that ordinary drawings on the Fund usually create reserves, although the Fund is passive in this particular process. They do so whenever the sale of a member's currency adds to the member's reserve position. Reserve positions, moreover, are close substitutes for SDR holdings, which leads Polak to make his main recommendation. The Fund should be based fully on the SDR by eliminating completely the distinction between the General Resources Account and the Special Drawing Rights Department and allowing the Fund to finance its credit operations by issuing SDRs.

But something more must happen once that starts to happen. The supply of SDRs cannot be permitted to depend too heavily on countries' balance of payments needs. The supply must conform to the need for reserves, to the extent that one can judge it. Therefore, the Executive Board of the Fund has eventually to function as an open-market committee for the international monetary system—to increase or decrease the supply of

SDRs on its own initiative.[25] That is why it is not time to take the next steps formally. Members are not ready to allow the Fund to create SDRs in a flexible manner, even to meet members' balance of payments needs. They are far from ready to go the rest of the way and allow the Fund to conduct open-market operations, even within guidelines set by its members.

Important progress can be made in that direction, however, without reorganizing the Fund formally. Until the Articles of Agreement are amended, the Fund cannot be empowered to create SDRs when meeting its members' balance of payments needs. By interpreting the Articles elastically, however, the Fund can be supplied with SDRs in amounts appropriate to meet those needs.

What Can Be Done in the Short Run

The proposal I make here ties in with those I made above designed to encourage members of the Fund to take SDRs when drawing on the General Resources Account. It is closely related to Polak's proposal, but it can be adopted right away without another amendment of the Articles of Agreement.

Let us look five years ahead to the next increase in quotas. Normally, a member would pay in one fourth of the increase in SDRs and the rest in its national currency. This procedure is cumbersome, to say the least. Quotas affect voting rights, drawing rights, and contributions of resources. Therefore, decisions regarding the size and distribution of a quota increase run into conflicting objectives—from the standpoint of each member and among the members. Furthermore, the Fund itself acquires "resources" it cannot use—currencies that members do not want to draw. Finally, some members encounter political problems because they must obtain legislative approval to transfer their currencies to the Fund.

Matters could be simplified and the SDR given a much larger role in the Fund itself by combining an increase in quotas with an allocation of SDRs large enough to pay in the *whole* quota increase in newly issued SDRs—or at least a fraction larger than one fourth of the increase, if an allocation equal to the increase was thought to be excessive, given the requirements of

---

[25] Reserve supplies could perhaps be regulated by allocations and cancellations rather than open-market operations. Lending and repayments, however, could cause large fluctuations in the stock of SDRs that would be hard to offset by adjusting allocations. They might have to be offset by open-market operations. The need for open-market operations was mentioned by Triffin (1960, p. 115), but Polak does not make provision for them in his plan for unifying the departments of the Fund. For more on open-market operations by the Fund, see the paper by Fischer (Chapter 4 in this volume), which makes a point germane to a main theme of this paper: the macroeconomic effects of those operations will be increased if the SDR is widely used as a unit of account and means of payment.

Article XVIII, Section 1(a) that govern allocations. Each member would obtain an increase in its reserve position equal to the increase in its quota; that is the form in which it would experience the increase in reserves produced by the SDR allocation. The General Resources Account would acquire SDRs that the Fund could use to finance subsequent drawings. No member of the Fund could be required to turn over the whole increase in its SDR holdings—only an amount equal to one fourth of the increase in its quota—but no great damage would be done if some of the smaller members kept most of their SDRs.[26]

There is, of course, one danger. Some governments object to allocations, which add to owned reserves; they object less strongly to increases in quotas, which add instead to the supply of conditional balance of payments credit. If the two were tied together, those who object to allocations might also object to increases in quotas. But the proposal made above is meant mainly to demonstrate that the operations of the Fund can be based more fully on the SDR without amending the Articles of Agreement. It does not say that *every* quota increase must be financed by issuing new SDRs. It does not say that allocations must take place *only* in conjunction with increases in quotas. In my view, allocations should resume right now, not on the occasion of the next quota increase, in order to combat the damaging effects of stagnation or decline in the stock of reserves.

REFERENCES

Bacha, Edmar Lisboa, and Carlos F. Díaz-Alejandro, *International Financial Intermediation: A Long and Tropical View*, Essays in International Finance, No. 147 (Princeton, New Jersey: International Finance Section, Princeton University, 1982).

Bergsten, C. Fred, and John Williamson, *The Multiple Reserve Currency System: Evolution, Consequences, and Alternatives* (Washington: Institute for International Economics, 1983).

Bilson, John F.O., and Jacob A. Frenkel, "International Reserves: Adjustment Dynamics," *Economics Letters*, Vol. 4 (1979), pp. 267-70.

Black, Stanley, "International Money and International Monetary Arrangements," Chapter 23 in *Handbook of International Economics*, ed. by Ronald W. Jones and Peter B. Kenen (Amsterdam: North-Holland, to be published in 1984).

---

[26] Defections would not be as serious as in the case of substitution (see footnote 22), where countries that kept their SDR allocations instead of turning them back to the Fund would be increasing their reserves, whereas those that turned them back and repurchased them with currencies would merely be changing the composition of their reserves.

Coats, Warren L., Jr., "The SDR as a Means of Payment," International Monetary Fund, *Staff Papers*, Vol. 29 (September 1982), pp. 422–36.

Cooper, Richard N., "The Gold Standard: Historical Facts and Future Prospects," *Brookings Papers on Economic Activity: 1* (1982), pp. 1–45.

Corden, W. Max, "The Logic of the International Monetary Non-System" (Canberra: Center for Economic Policy Research, Australian National University, Discussion Paper No. 24, March 1981).

de Vries, Tom, "Jamaica, Or the Non-Reform of the International Monetary System," *Foreign Affairs*, Vol. 54 (April 1976), pp. 577–605.

Eaton, Jonathan, and Mark Gersovitz, *Poor-Country Borrowing in Private Financial Markets and the Repudiation Issue*, Studies in International Finance, No. 47 (Princeton, New Jersey: International Finance Section, Princeton University, 1981).

Frenkel, Jacob A., "The Demand for International Reserves under Pegged and Flexible Exchange Rate Regimes and Aspects of the Economics of Managed Float," Chapter 7 in *The Functioning of Floating Exchange Rates: Theory, Evidence, and Policy Implications*, ed. by David Bigman and Teizo Taya (Cambridge, Massachusetts: Ballinger, 1980), pp. 169–95.

Group of Thirty, Reserve Assets Study Group, *Towards a Less Unstable International Monetary System* (New York, 1980).

_____, *How Central Banks Manage Their Reserves* (New York, 1982).

Heller, H. Robert, and Mohsin S. Khan, "The Demand for International Reserves Under Fixed and Floating Exchange Rates," International Monetary Fund, *Staff Papers*, Vol. 25 (December 1978), pp. 623–49.

International Monetary Fund, *International Monetary Reform: Documents of the Committee of Twenty* (Washington, 1974).

_____, *Annual Report 1982* (Washington, 1982).

Kenen, Peter B., "Techniques to Control International Reserves," in *The New International Monetary System*, ed. by Robert A. Mundell and Jacques J. Polak (New York: Columbia University Press, 1977), pp. 202–22.

_____, "Changing Views About the SDR and Implications for Its Attributes" (paper prepared for the Secretariat of the United Nations Conference on Trade and Development; International Finance Section, Princeton University, 1980).

_____, "The Analytics of a Substitution Account," Banca Nazionale del Lavoro, *Quarterly Review*, Vol. 34 (December 1981), pp. 403–26.

_____, "The Role of the U.S. Dollar as an International Currency" (paper presented at the annual meetings of the American Economic Association, December 1982; International Finance Section, Princeton University, 1982).

Khan, Mohsin S., "Inflation and International Reserves: A Time-Series Analysis," International Monetary Fund, *Staff Papers*, Vol. 26 (December 1979), pp. 699–724.

Kindleberger, Charles P., *Balance of Payments Deficits and the International Market for Liquidity*, Essays in International Finance, No. 46 (Princeton, New Jersey: International Finance Section, Princeton University, 1965).

McKinnon, Ronald I., "Currency Substitution and Instability in the World Dollar Market," *American Economic Review*, Vol. 72 (June 1982), pp. 320-33.

Polak, J.J., *Thoughts on an International Monetary Fund Based Fully on the SDR*, International Monetary Fund, Pamphlet Series, No. 28 (Washington, 1979).

Robertson, Dennis H., *Economic Commentaries* (London: Staples Press Limited, 1956).

Roosa, Robert V., and others, *Reserve Currencies in Transition* (New York: Group of Thirty, 1982).

Sachs, Jeffrey D., "The Current Account and Macroeconomic Adjustment in the 1970s," *Brookings Papers on Economic Activity: 1* (1981), pp. 201-68.

Sobol, Dorothy M., "The SDR in Private International Finance," Federal Reserve Bank of New York, *Quarterly Review*, Vol. 6 (Winter 1981-82), pp. 29-41.

Solomon, Robert, *The International Monetary System, 1945-1981* (New York: Harper and Row, 1982).

Suss, Esther C., "A Note on Reserve Use Under Alternative Exchange Rate Regimes," International Monetary Fund, *Staff Papers*, Vol. 23 (July 1976), pp. 387-94.

Triffin, Robert, *Gold and the Dollar Crisis: The Future of Convertibility* (New Haven: Yale University Press, 1960).

von Furstenberg, George M., "New Estimates of the Demand for Non-Gold Reserves under Floating Exchange Rates," *Journal of International Money and Finance*, Vol. 1 (1982), pp. 81-95.

Williamson, John H., "Exchange Rate Flexibility and Reserve Use," *Scandinavian Journal of Economics*, Vol. 78 (1976), pp. 327-39.

_____, *The Failure of World Monetary Reform, 1971-1974* (New York: New York University Press, 1977).

Comments

Richard N. Cooper

Sixteen years ago, the international community embarked on a bold and dramatic experiment—creation of a world money by fiat. Now, the special drawing right (SDR) is in danger of atrophying into irrelevance. The international community hesitates to create new SDRs (two allocational decisions have been made over the past 14 years), and it even shows some reluctance to use fully the SDRs it has created.

Two questions need to be asked about the present state of affairs: (1) How can the SDRs be made a truly effective international monetary medium? and (2) Is it still worthwhile to continue trying to make the SDR an effective international monetary medium?

With respect to the first question, Professor Kenen has argued in his paper that if the SDR is to have a meaningful future as a reserve asset, other than for use in transactions with the International Monetary Fund, it must be made usable as a means of international payment. That, in turn, will entail allowing the SDR to be used by private holders—at least by commercial banks—so that the SDRs can be used in the international financial system as it actually functions. Central banks must have reserve assets they can use in their everyday transactions with banks and exchange markets; and they are more likely to hold an asset in their reserves, the easier it is to use in such transactions.

If the SDR is successfully modified to make it a means of payment in the world of private finance, then central bank demand for SDRs will increase, and the supply will have to be increased commensurately. To this end, Kenen makes two proposals: (1) that whenever quotas are increased, SDRs be allocated to cover the hard-currency portion of the additional subscriptions; and (2) that a substitution account be created which will permit central banks to deposit other forms of reserve assets in exchange for SDRs.

I basically agree with Kenen's line of argument. Most "settlements" take place through financial markets, and demand for reserves is strongly linked to their usability for settlements. It is noteworthy that at the end of 1981, about a quarter of cumulative SDR allocations were in the Fund, even though total country reserves grew sharply over the preceding decade. That high proportion reflects the fact that although SDRs could readily be used in settlements with the Fund, they could not be used for other settlements, which take place in the exchange markets.

I also agree that SDR allocations should be made more routine and that a good way to do this would be to link SDR allocations, more or less automatically, to quota increases. This practice would have the disadvantage of removing the last inhibition on most Fund members, desire for quota increases, since these increases would be virtually free. But those inhibitions are not very great now; and, for the reasons to be given below, I believe that the growth of owned reserves is desirable and that, at the margin, it would be provided in large part by SDRs.

I am more doubtful about Kenen's other proposal for increasing the supply of SDRs, through a substitution account. As envisioned here, the account is quite different in form from the proposals for a substitution account made in the late 1970s, which would have created separate entities with no formal link to the Special Drawing Rights Department of the Fund. Kenen's proposal would integrate the substitution account into the Special Drawing Rights Department; it would be voluntary; and it would be a once-for-all undertaking (with a five-year period for action). Why not? What is the harm in that? My answer is that there would still be lengthy and unfruitful argument over who should bear the ultimate exchange risk for an account whose assets and liabilities would not match after the passage of time. More consequentially, the Fund might be obliged for long periods to pay out on its SDR liabilities more than it was earning on its foreign currency (mostly dollar) assets, or vice versa. If payments exceeded earnings, where would the additional resources come from? The obvious answer is that the Fund would simply create sufficient SDRs to make up the difference. But that would be reserve creation unrelated to world liquidity needs and would require possible adjustments to the normal allocations. Alternatively, the Fund could raise charges on its regular loans. In either case, there would be complaints from many Fund members, who would call for redress in other areas of Fund activity. If earnings exceeded payments, the Fund, by the same token, could lower charges on its regular loans. That move would be welcomed by many Fund members, but others would resist on the grounds that such reductions would encourage yield-induced drawings from the Fund.

These are not compelling objections, but they must be set against the alleged gains from the substitution account, which are likely to be small. The use of SDRs in international settlements will increase only gradually, and the resulting increase in demand for SDRs can probably be satisfied, over time, by new allocations. If that judgment proves incorrect, a substitution facility could be created when it was necessary.

Moreover, in the event that the demand for SDRs grows rapidly because of its attractiveness for settlements, the SDR would very likely also be used much more widely in private transactions as well; and central banks would then find it possible to hold SDR-denominated accounts in commercial banks. In other words, supply will grow in step with demand where, as here, the demand is stimulated by increased convenience in use. These private SDRs would be analogous to an increase in deposit money based on "base money" from the bank of issue, in this case the Fund. New SDR allocations would thus be leveraged by financial institutions.

So I agree with Kenen's proposals, except for the substitution account, and my objections to that are not fundamental, but rather reflect a judgment that the benefits will not be commensurate with the considerable costs of putting it in place.

The more fundamental question is why we should attempt to improve the SDR so that it becomes a functioning international money. The Second Amendment stipulates that Fund members will collaborate to make the SDR the principal reserve asset of the international monetary system, but that injunction is vague and needs to be examined in the context of likely developments over the next several decades.

Kenen does not address this question in any depth, but mentions two arguments, which he does not find compelling, for an SDR-based system: (1) that a move to such a system will introduce greater discipline into the system as a whole, by providing greater control over reserve creation; and (2) that an SDR-based system is desirable, since it would avoid the instabilities inherent in a multiple-reserve-currency system, the likely alternative to an SDR-based system. He points out that the correlation between money creation and reserve creation is weak under the present regime of floating exchange rates and highly developed capital markets. And he points out that the alleged instability of a multiple-reserve-currency system is based on a false analogy with bimetallism or other models in which the source of instability is the attempt to maintain fixed prices between two or more assets, not the mere existence of two or more attractive assets. Here again, I agree with Kenen, and, if anything, would be inclined to put his criticisms more strongly.

But if these are not adequate reasons for trying to strengthen the role of the SDR, are there adequate reasons? It is useful to recall the original rationale for SDRs, which, in my view, applies as well today as it did in the late 1960s, even though in two important respects the international financial system is very different: we have an extensive and well-functioning international capital market, and we have flexible exchange rates. The key assumption underlying SDR creation is that there is a governmental demand for *owned* reserves, and that this demand does not have to be satisfied by earning them—that is, the demand for owned reserves is not basically mercantilistic and can be satisfied by direct allocation. The rationale for SDR creation was that this demand for owned reserves could not be satisfied adequately and indefinitely either by gold or by national currencies.

The assumption of a demand for owned reserves is not overturned either by the move to flexible exchange rates or by the tremendous growth of international capital markets since the late 1960s. Most countries are unwilling to let their currencies float freely. In fact, 103 of the 146 members of the Fund formally tie their currencies to something—to another country's currency, to a basket of currencies, to the SDR, or—in the case of several European countries—to the European currency unit. Most of the remaining countries have internal (sometimes undeclared) rules or indicators linking their currencies to something else. There are important exceptions—in particular, Canada, Japan, the United Kingdom, and the United States—but even these countries have occasionally intervened heavily to influence their exchange rates. The demand for reserves remains under a regime of flexible exchange rates.

In normal times, this demand can be satisfied by borrowing; and indeed in the late 1970s, many countries borrowed to add to their reserves of foreign currencies—empirical evidence, if any is needed, for growth in the demand for reserves. But credit-based reserves tend to disappear when a country runs into serious difficulty, as Kenen points out. They do not provide the same security and assurance of availability as do owned reserves.

So there is a demand for owned reserves. Do they have to be earned? I believe not, but that is an empirical question, and the answer may well vary from time to time. Certainly many countries still welcome—and seek—export-led growth, but that by itself does not constitute sufficient evidence that their growing demand for reserves cannot be satisfied by direct allocation; rather, it may be evidence that the most severe constraint on growth is foreign exchange earnings. A demand for earned reserves, of course, poses a serious problem for the international monetary system as a whole if it is entertained by all countries, for all countries cannot earn (net) reserves simultaneously, and the system would be subject to a deflationary bias—something that has not been evident during most of the past decade.

If only high-income countries need to earn their reserves—that is, if their demand for reserves is mercantilistic in character—that demand could be satisfied by allocating SDRs to developing countries and allowing the industrialized countries to earn them through exports. This kind of notion seems to lie behind some of the proposals for an SDR-aid link and other forms of "massive transfer." Apart from a possible error in the underlying assumption (taking a long view, and abstracting from the current state of underemployment in the world economy), the trouble with this proposal is that perceived requirements for foreign aid would inevitably get mixed up with assessments of the need for additional world liquidity when it came to allocation of SDRs. Protestations to the contrary, however honest and well meant, are simply not credible. Once development planning comes to depend in a consequential way on SDR allocation, it is inconceivable that there would not be a major outcry against a Managing Director's proposal for no allocation, no matter what the state of the world economy.[1]

If there is a demand for owned reserves that can be satisfied by allocation, what should be the basis for allocation among countries? The current practice of using Fund quotas is perhaps imperfect, but these quotas at least represent attempts to capture the need for reserves. Perhaps this practice can be improved upon on the basis of future research into the long-run demand for owned reserves; but in the meantime, it seems superior to alternative formulas. Deliberate attempts to transfer resources through SDR allocations are likely to undermine whatever political support there is for SDRs in the industrialized nations.

Of course, SDRs are not necessary to satisfy the demand for owned reserves; this demand has been satisfied by gold in the past, and it has been, and can continue to be, satisfied by national currencies, provided the countries whose currencies are used are relaxed about their growing liquid liabilities to other countries.

Gold was abandoned as a viable reserve medium when the Second Amendment entered into force, and for good reasons. Gold remains a non-ferrous metal with many private uses, and it must be extracted from mines. On both counts, the price of gold has consequences on the real side of the world economy which, over time, would interfere, as it has historically, with gold's playing the role of a monetary medium conducive to economic stability. Furthermore, gold has the same disability as the current SDR: it is not a means of payment, and therefore must be mediated by currencies.

National currencies have emerged as the international means of payment and, consequently, as reserves—first the pound sterling; then the U.S. dollar and (in a limited realm) the French franc; and more recently the deutsche mark, the Swiss franc, and the Japanese yen. A currency-based

---

[1]When, in 1969, I raised an objection to the generalized system of tariff preferences on the grounds that they would create a vested interest by developing countries against the further liberalization of world trade on a most-favored-nation basis, the then Secretary General of the United Nations Conference on Trade and Development assured me that this was not so; developing countries would always see their interests lying in a general lowering of trade barriers by the industrialized countries, and consequently developing countries would not oppose further trade liberalization. During the Tokyo Round of General Agreement on Tariffs and Trade (GATT) negotiations, however, a number of developing countries objected to deep cuts in tariffs on the grounds that such cuts would dilute the tariff preferences they received under the Generalized System of Preferences (GSP). Officials and international civil servants cannot bind their successors when they are pleading current self-interest.

system can work provided, as noted above, the reserve-currency centers are not excessively anxious about the steady growth in their liquid liabilities. It is not intrinsically unstable, as is sometimes contended; and periods of currency turbulence can, if necessary, be dealt with through close cooperation between the central banks concerned.

On the other hand, large external holdings of a country's currency can make its monetary policy hostage to sentiment about the currency. The United States has avoided this so far by virtue of the large size of the U.S. economy and the scale of the U.S. financial markets relative to world holdings of dollars. The Federal Reserve System has sometimes adjusted monetary policy because of exchange rate developments. (In my view, it should pay more attention to exchange rate movements than it has in recent years.) But those adjustments were not mainly motivated by concern for the reserve-currency role of the dollar. Despite some selective diversification of reserve holdings by currency that have taken place in recent years, especially in 1977-79, the reserve-currency role of the dollar has, on the whole, helped to stabilize, rather than to destabilize, exchange rates vis-à-vis the dollar. In particular, in 1977-79, the European authorities added $40 billion to their dollar holdings. Other monetary authorities also added approximately $15 billion to their dollar reserves during this period. If other authorities had added more dollars and fewer marks to their reserves during this period, there would have been less pressure on the dollar-mark rate than there was, but that does not entitle one to characterize the reserve-currency role of the dollar as "destabilizing."

Still, over time, the relative position of the United States in the world economy will continue to decline as other countries develop, yet it will not yield primacy of place to any other single economy. So if world reserve needs are going to continue being satisfied by the dollar (supplemented by some other currencies) while growing at a rate faster than the nominal growth rate of the U.S. economy, external dollar holdings sooner or later will surpass domestic holdings of dollar assets; and long before that time, concern about shifts of dollar holdings will place constraints on, and then perhaps dominate, U.S. monetary policy. Some might welcome the discipline that this would impose on national monetary policy. I would consider this an undesirable development, however, not least because the "discipline" imposed would sometimes be of the wrong kind, motivated by desires for glory or other political considerations, such as wishes to influence foreign policies unrelated to economic policy, and sometimes it would conflict with the exercise of consistent national economic preferences, reached democratically.

These developments will take many years to mature. The development of an international money will also take a long time. I believe, therefore, that it is prudent to continue to improve and to allocate the SDR.

John Williamson

Peter Kenen has presented a wide-ranging paper which reflects on the evolution of the international monetary system in general and the special drawing right (SDR) in particular, and proceeds to prescribe reforms designed to promote the role of the SDR. I am in sympathy with his presuppositions and his objectives, but I believe that he understates his case in two important respects. First, he understates the case for seeking to enthrone the SDR. Second, he understates the contribution that the main original proposal made in his paper might make toward accomplishing that objective.

Advantages of an SDR System

Kenen mentions two traditional arguments for seeking to make the SDR the principal reserve asset, neither of which much impresses him. The first is that stable growth of the reserve supply promotes global macroeconomic stability. In my opinion, Kenen exaggerates the claims that have been made to this effect when he writes (p. 334) that he does not believe "that the world can avoid deflation and inflation merely by controlling the supply of international reserves." Orthodox opinion (as embodied in Article XVIII, Section 1(a)) claims no more than that reserve-supply policy can help hold a prudent balance between deflation and inflation, which is not obviously inconsistent with Kenen's own position. Before the international capital market seized up in the wake of excessive monetary stringency and the Mexican moratorium, reserves could be viewed as largely demand determined, so there seemed little role for reserve-supply policy (see Haberler (1977) and Williamson (1982 b)). But circumstances have now changed (perhaps only temporarily), and the criteria for determining allocations laid down in the Articles imply a far stronger case for an SDR allocation now than has existed at any previous time since the SDR was created. In my view, the need is for a large once-over allocation designed to help reliquify the world economy and to promote financial reconstruction, not for a series of grudgingly conceded small allocations that might raise hopes that adjustment efforts might be relaxed or fears that inflation might be rekindled. But this useful ability to supplement reserve supply at a time of liquidity shortage depends on the existence of the SDR rather than on its being the principal reserve asset, so I ultimately agree with Kenen that this provides no strong reason for seeking to displace currency reserves with SDRs.

The second traditional argument dismissed by Kenen is the concern for systemic stability—that is, the confidence problem. However, the form that the confidence problem takes under floating rates is reserve switching, which imposes costs insofar as those switches are destabilizing and amplify exchange rate misalignments. Kenen concedes that this appears to occur, which gives another modest argument for preferring an SDR system.

A third traditional argument, the seigniorage issue, is not mentioned by Kenen. This question has become less important in view of the increase in the SDR interest rate to a near-commercial level, but it is still not negligible: there are few countries, especially developing ones, that can borrow long term at anything like the SDR interest rate. This I consider an advantage of an SDR system, since requiring low-income countries to transfer real resources (or to borrow long term at commercial interest rates) in order to provide for their liquidity needs is surely perverse.

But the most persuasive case for seeking a move to an SDR system is quite distinct from these traditional considerations. It lies, rather, in the possibility of reducing the total amount of uncertainty in the system by adopting as vehicle currency a unit that represents an average of the major currencies, instead of using one or more of those currencies themselves.[1] One may identify at least three ways in which use of the SDR in place of the dollar could be expected to insulate a typical small country from the shocks to which it is subject as a result of exchange rate variations among the major currencies—variations that are, from its viewpoint, purely capricious.

(1) A peg to the SDR would reduce the shocks to the country's effective exchange rate, and thereby to output, the balance of payments, the distribution of income, and the rate of inflation. It is true that the "optimal peg" would, in general, depend on the weights attached to stabilizing one rather than another of those variables. It is also true that the optimal peg would, in general, be a currency basket tailored to the country's individual situation, rather than an exogenous composite like the SDR. Nevertheless, the evidence seems fairly conclusive that, with the exceptions of the Caribbean (where the dollar remains an acceptable peg) and francophone Africa (where the French franc still dominates), virtually all developing countries would be better off with an SDR peg than with any single-currency peg (see Williamson (1982 a), Section 5). More fundamentally, a peg to a basket—or to the SDR at present—involves furthering macroeco-

---

[1]The uncertainties that one is concerned with here stem largely from changes in *real* exchange rates, so the reduction in uncertainty would not be of much consequence if exchange rate changes simply served to neutralize differential inflation. But it is by now evident that this accounts for no more than a trivial part of the exchange rate variations among the major currencies.

nomic stability (by curbing capricious shocks to the effective exchange rate) at the expense of depriving one's traders of any stable link with a major international currency that they can use to denominate contracts (and cover their contracts denominated in other currencies). But whereas that microeconomic cost is inevitable when one pegs to a tailor-made basket, a peg to an SDR basket combined with emergence of the SDR as a major vehicle currency would yield the bulk of the macro benefit without the micro cost.

(2) Use of the SDR to invoice trade transactions, if combined with an SDR peg, would mean that the domestic-currency value of exporters' and importers' claims and liabilities would be at risk only from changes in their national pegs against the SDR, and not, as now, from variations in the exchange rate between their country's peg currency and the currency of invoice. (It is true that those variations can sometimes be covered forward, at a cost, but this merely diminishes, rather than eliminates, the potential gain from a move to an SDR system.)

(3) Use of the SDR to invoice trade transactions, as well as to denominate foreign assets and debts, would reduce the reserve level a country would need to hold to maintain a given level of security against reserve depletion. Soon after the move to generalized floating, I endeavored to calculate the increase in reserves that certain developing countries would need in order to offset the additional shocks they were suffering as a result of fluctuations among the major currencies (Williamson (1976)). I concluded that an increase of less than 1 percent in reserve holdings could compensate—that is, that the impact of developed-country floating on developing-country reserve needs was negligible. I no longer believe that conclusion. In part, this is because exchange rates have become far more variable (the variance of the sterling-dollar rate over the past two years has been more than six times that in the 1972–74 period on which my calculations were based). But the major reason is that I misspecified my model by assuming that each month's exchange rate is drawn randomly from a normal distribution, whereas we know that deviations of exchange rates from trend are highly autocorrelated. (Once again, countries can reduce the variability that comes from currency mismatches, by diversification. But, once again, the reduction cannot be complete, and it is costly, especially for a small country where the call on skilled manpower, or the cost of hiring foreign consultants, can be significant.)

As long as real effective exchange rates among the major currencies seemed likely to vary by no more than 5 percent or 10 percent, the advantages of replacing the dollar with the basket SDR as the world's principal vehicle currency could be considered marginal. Now that we know that floating plus ideologically motivated monetary policies can easily generate swings of 20 percent, 30 percent, or even more, such complacency is unwarranted.

Establishment of an SDR System

Why, it will doubtless be wondered by some, do markets not spring up that will allow these advantages to be gained?

A first answer points to what one may naturally term the "infant currency problem." It takes two to consummate an exchange, so there is not much point in holding as a medium of exchange something that no one else is holding. No atomistic agent has an incentive to pioneer the switch to a new medium of exchange.

The second answer is that the SDR lacks the financial infrastructure that would permit exchange of SDR claims in settlement of debts. The private sector is prohibited from owning official SDRs, and therefore from exchanging SDRs with the official sector (which rules out SDR intervention in support of an SDR peg). Private SDRs are marginally different from each other, as well as from official SDRs. The private sector has to convert SDRs into a vehicle currency and back again to effect an SDR transfer between the customers of different banks. Small wonder, then, that the SDR has not developed spontaneously.

This diagnosis suggests the actions that are needed to open the possibility of adoption of the SDR as a vehicle currency. The SDR must be standardized, made interchangeable between private and official sectors, and made transferable.

The obvious way to accomplish this would be to have the Fund accept SDR deposits from commercial banks and create a clearing mechanism. And the obvious snag is that this is explicitly incompatible with the Articles, which restrict SDR ownership to official holders. If one takes the view that anything requiring a third amendment to the Articles has to be reluctantly dismissed as social-science fiction, that would seem to be the end of the matter.

Peter Kenen presents a simple but ingenious proposal that would resolve this dilemma. He suggests the creation of a clearinghouse, not as a part of the Fund, but as a new international institution, which would be eligible for recognition as an "other holder" of SDRs. This clearinghouse would accept SDR deposits by commercial banks or other private-sector traders. Those deposits could be created by commercial banks using national-currency balances at their national central banks to "buy" official SDRs, and, instead of holding the SDRs, transferring them from the central bank's Fund account to the clearinghouse's Fund account, while the clearinghouse issued an SDR deposit.[2] In that way, official SDRs would never come into the ownership of the private sector, but interchangeability between official and private sectors would nonetheless be achieved. Central banks would, indeed, be able to intervene in SDRs instead of in dollars, settling such transactions by transferring SDRs from the Fund to the clearinghouse (or vice versa). Interchangeability would, as Kenen argues, be likely to lead to rapid standardization of private-sector SDRs on the official SDR. And the clearinghouse would, of course, clear SDR transactions, so that transferability would be achieved.

The proposal for creating a clearinghouse seems to me entirely admirable and potentially of the first importance. But one needs to think further about the central issues of the way in which SDR deposits at the clearinghouse would be created, how the value of the SDR would be ensured, and the implications for global monetary control.

Kenen describes how SDR balances at the clearinghouse could be established by the goodwill of a central bank facilitating a desired switch into the SDR without having on impact on exchange rates. The same end result would be achieved if central banks took the initiative and intervened in SDRs in order to influence exchange rates. But one cannot limit changes in the stock of SDR deposits at the clearinghouse to this channel. Suppose, for example, that commercial banks wished to increase their holdings of SDR deposits when no central bank was willing to reduce its SDR holdings: the market value of the SDR would then be bid up, with no force to prevent its value coming to exceed that of the five component currencies. A simple way to prevent that from occurring would be to have the clearinghouse also issue SDR deposits in exchange for a basket of the five currencies (plus a small premium, no doubt).[3] The SDR currency countries would need to concert their intervention policies to ensure that they were not acting in a manner collectively inconsistent with the SDR valuation, but that should not be difficult.

The right of the clearinghouse to create SDR deposits against a basket of the five component currencies, as well as to issue SDR deposits against a transfer of official SDRs, seems to me essential to establishment of the

---

[2]The idea of SDRs being transferred at the behest of commercial banks goes back to a Bank of England proposal presented to the Committee of Twenty's Technical Group on Intervention and Settlement: see International Monetary Fund (1974, pp. 122-25). Coats (1982) went a stage further and outlined a scheme that would allow commercial banks to hold SDR deposits with their central banks. Under this scheme, international, interbank transactions would be cleared through the respective central banks transferring SDRs between their Fund accounts.

[3]The inability to use this mechanism to ensure the maintenance of the value of the SDR would seem to be the main disadvantage of the Coats scheme in comparison with that of Kenen.

SDR as a major vehicle currency within an overall system in which ultimate monetary sovereignty remains with the major powers. And that is about as internationalist a solution as it might conceivably be realistic to aim for, at least in this century. The next need is to explore the feasibility and mechanics of a system in which the SDR-currency countries determine their joint rate of monetary expansion, but not its distribution among the SDR's component currencies or the (private) SDR, on the general lines advocated by McKinnon (1982). Perhaps SDR allocations should also follow a path designed to give reserve growth similar to the rate of monetary expansion agreed to be appropriate by the major countries. And perhaps the SDR-currency countries should use a part of their allocations to retire the balances of their currencies that the clearinghouse will acquire as the banks wish to build up their SDR deposits.

One other topic discussed by Kenen merits reconsideration in the light of the preceding discussion—substitution. Note first that a desire to increase the SDR component of official reserves could be accommodated through the private market under arrangements of the type discussed, since a central bank could use dollars (for example) to establish an SDR deposit at a commercial bank. To the extent that there was not a concomitant desire to redenominate commercial bank loans in SDRs rather than dollars, the commercial bank might wish to sell dollars for the other basket currencies, either in order to hold the basket currencies or in order to establish a matching SDR asset at the clearinghouse. That would exert downward pressure on the dollar in the exchange markets. If that downward pressure were undesired by the U.S. authorities, they might resist it by intervention. But, given the paucity of its reserves, the United States might lack the resources to intervene as much as it would wish. In these circumstances, it would be quite reasonable, indeed highly desirable, for the Fund to provide a substitution facility which allowed countries wishing to switch their dollar reserves into SDRs to do so directly. But since the reason for providing the facility would be to allow the United States to avoid the pressures on the value of its currency caused by desires to switch out of the dollar, it should surely be axiomatic that the U.S. liability to the substitution account should be an SDR liability carrying the SDR interest rate. As Kenen correctly notes, it was the failure to incorporate this principle in the 1979 proposals for substitution that doomed that scheme, although his discussion leaves one in some doubt as to whether he has fully absorbed the lesson. It cannot be said too strongly that substitution schemes that involve the Fund holding currencies rather than SDR claims are not worth consideration.

If substitution were to involve the United States accepting an SDR liability, then it would be natural for the United States to insist that countries have access to the substitution facility only when the U.S. authorities regarded a substitution of SDR liabilities for dollar liabilities as nationally advantageous. I see no reason why other countries should object to such a restriction, within the context of a system where they always had the alternative option of switching dollars into SDRs through the market. The United States and the Fund would have to agree on a value of the dollar above which the ingenious balance of substitution rights suggested in Kenen's paper would not apply.

Concluding Remarks

I have argued above that the case for seeking to enhance the role of the SDR is significantly stronger than is recognized by Kenen, primarily because of the reduction in uncertainty (especially to residents of the smaller countries) that could follow introduction of the SDR as a (or the) major vehicle currency. This step would not require countries to surrender their monetary sovereignty to the Fund. Kenen's paper has proposed creation of a clearinghouse as the essential step to initiate evolution in that direction. His proposal is one that deserves to be adopted.

REFERENCES

Coats, Warren L., Jr., "The SDR as a Means of Payment," International Monetary Fund, *Staff Papers*, Vol. 29 (September 1982), pp. 422-36.

Haberler, Gottfried, "How Important is Control over International Reserves?" in *The New International Monetary System*, ed. by Robert A. Mundell and Jacques J. Polak (New York: Columbia University Press, 1977), pp. 111-61.

International Monetary Fund, *International Monetary Reform: Documents of the Committee of Twenty*, report to the Board of Governors by the Committee on Reform of the International Monetary System and Related Issues (Committee of Twenty) (Washington, 1974).

McKinnon, Ronald I., "Currency Substitution and Instability in the World Dollar Standard," *American Economic Review*, Vol. 72 (June 1982), pp. 320-30.

Williamson, John, "Generalized Floating and the Reserve Needs of Developing Countries," in *The International Monetary System and the Developing Nations*, ed. by D. M. Leipziger (Washington: United States Government, Agency for International Development, 1976), pp. 75-86.

_____ (1982 a), "A Survey of the Literature on the Optimal Peg," *Journal of Development Economics*, Vol. 11 (January 1982), pp. 39-61

_____ (1982 b), "The Growth of Official Reserves and the Issue of World Monetary Control," in *The International Monetary System: A Time of Turbulence*, ed. by J. S. Dreyer, G. Haberler, and T. D. Willett (Washington: American Enterprise Institute for Public Policy Research, 1982), pp. 277-91.

What Are the Scope and Limits of Fruitful International Monetary Cooperation in the 1980s?

PAUL De GRAUWE

During the postwar period, the expectations of stable price levels lessened progressively in the major industrialized countries. It is now widely accepted that this change in attitude was due mainly to the change in the policy environment in these countries, where demand management and, in particular, monetary policy came to be pursued systematically for the purpose of domestic stabilization. This change in the policy environment made a system of rigidly fixed exchange rates difficult to sustain and led inevitably to a system in which the exchange rate would be allowed to vary more frequently. There is now a growing awareness, however, that the exchange rate movements that have occurred since the early seventies have been excessive and detrimental to the functioning of the international trade and financial system. In addition, it is now increasingly recognized that instead of facilitating national macroeconomic management, the variability of exchange rates has made independent macroeconomic policies more complex.[1]

Conflicts exist between major countries about how to deal with the extreme volatility of exchange rates. These conflicts exist on two levels. One is the more fundamental conflict about the degree of flexibility which is optimal for the macroeconomic stability of countries. Some countries favor more exchange rate flexibility than others. The most visible expression of these conflicting attitudes is the fact that some European countries have chosen

---

[1] See, for example, Rudiger Dornbusch (1983) for a recent statement of this view.

375

to peg their exchange rates within the EMS, whereas other countries have followed drastically different exchange rate regimes.

A second area of conflict relates to the question of how exchange rates can be stabilized, and how the task (or burden) of actually doing this should be distributed among countries. Resolving the first conflict (the desired degree of flexibility) still leaves open the question of how given exchange rate objectives should be attained using suitable mixes of intervention policies in the exchange market and in the domestic money market.

The discussion of this paper will be organized around these two major issues. There are other issues in the area of international monetary cooperation which will be given less attention here. One is the problem of the creation of international liquidity. This problem, which dominated discussion of international monetary reform in the past, has receded in importance since the inception of flexible exchange rates. It will be discussed at the end of the paper.

I. HOW MUCH EXCHANGE RATE FLEXIBILITY?

Theoretical Issues

A major issue confronting the international monetary system is the desirable degree of exchange rate flexibility. There is little disagreement that in today's policy environment, some degree of flexibility is inevitable. Yet the fluctuations of the exchange rates experienced since the early seventies are widely felt to be too large. They disrupt macroeconomic management in different countries and increase tensions between countries. While there is wide agreement that the exchange rate fluctuations have been excessive, there is much less agreement on how much flexibility (or how much management of the exchange rate) would be desirable. What are the reasons for these conflicting attitudes, and how can these conflicts be resolved?

There is now a growing literature on the issue of the optimal flexibility of exchange rates. Since the seminal paper of Mundell (1963), it has been recognized that the source of a disturbance to the economy should determine whether countries ought to react by pegging the exchange rate or by letting it change. This theme has been developed in a long list of recent papers (see Fischer (1977), Buiter and Eaton (1980), Turnovsky (1982), Marston (1981), Frenkel and Aizenman (1982), Canzoneri (1982), and Henderson (1982)). Given the diverse nature of the models, there is very little agreement, however, on specifics. For example, one of the major conclusions of the Mundellian analysis is that a flexible exchange rate should be used to deal with shocks originating in the domestic goods market and that a fixed exchange rate should be used to deal with a domestic monetary shock. This conclusion, however, is reversed by making different assumptions about price and supply behavior or about the policy objectives of the national authorities. When some agreement exists, for example, on how to react to a pure portfolio shift (see Henderson (1982)), it is recognized that in practice the exact nature of the shock is usually not known to policymakers. The most general conclusion one can draw from this literature is the following: Because economies are hit by many different shocks (monetary shocks, supply shocks) and because there is incomplete information on the nature of these shocks, neither a pure fixed nor a pure flexible exchange rate system is likely to be optimal (from the point of view of the stabilization of output or of aggregate spending). Instead, something between these two extreme exchange rate regimes—that is, some form of managed floating—will be optimal.

Despite these shortcomings, the recent literature on the optimal degree of flexibility of exchange rates can teach us something about problems of cooperation. One important insight that can be gained from this literature is that the covariance of the shocks across countries matters; a given disturbance hitting one country alone leads to quite a different optimal exchange rate response than a similar disturbance that hits other countries simultaneously. This point can best be illustrated by considering the effects of a supply shock. Suppose country A is hit by an unexpected and temporary disturbance that reduces domestic output. This will normally lead to a current account deficit. If country A alone is affected by such a disturbance, it can, by allowing its currency to depreciate, alleviate the negative output (and employment) effect. The reason is that the depreciation of the currency temporarily stimulates aggregate demand and output.[2]

If, however, many other countries are hit by the same supply shock, it is far from clear that the optimal response consists of letting the exchange rate adjust. The reason, of course, is that the depreciation of one currency is the appreciation of the other currencies. Thus, when supply shocks are positively correlated across countries, flexible exchange rates may easily lead to an exacerbation of policy conflicts between countries, as the depreciation of one currency aggravates the deflationary effects of the supply shock in other countries. Instead of facilitating the accommodation to a supply shock, an uncoordinated system of flexible exchange rates may make it more difficult for countries facing the same disturbance to adjust their economies. This paper will return to this issue later on when empirical evidence is discussed.

[2] Note that letting the currency depreciate may not be an optimal response if the authorities pursue an objective of stabilization of real consumption. In that case pegging the exchange rate will be optimal. This allows the country to compensate the shortfall of domestic output by increasing imports (see Frenkel and Aizenman (1982)).

Another way to look at the problem of the optimal degree of flexibility of the exchange rate is to start from the old debate between those emphasizing the need for domestic stability as a precondition for fixing the exchange rate and those emphasizing that exchange rates need to be pegged before one can stabilize the domestic economy. This debate has gone through many cycles in history. During the twenties, after a period of strong fluctuations of exchange rates, there was a widely held conviction that the paramount task in the field of international monetary cooperation was stabilizing the exchange rates of the major currencies. This was seen as a first step toward the successful stabilization of domestic economies (see Clarke (1967) for a history of central bank cooperation during 1924-31). The whole cooperative effort underlying the Bretton Woods system was inspired by the same idea. During the postwar period, as major countries relaxed the monetary discipline needed to sustain a fixed exchange rate system, the view that domestic stability was a precondition for exchange rate stability gained respectability. In the early seventies, this view had become predominant among academic economists. Now, after many years of volatile exchange rate behavior, the old view stressing the need to stabilize the exchange rates of major currencies as a first step toward achieving more domestic stability has regained respectability.

The conflict between these two viewpoints has not yet been settled. As a result, there is as yet no general agreement on how monetary cooperation should be organized in the eighties. In order to evaluate the merits of the two viewpoints, empirical data were collected for the sixties and seventies, and some lessons were drawn for the eighties. The next subsection provides details.

Some Stylized Facts

One piece of evidence is obtained from a comparison of inflation rates of the major industrial countries (see Table 1). This table shows the average yearly growth rate of the consumer price index during 1960-70 and 1971-81 and standard deviations. One can see that the average inflation rate was more than twice as high during the seventies than during the sixties in all countries (except Japan); in addition, the yearly variability (as measured by the standard deviation) was two or three times higher. Finally, the intercountry dispersion of inflation rates was almost three times higher in the seventies than in the sixties (see Table 1). One way to interpret these phenomena is along the lines of what proponents of flexible exchange rates have said all along: a flexible exchange rate system allows a country to choose its own long-run rate of inflation (see Laidler (1982)). It should, therefore, be no surprise that inflation rates differ across countries when

TABLE 1. SEVEN INDUSTRIAL COUNTRIES: MEANS AND STANDARD DEVIATIONS OF YEARLY INFLATION RATES, 1960–70 AND 1971–81

Country	1960–70		1971–81	
	Mean	Standard deviation	Mean	Standard deviation
United States	2.6	1.8	8.1	3.2
Canada	2.6	1.3	8.5	2.8
Japan	5.6	1.4	8.8	6.0
France	4.1	1.5	10.0	2.9
Germany, Fed. Rep.	2.5	0.8	5.2	1.3
Italy	3.8	1.9	14.3	5.3
United Kingdom	3.7	1.6	13.6	5.1
Average (across countries)	3.6		9.8	
Standard deviation (across countries)	1.1		3.2	

Source: International Monetary Fund, *International Financial Statistics.*

exchange rates are flexible. Some countries will have high rates of inflation, while others will have low rates of inflation.

This interpretation is surely only part of the story. It is difficult to see, for example, how and why all countries chose to double their long-run inflation rates in the seventies. Rather, if the previous explanation is to be taken seriously, one would have expected that some countries that were forced to accept higher inflation rates than they wanted during the fixed exchange rate system of the sixties should have been able to lower their long-run inflation rates in the seventies, since in the latter period the floating of their currencies should have allowed them to choose a lower inflation rate. The facts, however, show that such expectations were not justified.

Of course, the oil shocks which occurred during the seventies increased the rates of inflation in all countries. Although important, this factor fails to account for much of the acceleration of inflation rates observed in all countries during the seventies. From 1971–81, the consumer price index increased by 155 percent in the seven major industrialized countries versus only 43 percent during 1960–70. It is difficult to see how the oil shocks alone could account for this acceleration of inflation.[3]

[3] The Organization for Economic Cooperation and Development (OECD) has estimated that the mechanical effects of the oil shocks account for about half of the acceleration of inflation in the OECD countries during the years 1973-1974 and 1979-1980. During the other years, of course, the contribution of oil shocks to the acceleration of inflation rates was much lower.

Another explanation stresses that instead of facilitating domestic monetary management, the exchange rate system of the seventies made it much more difficult to manage domestic monetary systems. Wild swings in exchange rates led to large variations in inflation rates. In addition, since the monetary authorities were not indifferent to these exchange rate movements and consequently intervened heavily, money stock growth rates were highly variable during this period. This point has been stressed recently in McKinnon (1982) and also by the Bank for International Settlements in its annual reports.[4] In particular, the persistent and large depreciations of the dollar led the other industrialized countries to intervene heavily in exchange markets, thereby expanding their money stocks substantially. Thus, the managed floating exchange rate system led to higher money growth rates in the seventies. Evidence of this phenomenon is given in Table 2. This table shows the average yearly growth rates of money stocks (M_1) in the major industrial countries during 1960–70 and 1971–81. The most striking result is that whereas the growth rate of the money stock increased, on average, in the seven major industrial countries, the dispersion of the monetary expansion across countries narrowed from the sixties to the seventies.[5] Thus, despite more flexible exchange rates, countries

TABLE 2. SEVEN INDUSTRIAL COUNTRIES: MEANS AND STANDARD DEVIATIONS OF YEARLY GROWTH RATES OF MONEY STOCK (M_1), 1960–70 AND 1971–81

	1960–70		1971–81	
Country	Mean	Standard deviation	Mean	Standard deviation
United States	3.6	2.0	6.5	1.4
Canada	6.3	6.5	7.6	3.1
Japan	20.1	7.8	13.1	8.4
France	9.7	5.6	11.4	2.3
Germany, Fed. Rep.	7.7	2.2	8.5	4.6
Italy	14.7	3.4	18.3	5.1
United Kingdom	3.4	2.3	12.2	5.0
Average (across countries)	9.4		11.1	
Standard deviation (across countries)	6.1		4.0	

Source: International Monetary Fund, *International Financial Statistics*.

[4] See Bank for International Settlements (1980).

[5] Part of this decline in the average dispersion of the growth rates of the money stock is due to the fact that the GDP growth rates were less divergent during the seventies than during the sixties. This is discussed later on.

seem to have been disciplined in a particular way after all—intercountry *differences* in money growth rates were lower during the seventies than during the sixties.

This phenomenon is confirmed by analyzing the correlation matrix of the growth rates of the money stocks in the seven major industrial countries (see Table 3). It can be seen that the correlation of the growth rates of the money stocks between the countries (outside the United States) increased during the seventies. One can conclude that the managed floating rate system of the seventies may have led to less (rather than more) monetary independence in the industrial countries, with the sole exception of the United States. This is a paradoxical result, since it goes against the conventional wisdom about what a flexible exchange rate system allows countries to do.

How does the occurrence of large supply shocks during the seventies fit into this picture? Table 4 provides some clues. It shows the correlation matrix of the growth rates of (real) gross domestic product (GDP) during the sixties and the seventies. One can see that during the sixties, there was very little positive correlation of GDP growth rates across countries. During the seventies, however, the correlations increased dramatically. There is no question that this strong international synchronization of economic activity during the seventies has been caused by oil shocks which hit all countries simultaneously. However, this phenomenon of increased international synchronization of the business cycle can also be linked to the monetary phenomenon observed earlier. To the extent that the exchange rate system of the seventies led to substantial monetary dependence among countries, in the sense that monetary policies tended to be strongly correlated, it also reinforced the international synchronization of economic activity.

From the preceding analysis, one can derive the conclusion that the exchange rate system of the seventies tended to amplify the international transmission of monetary shocks. At the same time, instead of increasing the monetary independence of the major industrialized countries except the United States, it may have reduced it. (See also Dornbusch (1982) on this issue.) From this evidence, one can also conclude that there is some truth to the idea that there is too much flexibility in exchange rates, and that a major step toward the stabilization of monetary policies would be to stabilize exchange rates.

Does this mean that cooperative efforts during the eighties should be geared to returning to a fixed exchange rate system like the one used during the Bretton Woods period? The answer is, most probably, negative. In order to see this, it is important to realize that the degree of convergence of inflation rates and money growth rates during the sixties was insufficient to guarantee a durable fixed exchange rate system. The average

TABLE 3. SEVEN INDUSTRIAL COUNTRIES: CORRELATION MATRIX OF YEARLY GROWTH RATES OF MONEY STOCK (M_1), 1960–70 AND 1971–81

1960–70	United States	Canada	Japan	France	Germany, Fed. Rep.	Italy	United Kingdom
United States	1						
Canada	0.06	1					
Japan	−0.17	0.01	1				
France	−0.58	0.34	0.39	1			
Germany, Fed. Rep.	−0.31	−0.23	0.05	0.41	1		
Italy	−0.11	−0.40	−0.17	−0.22	−0.06	1	
United Kingdom	0.16	−0.04	0.39	−0.39	−0.39	0.13	1

1971–81	United States	Canada	Japan	France	Germany, Fed. Rep.	Italy	United Kingdom
United States	1						
Canada	0.06	1					
Japan	−0.03	0.79	1				
France	−0.36	0.03	0.44	1			
Germany, Fed. Rep.	−0.07	0.67	0.45	0.28	1		
Italy	0.57	0.18	0.42	0.22	0.20	1	
United Kingdom	0.10	0.51	0.26	0.22	0.78	0.27	1

Source: International Monetary Fund, *International Financial Statistics.*

TABLE 4. SEVEN INDUSTRIAL COUNTRIES: CORRELATION MATRIX OF YEARLY GROWTH RATES OF REAL GDP, 1962–70 AND 1971–81

1962–70	United States	Canada	Japan	France	Germany, Fed. Rep.	Italy	United Kingdom
United States	1						
Canada	0.95	1					
Japan	−0.28	−0.24	1				
France	−0.04	0.14	0.10	1			
Germany, Fed. Rep.	0.02	0.26	0.14	0.51	1		
Italy	−0.34	−0.37	0.20	−0.19	−0.53	1	
United Kingdom	0.10	0.04	0.56	−0.27	0.12	−0.42	1

1971–81	United States	Canada	Japan	France	Germany, Fed. Rep.	Italy	United Kingdom
United States	1						
Canada	0.67	1					
Japan	0.80	0.52	1				
France	0.71	0.83	0.59	1			
Germany, Fed. Rep.	0.79	0.64	0.72	0.84	1		
Italy	0.42	0.47	0.41	0.65	0.80	1	
United Kingdom	0.77	0.77	0.70	0.79	0.74	0.57	1

Source: Organization for Economic Cooperation and Development, *Main Economic Indicators*.

yearly divergence of inflation rates between the major industrialized countries was of the order of 2 percent during that decade. This turned out to be too great a divergence. It is useful to compare this to the situation which existed during the period of the international gold standard (1870–1913). Table 5 provides some evidence and compares the inflation divergences observed during that period with the Bretton Woods period. It can be seen that the long-run inflation differential across countries was almost zero when the international gold standard was in effect.[6] It is also noteworthy that the long-run inflation rate was practically zero during this

TABLE 5. FOUR INDUSTRIAL COUNTRIES: MEANS AND STANDARD DEVIATIONS OF YEARLY INFLATION RATES, 1870–1981[1]

(*In percent per annum*)

International Gold Standard Period	1870–1913		1870–92		1893–1913	
	Average	Standard deviation	Average	Standard deviation	Average	Standard deviation
France	−0.1	4.5	−2.0	3.6	2.0	4.3
Germany, Fed. Rep.	0.01	5.6	−1.6	5.4	1.6	4.8
United Kingdom	−0.8	3.9	−2.3	4.0	1.1	3.5
United States [2]	−0.9	5.8	−2.3	5.8	2.7	3.5

Postwar Period	1949–81		1949–71		1972–81	
	Average	Standard deviation	Average	Standard deviation	Average	Standard deviation
France	4.5	8.0	3.1	7.8	7.9	8.1
Germany, Fed. Rep.	2.3	4.1	1.1	4.0	5.0	3.3
United Kingdom	5.6	6.3	2.7	4.2	14.7	5.5
United States	3.4	4.8	1.2	2.7	9.4	4.2

Sources: France, Federal Republic of Germany, United Kingdom: Mitchell (1975) for 1870–1913; International Monetary Fund, *International Financial Statistics* for 1949–81.

United States: Williamson (1975) for 1870–1918; *Federal Reserve Bulletin* (January 1948) for 1919–38; International Monetary Fund, *International Financial Statistics* for 1949–81.

[1] The inflation rate is the rate of change of the *wholesale* price index.

[2] For the United States, the sample period starts in 1879 and ends in 1910; for France, the subperiods are 1879–96 and 1897–1913.

[6] The evidence also indicates that in the short run, large differences could exist. See Triffin (1964), Cooper (1982), and Bordo (1981) on this point.

period. This was not the case during the Bretton Woods period, and especially during the sixties. Creeping inflation and creeping inflation differentials existed, which undermined the fixed structure of exchange rates.

This evidence brings us back to the point stressed by the domestic-stability-first school of thought. The conditions for a successful maintenance of fixed exchange rates are very stringent. For all practical purposes, the international differences in long-run inflation rates should be close to zero. It is likely, although difficult to prove, that this can only be achieved by eliminating inflation in all countries participating in the system.

These stringent conditions are unlikely to be met soon. As a result, it would not be productive to come to an international agreement fixing exchange rates. Rather, cooperative efforts should be geared to reducing the volatility which now exists in the exchange market. The next section analyzes some of the problems associated with such attempts.

II. PROBLEMS OF COOPERATION IN FOREIGN EXCHANGE MARKET INTERVENTION

In this section, the issue of how intervention policies in the foreign exchange markets can be coordinated is analyzed. It is assumed that the problem of how much (or how little) flexibility of the exchange rate to allow has been settled. The problem then is to show how the implied exchange rate targets can most easily be attained. In order to analyze this issue, a simple two-country portfolio model is developed.

Theoretical Model

The model has two countries (A and B) and four assets: money issued by country A (A-money), government bonds issued by country A in currency A (A-bonds), money issued by country B (B-money), and government bonds issued by country B in currency B (B-bonds). The A- and B-bonds are imperfect substitutes. The degree of substitutability of the two bonds is an important parameter that influences the effectiveness of intervention policies. Monetary equilibrium is obtained in the two countries when

$$M_{sa} = P_a L_a(y_a, r_a) \tag{1}$$

and

$$M_{sb} = P_b L_b(y_b, r_b) \tag{2}$$

where

M_{sa} and M_{sb} = money supply in countries A and B, respectively
P_a and P_b = price level in countries A and B, respectively

L_a and L_b = demand for real money balances in countries A and B, respectively

y_a and y_b = level of real income in countries A and B, respectively

r_a and r_b = nominal interest rate on bonds of countries A and B, respectively

Since the bonds of countries A and B are imperfect substitutes, one can write that

$$r_a = r_b + \mu + \Pi \tag{3}$$

where

μ = the expected rate of depreciation of currency A—that is,

μ = $[E(S) - S]/S$, where $E(S)$ denotes the expectation held today about tomorrow's exchange rate, S (S denotes the price of currency B in units of currency A)

Π = risk premium paid to the holders of A-bonds in order to induce them to hold these bonds willingly.

The risk premium, Π, can be positive or negative. It is assumed here that the risk premium is a positive function of the supply of A-bonds and a negative function of the supply of B-bonds. This relationship is specified as follows:

$$\Pi = \Pi\left(\frac{B_a}{B_b}\right) \tag{4}$$

where B_a and B_b denote the supplies of A-bonds and B-bonds (held by the public), respectively. Note that both supplies are expressed in the currency of country A. It is assumed that

$$\frac{d\Pi}{d(B_a/B_b)} = \Pi_B > 0 \tag{5}$$

or, in words, that an increase in the supply of A-bonds relative to that of B-bonds necessitates a higher risk premium to induce economic agents to hold the government bonds issued in currency A. The degree of substitutability of A- and B-bonds is measured by the parameter Π_B. With greater substitutability, Π_B declines. This also means that when there is more substitution between A- and B-bonds, a larger change in the relative supply of A- and B-bonds must occur to affect the risk premium. In the limit of perfect substitutability, $\Pi_B = 0$—that is, the relative supplies of A- and B-bonds have no effect on the risk premium.

The equilibrium of the model is represented graphically in Figure 1.

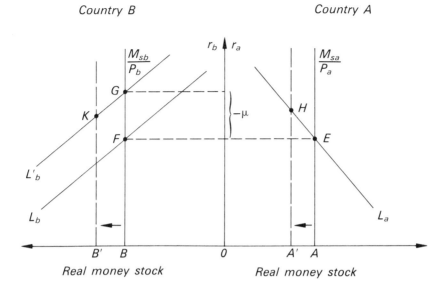

FIGURE 1. SYMMETRIC NONSTERILIZED INTERVENTION

The intersection of the L_a line with the supply of real money balances (M_{sa}/P_a) determines the point of monetary equilibrium in country A. Similarly, in country B, monetary equilibrium is obtained where the L_b line intersects the real money balances (M_{sb}/P_b).

This study makes the convenient assumption that initially the expected rate of depreciation μ is zero and that the relative supply of domestic and foreign bonds is such as to produce a zero risk premium ($\Pi = 0$). Points F and E then correspond to full asset market equilibrium, at which all four assets are willingly held by economic agents.

Let us now assume that this equilibrium situation is disturbed by a shock which raises the interest rate in country B. This could come about, for example, by an increase in liquidity preference in country B. Assume further that this shock is expected to be temporary, so that $E(S)$ is unchanged. (The next section analyzes problems of intervention when expectations change). Monetary equilibrium in country B is now obtained at point G. Clearly, some other variable will have to adjust in order to maintain full asset market equilibrium.

In a pure flexible exchange rate system, asset market equilibrium is maintained by an instantaneous increase in the exchange rate S over the expected exchange rate $E(S)$. This immediate increase in S is needed to produce an expectation of a future decline in the price of currency B. This increase in S will have to be such as to produce an expected decline in the exchange rate equal to the interest differential $(r_b - r_a = -\mu)$. In Figure 1, asset market equilibrium is obtained at points E and G. Since the monetary authorities do not intervene in the exchange market, money supplies remain unchanged in both countries. Asset market equilibrium is obtained because μ adjusts so as to reflect the change in r_b.

Instead of allowing the exchange rate to adjust freely, the monetary authorities may decide to manage the exchange rate. To make the analysis easier, suppose they peg the exchange rate at its initial value. Thus, the monetary authorities intervene in the exchange market so as to keep $\mu = 0.$[7] Obviously, some form of (implicit or explicit) cooperation will be necessary, since there is only one exchange rate to be managed by the two monetary authorities. The implications of nonsterilized and sterilized ("pure") intervention in this two-country model are analyzed consecutively.[8] The emphasis is on the different cooperative arrangements in which these intervention policies can be implemented.

Nonsterilized Intervention

Nonsterilized intervention means that the monetary authorities allow the money stock to be influenced by their foreign exchange market intervention. Thus, when they sell (buy) foreign exchange, the domestic money stock declines (increases). In the two-country model used here, every foreign exchange market intervention by one country influences the money stock in both countries. For example, when country A sells foreign exchange, it increases the money stock in country B and reduces the money stock in country A. Thus, one has to specify whether or not country B allows the intervention policy of the other country to affect its own money supply. A distinction will, therefore, be drawn between *symmetric* and *asymmetric* intervention policies.

The case of *symmetric* (nonsterilized) intervention is represented in Figure 1. Following the demand disturbance in country B, country A decides to sell foreign exchange (currency B), in order to avoid an exchange rate increase. In doing so, the money stock in country A declines

---

[7] This assumption is made for convenience and does not alter the essence of the analysis. For example, the purpose of the intervention policies might be to stabilize μ at a value different from zero.

[8] The effects of sterilized and nonsterilized intervention have been analyzed recently in the framework of one-country models by Obstfeld (1982 b), Branson (1982), and Genberg (1981). For a survey, see Mussa (1981). A model with more than one country is developed in Marston (1980).

(from OA to OA'), and the money stock in country B increases (from OB to OB'). Thus, country B does not sterilize the monetary effects of country A's intervention activities. A symmetric adjustment mechanism is now obtained. The interest differential disappears, so that $\mu = 0$, and the exchange rate does not change. Assuming that the money multipliers are constant and equal to 1, the amount of intervention by country A is given by the distance $A'A$.

If the intervention is *asymmetric*, a different result is obtained. Country B now sterilizes the domestic monetary effects of country A's intervention policies. This means that every unit of currency B sold by country A is bought again by country B through sales of domestic bonds (B-bonds) in the open market. The effects of this asymmetric intervention system are shown in Figure 2. Country B pegs its domestic money stock at the level OB. How much intervention must now be done by country A in order to peg the exchange rate at its initial level? There are two opposing effects. Since country B does not adjust its money stock, country A will have to intervene more extensively to reduce its money stock and to bring its interest rate closer to country B's interest rate. On the other hand, coun-

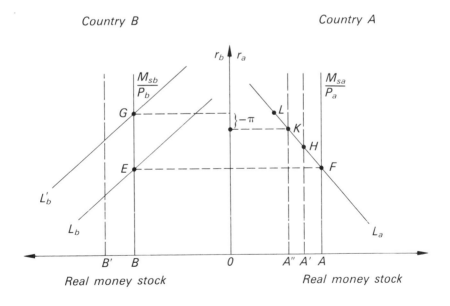

FIGURE 2. ASYMMETRIC NONSTERILIZED INTERVENTION

try B has increased the supply of B-bonds. It follows from equation (1) that the risk premium becomes negative. This reduces the need for country A to intervene in the foreign exchange market and to reduce its domestic money stock. The strength of this second effect depends on the degree of substitutability between A- and B-bonds. If this is high, the risk premium will be affected little by the change in the relative supply of A- and B-bonds. This is the case represented in Figure 2. As a result of the increase in the supply of B-bonds, the risk premium is equal to $-\Pi$. Country A has to deflate its money stock by the amount $A''A$.

It can be concluded that in this asymmetric case, intervention by country A is less effective than intervention under the symmetric (cooperative) arrangement. Put differently, country A must sell more foreign exchange to peg the exchange rate than it would have to under the symmetric arrangement. It now must sell an amount equal to $A''A$ (instead of AA' in the symmetric case). There are a number of real-world institutional arrangements that make the asymmetric intervention scenario more likely to be the rule than the exception. One such arrangement occurs when country A holds its exchange reserves in the form of B-bonds.[9] In that case, the intervention of country A in the exchange market will automatically be sterilized in country B's money market. The reason is that country A first has to buy B-currency by selling B-bonds in the open market of country B. The B-currency is then immediately sold in the exchange market. Thus, the money stock of country B remains unchanged. There is, however, a larger supply of B-bonds held by the private sector after intervention takes place. This is exactly the same situation as the one depicted in Figure 2. The conclusion here also is that such an asymmetric arrangement makes the foreign exchange market interventions of country A less effective.[10]

This section concludes by noting that cooperative arrangements influence the effectiveness of (nonsterilized) foreign exchange market interventions. In general, symmetric arrangements lead to enhanced effectiveness of intervention policies. Asymmetric arrangements (which can be labeled noncooperative, because one country refuses to adjust its money stock) reduce the effectiveness of foreign exchange market interventions.

Before turning to the issues relating to sterilized intervention, it is useful to ask to what extent it matters whether country A or country B carries out the intervention. To answer this question, it is helpful to have

---

[9] Note that central banks hold their dollar reserves mostly in the form of interest-bearing U.S. Treasury securities. See Balbach (1978) on the mechanics of this arrangement. See also Truman and Schafer (1981).

[10] See McKinnon (1974) on this problem. A similar asymmetric arrangement exists within the European Monetary System (EMS) when EMS countries buy and sell dollars to stabilize intra-EMS exchange rates. This also leads to reduced effectiveness of foreign exchange market interventions. See De Grauwe and Van den Bergh (1980).

another look at Figure 1. It can now be shown that the answer depends on the nature of the cooperative arrangment—that is, whether it is symmetric or asymmetric. In a symmetric (cooperative) intervention system, it is immediately clear that it does not make a difference which country intervenes in the foreign exchange market. In both situations, the same amount of B-currency will have to be sold and the same amount of A-currency will have to be bought to peg the exchange rate at the desired level. The fact that the central bank of country B sells its currency and buys the currency of country A does not change the analysis.

Things will be different if an asymmetric (noncooperative) arrangement exists. Suppose again that the liquidity preference schedule in country B shifts upward and that, instead of country A, country B intervenes in the exchange market. Assume also that the central bank of country B holds its international reserves in the form of interest-bearing assets (A-bonds). The intervention of country B now takes the following form: Country B sells its own currency and buys currency A, which it then uses to acquire A-bonds (on which it earns an interest rate). Thus, the money stock in country A remains unchanged, and the money stock in country B expands. This case is represented in Figure 3.

As a result of the intervention activity of country B the M_{sb}/P_b line shifts to the left, whereas the M_{sa}/P_a line does not shift. Note that the simultaneous buying and selling of A-currency by country B effectively sterilizes the foreign exchange market intervention *in country A*. This is exactly the opposite of what occurred when country A intervened in the foreign exchange market: country A was then effectively sterilizing its foreign exchange market intervention in country B.

How far should the money stock of country B expand? The answer again depends on the degree of substitutability of A- and B-bonds. As a result of the purchase of A-bonds by the monetary authorities of country B, the ratio B_a/B_b declines, so that the risk premium Π tends to decline (it becomes negative, assuming that initially it was zero). Asset market equilibrium is reached at point F. Note that because of imperfect substitutability, the authorities of country B can maintain a higher interest rate than the one prevailing in country A, reflecting the negative risk premium on A-bonds (which is a positive risk premium on B-bonds). With an increasing degree of substitution between A- and B-bonds, the risk premium is less affected. If A- and B-bonds are perfect substitutes, the risk premium will not decline. As a result, if the authorities of country B wish to avoid an appreciation of their currency, they will have to expand the money stock in order to bring the interest rate in country B back down to the level prevailing in country A. This is represented by point G in Figure 3.

It may be concluded from this analysis that it matters a great deal who

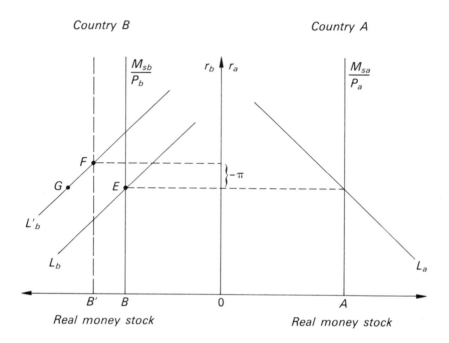

FIGURE 3. ASYMMETRIC STERILIZED INTERVENTION

intervenes in the foreign exchange market if the institutional arrangements are asymmetric (noncooperative). In general, if the country with the depreciating currency intervenes in the exchange market, there will be a net reduction in the money stock; if the country with the appreciating currency intervenes, there will be an increase in the money stock. Under a symmetric (cooperative) arrangement, however, this distinction disappears. It thus does not matter whether the country of the appreciating or of the depreciating currency intervenes. The monetary effects will be exactly the same.

It is worthwhile to point out here that this problem of choosing the country which has to intervene in the exchange market had an important influence on the design of the European Monetary System (EMS). It was generally believed that the snake arrangement was asymmetric and imposed a deflationary bias on the system (because, in fact, the country with the depreciating currency intervened). In order to avoid this problem, the European Currency Unit (ECU) indicator of divergence was instituted, which aimed at creating more symmetry in the adjustment mechanism.[11]

---

[11] For an evaluation of this system using a multicountry econometric model, see De Grauwe and Van den Bergh (1980).

Sterilized (Pure) Intervention

In the previous subsection, it was assumed that the country which intervenes in the foreign exchange market does not sterilize this intervention in its domestic money market. This subsection concentrates on issues relating to sterilized (pure) intervention. Two issues are analyzed. One is the effectiveness of this kind of intervention. The other deals with cooperative arrangements that increase (or reduce) the effectiveness of pure sterilization.

Assume again an upward movement of the liquidity preference schedule in country B. Country A now uses a pure sterilization policy—that is, it buys a certain amount of its own currency in the foreign exchange market and sells the same amount again in the domestic bond market. Thus, the money stock in country A is unaffected by country A's intervention policy.

How effective is this policy, and what are its effects on country B? The answer to this question also depends on whether or not the intervention activities of country A are sterilized in *country B*. Suppose, first, there is an asymmetrical situation where country B allows its money stock to increase as a result of the intervention by country A. This is exactly the same situation as the one depicted in Figure 3. The money stock expands in country B, and the size of this monetary expansion depends on the degree of substitution between the A- and B-bonds. Note the interesting implication that even with perfect substitutability of A- and B-bonds, sterilized intervention by country A is effective—that is, country A can peg the exchange rate by selling a finite amount of foreign exchange. The reason is that country B does not sterilize, so that with perfect substitution (II does not change), it has to expand its money stock up to the point where the interest differential disappears (point G in Figure 3). Thus, in this asymmetric institutional arrangement, country B allows its monetary policy to be dictated by the monetary authorities of country A. It is this feature which makes fully sterilized intervention by country A effective even if domestic and foreign bonds are perfect substitutes.[12]

The second, symmetric case arises when country B sterilizes the effects of country A's intervention activities. (Note that, as was indicated earlier, this occurs automatically if country A holds its international reserves in the form of B-bonds.) This situation is represented in Figure 4.

Following the sale of B-currency by country A, the authorities of country B buy their currency back by selling B-bonds. As a result, the money supply in country B remains unchanged. Since country A also pegs its money stock, an interest differential will be inevitable. This must come

---

[12] Note that in the recent literature on the effectiveness of pure sterilization, one-country models are often used. It is found that pure sterilization is ineffective when domestic and foreign bonds are perfect substitutes. See Mussa (1981).

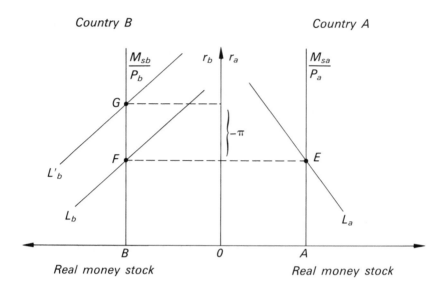

FIGURE 4. STERILIZED INTERVENTION

about because of a (negative) risk premium, $-\Pi$. Since country B sells B-bonds and country A buys A-bonds, the ratio B_a/B_b declines, thereby producing a negative risk premium. The question of the effectiveness of the interventions then simply boils down to the question of the degree of substitutability between A- and B-bonds. With high substitutability, the size of the sales of B-bonds and purchases of A-bonds will have to be large. In the limit of perfect substitution, no finite amounts will suffice to change the risk premium. In that case, sterilized intervention by the two countries becomes completely ineffective.

Does it matter which central bank intervenes, when the intervention is sterilized? What is obtained here is an answer similar to the one obtained for the nonsterilized intervention. If the pure intervention is symmetrical (both countries' money stocks are unaffected), it does not matter whether country A or B intervenes. In both cases, the money stock is pegged, and the risk premium $(-\Pi)$ will be the same.[13] Thus, the conclusion is the same as when the two authorities abstain from sterilization.

---

[13] If country B intervenes, it sells its own currency and buys currency A, and it simultaneously buys its own currency back by selling B-bonds. Thus, the same amount of B-bonds are sold as when country A was intervening in the foreign exchange market. Country A now has to buy A-bonds to bring the A-currency into circulation.

This conclusion will be different if we assume asymmetry in sterilization behavior. If a country does not sterilize the domestic monetary effects of the other country's intervention, the question of who does the intervention becomes important again. The analysis here is the same as in the previous section. This leads to a general proposition: It does not matter which central bank intervenes in the exchange market if the institutional arrangements are symmetric—that is, if *both* central banks abstain from sterilization or if *both* central banks fully sterilize. However, if the arrangements are asymmetric, it makes a difference who intervenes in the foreign exchange market.

This section can be summarized as follows. Intervention policies in the foreign exchange market by one country have quite different effects, depending on the way the other country whose currency is bought or sold conducts its monetary policies. This is true when a country engages in sterilized or nonsterilized intervention. It has also been emphasized that the degree of substitution between domestic and foreign bonds is important for the effectiveness of (pure) intervention policies. The discussion in this section, however, also stresses that for a given degree of substitution, a particular intervention policy followed by one country will be more or less effective, depending on such institutional arrangements as the form in which international reserves are held or the extent to which countries sterilize the interventions of other countries. It is clear that cooperative arrangements can be found that enhance the effectiveness of foreign exchange market interventions. In general, nonsterilized interventions will be more effective if they are symmetrical. Sterilized interventions, however, are more effective if they are asymmetrical.

III. ROLE OF EXPECTATIONS

The discussion in the previous section assumed static expectations. In this section, exchange rate expectations are allowed to vary. The existence of variable exchange rate expectations complicates the intervention policies. This is illustrated in Figure 5. Time is represented on the horizontal axis. The economy is at point A (in period 1). A change in expectations occurs: the exchange rate is now expected to increase to S_2 (in period 2). From the rational expectations literature, it is known that one may go from A to D in different ways, depending on the structure of the model and the source of the expectational change (see, for example, Branson (1982)). In general, one will not go from A to D along the straight line D, but will jump to B (or to C) and move along the path BD (or CD, in which case there will be overshooting).

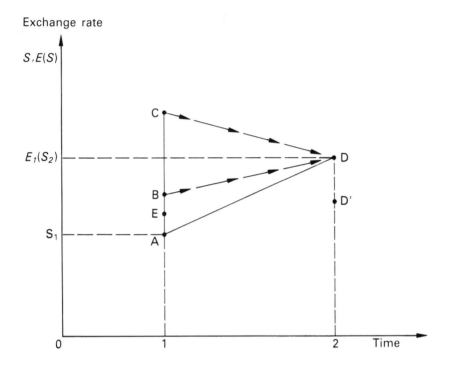

FIGURE 5. EXPECTATIONS AND INTERVENTION

The problem of foreign exchange market interventions now is the following. The authorities may intervene to reduce the size of the jump today to, say, from A to E. However, foreign exchange market intervention now has two effects. It changes the size of the initial jump (or even eliminates it), and it affects the expectations held today about the future exchange rate. The strength of the first effect depends on the degree of substitutability of domestic and foreign assets and on the nature of the sterilization practices, which were analyzed in the previous section. The second effect is largely independent of the degree of substitutability of domestic and foreign assets. It does, however, depend on the nature of the sterilization arrangements.

If the *two* countries involved use fully sterilized intervention policies, one can assume that expectations will not be affected. The reason is that under this intervention arrangement, the money stocks in the two countries are unaffected. In this case of pure intervention, the initial jump is reduced. The exchange rate jumps from A to E (instead of from A to B, or from A to C). Since the expected exchange rate is unchanged, the exchange rate has to move to D. As a result, pure intervention, if successful in reducing the initial jump, also changes the path the exchange rate subsequently follows. The currency may not depreciate much today (if sterilized intervention is effective in reducing the jump); it will, however, have to depreciate more in the future. Thus, sterilized intervention (by the two countries) will be ineffective even if there is a low degree of asset substitutability.[14]

Nonsterilized intervention policies have fundamentally different effects. In general, if intervention is not sterilized (or if one country sterilizes and the other does not), expectations are likely to be affected. Thus, when the authorities reduce the instantaneous jump of the exchange rate to AE, they reduce the domestic money stock and, if this is perceived as a permanent change in policy, it reduces $E(S)$. The point D in Figure 5 moves downward, say to D', and the subsequent depreciation of the currency is reduced. The same happens if the intervening country uses sterilized intervention, whereas the other country allows the intervention of the first country to affect its domestic money market. This expands the money stock in the other country and also shifts point D downward. Thus, by changing expectations, nonsterilized intervention by (at least) one country increases the effectiveness of intervention policies.

The general conclusion drawn from this analysis is analogous to the conclusion drawn in the previous section. When at least one country abstains from sterilization, foreign exchange market interventions are more effective than when the *two* countries fully sterilize. The difference between the two intervention strategies, however, is now more fundamental. It depends not only on the degree of substitutability of domestic and foreign assets but also on the fact that nonsterilized intervention changes expectations and, therefore, makes a more lasting effect on the exchange rate possible.

IV. INTERNATIONAL RESERVES AND THE MONEY SUPPLY PROCESS

From the analysis of the preceding sections, it will already be clear that the link between the stock of international reserves and the money supply in the two countries is a tenuous one. In this section, this matter is pursued.[15] Let us now call country B the reserve currency country. This means that the liabilities of country B are used as international reserves by coun-

---

[14] See Genberg (1981) on this issue; see also the recent empirical study of Obstfeld (1982 b) on the Federal Republic of Germany.

[15] This question has been analyzed by Swoboda (1978), among others.

try A. Assume that country B's money stock expands unexpectedly. As in Section II, it is assumed that expectations of the future exchange rate are unchanged.[16] This section analyzes the effects this has on the stock of international reserves and on the money stock in country A.

These effects depend on whether and how country A intervenes in the foreign exchange market. In a perfectly flexible exchange rate system (no intervention), the whole shock is absorbed by an appreciation of currency A. The money stock of country A and the stock of international reserves are unchanged.

Suppose, however, that country A intervenes in the exchange market. Again, several possible intervention arrangements can be analyzed. The number of possible cases is restricted by assuming that the reserve-currency country (country B) does not allow its money stock to be affected by the foreign exchange market interventions of country A.[17]

Country A can now use sterilized or nonsterilized intervention. In the nonsterilized case, country A buys currency B and sells its own currency. Since currency B is the reserve currency, the stock of international reserves (held by country A) increases, together with country A's money stock. Thus, the stock of international reserves and the money stocks increase. The monetary shock originating in country B is transmitted to country A through an increase in the stock of international reserves. This is the traditional (one may also call it the gold standard) transmission process.

A second possibility is for country A to use sterilized (pure) intervention. In that case, country A buys currency B (the reserve currency) and sells its own currency. This operation, however, is offset in the domestic money market of country A by a purchase of currency and a sale of A-bonds.[18] Thus, country A maintains its money stock unchanged. This money stock is now backed by a greater amount of B-bonds (international reserves) and a smaller amount of A-bonds (domestic assets). In fact, the whole operation consists of a switch in the bond portfolio held by the authorities of country A.[19] The result of this switch is that the stock of international reserves (B-bonds held by country A) increases without affecting country A's money stock.

The interesting point here is that in this case of sterilized intervention, the stock of international reserves increases more than in the previous case of nonsterilized intervention. This can be shown using Figure 6. Country B

---

[16] This amounts to assuming that the monetary shock is expected to be temporary.

[17] This is a realistic assumption, since it describes the behavior of the U.S. monetary authorities.

[18] Note that the reverse occurs in country B, since it was assumed that country B's money stock was unaffected by the purchase of B-currency by country A.

[19] For a recent analysis interpreting intervention policies as a form of management of the currency composition of the government debt, see Dooley (1982).

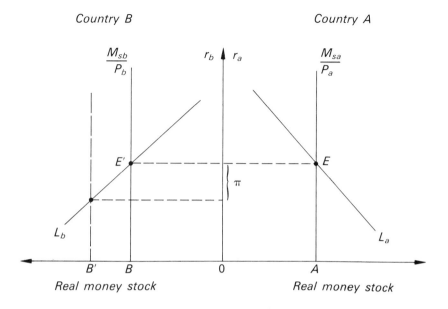

FIGURE 6. INTERVENTION AND INTERNATIONAL RESERVES

expands its money stock from OB to OB'. In order for country A to peg the exchange rate and the domestic money stock (at the level OA), it must be able to produce a positive risk premium, π. As has been shown

$$\pi = \pi\left(\frac{B_a}{B_b}\right)$$

where B_a and B_b denote the stocks of A- and B-bonds, respectively, held by the private sector. Thus, by increasing the ratio B_a/B_b, the authorities of country A increase the risk premium on A-bonds. They do this by purchasing B-bonds (international reserves) and by selling A-bonds. It is also known that the higher the degree of substitutability between A- and B-bonds, the more the authorities of country A will have to buy B-bonds and sell A-bonds to increase the risk premium by a given amount.

When there is nonsterilized intervention, however, country A allows its money stock to increase. This reduces the necessity of producing a positive risk premium, and thus country A will have to purchase fewer B-bonds (international reserves).

The interesting conclusion that can be drawn is that the more successful country A is in insulating its money stock from the expansionary shock originating in the reserve-currency country, the more international reserves will be "created" (that is, the more it will have to accumulate B-bonds). In addition, the growth of international reserves in this policy environment increases as the degree of substitutability between A- and B-bonds increases, becoming infinite if A- and B-bonds are perfect substitutes.[20]

The previous analysis makes clear that under a policy regime character-ized by many countries attempting to sterilize their interventions, the role of international reserves changes. These can no longer be interpreted as international base money "causing" the money stock and the price level to change in the different countries which participate in the international monetary system. Instead, the stock of international reserves can take on many different values for the same values of national money stocks.

A final note on the relation between international reserves and the money stock is the following. Country A in our model can, following the mone-tary expansion in country B, react by expanding its domestic money stock through an open market purchase of domestic bonds (A-bonds). If it does this in sufficient amounts, it will not have to intervene in the foreign exchange market. Thus, there will be an expansion of the money supply in country A without any change in the stock of international reserves.

One can conclude that under the present international monetary arrange-ments, there is no clear link between the stock of international reserves and the money stock, nor can it be said that the former causes the latter. The size of the international reserve stock (as measured officially) depends on many decisions of both the issuing country (the United States) and the other countries. The latter may change the composition of assets backing their domestic money supplies and, in so doing, affect the measured stock of international reserves without changing the money stock.

As a result, for any given set of money stocks, there are many different levels of international reserves. In addition, the more countries try to man-age their exchange rates without letting their domestic money stocks adjust, the more volatile the stock of international reserves can become. In a world of sterilized interventions and high substitutability between assets, the high variability of the international reserve stock also indicates the difficulties countries have in pegging their exchange rates.

The previous analysis also helps to explain the strong volatility of the international reserve stock observed during the seventies (which was dis-cussed recently in McKinnon (1982)). During 1972-73 and again during 1977-78, the stock of dollar reserves increased substantially.

During the same period, many countries were actively using sterilized intervention (Obstfeld (1982 a)). The previous analysis makes clear that

---

[20] For a more formal analysis in a multicountry framework, see De Grauwe (1975).

the volatility of international reserves observed during the seventies may also have been the result of systematic attempts by many countries to peg both their exchange rates and their money supplies.

V. INTERNATIONAL RESERVES AND WORLD MONEY STOCK: EMPIRICAL TESTS

The hypothesis of the role of international reserves in the international monetary process as developed in the previous section contrasts with another (and popular) view which sees the stock of international reserves as the equivalent of the international monetary base. Recent empirical studies (Heller (1976) and Khan (1979)) seem empirically to validate this view that the expanding stock of international reserves caused money stocks in the world to increase and, through this channel, has triggered an acceleration of world inflation. The logical extension of this view is that new international initiatives are needed to control the unbridled expansion of international reserves.

In this section, some empirical evidence on these two conflicting hypotheses is provided. The method which is used is a multivariate extension of the Granger "causality" test. Using these tests, one can determine whether a particular time series is a good predictor of one or more other time series. Thus, a test of the "international-monetary-base" hypothesis involves determining whether the time series of international reserves can be used to predict the time series of the money stock and the time series of the price level. The alternative hypothesis formulated in this paper implies that the time series of international reserves will, in general, not be a good predictor of the time series of the money stock, and vice versa.

The method used in devising these tests is explained more fully in the Appendix. In Table 6, the results are presented in summary form. The sample period, 1957–82, was divided into two subperiods, 1957–71 and 1971–82. The table should be read as follows. The first column gives the hypothesis about the direction of "causality" which is tested. The other columns indicate whether or not the hypothesis is accepted for different countries and for the world. Thus, for example, the hypothesis that international reserves, R, are a good predictor of the price level, P, and the money stock, M, is rejected for the Federal Republic of Germany and the world, and is accepted for Japan and the United Kingdom, during 1957–71 (see the first line of the table). A conclusion that can be drawn from this table is that the reserve stock is not a useful predictor of M and P for the Federal Republic of Germany in both subperiods, whereas it is a useful predictor for Japan. The evidence for the United Kingdom is mixed, because the joint test leads to acceptance, whereas the univariate test leads

TABLE 6. "CAUSALITY" TESTS: INTERNATIONAL RESERVES, MONEY STOCK,
AND PRICE LEVEL, 1957-71 AND 1971-82 [1]

(*Quarterly observations*)

Direction of Predictive Power	Germany, Fed. Rep.	Japan	United Kingdom	World
		1957-71		
$R \rightarrow P, M$	N	A	A	N
$R \rightarrow M$	A	A	N	N
$R \rightarrow P$	N	N	N	N
$M \rightarrow R, P$	A	A	A	A
$M \rightarrow R$	N	N	A	N
$M \rightarrow P$	A	A	A	A
$P \rightarrow R, M$	N	A	A	A
$P \rightarrow M$	N	N	A	N
$P \rightarrow R$	N	A	A	N
		1971-82		
$R \rightarrow P, M$	N	A	A	A
$R \rightarrow M$	N	A	N	N
$R \rightarrow P$	N	A	N	N
$M \rightarrow R, P$	A	A	A	A
$M \rightarrow R$	N	A	A	A
$M \rightarrow P$	A	A	A	A
$P \rightarrow R, M$	A	N	A	N
$P \rightarrow M$	N	A	N	N
$P \rightarrow R$	A	N	A	A

Source: International Monetary Fund, *International Financial Statistics*.

[1] These tests are explained in the Appendix. The confidence level for acceptance or rejection was set at 95 percent.

A = accepted
N = rejected
R = international reserve stock (excluding gold)
M = money stock (M_1)
P = price level (consumer price index)

to rejection. For the world as a whole, the reserve stock cannot be used as a predictor of M and P during 1957-71. For 1971-82, the evidence is mixed. The most robust relations are $M \rightarrow R$, P and $M \rightarrow P$. The hypothesis that M is a good predictor of R and P jointly is accepted for all countries in the two subperiods. Similarly, the hypothesis that M is a good predictor of the price level is accepted for all countries during the two subperiods. This is not the case for the hypothesis that M is a predictor of R, which is rejected half of the time.

The general conclusion that can be drawn from these tests is that although in some countries in some periods the "international-monetary-base" hypothesis cannot be rejected, the evidence is not very strong. The evidence of Table 6 suggests that for countries like the Federal Republic of Germany and the United Kingdom, and for the world as a whole, there is no clear causal link between international reserves and the money stock.

VI. CONCLUSION

During the seventies, exchange rates varied substantially. There is an increasing recognition that the wide swings in the exchange rates of the major currencies have made domestic monetary management extremely difficult. In this paper, some evidence has been provided indicating that the exchange rate regime of the seventies may have reduced the degree of monetary independence of the major industrial countries and may have contributed to the increased international synchronization of the business cycle. It has also been argued that in order to increase the effectiveness of domestic monetary management, international efforts to stabilize the exchange rates of the major currencies are needed. At the same time, however, a return to fixed exchange rates cannot be envisioned in the near future. The monetary regimes in the major countries which participate in the international monetary system are characterized by historically high and variable inflation rates. This excludes the possibility of a return to fixed exchange rates in the near future, unless inflation is eliminated from the system. As a result, international cooperative efforts should not be directed toward the establishment of fixed exchange rates but rather toward reduction of the extreme variability of exchange rates.

The second part of this paper has analyzed how intervention policies can be devised to become more effective in stabilizing exchange rates. This analysis has been carried out by developing a two-country model with imperfect substitutability of domestic and foreign assets. It has been shown that not only the degree of substitution between domestic and foreign assets but also the nature of the cooperative arrangements (or their absence) influences the effectiveness of intervention policies. In general, sterilized intervention by one country becomes less effective if the other country also sterilizes. Similarly, nonsterilized intervention by one country becomes more effective if the other country also abstains from sterilization.

This paper has also stressed that in a world where many countries sterilize and assets are highly substitutable, the observed stock of international reserves can become volatile. This volatility of the stock of international reserves can be viewed as resulting from the difficulties countries experience in managing their exchange rates and their money supplies at the same time.

This analysis has also cast some doubt on the view that the international reserve stock plays the role of an international monetary base that determines the world money stock and the world price level. On the basis of the evidence this paper has presented, one could not reject the alternative view that there is no clear causal link between international reserve stocks and money stocks. Money and international reserves can move in many different directions, depending on the nature of cooperative arrangements and, in particular, on the symmetry or asymmetry of sterilization policies. According to this view of the role of international reserves, there is not much scope for devising new schemes to control the supply of international reserves. Consequently, emphasis should be put on improving cooperative arrangements that make intervention policies in the foreign exchange markets more effective. If successful, these cooperative arrangements would also help to contain the explosion of international reserves that was observed during the seventies.

APPENDIX

Statistical Results

This appendix reports the results of the multivariate and bivariate Granger "causality" tests. The test of the hypothesis that the stock of international reserves is a predictor of the price level and the money stock was devised as follows: First, the following system of equations was estimated (with full information maximum likelihood (FIML)):

$$P_t = \sum_{i=1}^{T_1} \alpha_i P_{t-i} + \sum_{i=1}^{T_1} \beta_i M_{t-i} + \sum_{i=1}^{T_2} \gamma_i R_{t-i} + u_t \tag{6}$$

$$M_t = \sum_{i=1}^{T_1} \delta_i P_{t-i} + \sum_{i=1}^{T_1} \epsilon_i M_{t-i} + \sum_{i=1}^{T_2} \zeta_i R_{t-i} + v_t \tag{7}$$

where

P_t = price level in quarter t
M_t = money stock (M_1) in quarter t
R_t = stock of international reserves in quarter t

The same set of equations was then estimated without the lagged time series of international reserves, R_t. Thus,

$$P_t = \sum_{i=1}^{T_1} \alpha_i' P_{t-i} + \sum_{i=1}^{T_1} \beta_i' M_{t-i} + u_t' \tag{8}$$

TABLE 7. "CAUSALITY" TESTS (LIKELIHOOD RATIOS): INTERNATIONAL RESERVES, MONEY STOCK, AND PRICE LEVEL, 1957-71 AND 1971-82 [1]

(*Quarterly observations*)

Direction of Predictive Power	Germany, Fed. Rep.	Japan	United Kingdom	World
		1957-71		
Multivariate tests				
$R \rightarrow P, M$	15.42	23.45**	20.58**	10.46
$M \rightarrow R, P$	37.56**	32.56**	35.24**	42.91**
$P \rightarrow R, M$	3.27	12.38*	30.00**	15.60**
Univariate tests				
$R \rightarrow M$	12.30**	14.12**	1.29	5.60
$R \rightarrow P$	5.09	2.57	8.95	3.47
$M \rightarrow R$	8.46	5.55	16.00*	9.21
$M \rightarrow P$	32.82**	13.45*	21.11**	15.35*
$P \rightarrow R$	5.14	1.55	9.44**	0.30
$P \rightarrow M$	2.12	9.32**	21.35**	2.17
		1971-82		
Multivariate tests				
$R \rightarrow P, M$	12.52	42.27**	20.39**	19.35*
$M \rightarrow R, P$	48.13**	42.62**	46.63**	49.59**
$P \rightarrow R, M$	17.18**	9.38	14.88**	6.50
Univariate tests				
$R \rightarrow M$	4.80	10.42*	2.58	8.54
$R \rightarrow P$	5.78	14.84**	2.80	6.79
$M \rightarrow R$	12.28	14.72*	16.84**	15.65**
$M \rightarrow P$	23.31**	26.14**	20.94**	27.38**
$P \rightarrow R$	2.05	7.88*	5.19	8.07*
$P \rightarrow M$	8.75*	1.78	9.76**	4.52

[1] Two asterisks beside a number indicates that it exceeds critical value (at 99 percent probability). This means that the null hypothesis of no predictive power can be rejected with a confidence level of 99 percent. A single asterisk beside a number indicates that the ratios are high enough so that the null hypothesis of no predictive power can be rejected with a confidence level of 95 percent. These numbers underlie Table 6 in the text.

R = international reserve stock (excluding gold)

M = money stock (M_1)

P = price level (consumer price index)

$$M_t = \sum_{i=1}^{T_1} \delta_i' P_{t-i} + \sum_{i=1}^{T_1} \epsilon_i' M_{t-i} + v_t' \tag{9}$$

A test of the predictive power of R for M and P was obtained by means of a likelihood ratio test of the two models.[21] A similar procedure was devised for testing the predictive powers of M (for R and P) and P (for M and R).

The bivariate tests were devised as follows. To test whether R_t was a good predictor of P_t (alone), the following equation was estimated using ordinary least squares:

$$P_t = \sum_{i=1} \lambda_i P_{t-i} + \sum_{i=1} \eta_i R_{t-i} + w_t \tag{10}$$

The same regression was then run without R_{t-i}. A test of the predictive power of R_t was obtained in the same manner. Note that this is a bivariate Granger "causality" test. Similar bivariate tests were done to test for the predictive power of R on M, M on P, M on R, etc. Table 7 presents the likelihood ratios.

BIBLIOGRAPHY

Balbach, Anatol B., "The Mechanics of Intervention in Exchange Markets," Federal Reserve Bank of St. Louis, *Review*, Vol. 60 (February 1978), pp. 2-7.

Bank for International Settlements, *Fiftieth Annual Report* (Basle, June 1980).

Bloomfield, Arthur I., *Monetary Policy under the International Gold Standard: 1880-1914* (New York: Federal Reserve Bank of New York, 1959).

Bordo, Michael D., "The Classical Gold Standard: Some Lessons for Today," Federal Reserve Bank of St. Louis, *Review*, Vol. 63 (May 1981), pp. 2-17.

Branson, William H., "A Model of Exchange-Rate Determination with Policy Reaction: Theory and Empirical Evidence," paper presented at National Bureau of Economic Research Conference on Exchange Rate Theory and Policy, Bellagio, Italy, January 25-29, 1982.

Buiter, Willem H., and Jonathan Eaton, *Policy Decentralization and Exchange Rate Management in Interdependent Economies*, National Bureau of Economic Research, Working Papers Series, No. 531 (Cambridge, Massachusetts, August 1980).

Canzoneri, Matthew B., "Exchange Intervention Policy in a Multiple Country World," *Journal of International Economics*, Vol. 13 (November 1982), pp. 267-90.

Clarke, Stephen V.O., *Central Bank Cooperation 1924-1931* (New York: Federal Reserve Bank of New York, 1967).

Cooper, Richard N., "The Gold Standard: Historical Facts and Future Prospects," *Brookings Papers on Economic Activity: 1* (1982), pp. 1-46.

De Grauwe, Paul, "The Interaction of Monetary Policies in a Group of European Countries," *Journal of International Economics*, Vol. 5 (August 1975), pp. 207-28.

---

[21] Alternatively, one can perform an F-test on the coefficients γ_i and ζ_i.

_____, and Paul van den Bergh, "Monetary Policies and Exchange Rates in the E.C.-Countries," *European Economic Review*, Vol. 13 (May 1980), pp. 343-71.

Dooley, Michael, "An Analysis of Exchange Market Intervention of Industrial and Developing Countries," International Monetary Fund, *Staff Papers*, Vol. 29 (June 1982), pp. 233-69.

Dornbusch, Rudiger, *Flexible Exchange Rates and Interdependence*, National Bureau of Economic Research, Working Papers Series, No. 1035 (Cambridge, Massachusetts, November 1982).

_____, "Equilibrium and Disequilibrium Exchange Rates," *Zeitschrift für Wirtschafts- und Sozialwissenschaften*, No. 6 (1982), pp. 573-99.

Fischer, Stanley, "Stability and Exchange Rate Systems in a Monetarist Model of the Balance of Payments," Ch. 5 in *The Political Economy of Monetary Reform*, ed. by Robert Z. Aliber (London: Macmillan, 1977), pp. 59-73.

Frenkel, Jacob A., and Joshua Aizenman, "Aspects of the Optimal Management of Exchange Rates," *Journal of International Economics*, Vol. 13 (November 1982), pp. 231-56.

Genberg, Hans, "Effects of Central Bank Intervention in the Foreign Exchange Market," International Monetary Fund, *Staff Papers*, Vol. 28 (September 1981), pp. 451-76.

Heller, H. Robert, "International Reserves and World-Wide Inflation," International Monetary Fund, *Staff Papers*, Vol. 23 (March 1976), pp. 61-88.

Henderson, Dale W., *The Role of Intervention Policy in Open Economy Financial Policy: A Macroeconomic Perspective*, International Finance Discussion Papers, No. 202 (Washington: Board of Governors of the Federal Reserve System, February 1982).

Howson, Susan, "The Management of Sterling, 1932-1939," *Journal of Economic History*, Vol. 40 (March 1980), pp. 53-60.

Khan, Mohsin S., "Inflation and International Reserves: A Time-Series Analysis," International Monetary Fund, *Staff Papers*, Vol. 26 (December 1979), pp. 699-724.

Laidler, David, "The Case for Flexible Exchange Rates in 1980," Ch. 7 in *European Monetary Union: Progress and Prospects*, ed. by M. Sumner and G. Zis (London: Macmillan, 1982), pp. 152-67.

McKinnon, Ronald, *A New Tripartite Monetary Agreement or a Limping Dollar Standard?* Essays in International Finance, No. 106 (Princeton, New Jersey: International Finance Section, Princeton University, October 1974).

_____, "Currency Substitution and Instability in the World Dollar Standard," *American Economic Review*, Vol. 72 (June 1982), pp. 320-33.

Marston, Richard C., "Cross Country Effects of Sterilization, Reserve Currencies and Foreign Exchange Intervention," *Journal of International Economics*, Vol. 10 (February 1980), pp. 63-78.

_____, *Wages, Relative Prices and the Choice Between Fixed and Flexible Exchange Rates*, National Bureau of Economic Research, Working Papers Series, No. 793 (Cambridge, Massachusetts, October 1981).

Mitchell, Brian R., *European Historical Statistics 1750-1970* (New York: Columbia University Press, 1975).

Mundell, Robert A., "Capital Mobility and Stabilization Policy under Fixed and Flexible Exchange Rates," *Canadian Journal of Economics and Political Science*, Vol. 29 (November 1963), pp. 475-85.

Mussa, Michael, *The Role of Official Intervention*, Group of Thirty, Occasional Paper No. 6 (New York, 1981).

Obstfeld, Maurice (1982 a), *Can We Sterilize? Theory and Evidence*, National Bureau of Economic Research, Working Papers Series, No. 833 (Cambridge, Massachusetts, January 1982).

_____ (1982 b), *Exchange Rates, Inflation and the Sterilization Problem: Germany, 1975-1981*, National Bureau of Economic Research, Working Papers Series, No. 963 (Cambridge, Massachusetts, August 1982).

Solomon, Robert, *The International Monetary System, 1945-1976: An Insider's View* (New York: Harper and Row, 1977).

Swoboda, Alexander K., "Gold, Dollars, Euro-Dollars, and the World Money Stock under Fixed Exchange Rates," *American Economic Review*, Vol. 68 (September 1978), pp. 625-42.

Triffin, Robert, *The Evolution of the International Monetary System: Historical Reappraisal and Future Perspectives*, Studies in International Finance, No. 12 (Princeton, New Jersey: International Finance Section, Princeton University, 1964).

Truman, Edwin M., and Jeffrey R. Shafer, "International Portfolio Disturbances and Domestic Monetary Policy," Ch. 8 in *The International Monetary System under Flexible Exchange Rates*, ed. by Richard Cooper and others (Cambridge, Massachusetts: Ballinger, 1981).

Turnovsky, Stephen, "Exchange Market Intervention in a Small Open Economy," in *The International Transmission of Economic Disturbances*, ed. by J. Bhandari and B. Putnam (Cambridge, Massachusetts: MIT Press, 1982).

Williamson, Jeffrey G., *Late Nineteenth Century American Growth* (Cambridge, England: Cambridge University Press, 1975).

Comments

Emil-Maria Claassen

I would like to congratulate the author for his excellent paper. I learned quite a lot from his empirical findings and from his simple, and therefore elegant, model. Consequently, my comment will be complementary in nature. I shall concentrate my remarks on three points: (1) his empirical work on the level and variability of inflation rates and of growth rates of the money supply during regimes of fixed and floating exchange rates; (2) his theoretical contribution on symmetrical and asymmetrical intervention policies, which raises the question that is the title of his paper with respect to possible forms of international monetary cooperation in order to improve the functioning of the system; and (3) the interpretation of the nonexistence of a systematic link between international reserves and the world money stock.

The Need for Flexible Exchange Rates

One merit of Paul De Grauwe's paper is that it reminds us of the old, long-lasting, and still ongoing debate concerning the causal relationship consisting of either exchange rate stability first and domestic stability afterwards (claim for fixed exchange rates) or domestic stability first and exchange rate stability afterwards (claim for flexible exchange rates). Over the last 20 years, many attempts have been made to answer this fundamental question in a less crude, or more sophisticated, way.

(i) The currency-area discussion concluded that some countries, according to a long list of criteria, should opt for fixed rates among themselves and for flexible rates toward other countries, other currency blocs, or—finally—toward the United States. However, a question that is still open is whether fixity and flexibility should be interpreted in the absolute, "pure" sense.

(ii) The gold standard was a system of rigidly fixed exchange rates. The Bretton Woods system, on the other hand, was originally conceived as a regime of fixed rates within a narrow band in the shorter run; whereas in the longer run, rates were allowed to change when fundamental disequilibria arose. However, experience with the Bretton Woods system has shown that there were fewer changes in par values than were warranted, implying that there were unnecessarily strong external constraints on internal monetary and fiscal policies (see Argy (1982, pp. 1–2)).

(iii) Just as there is an *optimal degree of fixity* for a regime of fixed exchange rates, so there is an *optimal degree of flexibility* for a regime of floating rates, to which Paul De Grauwe devotes his Section I.

When De Grauwe arrives, on the basis of the empirical background of divergent inflation rates across countries during the 1970s (developed in Section II), at the conclusion that a return in the near future to a fixed-exchange-rate system should be excluded from consideration, he may have had in mind a fixity (within a given band) of 100 percent that applied to all countries concerned. However, as I see it, the political question is which countries should form a currency area, in which the optimal degree of fixity has to be determined along the lines of the idealized Bretton Woods system, whereas the question of the optimal degree of flexibility concerns the monetary relationship between the currency area and the rest of the world. When De Grauwe, after comparing the gold standard period with the Bretton Woods period, concludes (p. 385) that creeping inflation and creeping inflation differentials during the 1960s "undermined the fixed structure of exchange rates," then he is referring only to a rigid fixed-exchange-rate system and not to the above-mentioned original conception of the Bretton Woods system that permitted frequent changes in par values.

Based on observation of the 1970s, during which inflation rates were more than twice as high, and their variability across countries at least twice as great, as they were during the 1960s, one could advance the hypothesis that monetary discipline was loosened after the advent of the floating-exchange-rate regime and that, consequently, the world inflation rate and the volatility of national inflation rates increased, which, in turn, caused frequent changes in expected inflation rates among countries. Furthermore, inflationary expectations were stable during the international gold standard period despite the observed fluctuations in the price level, because exchange rates were fixed and because inflationary expectations depended primarily on the exchange rate and on the monetary "credibility" of the gold standard (even though on many occasions the monetary authorities did not follow the rules of the game). I agree that we shall never have a clear-cut answer to the question whether fixed- or floating-exchange-rate regimes are more inflationary, even though recent evidence favors of the post hoc, ergo propter hoc hypothesis that fixed rates are less inflationary. There is no doubt that the answer to this controversial question is extremely relevant to the issue of international monetary cooperation. If fixed rates are less inflationary *and* if international monetary cooperation is primarily concerned with a decrease in the *world* inflation rate (i.e., the inflation rate of the Organization for Economic Cooperation and Development (OECD) countries), then efforts should be made for a return to some kind of fixed-exchange-rate system (for instance, by forming a currency area between the United States, the Federal Republic of Germany, Japan, and some other countries—an area which the other OECD countries could join subsequently).

A rather puzzling empirical development during the 1970s which Paul De Grauwe discusses concerns the increased intercountry differences in inflation rates and the decreased intercountry differences in money supply growth rates, compared with rates recorded in the 1960s.[1] He interprets this phenomenon as evidence of an increased monetary dependence of a system of (too) flexible exchange rates, even though this statement completely contradicts the conventional professional wisdom. Even though I cannot give any definitive explanation of this puzzle, it might be solved by indicating that the supply shocks of the 1970s were common to all economies (in terms, for example, of the price increases for raw materials—in particular energy—and of the general slowdown in productivity growth), as was the effect on their monetary policies (or on their trade unions and, indirectly, on their monetary policies), which was to promote rapid monetary growth during some intervals and slowdowns in monetary growth during other intervals. Thus, it would not be astonishing to observe stronger international synchronization of the business cycle during the 1970s than was observed during the 1960s even if there had not been a change in the exchange rate regime.

How and By Whom Should Intervention Be Carried Out?

In order to avoid dealing with the question of when one should and when one should not intervene, the author assumes, throughout his lengthy model in Section III on "effective" intervention policies, that the monetary authorities want to maintain the existing exchange rate. The arguments he

---

[1] In De Grauwe's Table 1, the average inflation rate of the seven countries should be a *weighted* average. If—as a first, rather simple approximation—the United States were assigned a weight of 0.5 and all other countries equal shares in a total weight of 0.5, the average inflation rate would be 3.2 percent (instead of 3.6 percent) for 1960–70 and 9.1 percent (instead of 9.8 percent) for 1971–81. The same criticism applies to De Grauwe's Table 2, where the weighted average growth rate of the money supply would be 7.0 percent (instead of 9.4 percent) for 1960–70 and 9.2 percent (instead of 11.1 percent) for 1971–81. These revised figures would give a more reliable (quantity-theoretical) relationship between the average growth rate of the "world" quantity of money and the "world" inflation rate both for the 1960s, which were characterized by high growth rates of real national product, and for the 1970s, which were characterized by low growth rates of real national product. Furthermore, in order to render De Grauwe's Table 5 more comparable with his Table 1, the same price index should have been utilized, with preference given to the wholesale price index, since it is more concerned with tradable goods than the consumer price index is.

presents apply to a world of fixed exchange rates, represented by a two-country model. Using this model, De Grauwe tries to answer two questions: *How should one intervene?* and *Who should intervene* in the foreign exchange market?

How

The answer to the first question is relatively simple, since the exchange rate system is one of as-if-fixed rates under which the intervention rules of a fixed-rate system can be applied. In order for the system to work efficiently, the monetary authorities have to consider the exchange rate as the exogenous variable, and the interest rate and the money supply as the endogenous variables; when there is perfect substitutability between domestic and foreign bonds, the only endogenous variable will be the money supply. Thus, one rule of an efficient intervention policy is to avoid pursuing a sterilization policy when the central bank intervenes in the foreign exchange market, since in that case the exchange rate pressure would continue.[2]

Working with a two-country model raises the question of symmetrical versus asymmetrical sterilization policies. I have replaced the two anonymous countries of De Grauwe's model with the United States and the rest of the world (ROW). Furthermore, international reserves are U.S. dollars. In Table 1, I have classified different possible types of international monetary cooperation. Case 1 involves the lowest degree of cooperation, which is cooperation of degree zero. Cases 2 and 3 involve asymmetrical arrangements (which Paul De Grauwe labels noncooperative but which are, in my view, "imperfectly" cooperative). Case 4 involves the highest degree of cooperation.

(1) *Symmetrical Noncooperation.* The intervention policy used to influence the exchange rate is the most inefficient one. Under perfect substitutability of both countries' bonds, the policy is absolutely ineffective; whereas under imperfect substitutability, the sterilized intervention policy can, when it is combined with open market operations, succeed in influencing the exchange rate, but only after an extremely large amount of intervention. Since the quantity of money is not affected in either country, the world quantity of money also remains unchanged, which could be con-

---

[2]However—as De Grauwe shows, and as is discussed in various recent papers by Maurice Obstfeld (1980, 1982, 1983)—a sterilized intervention policy could still be efficient, even through the amount of intervention required would be far greater if it were coupled with open market operations (this is true only for the case of imperfect asset substitutability). These operations would imply changes in relative bond supplies that, in turn, would necessitate equilibrating interest-rate adjustments (De Grauwe's π) in the (desired) absence of equilibrating exchange-rate adjustments. I wonder whether the variable π is not also a function of the relative money supplies or of the relative wealth levels—a point which should be checked within a portfolio model.

TABLE 1. TYPES OF INTERNATIONAL MONETARY COOPERATION

Rest of the World (ROW) \ United States	Sterilization	Nonsterilization
Sterilization	Case 1. Symmetrical Noncooperation —Each "national" quantity of money remains unchanged. —Intervention policy is inefficient. —An extremely large amount of reserves is used. —World quantity of money remains unchanged.	Case 3. Asymmetrical Cooperation II —United States' quantity of money changes. —Intervention policy is efficient —A large amount of reserves is used. —World quantity of money changes.
Nonsterilization	Case 2. Asymmetrical Cooperation I —Rest of the world's quantity of money changes. —Intervention policy is efficient. —A large amount of reserves is used. —World quantity of money changes.	Case 4. Symmetrical Cooperation —Each "national" quantity of money changes. —Intervention policy is efficient. —A small amount of reserves is used. —World quantity of money remains unchanged.

sidered advantageous. However, since the intervention policy is the most inefficient compared with the other three cases, one should opt instead for a nonintervention policy, particularly in those countries with depreciating currencies, which generally lose a considerable amount of international reserves. Case 1 and the subsequent Case 2 are the representative cases of our past managed-floating system.

(2) *Asymmetrical Cooperation I.* One could defend the nonsterilized intervention policy of the ROW and the sterilization policy of the United States on the following grounds. Because, under the present system, the intervening country is generally the ROW and not the United States, the ROW-country is the one that fixes its exchange rate target, which may not be in the interests of the United States, but the U.S. authorities generally

accept it. If the intervening country can hit its own exchange rate target, it should also bear the adjustment burden by not sterilizing its intervention. As a matter of fact, the intervention amount and the subsequent change in the ROW's quantity of money will be higher (as Paul De Grauwe shows) than under a system where the United States also follows a nonsterilization policy.

As McKinnon (1982, p. 330) has shown, the sterilization policy of the United States is not consciously pursued but instead is "passive" to the extent that the Federal Reserve System does not know it is pursuing a sterilization policy, since it is induced by the ROW-country's willingness to hold international reserves in the form of U.S. Treasury bonds: the U.S. sterilization policy "is *passive* because the Federal Reserve is not consciously sterilizing with offsetting changes its own domestic asset position. Rather, the American money supply is insulated from changes in official reserves by the willingness of foreign central banks to hold nonmonetary U.S. government debt." Thus, for instance, if the ROW-country avoids an appreciation, it eventually uses, with the aid of the Federal Reserve System as a broker, its reserve inflows to purchase U.S. Treasury bonds or bills in the U.S. market.

The disadvantages of this asymmetrical type of cooperation are twofold. On the one hand, a relatively large amount of reserves is needed for intervention. On the other hand, the world quantity of money changes, since the intervening country's money supply varies.

(3) *Asymmetrical Cooperation II.* The outcome is identical to the preceding case, with only one exception: the United States' quantity of money changes. This case, as well as the following one, are not representative of our past managed-floating system.

(4) *Symmetrical Cooperation.* This case is the optimal one, or the "most fruitful" one, because the intervention policy for influencing the exchange rate is efficient, the need for international reserves is the lowest, the world quantity of money remains unchanged, and the adjustment burden is shared equally between the United States and the ROW-country.

The question one may now ask is whether such symmetrical cooperation could be brought about. Here again, I refer to the contribution of McKinnon (1982, pp. 331–33). Because the ROW-country represents, in principle, all members of the Fund except the United States, one could negotiate a "mutual nonsterilization pact," as McKinnon calls it, only among those that have *fully convertible* currencies, that have relatively *large* economies, and that are the best candidates to pursue a *stable monetary policy*. McKinnon mentions a pact between the United States, the Federal Republic of Germany, and Japan (and probably indirectly with their respective monetary satellites, such as the Netherlands and Austria in the case of Germany). Furthermore, in order to avoid money-supply shocks which increase the variability of the exchange rate, these countries should also agree on the rates of domestic credit expansion to be permitted in each country. Furthermore, passive sterilization by the United States could be avoided if central banks held their dollar reserves as deposits with the Federal Reserve System, on which the latter paid an interest rate equivalent to the yield on U.S. Government debt.

An extreme alternative to the above symmetrical cooperation scheme could be a mutual agreement among these same three countries, or among all industrial countries, not to intervene at all in the foreign exchange market so that there would be a pure regime of flexible exchange rates. Such a nonintervention pact could be in conflict with the "optimal degree of flexibility." However, the "optimal degree of flexibility" is only defensible when the *technique* of intervention follows the principle of asymmetrical cooperation or, at the best, of symmetrical cooperation.

By Whom

The author spends much time on the issue of which country should intervene in the foreign exchange market. He concludes that this question matters a lot when there are *asymmetrical* sterilization policies (our cases of asymmetrical cooperation). He is right on that point, to the extent he assigns to the intervening country the role of adjustment—that is, of refraining from sterilizing the monetary effect of intervention in the foreign exchange market. Thus, if the country with the depreciating currency intervenes (and does not sterilize), there will be a decrease in the world money stock. On the other hand, if the country of the appreciating currency intervenes (and does not sterilize), there will be an increase in the world money stock. However, if one separates the sterilization issue from the choice of the country which intervenes (in the sense that country A or our ROW-country does not sterilize and country B or the United States does sterilize, regardless of which member of both pairs of countries undertakes intervention), then the question of which country should intervene is without any importance as far as the adjustment process and the world quantity of money are concerned, but it certainly matters with respect to the question of which member of both pairs of countries should hold international reserves.

In our United States-ROW model, the symmetrical cooperation solution could also be achieved by according the intervention role in $(n - 1)$ foreign exchange markets to the United States and eventually coming up with a mutually agreed exchange rate target between the United States and ROW. Following the terminology of McKinnon (1982, p. 324) who calls

ROW's currency "rowa" and assumes that it is depreciating, the Federal Reserve System could create additional dollars and offer them in the foreign exchange market to purchase rowas. There would be an increase in the U.S. money stock and a decrease in ROW's money stock. Rowas would constitute one source of the U.S. monetary base. In order to prevent the Federal Reserve from investing rowas in ROW's domestic bond market (which would sterilize ROW's money supply), ROW could pay an interest rate on the Federal Reserve's holdings of rowas. On the contrary, if ROW's currency were appreciating and the Federal Reserve did not dispose of rowas, the latter should borrow them from ROW's central bank at an appropriate interest rate and sell them for dollars in the foreign exchange market. Again, both countries' money supplies would be adjusted. The eventual need for international reserves, now in terms of $(n - 1)$ currencies, would shift to the United States. But the exchange rate target could also be fixed by the United States which would pose the problem of "monetary sovereignty" for ROW.[3]

In the present context of the dollar standard, the question of who intervenes becomes relevant only for exchange rate adjustments between countries of the ROW area and, again, under the hypothesis of asymmetrical cooperation (of type I). If France faces a depreciation of 5 percent and the Federal Republic of Germany an appreciation of 3 percent, such that the French franc may depreciate by about 8 percent vis-à-vis the deutsche mark, and if the main exchange rate target of both countries is a depreciation of the French franc vis-à-vis the deutsche mark of 6 percent, then this result can be brought about by a variety of interventions conducted by the Banque de France and the Deutsche Bundesbank (for instance, a depreciation of the franc by 3 percent and an appreciation of the mark by 3 percent or a depreciation of the franc by 5 percent and an appreciation of the mark by 1 percent). Cooperation between the two countries is vital with respect to the exchange rate target between both countries, as with respect to monetary policy and the amount of intervention done by each country. The criterion used to determine who should intervene and to what extent does not depend on the choice made between the two countries to determine which of them will not sterilize, since neither country is allowed to sterilize if the intervention is efficient (and if the United States sterilizes). The criterion comprises three considerations. First, the adjustment burden created by changes in the quantity of money will be higher in the country which intervenes more. Sec-

---

[3]In November 1978, the United States abandoned its policy of benign neglect and intervened in the foreign exchange market in response to a depreciation of the dollar. However, during this episode, U.S. intervention was not in conflict with the exchange rate targets of other major countries (Federal Republic of Germany and Japan), but rather was supported by those countries.

ond, if the depreciation rate is higher (lower) than the appreciation rate, there will be a decline (rise) in the world quantity of money. Third, a special constraint on the country with the depreciating currency is the availability of international reserves.

The Link Between International Reserves and the World Quantity of Money

In a pure flexible-exchange-rate system, there is no relation whatsoever between international reserves and the money supplies of various countries, because the former simply remain constant (expressed in U.S. dollars). In a managed system of floating exchange rates, there is, again, no link at all when sterilized intervention policies are pursued, whereas there is a strong link when nonsterilized intervention policies are pursued. If, furthermore, the United States follows a policy of sterilization, the impact of nonsterilized intervention policies of other countries on the *world* quantity of money will be greatest.

The empirical evidence presented by De Grauwe indicating that there is no systematic link between international reserves and the national or world quantity of money during the period of floating exchange rates indicates simply that, as he correctly observes, there were many sterilized intervention policies.[4] And the same could be said for the period of fixed rates, when there was no systematic link either.

However, for the period of fixed exchange rates, the interpretation should be more subtle. Since the end of the 1960s, one has distinguished between a supply-determined growth rate of international reserves and a demand-determined growth rate. In the first case, there is a link between international reserves and the world quantity of money, and in the second case there is not. In both cases, it is assumed that the $n - 1$ intervening countries do not pursue a sterilization policy. According to the monetary approach of the balance of payments, if there is an expansionary monetary policy in the United States, world inflation tends to be higher, thus increasing the demand for money in the other countries. The excess demand for money creates a surplus in the balance of payments, an inflow of reserves (a supply-determined increase in international reserves), and an increase in

---

[4]However, by looking at yearly world data on growth rates (for the ten major industrial countries, the growth rates for the world money supply and for the world price level are weighted averages of national growth rates using gross national product weights of 1970), McKinnon (1982, pp. 321–24) finds strong evidence of a link between international reserves, the world quantity of money, and the world price level for two periods, 1971–72 and 1977–78 (when the dollar was under attack), as the figures reproduced in Table 2 indicate. There was only partial nonsterilization in the countries outside the United States and a sterilization of the U.S. quantity of money. The weight of the U.S. quantity of money within the world quantity of money is about 50 percent. The resulting world price inflation had a two-year lag.

TABLE 2. GROWTH RATES OF U.S. MONEY SUPPLY, OF INTERNATIONAL RESERVES, OF WORLD QUANTITY OF MONEY, AND OF WORLD PRICE LEVEL

(In percent)

Year	U.S. Money Supply (M_1)	International Reserves (Dollars)	World Money Supply (M_1)	World Price Level
1970	4.3	74.8	8.19	4.4
1971	6.5	142.0	11.77	3.1
1972	9.1	14.7	12.73	4.1
1973	5.7	8.9	7.65	12.9
1974	3.0	−0.8	6.51	21.9
1975	5.5	0.2	9.22	7.5
1976	5.9	6.2	7.36	6.6
1977	8.2	47.6	10.27	6.6
1978	8.2	33.5	10.98	5.6
1979	8.0	−19.9	7.60	11.1
1980	5.3	0.8	4.88	13.5

Source: McKinnon (1982).

the quantity of money. On the contrary, if, in the $n - 1$ countries, there is an increased demand for international reserves, their monetary policies will be restrictive in order to induce a surplus in their balances of payments. The consequent (demand-determined) inflow of reserves will compensate for the decrease in the internal-credit component of the monetary base, so that the total quantity of money (or its growth rate) will remain unchanged.

REFERENCES

Argy, Victor, *Exchange-Rate Management in Theory and Practice*, Princeton Studies in International Finance, No. 50 (Princeton, New Jersey: International Finance Section, Princeton University, October 1982).

McKinnon, Ronald I., "Currency Substitution and Instability in the World Dollar Standard," *American Economic Review*, Vol. 72 (June 1982), pp. 320–33.

Obstfeld, Maurice, "Imperfect Asset Substitutability and Monetary Policy under Fixed Exchange Rates," *Journal of International Economics*, Vol. 10 (May 1980), pp. 177–200.

———, "The Capitalization of Income Streams and the Effects of Open-Market Policy under Fixed Exchange Rates," *Journal of Monetary Economics*, Vol. 9 (January 1982), pp. 87–98.

_____, "Can We Sterilize? Theory and Evidence," *American Economic Review, Papers and Proceedings of the Ninety-Fourth Annual Meeting of the American Economic Association*, Vol. 72 (May 1982), pp. 45–50.

_____, "Exchange Rates, Inflation, and the Sterilization Problem: Germany, 1975–1981," *European Economic Review*, Vol. 21 (March/April 1983), pp. 161–89.

Niels Thygesen

Paul De Grauwe makes several interesting points in his wide-ranging and enjoyable paper. The three main ones of relevance to this final session of the conference, in the sense that they help to define a fruitful agenda for international monetary cooperation in the 1980s, are the following:

(1) The persistence of volatile inflationary expectations is likely to preclude the success of efforts to fix exchange rates among the major currencies.

(2) Since most of the issuers of these major currencies are unlikely to abandon a strategy of managed floating, an essential item on the international monetary agenda is how interventions can be made more efficient through internationally coordinated efforts. The paper contains a number of helpful suggestions in this area.

(3) Since there appears to be no clear causal link between international reserve stocks and national money stocks, there is little point in giving control of international reserve creation a prominent place on the future agenda; rather, the coordination of intervention policies should, as a by-product, yield more effective control of international reserve creation.

Put very simply, the author's three main points seem to me to illustrate three key words in the title of the paper: (1) identifies one *limit* on the agenda, which is that attempts to bring about fixity of exchange rates should not be undertaken prematurely; (2) outlines the *scope* of a major agenda item: the coordination of intervention policies; and (3) defines a side issue—the control of international reserve creation—the pursuit of which is unlikely to be *fruitful*.

While I have few comments on the author's outline of the need for better coordination of intervention in exchange markets and his substantive contribution to this subject, I believe that the agenda which he leaves us is too severely circumscribed, particularly if we think of the full span of what remains of the 1980s and not solely of the next one or two years. The author has, indeed, singled out the one area chosen by the policymakers of the main industrial nations for negotiations in 1982–83; we shall see, presumably at the time of the Williamsburg economic summit in May 1983, whether he has shown more foresight or courage than the officials to whom a study of the scope for intervention in the exchange markets among the world's major currencies was entrusted at the Versailles economic summit of 1982. I shall have some comments to add to his admirable analysis toward the end of my remarks. But my main concern is really with a broadening of the agenda to include some of the matters which De Grauwe considers to be either beyond the limits of feasibility or merely side issues.

How Much Exchange Rate Flexibility?

The author appears to regard the move toward exchange rate flexibility in recent years as irreversible, because it is the natural extension to the international economy of the monetary regimes which prevail in the major industrial countries. Over the past decade, these regimes have been characterized by high and variable—and hence internationally different— inflation rates. But it is not a foregone conclusion that the volatility of inflationary expectations which these experiences have understandably fostered will persist through the 1980s. In particular, the contribution tightly managed exchange rates could make to the dampening of volatile inflationary expectations should not be dismissed. Nor are they likely to be overlooked by governments and central banks.

To be more specific, I want to argue that the author is on more solid ground as an economic historian than as a policy analyst for the 1980s. By labeling the instability of exchange rates as the extension and interaction of unstable national monetary regimes, he has no doubt focused on the main cause of the breakdown of the Bretton Woods system. Widening divergences in monetary and other demand management policies between the United States and the Federal Republic of Germany over 1965-72 promoted a widening differential between observed (and expected) inflation rates in the two countries, which, in turn, eroded the credibility of a fixed, or even an administered, dollar/deutsche mark rate. Similarly, expansionary monetary policies in the United Kingdom starting in 1971, and the consequent additional inflation and external deficits, were reflected in the withdrawal of sterling, from 1972 onward, from any joint exchange rate management in the European Communities. Several other examples could be found to illustrate the same point; and the author's historical thesis would be strengthened by including in the analysis the years following the first oil price shock, when differences in policy responses to the mixture of inflationary and contractionary impulses arising therefrom perpetuated and widened the perceived and expected inflation differentials and other indicators of divergence in economic performance.

Nevertheless, much of this undoubtedly correct historical view of the causes leading to the adoption of exchange rate flexibility is not helpful in defining the agenda for the 1980s. Over the five years that have passed since the Second Amendment of the Fund's Articles of Agreement officially recognized the disappearance of exchange rate commitments, the pendulum has swung a long way back toward fixed exchange rates, so that re-establishment of the preconditions for a higher degree of exchange rate fixity is more likely today than it has been at any time during at least the past 15 years. While the author seems to echo the view, often heard from U.S. and German (Fed. Rep.) officials when negotiating with other countries more anxious to move toward fixity than they, that "stability begins at home," my main point is that stability in this sense is well on the road to being established. But in order to consolidate this progress, more explicit exchange rate commitments are required; the avoidance not only of erratic short-term movements in exchange rates but also of the longer-run swings in the value of the dollar, in terms of other main currencies, which we have seen during 1977–82 could be a major contribution to the restoration of noninflationary growth in the major industrial economies, though it would also involve risks. Let me examine, necessarily briefly and superficially, under four headings why it appears to me that, on balance, a somewhat bolder move toward exchange rate fixity than is envisaged by the author seems both feasible and fruitful.

Convergence of National Inflation Rates

The figures have indicated greater convergence of macroeconomic performances and policies in the major industrial economies for some time. Progress in inflationary performance in the United States and the United Kingdom over the past three years, since inflation peaked in both countries in early 1980, has been such as to narrow these countries' inflation differential above the Federal Republic of Germany and Japan to 2–3 percentage points. While some of this narrowing is due to the delayed impact of dollar and sterling appreciation of 1980–82, and consequently may be reversed in case of a subsequent decline in the remaining presumed overvaluation vis-à-vis the deutsche mark and the yen, the bulk of the observed convergence of inflation rates is attributable to domestic factors. Among the five economies whose currencies make up the special drawing right (SDR), only France has an inflation rate which is clearly out of line. Yet, paradoxically, France continues to be the strongest proponent among the main industrial countries of fixed exchange rates, a view which has survived a change in political regime.

Convergence of Macroeconomic Policies

Advocacy of a return to a high degree of fixity of exchange rates would be adventurous indeed if it rested solely on an observed, but possibly temporary, convergence of inflation rates. If the choice of policy mix varies greatly or is likely to do so among the main nations, formulation of any common policy becomes difficult, regardless of the exchange rate regime. The experiences of 1981–82 strongly suggest that flexible rates do not confer upon even the largest economy the autonomy it would need to change significantly its mix of monetary and fiscal measures without creating undesired side effects through movements in its real exchange rate. Several countries, in particular the United States, appear now to be in the process of modifying their policy mixes by tightening fiscal policies and loosening monetary policies. Policy adjustments are necessarily differentiated, as any careful analysis of the starting positions of individual countries and international requirements would suggest—see, for example, the recent statement on global economic strategy by 26 economists appearing in Institute for International Economics (1982). In this respect, the situation resembles that of 1977–78, when some international organizations and successive economic summits urged differentiated fiscal expansion in the industrial countries that was referred to as the locomotive approach and, subsequently, the convoy approach. The United States expanded first in 1976–78, while the Federal Republic of Germany and Japan lagged behind, claiming that their respective appreciations should be regarded as a substitute for domestic expansion. Subsequently, the latter two countries were persuaded to modify their policies, and Germany agreed at the Bonn summit in 1978 to undertake fiscal reflation. As these measures took effect in 1979–80, the German current and capital accounts swung sharply into deficit and the deutsche mark weakened remarkably. Memories of these experiences remain vivid in the minds of policymakers and will further complicate the already difficult task of reaching agreement on a differentiated policy response to promote recovery. The policy adjustments required to sustain a resumption of growth are more severely constrained under flexible exchange rates, the volatility of which is dampened only by individual and sporadic interventions, than in a situation where the structure of exchange rates has been broadly agreed among the major countries. The risk of aborting another recovery by creating unsustainable tensions in the exchange markets could well preclude any joint initiatives.

Beyond these issues relating to the outlook for the promotion of a non-inflationary recovery in 1983–84, the basic question about the desirability of a high degree of fixity is whether policy preferences have converged sufficiently to make feasible inthe 1980s what did not prove feasible prior to 1973. Provided sufficient control over international reserve creation can be exercised, as I shall argue in the following section, the continuation of a fairly cautious policy stance in the main countries seems to make largely fixed exchange rates among them a feasible option for the 1980s.

Pegged Exchange Rates as a Substitute for Monetary Targets

Most of the main industrial nations introduced target-constrained monetary policies in the mid-1970s. In the absence of the anchor of an exchange rate commitment, a number of central banks and other policy-makers felt the need to announce monetary targets in the form of one or more monetary aggregates. It was hoped that such a move would help to stabilize inflationary expectations domestically, while also providing guid-ance for the exchange markets. This is not the place to review the cumula-tive experience, except to say that the monetary targets have been more successful in carrying out the former task than the latter one. Despite a broadly similar monetary stance, interpreted as the relationship between a monetary target and projected growth of money incomes, exchange rates in the main countries became more volatile than ever. Thanks to the efforts of Dornbusch (1982) and several other participants of this conference, we have acquired a good understanding of the monetary factors that may pro-duce a severely misaligned exchange rate between two currencies which are apparently managed along similar lines: perceived minor policy changes are telescoped into large jumps in the exchange rate. Since so much depends on perceptions of policy, the ability to forecast how a particular constellation of monetary targets will affect the exchange rate is very limited.

To this disappointing external aspect of the experience with monetary targets, one may add the sheer technical difficulties of hitting the targets. It would not be an overstatement to say that the credibility of targeting has been eroding gradually. In the United States, the main monetary target (M_1) was recently suspended because financial innovations had made it an unreliable guide, and the subsidiary targets—the broader aggre-gates—have not been upgraded. In the United Kingdom, the main target ($£M_3$) was overshot so persistently in 1980–81 that confidence in the entire monetary strategy was badly shaken; more recently, the target has been de-emphasized. In the Federal Republic of Germany and, more clearly, in the other member countries of the European Monetary System (EMS), mone-tary targets have often been superseded by the need to observe the exchange rate objectives of the system. But whether the prime reason for the declining status of the monetary target is innovation in the domestic financial sector, rendering past definitions of an aggregate obsolete, or conflicts with more or less explicit exchange rate objectives, it seems a safe prediction that the monetary authorities in a number of countries will, over the next few years, be prepared to consider carefully alternative ways (to their present monetary targets) of presenting their longer-run price level objectives. Pegging the exchange rate is the simplest such alternative.

Differences in Economic Structure Causing Differential Responses to External Shocks

It would clearly be hazardous to try to peg exchange rates between countries that differ sufficiently with respect to economic structure, real or financial, to make divergent responses to external shocks likely. It is widely believed that an important role in explaining exchange rates and national inflation rates in the 1970s must be assigned to three such differences: (i) the degree of real-wage rigidity, (ii) the composition of exports, and (iii) the extent to which financial assets are traded internationally. To argue convincingly for largely fixed exchange rates among the main industrial countries, one has to demonstrate either that the structural differences (i)–(iii) are likely to be minor in the foreseeable future or, if they are not, that the external shocks which would make them relevant are unlikely to occur. Neither condition was met in the years following the first oil price shock. The degree of real-wage resistance was clearly greater in most European countries than in the United States and Japan (see, for example, Branson and Rotemberg (1980)), and the extent to which the industrial countries were able to export goods and services or financial assets to the oil exporters differed widely. These differences in real and financial structure produced divergent performance with respect to inflation rates, current accounts, and capital flows and, hence, with respect to exchange rates.

Experience following the second oil price shock indicates that at least some of these differences in real and financial structure have diminished in importance. The degree of real-wage resistance has been greatly reduced in Europe—even the most highly indexed economies, such as Belgium and Italy, have modified their systems—while spending by the oil exporters has been spread more widely. Even financial reflows have been better balanced, since both private capital flows and the diversification of official international reserves have increased the role of non-dollar currencies, particularly the hen and the deutsche mark, in private and official portfolios, as demonstrated in Group of Thirty (1982).

In contemplating possible external shocks that might, in the 1980s, once more blow away any prospect of stable exchange rates between the major currencies, one's imagination is regrettbly limited to a repetition of the supply shocks of the 1970s or to their partial reversal through a further decline in real oil prices. Though a further oil price decline would induce some depreciation of the currencies of the industrial countries which are relatively well-endowed with energy resources (Norway, the United Kingdom, Canada), the adjustments required on this account seem unlikely in themselves to undermine the feasibility of a largely stable exchange rate structure among the industrial countries.

My general conclusion, formed after surveying some of the main economic determinants of what must be the focus of international monetary cooperation in the 1980s—the exchange rate regime—is that one would be limiting the agenda unduly by leaving out the option of returning to a system of explicit exchange rate commitments. Improvements in intervention techniques, while obviously desirable, are only a first, very limited step toward stabilization of exchange markets. Such improvements could be useful in the initial phase of a graduation process that moved next to tighter managed floating without formal commitments; then to adoption of target zones for exchange rates; and, finally, to declared parities. Incidentally, a similar graduation process took place in 1976–78 among countries that are now members of the European Monetary System (EMS)—some might say prematurely, in view of difficulties encountered in keeping the EMS together during the subsequent turbulent years. Yet there would be little disagreement within Europe that the existence of the exchange rate commitments has prevented some dangerous illusions and policy mistakes.

It will surely be objected that such an agenda is utterly unrealistic in view of the difficulties encountered in reaching agreement at Versailles on the intervention study. It is clearly not a prediction of what is politically feasible over a short time span of one or two years—though the use of the word "fruitful" in the topic of this session ("What are the scope and limits of fruitful international monetary cooperation in the 1980s?") may appear to invite Mr. De Grauwe and his discussants to assess political feasibility Economists have often been too impressed with what appeared at the time to be political imponderables but shortly thereafter turned out to haven been temporary factors. The past decade of international monetary history—and, on a smaller scale, the past decade of European monetary integration—has seen too many reversals of positions to give observers without any official position excessive respect for the ability or political will of one or more main actors to eliminate items for discussion. (It is only necessary to recall how quickly the old allegiance to the two presumed pillars of the international monetary system—stable gold price and fixed exchange rates—disappeared ten years ago.) The question to ask in 1983 is whether interdependence of the main industrial countries is better accommodated by a high degree of exchange rate flexibility, even though dampened by occasional judicious interventions, or by a far more explicit structure of exchange rates.

If one takes the view that the latter option is more attractive, it is necessary to add a remark on what the pivot of such a re-emerging exchange rate structure would be. There are basically two scenarios which may be envisaged. The first entails a rebirth of the dollar standard, made possible by remarkable deceleration of the U.S. inflation rate. If that process were to continue and to reduce U.S. inflation to German and Japanese levels, it seems quite conceivable that the authorities of these two countries, as well as those of the United Kingdom and of the Federal Republic of Germany's EMS partners, could once more find it attractive to peg to the dollar. The other scenario entails the five countries whose currencies make up the SDR deciding to peg to that unit (or to derive bilateral intervention limits vis-à-vis each other from their SDR band). This choice might be important in determining the demand for international reserve assets, but otherwise it is clearly a matter of secondary importance relative to the main choice of the degree of exchange rate flexibility discussed above.

International Reserves and the World Money Stock

Paul De Grauwe's discussion of the interaction of international reserves and national money stocks is interesting, though inconclusive. He tends to see the volatility of international reserves as the result of systematic attempts by many countries to peg both their exchange rates and their money supplies. He does not find any clear evidence of a causative role for the growth of international reserves in the acceleration of national money stocks and inflation rates in the three countries selected.

To these sensible conclusions, I would add one general comment: international reserves have been growing at unprecedented speed since the late 1960s—at least 13 percent per annum, or even 21 percent per annum. if gold revaluation profits are included. The inclusion of the latter item is controversial, but it would be imprudent to think that these profits play no role at all in defining national perceptions of an external constraint or the absence thereof or that they do not constitute a tempting source of "financing" public sector deficits, as has been argued in Triffin (1983). Other reserves have been created largely in three different ways: (1) through international decisions to make SDR allocations and increase Fund reserve positions, (2) through the deficits of the United States, or (3) through the borrowing operations of countries wanting to supplement their reserves. Apart from brief periods during 1970-72 and 1977-78 when U.S. deficits were important, the dominant source by far has been the financing (usually excessive financing) of deficits by a large number of industrial and developing countries. Whether this process is regarded as the consequence of rapid growth rates of national money stocks or as a precondition for such growth is a semantic point unlikely to be clarified by Granger causality tests or the like. What is hardly in doubt is that the scope for financing persistently large deficits postponed domestic policy adjustments and kept inflation—and the level of economic activity—higher than it would otherwise have been. Internationally formulated guidelines for borrowing by deficit countries could, even under the rather flexible exchange rate regime in effect since 1973, have been developed into a powerful tool for influencing the world inflation rate.

In principle, making exchange rates less flexible emphasizes the importance of controlling the growth of international reserves. In practice, a somewhat less unbalanced international payments structure (which seems likely to exist during the next few years)—an important element in making more stable exchange rates possible—should slow down reserve creation. Nevertheless, an important complement to the stabilization of exchange rates would be putting control of reserve creation back on the international monetary agenda with a view to maintaining a stable and moderate reserve growth rate, with creation arising from international decisions and not from the other two sources.

Intervention and Sterilization

There is, I believe, little one can add to Paul De Grauwe's clear and useful graphical and verbal exposition of the main issues involved in intervention and sterilization, which extends the author's important earlier work on the proper role and limits of sterilized intervention. I merely want to underline two points the author makes and to add another.

The first relates to the role of expectations. Clearly interventions are typically designed not just to manage day-to-day movements in an exchange rate but also, and more importantly, to influence expectations or to make in the author's words (p. 397), "a more lasting effect on the exchange rate possible." Hence, models which assume the expected rate is independent of the intervention strategy would seem to miss the main point. There is, however (as is true of the market's perception of domestic monetary action), a high degree of indeterminacy in evaluating how expectations are influenced (see, for example, Mayer (1982)). If intervention is perceived to be temporary, half-hearted, and not part of any clear long-term strategy, its impact is likely to be small. When, on the other hand, intervention is perceived as supporting a more explicit strategy for the exchange rate, expectations are far more likely to change in such a way as to reinforce the strategy and to limit the need for large interventions. In other words, once the authorities have chosen a realistic target zone for the exchange rate, they need not engage in massive nonsterilized interventions to sustain it.

The second point is a clarification of what the author has to say about interventions in the snake and in the EMS. When two currencies are at their bilateral intervention limits under the EMS, the authorities in both countries have an obligation to intervene, as they had under the snake. If the central bank of the strong currency buys up the weak currency, the other central bank may lose reserves, since it has to buy back within 45 days the national currency by selling dollars or ECUs. Whether the system has a deflationary bias or not depends then on possible asymmetries in the monetary strategies pursued in the two countries. If the weaker one pursues a domestic credit target and the stronger one a money stock target, there will, indeed, be a deflationary bias. As an empirical matter, that seems to be the normal situation in the EMS, where countries such as Belgium, Denmark, and Italy pursue domestic credit targets while the prime target in the Federal Republic of Germany is the central bank money stock.

The third point is the simple one that once we talk of nonsterilized intervention between the dollar and other main currencies as a rather technical matter, a certain amount of hypocrisy creeps in. It would be fair to recognize that what is usually being asked for is the better monetary policy coordination that can be achieved by giving greater weight to external considerations. If the United States has now passed through the stage of inflationary deceleration through monetary restraint, perhaps improved monetary cooperation can be pursued more frankly and with better prospects of success.

REFERENCES

Branson, William H., and Julio J. Rotemberg, "International Adjustment with Wage Rigidity," *European Economic Review*, Vol. 13 (May 1980), pp. 309-41.

Bryant, Ralph C., *Money and Monetary Policy in Interdependent Nations* (Washington: Brookings Institution, 1980).

De Grauwe, Paul, "What are the Scope and Limits to Fruitful International Monetary Cooperation in the 1980s?" Chapter 8 in this volume.

Dornbusch, Rudiger, "Equilibrium and Disequilibrium Exchange Rates," *Zeitschrift für Wirtschafts- und Sozialwissenschaften* (No. 6, 1982), pp. 573-99.

Group of Thirty, *Reserve Currencies in Transition* (New York, 1982).

Institute for International Economics, *Promoting World Recovery*, A Statement on Global Economic Strategy (Washington, December 1982).

Mayer, Helmut, "The Theory and Practice of Floating Exchange Rates and the Role of Official Exchange-Market Intervention," BIS Economic Papers, No. 5 (Basle: Bank for International Settlements, 1982).

Triffin, Robert, "How to End the World 'Infession': Palliatives or Fundamental Reforms?" CEPS Working Documents, No. 1, Center for European Policy Studies (Brussels and Louvain, 1983).

Summary of Findings

A panel discussion between Executive Directors and the presenters of the eight papers contained in the previous chapters concluded the Conference on International Money, Credit, and the SDR. Utilizing many of the thoughts expressed by the panelists, this chapter attempts to characterize the main findings of the conference and some of the remaining differences in views. The topics covered in the wrap-up session ranged from evaluations of general aspects of the current international monetary system to consideration of the SDR, surveillance, and the role of the Fund. This chapter is organized according to these topics and avoids attributing views to individuals in summarizing positions taken on the subject matters discussed.

I. HOW THE SYSTEM HAS FUNCTIONED AND HOW IT CAN BE IMPROVED

The chief aspects of the prevailing international monetary system that were appraised related to the appropriateness of exchange rates and exchange arrangements, the harmonization of monetary policies, and the degree to which the system has facilitated international trade and the efficient transfer of resources between countries. Suggested improvements centered on ways of enhancing stability through increased policy coordination, with the possible assistance of Fund surveillance and of explicit exchange rate commitments. More pervasive changes of the kind that could conceivably produce an entirely new international monetary system received little attention. Some panelists welcomed this forbearance because they felt that monetary systems—like constitutions—should not casually be experimented with; major changes should be made infrequently and then only if there were good reason to expect substantial improvement. Others regretted the lack of consideration of the most far-reaching proposals for reform that would redress defects and asymmetries of the present system, particularly with regard to the developing world.

Fundamental disequilibria of the type that called for negotiated adjustments in exchange rates under the Bretton Woods system have not disappeared under floating rates. Although such disequilibria are now much more difficult to identify or to anticipate than formerly, a number of panelists cited recent episodes in which certain floating exchange rates had moved well beyond the range that might be regarded as compatible with efficiency in international trade and finance. There was widespread agreement that the exchange market is not always right and that, over time, private capital markets are not always efficient or stabilizing. However, opinions differed on whether better performance could be ensured by making major changes in the way the authorities operate under the present system.

It is difficult for many countries to have domestic stability without approximate stability of real exchange rates. Conversely, exchange rate stability is impossible to maintain over any extended period of time unless there is domestic stability. For these reasons, there has long been debate on which kind of stability should come first. Panelists put aside the question of whether domestic stability or exchange rate stability should be the starting point for achieving overall stability by arguing that countries should simultaneously pursue both.

Exchange rate intervention need not be ineffective or lacking in credibility if it is supported by an explicit commitment to an exchange rate target range that is consistent with macroeconomic policies, particularly money supply policies. Whether or not any such intervention should be sterilized depends very much on what exchange rate pressures or movements are believed to reveal about expected inflation differentials with other countries, transitory versus permanent changes in money demand, or structural changes in international competitiveness or in relative prices of a country's main exports and imports. At the very least, it was agreed, there is nothing to be gained by ignoring the information about desirable changes in domestic policies that exchange rate pressures can convey. For instance, rising nominal interest rates, if coupled with a tendency for the external value of a currency to depreciate, can signal a rapid rise in the expected inflation rate, falling real rates of interest, and the need to reduce the rate of money growth. If the United States and other countries had heeded such signals in the 1970s, price stability would not have deteriorated to such an extent as to require the painful and costly corrections made in the early 1980s, which have damaged trade, production, employment, and the international transfer of resources.

Since exchange rates are multilateral, the signals they convey should normally have implications not only for a single country but for all countries whose policies are important to the functioning of the international system of trade and finance. One of the factors affecting exchange rates is speculation about future monetary and macroeconomic policy in each of the countries involved. Hence, there is room for coordination; concerted intervention strategies and the harmonization of policies in the pursuit of common goals are clearly desirable in principle.

In reality, the macroeconomic decision-making processes within several major countries are compartmentalized; forecasts and the interpretation of signals are uncertain and contested; and perceptions about desirable trade-offs between objectives and about relations between policy instruments and goals keep changing. Given that internal coordination is incomplete, tentative, and easily upset by new political and economic developments, several panelists found it difficult to see how policy harmonzation between major countries could be promoted effectively through formal agreements between them. Though harmonization of macroeconomic policies can technically be achieved more easily the smaller the number of countries included in the negotiations, the political costs can be higher the greater the number of countries that are excluded. For these reasons, many panelists felt that surveillance by the International Monetary Fund might have a special role to play in harmonizing policies.

By contrast, panelists generally felt that there was little chance that policies could be harmonized by means of tight agreements among major countries' monetary authorities or through a return to fixed exchange rates. Although it is incontrovertible that inflation has been higher and the growth of trade and production lower in the floating-rate period of the seventies than in the fixed-rate period of the sixties, association does not prove causation. Many factors other than the floating system per se affected exchange rates, macroeconomic stability, and growth prospects in the seventies, most notably the two oil price shocks. Because of these episodes and differences in the lags with which industry structures and real wages tended to adjust, interest and inflation differentials arose which detracted from stability in a way that cannot be attributed simply to floating. In some situations, the adoption of floating may have facilitated the pursuit of undesirable policies; in other cases, it may have improved economic decision making and the economy's ability to cope with external shocks. Thus, most panelists appeared to feel that summary evaluations that abstracted from the particulars surrounding the choice of exchange rate regime—if, indeed, there is such a choice—were not very useful.

Nevertheless, there was also a feeling that in the present world of partial floating and emerging protective currency unions, it would be wishful thinking to assume that exchange rate volatility could be regarded as harmless and thus benignly neglected. Even if, in the past turbulent decade, the resulting ill effects of volatility did not seem particularly conspicuous, or if volatile exchange rates were somehow tolerated within the imperfect framework of the international system, it was felt that complacency about volatility would certainly be ill-advised.

At the present time, the international monetary system faces several pressing problems. The international debt crisis is probably the most urgent among them. Success in overcoming that crisis requires that there be (1) a robust and sustained recovery in all major industrial countries; (2) prolonged and painful adherence to austere policies in debtor countries; (3) a retreat from present protectionism; and (4) continued commercial bank lending and, for a sustained period, an increase of bank exposure.

In the short run, these requirements can only be met through increased cooperation between private, national, and international financial institutions. Beyond that, however, the need to meet these requirements may also spawn new information and management systems and arrangements for funding and the international transfer of resources that directly involve increased reliance on Fund conditionality, surveillance, and resources. The sense of several panelists' remarks thus appeared to be that innovations in the present international financial system derive primarily from what is learned in particular crises and that relatively little effort is made to anticipate or forestall possible future crises of different origin. Nevertheless, these improvised innovations may serve as building blocks in the construction of a reformed international financial system.

II. SDRS, SURVEILLANCE, AND THE ROLE OF THE FUND

Panelists expressed a fair amount of skepticism about how far one could push in the direction of making the SDR the principal reserve asset in the international monetary system. Even after it was explained that an asset need not be quantitatively the most important to be regarded as having a principal role to play, doubts remained about what the SDR's role would be. Hence, any practical steps taken with the SDR would have to be evaluated on their merits, rather than on how they enhanced the role of the SDR.

One of the practical steps that found almost unanimous support was to meet liquidity, funding, and reserve needs partly through SDR allocations. Whatever some might once have thought about the degree of excess liquidity in the system and how it should reflect on the desirability of SDR allocations, fears of any such excess and its inflationary potential would surely be groundless under current conditions. Rather, an SDR allocation would contribute to maintaining the international movement of funds and goods and reduce the drag on any world-wide recovery that would stem from attempts to rebuild depleted reserves by other, contractive means in the face of inelastic supplies of international credit. For these reasons, the idea of an SDR allocation, if conducted as in the past and not used as a substitute for bilateral aid, found very wide support among the panel.

Some panelists added the qualification that SDR allocations, no matter how important, should not take priority over increasing Fund resources for conditional lending, if there are only a limited number of things that can be accomplished at this time. Greater availability and use of SDRs in the conditionality programs of the Fund would, itself, deserve further study. Others emphasized that SDR allocations can never be viewed in isolation and that the Fund's conditionality and surveillance programs, if implemented evenhandedly, would ensure that the SDRs obtained through allocations, although containing elements of automaticity, would be used to support appropriate policy stances. Greater allocation and use of official SDRs under the overall supervision of the Fund would ensure availability and continuity of reserves and a more equitable distribution of Fund resources.

In addition to the SDR's use as official credit, panelists discussed its possible uses in intervention and in private capital markets as ways of getting industrial countries to take greater interest in the SDR. Major countries are not likely to want to use SDRs in intervention operations on a large scale unless they have first agreed on target zones for the external values of their currencies, some of which could be defined in SDRs. Even then, they could not do so unless there were fungibility between the Fund's SDR and SDR-denominated instruments in private markets. The institution of a clearinghouse was therefore discussed, in which official holders could deposit SDRs in return for claims that could be transferred to the private market. Since the rate of return that the clearinghouse could offer on its SDR-denominated deposits would be determined by the terms prevailing on its SDR assets, whose value in use is continuously assured by official valuation and by the transfer services provided by the Fund, measures to increase the attractiveness of the Fund's SDR would also increase the demand for SDR deposits. Hence, certain avenues of development came into view during the discussions along which the SDR could evolve from what some panelists characterized as a subsidiary international credit instrument into a full-fledged monetary asset.

Surveillance by the Fund has already been mentioned on a number of occasions in this chapter as an important aid in ensuring the appropriateness of policies, exchange rates, and the use of external resources. A number of panelists remarked, however, that surveillance, no matter how conducive to the smooth and efficient functioning of the system, tends to be more powerful when applied to some groups of countries than to others. They had no doubt that the Fund has been capable of appraising and influencing the exchange rate policies of many of the countries that have drawn on its resources over the years. However, they asked, can the Fund effectively influence the exchange rate and money supply policies of major countries, particularly if their currencies are floating against other major currencies under conditions of high capital mobility?

While the quality of the Fund's surveillance and conditionality programs, and hence the credibility of the Fund, were judged to be high, opportunities for extending that surveillance to major countries not in external difficulties were regarded as rather limited at present. Surveillance exercises might readily show that there are persistent, harmful, and costly disequilibria in exchange rates; yet no effective pressure apparently could be brought to bear on major countries to implement the policies required to eliminate these disequilibria. Some panelists saw in this a basic injustice of the present system that ought to be reduced by strengthening the hand of the Fund and focusing international concern on the policies pursued by major industrial countries.

Several more stressed that logical application of surveillance is inherently global and that surveillance has to be done within a system setting. The proposition "you look after your exchange rate, and we will look after ours" just does not work for the world as a whole. Thus, one cannot approach surveillance and exchange rate inappropriateness on a country-by-country basis, except possibly for very small countries. On the other hand, it was also recognized that even though surveillance has broader systemic applications, which should be strengthened, stabilization programs and adjustment loans are what earns surveillance its keep. Panelists found such programs to be the most important component of the Fund's regular business and one that needs to be expanded on account of its benefits to the system.

Regarding the size of the Fund, panelists appeared to agree that they would not like to see the major activities of the Fund curbed significantly by resource limitations at this time. No dissent was expressed from the view that the Fund should actively pursue lender-of-last-resort and rescue efforts and should engage on a much larger scale in conditional lending. Some panelists suggested that if quota increases and enlargement of the General Arrangements to Borrow should prove unequal to these tasks, other arrangements, including Fund borrowing in private markets, might have to be re-examined.

10

Special Drawing Rights and Plans for Reform of the International Monetary System: A Survey

ROBERT E. CUMBY*

The creation of a special drawing rights (SDRs) facility in the Fund, which was agreed upon by the Board of Governors at the 1967 Annual Meetings in Rio de Janeiro, followed nearly a decade of concern about the viability and desirability of the gold-exchange standard. This concern led to proposals for the reform of the international monetary system. This survey, which was one of four background papers distributed in advance of the conference, covers (1) the economics literature that provided part of the intellectual background for the creation of an international reserve asset, (2) assessments of the Rio agreement along with proposals for the further development of the SDR, (3) analyses of the changing role of an international reserve asset during a period of managed floating, and (4) proposals for a link between SDRs and development aid.

The development of thinking about the need for SDRs may be summarized as follows. During the early 1960s, the gold-exchange standard was viewed by many to be essentially unstable, since foreign exchange reserve accumulation (mainly in U.S. dollars) was projected to continue to grow more rapidly than the monetary gold stock. As official holdings of U.S. dollars represented a large and growing claim on the U.S. gold stock, conversions of dollars into gold could not be made without threatening a collapse of the system. A de facto dollar standard was then evolving that implied an important asymmetry between the United States and the rest of

---

* Mr. Cumby is Assistant Professor at New York University's Graduate School of Business Administration. This paper was substantially completed while the author was an Economist in the Fund's Research Department.

the world. These concerns led to the formulation of several plans to provide an international reserve asset that would help reduce dependence on the dollar by establishing a more symmetric system in which liquidity growth could be managed by international agreements.

A number of writers found the Rio agreement inadequate to deal with the fundamental problems of the gold-exchange standard. The confidence problem remained unsolved, and no provision had been made to remove the asymmetries of the dollar standard. While prospective SDR allocations could supplement reserve growth, no mechanism existed to control liquidity growth, especially in the face of large U.S. deficits, such as those encountered in the early 1970s. These considerations then led to proposals for further reform that involved the establishment of a new international monetary system, the evolution of which could be influenced more decisively by means of the SDR.

The adoption of floating exchange rates in 1973 substantially reduced academic writing concerning the SDR and questions relating to the fundamental reform of the international monetary system. Recently, dissatisfaction with the volatility of exchange rates has led to suggestions of more extensive exchange rate management and other modifications of the existing system. However, little has been written in the past few years about the SDR's role in a system with more exchange market intervention or on far-reaching alternatives to the present system. Instead, questions relating to the link between special drawing rights and development finance, to substitution among reserve assets under floating, and to the SDR's role in Fund operations have received most of the attention.

I. INTERNATIONAL MONETARY SYSTEM PRIOR TO THE RIO AGREEMENT: ASSESSMENTS AND PROPOSALS FOR REFORM

The survey begins with the important and influential *Gold and the Dollar Crisis* (1960), in which Triffin questioned the viability of the gold-exchange standard. The primary concerns raised by Triffin provide the framework for analyzing the pre-1967 literature. First, the overall level of gold reserves was projected to rise more slowly than the demand for reserves. In the absence of additional reserve supply, this excess demand would impart a contractionary or deflationary bias to monetary and balance of payments policies. Second, if this excess demand for reserves resulted in further accumulation of dollar claims by foreign official holders, there would be a concomitant increase in claims on U.S. gold reserves, which, in turn, would undermine confidence in the ability and preparedness of the United States to maintain convertibility of the dollar into gold at a fixed price. Third, the gold-exchange standard and the Bretton Woods system in general contained fundamental asymmetries owing to the dollar's special roles as the principal component of reserves and as the standard to which parities were pegged. If U.S. deficits were settled by increases in official foreign claims on the United States, the United States, unlike the rest of the world, faced no reserve constraint in formulating its demand policies. Thus, the burden of adjusting to current account imbalances generally fell on other countries, particularly deficit countries.

Reserve Adequacy

The notion of reserve adequacy has been developed from the early work of Triffin (1947), who assumed that reserve demand would grow with world trade and proposed the ratio of reserves to imports as a measure of adequacy. This measure was also used in *Gold and the Dollar Crisis* (1960), in which its movements over time provided the basis for Triffin's assessment of reserve adequacy. The ratio of monetary gold to imports was found by Triffin to be the same in 1957 as in 1913 and 1928 but, at 35 to 36 percent, this ratio was low in these three years relative to historical standards. The ratio of total reserves to imports for all countries other than the United States and the United Kingdom combined had fallen to a similar figure by 1957. From an examination of the distribution of reserves relative to imports across countries and over time, Triffin (1960) concluded that a level of 40 percent could be deemed adequate for the maintenance of convertibility. Countries with ratios of reserves to imports of less than 30 percent were found to be prone to payments restrictions.

Triffin next examined the projected behavior of the ratios of monetary gold to imports and of reserves to imports under alternative assumptions about the growth of monetary gold and trade during 1958–67 and found a large prospective gold shortage. This potential shortage would have had to be made up either by further accumulation of convertible currencies (mainly dollars) or by deflation, which was generally recognized as an evil to be avoided. Further accumulation of dollar balances had limited potential, according to Triffin, for reasons detailed in this paper's next section, which discusses the confidence problem.

Claims of reserve inadequacy were challenged by Jacobsson, Holtrop, Blessing, and others who argued that reserve growth had, if anything, been insufficiently restrictive to prevent an increase in the price levels in almost all countries (Machlup (1963)). Lutz (1965) agreed, and Triffin (1961) emphasized the importance of controlled liquidity growth rather than its prospective inadequacy. The Bellagio Group (Machlup and Malkiel (1964)) reached no consensus on the current state of reserve adequacy but agreed that the existing system of liquidity provision was inadequate. The increases in Fund quotas of 1959 and 1964, the creation of the Gold Pool in 1961, the growth of Roosa bonds and swap agreements since 1962, along with the conclusion of the General Arrangements to Borrow (GAB) in 1962, were held by the ministers of the Group of Ten to provide adequate means of dealing with any foreseeable liquidity problems (Roosa (1965, Appendix); Williamson (1977 b)).

On the other hand, Scitovsky (1965) and Harrod (1961, 1966) considered an increase in reserves to be desirable, so that smooth adjustment could be facilitated. Others pointed to the need for supplementary reserve creation in the event of a return of the U.S. balance of payments to surplus (Johnson (1964)).

The measurement of reserve adequacy was further refined by including considerations other than the ratio of reserves to imports. Triffin (1947) concluded that variability of export receipts also influenced reserve demand. The Bellagio Group (Machlup and Malkiel (1964)) reached the same conclusion. Kenen and Yudin (1965), Kelly (1970), Flanders (1971), Clark (1970 a, 1970 b), Frenkel (1974 a, 1978, 1980 a, 1980 b), Frenkel and Jovanovic (1981), Frenkel and Hakkio (1980), and Bilson and Frenkel (1979, 1980) later used variability measures in studies of reserve demand. Brown (1964) noted that reserves are used to finance payments imbalances and therefore used the ratio of reserves to net external balance in his analysis of adequacy. Similarly, Machlup (1966) examined the ratio of reserves to the largest annual reserve loss. The reserves-to-imports ratio remained popular, however (Machlup (1966), Thorn (1967), Heller (1968), and International Monetary Fund (1970)). Finally, Triffin's assumption of a unitary elasticity of desired reserves with respect to trade volumes was examined by Rhomberg (1966) and by Flanders (1971), who found an elasticity of 0.6. Polak (1970) concluded that the elasticity was unlikely to be less than 0.8 in the early 1970s, and von Furstenberg (1982) found a value of 0.6 for the floating rate period.

Machlup (1966) was less willing than Triffin to conclude that a drastic reserve shortage was imminent. He was skeptical about the ability to draw firm judgments from the historical record, likening the demand for reserves to his wife's demand for clothing: a little more than last year. Machlup was criticized, however, for failure to distinguish between need and demand (Grubel (1971), Williamson (1973)). Brown (1964) was also reluctant to predict a reserve shortage, since the ratio of reserves to imbalances remained relatively stable over the period 1953-63. Cooper (1968) and Williamson (1973) noted, however, that the use of ratios of reserves to imbalances might lead to a situation in which a country unable to finance a deficit because of a severe reserve constraint—and, consequently, unable to incur payments imbalances for lack of finance—would obtain an infinite measure of adequacy. Johnson (1970 b) offered the opinion that a liquidity crisis was not a serious problem, since central bankers had learned the lender-of-last-resort role and would prevent a crisis by using temporary short-term credit and swaps. He pointed to the need, however, for a deliberate and managed expansion of basic reserves.

The ratio analyses mentioned thus far lack any rigorous basis in theory, as Grubel (1971) pointed out. The adequacy of any level of reserves depends on the monetary, fiscal, and exchange rate policies pursued by various countries. A country willing to use demand policies for external balance would need smaller reserves for a given level of imports, imbalances, etc. than would a country more concerned with obtaining internal balance. If a country decides to use the exchange rate to adjust to external imbalance, its demand for reserves decreases. In the extreme, an authority that does not intervene needs reserves only for future contingencies (Yeager (1959), Sohmen (1970)). Finally, Clower and Lipsey (1968) noted that the capital account plays an important role in payments imbalances. They concluded that measures of adequacy based on trade data were insufficient and that making an assessment of adequacy under a policy regime that encouraged speculation against the authorities was impossible without an understanding of the economics and psychology of speculative crises.

The Confidence Problem

Triffin's (1960) analysis of the instability of the gold-exchange standard, which became known as the confidence problem, may be summarized as follows. If the growth in reserve demand in excess of any increased gold supply continued to be satisfied by increased official dollar claims, net U.S. reserves would decline to a point where confidence in the fixed dollar price of gold would be undermined. Once this point was reached, a large-scale attempt to exchange dollars for gold would result in a collapse of the system. Kenen (1960) presented a formal model of the gold-exchange standard along Triffin's lines in which reserves consisted of only gold and dollars. Kenen's model demonstrated that the system is not necessarily unstable. The gold supply may grow at a slower rate than desired reserves without inducing collapse. A stable path is less likely if account is taken of private holdings of dollars. Furthermore, the system becomes unstable if desired reserves grow at a constant percentage rate (rather than by a constant absolute amount), unless the gold supply grows at the same percentage rate.

Kenen (1963) pointed out that it was in the joint interest of reserve holders to prevent a collapse of the system and that this should increase their willingness to accumulate dollar balances above levels dictated by normal portfolio considerations. Johnson (1967) agreed that avoidance of a crisis of confidence was of primary concern to the large countries. These ideas were formalized by Officer and Willett (1969,1970), who concluded that stability would be greater, the deeper the system went into the "crisis zone," since each agent would perceive that his actions could have a direct and sizeable effect on the system and, consequently, alter the probability of collapse.

Kenen (1963) also examined empirical evidence on the reserve composition of central banks and found that while several small countries appeared to participate in a gold run in the fourth quarter of 1960, the central banks of the major industrial countries appeared to exercise restraint. Greene (1968) found substantial evidence of a move toward restraint by major industrial countries after 1960. Officer (1974) tested the Officer-Willett model and again found strong evidence of restraint, which peaked in 1964. He then offered an interpretation of this restraint as a "bribe" to the United States to engage in negotiations on the reform of the international monetary system. It appears, then, that both portfolio considerations and political considerations influenced the gold-conversion decision of central banks prior to the Rio agreement. These political factors increased the stability of the gold-exchange standard. However, as Officer suggested, the political restraint may have been linked with attempts to find a durable solution to the confidence problem.

Asymmetries

The third concern expressed in the literature involved the asymmetries in the (then) existing system. The first of these was an asymmetry between the United States and the rest of the world. If dollar balances were accumulated as the United States ran an official settlements deficit (whether or not the accumulators were reluctant), the United States would face no reserve constraint in the formulation of its monetary and fiscal policies. Other countries, however, would face a reserve loss if their demand management were overly expansionary. This asymmetry was recognized by Rueff (1961 a and b). Emminger (1973) placed great emphasis on it. Triffin (1978) noted in retrospect that he had placed too much emphasis on the potential of a reserve shortage and insufficient emphasis on this asymmetry in his 1960 classic.

The problems that arise from this asymmetry might be mitigated if, as Mundell (1968) suggested, gold conversions by the countries other than the United States were to be used to signal their reaction to the policy stance of the United States. The assignment of policy roles implicit in this idea was found by Mundell to lead to possible instability, however. In addition, this sort of signaling behavior is contrary to the evidence developed by Kenen, Greene, and Officer concerning restraint in gold conversion.

The absence of a reserve constraint was recognized by Mundell (1968), Whitman (1969), and Niehans (1973), among others, to imply that world aggregate demand is primarily determined by U.S. policy. Despres, Kindleberger, and Salant (1966) summarized the central role of the United States by stating that U.S. policy determined the general level of world interest rates, while other countries could only influence capital flows by altering their interest differentials with the dollar.

The absence of a reserve constraint on the United States reflected the evolution of the international monetary system toward a dollar standard rather than a gold-exchange standard. Accumulation of dollar balances increased to such an extent that the confidence problem ruled out even the gold conversions that would have occurred under a smoothly functioning gold-exchange standard. Had gold conversions occurred regularly without threatening the stability of the international monetary system, the United States would, in fact, have faced a reserve (gold) constraint.

The view of reserve creation implicit in the preceding discussion (as characterized by Williamson (1973)) treats the supply of dollar reserves as determined by U.S. policy and as independent of the reserve accumulation desires of the rest of the world. Johnson (1964); Kindleberger (1965); Despres, Kindleberger, and Salant (1966); McKinnon (1969); and Krause (1970) argued that the U.S. official settlements deficit was primarily determined by the portfolio decisions and reserve-accumulation desires of the rest of the world. This theory of U.S. deficits under a de facto dollar standard was termed a demand-oriented theory by Aliber (1969 a), as opposed to the supply-oriented theories implicit in the work of Triffin and others. Aliber examined the evidence accumulated during the 1960s and found that it supported the demand-oriented approaches. Machlup (1968 b) and Williamson (1971) found that the evidence supported the supply-oriented theories. While the demand-oriented approach might, at times, have had merit, Williamson (1977 b) made the observation that the large U.S. deficits in the early 1970s resulted from a relaxation of monetary policy in the United States and not from a sudden desire on the part of other countries to increase reserve holdings.

The discussion of supply-determined versus demand-determined reserve accumulation, while possibly useful in analyzing specific historical episodes, is somewhat misleading. A more general-equilibrium view would attribute observed deficits to policies pursued in both the United States and other countries. Such a view was adopted by Mundell (1971, chapter 16). One point derived from the demand-oriented theories deserves emphasis, however. The inability of countries to engage in gold conversion on a large scale without threatening the stability of the system severely limited their ability to impose any constraint on U.S. policy. This point is important to keep in mind when analyzing the shortcomings of the gold-exchange standard, regardless of whether, at any particular point during the 1960s, the official settlements deficit desired by the United States differed from the desired reserve accumulation of the rest of the world.

The second asymmetry involved the assignment of responsibility for adjustment to payments imbalances. In the absence of agreed guidelines, deficit countries bore the primary responsibility for adjustment, as they faced a loss of reserves (Cooper (1970) and Roper (1972), among others). This asymmetry resulted from the ability of a surplus country to sterilize its reserve accumulation and thereby avoided the automatic adjustment provided by an increase in its monetary base. Wilms (1971), Argy and Kouri (1974), Herring and Marston (1977), and Obstfeld (1980 b) have provided evidence that a policy of systematic sterilization was pursued by the Federal Republic of Germany during the 1960s. Argy and Kouri (1974) found that a policy of sterilization was also followed in Italy and the Netherlands during this period. While sterilization allows a monetary authority to insulate the monetary base from the effects of payments imbalances in the short run, Obstfeld (1980 a) has concluded that, in general, sterilization is not a feasible long-run policy. The 1969 revaluation of the deutsche mark provides evidence of the inability of a monetary authority to sterilize persistent imbalances successfully.

Plans for Reform

Triffin (1960) set forth a detailed proposal for the reform of the international monetary system in which the Fund would play a central role in the creation and management of international liquidity. The plan modified Keynes's (1943) proposal for an international clearing union and was, in turn, followed by a series of derivative proposals. The proposals all envisage an expanded role for the Fund. Under several plans, the Fund would create additional deposit liabilities that would be accepted by central banks as part of their reserves. Machlup (1963) provided a detailed analysis of the various plans.

The Keynes Plan involved the creation of deposits in Bancor, a new international currency unit, at the (proposed) International Clearing Union (ICU). Bancor would have a fixed (but adjustable) price in terms of gold, and Bancor deposits would be used by central banks only for transfer to other central banks. Currencies would not be permitted as part of reserves. Bancor deposits could be created or augmented by sales of gold to the ICU or by the use of overdraft privileges by deficit countries. Each country would be assigned a quota, which would set an upper limit on the country's use of the overdraft privilege. These quotas would be adjusted annually as foreign trade increased. Both overdrafts and credit balances would be subject to charges determined by the relationship between (positive or negative) Bancor balances and a country's quota. In addition to overdrafts, a deficit country could acquire Bancor in an active credit market for these claims. Girton (1974), drawing an analogy to the real-bills doctrine, pointed out that tying reserve creation to a nominal magnitude, such as the value of trade, would lead to instability.

The Triffin Plan (1960) differed from the Keynes Plan, in that it allowed for a more deliberate expansion of reserve assets through open-market operations by an expanded International Monetary Fund (XIMF). An upward limit on reserve creation of 3 to 5 percent per annum would be set. Initial (interest-bearing) deposits would be created through sales of gold and foreign exchange to the XIMF. The confidence problem would be overcome as holders of reserve currencies (dollars and sterling) exchanged their balances for XIMF deposits. In addition, an initial minimum proportion (20 percent) of reserves to be held in XIMF balances would be established. The Triffin Plan thus provided for both a controlled but steady growth in liquidity and a substitute for reserve currencies in central bank portfolios.

Stamp (1958) suggested the creation of International Monetary Fund certificates that would be accepted by central banks as payment from other central banks. These certificates would be distributed to developing countries, thus providing an early proposal of a link between reserve creation and development finance. Machlup (1963) pointed out that these certificates would be much less saleable than the XIMF investments envisaged by Triffin, exposing the Fund to the risk of loss on its investments. Day (1960) and Angell (1961) proposed modified Keynes-Triffin plans according to which initial deposits at the XIMF would be voluntary rather than required. Harrod (1961) discussed several proposals along these lines, none of which he endorsed. The proposals discussed thus far all involve an expanded International Monetary Fund whose liabilities represent reserve assets of central banks and are intended to replace reserve currencies.

Bernstein (1963, 1965) proposed that a limited group of key-currency countries create Composite Reserve Units (CRUs) by depositing their currencies at the Fund. These would become a supplement to gold, and the participants would be obliged to accept CRUs up to a specified proportion of their gold stocks. This plan essentially involved mutual assistance among the central banks of the major industrial countries, with the Fund acting as a trustee. The Ossola Report (Group of Ten (1965)) discussed a

CRU proposal similar to Bernstein's but without Fund participation. Similar plans for mutual assistance were proposed earlier by Zolotas (1961), Bernstein (1962), and Jacobsson (1962) (described in Machlup (1963) and Hawkins and Rolfe (1965)). These plans all involved extension of the (then) existing system through additional liquidity creation and resemble the GAB.

Roosa (1962) advanced a plan for the extension of the existing system involving the expanded use of swap networks and the announcement that the United States would move toward a multiple reserve currency system by acquiring foreign exchange when the U.S. overall balance moved back into surplus. Zolotas (1961) and Lutz (1962, 1963) also made proposals favoring the establishment of a multiple reserve currency system. Roosa (1965) proposed that the use of long-term loans between surplus and deficit central banks be expanded and that access to these loans be formalized. Hawkins and Rolfe (1965) characterized the Roosa proposal as extending Roosa bonds to a multiple-reserve-currency system. While the proposals for reinforcing the gold-exchange standard responded to concerns of inadequate liquidity growth, they failed to deal adequately with the confidence problem or with the fundamental asymmetry between the United States and the rest of the world entailed by that system.

A third set of proposals involved a uniform increase in par values or a revaluation of gold as part of a return to a gold standard (Rueff (1961 a and b), Heilperin (1962)). Harrod (1953, 1961, 1966) doubted the feasibility of alternative schemes and supported the revaluation of gold as a means of allowing more expansionary credit policies to be pursued. Gilbert (1968) and Oppenheimer (1969) emphasized the advantages of monetizing the flow of new gold at a higher price rather than the effects of revaluing the existing stock of monetary gold. Mundell (1971), however, questioned whether such changes in nominal reserves would be effective in raising the real stock of reserves or would, instead, raise the level of world prices proportionately.

Critics of the proposed revaluation of gold pointed out that a simple revaluation would make no sense unless it were part of a general program for the abolition of the reserve-currency system (Mundell (1973)). With the value of the U.S. gold stock augmented, the confidence problem would ease for a short while, but would certainly not go away. Williamson (1977 b) made the point that restoration of a gold standard is unlikely to be successful, since, unless confidence is in question, countries prefer interest-bearing dollar balances to non-interest-bearing gold. Machlup (1964) raised the possibility that the revaluation of gold would be repeated, generating speculation on gold price changes. The Bellagio Group (Machlup and Malkiel (1964)) noted that this speculation could result in a "run" on gold that would make the speculation self-fulfilling. Hawkins and Rolfe (1965) questioned the credibility of any guarantee that further revaluations would not be forthcoming, since there was no guarantee that gold production would keep pace with liquidity demand in the future. Gold revaluation, like reserve supplements, would at best have solved only the problem of reserve inadequacy. Both the confidence problem and the fundamental asymmetry of the gold-exchange standard would persist unless a full gold standard were restored.

II. RIO AGREEMENT

As Machlup (1968 a) pointed out, the Rio agreement creating special drawing rights was reached despite conflicting national aims and goals. According to Machlup, the French opposed the creation of a new reserve asset, while the Anglo-American position favored the creation and allocation of assets to be held by monetary authorities as owned reserves with no repayment obligation. A detailed account of the negotiations leading up to the Rio agreement has been provided by Stephen Cohen (1970). The product of this political compromise differed substantially from the plans for reform described earlier in this paper. The following section deals with assessments of the ability of the newly created SDR to alleviate various problems of the gold-exchange standard.

Reserve Adequacy and Control of Liquidity Creation

The ability to allocate SDRs allowed the Fund to supplement international liquidity if this were judged necessary in the event of a return by the United States to an official-settlements surplus. Conversely, SDR allocations could not cope with problems of liquidity control implied by U.S. deficits (Williamson (1977 b), Willett (1980 a)). McKinnon (1969), Johnson (1970 a), and Hirsch (1971, 1973) have pointed out that as long as SDRs and reserve currencies are held in central bank portfolios, allocations cannot control the overall level of reserves but can only influence the composition of reserves between SDRs and other reserve assets. The liquidity explosion of 1971-73 provided strong evidence on this point. While the newly-created SDR could have provided a solution to the problem of inadequate liquidity growth under the gold-exchange standard discussed by Triffin in 1960, allocations of SDRs were discouraged, after the first basic period ended in 1972, by the unforeseen problems posed by the rapid growth of international liquidity in the early seventies.

The SDR agreement also failed to remove the asymmetries of the gold-exchange standard. Instead, the evolution toward a dollar standard continued (McKinnon (1969)). Willett (1980 a) concluded that the dollar was already de facto inconvertible into gold by the time of the Rio meetings. In March 1968, a two-tier gold market was created, and official conversions into gold were regarded as acts of political hostility to the United States. The perception was widespread that any major conversions would result in the United States closing the gold window. Accumulation of dollar reserves continued despite some reluctance on the part of the accumulators (Williamson (1977 b)). The last vestige of a reserve constraint on the United States was eliminated when it officially suspended convertibility in August 1971. The large increase in the U.S. balance of payments deficit that occurred during the early 1970s was reflected in the accumulation of official dollar claims in foreign central bank portfolios.

The Confidence Problem

The SDR agreement and subsequent allocations failed to solve the confidence problem. Indeed, had SDR use not been prohibited in the absence of balance of payments need, SDRs might have provided an additional primary reserve asset for reserve switching (Machlup (1968 a), Williamson (1973, 1977 b)). The problems of a system in which gold, SDRs, and reserve currencies coexisted was addressed by Aliber (1967), who raised concerns of instability owing to Gresham's law. Similar issues were later discussed in Henry Goldstein (1969), Aliber (1969 b), and Hirsch (1971) and formalized in Makin (1972). One of the possibilities considered was that payment of interest, coupled with a gold-value guarantee, would make the SDR a superior asset compared with one of the others in reserve portfolios, causing the inferior asset to disappear from portfolios. Henry Goldstein (1974) pointed out that under the Articles of Agreement, the use of SDRs required balance of payments need; this limited the extent of reserve substitution, and therefore concerns about the operation of Gresham's law were misplaced. Kenen (1980) and Willett (1980 a) argued that Gresham's law would not apply under a regime of freely floating exchange rates, since no attempt would be made to maintain a fixed (disequilibrium) set of exchange rates among the various reserve assets. Aliber (1973) discussed the problems that would arise in a system in which the SDR played an expanded role.

Further Proposals for Reform

The creation of an international monetary system based on a single reserve asset requires the solution of two problems (Williamson (1977 b)): first, what should the system look like and, second, how should the transition be achieved? As regards the first question, the main issue is the choice of the central reserve asset. One possible choice is gold. The case against gold has been made forcefully several times and is summarized in Williamson (1977 a, 1977 b) and Cooper (1982). Hirsch (1971, 1973) and Williamson (1973, 1977 a, 1977 b) also expressed doubts, based on Friedman's (1951) arguments, about the feasibility of maintaining a pure gold standard. Gold is costly to produce, and consequently there is always an incentive to find substitute reserve assets. Barro (1981) proposed a "monetary constitution" that would provide constraints on the behavior of a monetary authority and entail advance commitment to a long-run growth path of monetary aggregates. Such a system would provide the "discipline" of a gold standard without the resource costs of commodity reserves. Fischer (1982) provided a model that demonstrates that, from the point of view of a small country, the benefits derived from the "discipline" imposed by a monetary standard based on gold or foreign exchange must be weighed against the resulting seigniorage loss the country experiences and the deadweight welfare loss owing to the country's inability to choose an optimal rate of money growth.

Machlup (1968 a) and Fleming (1971) have described an SDR-based international monetary system. The creation of an SDR standard received important official support during the Fund's 1971 Annual Meetings. Anthony Barber, then the British Chancellor of the Exchequer, made a speech calling for the SDR to become the principal reserve asset, with reserve currency holdings limited to working balances and the remainder converted into SDRs through substitution. He also proposed that the SDR become the standard against which par values were expressed. Williamson (1977 b) emphasized that while this proposal was a slightly-revised version of the Triffin plan, it was of enormous political importance.

The transition to such a system, which would involve the reduction of reserve currency holdings in central bank portfolios, could be facilitated by the establishment of an account (at the Fund) in which countries would pool their reserves and hold deposits as their primary reserves (Mundell (1969)). Machlup (1968 a) pointed to the inconsistency of funding as existing overhang while allowing further accumulation of reserve currencies. He therefore proposed prohibition of further accumulation of reserve currencies as a final solution to the confidence problem. Machlup (1968 a) also proposed that gold be removed from central bank portfolios and deposited at the Fund in return for reserve deposits in order to prevent a confidence problem that could arise in a system based on both gold and the SDR. The Fund reserve settlement account could later sell gold to industrial users and private consumers when its price rose above $35 per ounce.

Hirsch (1973), van Ypersele (1977), Sacchetti (1979), and Kenen (1980) have pointed out that certain technical changes, such as an increase in the rate of interest on SDRs (as later adopted by the Fund), would be necessary in order to enhance the attractiveness of the SDR sufficiently to allow it to play a larger role in reserve portfolios. Makin (1974) presented a formal model of the equilibrium interest rate on hypothetical SDRs with a constant real value. As emphasized by van Ypersele (1977), a system in which enhanced SDRs were accepted freely, rather than with designation, would make the SDR more attractive. Kenen (1980) and UNDP/UNCTAD (1981) also pointed to changes that would make SDRs more freely transferable. Both proposed that the practice of designation be phased out over time (as it since has). The UNDP/UNCTAD (1981) report also suggested the immediate removal of the requirement of balance of payments need. Additional details and recommendations are found in Chapter 12, "Further Improvements in the Existing SDR," later in this volume. Chrystal (1978) attributed the SDR's failure to make progress toward becoming the principal reserve asset of the international financial system to its being a less attractive asset than the dollar and suggested reforms to make it more desirable. More fundamental questions have been raised by Mundell (1971), who argued that a pure fiduciary SDR would not be widely accepted owing to its lacking the "psychological elements of trust and confidence based on historical considerations."

The creation of a substitution account to fund the replacement of reserve currencies by SDRs was discussed by Fleming (1971, 1972) and Hirsch (1973). Gold (1980) provided a summary of the history of substitution proposals. Aliber (1973) discussed political problems involved in the creation of a reserve substitution account and technical problems in designing a system in which SDRs would become the principal reserve asset. The problems involved in removing incentives to accumulate reserve currencies and to switch among reserve assets were given particular attention.

Williamson (1977 b) discussed the difficulties experienced in reaching agreement on a substitution account during the period 1971–74 owing to divergent national interests. A Triffin-like account was not feasible owing to the reluctance of the United States to eliminate the reserve-currency role of the dollar. In addition, developing countries desired the freedom to switch among assets in order to improve the yields on their reserve portfolios. Additional problems existed with less far-reaching proposals. First, Williamson (1977 b) summarized the Indian position as expressing concern that the increased supply of SDRs obtained through substitution would lead to a reduction in the size of subsequent allocations. Second, the United States favored a once-and-for-all substitution because it feared that the continuously available, European-backed account would create opportunities for one-way speculation against the dollar, giving rise to U.S. exchange losses if its obligations to the account were SDR-denominated. A continuously available account in which reverse substitution was possible would create the same potential for reserve switching that existed under the gold-exchange standard.

Willett (1980 a) agreed that a reversible account would have increased incentives for reserve switching. In addition, an open-ended, or continuously available, account would obligate a reserve center to swap SDRs for liabilities it had acquired in intervention initiated by others, possibly without regard to the reserve center's interest. However, a once-and-for-all account would satisfy only present (and not future) desired reserve accumulation. Willett therefore suggested a nonreversible account that would be open ended and accompanied by increased Fund surveillance of intervention. Only reserves acquired through Fund-sanctioned intervention would be eligible for substitution.

Kenen (1981) investigated potential imbalances that could arise in a substitution account owing to a difference in the currency denomination of the account's assets and liabilities. A substitution account would have dollar-denominated assets and SDR-denominated liabilities. A flow deficit (an excess of interest payments over interest income) in the account would arise if the dollar interest rate were lower than the SDR interest rate. A stock deficit (an excess of liabilities over assets) could arise as a result of either persistent flow imbalances or a depreciation of the dollar relative to the SDR. In the latter case, if the account were liquidated, participants could not be paid in full. Using simulations of a hypothetical substitution account begun in the mid-1960s, Kenen found that persistent flow deficits and stock deficits resulting from depreciation of the U.S. dollar would have been sizeable. Participation would have been beneficial to depositors and costly to the United States whether the costs were shared or were borne fully by the United States. The allocation of financial responsibility for these imbalances has not yet been resolved.

Hirsch (1973) argued that a full SDR system—along the lines proposed by Triffin (1960), Machlup (1968 a), and others—in which exchange rates were pegged required policy decisions to be more highly integrated than was politically feasible or, in his view, desirable. The adoption of such a system would have involved a move toward a world central bank when prevailing sentiment was toward greater policy autonomy and greater flexibility of exchange rates. He went on to outline what he considered to be a politically feasible system in which exchange rates would become more flexible, with the SDR serving as the intervention currency. Intervention would occur according to guidelines, with clearly defined responsibilities agreed upon by all participants. A substitution account for reserve currencies would be set up along with a voluntary parallel reserve substitution facility for gold. The system would contain provisions discouraging any accumulation of reserve currencies.

III. RESERVE NEEDS UNDER MANAGED FLOATING

Problems concerning the creation and control of international liquidity received less attention after the mid-seventies than before managed floating became the accepted order. Several authors have concluded that when exchange rates are flexible, controlling international reserves plays a less important role in determining the average inflation rate across countries than when rates were fixed, since countries are less constrained in domestic credit creation. Other authors have noted that the conventional confidence problem no longer exists, although some have expressed concern over the potential effects of reserve-currency switching in official portfolios. These concerns have given rise to proposals for a substitution account in the Fund to help stabilize exchange rates, although doubts have been expressed about whether creation of a substitution account would lead to achievement of this objective. Considerable attention has been paid to the functioning of the managed floating system and to the volatility of exchange rates that has been experienced since 1973. This concern has led to proposals for more coordination of government policies and for a more tightly controlled international monetary system with well-defined exchange market intervention rules. However, many observers have remained skeptical about the desirability and political feasibility of such a system.

While, in principle, greater exchange rate flexibility should reduce the need for reserves, Williamson (1976) and Knight and Salop (1977) presented evidence that intervention during 1973–76 was substantial, especially in the period shortly after the move to floating. Bilson and Frenkel (1979) and Frenkel (1978, 1980 a, and 1980 b) have found that reserve-holding behavior showed little change after the adoption of managed floating. Von Furstenberg (1982) found reserve holding under floating is still linked to fundamentals, including money supply and trade developments. Heller and Knight (1978) provided evidence that intervention arrangements have influenced reserve portfolio composition.

Several authors have studied the determinants of exchange market intervention. They have found that central banks have attempted to smooth short-run fluctuations in exchange rates. Branson and others (1977), Black (1979), Dornbusch (1980), and O'Toole (1981) have presented evidence of leaning against the wind in the Federal Republic of Germany's intervention policy. Quirk (1977), Black (1979), and Dornbusch (1980) found the same to be true of Japanese policy. Similar findings have been reported by Black (1979) for the United Kingdom, Italy, France, and Belgium; by O'Toole (1981) for the United States; by Longworth (1980) for Canada; and by Dornbusch (1980) for the major industrial countries as a group. Exchange market intervention has been used as a component of anti-inflationary policies in the Federal Republic of Germany, according to Black (1979). Dornbusch (1980) was unable to find any evidence of intervention aimed at promoting competitiveness in the countries he studied, but Black (1979) found evidence of competitiveness targets in Belgium, Canada, Japan, the Netherlands, and the United States. Exchange rates, then, have not ceased to be of concern to policymakers, since some have used exchange rate policy to promote competitiveness while others have used exchange rate policy to influence domestic inflation rates.

The removal of the obligation to intervene has, in principle, allowed monetary authorities to exert greater control over the monetary base by bringing its foreign source component under their control. The degree to which this potential control of the high-powered money stock has given monetary authorities additional autonomy to conduct policy has received considerable attention. The general conclusion reached is that the move to flexible exchange rates has increased somewhat the ability of monetary authorities to pursue independent policies, but that domestic economies have in no way been insulated from either real or financial disturbances abroad (Willett (1982), Morris Goldstein (1980)). Bryant (1980) concluded that the increased ability to pursue independent policies has not led to greater "controllability" of the domestic economy; Mussa (1979 b) demonstrated that the mobility of capital provides an important mechanism for the international transmission of disturbances. Willett (1982) concluded that foreign monetary disturbances are likely to have significant effects in the short run, even under floating exchange rates, especially if these disturbances are unanticipated. Floating, he concluded, however, does provide greater insulation from foreign nominal disturbances in the long run, allowing countries to choose their own trend inflation rates.

Since floating exchange rates have not insulated economies from external disturbances, monetary policy can be used for internal balance only if a monetary authority is prepared to accept the exchange rate consequences of its policy. Kindleberger (1969) argued that this was unlikely to be the case, since "along with one more variable [the money supply] there is one more target—the exchange rate." McKinnon (1981) concluded that the pursuit of exchange rate targets has been an important determinant of monetary policy; countries have been unwilling to allow their exchange rates to be determined solely by the market's reaction to external developments or shocks and have therefore intervened extensively, which has caused them to lose control over their money supplies. Mussa (1981) found that exchange rate movements have initiated important changes in monetary policy when the exchange rate was viewed by the authorities to have moved out of acceptable bounds. Black (1983) studied the determinants of monetary policy in ten industrial countries and found that internal and external factors were both important, although their relative importance differed among countries. The effect of external factors was found to be less important during the floating-rate period than during the fixed-rate period in Belgium, the Federal Republic of Germany, Japan, and the United States, indicating that greater monetary independence has accompanied greater exchange rate flexibility.

Since both exchange rates and money supplies have been found to be policy targets, questions concerning the use of sterilized intervention have naturally arisen. Artus (1976), Branson and others (1977), and Obstfeld (1983) have all found that separate exchange rate and money supply targets were pursued systematically through the use of sterilized intervention in the Federal Republic of Germany during the recent floating-rate period. Willett (1980 a) concluded that sterilized intervention has been used for short-run management during the floating-rate period, but that it has played a limited role. Obstfeld (1983) found the exchange-rate effect of sterilized intervention in the Federal Republic of Germany during recent years to be much smaller than that of intervention affecting the monetary base. Mussa (1981) emphasized that any effects of sterilized intervention are limited to the short run. In the long run, either the exchange rate target or the money supply target must be abandoned.

Haberler (1977 a and b) has argued that the control of international liquidity is less important under generalized floating, since no clear link exists between reserves and inflation. Under a regime of floating rates, a country may determine its own long-run inflation rate by setting a growth rate for domestic credit and then allowing the exchange rate to adjust to any resulting excess demand or excess supply in the exchange market. Reserve losses do not offset domestic credit growth that exceeds or falls short of "world" rates of money growth. Williamson (1980) reached the same conclusion, noting that no contraction in domestic credit is required when reserves become scarce. Khan (1975) found that reserve growth lagged behind inflation in the industrial countries during 1973-77. The reverse relationship was found to hold during 1957-72. He also found the observed relationship in the developing countries to be contemporaneous during both periods. Williamson (1982) pointed out that, provided a monetary authority accepts the exchange rate movements consistent with its money supply target, reserves and domestic credit are substitute tools for attaining that target. Willett (1980 a) has also concluded that control of international liquidity is only loosely related to control of inflation and that SDR allocations are therefore unlikely to be inflationary.

The abandonment of fixed parities, according to Williamson (1977 b), provided the final resolution of the confidence problem. Haberler (1977 a) agreed that the conventional confidence problem no longer exists but noted that confidence in the stability of individual currencies—particularly the dollar, owing to its widespread use as a reserve currency—may still be important. Willett (1977) reached the same conclusions as Haberler but found concerns about changes in official and private asset preferences to be of a different order of magnitude from the concerns underlying the conventional confidence problem. Kenen (1977) also expressed concern over the consequences of a widespread attempt to unload dollar balances following a decline in confidence in the exchange value of the dollar. The substitution of SDRs for dollars in reserve portfolios, he argued, would reduce the potential for this sort of instability.

Questions have been raised, however, about the ability of a substitution account to stabilize exchange rates. Willett (1980 a) reasoned that owing to the high degree of capital mobility in world markets, the potential pressure on the exchange value of the dollar is only loosely related to any "overhang" in official dollar claims. Von Furstenberg (1981) also concluded that major disturbances are unlikely to result from changes in official holdings of reserve center currencies in a multiple reserve currency system, since private holdings dwarf official holdings. Roosa (1982) conservatively estimated that private claims in Euromarkets (broadly defined as extraterritorial money markets) outweigh official claims by three to one. Williamson (1981) concluded from data on the currency composition of aggregate reserve portfolios of industrial and nonindustrial countries that, on the whole, central banks increased their holdings of currencies that, though they were depreciating, had appreciated relative to trend. He interpreted this as evidence that official portfolio shifts have been destabilizing. Dornbusch (1982) pointed out that official speculation against a weakening dollar could still occur at the margin, even if a larger proportion of reserves were "locked up" in SDRs, and that locking reserves up would aggravate matters if the dollar were rising. He concluded that the substitution account is "one gimmick we can do without."

A survey of central bankers conducted by the Group of Thirty (1982) found that those officials almost uniformly expected the role of the SDR in the international monetary system to remain modest. Among the perceived disadvantages of the SDR as a reserve asset were the acceptance and designation rules, the balance of payments need requirement, the lack of transferability to the private sector, and its lack of usability as an intervention asset. Some pointed to the lower yield on the official SDR compared with that on similarly composed Eurocurrency bundles. Others found that its currency composition was inappropriate for the composition of their foreign trade or external debt.

Kenen (1981) asked what steps could be taken to make the SDR the principal reserve asset in the international financial system. He noted that, apart from its role as the Fund's unit of account, the SDR was not being widely used as a unit of account in international transactions, as a standard against which par values were defined, or as an intervention currency, and concluded that the extensive changes required to achieve the status of principal reserve asset might not be worth the effort and costs involved in making them. In addition to changes that would make the SDR more marketable, such as phasing out designation, Kenen (1980) concluded that large-scale substitution and restrictions on accumulation of reserve-currency holdings would be required. Mandatory asset settlement would limit reserve-currency accumulation but would not be feasible under the current system of managed floating. Asset settlement would limit the freedom of choice of a reserve center by obliging it to exchange SDRs for liabilities it had acquired through intervention by other official institutions over which the reserve center had no control. Williamson (1977 b) pointed out that a reserve center is likely to be reluctant to provide SDRs in exchange for liabilities that were acquired in exchange-rate-support operations of which it disapproves. The successful substitution of SDRs for reserve currencies would thus require more fundamental changes in the international monetary system, including, as a minimum, more clearly defined intervention rules.

Kenen (1981) also suggested that increased private use of the SDR and the creation of markets in SDR-denominated assets would be necessary for the SDR to play a more central role in the international financial system. Some members of the UNDP/UNCTAD committee reporting on measures to strengthen the SDR proposed encouraging increased private holdings of SDRs and the creation of a Fund-administered clearinghouse in SDR claims. Without such an increase in private SDR holdings and growing markets in SDRs, the SDR would be unlikely to assume a central role as an intervention asset or as a standard for the definition of par values.

The recent experience with floating exchange rates has led observers to emphasize the short-run volatility of exchange rates ((Mussa (1979 a), Artus and Young (1979), and Frenkel (1981)). Day-to-day and week-to-week exchange rate changes have frequently been large and have often been reversed (Williamson (1977 b) and Willett (1980 a)). Flood (1981) found observed volatility to be consistent with models characterized by flexible prices that emphasize the role of new information (Frenkel (1976, 1981)) and models that emphasize the effects of efficient asset (exchange) markets and sticky prices in the goods market (Dornbusch (1976)).

Recent exchange rate volatility has been viewed by some as excessive. Williamson (1977 b) has argued that such volatility inevitably depresses foreign trade. The Brandt Commission (Brandt and others (1980)) accepted the harmful effects of exchange rate volatility as a premise. However, Willett (1977, 1980 a), Williamson (1977 b), and Artus and Young (1979) found no evidence to support the proposition that exchange rate volatility has reduced trade volumes. J. Carter Murphy (1979) pointed out that during 1973–77, trade volumes grew twice as fast as production. The reason given by most analysts for the absence of any measurable effect of short-run exchange rate volatility on trade volumes is the existence of forward markets, which allow traders to hedge their exchange risks (Williamson (1977 b), Willett (1977, 1980 a and b), and Artus and Young (1979)). Williamson (1977 b) suggested that the evidence was inconclusive, however, since insufficient time had elapsed to assess the long-run effects on investment. Willett (1977) concluded that floating has had positive long-run effects by curbing the persistent overvaluation of exchange rates that characterizes a fixed-rate world with divergent national policies.

Dissatisfaction with the volatility of floating exchange rates has led some to propose coordinated exchange market intervention to help smooth fluctuations. Williamson (1977 b) placed great emphasis on the importance of well-defined guidelines for exchange rate adjustment. In his view, the ultimate breakdown of the fixed-rate system resulted from the inability to devise a crisis-free means of adjusting exchange rates in a world of high capital mobility. He reiterated his longstanding proposal (Williamson (1965)) for exchange rate flexibility in the form of a crawling peg and described a possible set of intervention rules in the form of the reference-rate system of Ethier and Bloomfield (1975). Kenen (1977) suggested that specific rules governing intervention be established. Coordinated exchange rate management is also an important part of the Brandt Commission's (Brandt and others (1980, 1981)) proposals for monetary reform.

Others (notably Haberler (1977 a) and Willett (1977)) have been skeptical of the Ethier-Bloomfield proposal and other proposals for increased exchange market intervention. Haberler (1977 a) argued that, given the extreme uncertainties during 1973–77, it was not surprising that exchange rates were so volatile. He and Willett (1977) both concluded that exchange rate volatility was a symptom of turmoil and uncertainty in the underlying economic environment, rather than a cause of uncertainty. Their arguments apply equally well to 1978–81. Haberler concluded that it is extremely difficult both for policymakers and for private exchange market participants to identify an "appropriate" exchange rate in an uncertain environment. Intervention was therefore likely to be misguided. Willett (1980 a and b, 1982) agreed that the best way to achieve more stable exchange rates was to adopt more stable policies. He also concluded (Willett (1982)) that economists and policymakers lacked sufficient knowledge to identify unnecessary exchange rate changes ex ante except perhaps when the exchange rate was far "out of bounds." Mussa (1981) found identifying proper circumstances for intervention extremely difficult and pointed to a general inability to define an "economically-appropriate exchange rate." Dornbusch (1981) emphasized that, unlike day-to-day exchange rate changes, medium-run swings (lasting two or three quarters) have had important effects on inflation and real activity; he concluded, therefore, that it may be beneficial to dampen them. However, he judged the swings to be too long and the pressures behind them too strong for intervention to be successful. In addition, they were found to be distinguishable from changes in the equilibrium real exchange rate only with the benefit of hindsight.

Greater coordination of monetary policies is widely held to be a necessary condition for greater exchange rate stability (Willett (1982)). McKinnon (1974) and Williamson (1982) have both stressed the importance of coordination in monetary policies. Whitman (1976) termed the level of policy coordination experienced under floating exchange rates "negative" coordination—that is, coordination aimed at avoiding beggar-thy-neighbor policies. She argued, however, that a higher level of coordination, which has proven difficult to attain, is necessary to avoid the pursuit of contradictory policies. Willett (1980 b) agreed that so long as countries are interdependent, policy coordination remains a live issue but also noted that determination of the optimal degree of integration is a difficult problem that still lacks a solution. Polak (1981) cautioned that "once it is realized that international decision making is indeed very difficult, one can hardly argue that any economic policies that have 'significant international effect' should be brought into harmonization."

Should the requisite degree of stability and coordination of policies be established and a symmetric set of intervention rules be adopted, the intervention currency and reserve currency would need to be established. The benefits of an international reserve and intervention asset such as the SDR, which were described previously in connection with the Bretton Woods system, remain important. Willett (1980 a) concluded that the arguments for an SDR-based system are exactly the same as those for a centralized international financial system with tight international controls. In addition, if the United States had intervention requirements that were symmetric with those of the rest of the world, it is possible that under a dollar standard, the U.S. deficit implied by intervention requirements would be inconsistent with the reserve demand of the rest of the world. This, of course, is just the "(N-1) problem" in the setting of managed floating (Williamson (1977 b)). The case for an international intervention and international reserve asset is strengthened by Niehans' (1976) point that such an asset would minimize the effect of intervention by one country on the national monetary policies of other countries. Willett (1977) speculated, however, that countries would be unwilling to give up whatever degree of autonomy they had gained in recent years, so that any movement toward a centrally controlled international financial system would be unlikely.

In addition to proposals for increased intervention, recent exchange rate volatility has given rise to interest in using currency bundles in denominating international trade. Schulenburg (1981) presented a theoretical model of the choice of currency bundles. He found that an optimal bundle would assign large weights to the currencies of both trading partners, so that SDR-denominated trade would be inferior to trade denominated in other (hypothetical) bundles. The availability of forward foreign exchange markets was found, however, to make the choice of a bundle irrelevant. Helleiner (1981) advocated expanded use of SDR denomination in trade involving developing countries in order to reduce the exchange risk they bear. Since, for many of them, opportunities for hedging exchange risk are limited, Helleiner (1981) argued that the reduced real exchange rate volatility that could derive from greater use of SDR invoicing could be of great benefit. He also pointed to scattered evidence suggesting that the external trade of developing countries, unlike that of developed countries, was impaired by exchange rate volatility.

IV. THE LINK BETWEEN SPECIAL DRAWING RIGHTS AND DEVELOPMENT ASSISTANCE

The substitution of fiat money for commodity money involves a social saving, since commodity money is costly to produce. In the case of a gold standard, the resource costs have been estimated to be substantial (Oppenheimer (1969) and Laidler (1969)). Hart (1966) and Grubel (1965) estimated the cost of a "commodity-reserve currency" based on a stockpiled bundle of commodities to be greater, owing to larger storage costs and depreciation, than that of a gold-backed monetary system. The use of national fiat money and SDRs as reserves both represent a saving, although its distribution is, of course, very different for the two types of assets. The Brandt Commission (Brandt and others (1981)) pointed to political considerations in favor of an SDR-based system. Such a system would involve broadly based participation in the decision-making process and would provide for greater equity in the distribution of seigniorage (the net value of resources accruing to the issuer of money) than would a multicurrency reserve system.

The distribution of the social saving under various plans has been analyzed by Machlup (1965, 1968 a) and Grubel (1969) and was summarized by Williamson (1973) as follows. To the extent that market rates of interest were paid on balances of fiat money, the social saving would be distributed as interest payments to net holders. If below-market rates were paid, the saving would accrue as seigniorage to the first recipients. Prior to the increase in the SDR rate of interest in 1981, the saving accrued mainly to net users of SDRs. Grubel (1972), Williamson (1972, 1973), Hirsch (1973), Murphy and von Furstenberg (1981), and UNDP/UNCTAD (1981) have all pointed out that an element of seigniorage might still exist if the SDR paid an interest rate equal to that on government or interbank debt in the countries whose currencies make up the SDR, since most countries would find themselves unable to borrow at such favorable rates. While allocated SDRs held as reserves would be virtually costless to participants, reserves would be borrowed at a rate determined by the borrower's credit rating while earning a lower deposit rate. Hirsch (1973) also speculated that many countries might prefer owing the SDR account to owing a large commercial bank.

The case for paying a market rate of interest on SDRs has involved three arguments. Doing so would minimize the transfer of real reserves from net holders to net users. Machlup (1968 a) argued that one first principle of liquidity creation is the absence of long-run transfers of real reserves. Williamson (1977 b) argued that distributional neutrality is desirable to preserve the stature of the SDR as a reserve asset and to prevent the issue of SDR allocation from causing conflict between probable net users and probable net holders. Hirsch's (1973) analysis of the likely evolution of an SDR-exchange standard if net holdings of SDRs carried below-market rates provided an additional argument for the payment of market rates, according to Williamson (1973). SDRs would have to be preferable to reserve-currency balances if further acquisition of these balances were to be prevented. On the one hand, Johnson (1967) and Clark (1973) have argued that a socially optimal level of reserve holdings would result from the payment of market rates on SDR holdings. Scitovsky (1965), on the other hand, argued that payment of market rates would have the undesirable consequence of reducing the incentive for surplus countries to adjust.

The potential seigniorage gains from the creation of SDRs, whether resulting from below-market rates or simply from the spread between the relevant borrowing and lending rates, have led to several proposals for a link between SDR allocation and development aid. The earliest was that of Stamp (1958), who proposed creating Fund certificates and issuing them to developing countries. An interesting aspect of the Triffin plan (1960) is that a portion of open-market purchases by an expanded International Monetary Fund would involve World Bank bonds, thereby linking liquidity creation with development finance. A similar proposal may be found in the Keynes (1943) plan. One recommendation of the Brandt Commission (Brandt and others (1980)) was the creation of a World Development Fund

(WDF) to aid in the financing of economic development. Background papers contained proposals that reserves be created and allocated to the WDF to help provide resources. Proposals were also advanced that the WDF be granted exemption from the payment of interest on its use of these reserves. Haan (1971) and Park (1973) have provided summaries of the history of link proposals.

Grubel (1972) and Williamson (1977 b) argued that the existing system, under which the seigniorage remaining after the payment of interest is distributed in proportion to Fund quota, is distributionally neutral. To the extent that quotas measure the long-run demand for reserves, countries will tend to be neither long-run net users nor long-run net holders. Hawkins and Rangarajan (1970) concluded that quotas provided an inadequate criterion for SDR allocation, since the original quota formula reflected economic relationships during the prewar period and reserve holdings in 1943. Subsequent changes were found to have been based on political pressures rather than systematic analysis. Maynard and Bird (1975) found arguments concerning the appropriateness of quotas as a criterion for SDR allocation unrealistic. The Brandt Commission concluded that the use of the quota criterion was inappropriate, since quotas were based on the perceived economic and political importance of countries, not on prospective reserve needs.

Some proponents of the link have argued that developing countries suffer from greater instability in export earnings than do the developed countries, and distributing new reserves to them would provide a more equitable distribution of the adjustment burden (Benjamin Cohen (1966) and Marquez (1970)). Erb and Schiavo Campo (1969), Glezakos (1972), and Lawson (1974) have provided evidence that, on the whole, developing countries have a relatively large demand for reserves owing to their greater export instability. Using alternative models of reserve holdings, Hawkins and Rangarajan (1970) concluded that allocation according to quota is systematically disadvantageous to primary producing countries. The UNDP/ UNCTAD (1981) report suggested that since the need for reserves was relatively higher in developing countries than in developed countries, developing countries should receive allocation shares based upon 150 percent of their quotas, with the allocation shares of the developed countries reduced correspondingly.

Williamson (1973, 1977 b) found the most important argument for the establishment of a link to be egalitarianism. In the absence of compelling arguments against a link, more redistribution is to be preferred to less.

Several arguments have been advanced in opposition to the link. First, the link might undermine the integrity of the SDR in one of two ways. Pressures for allocations could lead to an undesirably rapid rate of reserve creation (Haberler (1971)). Large allocations would then be inflationary (Bauer (1973)). Fleming (1971) and Johnson (1972 a and b) argued that, on the contrary, the developed countries might try to restrain allocations unduly under the link. Haan (1971) agreed that the developed countries would restrain SDR creation, but he found this desirable. The potential inflationary consequences of the link have been estimated to be small by Maynard (1972, 1973) and Dornbusch (1981). However, the link might undermine the integrity of the SDR by increasing the probability of default on interest payments if all net users were low-income countries. Williamson (1972, 1973, 1977 b) raised this possibility and suggested possible remedies.

A second argument is that the link would be unsuccessful in raising the total quantity of aid to developing countries. Salin (1970), Haberler (1971), and Johnson (1972 b) have argued that national governments, unless "tricked," will reduce conventional aid by an amount equal to the aid component in linked SDR allocations. Williamson (1973) offered the view, however, that governments might be more favorably disposed toward increases in multilateral aid than toward growth in bilateral aid.

Johnson (1972 b) argued that potential aid recipients under the link would be better off without the link and should oppose it. Developing countries would benefit from the increased stability and growth that would derive from a reformed international monetary system. However, under a linked SDR standard, the developed countries would not benefit from SDR allocations and would find it as costly to acquire reserves under such a system as under a dollar standard. He judged that they would therefore be less likely to reform the international monetary system adequately.

Advocates of the link failed to be convinced by the arguments of link opponents (Grubel (1972), Maynard (1972, 1973), and Kahn (1973)). Williamson found the arguments "secondary and unpersuasive" (Díaz-Alejandro (1975) and Williamson (1977 b)).

V. CONCLUDING REMARKS

The perceived inadequacies of the Bretton Woods system led to several proposals to replace the gold-exchange standard with an international monetary system utilizing an international reserve asset. Special drawing rights, which were created by the Fund in 1967, failed to resolve the problems inherent in the gold-exchange standard, and in 1973, the Bretton Woods system was finally abandoned. The adoption of floating exchange rates has restricted academic interest in the SDR mainly to issues concerning substitution among reserve assets and the link between SDRs and development assistance. The functioning of exchange markets under floating and the volatility of exchange rates have received considerable attention. Some authors have advanced proposals concerning a return to a more tightly controlled system involving more extensive exchange rate management and a central role for SDRs. Others, however, have expressed doubts about the desirability and political feasibility of a more closely controlled system.

BIBLIOGRAPHY

Aliber, Robert Z., "Gresham's Law, Asset Preferences, and the Demand for International Reserves," *Quarterly Journal of Economics*, Vol. 81 (November 1967), pp. 628-38.

_____(1969 a), *Choices for the Dollar: Costs and Benefits of Possible Approaches to the Balance-of-Payments Problem* (Washington: National Planning Association, 1969).

_____(1969 b), "Gresham's Law and the Demand for NRU's and SDR's: A Reply," *Quarterly Journal of Economics*, Vol. 83 (November 1969), pp. 704-705.

_____, *National Preferences and the Scope for International Monetary Reform*, Essays in International Finance, No. 101 (Princeton, New Jersey: International Finance Section, Princeton University, 1973).

_____, ed., *National Monetary Policies and the International Financial System* (Chicago: University of Chicago Press, 1974).

Angell, James W., "The Reorganization of the International Monetary System: An Alternative Proposal," *Economic Journal*, Vol. 71 (December 1961), pp. 691-708.

Argy, Victor, and Pentti J. K. Kouri, "Stabilization Policies and the Volatility of International Reserves," in *National Monetary Policies and the International Financial System*, ed. by Robert Z. Aliber (Chicago: University of Chicago Press, 1974), pp. 209-30.

Artus, Jacques R., "Exchange Rate Stability and Managed Floating: The Experience of the Federal Republic of Germany," International Monetary Fund, *Staff Papers*, Vol. 23 (July 1976), pp. 312-33.

_____, and John H. Young, "Fixed and Flexible Exchange Rates: A Renewal of the Debate," International Monetary Fund, *Staff Papers*, Vol. 26 (December 1979), pp. 654-98.

Barro, Robert J., *U.S. Inflation and the Choice of Monetary Standard*, National Bureau of Economic Research, Conference Paper No. 91 (January 1981).

Bauer, Peter T., "Inflation, SDRs and Aid," *Lloyds Bank Review*, No. 109 (July 1973), pp. 31-35.

Bernstein, Edward M. (1963 a), "Proposed Reforms in the International Monetary System," in *World Monetary Reform*, ed. by Herbert G. Grubel (Stanford, California: Stanford University Press, 1963), pp. 187-202.

_____ (1963 b), "A Practical Program for International Monetary Reserves," *Quarterly Review and Investment Survey*, Model, Roland and Co., New York (Fourth Quarter 1963).

_____, "Further Evolution of the International Monetary System," in *A Compendium of Plans for International Monetary Reform*, ed. by Robert G. Hawkins (New York: C.J. Devine Institute of Finance, New York University, 1965), pp. 83-95.

Bigman, David, and Teizo Taya, eds., *The Functioning of Floating Exchange Rates: Theory, Evidence and Policy Implications* (Cambridge, Massachusetts: Ballinger, 1980).

Bilson, John F. O., and Jacob A. Frenkel, *Dynamic Adjustment and the Demand for International Reserves*, National Bureau of Economic Research, Working Paper No. 407 (November 1979).

_____, "International Reserves: Adjustment Dynamics," *Economics Letters*, Vol. 4 (June 1980), pp. 267-70.

Black, Stanley W., "Central Bank Intervention and the Stability of Exchange Rates" (unpublished, Vanderbilt University, December 1979; and Institute for International Economic Studies, University of Stockholm, Seminar Paper No. 136).

_____, "The Use of Monetary Policy for Internal and External Balance in Ten Industrial Countries," in *Exchange Rates and International Macroeconomics*, ed. by Jacob A. Frenkel (Chicago: University of Chicago Press, forthcoming in 1983).

Brandt, Willy, and others, *North-South: A Program for Survival*, report of the Independent Commission on International Development Issues ("Brandt Commission") (Cambridge, Massachusetts: MIT Press, 1980).

_____, *The Brandt Commission Papers* (Geneva: Independent Commission on International Development Issues, 1981).

Branson, William H., and others, "Exchange Rates in the Short Run: The Dollar-Deutschemark Rate," *European Economic Review*, Vol. 10 (December 1977), pp. 303-24.

Brown, Weir M., *The External Liquidity of an Advanced Country*, Studies in International Finance, No. 14 (Princeton, New Jersey: International Finance Section, Princeton University, 1964).

Bryant, Ralph C., *Money and Monetary Policy in Independent Nations* (Washington: Brookings Institution, 1980).

Chrystal, K. Alec, *International Money and the Future of the SDR*, Essays in International Finance, No. 128 (Princeton, New Jersey: International Finance Section, Princeton University, 1978).

Clark, Peter B. (1970 a), "Optimum International Reserves and the Speed of Adjustment," *Journal of Political Economy*, Vol. 78 (March-April 1970), pp. 356-76.

_____(1970 b), "Demand for International Reserves: A Cross-Country Analysis," *Canadian Journal of Economics*, Vol. 3 (November 1970), pp. 577-94.

_____, "Interest Payments and the Rate of Return on an International Fiat Currency," *Weltwirtschaftliches Archiv*, No. 108 (December 1973), pp. 537-64.

Clower, Robert W., and Richard G. Lipsey, "The Present State of International Liquidity Theory," *American Economic Review, Papers and Proceedings of the Eightieth Annual Meeting of the American Economic Association*, Vol. 58 (May 1968), pp. 586-95.

Cohen, Benjamin J., *Adjustment Costs and the Distribution of New Reserves*, Studies in International Finance, No. 18 (Princeton, New Jersey: International Finance Section, Princeton University, 1966).

_____, "International Reserves and Liquidity," in *International Trade and Finance: Frontiers for Research*, ed. by Peter B. Kenen (Cambridge, England: Cambridge University Press, 1975), pp. 411-51.

Cohen, Stephen D., *International Monetary Reform: The Political Dimension 1964-1969* (New York: Praeger, 1970).

Cooper, Richard N., "The Relevance of International Liquidity to Developed Countries," *American Economic Review, Papers and Proceedings of the Eightieth Annual Meeting of the American Economic Association*, Vol. 58 (May 1968), pp. 625-36.

_____, "International Liquidity and Balance of Payments Adjustment," in International Monetary Fund, *International Reserves: Needs and Availability* (Washington, 1970), pp. 125-45.

_____, "The Gold Standard: Historical Facts and Future Prospects," *Brookings Papers on Economic Activity: 1* (1982), pp. 1-45.

Day, A.C.L., "The World Liquidity Problem and the British Monetary System," in *Principal Memoranda of Evidence Submitted to the Committee on the Working of the Monetary System*, Vol. 3 (London: Her Majesty's Stationery Office, 1960).

Despres, Emile, Charles P. Kindleberger, and Walter S. Salant, "The Dollar and World Liquidity—A Minority View," *Economist*, Vol. 218 (February 5, 1966), pp. 526-29.

Díaz-Alejandro, Carlos F., *Less Developed Countries and the Post-1971 International Financial System*, Essays in International Finance, No. 108 (Princeton, New Jersey: International Finance Section, Princeton University, 1975).

Dornbusch, Rudiger, "Expectations and Exchange-Rate Dynamics," *Journal of Political Economy*, Vol. 84 (December 1976), pp. 1161-76.

_____, "Exchange-Rate Economics: Where Do We Stand?" *Brookings Papers on Economic Activity: 1* (1980), pp. 143-206.

_____, "Oversight Hearings on U.S. International Monetary Policies," in U.S. Congress, Committee on Banking, Finance, and Urban Affairs, Subcommittee on International Trade, Investment and Monetary Policy, 97th Congress, First Session, November 4, 1981 (Washington: Government Printing Office, 1982), pp. 21-40.

_____, and Jacob A. Frenkel, eds., *International Economic Policy: Theory and Evidence* (Baltimore: Johns Hopkins Press, 1979).

Emminger, Otmar, *Inflation and the International Monetary System* (Washington: Per Jacobsson Foundation, 1973).

Erb, Guy F., and S. Schiavo-Campo, "Export Instability, Level of Development and Economic Size of Less Developed Countries," *Bulletin of Oxford University Institute of Economics and Statistics*, Vol. 31 (November 1969), pp. 263-84.

Ethier, Wilfred, and Arthur I. Bloomfield, *Managing the Managed Float*, Essays in International Finance, No. 112 (Princeton, New Jersey: International Finance Section, Princeton University, 1975).

Fellner, William, ed., *Contemporary Economic Problems* (Washington: American Enterprise Institute for Public Policy Research, 1976).

Fischer, Stanley, "Seigniorage and the Case for a National Money," *Journal of Political Economy*, Vol. 90 (April 1982), pp. 295-313.

Flanders, M. June, *The Demand for International Reserves*, Studies in International Finance, No. 27 (Princeton, New Jersey: International Finance Section, Princeton University, 1973).

Fleming, J. Marcus, "The SDR: Some Problems and Possibilities," International Monetary Fund, *Staff Papers*, Vol. 18 (March 1971), pp. 25-47.

_____, "Towards a New Regime for International Payments," *Journal of International Economics*, Vol. 2 (September 1972), pp. 345-73.

Flood, Robert P., "Explanations of Exchange-Rate Volatility and Other Empirical Regularities in Some Popular Models of the Foreign Exchange Market," in *The Costs and Consequences of Inflation*, ed. by Karl Brunner and Allan H. Meltzer, Carnegie-Rochester Conference Series on Public Policy, Vol. 15 (Amsterdam: North-Holland, 1981), pp. 219-50.

Frenkel, Jacob A. (1974 a), "The Demand for International Reserves by Developed and Less-Developed Countries," *Economica*, Vol. 41 (February 1974), pp. 14-24.

_____(1974 b), "Openness and the Demand for Reserves," in *National Monetary Policies and the International Financial System*, ed. by Robert Z. Aliber (Chicago: University of Chicago Press, 1974), pp. 289-300.

_____, "A Monetary Approach to the Exchange Rate: Doctrinal Aspects and Empirical Evidence," *Scandinavian Journal of Economics*, Vol. 78 (May 1976), pp. 200-24.

_____, "International Reserves: Pegged Exchange Rates and Managed Float," in *Public Policies in Open Economies*, ed. by Karl Brunner and Allan H. Meltzer, Carnegie-Rochester Conference Series on Public Policy, Vol. 9 (Amsterdam: North-Holland, 1978), pp. 111-40.

_____(1980 a), "The Demand for International Reserves Under Pegged and Flexible Exchange Rate Regimes and Aspects of the Economics of Managed Float," in *The Functioning of Floating Exchange Rates: Theory, Evidence and Policy Implications*, ed. by David Bigman and Teizo Taya (Cambridge, Massachusetts: Ballinger, 1980), pp. 169-95.

_____(1980 b), "International Reserves Under Pegged Exchange Rates and Managed Float," *Journal of Monetary Economics*, Vol. 6 (April 1980), pp. 295-302.

_____, "Flexible Exchange Rates, Prices and the Role of 'News': Lessons from the 1980s," *Journal of Political Economy*, Vol. 89 (August 1981), pp. 665-705.

_____, ed., *Exchange Rates and International Macroeconomics* (Chicago: University of Chicago Press, 1983).

_____, and Craig S. Hakkio, "Country-Specific and Time-Specific Factors in the Demand for International Reserves, *Economics Letters*, Vol. 5 (March 1980), pp. 75-80.

Frenkel, Jacob A., and Boyan Jovanovic, "Optimal International Reserves: A Stochastic Framework," *Economic Journal*, Vol. 91 (June 1981), pp. 507-14.

Friedman, Milton, "Commodity-Reserve Currency," *Journal of Political Economy*, Vol. 59 (June 1951), pp. 203-32.

Gilbert, Milton, *The Gold-Dollar System: Conditions of Equilibrium and the Price of Gold*, Essays in International Finance, No. 70 (Princeton, New Jersey: International Finance Section, Princeton University, 1968).

Girton, Lance, "SDR Creation and the Real-Bills Doctrine," *Southern Economic Journal*, Vol. 41 (July 1974), pp. 57-61.

Glezakos, Constantine, "Export Instability and Economic Growth: A Statistical Verification," *Economic Development and Cultural Change*, Vol. 21 (July 1973), pp. 670-78.

Gold, Joseph, "Substitution in the International Monetary System," *Case Western Reserve Journal of International Law*, Vol. 12 (Spring 1980), pp. 265-326.

Goldstein, Henry N., "Gresham's Law and the Demand for NRU's and SDR's," *Quarterly Journal of Economics*, Vol. 83 (February 1969), pp. 163-66.

_____, "Can SDRs and a Reserve Currency Coexist?" *Journal of Money, Credit and Banking*, Vol. 6 (November 1974), pp. 567-70.

Goldstein, Morris, *Have Flexible Exchange Rates Handicapped Macroeconomic Policy?* Special Papers in International Economics, No. 14 (Princeton, New Jersey: International Finance Section, Princeton University, 1980).

Greene, Margaret L., "Reserve-Asset Preferences Revisited," in *The Open Economy: Essays on International Trade and Finance*, ed. by P. B. Kenen and R. Lawrence (New York: Columbia University Press, 1968), pp. 355-85.

Group of Ten, *Report of the Study Group on the Creation of Reserve Assets: A Report to the Deputies of the Group of Ten, 31st May 1965* ("Ossola Report") (Rome: Bank of Italy Press, and Washington: Government Printing Office, 1965).

Group of Thirty, *How Central Banks Manage Their Reserves: A Study* (New York, 1982).

Grubel, Herbert G., ed., *World Monetary Reform* (Stanford, California: Stanford University Press, 1963).

_____, "The Case Against an International Commodity Reserve Currency," *Oxford Economic Papers*, Vol. 17 (March 1965), pp. 130-35.

_____, "The Distribution of Seigniorage from International Liquidity Creation," in *Monetary Problems of the International Economy*, ed. by Robert A. Mundell and Alexander K. Swoboda (Chicago: University of Chicago Press, 1969), pp. 269-82.

_____, "The Demand for International Reserves: A Critical Review of the Literature," *Journal of Economic Literature*, Vol. 9 (December 1971), pp. 1148-66.

_____, "Basic Methods for Distributing SDRs and the Problem of International Aid," *Journal of Finance*, Vol. 27 (December 1972), pp. 1009-22.

Haan, Roelf L., *Special Drawing Rights and Development* (Leiden: Stenfert Kroese N.V., 1971).

Haberler, Gottfried, "The Case Against the Link," Banca Nazionale del Lavoro, *Quarterly Review*, Vol. 24 (March 1971), pp. 13-22.

_____(1977 a), "The International Monetary System After Jamaica and Manila," *Weltwirtschaftliches Archiv*, No. 113 (1977), pp. 1-30.

_____(1977 b), "How Important Is Control over Reserves?" in *The New International Monetary System*, ed. by Robert A. Mundell and J. J. Polak (New York: Columbia University Press, 1977), pp. 109-32.

Harrod, Roy, "Imbalance of International Payments," International Monetary Fund, *Staff Papers*, Vol. 3 (April 1953), pp. 1-46.

_____, *Alternative Methods for Increasing International Liquidity* (London: European League for Economic Cooperation, 1961).

_____, "Liquidity," in *World Monetary Reform*, ed. by Herbert G. Grubel (Stanford, California: Stanford University Press, 1963), pp. 203-26.

_____, *Reforming the World's Money* (London: Macmillan, 1965).

Hart, Albert G., "The Case for and Against International Commodity Reserve Currency," *Oxford Economic Papers*, Vol. 18 (July 1966), pp. 237-41.

Hawkins, Robert G., ed., *A Compendium of Plans for International Monetary Reform* (New York: C. J. Devine Institute of Finance, New York University, 1965).

_____, and C. Rangarajan, "On the Distribution of New International Reserves," *Journal of Finance*, Vol. 25 (September 1970), pp. 881-91.

Hawkins, Robert G., and Sidney E. Rolfe, *A Critical Survey of Plans for International Monetary Reform* (New York: C. J. Devine Institute of Finance, New York University, 1965).

Heilperin, Michael A., "The Case for Going Back to Gold," in *World Monetary Reform*, ed. by Herbert G. Grubel (Stanford, California: Stanford University Press, 1963), pp. 329-42.

Helleiner, G. K., "The Impact of the Exchange Rate System on the Developing Countries," in *Measures to Strengthen the SDR, Report to the Group of Twenty-Four*, United Nations Development Program, United Nations Conference on Trade and Development (New York, 1981).

Heller, H. Robert, "The Transactions Demand for International Means of Payment," *Journal of Political Economy*, Vol. 76 (January 1968), pp. 141-45.

_____, and Malcolm A. Knight, *Reserve-Currency Preferences of Central Banks*, Essays in International Finance, No. 131 (Princeton, New Jersey: International Finance Section, Princeton University, 1973).

Herring, Richard J., and Richard C. Marston, *National Monetary Policies and International Financial Markets* (Amsterdam: North-Holland, 1977).

Hirsch, Fred, "SDRs and the Working of the Gold Exchange Standard," International Monetary Fund, *Staff Papers*, Vol. 18 (July 1971), pp. 221-53.

_____, *An SDR Standard: Impetus, Elements and Impediments*, Essays in International Finance, No. 99 (Princeton, New Jersey: International Finance Section, Princeton University, 1973).

Hufbauer, Gary C., ed., *The International Framework for Money and Banking in the 1980s* (Washington: International Law Institute, Georgetown University, 1981).

International Monetary Fund, *International Reserves: Needs and Availability* (Washington, 1970).

Jacobsson, Per, "The Two Functions of an International Monetary Standard: Stability and Liquidity," National Bank of Belgium, *Bulletin d'Information et de Documentation*, Vol. 37, Part 1 (April 1962), pp. 346-51.

Johnson, Harry G., "The International Competitive Position of the United States and the Balance of Payments Prospect for 1968," *Review of Economics and Statistics*, Vol. 46 (February 1964), pp. 14-32.

_____, "Theoretical Problems of the International Monetary System," *Pakistan Development Review*, Vol. 7 (Spring 1967) pp. 1-28.

_____(1970 a), "International Liquidity and Balance of Payments Adjustment: Comment," in International Monetary Fund, *International Reserves: Needs and Availability* (Washington, 1970), pp. 147-51.

_____(1970 b), "Toward a World Central Bank?: Comment," in *Toward a World Central Bank* (Basle: Per Jacobsson Foundation, September 1970), pp. 42-49.

_____(1972 a), *Inflation and the Monetarist Controversy* (Amsterdam: North-Holland, 1972).

_____(1972 b), "The Link that Chains," *Foreign Policy*, Vol. 8 (Fall 1972), pp. 113-20.

_____, and Alexander K. Swoboda, eds., *The Economics of Common Currencies* (London: Allen and Unwin, 1973).

Kahn, R. F., "SDRs and Aid," *Lloyds Bank Review*, No. 110 (October 1973), pp. 1-18.

Kelly, Michael G., "The Demand for International Reserves," *American Economic Review*, Vol. 60 (September 1970), pp. 655-67.

Kenen, Peter B., "International Liquidity and the Balance of Payments of a Reserve-Currency Country," *Quarterly Journal of Economics*, Vol. 74 (November 1960), pp. 572-86.

_____, *Reserve-Asset Preferences of Central Banks and Stability of the Gold Exchange Standard*, Studies in International Finance, No. 10 (Princeton, New Jersey: International Finance Section, Princeton University, 1963).

_____, ed., *International Trade and Finance: Frontiers for Research* (Cambridge, England: Cambridge University Press, 1975).

_____, "How Important is Control of International Reserves?" in *The New International Monetary System*, ed. by Robert A. Mundell and Jacques J. Polak (New York: Columbia University Press, 1977), pp. 202-22.

_____(1981 a), "Changing Views about the Role of the SDR and Implications for its Attributes," in *Studies on International Monetary and Financial Issues for the Developing Countries: Measures to Strengthen the SDR*, Supporting Papers, UNDP/UNCTAD, April 1981 (Document UNCTAD/MFD/TA/11).

_____(1981 b), "The Analytics of the Substitution Account," Banca Nazionale del Lavoro, *Quarterly Review*, Vol. 34 (December 1981), pp. 403-26.

_____, and Roger Lawrence, eds., *The Open Economy* (New York: Columbia University Press, 1968).

Kenen, Peter B., and Elinor B. Yudin, "The Demand for International Reserves," *Review of Economics and Statistics*, Vol. 47 (August 1965), pp. 242-50.

Keynes, John Maynard, "Proposals for an International Clearing Union," in *World Monetary Reform*, ed. by Herbert G. Grubel (Stanford, California: Stanford University Press, 1963), pp. 55-79.

Khan, Mohsin S., "Inflation and International Reserves: A Time-Series Analysis," International Monetary Fund, *Staff Papers*, Vol. 26 (December 1979), pp. 699-724.

Kindleberger, Charles P., *Balance-of-Payments Deficits and the International Market for Liquidity*, Essays in International Finance, No. 46 (Princeton, New Jersey: International Finance Section, Princeton University, 1965).

_____, "The Case for Fixed Exchange Rates, 1969," in *The International Adjustment Mechanism*, Federal Reserve Bank of Boston Conference Series, No. 2 (Boston: Federal Reserve Bank of Boston, 1969), pp. 93-108.

Knight, Malcolm A., and Joanne Salop, "The New International Monetary System: Some Issues," *Finance & Development*, Vol. 14 (June 1977), pp. 19-22.

Krause, Lawrence B., "A Passive Balance-of-Payments Strategy for the United States," *Brookings Papers on Economic Activity: 3* (1970), pp. 339-60.

Laidler, David E. W., "The Case for Raising the Price of Gold: A Comment," *Journal of Money, Credit and Banking*, Vol. 1 (August 1969), pp. 675-78.

Lawson, C. W., "The Decline of World Export Instability—A Reappraisal," *Oxford Bulletin of Economics and Statistics*, Vol. 36 (February 1974), pp. 53-65.

Longworth, David, "Canadian Intervention in the Foreign Exchange Market: A Note," *Review of Economics and Statistics*, Vol. 62 (May 1980), pp. 284-87.

Lutz, Friedrich A., *The Problem of International Economic Equilibrium* (Amsterdam: North-Holland, 1962).

_____, *The Problem of International Liquidity and the Multiple-Currency Standard*, Essays in International Finance, No. 41 (Princeton, New Jersey: International Finance Section, Princeton University, 1963).

_____, "World Inflation and Domestic Monetary Stability," Banca Nazionale del Lavoro, *Quarterly Review*, Vol. 18 (June 1965), pp. 111-26.

Machlup, Fritz, "Reform of the International Monetary System," in *Outlook for U.S. Balance of Payments*, U.S. Congress, Joint Economic Committee, Subcommittee on Exchange and Payments, 87th Congress, Second Session, December 1962, reprinted in *World Monetary Reform*, ed. by Herbert G. Grubel (Stanford, California: Stanford University Press, 1963), pp. 253-60.

_____, *Plans for Reform of the International Monetary System*, Special Papers in International Economics, No. 3 (Princeton, New Jersey: International Finance Section, Princeton University, 1963).

_____, *International Payments, Debts and Gold* (New York: Charles Scribner's Sons, 1964).

_____, "The Cloakroom Rule of International Reserves: Reserve Creation and Resource Transfer," *Quarterly Journal of Economics*, Vol. 79 (August 1965), pp. 337-55.

———, "The Need for Monetary Reserves," Banca Nazionale del Lavoro, *Quarterly Review*, Vol. 19 (September 1966), pp. 175-222.

———(1968 a), *Remaking the International Monetary System: The Rio Agreement and Beyond* (Baltimore: Johns Hopkins Press, 1968).

———(1968 b), "The Transfer Gap of the United States," Banca Nazionale del Lavoro, *Quarterly Review*, Vol. 21 (September 1968), pp. 195-238.

———, "Speculation on Gold Speculation," *American Economic Review, Papers and Proceedings of the Eighty-First Annual Meeting of the American Economic Association*, Vol. 59 (May 1969), pp. 332-43.

———, and Burton G. Malkiel, eds., *International Monetary Arrangements: The Problem of Choice* (Princeton, New Jersey: International Finance Section, Princeton University, 1964).

Makin, John H., "The Composition of International Reserve Holdings: A Problem of Choice Involving Risk," *American Economic Review*, Vol. 61 (December 1971), pp. 818-32.

———, "The Problem of Coexistence of SDRs and a Reserve Currency," *Journal of Money, Credit and Banking*, Vol. 4 (August 1972), pp. 509-28.

———, "Equilibrium Interest on Special Drawing Rights," *Southern Economic Journal*, Vol. 41 (October 1974), pp. 171-81.

Márquez, Javier, "Reserves, Liquidity, and the Developing Countries," in International Monetary Fund, *International Reserves: Needs and Availability* (Washington, 1970), pp. 97-111.

Maynard, Geoffrey, *Special Drawing Rights and Development Aid*, Occasional Paper No. 6 (Washington: Overseas Development Council, September 1972).

———, "Special Drawing Rights and Development Aid," *Journal of Development Studies*, Vol. 9 (July 1973), pp. 518-43.

———, and Graham Bird, "International Monetary Issues and the Developing Countries: A Survey," *World Development*, Vol. 3 (September 1975), pp. 609-31.

McKinnon, Ronald I., *Private and Official International Money: The Case for the Dollar*, Essays in International Finance, No. 74 (Princeton, New Jersey: International Finance Section, Princeton University, 1969).

———, "Sterilization in Three Dimensions: Major Trading Countries, Eurocurrencies, and the United States," in *National Monetary Policies and the International Financial System*, ed. by Robert Z. Aliber (Chicago: University of Chicago Press, 1974), pp. 231-49.

———, "The Exchange Rate and Macroeconomic Policy: Changing Postwar Perceptions," *Journal of Economic Literature*, Vol. 19 (June 1981), pp. 531-57.

Mundell, Robert A., *International Economics* (New York: Macmillan, 1968).

———, "Real Gold, Dollars and Paper Gold," *American Economic Review, Papers and Proceedings of the Eighty-First Annual Meeting of the American Economic Association*, Vol. 59 (May 1969), pp. 324-31.

———, *Monetary Theory: Inflation, Interest and Growth in the World Economy* (Pacific Palisades, California: Goodyear Publishers, 1971).

_____, "The Economic Consequences of Jacques Rueff," *Journal of Business*, Vol. 46 (July 1973), pp. 368-73.

_____, and Jacques J. Polak, eds., *The New International Monetary System* (New York: Columbia University Press, 1977).

Mundell, Robert A., and Alexander K. Swoboda, eds., *Monetary Problems of the International Economy* (Chicago: University of Chicago Press, 1969).

Murphy, J. Carter, *International Monetary System: Beyond the First Stage of Reform* (Washington: American Enterprise Institute for Public Policy Research, 1979).

Murphy, Robert J., and George M. von Furstenberg, "An Analysis of Factors Influencing the Level of SDR Holdings in Non-Oil Developing Countries," International Monetary Fund, *Staff Papers*, Vol. 28 (June 1981), pp. 310-37.

Mussa, Michael (1979 a), "Empirical Regularities in the Behavior of Exchange Rates and Theories of the Foreign Exchange Market," in *Policies for Employment, Prices and Exchange Rates*, ed. by Karl Brunner and Allan H. Meltzer, Carnegie-Rochester Conference Series on Public Policy, Vol. 11 (Amsterdam: North-Holland, 1979), pp. 9-58.

_____(1979 b), "Macroeconomic Interdependence and the Exchange Rate Regime," in *International Economic Policy*, ed. by Rudiger Dornbusch and Jacob A. Frenkel (Baltimore: Johns Hopkins Press, 1979), pp. 160-203.

_____, *The Role of Official Intervention*, Group of Thirty, Occasional Paper No. 6 (New York, 1981).

Niehans, Jürg, "The Need for Reserves of a Single Country," in International Monetary Fund, *International Reserves: Needs and Availability* (Washington, 1970), pp. 49-85.

_____, "The Flexibility of the Gold-Exchange Standard and Its Limits," in *The Economics of Common Currencies*, ed. by Harry G. Johnson and Alexander K. Swoboda (London: Allen and Unwin, 1973), pp. 46-64.

_____, "How to Fill an Empty Shell," *American Economic Review, Papers and Proceedings of the Eighty-Eighth Annual Meeting of the American Economic Association*, Vol. 76 (May 1976), pp. 177-83.

Obstfeld, Maurice (1980 a), "Imperfect Asset Substitutability and Monetary Policy under Fixed Exchange Rates," *Journal of International Economics*, Vol. 10 (May 1980), pp. 177-200.

_____(1980 b), *Sterilization and Offsetting Capital Movements: Evidence from West Germany 1960-1970*, National Bureau of Economic Research, Working Paper No. 494 (June 1980).

_____, "Exchange Rates, Inflation, and the Sterilization Problem: Germany, 1975-1981," *European Economic Review*, Vol. 20 (May-June 1983).

Officer, Lawrence H., and Thomas D. Willett, "Reserve Asset Preferences and the Confidence Problem in the Crisis Zone," *Quarterly Journal of Economics*, Vol. 83 (November 1969), pp. 688-95.

_____, "The Interaction of Adjustment and Gold-Conversion Policies in a Reserve Currency System," *Western Economic Journal*, Vol. 8 (March 1970), pp. 47-60.

_____, "Reserve Asset Preferences in the Crisis Zone, 1958-1967," *Journal of Money, Credit and Banking*, Vol. 6 (May 1974), pp. 191-211.

Oppenheimer, Peter M., "The Case for Raising the Price of Gold," *Journal of Money, Credit and Banking*, Vol. 1 (August 1969), pp. 649-65.

O'Toole, Thomas P., "Central Bank Intervention in Foreign Exchange Markets: An Empirical Investigation" (unpublished, University of North Carolina, December 1981).

Park, Y. S., *The Link Between Special Drawing Rights and Development Finance*, Essays in International Finance, No. 100 (Princeton, New Jersey: International Finance Section, Princeton University, 1973).

Polak, J. J., "Money: National and International," in International Monetary Fund, *International Reserves: Needs and Availability* (Washington, 1970), pp. 510-20.

_____, "The SDRs as a Basket of Currencies," International Monetary Fund, *Staff Papers*, Vol. 26 (December 1979), pp. 627-53.

_____, *Coordination of National Economic Policies*, Group of Thirty, Occasional Paper No. 7 (New York, 1981).

Quirk, Peter J., "Exchange Rate Policy in Japan: Leaning Against the Wind," International Monetary Fund, *Staff Papers*, Vol. 24 (November 1977), pp. 642-64.

Rhomberg, Rudolf R., "Trends in Payments Imbalances, 1952-64," International Monetary Fund, *Staff Papers*, Vol. 13 (November 1966), pp. 371-97.

Roosa, Robert V., "Assuring the Free World's Liquidity," in *World Monetary Reform*, ed. by Herbert G. Grubel (Stanford, California: Stanford University Press, 1963), pp. 261-74.

_____, *Monetary Reform for the World Economy* (New York: Harper and Row, 1965).

_____, "The Multiple Reserve Currency System," in *Reserve Currencies in Transition* (New York: Group of Thirty, 1982).

Roper, Donald E., "On the Theory of the Devaluation Bias," *Kyklos*, Vol. 25 (1972), pp. 315-25.

Rueff, Jacques (1961 a), "Gold Exchange Standard a Danger to the West," *The Times* (London), June 27-29, 1961, reprinted in *World Monetary Reform*, ed. by Herbert G. Grubel (Stanford, California: Stanford University Press, 1963), pp. 320-28.

_____(1961 b), "The West is Risking a Credit Collapse," *Fortune*, Vol. 64 (July 1961), pp. 126-27.

Sacchetti, Ugo, "The SDR: Ten Years of Experience," Banca Nazionale del Lavoro, *Quarterly Review*, Vol. 32 (December 1979), pp. 391-405.

Salin, Pascal, referred to in International Monetary Fund, *International Reserves: Needs and Availability* (Washington, 1970), p. 120.

Schulenburg, J. Matthias Graf, "The Use of Currency-Baskets in International Transactions: A Risk-Theoretical Study" (unpublished, Woodrow Wilson School of Public and International Affairs Discussion Paper, Princeton University, October 1981).

Scitovsky, Tibor, *Requirements of an International Reserve System*, Essays in International Finance, No. 49 (Princeton, New Jersey: International Finance Section, Princeton University, 1965).

Sohmen, Egon, "General Reserve Supplementation: Some Central Issues," in International Monetary Fund, *International Reserves: Needs and Availability* (Washington, 1970), pp. 12-31.

Stamp, Maxwell, "The Fund and the Future," *Lloyds Bank Review*, No. 50 (October 1958), pp. 1-20.

_____, "The Stamp Plan—1962 Version," in *World Monetary Reform*, ed. by Herbert G. Grubel (Stanford, California: Stanford University Press, 1963), pp. 80-89.

Thorn, R. S., "The Demand for International Reserves: A Note in Behalf of the Rejected Hypothesis," *Review of Economics and Statistics*, Vol. 49 (November 1967), pp. 623-26.

Triffin, Robert, "National Central Banking and the International Economy," *Review of Economic Studies*, Vol. 14 (February 1947), pp. 53-75.

_____, *Gold and the Dollar Crisis* (New Haven, Connecticut: Yale University Press, 1960).

_____, "After the Gold Exchange Standard?" in *World Monetary Reform*, ed. by Herbert G. Grubel (Stanford, California: Stanford University Press, 1963), pp. 422-39.

_____, *Gold and the Dollar Crisis: Yesterday and Tomorrow*, Essays in International Finance, No. 132 (Princeton, New Jersey: International Finance Section, Princeton University, 1978).

United Nations Development Program, United Nations Conference on Trade and Development, *Measures to Strengthen the SDR, Report to the Group of Twenty-Four* (New York, 1981).

van Ypersele, J., "A Central Position for the Special Drawing Right in the Monetary System," Banca Nazionale del Lavoro, *Quarterly Review*, Vol. 30 (December 1977), pp. 381-97.

von Furstenberg, George M., "The Multiple Reserve Currency System in the 1980s: Comment," in *The International Framework for Money and Banking in the 1980s*, ed. by Gary C. Hufbauer (Washington: International Law Institute, Georgetown University, 1981), pp. 78-92.

_____, "New Estimates of the Demand for Non-Gold Reserves Under Floating," *Journal of International Money and Finance*, Vol. 1 (April 1982), pp. 81-95.

Whitman, Marina v. N., "The Crisis Problem: Comment," in *Monetary Problems of the International Economy*, ed. by Robert A. Mundell and Alexander K. Swoboda (Chicago: University of Chicago Press, 1969), pp. 351-56.

_____, "International Interdependence and the U.S. Economy," in *Contemporary Economic Problems*, ed. by William Fellner (Washington: American Enterprise Institute for Public Policy Research, 1976), pp. 183-224.

Willett, Thomas D., *Floating Exchange Rates and International Monetary Reform* (Washington: American Enterprise Institute for Public Policy Research, 1977).

_____(1980 a), *International Liquidity Issues* (Washington: American Enterprise Institute for Public Policy Research, 1980).

_____(1980 b), "Policy Research Issues in a Floating-Rate World: An Assessment of Policy-Relevant Research on the Effects of International Monetary Institutions and Behavior on Macroeconomic Performance," *International Economic Policy*

Research, proceedings of a colloquium held in Washington, October 3-4, 1980 (Washington: National Science Foundation, 1980), pp. I-24 to I-58.

————, "The Causes and Effects of Exchange-Rate Volatility," ed. by Jacob S. Dreyer, Gottfried Haberler, and Thomas D. Willett, *The International Monetary System: A Time of Turbulence* (Washington, American Enterprise Institute for Public Policy Research, 1982), pp. 24-64.

Williamson, John, *The Crawling Peg*, Essays in International Finance, No. 50 (Princeton, New Jersey: International Finance Section, Princeton University, 1965).

————, *The Choice of a Pivot for Parities*, Essays in International Finance, No. 90 (Princeton, New Jersey: International Finance Section, Princeton University, 1971).

————, "SDRs, Interest and the Aid Link," Banca Nazionale del Lavoro, *Quarterly Review*, Vol. 25 (June 1972), pp. 199-205.

————, "International Liquidity: A Survey," *Economic Journal*, Vol. 83 (September 1973), pp. 685-746.

————, "Exchange-Rate Flexibility and Reserve Use," *Scandinavian Journal of Economics*, Vol. 78 (June 1976), pp. 327-39.

————(1977 a), "The Problem of Remonetizing Gold," Banca Nazionale del Lavoro, *Quarterly Review*, Vol. 30 (June 1977), pp. 171-86.

————(1977 b), *The Failure of World Monetary Reform, 1971-1974* (New York: New York University Press, 1977).

————, "The Multiple Reserve Currency System and Exchange Stability" (unpublished, December 1981).

————, "The Growth of Official Reserves and the Issue of World Monetary Control," in *The International Monetary System: A Time of Turbulence*, ed. by Jacob S. Dreyer, Gottfried Haberler, and Thomas D. Willett (Washington: American Enterprise Institute for Public Policy Research, 1982), pp. 277-91.

Wilms, Manfred, "Controlling Money in an Open Economy," Federal Reserve Bank of St. Louis, *Review*, Vol. 53 (April 1971), pp. 10-27.

Yeager, Leland B., "The Misconceived Problem of International Liquidity," *Journal of Finance*, Vol. 14 (September 1959), pp. 347-60.

Zolotas, Xenophon, *Towards a Reinforced Gold Exchange Standard* (Athens: Bank of Greece, 1961).

The Evolving Role of the SDR in the International Monetary System

This paper, which was prepared by Fund staff in 1982, served as background for conference discussion of the various actual and potential roles of the SDR in the functioning of the international financial system. The first part deals with past developments and their implications for the SDR; the second considers how the role of SDRs and SDR-denominated claims could usefully be broadened under the existing international monetary system and under a conceivable future system that is characterized by greater stability of exchange rates and national price levels.

In the first part, elaboration of past discussions and deliberations is arranged largely chronologically, starting with those on the establishment of the SDR in 1967 and ending with those pertaining to the substitution account that was proposed in 1979–80. Section I surveys the problems that led to the creation of the SDR as a possible solution and then reflects, in broad terms, on how the SDR might evolve to meet needs other than those originally perceived. Section II describes how the SDR and SDR allocations have already been adapted to major changes in the international monetary system during the 1970s. Discussions that are summarized in Section III deal with extension of the role of the SDR through substitution. These discussions started in the first half of the past decade and resumed in 1979–80 under changed conditions.

In the second part of the paper, a discussion of the future of the SDR opens with a short introduction that establishes the approach used in this part. Section IV then takes up the anticipated development of the SDR in conditions of economic instability such as those now prevailing in the world. Section V, the most speculative and tentative in the paper, turns to the expected evolution of the SDR under more stable prices and exchange rates than those of the early 1980s. The paper closes with a short list of issues for further discussion.

Part One: Past Developments and Their Implications for the SDR

I. THE INTERNATIONAL MONETARY SYSTEM, 1960-1980, WITH IMPLICATIONS FOR THE FUTURE ROLE OF THE SDR

During the 1950s, the international monetary system developed in accordance with the form set forth at Bretton Woods in 1944. Until the late 1950s, the foundation appeared to remain stable as the liberalization of trade and payments progressed rapidly and as European currencies regained exchange convertibility. Any contradictions inherent in the gold exchange standard were not keenly felt, as long as the resulting redistribution of gold and the accumulation of claims on the United States were judged desirable. Even as late as 1958, gold and reserve currency balances were generally regarded as capable of yielding satisfactory growth in international reserves in future years, "provided that further progress is made, by sensible policies, in restoring and maintaining balance in the individual economies, in avoiding increased obstacles to trade, and in strengthening the international credit system" (International Monetary Fund (1958), p. 93).

In the early 1960s, however, alternative methods of reserve creation and the introduction of new international reserve assets were being discussed increasingly, as the need for supplementing existing reserves began to be felt (de Vries (1976), Vol. I, pp. 193-95). The decision to create SDRs reflected a changed appraisal of what was required to maintain confidence in reserve media and their ability to grow at an adequate rate. Thus, the First Amendment to the Articles of Agreement, which took effect in 1969, authorized the Fund—in Article XXI, Section 1—to allocate SDRs "to meet the need, as and when it arises, for a supplement to existing reserve assets" (International Monetary Fund (1969 a), p. 50).

This section first presents some of the needs perceived and the solutions proposed up to the establishment of the SDR at the 1967 Annual Meeting of the Board of Governors of the Fund in Rio de Janeiro. It then surveys developments and deliberations extending from the 1967 outline of the First Amendment to the first SDR allocation in 1970. Finally, it recounts the major changes in both the world economy and the international monetary system during the 1970s and sets out, in broad terms, the questions concerning the future role of the SDR raised by the loss of stability in exchange relations and domestic prices.

Envisaged Role of the SDR Before Its Establishment

The decade leading up to the adoption of the SDR as a reserve asset was one of considerable turmoil in the international monetary system. During that period, the United States built a ring of defense for the U.S. dollar, which had been weakened in part by the domestic inflation associated with the Viet Nam conflict, by attempting to stem capital and gold outflows through instruments such as the interest equalization tax, through operations designed to affect the term structure of interest rates,[1] and through Roosa bonds and gold market arrangements like the gold pool. There were also recurring exchange market crises affecting the pound sterling and other currencies, with exchange markets even closed for an entire week on one occasion in November 1968.

As signs of stress in the international financial system began to multiply in the 1960s, creation of a new international reserve asset was considered a matter of urgency. Government policies became increasingly incompatible with the goal of maintaining internationally agreed parities and the official U.S. dollar price of gold. The demand for more reserves and their supply were difficult to keep in broad balance, and reliance on a single major source of reserve growth—U.S. payments deficits on the official settlements basis—gave rise to problems relating to the composition of reserves and the safety of their value.

Robert Triffin (1961, p. 9) was among the first to articulate the resulting policy dilemma:

> ...the elimination of [the] overall balance of payments deficits [of the United States] would, by definition, put an end to the constant deterioration of [U.S.] monetary reserves and deprive thereby the rest of the world of the major source by far—two thirds to three fourths—from which the international liquidity requirements of an expanding world economy have been met in recent years, in the face of a totally inadequate supply of monetary gold.

Worthy arguments were made for resolving the dilemma inherent in the gold exchange system by raising the official price of gold. This approach was opposed by those who regarded gold as a "barbarous relic," as well as by many who felt that the distribution by countries of the benefits derived from an increase in the price of gold would be politically unacceptable. There was also concern about generating windfall gains for private holders and encouraging speculation on future increases in the price of gold.

A variety of schemes for adjusting pegs were also studied, and free float-

---

[1] To reconcile internal and external policy objectives, an attempt was made to raise short-term interest rates relative to long-term rates through open-market operations, known as "nudge and twist," designed to discourage short-term capital outflows without dampening domestic fixed investment.

ing was widely discussed. One of the most telling arguments was that if the demand for reserves with which to defend exchange rates were growing more rapidly than the supply, that demand should be lessened by reducing the need for defending exchange rates through foreign exchange market intervention. Adjusting policies more promptly in order to reduce payments imbalances without recourse to exchange depreciation was viewed as the most desirable means of husbanding scarce reserves and keeping down inflation.

In this connection, the role of the Fund in providing liquidity to members on condition that they adopt policies conducive to balance of payments adjustment was much discussed and clarified, as was the relationship of conditional to unconditional liquidity in the functioning of the Fund and of the entire international monetary system. The imperative worldwide need for development finance was reflected in the debate about a new reserve asset during this period. The possibility that a new system of reserve creation might in some way be linked to the provision of development finance encouraged many members to support the idea of the SDR. But this possibility also worried other members, many of which inclined to the view that the world's need for reserves was separate and distinct from the need for development finance and that it would be unwise to risk influencing decisions concerning the former by considerations pertaining to the latter.

Discussion of these matters took place in many circles, resulting in a number of proposals that promised alternate choices while continuing to adhere to the gold exchange standard. Most of these alternatives were considered by two major study groups, known as the Ossola Committee and the Bellagio group of economists, both of which prepared the way for the creation of the SDR as an important adjunct of the fixed exchange rate system.[2] The Group of Ten, which was organized in 1961 to discuss new borrowing arrangements for providing the Fund with resources to help counter the disruptions caused by unusually large short-term capital flows, became the focal point of far-reaching discussions among the authorities of major countries. These discussions culminated in 1965, when the Ossola Committee presented its report on the creation of reserve assets (Group of Ten (1965)) to the Deputies of the Group of Ten. At about the same time, the choice of international monetary arrangements was considered in the report on a conference by an international study group meeting in Bellagio (Machlup and Malkiel (1964)).

---

[2] Since a comprehensive survey of the literature is provided in the preceding chapter of this volume, only studies bearing most centrally on the establishment of the SDR are considered here. For a synopsis of how the SDR evolved, see de Vries (1976, Vol. I, Chapter 9).

With respect to the issues of international liquidity and confidence already identified by Triffin (1961), the Bellagio group first noted that, for an individual country, "international liquidity" could include not only owned assets convertible into foreign exchange and borrowed reserves but also reserves obtainable under existing or ad hoc borrowing arrangements—and even contingent reserves available through restrictive monetary policies and central bank action directed at interest rates and forward foreign exchange rates. After narrowing the definition of reserves to the sum of owned reserves and unconditional drawing rights, the private study group cited the disproportionate growth of U.S. dollars in international reserves as evidence of the inadequacy of gold supplies at a fixed price. The resultant weakening of the U.S. position, which had been intensified by the large balance of payments deficits of the United States over the period 1958-64, had contributed to the twin problems of international liquidity and confidence in reserve media. All members of the Bellagio group thus agreed on the desirability of reforms to provide for better control and steadier growth of international reserves if the system of relatively rigid exchange rates was to be maintained. Some members were also in favor of replacing the fixed exchange rates with freely floating exchange rates, which in their opinion would eliminate the problem of international liquidity by providing an automatic mechanism for instant adjustment of international balances.

The Bellagio group further described the problem of confidence in reserve media as arising from the Fund's insufficiency of resources to enable it to act as "lender of last resort" and as the organizer of internationally agreed approaches to liquidity creation and reserve management. It considered that official holders of reserves might be influenced not only by concern over the value of their assets but also by political considerations and that an "overhang" of dollar and sterling claims held as reserves by other monetary authorities might precipitate conversions of dollars into gold on a large scale. Substitution arrangements in the Fund or funding by the issuers of reserve currencies were therefore discussed as solutions to reduce such overhangs (see Section III). Even if central banks would not initiate destabilizing action to adjust the composition of reserves, there might be massive private outflows of dollars or sterling, which would transfer more dollars or sterling to foreign central banks than they cared to hold or felt able to sterilize. In these as in other respects, "the speed and character of adjustment are likely to be affected by the magnitude of the available reserves and the ease with which gross reserves can be replenished" (Machlup and Malkiel (1964, p. 36)).

Although none of the plans of the Bellagio group for reducing the conflicts between adjustment, liquidity, and confidence discussed implementation, several of them envisaged an important role for the Fund. Most notably, under a plan for centralization of international reserves, credit reserves would no longer consist of national currencies but of gold-value-guaranteed sight deposits at a reorganized Fund. These deposits would replace Fund capital subscriptions (see Section IV). Members might undertake to hold an agreed proportion of their gross monetary reserves in the form of Fund deposits,[3] and these deposits would be increased or decreased over time, in accordance with the requirements of noninflationary growth in the world economy, by direct lending to (repayments by) member countries, by open market operations, and by purchases (sales) of bonds issued by the International Bank for Reconstruction and Development (World Bank).

More detailed discussions of alternative plans appeared in the Ossola Committee's report of the Study Group on the Creation of Reserve Assets. When preparation of that report was authorized by the Ministers and Governors of the Group of Ten countries in 1964, they called for examination of various proposals regarding the creation of reserve assets through the Fund or otherwise. Interestingly, however, the proposal for Collective Reserve Units (CRUs), which was not thought to involve the Fund directly, came closest to anticipating the type of generation adopted for the SDR in 1967. Therefore, this plan, which had been proposed by Edward Bernstein in 1963 and then modified, will be described in detail before proceeding to the agreement reached at the 1967 Annual Meeting of the Fund.

As outlined in the 1965 Ossola Committee's report, the CRU scheme would provide for the creation of reserves directly in the hands of monetary authorities on the basis of a collective appraisal of global need. CRUs could be distributed to participants, thought to be a limited group of industrial countries,[4] in proportion to their gold reserves or in some other manner independent of their balance of payments situations. No matter how CRUs were distributed initially, periodic transfers of gold and CRUs would ensure maintenance of a uniform ratio of CRUs to gold. This would make CRUs a strict quantity supplement to gold reserves, which countries could use in fixed proportion to their official gold holdings and which would lessen their dependence on additional production and also lessen private destocking of gold that might otherwise have to be induced by an increase in its price.

The CRU scheme advanced the concept that international reserve assets

---

[3] As described in Section III, this proposal was applied about a decade later to SDRs rather than to Fund deposits.

[4] Throughout this debate, the Fund emphasized the importance of a solution involving the entire membership which would indicate that international liquidity was the business of the Fund.

could be created through book entry by common agreement on their acceptance and use, rather than by acquiring claims on any one country or international organization. The scheme was abandoned when the position taken by France—that CRUs be distributed in proportion to the gold holdings of ten major countries—met with opposition. Subsequently, when all the members of the European Community in the early months of 1967 endorsed a position opposed to the creation of new reserve assets, conceding only the possible extension of credit to monetary authorities, chances for agreement on the creation of a new international reserve asset, as opposed to additional credit facilities, further diminished.[5] Soon thereafter, however, formulas and wording were found that allowed some members to claim that the proposed SDR scheme provided only for the possible extension of credit facilities, while others could claim that it provided for the creation of a new reserve asset that would be available unconditionally and automatically and would be permanent in character. Some members emphasized the reconstitution requirement and confinement of the use of SDRs to situations of balance of payments need, while others pointed to its acceptability as an international medium of exchange (see Section II).

Developments Leading up to the First Allocation of SDRs

The Outline as agreed at the 1967 Annual Meeting of the Fund, which was called the Rio agreement, led to the First Amendment of the Articles,[6] which took effect in 1969, and then to a proposal for an allocation of SDRs in the first basic period, which started in 1970. As the time approached for the first SDR allocation, none of the exchange rate developments and trends in international liquidity appeared to reduce the need for a new international reserve asset. After noting some of these developments, this discussion analyzes the reasoning behind the determination of the appropriate size of SDR allocations in the first basic period.

During the second half of the 1960s, international liquidity became increasingly strained. The official settlements deficit of the United States and the excess of the gold supply over the net private acquisition of gold contributed less and less to the growth of international reserves. The traditional sources of reserve growth under the gold exchange standard began to disappear, and diverse sources of reserve growth and financial alternatives were stimulated. In the first half of the 1960s, rising official claims on

[5] For more detailed characterizations of positions, see Machlup (1968, pp. 8-12) and Cohen (1970, especially pp. 169-73).

[6] The resolution adopted by the Board of Governors at the 1967 Annual Meeting, containing that outline and the proposed amendment of the Articles, is reproduced in de Vries (1976, Vol. II, pp. 54-94).

the United States still yielded more than half of the average annual growth of reserves, and the increase in the official gold holdings of countries accounted for most of the remainder (International Monetary Fund (1970, p. 19)). By contrast, from the end of 1964 to the end of 1969, official holdings of Eurodollars and of currencies other than the U.S. dollar and pound sterling, together with growing reserve positions in the Fund, provided the little growth in reserves that there was. Over the 1960s as a whole, reserves grew far less than the volume of trade, with about two thirds of the growth of reserves occurring in the first half of the decade.

Partly reflecting this growing stringency and diversification, exchange crises in the existing system of parities began to multiply during the second half of the 1960s, as did cooperative efforts to resolve them. The network of swap arrangements and short-term credit facilities between central banks and treasuries, which was principally used to support sterling and the U.S. dollar, expanded rapidly beginning in 1965 (International Monetary Fund (1970, pp. 24-25)). By the end of 1969, the credit ceiling under all these arrangements between national authorities had reached $20 billion, while the foreign exchange reserves of all countries amounted to $33 billion. In addition, the General Arrangements to Borrow, initiated in 1962, provided the Fund with loan commitments equivalent to $6 billion in the currencies of ten industrial member countries called the Group of Ten. Mutually agreed loan resources, Eurodollars, and reserve currencies other than the U.S. dollar and sterling thus began to contribute importantly to the supply of reserves and to the means for intervention. Furthermore, the Eurodollar market became a major link between national short-term money markets, providing escape from national banking regulations and improved access to foreign borrowers.

As the growth of actual, as opposed to potential, reserves in the form of undrawn swap arrangements, etc. had remained extremely modest and as rapid expansion of international credit agreements was itself interpreted as a sign of stress, the Fund judged that reserves were likely to remain in short supply during the early 1970s. The additional supply of reserves estimated to be forthcoming under the existing par value system during those years was deemed insufficient to meet the projected increase in demand accompanying acceptable growth in the volume of trade without allowing for inflation. The projected inadequacy of the supply of reserves for such growth was therefore the main argument used to justify the first round of SDR allocations. In the First Amendment to the Fund's Articles of Agreement, which became effective in 1969, the value of the SDR had been defined by reference to a fixed quantity of gold that was worth one U.S. dollar at the old official price of $35 per troy ounce. Deliberations about SDR allocations proceeded on the assumption that the official U.S. dollar price of gold would not be changed, so that one SDR would equal one U.S. dollar throughout the first basic period, 1970-72.[7]

The arguments for the first allocation of SDRs were set forth in the report to the Fund's Board of Governors, dated September 12, 1969, which contains the Managing Director's proposal (International Monetary Fund (1969 b, pp. 276-95)). The Managing Director first provided broad historical perspectives, noting that reserves had declined by over 50 percent relative to world trade since the early 1950s. Over most of the period, any effect of declining reserve ratios in impairing reserve ease of most countries had been offset, if not outweighed, by a marked improvement in the distribution of reserves, in the sense of a shift from countries (notably the United States) where reserves had been abundant in the 1950s to other countries where they had been inadequate at that time. Also, there may have been some decline in the magnitude of payments imbalances relative to international transactions. About 1964, however, the situation began to change. Growth of reserves had flattened markedly; the ratio of reserves to trade had declined more rapidly; the transfer of reserves from deficit to surplus countries had ceased to act as a force tending to equalize reserve ratios; and there had been increasing resort to international credit as a means of relieving the tightness of reserves.

The Managing Director then noted that the main indications of reserve inadequacy in those years lay in the increased reliance on restrictions in international transactions and the increased recourse to international financial assistance (bilateral and multilateral) for the purpose of meeting payments deficits and sustaining reserves. After due consideration, less weight was given to evidence—such as high levels of domestic demand, rising rates of inflation, and the absence of competitive or excessive devaluations—that could have suggested that reserve levels were adequate or even excessive. On balance, the Managing Director concluded that some supplement to reserves was required. Otherwise, he argued, the balance of payments adjustment policies adopted by deficit countries could well be frustrated by the attempts of others to increase their reserves. He therefore proposed that the prospective growth in the supply of reserves of SDR 1 billion to SDR 1.5 billion per annum, which was assumed to be produced by U.S. payments deficits on the official settlements basis, be supplemented by allocations of SDR 3 billion to SDR 3.5 billion per annum to meet annual increases in the need for reserves, which were estimated to range from SDR 4 billion to SDR 5 billion per annum under noninflation-

---

[7] In fact, SDR allocations were viewed by some as lessening conversion pressures on the U.S. dollar by reducing reliance on dollar claims for the needed growth of reserves. Nevertheless, the official U.S. dollar price of gold was increased from $35 to $38 per troy ounce in December 1971, well before the end of the first basic period.

ary conditions. The decision subsequently adopted was to allocate SDR 3 billion at the start of each year during the three-year period 1970–72.

Major Changes in the International Monetary System and the Role of the SDR

The decade of the 1970s brought fundamental changes that raised profound questions concerning the role that the SDR might play in the international monetary system. The conditions on which the planning of the first round of SDR allocations had been predicated were not realized. Instead, rising rates of money creation in the United States and in some other major countries caused unexpectedly large growth in international liquidity and fueled inflation. At the same time, differences in inflationary pressures on these countries contributed to large capital movements and payments imbalances, which were followed by exchange rate adjustments. This discussion tells how these developments led to the suspension of the convertibility of the U.S. dollar into gold and to the widespread adoption of managed floating and how they clouded the case for SDR allocation. It also considers how the growing integration of international financial markets for both private and official asset holders and borrowers changed the determinants of international liquidity and reserves. At the same time it reflects, in broad terms, on the possible implications of these and related developments for the future role of the SDR.

The first major change that occurred during the 1970s was the suspension of the convertibility of the dollar into gold for official holders in August 1971. This change freed the international liquidity and reserve creation process from the restraints of convertibility and signaled the end of the Bretton Woods system. It was the harbinger of major changes in the investment characteristics attributed to gold by both private and official holders and of fluctuations in the price of gold, which was increasingly sought as a hedge against rising inflation. Although these developments raised a number of questions relating to the measurement and adequacy of reserves and to the formal reintroduction of gold into national monetary systems, such questions are not analyzed here.[8]

The second major change in the 1970s was the abandonment of the system of fixed exchange rates by the major countries. The de facto disintegration of that system, which was hastened by the unwillingness to accept fixed external constraints on domestic policies and by the continuing overvaluation of the U.S. dollar, was arrested temporarily by the multilateral

---

[8] For detailed analyses, see United States, Commission on the Role of Gold in the Domestic and International Monetary System (1982) and Cooper (1982).

realignment of exchange rates negotiated in the Smithsonian agreement of December 1971. That agreement sanctioned the widening of the permissible margins from 1 percent to $2^{1/4}$ percent on either side of the announced parity or central rate with the U.S. dollar. The pound sterling soon moved outside this widened range and was joined by a number of other currencies early in 1973, until in February of that year the governments of most major countries suspended their commitments to maintain exchange rates within fixed margins of parity. Less than a year later, in January 1974, the French authorities severed the tie between the franc and other currencies of the European Community, so that the franc continued to float jointly against the dollar. After 1973, most smaller countries continued to peg their currencies to a major currency or basket of currencies. The large industrial countries continued to intervene in foreign exchange markets, but with the intent to maintain orderly markets rather than a parity rate.

The SDR was conceived in the framework of the fixed-rate system. Manifestly, the abandonment of that system required and continues to require a reappraisal of the role of the SDR. How has the change of the exchange rate regime modified reserve demand and supply and hence the need for a supplement to existing reserve assets? Can an internationally created and managed asset play a useful unifying or integrating role in a system with floating rates among major currencies or in other systems that might emerge? These questions, which are posed for the SDR by the choice of the exchange rate regime, are discussed in Section II for the 1970s and in Section V for the period beyond.

A third major change of the 1970s has been the growing willingness of countries to hold their currency reserves in assets denominated in currencies other than the U.S. dollar.[9] The multicurrency reserve system, as it has come to be known, also raises questions concerning the role of the SDR. If the practical choice among denominations in which currencies and reserves may be held is widened, does this lessen the need for an asset like the SDR as a supplement to existing reserve assets and as a monetary alternative? Or does the possibility of shifts between currencies raise the risk of instability and, therefore, give added impetus to the provision of the SDR as an alternative form in which currencies and reserves may be held? Section III explores how these and other questions were addressed, particularly in connection with proposals for a "substitution account" in the Fund.

Closely related to the emergence of the practice of diversifying exchange

---

[9] A tabulation of the changing shares of national currencies in the SDR value of total official holdings of foreign exchange is given for various dates from early 1975 to the end of 1980 in the Fund's *Annual Report* (International Monetary Fund (1981, p. 69)).

reserves among currencies has been the almost uninterrupted expansion of integrated international capital markets since 1960. One effect of the growing maturity of international capital markets has been to improve possibilities for national monetary authorities to use these markets as channels for the investment of their reserves, thereby facilitating diversification of reserves. At the same time, opportunities for countries to borrow in the international capital markets for increasing or sustaining their reserves, as well as for other purposes, have improved. These developments raise questions relating to the use of the Fund's resources, as well as to the need for SDR allocations.

Furthermore, the evolution of international capital markets has led to much more widespread private holding of foreign currencies and greater integration of the major money markets of the world. As private foreign reserves are now important adjuncts to domestic monetary and banking systems and as credit markets are more open to foreign and nonresident borrowers, movements of funds can tie these systems more closely together. With global liquidity more directly a result of the monetary policies of major countries than in the past, it may be difficult to focus on global liquidity as an issue separate from such policies.

The use of privately issued assets denominated in a basket of currencies linked to the SDR has begun but has not yet spread widely. A question for discussion is whether further development of this kind would be helpful. If so, would commercial SDRs be accepted in the market more readily if national monetary authorities and governments issued liabilities denominated in currency baskets that could be purchased and traded widely? More to the point, would such developments reinforce the demand by monetary authorities for SDRs created by the Fund? Could the Fund itself make greater use of the SDR and unify its operations in SDRs to be of greater service to members? If SDRs created by the Fund were capable of being held and traded by private banks and others in the private sector as well as by national authorities, would this lead to greater use of the Fund's SDRs and other SDRs and would the international monetary system then benefit? These questions are discussed in Section IV.

A final aspect of the changes during the 1970s that could have lasting effects on the future of the SDR is the severe inflation that has gripped the world for much of the decade. One effect of the reaction to inflation has already been to limit the creation of SDRs through allocation, mainly because of apprehension by some authorities that the creation of SDRs in an inflationary period might signal an official lack of concern with inflation and thereby intensify inflation (see Section II). Another reason is that, in an inflationary period during which structural changes in economies are needed and countries have different rates of inflation, the Fund had to emphasize conditional lending rather than the provision of unconditional resources through SDR allocation. A broader general question, introduced below and discussed further in Section II and Part Two, pertains to the influence of the worldwide experience with inflation on the future evolution of the international monetary system.

Inflation and the Search for Stability

In the early 1970s, many countries expected that the abandonment of fixed exchange rates with the dollar would facilitate independent monetary policy and would insulate them from inflationary pressures originating elsewhere. Many of these expectations were not realized, because inflation rose higher and monetary control became weaker in most major countries. This experience led to worldwide attempts to get the domestic money supply under control through the adoption of improved procedures and then to reduce its target rate of growth in a resolute manner designed to instill confidence that inflationary pressures would subside. Restoration of the approximate stability of domestic and international prices prevailing in the 1950s and 1960s might not only reduce exchange rate instability of its own accord but also encourage a return to exchange rate commitments in which the SDR could play a major part.

During the 1970s, many major countries found that the adoption of floating had not boosted their resistance to inflationary impulses generated by other major countries, particularly the United States, nor had it strengthened their resolve to pursue noninflationary policies on their own. Because of the growing interconnections among financial markets, it became increasingly difficult for money to be kept "tight" in one major country and "easy" in another without precipitating exchange rate overshooting and/or a diversion of international capital flows that would drive interest rate differentials back into line with expected inflation differentials. An environment in which countries keenly experienced their exposure to worldwide inflationary forces and to the difficulties of controlling or separating the creation of national and international liquidity was clearly not propitious for enhancing the use of the SDR as a supplement to existing reserve assets through allocation.

In view of this past record of instability, questions have increasingly been raised in recent years as to whether managed floating, no matter how inevitable at the time of its adoption, has served the international community well enough to discourage the search for superior alternatives, in which currency baskets could assume new and important roles. A number of European countries have obviously embarked on such a search—first, through participation in the European joint float and then through the founding of the European Monetary System (EMS), whose first stage was implemented in 1979. This quest for greater exchange stability and monetary integration in a major area of the world could spread to other countries that are increasingly buffeted by developments in international trade and finance. Reasons why some of the smaller European countries chose not to float independently throughout the 1970s could be instructive in this regard, as they may apply increasingly to larger countries as well. One of the reasons may be that instability of real exchange rates of small countries with larger competing countries can disturb price/cost relationships and hence output and investment to a greater extent in small countries than in countries that are either less dependent on foreign trade or have more pricing power in international markets. To the extent floating is more likely to be associated with disturbances of real exchange rates than pegging supported by harmonization of monetary policies, the latter system may be preferred.

It is argued in Section V that if movements toward lessening exchange rate volatility should spread from a regional to a global basis, as more countries seek to reduce their rates of inflation to a low common level, the SDR and SDR claims might be called upon to play a greater role than they would if the current system were continued without major changes. Whether the Fund should prepare for the possibility that the SDR will assume additional functions in the future evolution of the international monetary system through allocations, substitution, or greater use of SDRs in the Fund's own operations and in private markets are among the questions addressed in the remainder of this paper.

II. CHANGES IN THE SDR AND IN THE ROLE OF SDR ALLOCATIONS AFTER THE FIRST BASIC PERIOD

During the early years of the 1970s, the international monetary system underwent major changes that helped trigger a series of adaptations in the SDR and a re-examination of the role of the SDR and of SDR allocations. Particularly after the widespread adoption of managed floating in February 1973, new ideas emerged regarding the functions of the SDR and its use.

The initiatives and proposals surveyed here are grouped into three categories: (1) those concerning the characteristics of the SDR, (2) those relating to allocations after the first basic period, and (3) those concerning the link between SDR allocations and development aid or finance. The "link" proposal that has received most attention to date involves allocation of SDRs to members, not in proportion to quotas, as prescribed under the Articles of Agreement, but disproportionately to developing countries.

However, other ideas, such as allocation of SDRs by the Fund to itself or issuance of SDRs by the Fund to finance its lending to developing countries, are also covered in the last part of this section. The issuance of SDRs by a Fund based fully on the SDR is considered further in Section IV.

Evolving Characteristics of the SDR

External developments in the 1970s had a profound effect on the design of the SDR and its function in the international monetary system. From its inception, the SDR was intended to help satisfy the growing demand for reserves, by providing an alternative to increased reliance on gold and foreign exchange reserves. For this reason, the SDR was equipped with characteristics that would make it competitive with one or more of these reserve assets. As long as gold and U.S. dollars were the reserve assets, the SDR shared characteristics of those assets. The SDR then adapted to the de-emphasizing of gold, to more flexible exchange rates, and to the open-ended multiple currency system. Changes in the definition of the SDR were accompanied by changes in its yield and in the rules for transfer and reconstitution until it had evolved from a comparatively illiquid, low-yielding asset akin to gold to an instrument competitive with balanced holdings of all major foreign exchange components of the multiple currency reserve system. This discussion relates how changes in the exchange rate system and the growing variety and liquidity of reserves, as well as their higher nominal yield, set the SDR on a course that led from the protected administrative environment of its creation to the threshold of the open market.

Although the value of the SDR was originally given by the official U.S. dollar price of a fixed quantity of gold worth one U.S. dollar, the relation between gold and the SDR was tenuous from the start. Because official interventions in the London gold market had been suspended since March 17, 1968, the market price of gold ceased to be controlled by the authorities on the basis of the official price well before the first SDR was ever allocated. While official holders were still nominally free to demand conversion of U.S. dollar holdings into gold, they recognized that any attempt to do so on a large scale would jeopardize continued convertibility. When the United States nevertheless suspended the convertibility of the dollar into gold for official holders on August 15, 1971, gold became entirely unavailable at the official price. As a result, the physical link between currencies and gold was severed. The gold value guarantee of the SDR retained its meaning only with respect to the official dollar price of gold, as subsequent dollar devaluations were expressed as increases in the official accounting price of gold. Consequently, the official dollar value of the SDR was raised to $1.08571 in December 1971 and then to $1.20635 in February 1973, when such devaluations occurred. However, since the market price of gold had risen by much more than 21 percent over this period, these increases in the dollar value of the SDR did not maintain its purchasing power over gold.

About two years later, the official valuation link between the SDR and gold was broken too. The Interim Committee of the Fund's Board of Governors on the International Monetary System reported widespread agreement at its meeting of June 10-11, 1975 on the abolition of the official price of gold and on a reduction of the role of gold. To this end, a two-year agreement, concluded by the Group of Ten in August 1975 and effective on February 1, 1976, provided that there should be no action to peg the price of gold and that the total stock of gold then held by the Fund and the monetary authorities of the Group of Ten should not be increased. One sixth of the gold holdings of the Fund were to be sold to members at the official price in proportion to their quotas, and another one sixth was to be sold at auction over a four-year period, with the proceeds in excess of the official price to be used to finance a Trust Fund for the benefit of the least developed member countries.

Soon after the Group of Ten agreement had expired on January 31, 1978, the United States began to schedule regular sales of small quantities of gold from official stocks. The Second Amendment to the Fund's Articles of Agreement, effective April 1, 1978, formally eliminated the official price of gold and lifted the former prohibition on gold purchases by members at prices exceeding the official price by more than the margin established by the Fund. As a result, gold became a completely deregulated international asset that members could buy and sell subject only to the general obligations of Article VIII. Section 7 of Article VIII (International Monetary Fund (1978, p. 33)) further provides that:

> Each member undertakes to collaborate with the Fund and with other members in order to ensure that the policies of the member with respect to reserve assets shall be consistent with the objectives of promoting better international surveillance of international liquidity and making the special drawing right the principal reserve asset in the international monetary system.

Contrary to the objectives implicit in the Second Amendment to the Fund's Articles, a reduction in the role of gold and an enhancement of the role of the SDR did not accompany these developments. Rather, the SDR lost whatever ability it was originally designed to have to provide a close alternative to official gold holdings. Instead it became an increasingly close substitute for currency holdings in several steps that started in 1973 and continued into the 1980s.

The de facto development of a purely currency-based SDR dates back to February 1973. Although the SDR was still officially linked to gold when floating became widespread, in practice its value came to be linked to, and to float with, the U.S. dollar. Once the SDR had lost its gold value characteristics, continuation of the low nominal yield of $1\frac{1}{2}$ percent per annum, which had been fixed for the SDR at its inception, appeared questionable if the SDR was to remain an attractive international reserve asset. Furthermore, the SDR's lack of diversification and representativeness as an instrument whose price was fixed in terms of the U.S. dollar but flexible in terms of all other major currencies not linked to the dollar became a major cause for concern. If the SDR was to compete in the emerging multiple currency reserve system, it could not be expected to do so successfully by offering holders the exchange characteristics of the U.S. dollar and a lower yield.

In the debate that led to the adoption of the first SDR basket in July 1974, representativeness took on political as well as financial connotations, as the currencies of 15 major trading countries and the U.S. dollar were included in that basket, irrespective of whether these currencies were also important in international reserve holdings and in international finance. Some of the smaller currencies selected were pegged to the U.S. dollar, the deutsche mark, or the SDR, while currencies of other countries that were included in the basket floated independently. However, suitable national series of market-determined interest rates, well-developed forward markets, and participation in international finance and reserves were available to only a few of the currencies included in the first valuation basket. Although two currencies were added and two were eliminated in the second valuation basket, which took effect on July 1, 1978, the SDR remained, for a time, more broadly representative of members' shares in the volume of international trade than of the principal currencies used in their external transactions and finances.

The discrepancy between the 16-currency valuation baskets and the 5-currency interest rate baskets used to determine the yield on the SDR since July 1, 1974 gave evidence of some of the difficulties arising from inclusion in the SDR basket of currencies that are not widely used in international trade or finance. The private sector would find it difficult to hedge the obligations in such currencies that would be implied by denominating liabilities in SDRs. Furthermore, private SDR-denominated contracts would have to be negotiated with extreme care to cover contingencies, such as the unavailability of one or other of the underlying currencies and the determination of its fair market exchange value after the imposition of exchange restrictions or the loss of convertibility. Such complications greatly discouraged the private use of SDR-denominated instruments. They also would have made it difficult and more costly for the Fund to borrow in private markets, a step that was explored in 1980 and 1981.

Considerations such as these led to the selection of the five principal world currencies for the third basket, which became effective on January 1, 1981, and thereby also led to the unification of the interest rate and valuation baskets. On that date, currency amounts were fixed so that the U.S.

dollar would have a weight of 42 percent in the total at the average exchange rates of the three-month period ended December 31, 1980, and the deutsche mark a weight of 19 percent. The French franc, Japanese yen, and pound sterling were given weights of 13 percent each. The weight of the fixed currency amounts so determined in the SDR changes continuously with the SDR price of these currencies. The percentage weights are subject to revision at five-year intervals as necessary to correspond with the relative importance of the five major currencies in international trade and reserves.

With this last change in its composition, the SDR had been fully adapted to the multiple currency reserve system. The adaptation of its yield characteristics to the market also took about seven years. As already noted, the interest rate on the SDR had been fixed at a mere $1\frac{1}{2}$ percent from the start of 1970 to mid-1974, although devaluation of the U.S. dollar against gold raised the rate of return on two occasions. The complex formula for determination of the SDR interest rate for the two years thereafter yielded a rate equal, on average, to about 55 percent of the combined rate before it was raised to 60 percent of the combined rate, effective July 1, 1976, and to 80 percent, effective January 1, 1979. Finally, in May 1981, the attractiveness of the SDR to holders (and its cost to users) was further enhanced by raising its yield to 100 percent of the weighted average of the rates selected on liquid national instruments, all of which are, in practice, free of default risk. Although the rates on comparable Eurocurrency deposits would generally be somewhat higher, the SDR thus became broadly competitive with balanced holdings of the major currencies in the multiple currency reserve system in both character and yield. However, the adequacy of yield on one issue relative to another depends on all the financial characteristics of competing issues as they are weighed in the market.

The liquidity and usability of the SDR were also improved, particularly for net users holding substantially less than their cumulative allocations. During the period 1970-78, a sizable reconstitution was required to prevent average daily holdings, as a percentage of average daily cumulative allocations over five-year periods ending with successive quarters, from falling below a set percentage of 30 percent. Although the first such average applied to year-end 1975, countries knew that they had to compensate for holdings below the percentage set by the reconstitution requirement at one time by more holding at other times, thereby reducing the extent and flexibility of SDR use. These constraints were phased out in two successive steps as the reconstitution limit was lowered from 30 percent to 15 percent at the beginning of 1979 and was eliminated in May 1981.

Other constraints on net users and net acquirers of SDRs were also relaxed gradually. Prior to August 1976, SDR transactions by agreement between participants normally required that the user in the transaction have a balance of payments need. After that date, the requirement of need was waived, provided that the transaction brought both parties' holdings of SDRs closer to their cumulative allocations. The Second Amendment of the Fund's Articles, which became effective April 1, 1978, put an end to all specific restrictions governing transactions by agreement. Nevertheless, net holders of SDRs in excess of allocations do not necessarily hold such excess amounts voluntarily but rather because they are required to accept up to three times the SDRs allocated to them under rules for transactions with designation that channel SDRs to countries with strong balance of payments and gross reserve positions. Members that find themselves in these circumstances may thus continue to be constrained by designation in exercising their preferences regarding the composition of reserves. Although holding SDRs that can be managed less freely and used less widely than foreign exchange reserves has been made progressively less costly for net acquirers, allowing the yield on the SDR to rise above 100 percent of the combined rate would be one way of widening the scope for acceptance by agreement until acceptance obligations become dispensable in fact.

While the SDR has certain disadvantages at the present time,[10] the SDR, as currently constituted, also has unique advantages from the standpoint of the international monetary system. Because the SDR is defined as a representative basket of major currencies, creating SDRs is unlikely to affect the exchange rates between the component currencies, while creating non-gold reserves through any other process is tied to intervention operations and changes in relative prices. Hence, while the SDR has been and must remain equipped to prove itself in freely functioning asset markets, it also provides a means by which decisions on international liquidity can be insulated from some of the immediate pressures arising in foreign exchange markets and can be focused instead on the concerns of the membership of the Fund as a whole. As described below, these decisions have centered around the question of SDR allocations.

Considerations Relating to SDR Allocations After the First Basic Period

In 1969, it was thought that allocations ranging from SDR 3 billion to SDR 3.5 billion in each of the succeeding three years of the first basic

---

[10] For a longer list of disadvantages attributed to the Fund's SDR by central banks responding to a recent survey, see Group of Thirty (1982, pp. 19–20). Apart from limited usability and a below-average yield, lack of a range of maturities, relative lack of liquidity, and "lack of anonymity" were among the disadvantages cited. For a more detailed description of these and other possible disadvantages and for recommendations on how many of them could be ameliorated, see "Possible Further Improvements in the Existing SDR," Chapter 12 in this volume.

period (1970-72) would be sufficient to account for most of the growth of international reserves. If SDR allocations had accounted for most of the growth of reserves in these and subsequent years, the SDR would have been started on the road to becoming the principal reserve asset in the international monetary system as its originators had intended. However, matters turned out differently, and allocations ceased until a new understanding was reached about the role of SDR allocations in view of the changed international reserve situation.

At the end of the first basic period, the U.S. deficit on official settlements had averaged SDR 17 billion per annum in the years 1970 through 1972, rather than from SDR 1 billion to SDR 1.5 billion as projected by the Fund at the start of that period. The cumulative allocations of SDR 9 billion during the first basic period thus contributed to a growth in reserves that would clearly have been excessive, rather than inadequate, even without such allocations. No proposal was made to cancel or suspend allocations as these developments became apparent. However, in view of the unexpectedly large growth of reserves and the rising inflation during the early 1970s, no allocations were proposed for 1973-77, the second basic period. As noted in the Fund's 1973 Annual Report, the symptoms of reserve ease were now acknowledged to predominate over those of stringency. Under these circumstances, SDR allocation could no longer be justified by the need to supplement the growth of reserves in quantitative terms.

The early 1970s brought other changes that would have made it difficult to justify SDR allocations by the need to avert a projected inadequacy of reserve supply after the mid-1970s. These changes included the adoption of managed floating by the major industrial countries and the growing integration of national and international financial markets. Reflecting on the implications of these developments, J.J. Polak (1980, pp. 337-38) wrote:

> With the expansion of international banking, the control of the level of international liquidity has mostly ceased to be a separate problem; the central issue for attention is the control of domestic liquidity in the main industrial countries, in particular the United States. Within the total of liquidity provided by the banking systems of the main industrial countries, the great majority of countries can arrange their asset and liability structure so as to have the amount of reserves they want to hold at prevailing interest rates.

Hence, consideration of global reserve adequacy in purely quantitative terms no longer provided a powerful rationale for SDR allocations. Before SDR allocations could be resumed, this rationale had to be supplemented by reference to the qualitative considerations set forth in the Fund's Articles, as well as by considerations with respect to the broader functioning of markets and the differences between reserve center countries and non-oil developing countries in the cost of acquiring reserves and of financing deficits.

The Managing Director's 1978 proposal for allocation of SDRs in the third basic period acknowledged the changes in the reserve creation process that had taken place in the 1970s by noting that most countries have a means for satisfying their need for reserves when international capital markets are as free as they are today.[11] As a result, SDR allocations were no longer justified by a long-term global need for reserves that cannot be met except by allocation. Rather, the Managing Director pointed to qualitative improvements, noting that some of the difficulties associated with a system in which countries add to their international indebtedness as they increase their gross reserves can be overcome through allocation. In particular, if developing countries substituted a substantial part of any SDR allocation for increases in official holdings of foreign exchange that would otherwise have taken place, so that total borrowing would fall, any expansionary effects of allocation would be limited. If non-oil developing countries borrowed less but also held smaller deposits in the Eurocurrency market, as here assumed, the supply of loans to other groups of countries in that market would not rise directly but only in response to a favorable change in the risk composition of the banks' remaining assets. The desire to change the composition of gross reserves by additions of SDRs, thereby improving the terms and conditions on which such additions are supplied, rather than the need to provide adequate growth of total non-gold reserves now provided the main rationale for renewing SDR allocations. Also, the international symmetry and exchange neutrality of reserve creation through SDR allocation could make it a substitute for reserve creation by other less efficient and potentially more inflationary means. For example, reserve creation through intervention often has undesirable consequences for money supply growth and inflation in industrial countries, and continued liability settlement by reserve center countries usually implies an exchange rate structure with other countries that is inefficient for trade and the appropriate transfer of resources toward their internationally most profitable uses.

Possible effects of a decision to allocate SDRs on expectations with respect to inflation caused the Fund to keep the allocations modest. The total of SDR 4 billion allocated each year over the period 1979-81 was estimated to amount to only a small fraction of the average annual growth of non-gold reserves, conservatively estimated as SDR 20 billion per year. While the actual growth of non-gold reserves from the end of 1978 to the

---

[11] For this and subsequent references to the Managing Director's proposal, see International Monetary Fund (1979, pp. 123-28).

end of 1981 was eventually almost twice as high as projected, this fact alone would no longer automatically have diminished the size of the SDR allocations indicated under the criteria followed in 1978, as opposed to those applied in 1968-69, to determine the appropriate size of allocations.

Both the effects on inflationary expectations and the state of international liquidity resurfaced as major issues in the debates surrounding the still unresolved question of allocations in the fourth basic period, starting in 1982. After a series of qualitative improvements, the interest rate on SDR holdings had finally been raised to the full combined rate by May 1981. This step had completed the transformation of the SDR from its earlier likeness to paper gold or "outside" money to "inside" money issued against the obligation to pay market-related interest on allocations by those who receive them.[12] Instead of representing to a large degree a gift of money that some could use at very low cost, allocations thus became an offer of money on credit. As the interest rate on the SDR is now high enough to prevent an SDR allocation from increasing the net worth of the recipient to any great extent, SDR allocation can also be likened to the establishment of a guaranteed line of credit. Members can draw on this line unconditionally to the limit of their cumulative allocation at interest rates linked to a basket of interest rates on riskless national instruments, but if they retain SDRs allocated to them, the net cost is zero.[13] In spite of this transformation, qualitative issues received less weight in the 1981 discussions than in 1978. Major debates centered on the possible inflationary effects of SDR allocations and on the influence of pre-existing inflation on international liquidity and on the advisability of further allocations.

In a previous investigation of the channels through which SDR allocations could conceivably raise inflationary pressures, Fund staff considered a variety of possible SDR uses and mechanisms of transmission. Since it was found difficult to conceive of SDR allocations raising the rate of growth of the money supply in major industrial countries, only modest effects on the velocities of those moneys were pointed to as possibly having worldwide inflationary implications if resource constraints were tight. Some outside investigators have concluded that the actual effects of rais-

---

[12] Inside money is created through the purchase of claims on those who receive it, so that the sector holding more inside money also has greater debts to the issuer. Hence, wealth is created by the issuance of inside money only to the extent these debts are incurred on unusually favorable terms or there are efficiency gains from monetization.

[13] The analogy with a guaranteed line of credit is used only to elucidate certain features or possible uses of the SDR, in this case the saving of commitment fees afforded by allocations, to the extent they are substituted for lines of credit from banks. The fact that the credit is paid out even to countries not in a position to use it is one of the formal differences between the establishment of a guaranteed line of credit and the SDR allocation mechanism, as further discussed in Section IV.

ing the ceiling on a line of credit that involves the payment of interest at the full combined rate upon use does not have significant macroeconomic consequences on variables such as worldwide inflation,[14] even if the raising of such ceilings permits increased resource absorption or spending that could be unwise in individual cases. Others have pointed out that the answer depends very much on what SDR allocations are compared with, and that SDR allocations may be less inflationary than other ways of adding to reserves. Thomas D. Willett (1980, p. 78) has commented:

> For example, the creation of international liquidity through the undesired payments imbalances associated with the breakdown of the Bretton Woods system placed much greater direct inflationary pressure on recipient countries—that is, they were more difficult to sterilize—than do SDR allocations and increases in the market price of gold.

Nevertheless, a decision to resume allocation of SDRs could, under certain conditions, give the wrong signal. For instance, if governments agree to allocations and these actions are construed by the public as signals of a more relaxed attitude to domestic liquidity creation or a reversion from tight monetary control over national monetary targets programmed for deceleration, SDR allocations may be associated with higher inflation or with greater perceived tolerance of it.

The allocation of SDRs raises other problems of adjustment. The line of credit provided by allocations is more favorable than commercial credit, particularly for those members that plan to use allocations not only to reduce foreign borrowing but also to increase imports.[15] Increasing imports by drawing on SDR holdings rather than by resorting to additional borrowing in international financial markets thus lowers the cost of financing those added imports. Also, countries might not have been able to raise their bank borrowing without having to accept wider spreads and being subjected to other disciplines of the market, such as credit rationing, which do not apply to the use of allocated SDRs. However, recognizing that the use of the line of credit provided by SDR allocations implies increased indebtedness and interest obligations, banks take account of SDR allocations and holdings and of other components of gross reserves in setting their own terms. For this reason, it is debatable to what extent SDR allocations provide an escape from market discipline for countries with continuing banking relationships.

[14] See, for instance, *Balance-of-Payments Problems of Developing Countries* (Group of Thirty (1981, p. 22)).

[15] The economic and financial uses made of SDR allocations can be determined only by looking at the totality of external financing relationships and reserve holdings and by examining how balance sheets and the balance of payments may have changed as a result of allocations. Such uses are not necessarily revealed by the statistical measure of "net use," which is simply the excess of cumulative allocations over a country's holdings of SDRs. Net use that is not associated with increased balance of payments deficits merely involves the rearrangement of assets and liabilities in the portfolio of gross reserves.

Since SDRs can now be used unconditionally and indefinitely, any use of SDR allocations to finance larger balance of payments deficits than would otherwise be financed could entail a potentially permanent transfer of resources to user countries at a cost below that incurred on borrowing in international financial markets. Although SDR allocations may be used in this way by some non-oil developing countries, the amount of such use is likely to be small in relation to the total size of the allocations, in part because only about one fourth of allocations go to non-oil developing countries under the existing distribution of Fund quotas.

Whether the transfer of allocated SDRs is now best likened to borrowing and lending or to a transaction involving the use of international reserve money as a medium of exchange depends on the usefulness of either analogy. Net users may feel that the use of allocated SDRs increases their obligation to pay interest, much as the use of credit does. Net acquirers, on the other hand, may find that the SDR is much more liquid than loan assets and always transferable at par very much like deposit money. Hence, it is quite possible that the Fund intermediates in the process of net use and net acquisition of SDRs in a way that distinguishes the economic characteristics of SDRs held by net acquirers from those of the corresponding liabilities incurred by net users. As one of the finance ministers participating in the introduction of the SDR scheme remarked in 1967, "as in the national field, money is created by credit." Applied to the SDR, it could be said that the "money" held by net acquirers provides "credit" to net users of allocated SDRs. A third function of the SDR—for participants to the extent they are neither net users nor net acquirers—is that of a line of credit. All things considered, it may be difficult to generalize about the monetary characteristics of the SDR and how they have developed. Indeed, through the liberalization of its use and return, the SDR may have become more like interest-bearing deposit money for some while becoming a more permanent but also a more costly means of credit for others. This could affect attitudes toward the "link," which is discussed below.

Proposals for a Link

Because of the multiple potentialities of the SDR, attempts have been made by various groups to emphasize particular characteristics of its use in preference to others. The originally tight restriction of net use of SDRs to situations of balance of payments need and the former reconstitution requirement had been seized upon in the deliberations leading up to the establishment of the SDR as means of emphasizing its affinity to repayable credit and its distance from international reserve assets. The proposals for a link between SDR allocations and development finance emphasize other credit aspects, in that they are based, in part, on representations of the special needs of developing countries for unconditional resource loans from the rest of the world.[16]

The case for a link was clearly stated on several occasions in the second half of the 1960s. As the Governor for Indonesia, commenting on the proposal for allocations in the first basic period, stated in 1969:

> [A] rather striking feature is that developed countries not in need of extra liquidity are receiving SDR's as well. It is true that their use is dependent on balance of payments needs, but, in ordinary life, an enterprise neither seeks nor obtains extra credit facilities from a bank if it has already ample means at its disposal. Instead of the present system of distribution, conceptually at least, it seems feasible to allocate SDR's only to countries in need of additional liquidity. (International Monetary Fund (1969 b, p. 83))

As was pointed out much earlier:

> A world-wide distribution of monetary reserves in accordance with the apparent need for them is incompatible with the yet more fundamental consideration of the distribution of the real resources *of each country* in accordance with the highest priority for their use. If the monetary reserves of the world were completely redistributed in accordance with apparent need, they would soon be re-redistributed, as each country would soon (quite properly) rearrange the changed amount of real resources at its disposal in accordance with its scale of preferences. (International Monetary Fund (1953, p. 43))

Nevertheless, there could be force to the argument that if SDR allocations can be likened to the establishment of a guaranteed line of credit for acquiring internationally accepted means of payment to hold or to draw on, it is unclear why this credit should be paid out to countries that may have no desire to activate the line of credit on account of strength in their balance of payments and gross reserve position but still wish to contribute to the success of the SDR scheme in other ways.

Since 1969, representatives of developing countries have repeatedly argued that the principle of establishing a link between the allocation of SDRs and development finance would best be served by an increase in their share of SDRs by means of direct SDR allocations by the Fund to be used for development purposes.[17] Thus, it was stated in 1973 that, whereas reserve creation has in the past involved resource transfers to gold producers and reserve centers, it would be appropriate in a reformed system that a greater part of the benefit derived from the switch to reserve creation in the form of SDRs should be channeled on an agreed basis to developing countries (International Monetary Fund (1974, p. 96)). Essentially the same conclusion was repeated in 1980 when the Brandt Commission recommended that SDRs be allocated to those countries most likely to experi-

---

[16] A taxonomy of developing countries' needs for reserves is provided in Javier Márquez (1970, pp. 104-107).

[17] See the report of the Technical Group on the SDR/Aid Link and Related Proposals in the Committee of Twenty's report (International Monetary Fund (1974, pp. 95-109)).

ence balance of payments deficits and high domestic costs of adjustment and least likely to be able to finance them from alternative sources (Brandt (1980, p. 212), and United Nations (1982, p. 48)).

Use of the SDR for the additional objective of resource transfer to the developing countries in a more concentrated fashion than is possible through allocations in proportion to quota can take several different forms (International Monetary Fund (1974, p. 101)). Direct allocations to developing countries—the scheme preferred by such countries—would involve the adoption of a new formula for the allocation of SDRs among participants that would channel to the developing countries a share of total allocations larger than their share in Fund quotas. Direct allocations to development finance institutions (or, alternatively, to the General Department of the Fund) would involve making available to development finance institutions (or to the Fund) a portion of the SDRs created, determined either as a percentage of the total SDR allocation or as an absolute amount. Indirect allocations to development finance institutions (or to the Fund) would leave unaltered the principle of SDR allocations to participants on a basis strictly proportional to Fund quotas, but it would be complemented by agreement among developed countries to transfer to development finance institutions (or to the Fund) either part of the SDRs allocated to them or the equivalent in currencies. Of these three alternatives, only elements of the first two—direct allocations to developing countries and direct allocations to the General Department of the Fund—are discussed here.

Direct allocations to developing countries help economize on two types of cost. First, increasing gross reserves through SDR allocation rather than through borrowing in the international capital market saves the spread between the rate at which developing countries can borrow in that market and the London interbank bid (LIBID) rate, at which the proceeds are deposited. This spread typically is 0.5 to 1.5 percentage point, depending on the risk class of the borrower. Alternatively, if the SDR holdings deriving from allocations are viewed as equivalent to an unused line of credit, the holder would save the commitment fees that would otherwise be incurred if such a line of credit were established with banks. Second, there may be profit in using allocated SDRs to increase Eurocurrency deposits, since the interest rate on these deposits, combined as in the SDR, is 1 to 1.5 percentage point above the interest rate on the SDR as currently determined.

Overall, therefore, SDR allocations year after year may entail annual interest savings for developing countries of between 1.5 and 3 percentage points of the amount of such allocations, if they are fully used. As of April 30, 1982, about half of all non-oil developing countries held less than 10 percent of their cumulative allocations, with interest savings within the range indicated. Such savings can be obtained by all countries operating under similar financial circumstances by merely letting the composition of their gross reserve portfolio change over time and by not letting either reserves or imports grow faster than they otherwise would. Under certain conditions, countries whose reserves or imports have been constrained to lower levels than they desire on account of credit rationing and risk perceptions in international financial markets could reap even greater benefits from SDR allocations. Availability and the absence of advance limitations on maturity would be beneficial under conditions of credit rationing to some countries, even in the unlikely event of SDR cancellation, particularly since reconstitution for the purpose of cancellation could be financed by the Fund.

Allocating SDRs to the Fund for relending to non-oil developing countries rather than allocating them disproportionately to such countries themselves would provide for conditional resource transfers, as SDR holdings of members would then be created through the Fund's lending rather than unconditionally by allocations. The scope for conditionality would be broadened, although the Fund already has the means for influencing the resource use of those developing countries that borrow from the Fund under its conditionality programs. Direct allocations to developing countries and allocations to the General Department of the Fund for lending and relending mainly to non-oil developing countries could differ also in terms of the initial distribution and subsequent circulation among such countries according to the use made of SDRs in repayments (repurchases). The expansion of conditional lending by the Fund would not increase the resources available to individual non-oil developing countries as promptly or as predictably as a linked allocation. Nevertheless, if the combined amount of resources transferred to such countries—and hence the total addition to SDRs held in the international reserves of all countries—was identical under the two schemes over some period of time, global liquidity would be about the same.

The surplus countries that would be the net acquirers of the SDRs used by non-oil developing countries would have somewhat more influence on the policies governing such use if SDRs were allocated to the Fund rather than directly to non-oil developing countries. Under either scheme, they might view any obligation to acquire more SDRs than had been allocated to them as interfering with their freedom to manage the composition of their reserves. Since SDRs continue to be transferred not just by agreement but also with designation, net acquirers cannot always choose the amount of SDRs that they hold. They may have the opportunity of partially offsetting increased SDR holdings by selling U.S. and U.K. treasury bills. But they can rarely sell instruments denominated in deutsche mark, Japanese yen, and French francs that are strictly comparable with those whose yield is used in deriving the combined rate. As a result, they cannot view increased SDR holdings as a one-to-one substitute for non-gold reserves. Hence, in addition to questions about the appropriate scope of conditionality, there is a close relation between the interest rate and holding regulations of the SDR and the degree to which a direct or indirect link to development finance may be acceptable to those industrial and oil exporting countries that are the prospective net acquirers.

Broader problems could arise in connection with authorization to the Fund to issue SDRs for financing its own lending to developing countries. Since the evolutionary implications of such a step are rather distant, only a brief discussion is provided here (see Section IV for further discussion). Conceptually, SDR deposits created by Fund lending could involve an expansion of international reserves in much the same way as central bank purchases of government securities in the open market increase the reserves of the domestic banking system. If some countries acquired more SDRs from other countries *and* let their total reserves grow more rapidly than they otherwise would, they would have to offset faster growth of the foreign component of their monetary base with slower growth in the domestic component if they wished to adhere to their domestic money supply targets. If the Fund was empowered to issue SDRs for the special purpose of financing its lending for balance of payments adjustment in the developing countries, it would acquire powers exceeding those of central banks. Central banks are not generally authorized to acquire assets that may be subject to default and liquidity risks by issuing their own liabilities to captive holders under their jurisdiction. A variety of safeguards would thus have to be considered, once it is clear what, if any, central banking functions and responsibilities members might be willing to delegate to the Fund. Nevertheless, for the Fund to provide SDRs to some countries for transfer to others is part of the essence of the link, whether the SDRs are created directly in the process of Fund lending or through allocations to countries or groups of countries that are likely to remain net users.

III. PROPOSALS FOR EXTENDING THE ROLE OF THE SDR THROUGH SUBSTITUTION

The hectic and uncoordinated growth of reserves, as well as uncertainty about the future working of the exchange rate system, contributed to a general unwillingness by Fund members in the years following 1972 to endorse any particular calculation of an appropriate level of global reserves that could have formed the basis for further SDR allocations in proportion to quota. Instead, attention shifted to the question of how the role of the SDR could be enhanced through substitution without contributing to the growth of international liquidity on a global basis. Indeed, some proposals were made to restrict and control the growth of international liquidity by means of the SDR, although in a manner least harmful to non-oil developing countries.

Although many of these issues had already been raised at the time the SDR was created in 1969 (International Monetary Fund (1969 b)), they were first aired fully in the documents of the Fund's Committee on Reform of the International Monetary System and Related Issues (Committee of Twenty) published in 1974. Intensive discussions of a substitution account recurred in 1979–80, but the once keen interest in using the SDR to control the growth of international liquidity dwindled after the mid-1970s. This section surveys the major proposals on substitution, the conditions under which they were made, and the problems they addressed. It deals with ideas pertaining to the substitution of SDRs or SDR-denominated assets for other reserve assets, including substitution associated with a general regime for the settlement of balance of payments deficits through the transfer of assets as well as substitution processes designed to lessen the unwanted effects of the operation of a multiple currency reserve system.

Substitution as Viewed by the Committee of Twenty

Ideas on substitution have been put forward intermittently since before the founding of the Fund.[18] The most detailed and far-ranging discussions since the establishment of the SDR were those of the Committee of Twenty, which was constituted in 1972 to report to the Board of Governors with respect to all aspects of reform of the international monetary system. Some participants in the deliberations of the Committee of Twenty had a keen appreciation of the fact that any increase in official holdings of SDRs would reduce the demand for other reserve assets and thereby provide for substitution as long as there was no change in the demand for reserves in total (International Monetary Fund (1974, p. 166)). However, it was thought that rapid progress toward the goal of enhancing the role of the SDR in the international financial system would require more direct measures of substitution.

In the report of the Committee's Technical Group on Global Liquidity and Consolidation headed by Alexandre Kafka, substitution was defined as the replacement of short-term currency assets by liquid claims on the

---

[18] For a detailed historical account, see Gold (1980, pp. 265–326).

international community in the form of SDRs; its principal effect would be to change the composition of reserves while the volume remained the same (International Monetary Fund (1974, pp. 167–76)). Elements of reserve creation would remain only to the extent that the proposed substitution account would issue SDRs to reserve centers against payments of their own currencies, as it might be authorized to do if reserves should ever decline below predetermined levels, initially those outstanding at the outset of the reform (International Monetary Fund (1974, p. 169)). Principally, however, the proposed substitution account was designed to convert official holdings of "old" foreign currency balances into an internationally accepted and nonredeemable asset. In 1974, such a step was thought to facilitate the restoration and subsequent maintenance of general convertibility by reducing the strains on the system that might result if reserve centers were faced with demands for the net conversion of existing balances of their currencies (International Monetary Fund (1974, p. 170)).

There was, however, some concern that voluntary substitution on a continuing basis could adversely affect foreign exchange markets and that the SDR could become the preferred alternative to whatever reserve currency was least desired, with purely speculative movements out of reserve currencies induced by the availability of substitution (International Monetary Fund (1974, p. 173)). The adverse effects of substitution in discouraging adjustment of reserve centers were to be reduced by requiring that currency balances surrendered to a substitution account be eliminated gradually over time by asset settlements on the part of the issuers of the currencies (International Monetary Fund (1974, p. 174)). These settlements could take the form of earmarking some portion of SDR allocations received by the reserve centers for amortization. It was thought that for the Fund to lend out the currency balances obtained by substitution would defeat the purpose of substitution—achievement of a reduction in existing currency balances—and would also have inflationary effects by adding to existing reserves (International Monetary Fund (1974, p. 175)).

Because "old" balances outside the scope of substitution would still be convertible and because "new" balances could pile up in the future, SDR substitution had to be buttressed by measures designed to control the growth and composition of international reserves. Thus, funding short-term currency assets with longer-term and less liquid claims and substituting SDRs for short-term currency assets were both considered in relation to the control of international liquidity. If the uncontrolled growth of liability settlement was to be discouraged, the SDR could be given a role in intervention, particularly if the major countries would choose to define par values of their currencies in terms of the SDR (International Monetary Fund (1974, pp. 122–23)). Any additional foreign exchange acquired by official holders would be immediately presented to the issuer for conversion into SDRs. Control over the growth of SDRs in the international financial system would then confer a large measure of control over the growth of international reserves (International Monetary Fund (1974, pp. 124–26)). It was also proposed that countries could go directly to a substitution facility to purchase SDRs in exchange for reserve currency balances, as an alternative to presenting the balances to the reserve center (International Monetary Fund (1974, p. 127)). In either event, the basic asset used in settlement would be the SDR.

Under these strict rules, asset settlement could imply tight limits on intervention because countries might soon exhaust their reserves of SDRs and foreign exchange convertible into SDRs. Proposals were made to provide additional resources through official lending to members needing to defend the external value of their currency against private capital outflows that were considered to be disequilibrating (International Monetary Fund (1974, p. 79)). It was agreed that official currency balances arising out of such short-term assistance should be disregarded in the calculation both of settlement obligations and of the amount that could be drawn on the proposed substitution account (International Monetary Fund (1974, p. 128)). The credit facilities that were to provide this elasticity would include bilateral swaps as well as Fund credit obtained by drawings on the General Resources Account. Proposals were also made for a new facility under which the Fund would borrow SDRs from surplus countries and lend to deficit countries (International Monetary Fund (1974, p. 128)), thereby recycling SDRs and building SDR claims on the SDR.

To retain some measure of control under these more flexible arrangements for asset settlement, under which rules would be relaxed by members being allowed to borrow for intervention purposes from the Fund and from each other under certain conditions, the Fund was to exercise general surveillance over the trend of official currency holdings.[19] In the last analysis, the Fund was to be prepared to make recommendations with respect to countries' behavior, including procedures for orderly reductions in such holdings. It was also envisaged that an issuing country should have the right to place limits on further accumulation of balances of its currency by other countries. Conversely, the surplus countries were to be subjected to holding limits for acquiring further primary reserves other than by allocation of SDRs. To observe those limits, countries would be forced either to

---

[19] General surveillance obligations of the Fund are reflected in the present Articles of Agreement. According to Article IV, Section 3(a): "The Fund shall oversee the international monetary system in order to ensure its effective operation, ..." The corresponding obligations of members are elaborated in Section 7 of Article VIII, which is quoted in Section II of this paper.

fund their claims on the issuers of reserve currencies or to adjust to them by varying their monetary policies or exchange rates (or their capital controls and tariff and nontariff barriers to trade).

Owing to the diverse interests and economic circumstances of Fund members, to concerns about the infringement of government authority that would be implied by controlling the growth of international reserves, as well as to uncertainty about the effects of the more mandatory forms of asset settlement on the international adjustment process, no agreement was reached on any global formula or on its application to individual countries. While the development of the SDR as the principal reserve asset and the reduction of the role of reserve assets other than SDRs suggested a reduction in the proportion of global reserves held in the form of currency balances, it was recognized that official attitudes toward such a reduction "would depend on several factors, including the future characteristics of SDRs, the timing and extent of the reduction, and the method employed to achieve it" (International Monetary Fund (1974, p. 166)). There was a wide variation in the views concerning the degree to which currency balances should be reduced, with some countries being particularly concerned about possible contractive effects of substitution. Widespread substitution might reduce the liquidity of reserve holdings and eliminate any pyramiding of reserves through Eurocurrency markets. Hence there were fears, first voiced in 1974 and repeated in 1979–80, that the establishment of a substitution account would divert credit from the international credit markets to the reserve center country, since not only official claims on the United States but also Eurodollar assets, would, in effect, be sold for SDRs. Some non-oil developing countries, for example, emphasized their need to hold currency balances with commercial banks that provided a multiple of these balances in credit lines that could be used for commercial purposes, as well as in support of development programs. In that respect, SDRs could not perform the role of currency holdings as long as they could not be held in the private sector. Moreover, it was argued that some countries' currency holdings were partly the counterpart of foreign debts incurred in order to enable them to hold reserves (International Monetary Fund (1974, pp. 166–67)). For these reasons, some countries expressed reservations about the establishment of a substitution account and other proposed measures to fund currency balances.

Substitution Account Proposed in 1979–80

While consideration of possible substitution arrangements for both gold and the U.S. dollar continued after 1974, high-level discussions were not resumed until several years later, when the U.S. dollar began to weaken against most major currencies. Meanwhile, difficulties in quantifying and preserving the appropriate degree of international liquidity were compounded when the official U.S. dollar price of gold was abolished on August 31, 1975.[20] To regain control, a gold substitution account was mentioned as one possibility. Concentration in the Fund of a large proportion of the gold now held in individual countries was compared with the historical phasing out of gold as a domestic means of payment by its transfer from the private sector to central banks. Furthermore, proposals were made to elevate the Fund to exclusive, or at least controlling, issuer of official reserve assets and to lender of last resort to central banks (Witteveen (1975, pp. 313–16)). One of the proposals involved the Fund regulating international liquidity by obtaining agreement that countries would hold a certain minimum proportion of their international reserves in the form of SDRs. Adjustments in the aggregate volume of SDRs and/or in the required minimum ratio of SDRs to total (non-gold) reserves could then also bring about international management of the global amount of international reserves. (If this ratio were set equal to one, the Fund would become the exclusive issuer of additions to (non-gold) reserves.) Under an approach of this kind, the SDR would become the center of the international reserve system without necessarily being the exclusive or even the main reserve asset, yet there would be safeguards against an uncontrolled expansion of international reserves and the resulting inflationary potential. However, none of these proposals, which might have pointed the way to providing a pivotal role for the SDR even without large-scale substitution, received wide attention or consideration with a view to implementation.

In the closing years of the 1970s, the international monetary system experienced strains that reminded some observers of the recurring dollar crises and other systemic defects that had been evident when the decision to create the SDR had been taken in 1969. The first round of SDR allocations had done little to modify a reserve system depending overwhelmingly on the U.S. dollar and on a continuous growth in the stock of dollars held abroad. Furthermore, a multiple currency reserve system was widely considered an undesirable alternative because the process of moving toward such a system through reserve diversification could disrupt exchange markets and, once completed, that system could be an ever-present source of exchange rate instability. Some observers therefore regarded SDR substitution as the only feasible means of checking excessive dependence on the U.S. dollar and of providing an alternative to the development of a multiple currency reserve system.

Renewed interest in the substitution account arose from a number of sources. The increasingly rapid depreciation of the U.S. dollar before sta-

---

[20] This abolition was ratified by the international community as a whole when the Second Amendment to the Articles became effective on April 1, 1978.

bilizing measures were announced on November 1, 1978 was taken as a sign of unsatisfied demands for reducing the share of the U.S. dollar in reserve portfolios. Unless countries had an opportunity to shift part of their reserves into SDR-denominated assets without going through the exchange markets, many of them, it was feared, might further diversify their reserves by purchasing in the market currencies that had already substantially appreciated in real terms against the U.S. dollar. The issuers of these currencies were, however, reluctant to see a major increase in their roles as suppliers of reserve currencies, since this would interfere with control over their money supplies if nonsterilized intervention were involved or might lead to an excessive appreciation of their currencies if central banks did not enter the market. Moreover, a system based on a number of major reserve currencies would be vulnerable to shifts among them. Under these circumstances, it was felt that the use of the SDR in substitution for currencies would not only help avert undesired pressures on currencies but would also contribute to making the SDR the principal reserve asset in the international monetary system—an objective that countries had accepted as part of the Second Amendment to the Fund's Articles.

These goals were modest compared with those envisaged in 1974. SDR substitution had then been proposed as part of an asset settlement system in which balance of payments adjustment and stable growth were to be promoted by controlling the generation and use of international reserves by means of the SDR. The voluntary substitution account proposed in 1979-80, however, would provide directly only for adjustments in the portfolio of international reserves. While it might dampen exchange rate pressures by taking any dollar overhang out of official holdings and thus enhance the role of the SDR, the immediate impact of such an account on the working of the international monetary system would be quite limited, unless accompanied by national measures promising greater price stability and international adjustment. In this regard, the Executive Board, in its report to the Interim Committee on a substitution account, dated August 3, 1979, noted the longer-range potential that "this development could over time bring about conditions more conducive to international influence over the growth of international liquidity," although there was some doubt about these results.

Studies around this time focused on a single substitution of SDR claims for dollars, although it was noticed that, in the long run, the SDR could be envisaged as a substitute for any reserve currency or group of currencies. It was generally agreed that in order for the account to achieve widespread participation on a voluntary basis and on a large scale, the account should contain satisfactory provisions with respect to the liquidity of the claims, their rate of interest, and the preservation of their capital value. Furthermore, the claims should have a yield that would make them sufficiently attractive in comparison with other major reserve components, implying that they should yield a market-oriented return.

Payment of such a yield and the maintenance of capital value had to be assured through arrangements covering two sources of risk in the trust in which the substitution account might be lodged. First, that trust was exposed to exchange risk that could cause the SDR value of its U.S. dollar investments to deviate from the SDR value of its interest-bearing SDR obligations to members, thereby creating a stock discrepancy. Second, the SDR value of the interest received in U.S. dollars could differ from that of interest payable on SDR obligations, thereby giving rise to a flow discrepancy. While flow discrepancies could compensate for stock discrepancies under certain conditions (for instance, if the interest rate on the U.S. dollar investments of the Fund exceeded the interest rate on its SDR obligations when the dollar depreciated against the SDR), there was no assurance of such matching. For this reason, a substantial amount of uncovered risk had to be provided for (for details, see Kenen (1981)).

As presented in the beginning months of 1980, the substitution account was designed to promote development of a stable international monetary system and of the SDR as the principal reserve asset in that system. To this end, participating countries would be able, on a voluntary basis, to deposit U.S. dollars in the account and receive in exchange obligations denominated in SDRs issued by the account (SDR claims). The dollars deposited in the account would be held in a special account in the U.S. Treasury, with the United States paying interest on the dollar balances in this account at a floating rate to be determined on the basis of one or more market interest rates for U.S. government securities. The substitution account would pay interest to the holders of SDR claims at a floating interest rate equal to the combined market interest rate used by the Fund to determine the interest payable on SDRs.

Any difference between the interest rates on the SDR and on dollar claims and in the exchange value between them would have to be compensated, and capital value would have to be maintained by mechanisms on which no agreement was reached. The United States continued to argue, as it has since 1974 (International Monetary Fund (1974, p. 175)), that if a substitution account provided important advantages for the international community, its benefits and risks should be shared among the membership in proportion to quotas, or in relation to the amounts of currency that individual members substituted for SDRs, or in relation to countries' shares in total currency holdings, or by pledging some of the Fund's gold to provide a reserve equity for the account. The possibility of providing such a backup through issuing SDRs to the substitution account was also considered. While this recent attempt to construct a substitution account envisaged an account *administered by the Fund*, it has since been proposed to consider the establishment of such an account *in* the Fund so as to avoid the complications of committing specific Fund resources to back up such an account (see Polak (1980, pp. 337–38)).

Lessening of the problems associated with an alleged dollar overhang and with sudden and disruptive switches between reserve media continued to fall under the broader rationale of improving the functioning of the international monetary system by promoting the role of the SDR through establishment of a substitution account (Gold (1980, p. 313)). There was an underlying presumption that the desired or appropriate share of U.S. dollars in foreign exchange reserves had fallen faster than the actual decline of the relative importance of the United States in international trade. Some also viewed the share of U.S. dollars in private finance as unsustainably high. As a result, it was widely thought that there was a potential excess supply of U.S. dollars that the market might be unable to absorb without excessive depreciation of the U.S. dollar. Had this diagnosis been as accurate as it appeared to be before the major change in U.S. monetary policy and the turnaround of the U.S. dollar in October 1979, removal of this excess through the nonmarket process of SDR substitution would have made an immediate contribution to stability.

Appraisal of Proposals for Substitution

This section has discussed the roles envisaged for substitution in helping to meet the generally agreed objective of making the SDR the principal reserve asset in the international monetary system. Most of the ideas on substitution in the two years immediately following the widespread adoption of floating were based on the premise that, in a highly structured, centralized system with tight international controls, the SDR would be the obvious choice for the major reserve asset, and holdings of other reserves beyond working balances would best be phased out (Willett (1980, pp. 87–88)). Through substitution, the SDR would then become the major asset for settlement and reserve holding in an internationally agreed framework, organized around mandatory asset settlement or around less stringent norms affording global control over international reserve aggregates.

When the premise for the proposals discussed by the Committee of Twenty failed to materialize and centrifugal tendencies continued, substitution came to be viewed as a desirable alternative to the further spread of multiple currency reserve holdings through the market, even if substitution was no longer an integral part of more fundamental reforms of the international monetary system. Commenting on the 1979–80 approach, Walter O. Habermeier (1980, p. 42) stated: "A comprehensive reform is no longer at issue. Rather, the aim is to curtail the destabilizing shifts of U.S. dollars into 'new' reserve currencies and to issue for this purpose a new kind of SDR paper as an alternative reserve instrument." Many still felt that substitution would work best if it were accompanied by a shift to tighter control of money supply growth in the United States, so that both the initial stocks and new flows of dollars could be reduced. However, a major change—the adoption in October 1979 of new operating procedures for achieving the intended slowing of money supply growth in the United States—occurred long before agreement on a substitution account could be reached. As a result, changes in the behavior of interest and exchange rates were set in motion (Greene (1981)) that militated against the introduction of a substitution account. The sharp increase in nominal and real interest rates in the United States during the first quarter of 1980 and the accompanying appreciation of the dollar helped prevent agreement on the proposed substitution account when it was fully considered at the April 1980 meeting of the Fund's Interim Committee on the International Monetary System in Hamburg.

It can be argued, based on the experience after 1979, that the alleged dollar overhang has now ceased to be a problem. In the second half of 1980, the U.S. dollar was again appreciating relative to all major foreign currencies, providing monetary authorities with an opportunity to decrease any undesired holdings of dollar assets by defending their currencies. Instead, countries substantially increased their aggregate holdings of dollars. At the same time, those industrial countries that reduced their dollar holdings argued in 1980 and again in 1981 that the United States should increase the supply of dollars by purchasing their currencies in intervention operations—clearly indicating that they wished to conserve, rather than unload, their own dollar holdings. These facts provide prima facie evidence that total dollar holdings were approximately equal to desired holdings. Starting the proposed substitution account in 1980 or 1981 to take official dollars out of the international financial system would have reduced the supply of dollar reserves at a time when the demand for official dollar holdings appears to have been firm. However, the broader goal of promoting the use of the SDR in reserve asset management, discussed above, would still have been served.

The question is whether a substitution account might appear attractive at some future time, even if no major changes are made in the existing system of floating. Some considerations seem to militate against such a revival. There is a strong possibility that interest rates and exchange rates have adjusted and will continue to adjust so as to eliminate any incipient excess supply of foreign exchange by private and official holders. Moreover, a substitution account for official holders could interfere with the market's evaluation of exchange prospects, imperfect as it is, if expectations were raised that substitution opportunities might be provided on future occasions of dollar weakness, even if the account initially negotiated were not an open-ended one. The prospect of any currency overhang being taken off the market could lower the cost of monetary and intervention policies leading to such an overhang by reducing the risk of subsequent exchange valuation losses. Substitution arrangements could thus amount not only to reserve switching designed to provide for the diversification of international reserves out of the dollar through nonmarket means but could also encourage intervention and increase uncertainty if the possibility remained that the Fund might, in effect, take open positions in a currency in excess supply.

The broader aims of a substitution account are, however, still relevant. It is clear from the discussion of the account proposed in 1979–80 that it was widely regarded as a first step that could contribute to an important change in the international monetary system, even if greater international control over international liquidity could not be asserted immediately, as had been envisaged by the Committee of Twenty in 1974.[21] Once the necessary experience with the account had been gained, it was to be permitted to sell SDR-denominated claims to the private sector, with the Fund assisting in the development of a secondary market in SDR claims. Any such development, by making the SDR a more substantial competitor with both private and official holdings of monetary assets and financial claims denominated in national currencies, could have carried the seeds of further change by making policies on national and international liquidity creation compatible with greater stability of exchange rates.

Although no such developments have been set in motion so far, some degree of substitution is induced by SDRs regardless of the way in which they are created. This indirect substitution occurs over time to the extent that the foreign currency claims desired by official holders fall when SDRs are generated through the Fund's operations. It can be induced not only by allocation of SDRs but also by SDR-denominated claims issued when the Fund borrows from some of its members. Even if the Fund does not hold and fund the foreign exchange it obtains from certain of its members, as under direct substitution, but relends it to other members, a large part of the foreign exchange that is moved out of official holdings through the issuance of SDR claims on the Fund may not, once it is spent, get back into official currency holdings. Thus, under floating, indirect substitution is a normal concomitant of the operations of the Fund in SDRs or SDR-

---

[21] See, for instance, the exposition in the Managing Director's statement to the Board of Governors of the Fund at the Annual Meeting in Belgrade, October 2, 1979 (de Larosière (1979, p. 312)), as well as the commentaries by Polak (1979 a, p. 336), and the Group of Thirty's Reserve Assets Study Group (1980).

denominated assets. However, the extent of such substitution is small, compared with substitution on the order of SDR 50 billion that had been envisaged in connection with the substitution account proposed in 1979–80.

At the end of March 1982, Fund-related assets, which take the form of SDR holdings by members and SDR-denominated reserve positions in the Fund, amounted to SDR 39 billion, or less than 12 percent of total non-gold reserves of all countries. In the absence of large-scale substitution, there is little prospect that this percentage will rise appreciably in the near future, and it could decline. If direct substitution remains the only currently viable means of progressing rapidly toward the goal of making the SDR the principal reserve asset in the international monetary system, one may ask what would have changed if the proposal discussed by the Interim Committee at Hamburg had been adopted and Fund-related assets had grown from less than one eighth to about one fourth of total non-gold reserves. Would countries in a position to change the currency composition of their reserves without directly affecting the exchange rates with which they are most concerned have chosen to participate in the scheme, and would their ability or willingness to make portfolio adjustments at the margin have been significantly reduced if they had? Would other participants have been able to use the SDR-denominated claims on the Fund in intervention with the private sector as easily as foreign exchange, or would they have chosen to intervene less actively on account of reduced means for doing so? Would the behavior of the private sector have changed, and would exchange rate volatility have been reduced in the existing system? Would further changes have followed, for instance, through encouragement to create more privately held SDR claims and to use the SDR more widely as a unit of account in finance and trade?

For lack of a relevant experiment, there can be no firm answers to these questions. The second part of this paper suggests, however, that it may take considerably more than a substitution operation engineered from the top to provide a setting in which SDRs and SDR-denominated claims could come into wide use and play a broad, integrative role in an international monetary system that would provide greater stability than the present system. How an international system that is based more fully on the SDR as unit of account could emerge and what developments could bring about such an evolution are the main topics in Part Two.

Part Two: Possible Future Evolution of the SDR

Part One was devoted to the circumstances and expectations surrounding the establishment of the SDR and subsequent SDR allocations, as well as to extensions of the role of the SDR that have been considered during the past decade. Part Two is concerned with the opportunities to broaden the role of the SDR in present and future settings.

This introduction reviews very briefly the current status of the SDR as an international monetary unit. Section IV considers the evolution of the SDR in the conditions of price and exchange rate instability in the world today. It is argued that while considerable scope exists for broadening the use of SDRs in the Fund and beyond the Fund in these circumstances, the instabilities currently troubling the international economy substantially limit the evolution of the SDR. Section V argues that stable economic conditions, such as might permit the emergence of stable exchange rates, favor a more comprehensive evolution of the SDR as an international monetary standard, as a reserve asset, and as a denomination commonly used not only in transactions with the Fund but in other international transactions as well.

As a standard of value, the SDR, defined under the Fund's Articles of Agreement in decisions of the Executive Board, is a basket of currencies whose composition is reviewed every five years, unless the Board decides otherwise. As a store of value, the SDR thus rests on the performance of its constituent currencies. If the underlying currencies lose their purchasing power at high and uneven rates and if national policies and future inflation rates remain far less predictable in some major countries than in others, it will be very difficult for the SDR to gain acceptance as either a standard or store of value in transactions outside of the Fund in competition with the superior performers among national currencies.

The SDR has not yet matured in its role as a medium of exchange. This is not because the number of parties that may hold SDR accounts with the Fund is small. It is normal, even in a national monetary system, to limit the number of parties holding accounts with the monetary authority. The role of the SDR as a medium of exchange is limited because of constraints by the Fund itself upon the use of the SDR accounts and because the use of SDR-denominated assets and liabilities by institutions other than the Fund and the monetary authorities that deal with the Fund has not yet developed to more than a limited extent.

The SDRs that are allocated by the Fund may be used in certain transactions with the Fund—for example, in the payment of charges. The Fund's Articles provide that SDRs may be used by one "participant" in the Special Drawing Rights Department to obtain money from another "participant"—either one designated by the Fund or one with which the user has made an agreement. In the former case, the user must demonstrate a balance of payments need to obtain currency and the designated participant has a limited obligation to accept SDRs in exchange for currency. The

Articles authorize the Fund to prescribe the terms and conditions on which participants and the Fund may enter into operations and transactions in SDRs with prescribed holders. Prescribed operations in SDRs currently include the use of SDRs in loans, swaps, forward transactions, settlement of financial obligations, donations, and as security for the performance of financial obligations.

It may be observed that a market for short-term borrowing and lending of SDRs, which would function somewhat like the Federal funds market, has not developed among participants in the Special Drawing Rights Department and other holders of SDRs. The reasons for this are to be found not only in the remaining restrictions on the use of the SDR but also in more general factors governing the attitudes of monetary authorities toward holding SDRs as an investment or as an asset to be liquidated before exchange market intervention. As has been described in Section II, some of the features that determine the attractiveness of the SDR as an investment have been improved substantially since the SDR was first introduced into the international monetary system. Nevertheless, the SDR remains comparatively illiquid.

The connection between the issue of SDRs or SDR-denominated claims and the other functions of the Fund is weaker than the connection between the lending and money creation engaged in by central banks and commercial banks. In most money-creating institutions, the creation of money in the form of a liability of that institution is a direct counterpart of the act of extending credit. In the Fund, the SDR is created by a deliberate act of allocation that may be described as an exchange of rights and obligations by the Fund with each of its members participating in the Special Drawing Rights Department, the result of which is that a member receives a credit in the Fund that may be transferred to other participants and other holders of SDRs in accordance with prescribed procedures. In normal lending by the Fund, the process is an exchange in the Fund of the currency of the borrower for another currency held by the Fund. The use of a member's currency in extending a Fund loan to another member enhances the creditor position of the country whose currency is used (except when the effect is to reverse a previous debtor position). Such creditor positions—now denominated in SDRs—are deemed to be reserve assets usable by the member country in the case of a demonstrable balance of payments need.

The role of the SDR as a medium of exchange remains moderate not only because of restraints on its use that derive from present Fund prescriptions, practices, and procedures but also, and indeed probably to a greater degree, because the use of SDR-denominated assets outside the Fund has evolved to only a limited extent. The effective performance of a monetary unit depends not only on the adequate financing of the official institution that creates it but equally on the willingness of other institutions to issue their own liabilities denominated in it. These other institutions include central banks, commercial banks, brokers, dealers—indeed, all those whose readiness to transact business in the SDR would contribute to its general acceptability as well as its ease of transfer and clearance.

In the sections that follow on the possible evolution of the SDR in existing economic circumstances and in a more stable world, no attempt is made to distinguish evolutionary steps that are consistent with the present Articles of the Fund from those that are not.

IV. EVOLUTION OF THE SDR IN TODAY'S WORLD OF FLOATING CURRENCIES

Changes in the characteristics of the SDR, in the functioning of the Fund, and in the institutions and practices of the private markets could lead to a more prominent role for the SDR and thus could be the foundation for more basic changes in the international monetary system if circumstances were to warrant them at a later date. Attention is directed in this section to the more immediate possibilities.

Characteristics of the SDR Issued by the Fund

The report on "Possible Further Improvements in the Existing SDR," Chapter 12 in this volume, suggests a range of improvements in the SDRs issued by the Fund that could be effected in present circumstances and thus could extend the improvements in the SDR. These suggestions relate to the following:

(1) To bring the yield on the Fund's SDR more closely in line with rates of return on other competing reserve assets and with yields on SDR claims issued outside the Fund;

(2) To enhance the liquidity of the SDR by improving its usability and voluntary acceptance;

(3) To facilitate the use of the SDR by the Fund in a variety of transactions;

(4) To further extend the Fund's efforts to have more official entities prescribed as other holders.[22]

Implementation of such suggestions would encourage frequent use of the SDR in a variety of official transactions. Such an effect might acceler-

---

[22] The more far-reaching issue of amending the Fund's Articles to allow the opening of accounts in the Special Drawing Rights Department by a wider range of institutions, such as commercial banks, has also been raised.

ate the evolution of the SDR and might lead to broader use of SDR-denominated claims outside the Fund.

Functions of the SDR in the Fund

Use by the Fund of its own currency basket for the SDR facilitates the conduct of its programs and its dealings with members. In comparison with transactions, allocations, or loans denominated in a single national currency or its equivalent,[23] use of the SDR basket unit lowers the risk of conflict with national authorities and of interference with their exchange rates, money supply control, and borrowing. SDR-denominated Fund transactions and operations also conveniently eliminate exposure by the Fund to exchange and interest rate risks.

The Fund could accord a larger role to the SDR and a smaller role to currencies in its activities. It could accomplish this without altering present priorities of its key functions or of the services now provided. The immediate objective in making these adjustments would be the promotion of wider use of the SDR as an international monetary asset.

One method that the Fund could use to assign a larger role to the SDR in its operations would be to lay the foundation for a much closer association between the extension of credit by the Fund and the creation of SDRs. The Fund's Articles now provide that members should pay in SDRs 25 percent of any increase in quota subscriptions, but payment in SDRs is not mandatory. A first step toward greater use of the SDR in Fund operations would be to insist on the payment of 25 percent of quota increases in SDRs. This would provide the Fund with SDRs to use in its lending operations, although currencies would continue to be the predominant means of payment in purchases and repurchases by members.

It is possible that the amount of SDRs outstanding would not be adequate to permit payment of 25 percent of quota subscriptions in SDRs without borrowing or purchasing them first from the Fund or from other members. This situation could be remedied by a special allocation of SDRs in an amount sufficient to permit the payment of the quota subscription in SDRs to the extent of 25 percent. The special allocation could be for the full 25 percent of the quota or a lesser amount. A further step might be to require that more than 25 percent of a quota increase be paid with SDRs specifically allocated for the purpose.

These suggestions for tying allocations to quota subscriptions would

---

[23] For instance, prior to the First Amendment, which took effect in 1969, the accounting unit of the Fund was the U.S. dollar. During the period February 1973 to June 1974, the SDR could again be viewed as equivalent to the U.S. dollar in its exchange characteristics, since it was no longer effectively related to gold and not yet related to other currencies.

have different effects on the reserve positions of members. If 25 percent of a quota subscription is paid out of existing holdings of SDRs, members as a group substitute a reserve tranche position in the Fund for SDRs in their reserve portfolio. If members are allocated SDRs for the purpose of making the 25 percent subscription payment, they retain their existing SDR holdings and in addition acquire reserve tranche positions in the Fund. If members are provided, through allocations, more than 25 percent of quota increases and subscribe these SDRs to the Fund, they again obtain reserve tranche positions in the Fund in exchange for SDRs, and their total reserves are increased by the total of the allocation. In assuring the liquidity of the Fund, greater reliance would be placed on acceptance obligations of members and less on usable currencies, the greater the degree to which a quota increase was paid in SDRs allocated at the time of the increase. The extent to which acceptance obligations would have to be adjusted in such circumstances would be a matter for study.

One disadvantage is evident in linking the allocation of SDRs and payment of quota increases. The increase in members' reserves involved may be considered inappropriate—if not on every occasion of a quota increase, then at least on some such occasions. To meet that objection but at the same time achieve the goal of exposing the international monetary system to greater use of the SDR and lesser use of currencies in the Fund's transactions, another possibility could be considered: requiring no payment of SDRs or currencies to the Fund at the time of further quota increases. Quota increases, selective and proportional, would take place as at present to determine the limits of members' access to Fund resources, the voting rights of members, and their shares of SDR allocations but not to determine their obligations to provide resources to the Fund in the form of currency or SDR subscriptions. A member's obligations to assist the Fund in extending credit to other members would still be based on its quota, but the additional resources required by the Fund following an increase in quotas would be generated by the issue of SDRs (as opposed to allocation of SDRs) at the time of, and to the extent of, the extension of credit. Thus, a drawing by a member would be a drawing of SDRs expressly created for that purpose. Similarly, a repurchase by a member would be effected in SDRs that would subsequently be canceled. In this respect, the Fund would perform in the manner of other financial institutions in creating money through the extension of credit.

The obligation of members to assist in this process would emerge as an acceptance obligation, which would have to be raised at the time of a quota increase. The quota limits on access to Fund resources under Fund facilities would remain the basic control on the expansion of Fund credit and on the associated SDR creation by the Fund, with the acceptance obligation, linked to quota, setting the upper bound on the general resources that could be created to support Fund lending. To the extent allocated SDRs were retained in the system, the acceptance limit on any country would be equal to its quota (or to increases in its quota, if the new system were applied only to the quota increments subsequent to the system's adoption) *plus* three times the net cumulative allocations it has received. However, there need be no difference in the reserve asset characteristics of the SDRs created by allocation and those created in the process of Fund lending under the new system; a single acceptance limit could apply without distinction between them.

Use of the technique of financing Fund lending by issuing SDRs would not preclude borrowing by the Fund as an alternative means of issuing SDR-denominated liabilities. Nor would it imply abandoning the existing allocation system, which, as now, could be used to effect a general increase in members' reserves.[24] Adoption of the technique would not require merging the Special Drawing Rights Department and the General Department of the Fund. However, particularly if this technique were applied not only to quota increases but also to past subscriptions, such a simplification of the Fund's structure might be a natural consequence (see Polak (1979)).

The above are some examples of changes in Fund practices that, while they would not change the basic priorities of the Fund's operations, could assist in the further development of the SDR in the Fund's dealings with its members and thereby could help to broaden the use of SDR claims in official finance. However, the evolution of the SDR depends as much on developments in private markets and on the practices of institutions other than the Fund as it does on developments in the SDR claims issued by the Fund and in the operations of the Fund.

The SDR Outside the Fund

The major national currency denominations in the international monetary system are used in a network of central banking relationships that

---

[24] The question might even be raised as to whether SDR allocations would need to be made, once SDRs were created through Fund lending to meet particular needs, subject to global constraints. If SDR allocations to member countries were viewed as equivalent to the establishment of guaranteed lines of credit for them, there would be little change in substance if those lines were replaced by unconditional drawing rights on the Fund up to a specified percentage of quotas. Like net users of SDRs under the present system, the drawers would incur an obligation to pay interest when the line of credit was actually used. Furthermore, members that wished to hold on to some of the SDRs obtained by borrowing from the Fund would be free to do so and would incur little or no net interest cost in the process (the precise balance depending on the difference, if any, between the interest rate on the SDR and the rate of charge on unconditional borrowing from the Fund). However, it is unlikely that members that had no intention of increasing reserves on hand for possible use would have recourse to their unconditional right to borrow SDRs. It may be noted, however, that these unconditional borrowing rights could be treated as reserves, as is currently the case with reserve positions in the Fund.

extends to commercial banks and then to other financial and commercial entities, including individual transactors and contractors. However, there is no comparable infrastructure supporting the Fund's SDRs or linking them to SDR-denominated claims in the private sector. Unlike the national currencies that are widely used in international trade and finance, the SDR is neither a medium of exchange nor a standard unit of account in any country. Rather, private dealings in SDR-denominated assets are a minor adjunct to foreign exchange dealings, for which only limited transfer and clearance facilities have been provided. As a unit of account, the SDR has remained a comparatively rare convenience in international banking and commerce, since payments, terms, and obligations are not yet specified in SDR units very often.

While use of the SDR to denominate international assets, loans, and values and to establish prices has hitherto been comparatively rare in the private sector, compared with the use of national currency denominations internationally, its use could rise appreciably. Since there is a separate chapter on "Evolution of the SDR Outside the Fund," Chapter 13 in this volume, only a brief overview of the SDR's present use outside the Fund and of possible changes is given here.

Outside the Fund, the SDR functions as a unit of account and as a valuation basis for privately issued claims. The SDR can be useful as a unit of account in a variety of applications because the SDR represents an internationally sanctioned basket of currencies and a legally accepted unit of contract and value, for which decision makers in the private or public sectors do not have to assume responsibility. Private or government contracts made in SDRs are enforceable in currency components or their equivalents, all of which can now readily be obtained, traded, and covered in the open market (see Gold (1981, pp. 26-43)). Furthermore, growing familiarity with the SDR, with the relation of its value to that of other currencies, and with its past uses as a unit of account facilitate the adoption of new uses, including any possible use of the private market by the Fund that may be authorized.

Some countries hold in their reserves SDR-denominated deposits issued by the Bank for International Settlements (BIS) or by Eurobanks. Although the precise total is unknown, private holders are believed to hold at least half of the SDR-denominated deposits of Eurobanks. The SDR-denominated deposits outstanding at such banks, net of interbank deposits, were reported to be SDR 3-5 billion in mid-1981 [25] and SDR 5-7 billion at the end of that year (Sobol (1981-82)). For comparison, at the end of 1981, the holdings of SDRs derived by countries from cumulative allocations of SDR 21

[25] See Morgan Guaranty Trust Company of New York (1981, pp. 6-11); Rodriguez (1981, pp. 169-79); and Naudin (1981, pp. 118-20).

billion amounted to SDR 16 billion, and SDR-denominated reserve positions in the Fund accounted for another SDR 21 billion of Fund-related assets. While Fund-related assets amounted to about 11 percent of the total non-gold reserves of members (SDR 341 billion), SDR-denominated deposits by official holders in the private market may have amounted to less than 4 percent of identified official holdings of Eurocurrencies (SDR 94 billion) at the end of 1981. Furthermore, less than 1 percent of all Eurocurrency deposits (net) were denominated in SDRs. External claims of banks in the BIS reporting area alone, net of interbank deposits, amounted to $940 billion (SDR 808 billion) at the end of 1981.

Although the total amount of SDR claims in the private market is still small, compared with that of SDRs proper, such claims appear to have grown rapidly for a time in 1981, soon after the SDR basket was reduced from 16 to 5 currencies. While Eurobanks can hedge their SDR deposit liabilities through appropriate currency diversification of their assets and through forward contracts, they may prefer direct matching in SDRs. However, generation of SDR-denominated loan instruments that are available to private banks has lagged behind that of SDR-denominated deposits, with SDR-denominated Eurocredits (syndicated credits, Eurobonds, and floating-rate notes) outstanding at the end of 1981 amounting to SDR 1.5–2 billion.

Considerable complications are encountered in negotiating such loans, each of which contains safeguard clauses to cover situations arising from the unavailability of one or more of the constituent currencies or changes in the composition of the SDR basket. Although continuity of valuation is provided by the Fund at the moment of changeover to a new basket, private contractors in SDRs may have to adjust their cover if the contract stipulates that the tie to the Fund's definition of the SDR is to be maintained. Stipulating the use of this "open basket" would make all SDR-denominated assets refer to the same (current) basket, regardless of when they were created. By contrast, use of the "closed-basket" SDR, whose currency composition is fixed at time of issue for the duration of the contract, would contribute to heterogeneity when the Fund's definition of the SDR is changed. Because the settlement currency is still usually the U.S. dollar rather than the commercial SDR itself, precise conversion points have to be stipulated in each contract. In addition, the floating interest rates on SDR-denominated loans have been negotiated in a heterogeneous manner (see Möller (1981, pp. 77–83) and "Evolution of the SDR Outside the Fund," Chapter 13 in this volume). So far, SDR-denominated obligations of the Fund that could, in principle, provide an alternative source of supply of SDR-denominated assets have not been sold in the private market.

In sum, information and transaction costs associated with active use of SDR claims are still considerable. Private users who transfer such claims through the U.S. dollar incur exchange costs. Converting SDRs into dollars at the bid rate, transferring dollars, and then converting them back into SDRs at the asked rate involves a loss of spread. Even if banks are willing to make the transfer at a central rate, the costs will still be charged to SDR depositors, for instance, by offering a lower interest rate on SDR deposits. In addition, the growth of the private SDR deposit market may have been impeded somewhat by difficulties in generating SDR-denominated assets for banks caused by the reluctance of some non-bank borrowers, both private and public, to have their liabilities denominated in that unit. Although a start has been made in the development of markets in SDR claims and an increasing number of institutions have exhibited a readiness to deal in such claims by issuing and acquiring them, it would have to be concluded that this activity has not yet produced a significant change either in the behavior of exchange rates or in the efficiency and transfer aspects of the international monetary system.

More complementary relations between official SDRs and nonofficial SDRs could be envisaged if central banks were brought into the process of intermediating between the Fund's SDRs and commercial SDR claims. A development that could assist in opening the way to broader use of SDR-denominated claims outside the Fund would be for central banks in key member countries to permit commercial banks in their jurisdictions to open SDR-denominated accounts with them.

Such a step might have a number of technical advantages:

(1) Banking institutions in the private sector would gain access to a riskless and transferable reserve base in SDRs with their central bank, on which a structure of SDR-denominated assets and liabilities and a market for overnight reserve funds could safely be based under the supervision and regulation of national banking authorities.

(2) By facilitating currency substitution at home rather than abroad, central banks would gain a clearer view of the money supply to domestic residents and of how best to control it, assuming that SDR deposits at home would compete with foreign currency deposits held by domestic residents abroad.

(3) By bringing SDR deposits in domestic banks under the normal reserve requirements, the seigniorage benefits of national authorities would be unaffected by residents' switching between deposits in home currencies and in SDRs.[26]

---

[26] SDR deposits would have an unfair competitive advantage over other domestic deposits if they were not subject to reserve requirements, although imposition of reserve requirements would weaken the ability of SDR deposits to compete with foreign currency and SDR-denominated deposits in Eurocurrency markets.

(4) Central clearance facilities in SDR claims could be furnished by central banks for their domestic banks, thereby providing a convenient means of transferring SDR funds directly without having to use another currency (see United Nations (1981, pp. 12-13) and "Evolution of the SDR Outside the Fund," Chapter 13 in this volume). In addition, the central bank would ensure that reserves in home currencies and SDR-denominated reserves held with it by member banks are exchangeable at low cost upon demand.

(5) Central banks could cover their SDR-denominated liabilities to domestic banks by holding the Fund's SDRs to the extent they wished to hedge against exchange risk. If central banks agreed to apply a 100 percent reserve requirement to their SDR-denominated deposit liabilities, they would, in effect, be converting the Fund's SDRs to local currency when they accepted SDR-denominated deposits from private financial holders against payment in domestic currency. While private holders could view any SDR-denominated reserves they may be allowed to hold with their central bank as just as riskless and officially supported as the Fund's SDRs, the interest, if any, that central banks would pay on such deposits would be set at their own discretion.

By contrast, there are at least two possible disadvantages that may incline national authorities not to sell SDR-denominated deposits to banks and not to authorize such banks to create SDR deposits for domestic holders.

(1) Greater ease of currency substitution at home, through a greatly increased number of depositors who could readily switch between home currencies and SDR-denominated deposits at their local banks, could increase exchange instability if the additional speculation were destabilizing. If the residents of one country whose currency is included in the SDR switch into the SDR, while the residents of another country switch out of the SDR—say because both U.S. and German residents expect the dollar to depreciate (more rapidly than would be predicted by prevailing interest rate differentials) against the deutsche mark, dollars will be exchanged for marks somewhere in the international financial system to square positions. Thus, exchange stability could be reduced if more speculators were drawn into the market. On the other hand, it could just as plausibly be argued that broadening the market for currencies and making conversion easier and less costly could be stabilizing and beneficial partly because it would prompt timely adjustment of national policies. The pros and cons are summarized by Sobol (1981-82, pp. 40-41):

> To the extent that the official community views the SDR markets as a means for private participants to circumvent government regulations and acquire currencies which are otherwise difficult to obtain, it might be inclined to try to thwart their development. On the other hand, to the extent that it views the SDR markets as an indirect approach to currency diversification which presents less of a threat to domestic policy and international stability than explicit currency diversification, it may be more tolerant of the markets and

willing to promote their development ... Because the SDR offers private market participants a diversified instrument, the SDR may reduce the incentive to manage a portfolio actively on the exchange markets after a transitional period ... But to the extent that the SDR encouraged those to diversify who would otherwise not be disposed to doing so and to manage actively a portfolio of home currency and SDRs, further development of SDR markets would tend to hinder exchange market stability.

(2) Any depreciation of the local currency against the SDR would immediately increase the national money supply, reckoned in domestic currency, if SDR-denominated deposits at home were counted as part of that supply. They should be so counted if SDR deposits held by residents at home serve substantially the same transaction functions as domestic money holdings, so that velocity is more predictable for the aggregate than for the home currency component alone. The resulting indexation of a portion of the domestic money supply could make it more difficult to counteract undesirable or excessive depreciations. (An example of indexation of a component of international reserves is the amount of ECUs issued against gold being expanded or contracted with the moving-average market value of official gold holdings.) The same applies to appreciation that lowers the domestic currency value of SDR deposits and thereby contributes to further appreciation through the induced tightening of the money supply. Exchange rate changes would impinge immediately on the conduct and effects of national monetary policies. Particularly for the latter reason, many national authorities may be unwilling to contemplate a parallel money in their jurisdiction. Nevertheless, it is likely that for the SDR denomination to spread through the international monetary system, central banks would have to be prepared to deal in that denomination not only with the Fund (and to some extent with each other and with Eurobanks) but also with commercial banks under their jurisdiction.

V. EVOLUTION OF THE SDR IN A WORLD OF MORE STABLE PRICES AND CURRENCY VALUES

This section considers the possible evolution of the SDR in circumstances most favorable to its emergence as the principal reserve asset of the international monetary system—that is, in a world characterized much more by economic stability than instability, reasonably steady economic performance of major countries, and trust in money fostered by a favorable economic climate and the withering of inflationary expectations.

Opportunities for the SDR in a More Stable Environment

It is recognized in this paper that if SDR-denominated assets are to be widely used in international commerce, they must successfully compete with the major national currencies used in international trade, finance, and investment. Such competition is likely to be more successful in a stable environment than in today's unstable one in which the purchasing power of the currencies underlying the SDR continues to erode at high and uneven rates and exchange and interest rates continue to gyrate. It is by no means contended that more stability will guarantee that the SDR will flourish as an international currency; it is contended only that more stability is a necessary condition for evolution of the SDR beyond what was discussed in the preceding section.

The contention that more stability is necessary rests on two lines of argument: one negative and one positive. The negative line of argument is to the effect that if instability promotes resort to currency baskets, the SDR should have flourished in the present period. As was detailed earlier in this paper, there has been some advance in private use of the SDR, but it has not been outstanding. Also, while the ECU has been born and has survived its infancy, it has not become prominent as a denominator of assets in private hands. These facts may seem surprising, for a resort to the SDR denominator is a resort to an average performance of asset value and yield (neither the worst nor the best). However, it appears that the need for precise hedging of positions is generally felt to be greatest when fluctuations of values and returns are expected to be greatest. Denomination in SDRs will be a precise hedge only when the distribution by currency of the risks to be hedged matches the weighting of currencies in the SDR. Only rarely in commercial life does this matching occur even reasonably closely.

This leads to the positive argument that in more stable conditions the need to hedge is felt less keenly and the need to hedge precisely is felt less keenly still. Therefore, in those conditions, there is a greater prospect of a composite unit competing successfully with any or all of the constituent currencies. But even in these circumstances it is not certain that the SDR would be more widely used. Many developments would still have to converge to make the SDR more convenient and financially advantageous in order to permit the SDR to evolve into a more widely used instrument in international transactions, both private and public. At best, the evolution would be gradual. Once there were a basis for believing that the SDR would be as good as the major currencies making up the unit, it would become convenient for a much greater number of transactors to do business, to bank, to create liquidity, and to store wealth in SDRs. International transaction and settlement costs could be reduced by avoiding currency conversion and using the SDR as the uniform denominator of international transactions. An SDR standard could thus evolve if the SDR were expected to maintain its value as well as all other major national currencies and also provided users with a means of spreading risks and reducing the information and transactions costs that remain.[27]

In the more favorable circumstances discussed here, the improvements in the character of the SDR and the wider use of the SDR in transactions with the Fund that can be effected even under present-day conditions could be made more easily, thus facilitating the asset's further evolution.

If the major countries, particularly those whose currencies make up the SDR, succeeded through appropriate policies in stabilizing their domestic price levels, then they would calm exchange rates, which are now disturbed by volatile expectations about prices, interest rates, and policies. In these circumstances, the countries whose currencies are embodied in the SDR (as well as other countries) might choose to establish parities with each other's currencies or groups of currencies that they would be willing to defend within some range. Pegging to the SDR would put all such countries on a more equal footing in their international and domestic policy obligations than would pegging to a single currency. Even if par values were fixed in terms of the SDR, countries whose currencies are included in the SDR basket might choose to continue using individual foreign currencies underlying the SDR to meet any intervention objectives or obligations they might have, rather then buying SDR claims with, or selling them for, domestic currency.

Pegging to the SDR could be an important factor contributing to the willingness to use the SDR in international transactions, but it is not contended here that it is essential. What is contended is that a history of stability is required that would reduce the need for constant reappraisals of exchange prospects and of future policies likely to affect exchange rates—a need and responsibility currently felt by many private participants in international trade and finance. For businesses, the saving of information, transfer, and management costs, as well as the convenience and efficiency of worldwide standardization that is associated with using a single and common standard of denomination in diverse transactions with many countries, could then outweigh any opportunity losses associated with ceasing to adjust and manage day by day the currency composition of contracts, exposures, and positions. Financial investors might also be more comfortable holding SDR claims if their value in terms of most cur-

---

[27] In theoretical discussions, money has been described as a commodity or an asset with a comparative advantage in absorbing and disseminating information concerning transactions. The degree of predictability of the exchange rate for commodities determines this comparative advantage. Moneys possessing lower costs of information on account of shorter transaction chains and a smaller variance of price quotations replace moneys with higher costs of information. Hence, stability, predictability, and uniformity of purchasing power in the international arena would be among the prerequisites for the SDR to emerge as the dominant money. See Brunner and Meltzer (1971, pp. 784-805).

rencies were likely to remain stable, even though small devaluations of particular currencies against the SDR might occur from time to time that would increase the value of the SDR in terms of those currencies.[28] Thus, it is argued that the SDR would become a major competitor of the national currencies that are currently dominant in the international monetary system if, as a result of price level and exchange rate stability, the SDR first became an acceptable substitute for each of those currencies in international use. But, as noted above, to be successful in such competition, the SDR must compare favorably with national currencies in terms of convenience and transaction costs.

Development of Institutions and Practices Outside the Fund

There is no reason to suppose that the preference for using national currencies in domestic transactions would in any way be reduced in the more stable conditions under consideration. However, if the SDR became the money and unit of account favored in international applications, many private parties across the world would need SDR-denominated assets and liabilities, including assets that could serve as banking reserves. Just as domestic banks in many countries now do business in U.S. dollars, one could envisage the development of domestic banking in SDRs to facilitate the international transactions of banks and their customers.

If the banks required assets denominated in SDRs, the basis would exist for lending, particularly in support of international trade, in SDRs. Some national authorities might also be willing to issue SDR-denominated debt to the domestic private sector as an alternative to national debt denominated in the home currency. Alternatively, the Fund might at some future date make SDR-denominated assets available for investment by banks. Banking reserves denominated in SDRs might be provided in more than one way. Smaller banks in a given country would hold reserves against their SDR deposit liabilities with banking institutions in the larger countries. At some point in the structure, access to central bank credit in SDRs would be

---

[28] To prevent the value of the SDR from falling in terms of the stronger currencies contained in it when a devaluation occurs, an "asymmetrical basket" technique of valuation for the SDR of the kind that was already considered by the Committee of Twenty (International Monetary Fund (1974, p. 44)) could conceivably be introduced. Application of such a technique could imply that par value changes were always expressed as devaluations of a particular currency against the SDR, with the resulting decline in the share of its value in the SDR compensated for by raising the amount of that currency in the SDR. Under such a valuation adjustment rule, the SDR would retain its value as well as the hardest currency, or succession of hardest currencies, within it. The interest rate that would be appropriate on such an SDR would normally be below the weighted average of interest rates on the five national instruments currently used. There would be numerous other implications, including an increased ability of the SDR to compete with official gold holdings as a possible hedge against inflation, as well as possible complication of private use of SDR-denominated claims, neither of which can be further discussed here.

needed. Central banks in some countries might ultimately be prepared to accept SDR-denominated deposits from domestic banks that offered such deposits commercially, thereby providing reserve facilities for the latter. Indeed, central banks could impose reserve requirements on SDR-denominated deposits at commercial banks. On the other hand, use of formal reserve requirements might not be widespread, and the availability of central bank credit in SDRs and the opportunity to open SDR accounts might be offered by a rather limited number of central banks to only a few financial institutions in the system.

To the extent that central banks offered deposit liabilities to commercial banks in SDRs, the former might wish to have access to SDR-denominated assets. SDRs issued by the Fund would be the natural ultimate source of such assets. If central banks having SDR liabilities made a practice of keeping a reserve against those liabilities in the form of SDRs or SDR-denominated claims on the Fund, then the Fund could, in theory, acquire leverage over the high-powered SDR liabilities of those central banks and, through their reserve requirements, over the SDR liabilities of commercial banks.

This structure of assets and liabilities in the international monetary system is perhaps conceivable in a well-integrated international economy marked by stability of prices and exchange rates. The further step of achieving leverage over the creation of money generally, and not just over a particular form of money, through the direct control of high-powered money within member countries, is not conceivable at all. Nevertheless, the commitment to stability of prices and exchange rates by countries implies a commitment by the major central banks to control their money supplies that is compatible with those goals. The Fund would gain leverage by virtue of those commitments and by the exercise of firm surveillance, and it could assist countries in carrying out their commitments by making resources available to them under suitable conditions.

Implications for Functions of the Fund

If the role of the SDR evolves in the general direction indicated in the earlier part of this section, the Fund would continue to perform all of the functions it performs today. The international monetary system's needs for some functions would clearly be greater than today, while the need for other functions might show little change. Flexibility in the evolution of the Fund would permit emphasis to shift from one function to another. Key functions and their importance in today's world situation are briefly reviewed here.

(1) The function of SDR allocation, or of equivalent ways of creating unconditional liquidity by means of the Fund's SDRs, could be relatively more important in the international monetary system envisaged in this

section than it is today. With the underlying commitment to stability, the need for international reserves to protect the external value of national currencies relative to the SDR could grow, even though intervention would have to be coupled with timely adjustment. SDR-denominated claims could be generated by members through lending to the Fund or substituting foreign exchange for SDR-denominated claims on the Fund during a transition period, but all countries might feel a continuing need for the supply of SDRs or SDR-denominated reserve assets to grow along with the volume of trade.

Under the circumstances envisaged in this section, there are more specific reasons for anticipating an increased emphasis on allocation. If monetary policies of the major reserve currency countries are restrained so as to maintain reasonable stability in their domestic price levels and if there is no specific inducement to the expansion of Eurocurrency markets, such as there was at the time of the growth of the surpluses of the members of the Organization of Petroleum Exporting Countries, the apparatus for the supply of reserves in the form of reserve currencies may not be adequate to meet countries' needs for reserves. In such circumstances, the need for allocations of SDRs will certainly be more apparent than it has been under recent world conditions. Indeed, these stabler circumstances were what was envisaged when the SDR was created. In addition, the need for allocations could be further enhanced to the extent that the practice of asset settlement is adopted in the monetary system.

(2) The function of credit extension by the Fund would remain important. Countries' needs for additional reserves in periods of pressure on exchange rates would continue, even though the international monetary system's performance would be characterized by greater stability of exchange rates than it is today. As now, there would be alternative means for countries to supplement their international reserves through recourse to international markets and other monetary authorities. But the Fund would continue to offer short-term balance of payments financing on varying degrees of conditionality. All countries, even the major industrial countries, might readily come to the Fund for supplementary balance of payments financing. Once an SDR standard evolved, the Fund would almost certainly finance credit extension through creation of SDRs rather than through currencies as it does today.

(3) The Fund's surveillance over exchange rate policies would also continue to be exceedingly important. It is sometimes asserted that the surveillance function of the Fund is accented most heavily when there is widespread instability and a limited commitment to the restoration and maintenance of stability, as is the case now. The international monetary system today lacks the discipline of a commitment to stable exchange rates which it would have in the circumstances discussed in this section. On the other hand, in a

tighter system of more stable prices and exchange rates, economies could find it just as difficult to stay on track. In addition, a track more clearly marked with rules would provide agreed criteria and lines of orientation for national policies and for consultations between national authorities and the Fund. In view of these considerations and in view of the increasing experience of the Fund, surveillance by the Fund could be more effective in a more structured system of stable exchange rates than it is today. It could effectively apply to industrial countries to a much greater degree than at present, since countries whose currencies are included in the SDR would acquire special powers and responsibilities in the process of international liquidity creation in conjunction with the Fund. International capital markets would remain as free as they are today, and national and international capital markets could become even more integrated through common use of SDRs and SDR-denominated assets. As part of this integration, clearing for central banks—and, indirectly, for the private sector—might be added to the transfer services if the SDR became the principal monetary asset in international use. Nevertheless, the total growth of international reserves would have to be closely monitored and reconciled with the requirement of approximate price stability in the major countries, on which the potential usefulness and feasibility of the entire system envisaged in this section would depend.

VI. ISSUES FOR DISCUSSION

A major theme of this paper is the adaptation of the SDR to the changing needs of the international community under different conditions in the world economy and the international monetary system. The gradual adaptation of the SDR will no doubt continue as these needs evolve, so that this important international financial instrument—the only such instrument under the control, and at the disposal of, the world community—can better perform the tasks for which it is intended. A conscious assessment of possible future developments in the international monetary system may speed up this process and help to guide the SDR through an appropriate evolution. The discussion of the issues raised in this paper, some of which are set out below, provides an opportunity for initiating such an assessment.

(1) The contention in the foregoing preamble that the SDR is the appropriate principal instrument to be used in the conduct of international financial relations may be regarded as the first, and perhaps most central, issue for discussion.

(2) International monetary cooperation may be viewed as having two closely linked objectives: to facilitate the conduct of trade and financial transactions among countries, and to safeguard international financial

stability. There may be comments on the view that the SDR should, as much as possible, be made to serve both objectives.

(3) One question, which was considered in Section IV, is whether international financial relations conducted through the Fund could be simplified in important ways, without being changed in broad substance, by basing the Fund's activity largely or entirely on the SDR. This could be done by extending Fund credit to members, under the appropriate safeguards, in the form of newly issued SDRs up to agreed "quota" limits rather than through the exchange of member currencies, as under the present Articles.

(4) Commentators may also wish to address the view implicit in this paper that the SDR as an instrument is, by itself, neutral with respect to the provision of conditional and unconditional liquidity. SDR allocation (or an unconditional tranche in quota increases under the alternative system discussed in paragraph (3) above) provides unconditional liquidity to members, while use of SDRs held by the present General Department (or newly issued under the alternative system) in the extension of Fund credit provides conditional liquidity. The proportions in which the two types of liquidity should be provided depend on world economic conditions and developments in the international monetary system (see also paragraph (8) below); they must, therefore, be left for determination from time to time, as they are at present.

(5) Emphasis has been given in the paper to the importance of the supporting role of private institutions and practices in any evolution of the SDR that would put it in a position of greater prominence in the international monetary system. Improvements in the financial characteristics of the SDR since its inception have made private transactors and markets more receptive to the use of the SDR as a unit of account and to transactions in SDR-denominated instruments. There may be expressions of views on the extent to which increased private use of the SDR may support its liquidity, so as to diminish the need for the active use of control mechanisms, such as designation procedures and acceptance limits.

(6) It may be argued that the recent expansion of international banking, while involving mainly Eurocurrencies rather than SDR-denominated assets, nevertheless makes the international monetary system more receptive to the evolution of the SDR. The shift in banking practice from Eurocurrencies to SDR-denominated assets and liabilities could, in suitable circumstances, be easier than a transition from a primarily domestic banking system to one oriented to dealing in units other than domestic units.

(7) It is contended in the paper that stability of prices and exchange rates provides a more favorable climate for the evolution of the SDR than do conditions of instability. As opposed to this view, it may be argued that it is precisely when exchange rates are unstable that countries seek refuge

in currency baskets. In support of this opposing view, it may be argued that the multiple currency reserve system, based upon a diversification of the currency composition of reserve portfolios, has evolved essentially in the period of exchange instability and more particularly in periods of weakness of the U.S. dollar.

(8) It is noted in Section IV that, in a period of instability of exchange rates such as the world has recently been experiencing, the extension of conditional credit receives a great deal more emphasis in the Fund's activity than does the provision of unconditional liquidity (through the allocation of SDRs). By contrast, in Section V, where the possible evolution of the SDR in an atmosphere of stability is discussed, the view is taken that the role of the Fund in providing reserves (through allocation and cancellation, or in other ways) would be considerably more important in a more stable environment than it is today.

(9) The paper has developed the view that the further evolution of the SDR and its uses should be guided in the direction of establishing a generally acceptable and widely usable financial instrument, one which can facilitate the conduct of the world's business and achieve the agreed purposes of members, whatever they may be at a particular time. In this connection, ad hoc responses to transitory problems, such as the absorption of a temporary excess supply of particular member currencies or the transfer of resources from some members to others in certain circumstances, have not been stressed in the second part of this paper. This does not mean, of course, that a fully developed SDR system could not be used for such purposes. It does mean, however, that the establishment of the SDR system should not be made to depend on accidental temporary requirements and exigencies.

(10) A related suggestion deserving of comment is that, even though the times may not now be particularly favorable for a full development of the SDR as the principal asset in the international monetary system and as an instrument for the exercise of surveillance over international liquidity, care should be taken not to limit or close options that might be viewed as desirable when better opportunities to develop the role of the SDR are available.

REFERENCES

Brandt, Willy, and others, *North-South: A Program for Survival*, report of the Independent Commission on International Development Issues ("Brandt Commission") (Cambridge, Massachusetts: M.I.T. Press, 1980).

Brunner, Karl, and Allan H. Meltzer, "The Uses of Money: Money in the Theory of an Exchange Economy," *American Economic Review*, Vol. 61 (December 1971), pp. 784-805.

Cohen, Stephen D., *International Monetary Reform: The Political Dimension, 1964–69* (New York: Praeger, 1970).

Cooper, Richard N., "The Gold Standard: Historical Facts and Future Prospects," *Brookings Papers on Economic Activity:1* (1982), pp. 1–45.

Cumby, Robert E., "Special Drawing Rights and Plans for Reform of the International Monetary System: A Survey," Chapter 10 in this volume.

de Larosière, J., "Struggle Against Rampant Inflation a Precondition for Healthy Growth," address of the Managing Director of the International Monetary Fund to the Board of Governors, Belgrade, October 2, 1979, *IMF Survey*, Vol. 8 (October 15, 1979), pp. 309–13.

de Vries, Margaret G., *The International Monetary Fund, 1966–1971: The System Under Stress: Vol. I: Narrative,* and *Vol. II: Documents* (Washington: International Monetary Fund, 1976).

Gold, Joseph, "Substitution in the International Monetary System," *Case Western Reserve Journal of International Law*, Vol. 12 (Spring 1980), pp. 265–326.

———, *SDRs, Currencies, and Gold: Fifth Survey of New Legal Developments*, IMF Pamphlet Series, No. 36 (Washington, 1981).

Greene, Margaret L., "The New Approach to Monetary Policy: A View from the Foreign Exchange Trading Desk at the Federal Reserve Bank of New York," in Vol. I of *New Monetary Control Procedures: Federal Reserve Staff Study*, Board of Governors of the Federal Reserve System, 2 vols. (Washington, 1981).

Group of Ten, *Report of the Study Group on the Creation of Reserve Assets: A Report to the Deputies of the Group of Ten, May 31, 1965* ("Ossola Report") (Rome: Bank of Italy Press, and Washington: Government Printing Office, 1965).

Group of Thirty, *Towards a Less Unstable International Monetary System*, report of the Reserve Assets Study Group, chaired by H. Johannes Witteveen (New York: Group of Thirty, 1980); summary of report in *IMF Survey*, Vol. 9 (March 3, 1980), pp. 65 and 71.

———, *Balance-of-Payments Problems of Developing Countries: A Report*, report of a Study Group chaired by J.J. Polak (New York: Group of Thirty, 1981).

———, *How Central Banks Manage Their Reserves: A Study*, report of the Multiple Reserve Currency Study Group, chaired by H. Johannes Witteveen (New York: Group of Thirty, 1982).

Habermeier, Walter O., "Substitution Account Plan Sought to Enhance SDR, Help Stabilize Composition of Exchange Reserves," *IMF Survey*, Vol. 9 (February 4, 1980), pp. 33 and 42–44.

International Monetary Fund, *The Adequacy of Monetary Reserves: An Analysis*, prepared by the International Monetary Fund for the Economic and Social Council of the United Nations (Washington, 1953).

———, *International Reserves and Liquidity: A Study by the Staff of the International Monetary Fund* (Washington, 1958).

——— (1969 a), *Articles of Agreement* (Washington, 1969).

——— (1969 b), *Summary Proceedings of the Twenty-Fourth Annual Meeting of the Board of Governors, September 29–October 3, 1969* (Washington, 1969).

——— *Annual Report of the Executive Directors for the Fiscal Year Ended April 30, 1970* (Washington, 1970).

———, *International Monetary Reform: Documents of the Committee of Twenty*, report to the Board of Governors by the Committee on Reform of the International Monetary System and Related Issues (Committee of Twenty) (Washington, 1974).

———, *Articles of Agreement* (amended effective April 1, 1978) (Washington, 1978).

———, *Annual Report of the Executive Board for the Financial Year Ended April 30, 1979* (Washington, 1979).

———, *Annual Report of the Executive Board for the Financial Year Ended April 30, 1981* (Washington, 1981).

Kenen, Peter B., "The Analytics of a Substitution Account," Banca Nazionale del Lavoro, *Quarterly Review*, Vol. 34 (December 1981), pp. 403-26.

Machlup, Fritz, *Remaking the International Monetary System: The Rio Agreement and Beyond* (Baltimore: Johns Hopkins Press, 1968).

———, and Burton G. Malkiel, eds., *International Monetary Arrangements: The Problem of Choice*, International Finance Section (Princeton University, 1964).

Márquez, Javier, "Reserves, Liquidity, and the Developing Countries," in International Monetary Fund, *International Reserves: Needs and Availability* (Washington, 1970), pp. 97-111.

Möller, George, "Calculating Interest Rates on SDR Denominated Loans and Deposits," *Banker*, Vol. 131 (November 1981), pp. 77-83.

Morgan Guaranty Trust Company of New York, "The Private SDR and Its Implications," *World Financial Markets* (April 1981), pp. 6-11.

Naudin, Thierry, "Le marché des certificats de dépôts en D.T.S.," *Agence Economique et Financière*, special 1981 edition (December 1981), pp. 118-20.

Polak, J.J. (1979 a), "The Evolution of the International Monetary System," commentary on the 1979 Per Jacobsson Foundation Lecture, Belgrade, September 30, 1979, in Proceedings of the Foundation (Washington: Per Jacobsson Foundation, September 30, 1979), pp. 37-43; also excerpted in *IMF Survey*, Vol. 8 (October 29, 1979), p. 336.

——— (1979 b), *Thoughts on an International Monetary Fund Based Fully on the SDR*, IMF Pamphlet Series, No. 28 (Washington, 1979).

——— "Hope for Substitution Account May Lie in a Simpler Scheme, Embodied in IMF," *IMF Survey*, Vol. 9 (October 27, 1980), pp. 337-39.

Rodriguez, Rita M., "The Increasing Attraction of the SDR to Business Corporations," *Euromoney* (December 1981), pp. 168-79.

Sobol, Dorothy M., "The SDR in Private International Finance," *Federal Reserve Bank of New York Quarterly Review*, Vol. 6 (Winter 1981-82), pp. 29-41.

Triffin, Robert, *Gold and the Dollar Crisis: The Future of Convertibility*, rev. ed. (New Haven, Connecticut: Yale University Press, 1961).

United Nations, *Studies on International Monetary and Financial Issues for the Developing Countries: Measures to Strengthen the SDR*, report to the Group of Twenty-Four, UNDP/UNCTAD Project INT/75/015, Document UNCTAD/MFD/TA/11, dated March 1981.

———, *Towards the New International Economic Order: Analytical Report on Developments in the Field of International Economic Cooperation Since the Sixth*

Special Session of the General Assembly, report of the Director-General for Development and Economic Cooperation, UN Document A/S-11/5, dated August 7, 1980 (New York, 1982).

United States, Commission on the Role of Gold in the Domestic and International Monetary System, *The Role of Gold in the Domestic and International Monetary System*, report to the U.S. Congress, 2 vols. (Washington, March 1982).

Willett, Thomas D., *International Liquidity Issues* (Washington: American Enterprise Institute for Public Policy Research, 1980).

Witteveen, H. Johannes, "The Control of International Liquidity," address of the Managing Director of the International Monetary Fund before a meeting of the Conference Board in Frankfurt, October 28, 1975, *IMF Survey*, Vol. 4 (October 28, 1975), pp. 313-16.

12

Possible Further Improvements in the Existing SDR

Since 1970, the International Monetary Fund has made a number of evolutionary changes in the characteristics of the official special drawing right (SDR) with a view of improving its attractiveness as a reserve asset. This background paper, prepared by Fund staff in 1982, lists a number of possible further steps along that path. It explores in a general way certain refinements in the SDR's characteristics, most of which are limited but nonetheless collectively may contribute materially to its attractiveness. It does not re-examine the principle of valuation (i.e., the "basket"), nor does it deal with the amount and distribution of allocations or the issue of how to fit an operationally improved SDR into the international monetary system.

Improvements in the SDR will be helpful whether there are additional allocations or not, although changes in the international monetary system or a more fundamental examination of the SDR will no doubt require further re-examination of the issues taken up here. Except where otherwise noted, the potential improvements mentioned here are limited to changes that it is believed could be made under the Fund's existing Articles of Agreement. They are not put forward as recommendations at this time but are raised to stimulate discussion. Some might be appropriate only in the more distant future, while others could, if desired, be implemented immediately.

Under the First Amendment to the Fund's Articles of Agreement, SDRs were created to supplement existing reserve assets, and their use other than with the Fund was limited to periods of need arising from balance of payments and reserve developments. With the adoption of the Second Amendment in 1978, members re-expressed their intention of "making the special drawing right the principal reserve asset in the international monetary system" and broadened its uses. Achievement of this

537

objective requires making the SDR sufficiently attractive in those characteristics that hitherto have been associated with reserve assets and creating a sufficient, but not excessive, amount of SDRs.

Historically, only a limited number of instruments have emerged as international reserve assets. They generally share certain characteristics, which include (i) the relative stability of their real value, (ii) the ease and safety with which they could be invested, (iii) the ease with which these investments could be liquidated, and (iv) their global acceptability in settlement of financial and commercial obligations.

While allocations had created SDRs equal to less than 6 percent of members' non-gold foreign exchange reserves by the end of 1981, the usefulness of the concepts underlying the official SDR allocated by the Special Drawing Rights Department can be seen by its growing use outside the Fund as a unit of account, a store of value, and a means of payment. The growth of SDR-denominated instruments, so-called commercial SDRs, and other uses of the denomination are important complements to the growth of the Fund's official SDRs and could contribute to making the SDR the principal reserve asset. (See "The Evolving Role of the SDR in the International Monetary System," Part II, and "Evolution of the SDR Outside the Fund," Chapters 11 and 13 in this volume.)

While central banks are not generally oriented to maximizing their profits and do generally cooperate with each other for their common good, they are accountable to their governments for the prudent and beneficial management of their countries' foreign exchange reserves. Their decisions in regard to acquiring, holding, and using SDRs must meet these criteria. The attributes of the SDR are therefore seen and judged relative to those of possible alternative reserve assets, including commercial SDRs. It is a well-known proposition that for an asset to circulate as a medium of exchange, it must enjoy approximate equality between its supply and demand. If it is so attractive that it is hoarded or so unattractive that it is held only forcibly, it will not circulate as money, and other means of payment will tend to be used in its place. It is assumed in the following discussion that for the SDR to achieve the broader role envisioned by the Second Amendment, its yield and value must be market-related and its uses must be wide ranging, simple, and as well understood as possible. Suggestions are made in the following sections as to how the SDR's liquidity, acceptability, and characteristics as an investment asset might be improved in relation to other reserve assets.

Section I discusses possible changes in the method of determining the rate of interest on the SDR. Section II deals with changes that might be considered in the procedures for determining the daily valuation of the SDR in terms of currencies and the exchange rates used in operations and transactions in SDRs. Section III puts forward some ways in which the liquidity of the SDR might be improved by the development of a more active market among official holders. Section IV considers some ways in which the role of SDRs in the Fund might be increased and additional promotional steps that the Fund might usefully take. The list of possible improvements is presented topically and not in order of importance. While possible improvements can be considered individually, the relative "attractiveness" of the SDR, which reflects the combination of all its characteristics, will depend on the collective impact of the individual improvements undertaken.

I. INTEREST RATE

If SDRs are to be actively used for making international payments, they must be neither hoarded nor shunned. Taking account of all the SDR's attributes, its rate of interest should be such as to make holders just willing to hold the quantity available.[1] The "equilibrium" interest rate must be related to the yield on alternative reserve assets and therefore must reflect current market conditions, including the rate at which the exchange value of the SDR is expected to change in relation to other reserve assets. The determination of the equilibrium level of the interest rate is by no means self-evident.[2] Central banks have widely different policies with respect to the form in which they hold their reserves. Therefore, it is impossible to know exactly with which particular assets the official SDR compares directly, or to set an interest rate that each central bank will find sufficiently competitive in the light of all the other characteristics of the SDR. Furthermore, as many central banks are substantial borrowers, their decisions whether to use SDRs to finance their deficits may be strongly influenced by the rates they are paying on borrowing relative to the rate of interest (charge) on SDRs.

What is clear is that marginal adjustments in reserve portfolios are necessarily made in light of the conditions, such as relative interest rates, that prevail at the moment. The SDR, like cash or a consol, is an asset without a specific maturity. A consol maintains an ever-changing equilib-

---

[1] The report of the Committee on Reform of the International Monetary System and Related Issues (hereinafter referred to as the Committee of Twenty) sets out the general objective for the interest rate on the SDR as follows: "The effective yield on the SDR will be high enough to make it attractive to acquire and hold, but not so high as to make countries reluctant to use the SDR when in deficit." Committee of Twenty (1974), p. 15.

[2] The concept of an equilibrium interest rate leaves aside the possibility of deliberately setting the SDR interest rate through some suitable mechanism above or below that rate to encourage or discourage use or retention of SDRs. (See also the subsection entitled "Brokerage Service.")

rium yield by means of adjustments in its price. Having excluded from consideration, in this paper, adjustments in the value of the SDR against all currencies, continuous adjustment of the interest rate is the only means of keeping the SDR's yield in line with those on alternative assets. Without such adjustments in the face of ever-changing market conditions, the SDR's liquidity will be impeded.

The following paragraphs discuss possible changes in the method of determining the SDR interest rate that would affect its relationship to rates on other assets. These include changes in the frequency of adjustment of the SDR rate, in the frequency of posting net interest earned (owed), in the level of the rate in relation to the currently defined "combined market rate," and in the reference basket to which the level is related.

The Articles of Agreement allow any rate of interest on the SDR to be determined by a 70 percent majority, but the same rate must apply to all holdings and the rate of charge on net cumulative allocations must be equal to the rate of interest. In addition, the Articles link the rate of remuneration to the interest rate; it must be within a range of 80 percent to 100 percent of the SDR interest rate. Accordingly, the possible impact of the alternatives discussed here on the rate of remuneration, and indirectly on the rate of charge on the use of the Fund's ordinary resources, needs to be borne in mind throughout.

Timing and Frequency of Interest Rate Adjustments

More Frequent Determination of SDR Interest Rate

Currently, the SDR interest rate for each calendar quarter is determined by reference to the average yield on the instruments comprising the interest rate basket (i.e., the combined market rate) for the 15 business days preceding the last 2 business days of the previous calendar quarter. Wide divergences are therefore possible between the current combined market rate and the SDR interest rate during the course of a quarter. For example, a participant deciding the form in which to hold an addition to its reserves in November 1981 faced an SDR interest rate of 13.99 percent per annum, whereas the combined market rate averaged only 11.86 percent per annum during that month. Thus, the aim of keeping the interest rate on the SDR closely related to current market rates is not fully achieved by the present method.

One technique that would keep the SDR's interest rate closer to market rates would be to adjust the rate more frequently—monthly, weekly, or even daily. More frequent adjustment of the rate could be combined with a shorter lag between the period on which the rate is based and the period to which it applies. At the extreme of timeliness, the rate might be set daily on the basis of the previous business day's combined market interest rate. As interest and charges are already computed on the basis of average daily positions, this proposal does not pose any unmanageable operational problems. The daily interest rates could be published along with the daily exchange rates.

There would be no need to adjust the rate of remuneration every time the interest rate on the SDR changed if it were judged to be undesirable to do so, as long as the former remained between 80 percent and 100 percent of the latter. The issues that more frequent adjustments in the SDR rate would raise for the rate of remuneration are not further examined here.

More Frequent Payment of Interest

Interest and charges on the SDR are currently paid as of the end of the Fund's financial year (April 30) on the basis of the five quarterly SDR interest rates that prevailed over that period (i.e., those for May and June, July to September, October to December, January to March, and the month of April). Given that the standards of comparison in the interest rate basket are three-month obligations held to maturity, it would be reasonable to consider the quarterly payment of interest and charges on SDRs, which, owing to compounding, would make the interest rate on the SDR closer to the average rate on holdings of the component currencies invested in the instruments in the interest rate basket.

If the interest rate on the SDR were to be adjusted more frequently than it is currently, as discussed in the preceding subsection, interest (and charges) might also be credited (debited) more frequently. Monthly postings to the accounts of individual holders would be operationally convenient, as monthly statements of accrued interest and charges are already prepared. These changes would have the drawback that participants needing to acquire SDRs to pay net charges in the Special Drawing Rights Department would have to do so quarterly or monthly rather than annually as at present; however, they have the potentially important advantage that the amounts required on each occasion would be smaller.

Adjustments in SDR Interest Rate in Relation to Combined Market Rate

The adjustments discussed earlier would keep the interest rate on the SDR closer to 100 percent of the combined market rate of the five instruments currently in the interest rate basket. However, there is no guarantee that this will be the equilibrium rate. If there is any evidence based on experience, it is that very few participants actively seek to acquire SDRs and that certain others have at times been unenthusiastic about being included in the designation plan.[3] This fact suggests that the rate might be too low in present circumstances.

A number of factors other than the interet rate also tend to reduce the relative attractiveness of the SDR. Owing to the somewhat limited uses prescribed by the Fund for the SDR, the inability of participants always to maintain holdings of SDRs at desired levels as a result of the designation mechanism, and the lack of an active market in them, SDRs are less liquid than many alternative reserve assets. Again, this situation suggests that a rate higher than 100 percent of the current combined market rate would represent the equilibrium position.

Should these shortcomings be reduced or eliminated, however, the need for the SDR rate to be competitive if it is to circulate freely does not necessarily require full parity with interest rates on commercial SDRs, which tend to be based on rates obtainable in the higher-yielding Eurocurrency market. The official SDR has several potential advantages over either of these alternatives or over other homemade currency cocktails. These include international rather than national control of the characteristics, quantity, and uses of the asset and better protection against the dangers of sovereign risk. In addition, participants hold official SDRs in the spirit of international cooperation.

SDRs of both the official and the commercial type enjoy two other advantages over currency cocktails or other forms of portfolio diversification. (1) While the SDR's value is derived from a well-defined basket of currencies, all those currencies are not necessarily freely available in the market. This helps to distinguish the SDR from a portfolio of its components. (2) A prepackaged, widely accepted composite currency should involve lower transactions costs than homemade currency cocktails. For these reasons, the equilibrium interest rates for the official SDR should tend to be lower than the comparable combined Eurocurrency market rates. However, there are limits to the appropriate rate spreads between the official SDR and the commercial SDR or Eurocurrencies. While the interest rate is only one of several factors that prudent reserve portfolio managers must take into account, it is almost invariably an important one.

[3]The rate of interest on the SDR has been at the 100 percent level for only one year, so that experience with that level is minimal.

Revision of SDR Interest Rate Basket

Maturities of Instruments

The relationship between the yield on the official SDR and on alternative, potentially competitive reserve assets depends not only on the relationship chosen with respect to a reference basket of assets but also on the assets included in the basket. Straightforward comparisons between the SDR and other reserve assets are suspect, as the official SDR has a number of unusual properties. For one thing, reserve currencies can be readily placed in a wide range of investments with different characteristics and different rates of interest, while the official SDR itself is the investment. For another, official SDRs are more liquid for one set of holders than for others. Holders with a balance of payments need to use their SDRs receive the same interest rate on an asset that can be converted at short notice through the designation mechanism as do holders without a balance of payments need for an asset that is (for them) less liquid than the assets included in the interest rate basket.

While holdings of commercial SDRs may eventually take the same variety of forms as do holdings of instruments denominated in currencies, the official SDR under its present legal constitution can have only one form and one interest rate. Hence, the choice of a single interest rate must balance all considerations. Interest rates on assets of different maturities are linked; however, the rates on longer-term assets tend to reflect the average of the overnight rates expected over the same term *plus* a risk premium. Use of the average actual overnight rates for any particular holding period removes the risk of unforeseen rate movements and, with it, the risk premium. If measures could be taken to improve the opportunities for holders with no balance of payments need to sell their SDRs when they wish, it is possible that overnight interest rates would be more appropriate than three-month rates. As indicated in the subsection entitled "More Frequent Determination of SDR Interest Rate," (in Section I), if the SDR's interest rate were adjusted daily, each day's rate (taken from the previous day) could be published with the SDR exchange rate. On the other hand, for special or extraneous reasons, one-day interest rates tend to be more volatile than longer-term rates.

Domestic versus International Instruments

The assets currently comprising the interest rate basket are domestic instruments in the five countries whose currencies comprise the valuation basket. Certain members, however, hold a substantial portion of their reserves in the Eurocurrency market, where interest rates are generally higher. In addition, a number of banks accept SDR-denominated deposits carrying interest rates that reflect covered investments in the Euromarkets for the component currencies, which are therefore higher than the official SDR rate. These deposits compete directly with the official SDR for inclusion in members' reserves (Heller and Knight (1978); Fawzi (1982)). However, as argued earlier, the official SDR has advantages that might ultimately justify some differential between its interest rate and the rates on commercial SDRs.

Market-Determined Interest Rate

There is obviously no readily apparent formula for establishing the appropriate SDR interest rate. A more far-reaching possibility, therefore, would be to establish some form of "market process" for SDRs that determined the equality interest rate for the SDR in an ongoing process. Such a scheme is explained in the subsection entitled "Market Making" (in Section III), in conjunction with a discussion of the idea of the Fund's buying and selling SDRs in order to make a better market for them.

II. VALUATION

Determination of the exchange value of the SDR against a currency, and particularly against the main reserve and invoicing currencies, depends, in addition to the composition of the basket itself, on the particular exchange rates used in computing it. The composition of the basket and the principles underlying its determination are not discussed here, but the other technical aspects of determining the SDR's value are examined from the perspective that divergences between the official value and the market value of the SDR give rise to undesirable opportunities for arbitrage and diminish the usefulness of the SDR as a unit of account in private financial markets.

If exchange rates obtainable in foreign exchange markets differ from those used by the Fund, a participant could obtain different amounts of SDRs for its own currency by going through different third currencies.[4]

---

[4]If Country A desires 10 million pesos worth of SDRs, it will generally first need to acquire a freely usable currency with which to make payment for the SDRs. Assume that at noon London time, this sum would purchase about SDR 10 million going through any freely usable currency. However, as the day moves on, the rates of exchange for Country A's pesos against the deutsche mark and the French franc, for example, will generally change in different directions from the peso's exchange rate against the dollar. Assume that by 4:00 p.m. London time, the deutsche mark/peso rate would have risen from 2.40 to 2.41 and the French franc/peso rate would have fallen from 6.01 to 6.00, while the U.S. dollar/peso rate would

This would be at variance with current interpretations of the equal-value provision of Article XIX, Section 7(a), which states that the exchange rates for transactions "shall be such that participants using special drawing rights shall receive the *same value whatever currencies might be provided...*" (italics added). This principle could be more closely observed than it is at present with official SDR rates by using SDR rates based on exchange rates obtainable at the time of individual transactions. This could be done as long as foreign exchange markets were always reasonably well arbitraged.

The use of the SDR as a unit of account ultimately requires the conversion of SDR values into national currency values, whether for determining the currency equivalent of the insurance liability on an internationally shipped parcel that is lost or damaged, of a maturing SDR-denominated bond, or of a maturing SDR-denominated deposit. If the Fund's official value of the SDR differs much from the values obtainable in the market, the official value will tend to be avoided by the market. The need in the market to cover costs and to compensate risk with a spread between buying and selling rates by itself makes the Fund's mid-rate quote unpopular with dealers, and consequently it is often replaced by private quotations in the bank deposit market. Nonetheless, there is an advantage to the market in having an objective official rate in which all can have some confidence; hence, SDR-denominated bonds and syndicated bank loans invariably use the official rate at maturity. The current valuation procedures of the Fund, however, can on occasion produce rates that differ significantly from market values and thereby jeopardize the usefulness of the official rate as a unit of account.

Relationship of Official and Market Values of SDR

The Fund's official SDR/U.S. dollar rate is currently based on the midpoint rates of the currencies in the SDR basket in the London market at noon, as assessed and supplied to the Fund by the Bank of England. SDR transactions with designation and with the Fund entail use of the exchange rate so determined three business days prior to the value date.

---

have remained unchanged at 1.0. At that time, Country A would still be able to acquire SDR 10 million by going through U.S. dollars. However, if francs were used as the vehicle currency, 10 million pesos would purchase SDR 9,983,361, while if deutsche mark were used instead, the same amount of pesos would purchase SDR 10,041,667 at the Fund's official SDR exchange rates. Furthermore, Country A could sell this larger amount of SDRs (by agreement, if it could find a willing taker, or with designation, if it had a balance of payments need) for 60,350,419 French francs, which at 4:00 p.m. would be equivalent to 10,058,403 million pesos, for an arbitrage gain of 58,403 pesos (or SDR 58,403, if the pesos were converted back into SDRs via the U.S. dollar).

Transactions and operations by agreement[5] may be for value either three days or two days after setting the exchange rate. Official SDR rates against other currencies are determined on the basis of the representative exchange rates of those currencies, which are not generally London noon rates.

The official SDR exchange rates may differ from rates used for SDR-denominated deposits with commercial banks for several reasons: (1) noon rates in the London market are not likely to be the same as the rates in the markets in which transactors might actually be dealing or in which the representative rates are determined; (2) noon rates in London will differ from market rates at other times during the day, especially under a system of floating exchange rates; and (3) rates computed for three days' value will generally differ from rates used in exchange market transactions that are taken from two days before the value date. Any such differences could be reduced by having the Fund fix the value of the rate more than once daily, or they could be eliminated by giving transactors the freedom to determine their own rates.

More Frequent Determination of SDR Exchange Rates

In considering the above-mentioned imperfections in the fixing of official exchange rates for currencies against the SDR—that is, the question of how the principle of equal value for the SDR could be achieved more realistically under the present valuation system for the SDR—it is useful to divide transactions in which an exchange rate for the SDR is needed into two broad categories—those in which the Fund itself is directly involved and those in which transactions by agreement or operations are between two participants or prescribed holders. The first category includes transactions and operations in which the Fund itself is a principal (e.g., transactions in the General Resources Account) and those in which the Fund designates participants to receive SDRs. The second category—transactions by agreement and operations—are those in which the members themselves agree on the basis for a transaction or operation by direct negotiation.

For transactions in the first category, it is essential to have a standard method of establishing the exchange rate at which they will be executed, and the Fund's official rate should continue to be used for this purpose.[6]

---

[5]Transactions in SDRs are defined by the Fund's Article XXX(i) as spot "exchanges of special drawing rights for other monetary assets. Operations in special drawing rights means other uses of special drawing rights." Operations prescribed by the Executive Board currently include the use of SDRs in: (a) loans, (b) swaps, (c) settlement of financial obligations, (d) forward operations (i.e., transactions for value in more than three business days), (e) donations, and (f) as security for the performance of financial obligations.

[6]This rate would also apply to those transactions by agreement in which the Fund acts as an intermediary and in which there is little or no direct communication between two parties to the transactions.

As far as the second category is concerned, there is already some freedom for holders to select the exchange rate to use. In these transactions and operations, the holders are permitted to use the official SDR rate for either the second or the third business day prior to the value date. Moreover, as experience has accumulated with the evolving SDR, the most recent decisions on prescribed operations have dropped the equal value requirement altogether. For example, holders are permitted to use any exchange rate for forward operations, which are defined as being for value more than three business days ahead. (See Executive Board Decisions Nos. 6337-(79/178) S, adopted November 28, 1979, and 6437-(80/37) S, adopted March 5, 1980 (International Monetary Fund (1981), pp. 258-59).) The question therefore arises as to whether it would be helpful to allow for transactions and operations by agreement to take place at exchange rates determined by and agreed between the two parties. The Fund's definition and valuation methodology would be used, but the transacting parties would determine the current value of the exchange rates needed in computing SDR rates at the time that a deal is struck. There is, unfortunately, no practical way in which the Fund could ensure that this procedure would not be abused or used to effectively alter the exchange value of the SDR, should there be an incentive to do so. Therefore, this degree of freedom might be approached more gradually; the Fund might allow the parties to a negotiated transaction or operation to agree on a rate that fell within a range around the official rates.[7]

Once the SDR is seen as fully competitive with alternative reserve assets (in interest rate, liquidity, etc.) it may be desirable to allow self-determination of the exchange value of the SDR. Any rate agreed between the two parties would be the equilibrium price at that time. The extent to which the price established in this way differed from the official value of the SDR would reflect imperfections in the SDR; in particular, if the SDR lost or gained in value against currencies generally (i.e., floated), the interest rate of the SDR or possibly even the volume of SDRs outstanding, or both, would probably need to be reconsidered.[8]

Alternatively, differences between the official and market rates could be reduced in negotiated transactions or operations by the use of the most current of multiple daily fixings of the official rates. Multiple fixings of the official rates might be computed by geographically scattered central banks acting as the Fund's agents. Three fixings might adequately serve

[7]See the discussion of commissions in Section III, especially the subsection entitled "Market Making." The flexibility to allow this practice under the existing Articles is, however, limited, particularly for transactions.

[8]This more radical proposal would have to wait until either the market for voluntary transactions in SDRs developed sufficiently to make designation no longer necessary or additional safeguards were developed against the use of designation to subject SDRs acquired at a discount to arbitrage.

the 24-hour day—for example, in London (Frankfurt), New York, and Tokyo.[9] The advantages will vary, depending on the type of transaction or operation and the transactors involved. If applied to those transactions involving the Fund, decisions would be needed whether such transactions would take place at the most recently determined rate—giving rise to the possible use of several rates in the same day—or whether only one of them that is in the same time zone as the Fund's headquarters should be used for this purpose.

Another problem with the Fund's official SDR rates that affects the usability of the SDR as a unit of account is the fact that the official SDR rate for three of the five currencies in the SDR basket—the deutsche mark, the French franc, and the Japanese yen—are obtained by using representative U.S. dollar rates for these three currencies taken from the local market of each. These rates generally differ from the noon London rates of these currencies, which are used in establishing the value of the SDR basket. These differences make it difficult to cover in the exchange markets commercial SDRs that are placed at the official SDR rates, even to the point that firm interest rate quotations sometimes cannot be obtained. This problem is often resolved by avoiding the use of the official rates of the Fund. It could also be corrected by making the so-called representative rates identical with the rates used in valuing the SDR basket. Therefore, the Fund might adopt the market rates used in computing the official value of the SDR basket as the representative rates for all currencies in the basket.

Delivery Period

As mentioned, market practice is normally that spot exchange rates are for value two business days hence. Ideally, there would be advantages if transactions with designation and transactions in the General Resources Account were carried out with two-day value. However, there are technical difficulties in the General Resources Account with respect to currency transfers, and the experience has been such that three-day value has been adopted and is reflected in existing decisions and in borrowing agreements; there are likely to be operational problems in a reversion to two-day value. As technical advances are made in communications, it may nevertheless prove possible to move back to two-day value, and the Fund staff will keep this possibility in mind. In transactions and operations by

---

[9]Multiple fixings of the SDR/U.S. dollar rate could actually move transactions away from the equal-value condition with regard to the SDR rate against other currencies unless similar multiple fixings of these other currencies were also used. This would require modification of the current representative rate arrangements, which often reflect conditions at a different time of day than prevailed in fixing the SDR/U.S. dollar rate.

agreement, there is already such a degree of freedom, and this could be extended by permitting the parties to agree to one-day value or same-day value.

III. LIQUIDITY

Liquidity refers to the ease and speed with which SDRs can be used for whatever financial needs their holders might have. From the beginning of the scheme, the liquidity of the SDR was assured by the designation process for those participants having a balance of payments need. The ability to designate a participant who must provide a freely usable currency in exchange for SDRs was considered essential to the establishment of the liquidity of a newly created asset, and it continues to function quantitatively as the backbone of the scheme. However, designation also gives the SDR an unattractive quality, in that within the acceptance limit of the Fund's Articles of Agreement, participants cannot freely choose the quantity of SDRs they will hold in their reserve asset portfolios.

The SDR's liquidity ultimately rests on the willingness of participants and other holders voluntarily to acquire and hold it, and this depends on its attractiveness in all dimensions relative to alternative reserve assets. Over time the Fund has attempted to improve the liquidity of the SDR by cautiously expanding the number of uses to which it could be put and by diminishing the restrictions that inhibit such uses. Currently, the SDR may be used in a wide range of financial operations and transactions. The need to rely on designation as a source of liquidity for the SDR could be reduced as a result of increased use of transactions by agreement. The following subsection lists a number of steps to increase the SDR's liquidity that generally move in this direction.[10]

Freer Use

Under the Second Amendment of the Fund's Articles of Agreement, SDRs can be used fairly freely in transactions by agreement and, as a result of a series of Executive Board decisions, in operations. While these decisions have considerably expanded the authorized uses of the SDR, holders contemplating an operation with SDRs must carefully examine the several Board decisions that relate to such operations in search of specific authorization. Furthermore, when an amount of currency or some other unit is to be equated with an SDR amount (e.g., as the principal amount of a loan, or the amount of a financial obligation), the exchange

---

[10]The voluntary acceptability of the SDR will, of course, also depend significantly on all its other qualities, in particular the relative level of its interest rate.

rate against the SDR is often required to be the Fund's official rate, with the choice of two-day or three-day value left to the transactors.

To date, the only prescribed operations in SDRs that have occurred have been in regard to loans and the settlement of financial obligations. The amounts involved are very small. For the SDR to realize its potential as a reserve asset, it would be desirable to consider a further broadening and simplification of the authority to use SDRs in operations. The series of Board decisions authorizing specific operations in SDRs could be replaced by the single authorization for all participants and other holders to engage in any transaction or operation by mutual agreement, subject only to the specific limitations imposed by the Articles of Agreement. These limitations are (i) the use of equal-value exchange rates in spot SDR transactions; (ii) restrictions on the use of gold; and (iii) the requirement to "collaborate" and the reporting of pertinent information that is part of collaboration.[11]

Such a simplified statement of uses of SDRs would assure holders that they may undertake any type of mutually acceptable transaction or operation, except those that the Fund might wish specifically to prohibit or restrict. This step would thereby remove any doubts about just what is allowed under the current decisions, while broadening the range of uses of SDRs and the terms and conditions associated with those uses. Protection against possible abuse can be found in the obligation of each participant under Article XXII to "collaborate with the Fund and with other participants in order to facilitate the effective functioning of the Special Drawing Rights Department and the proper use of special drawing rights...."

A further simplification of the use of SDRs in operations would be achieved by reducing the current reporting requirements. At present, communications informing the Fund of intended SDR operations are required to read more like legal documents than instructions for making payments. For example, the Executive Board decision authorizing the use of SDRs in loans requires that *both* parties to such an operation inform the Fund of the denomination, amount, rate of interest, maturity, means of repayment, and intended value date of the operation; in addition, *both* parties must declare that the intended use of SDRs is in accordance with the appropriate prescription.

Requiring instructions from only the holder transferring SDRs and dropping the declaration would simplify communications without any loss

---

[11]Two Executive Board decisions go beyond prescribing operations and establish special facilities or services—No. 6053-(79/34) S and No. 6054-(79/34) S, adopted February 26, 1979, as amended by No. 6438-(80/37) S, adopted March 5, 1980 (International Monetary Fund (1981), pp. 252–56). These decisions (use of SDRs in pledges and in transfers as security for the performance of financial obligations) should remain in place.

of information. The amount and value date are the only other essential items of information. While information on the maturity and interest rate of loans, for example, might be useful to the Fund in carrying out its responsibility of assessing whether the SDR system is functioning smoothly, the possible benefits derived from requiring this information must be weighed against the inconvenience to the user. The Fund's need to be kept informed could be met in other ways—for example, through periodic reports from holders on the type, volume, and other characteristics of SDR operations.

Another simplification of SDR operations would be the omission of the equal-value requirement to the full extent allowed for in the Articles of Agreement. There may be occasions when small differences in calculating SDR rates would impede the use of SDRs, as, for example, if financial obligations have to be valued in SDRs at the official rate. Such differences are likely to be small, although the possibility of split pricing would exist. The fact that transactions would continue to be made at the official rate, however, means that arbitrage possibilities would minimize any difference that might otherwise emerge. In any event, should actual experience suggest that such a change were proving detrimental to the smooth functioning of the SDR system, the Fund could reimpose the equal-value requirement.

These several changes would, for example, enable two participants to settle a financial obligation between themselves in SDRs by a simple instruction from the user to transfer a stipulated amount of SDRs to the recipient on a particular day in settlement of the obligation.

The liquidity of the SDR is to some extent affected by the Fund's fairly prompt report of the use of SDRs by individual holders. Some participants and other holders have expressed reservations about having their use of SDRs reported to the public. The Fund might consider ways of maintaining a greater degree of confidentiality of individual usage, such as making public reports that are more aggregated and do not identify the use by individual holders.

Promoting a Market in SDRs among Participants and with Prescribed Holders

Authorization for freer use of SDRs is an essentially meaningless step unless holders can readily find transacting partners. The ability to buy or sell SDRs on short notice is central to their liquidity. Outside the designation mechanism and its use in settling financial obligations to the Fund, the SDR has remained a relatively illiquid asset. Along with considerations of yield, valuation, relative newness of the asset, and heavy regulation of its uses, this characteristic both results from and contributes to the market in official SDRs being a very limited one.

Current Fund rules prohibiting the charging of commissions by participants and prescribed holders with respect to SDR transactions are a double-edged sword in this regard. The lack of a bid/ask spread gives the SDR an advantage relative to alternative reserve assets by reducing the cost of transacting in it. On the other hand, it removes an important financial incentive for any holder either to deal in or make a market for SDRs. One of the roles that the Fund can play in promoting the liquidity of the SDR is that of broker between prospective buyers and sellers. This role could range from the rather limited form that has characterized the Fund staff's activity since 1976 (guiding participants needing to acquire SDRs for the payment of charges to the several holders known to be willing to sell them) to a more active form of service; ultimately, it might involve the Fund making a market for SDRs and standing ready in the last resort to clear it, thereby making designation unimportant as a source of liquidity.

Brokerage Service

The role of the Fund as broker currently involves the occasional service of providing prospective buyers and sellers with knowledge of their respective interests and acting on their behalf at no cost. The Fund staff monitors participants' needs to acquire SDRs to discharge obligations to the Fund and informs them of known sources. Thus, the staff assists participants in the management of their SDR holdings in such a way that adequate balances are generally on hand to meet pending obligations, and it helps to provide participants with some outlet for their SDRs.

In addition to monitoring the demand side, the staff periodically surveys participants and other holders who might be potential sellers to ascertain their willingness to provide SDRs. This is done informally through telephone contacts with central banks or Executive Directors and, occasionally, by means of telex communications to such participants and prescribed holders.

The Fund staff can perform a more active brokerage service by establishing and maintaining more active contact with potential transactors. In doing so, the staff would attempt to anticipate current demand for, and supply of, SDRs in all types of SDR transfers and, as at present, would help to arrange most of these transfers between buyers and sellers so as to meet their respective needs. In fact, the staff has already been moving in this direction.

Brokerage activities presume an underlying balance between buyers and sellers (demand and supply) who simply need information. In fact, to date, the demand for SDRs has been derived largely from the need to acquire SDRs for immediate use (i.e., for the payment of charges to the Fund) rather than for holding in the purchaser's reserves as an attractive asset. The truly "voluntary" transactors have almost all been sellers, which is at least a partial, although not a conclusive, indication that the SDR is not yet as attractive as alternative assets.[12]

Market Making

The roles just described do not presuppose that the Fund would supply or absorb SDRs to clear the market on its own. Beyond the designation mechanism, which has the limitation of being subject to a balance of payments need, liquidity requires an active market in SDRs with a buyer and a seller of last resort to clear the market when necessary. An institution that stood ready to buy or sell SDRs in exchange for freely usable currencies would thereby ensure a market for SDRs and, hence, their liquidity. The Fund's current restriction on commissions makes it unprofitable for any participant or prescribed holder to undertake such a role. Commissions, or their equivalent, compensate for the risk of taking a position in an asset and generate the return that induces traders to make a market. Furthermore, potential market makers cannot generally set or in any way adjust the spot price or the interest rate of SDRs so as to clear the market.

The Fund, however, is uniquely positioned to provide a market-making service for holders in the interest of promoting the role of the SDR. If the SDR's liquidity were assured in this way, the designation mechanism might then serve as a seldom-used safety net. Should the SDR evolve into a widely used means of settling international financial obligations, its liquidity would be further enhanced, and the need or desire to convert it into a domestic vehicle currency (in either a transaction with designation or a transaction by agreement) would be reduced.

As a market maker, the Fund might bridge the gap between the transactors in SDRs in several different ways. The *Fund could manage a pool of SDRs and freely usable currencies* or credit lines provided for that purpose by some of its members and other holders from which the Fund would buy and sell SDRs. The assets of the pool would continue to be owned by the participants and other holders that initially provided them.

Alternatively, as the Articles of Agreement provide for the General Resources Account to hold, buy, and sell SDRs from participants, a somewhat more restricted approach would be for *the Fund itself to make a*

---

[12]Two participants have provided over three fourths of the SDRs acquired by others in transactions by agreement. Both of these participants entered into standing agreements with the Fund to sell SDRs on demand in transactions by agreement arranged by the Fund staff in order to facilitate their acquisition by participants needing SDRs to meet obligations to the Fund. Sales of SDRs took this particular form, partly as a result of the desire of these participants to cooperate so as to improve the functioning of the SDR scheme.

market in SDRs through its General Resources Account.[13] This would mean, however, that the members whose currencies were used would need to be willing (perhaps within certain limits to be agreed from time to time) to allow their reserve tranche positions, and hence the amounts of currency held in their reserves, to fluctuate at the initiative of buyers and sellers of SDRs whose wishes to buy and sell could not be met with transactions by agreement. At the same time, the Fund itself would see the composition of usable assets in the General Resources Account changing, at least in the short run, as between currencies and SDRs.

Either of these approaches is intended to provide a buffer, or bridge the time gap, between the supply of, and demand for, SDRs in such a manner that the composition of assets in the General Resources Account or in the "pool" would not change, on average, over time. Therefore, if the Fund were to stand ready to buy and sell SDRs in either of these ways, it would need the ability to influence supply and demand so as to clear the market over time without unbounded variations in its "own" holdings.

To clear the market without floating the exchange value of the SDR, the Fund would have to adjust the interest rate on SDRs. For example, if demand were to exceed supply by more than the Fund wished to reduce its stock, the Fund would lower the interest rate; conversely, if an excess supply were to raise the Fund's holdings above a desired level, it would increase the interest rate. There might need to be small and frequent changes in the interest rate if a particular trend seemed to be developing. There would no longer be a need to set the interest rate by reference to rates on other assets; like other assets, the SDR would have an interest rate that would bring about equilibrium in its own market and would reflect participants' and other holders' assessments of its characteristics.

The absence of a market of significant size may be an impediment to this approach. The possibility of wide swings in market-clearing interest rates would require some care in adjusting the SDR interest rate. The experience with other financial assets, however, has been that unless their yields were kept at ever-changing equilibrium levels, no markets ever developed for them.

Another change that could promote a broader market for SDRs might be to permit techniques that would effectively allow the charging of commissions by participants and prescribed holders when transacting between themselves, to the extent permissible under the Articles. The Fund might

---

[13]This action would be subject to a number of limitations imposed by the Articles. These limitations are (i) that such dealings would have to be for currencies other than that of the participant; (ii) the need for concurrence of the member whose currency is used; and (iii) the requirement that all the transactions occur at the official value.

also consider charging commissions on its SDR dealings,[14] particularly with regard to the market-clearing transactions in SDRs described earlier. The use of middle rates without charge for this purpose would give the Fund a competitive advantage in making a market for SDRs, which it probably should not seek.

A further important step in this direction would be the extension of the Fund's market-making activities to forward contracts and swaps for SDRs to the extent permissible under the Articles. The timing and amounts of certain flows of SDRs between the Fund and participants are predictable. These include remuneration payments, repayments of borrowing by the Fund, and the use of SDRs in repurchases and charges. Since central banks, in dealing among themselves or with the market, are able, if they choose, to offset expected flows through their investment portfolios by swaps and forward transactions, this step would represent an extension of this practice in their dealings with the Fund.

Enhancing the liquidity of the SDR may, however, conflict with the aim of stability in the international financial system, which requires the avoidance of major swings into and out of reserve currencies. While increased liquidity makes shifts between SDRs and other reserve assets easier, it makes them less likely if the attractiveness of the asset is sufficiently improved so that the demand for it is fairly stable. In any event, maintaining controls on the uses of the SDR that reduce its usability for speculation does not reduce the potential instability between the remaining reserve assets, while it does discourage the broader use of a potentially stabilizing asset with hedging characteristics, such as the SDR.

Widening and Clearing the SDR Market

The settlement of SDR payments is a straightforward process, inasmuch as all official SDR accounts are maintained by the Fund in the Special Drawing Rights Department. The use of SDRs for this purpose has the advantage of lower cost, owing to the absence of margins. A possible shortcoming is that such payments and transfers are limited to those between Fund members, all of whom are participants, and other holders prescribed by the Fund. Broadening the number of holders would increase the usefulness of the SDR in settling international payments. The Fund might further extend its efforts to have more official entities prescribed as holders. Immediate candidates would be those official entities that already have adopted the SDR unit of account. This effort could usefully

---

[14]It currently does so with respect to the use by its members of Fund resources other than the reserve tranches.

be carried on in conjunction with efforts to broaden the use of the SDR as a unit of account.

A more far-reaching issue is whether the Fund's Articles should be amended to allow the opening of accounts in the Special Drawing Rights Department by a wider range of institutions, such as commercial banks, or whether use of the SDR in the settlement of international payments can be further advanced in ways that are in keeping with the current Articles (Coats (1982); see also Peter B. Kenen, "Use of the SDR to Supplement or Substitute for Other Means of Finance," Chapter 7 in this volume, and "Evolution of the SDR Outside the Fund," Chapter 13).

IV. FUND OPERATIONS

General Resources Account

The Fund denominates its accounts and financial obligations in SDRs, and accepts and makes payments in this medium. Since the inception of the SDR scheme in 1970, SDR 27 billion has flowed to and from the General Resources Account; this represents about one third of all transfers to and from the General Resources Account during the last 12 years. Use of the SDR by the Fund not only has simplified its financial dealings but also has had educational value, in that member countries have been exposed to the SDR and to transactions in SDRs. Convenience is an important factor in the choice of a transactions currency in international finance. Familiarity and habit are major components of convenience. The more frequently central banks engage in SDR transactions, the more familiar they become with the SDR and, hence, the more likely they are to use SDRs in making other transactions.

There are several ways in which the Fund could broaden its uses of SDRs, short of basing the Fund entirely on SDRs by way of amending the Articles (Polak (1979)).

Currently, the Fund may sell SDRs from its General Resources Account to members needing them for charges due the Fund or for payment of quota increases. For both of these purposes, SDRs can at present be sold only in the estimated net amount needed by the member and within 30 days preceding the date those payments are due. One of these limitations could be relaxed without altering the basic purpose of such sales by allowing the sale of the amount of estimated charges falling due over some longer period—say, the next 6 to 12 months. In addition, if full-fledged market-making activity (as discussed earlier) were not desired, there would still be scope for exploring the buying and selling of SDRs by the General Resources Account; for example, the Fund could encourage the use of SDRs in repurchases and purchases and thereby reduce the use of currencies in its operations and transactions. Finally, the Articles do not allow the Fund to borrow official SDRs or allow the Borrowed Resources Suspense Accounts to hold or to transact in them. Finding practical ways to handle these anomalies would benefit the SDR and would simplify Fund operations.

Administered Accounts

The Second Amendment of the Articles did not provide for the administered accounts to hold SDRs. It is, however, paradoxical that participants and prescribed holders can engage in transactions or operations that are not possible for the Fund or for the administered accounts. A number of possible ways exist for resolving this anomaly, some of which, however, may raise difficult legal issues.

There are several indirect ways of making it possible for these accounts to use SDRs without holding them directly. The administered accounts might operate on the basis of indirect claims on official SDRs through the account of a participant or prescribed holder. A holder might establish SDR-denominated accounts for the Fund's respective special accounts, holding as their counterparts earmarked SDRs in its own account with the Special Drawing Rights Department. While this technique would allow, for example, a subsidy account to receive and to disburse SDRs through an intermediary's account, it would rely upon, and require the cooperation of, the intermediary for this purpose. The practical differences between this technique and prescribing the Borrowed Resources Suspense Accounts and the Fund's three administered accounts as holders would be matters of cost, since the circuitous route involving an intermediary could involve service fees, and of risk.

In the absence of one of these or some other legally acceptable approaches, the Fund's special accounts would not be able to hold SDRs without amendment of the Articles.

Promotional Activities

Inadequate awareness of just what the SDR is and how it can be used may partly explain its limited importance to date. Along with improving the characteristics of the asset itself, the Fund could contribute to the enhancement of its role by more actively communicating the nature and advantages of the improved SDR to participants and prescribed holders through publications, seminars, press releases, etc.

The SDR is shackled with an unfortunate name. To explain that an SDR is a "special drawing right" is, in the staff's experience, invariably counterproductive. Yet the term "SDR" has now been in use for over a decade and has acquired some recognition and goodwill. A sharpening of this recognition would result from an Executive Board decision to use the letters "SDR" in all official references rather than the full description, "special drawing right."

A number of other steps could usefully be taken, such as more frequent exchanges of views among holders of SDRs, particularly among those officials who manage the reserve assets of their authorities. Such exchanges are already encouraged, thus far on an annual basis, among prescribed holders; meetings between senior officials of these entities and the Fund staff have been well received in recent years and have helped in the involvement of these institutions in more recently authorized operations.

V. SUMMARY

The attractiveness of the SDR to holders or potential users reflects all its various attributes. Efforts to improve further its attractiveness should address all its characteristics. Relatively minor refinements, if achieved for enough of its characteristics, may be sufficient to put the SDR on a par with established reserve assets, leaving aside the issue of the volume at which it is supplied.

The possible steps discussed in this paper are summarized here by section.

I. To bring the interest rate of the Fund's official SDR more closely into line with market rates for commercial SDRs or with rates on competing reserve assets: (1) the interest rate could be fixed more frequently than once a quarter; (2) interest earnings (and charges) could be paid more frequently to raise the effective rate somewhat; (3) the level of the rate could be reassessed; and (4) the basket of instruments on which it is based could be reappraised.

II. To bring the value of the Fund's official SDR more into line with market values for commercial SDRs or for other alternative reserve assets, parties to transactions and operations by agreement in SDRs could be allowed to use (1) exchange rates that fall within a fixed range around the official rate, or (2) the most current of multiple daily fixings by the Fund. Such transactions and operations could also be settled on a one-day value or same-day value basis.

III. The SDR could be made more liquid by freeing up and simplifying its uses in transactions and operations, which could include (1) a single Executive Board decision allowing all that is not prohibited and (2) simplifying the reporting requirements. Liquidity would also be enhanced by assisting the development of a more active market in SDRs, which could include: (1) increased brokerage activity; (2) a Fund role in creating a market for SDRs; (3) a market-determined interest rate for the SDR; and (4) allowing commissions.

IV. Fund operations could also be improved and simplified by more use of SDRs by the Fund, which would also serve to accustom further the financial world to the uses of SDRs. More SDR use by the Fund might include: (1) more extensive use for purchases and repurchases from the Fund's General Resources Account; (2) allowing the Borrowed Resources Suspense Accounts and the administered accounts to hold SDRs; (3) borrowing of SDRs by the Fund; (4) use of the abbreviation "SDR" in all references to special drawing rights; and (5) other steps that might be taken to enhance the SDR's usefulness as a unit of account, a means of payment, and a reserve asset.

REFERENCES

Coats, Warren, L., Jr., "The SDR as a Means of Payment," International Monetary Fund, *Staff Papers* (Washington), Vol. 29 (September 1982), pp. 422-36.

Committee of Twenty (Committee on Reform of the International Monetary System and Related Issues), "Outline of Reform" in *International Monetary Reform: Documents of the Committee of Twenty* (Washington: International Monetary Fund, 1974), pp. 7-48.

Fawzi, Samir I., "Has the SDR Been Used as the First Line Reserve Asset?" (unpublished, International Monetary Fund, January 27, 1982).

Heller, H. Robert, and Malcolm Knight, *Reserve-Currency Preferences of Central Banks*, Essays in International Finance, No. 131 (Princeton, New Jersey: International Finance Section, Princeton University, 1978).

International Monetary Fund, *Selected Decisions of the International Monetary Fund and Selected Documents*, Ninth Issue (Washington, June 15, 1981).

Polak, J. J., *Thoughts on an International Monetary Fund Based Fully on the SDR*, IMF Pamphlet Series, No. 28 (Washington, 1979).

13

Evolution of the SDR Outside the Fund

This background paper, prepared by Fund staff, examines the major uses of the special drawing right (SDR) as a unit of account outside the Fund. It does not discuss the SDRs created by the Fund through the Special Drawing Rights Department, nor such SDR-denominated Fund-related assets or obligations as reserve tranche positions, repurchase obligations, or loan claims other than to distinguish them from other forms of SDRs. It is concerned mostly with the use of the SDR as a unit of account in commercial and financial markets but also refers to the use of the SDR as a means of payment and as a unit of account by official entities other than the Fund. After a brief discussion of certain issues raised by the advent and growth of these uses, subsequent sections review SDR developments in private financial markets and other uses of the SDR as a unit of account. A final section explores a variety of ways in which the Fund might promote the uses of the SDR outside the Fund.

I. SDRs ISSUED BY THE FUND AND OTHER FORMS OF SDRs

At the beginning of 1981, the number of currencies in the SDR valuation basket was reduced from 16 to 5. Since that time, the volume of SDR-denominated bank deposits has grown substantially; SDR-denominated certificates of deposit totaling at least SDR 500 million have been issued or rolled over; five bonds or notes totaling SDR 300 million have been issued or announced; and seven syndicated loans, together amounting to almost SDR 1.2 billion have been organized (see Tables 1–3). These activities had no direct relation to the balances of holdings recorded in the Fund's Special Drawing Rights Department—that is, to official SDRs. These are but a few of the uses of SDR-denominated financial obligations

561

issued by entities other than the Fund, which for convenience are called commercial SDRs in this paper.

The SDR monetary unit is any unit defined (i.e., valued) in terms of the basket of currencies selected by the Fund for that purpose. It may be used commercially or officially for invoicing and pricing goods and services, in contracts establishing or defining financial obligations, and as the unit in which deposits, bonds, or other financial assets or liabilities are denominated or in which accounts are maintained or reported. The SDRs recorded in the Fund's Special Drawing Rights Department have a daily exchange value, an interest yield, rules for use, and an aggregate quantity, all determined by the Fund. SDR-denominated deposits with commercial banks, the commercial asset most like the Fund's official SDR, have different yields, maturities, and uses. However, they all share a value in terms of currencies that is related in some well-defined way to the Fund-determined basket of currencies.

These developments raise the issues of the Fund's attitude toward these uses of the SDR and whether the Fund should encourage, or attempt to redirect, these developments where it is able. The following brief summaries of some of the SDR's characteristics are intended to assist readers in assessing this issue.

(a) There is a private market in SDR-denominated financial assets, and it has grown substantially since the simplification of the SDR valuation basket in January 1981.

(b) The growth of commercial SDRs has been in response to evolving preferences for more diversified, multicurrency portfolios as a means of managing the increased risk of exchange losses in a world of widespread floating. Moreover, expansion of either official or commercial SDRs potentially provides many official depositors with a reserve asset superior to national currencies or gold in terms of exchange stability. As such, the availability of SDRs may reduce switching among currencies by both official reserve holders and private markets, thereby contributing to more orderly exchange markets. The SDR is advantageous primarily to those with a conservative portfolio management strategy. Those with an aggressive strategy will be prepared to arrange and rearrange their holdings in the hope of earning a higher return than would be yielded by a prepackaged basket, even at the risk of receiving a lesser return if their expectations are incorrect.

(c) In international financial markets and under international agreements, the SDR has thus far been used primarily as a unit of account. The basket method of valuation is used to determine the value of an asset or an obligation, but payments are made by transfer of a currency, most often the U.S. dollar—that is, the SDR is not generally used as a means of payment. Its development as a means of payment is, as yet, in the initial stages. Further development in this direction is required before the SDR unit can be viewed as being akin to a currency rather than a basket of five currencies.

(d) Use of the commercial SDR as a means of payment would in all likelihood increase the utility of the official SDR to monetary authorities and other official entities holding SDRs. Liquidity is enhanced by familiarity. As routine procedures are developed, transacting in SDRs tends to become quicker and less costly, thereby enhancing the demand for official as well as commercial SDRs.

(e) With some exceptions, the arguments in support of the usefulness of official SDRs also generally support the development of commercial SDRs. While official and other entities are free to hold any mix of currencies they desire and thereby fashion their own currency baskets, the Fund's unit of account has the advantages of international standing and, to the extent its use achieves wide acceptance, of lower transactions costs. The SDR has the potential to provide the world with a relatively more stable standard and store of value in an environment of widespread floating. As such, it could contribute to the evolution of more viable monetary arrangements than would exist in its absence.

Normally, commercial SDRs do not add to official foreign exchange reserves, since, at present, commercial SDRs are created mostly by substituting SDR deposits for other reserve assets, primarily U.S. dollars. However, if the commercial banks accepting SDR-denominated deposits increase the credit they extend to central banks as a result of accepting these deposits, it is possible that international reserves will be augmented. Moreover, commercial SDRs (particularly SDR-denominated deposits) potentially compete with official SDRs in reserve portfolios of Fund members. This competition does not prevent the issuance of additional official SDRs, since allocations are made on the basis of a global need to supplement existing reserve assets. However, it could impair the evolution of the official asset if the commercial SDR were considered by participants to be an asset superior to the official SDR, with the result that countries would be reluctant to add to their holdings of official SDRs. If necessary, the Fund could overcome this reluctance by making appropriate adjustments in the official SDR to establish and maintain its attractiveness relative to the commercial SDR. (See the specific suggestions in the companion paper, "Possible Further Improvements in the Existing SDR," Chapter 12 in this volume.)

A further reason for the Fund to maintain the attractiveness of the official SDR relative to the commercial SDR is the possibility of switching between the assets based on the relative yields. The differences in yield arise for four reasons: (1) because interest rates paid on privately issued SDR-denominated assets are determined on a continuous basis in the financial markets and will therefore generally differ from the official interest rate presently set once each quarter by the Fund; (2) because exchange rates between major currencies and the SDR vary throughout the day, while the official rates are calculated only once daily by the Fund; (3) because the interest rates on SDR-denominated deposits are close to the weighted average of Eurocurrency deposit rates for the same term to maturity, while the interest rate on the official SDR is a weighted average of rates on national instruments, which are generally lower; and (4) because of the existence of commercial risk with respect to private SDR deposits.

II. USE OF THE SDR IN INTERNATIONAL FINANCIAL MARKETS

The SDR is now used to denominate a wide range of financial instruments and obligations, ranging from current accounts to ten-year syndicated credits. This section contains a brief description of the different types of SDR-denominated obligation and discusses the advantages and shortcomings of the SDR as a financial unit of account in the light of experience with these obligations.

SDR-Denominated Obligations

Bond and Note Issues

The first SDR-denominated obligation was a 1975 bond issue. There have subsequently been 12 further issues of bonds or notes, the details of which are given in Table 1. These issues totaled SDR 563 million, of which SDR 479.3 million is currently outstanding. The issuers are primarily official institutions, although two private corporations have also made issues. The first nine issues carried a fixed interest rate that was usually about $\frac{1}{2}$ of 1 percentage point below the weighted average rate for domestic instruments of comparable maturity in the underlying currencies. This discount was based on the advantages of the SDR denomination in spreading exchange risk for the lender. The four most recent issues have been floating-rate issues. (The method of setting the interest rate on floating-rate issues is discussed below.) Most of the bonds and notes are quoted on the Luxembourg stock exchange, but secondary market activity has apparently been limited, since most investors have held their bonds to maturity.

Syndicated Bank Loans

The first syndicated loans denominated in SDRs did not appear until after the reduction of the SDR valuation basket to five currencies in January 1981. Since then, there have been seven such syndicated credits, totaling approximately SDR 1.2 billion—a small amount relative to the total of syndicated credits in all denominations, which amounted to SDR 104.3 billion in 1981 (Bank of England (1982)). All the SDR-denominated credits have borne a floating interest rate. Details of these credits are given in Table 2. Part of the reason for the introduction of credits denominated in SDRs was the generally high rate of interest on credits denominated in U.S. dollars in 1981.

Deposits

The first deposit facility in SDRs was offered by a London bank in June 1975. By the end of 1978, 20 banks were prepared to accept SDR-denominated deposits, although it is not certain how many of them had actually taken deposits at that stage. The rates offered were generally not very attractive, and there was little demand from borrowers for loans denominated in SDRs. To cover their exchange risk, banks had to break up the SDR basket into its component currencies. This entailed heavy transactions and organizational costs, particularly as money markets and forward markets were not well developed for some of the component currencies of the 16-currency basket. However, the size of the SDR deposit market grew gradually, with both official institutions and private organizations making deposits. By December 1980, at least 30 banks were offering SDR-denominated deposits, typically with maturities of 3, 6, and 12 months and a typical minimum of US$1 million.[1] No statistics are collected on the size of the SDR deposit market, and banking data do not generally show SDR-denominated liabilities separately. Impressions derived from conversations with bankers and depositors indicate that the size of the market in December 1980 was about SDR 2–3 billion.

The advent of the five-currency basket made it easier for banks to cover their SDR deposit obligations. In particular, it was now profitable for them to accept deposits of shorter maturity because transactions costs were much lower. Of 17 banks surveyed in February 1981, 8 were willing to accept SDR deposits for periods of as short as one week, with some, however, requiring a higher minimum deposit on the shorter maturities. The final step of this trend was the introduction of the SDR current account, which is discussed below.

[1] This information is taken from Hambros Bank Limited, "Investing in Currency Baskets" (undated) and from conversations with bankers.

TABLE 1. COMPARISON OF EURONOTE AND EUROBOND ISSUES DENOMINATED IN SDRs

Offering Date	Issuer (Guarantor),[1] Coupon, and Maturity	Lead Manager	Amount Issued	Amount Out-standing	Initial Yield	Yield to Maturity as of 2/10/82	Denomi-nation of Issue	Final Maturity	Percentage to be retired prior to maturity	Average life	Callable after year	Initial call price
			million SDRs		*percent*		*SDRs*	*years*		*years*		*percent*
12/18/81	Red Nacional de los Ferrocariles Españoles (Kingdom of Spain) Floating rate note, mini-mum 5 percent coupon, 0.25 percent above 6-month SDR London Inter-bank Offered Rate (LIBOR), due 1989	Orion Bank	50	50	13.769	14.360	100,000	8	—	6.5	—	—
11/30/81	Ferrovie dello Stato (Rep. of Italy) Floating rate note,	Dillon Read and Orion Bank	80	80	14.0625	14.534	100,000	4	—	—	1	100.0

Date	Issue / Borrower										
	minimum 5 percent coupon, 0.25 percent above 6-month SDR LIBOR, due 1985	50	50	16.1875	17.638	1,000	7	48.0	6.0	3	100.0
5/7/81	Pechiney Ugine Kuhlmann Floating rate note, due 1988[2]										
4/8/81	Enel (Rep. of Italy) Floating rate debenture, minimum 5 percent coupon, due 1989[2]	100	100	15.1875	16.999	5,000	5 (extendable to 8)	—	—	3	100.0
	Dillon, Read Overseas Corp.										
1/16/81	Nordic Investment Bank 11½ percent due 2/15/86	20	20	11.50	14.432	10,000	5	—	5	3	—
	Orion Bank										
2/26/80	Svenska Handelsbanken 11 percent bonds due 3/15/85	15	15	11.00	13.906	5,000	5	—	—	2	102.0
	Kuwait International Investment Co.										
8/23/79	Nordic Investment Bank 9¼ percent notes due 9/15/84	13	13	9.25	15.637	10,000	5	—	5	3	—
	Credit Suisse, First Boston Ltd.										

Banque de l'Indo-Chine et de Suez, Kredietbank International Group

TABLE 1 (concluded). COMPARISON OF EURONOTE AND EUROBOND ISSUES DENOMINATED IN SDRs

Offering Date	Issuer (Guarantor), Coupon,[1] and Maturity	Lead Manager	Amount Issued	Amount Outstanding	Initial Yield	Yield to Maturity as of 2/10/82	Denomination of Issue	Final Maturity	Mandatory Redemption Provision		Optional Redemption Provisions	
									Percentage to be retired prior to maturity	Average life	Callable after year	Initial call price
4/11/79	Republic of Finland 8 3/4 percent notes due 9/15/84	Credit Suisse, First Boston Ltd.	50	50	8.88	14.361	1,000	5	—	5	3	—
3/2/79	Nordic Investment Bank 9 percent notes due 3/15/84	S.G. Warburg and Co. Ltd.	20	20	9.00	14.229	10,000	5	—	—	3	101.0
11/22/78	Swedish Investment Bank 9 percent bonds due 12/1/85	Credit Suisse, First Boston Ltd.	25	21.33	9.00	14.349	1,000	7	48.0	5.3	4	101.5
7/8/75	Electricité de France (Republic of France) 9 percent bonds due 7/17/83	Kredietbank Luxembourgeoise	50	50	9.00	15.501	1,000	8	—	—	—	101.0

| 6/19/75 | Swedish Investment Bank 9 percent bonds due 7/1/82 | Credit Suisse, White Weld Ltd. | 40 | 10 | 9.00 | 15.625 | 1,000 | 7 | 75.0 | 5.5 | 4 | 102.0 |
| 6/11/75 | Alusuisse Int. N.V. (Swiss Aluminum Ltd.) 9 percent bonds due 6/15/80 | Credit Suisse, White Weld Ltd. | 50 | 0 | 9.00 | — | 1,000 | 5 | — | — | 3 | 102.0 |

Source: Chemical Bank International Limited and Luxembourg Stock Exchange.

[1] Coupons are payable semiannually.

[2] Interest will be payable semiannually from the issue date, with interest payment dates falling in November and May. The rate for each interest period will be $\frac{1}{4}$ percent per annum above the average (weighted in the proportions which each currency from which the value of an SDR is determined bears to one SDR in terms of the U.S. dollar) of the rates at which six-month deposits in each such currency are offered by the reference bank to prime banks in the London interbank market at or about 11:00 a.m. (London time) two days prior to the commencement of each interest period. The weighted average is, if necessary, to be rounded upward to the nearest whole multiple of $\frac{1}{16}$ percent.

[3] Not callable.

TABLE 2. SYNDICATED SDR CREDITS

Borrower	Date Agreed	Lead Manager	Amount	Final Maturity	Procedure for Setting Interest Rate	Repayment Provisions	Other Provisions
			million SDRs	*years*			
African Development Bank	February 1982	Chase Manhattan	200	8	$1/2$ percent above 6-month SDR London Interbank Offered Rate (LIBOR) for first 3 years, $5/8$ percent for remaining 3 years	5 years grace, $1/16$ of principal semiannually thereafter	
Fuerzos Eléctricas del Noroeste S.A. (Spanish Utility)	January 1982	Orion Bank	100	8	$5/8$ percent above SDR LIBOR for first 5 years, $3/4$ percent for remaining 3 years	5 years grace, $1/7$ of principal semiannually thereafter	
Nacional Financiera S.A. (Mexico)	December 1981	Chemical Bank International	220	8	$5/8$ percent above 6-month US$ LIBOR adjusted for forward premium or discount of other four currencies	9 equal semiannual installments beginning after 4 years	
Compañia Anónima de Administración y Fomento Eléctrico (Venezuelan Government utility)	July 1981	Chemical Bank International	47.5	6	$5/8$ percent above 6-month SDR LIBOR	Interest payable at 3- or 6-month intervals (borrower's discretion), principal due at maturity	
Government of Ireland	June 1981	National Westminster Bank	Equivalent of $90 million	10	$3/8$ percent above 3-, 6-, or 12-month (borrower's discretion) SDR LIBOR for first 5 years; $1/2$ percent margin for last 5 years	Principal due at maturity	Borrower can switch denomination to any freely available Eurocurrency
Republic of Ivory Coast	May 1981	Chase Manhattan	Equivalent of $50 million	8	Average of middle 3 of 6-month SDR offered rates by 5 reference banks	Semiannually in installments equal to 1/7 of SDRs borrowed, paid in U.S. dollars valued by Fund on repayment date, payments to begin 5 years after signing	10 percent ceiling on appreciation of SDR against U.S. dollar
Kingdom of Sweden	April 1981	Morgan Guaranty	500	5	$3/8$ percent above 3- or 6-month (borrower's discretion) SDR LIBOR for first 3 years, $1/2$ percent for remaining 2 years	Interest payable at 3- or 6-month intervals (borrower's discretion), principal due at maturity	

The volume of SDR-denominated deposits grew rapidly in early 1981. With the higher interest rate on U.S. dollar deposits, the growth in the size of the SDR deposit market slowed in mid-1981, even though the basket had been simplified. However, activity appears to have picked up late in the year. Conversations with bankers and with some depositors indicate deposits at the end of 1981 of SDR 5-7 billion net of interbank deposits.[2] It is estimated that between 40 and 50 banks now have the organizational capability to accept and manage SDR deposits (Godsell and Company (1981)). The largest depositors are private corporations, but a number of central banks and other official institutions are also depositors.

Banks usually cover the exchange risk involved in accepting an SDR deposit either by acquiring an asset denominated in SDRs (e.g., by making a loan denominated in SDRs) or by breaking down the proceeds of the investment into the component currencies. The latter can be done in two ways—by breaking down the proceeds of the deposit into the five component currencies and investing them in the appropriate amounts or by investing all the proceeds in one currency and selling the proceeds of the investment forward for the component currencies, again in the appropriate amounts. The yields on these investments and the transactions costs associated with them determine the interest rates that banks can offer on SDR-denominated deposits.

Certificates of Deposit

The first certificate of deposit (CD) denominated in SDRs was issued in June 1980 at a fixed rate of interest. Since then, there have been a number of issues, bringing the total value of such CDs issued to SDR 500-700 million (Wragg (1981 b)). The most important development was the announcement in January 1981 by a group of seven London banks that they would issue and trade in London CDs denominated in SDRs. The market is wholesale and short term, with a minimum denomination of SDR 1 million and maturities of less than one year. The group adopted general guidelines for procedures in the secondary market and uniform documentation for the CDs. A copy of the SDR CD agreed upon by those banks is reproduced in Appendix I. The number of participating banks has subsequently risen to about 20 (Wragg (1981 b)). It is estimated that these banks have made "tap" issues of CDs (i.e., issues in exact amounts demanded by investors rather than in so-called tranche offerings of fixed amounts) of between SDR 350 million and SDR 550 million. Initially, there was little secondary market activity, since issues were generally held to maturity.

---

[2]It is estimated that about one half of gross deposits were interbank deposits.

The view has been expressed that investors may prefer the CD to the deposit for reasons of convenience, but have no intention of testing the former's liquidity before the maturity date (Naudin (1981)). There was, however, some increase in secondary market trading in early 1982. Details of the "tranche" offerings of CDs are given in Table 3. It will be noted that all the issues made in 1981 were floating-rate issues.

Forward Market

There was no forward market activity in SDRs before the simplification of the SDR valuation basket in January 1981. It is now possible, however, to buy and sell SDRs forward against U.S. dollars for periods of up to one year (including broken periods) and in amounts of up to SDR 50 million. At least ten banks deal in forward SDRs, and as business has grown, the spread between bid and offered forward rates has narrowed. Banks making loans denominated in SDRs—for example, participants in syndicated credits—may use deposits denominated in U.S. dollars to finance their extension of these credits while covering their exchange risk by buying U.S. dollars forward against SDRs. In these respects, the SDR is a currency like any other. This technique is particularly useful to banks that have not yet fully developed in-house experience in dealing in SDRs or expect to be active relatively infrequently (Wragg (1981 b)).

Current Accounts and Other Short-Term Accounts

Two commercial banks offer current accounts denominated in SDRs. In addition, participants in Euroclear—a clearing system for Eurobonds—are able to purchase SDR-denominated bonds by debiting SDR-denominated current accounts held with Euroclear. Demand for these current accounts is mostly from banks and multinational corporations that have receipts and expenses in some or all of the component currencies. Sometimes they use all five currencies as vehicles for deposits or withdrawals. The issue of SDR-denominated loans and bonds has generated many transactions denominated in SDRs (e.g., brokerage fees and interest), for which these accounts are used to make payments. Some securities have a requirement that subscription payments be made in SDRs and that payment of interest and repayment of principal be made in SDRs, that is—by transfers from and to an SDR account. The turnaround of funds in current accounts is rapid, since depositors with funds at their disposal for more than a few days deposit them in interest-bearing "call" deposits that require two days' notice of withdrawal. Current accounts pay no interest.

TABLE 3. BASIC INFORMATION ON SDR CERTIFICATES OF DEPOSIT[1]

Issuers	Issue Date	Amount	Maturity of Issue	Initial Interest Rate	Procedure for Setting Interest Rate	Minimum Denomination of Issues	Other Characteristics	Managed by:
		million SDRs		percent 2		million SDRs		
Sumitomo Bank	7/30/81	10	3 years		1/4 percent above 6-month SDR London Interbank Offered Rate (LIBOR)	0.5		Chemical Bank International
Bank of Tokyo (London Branch)	4/27/81	15	6 months	13.75	Offered rate of three reference banks	1	Rollover for up to 3 years	Swiss Bank Corporation International
Fuji Bank Ltd.	4/2/81	15	3 years	13.32	1/4 percent above offered rate of five reference banks	0.5		Credit Suisse, First Boston Ltd. (London)
Sanwa Bank Ltd.	2/19/81	20	3 months	14.30	The offered rate on Chemical Bank's SDR deposits	1	Rollover for up to 3 years	Chemical Bank International
Gulf Bank (Kuwait)	2/17/81	15	3 years	14.3125	1/4 percent above 3-month SDR-denominated deposit rates of five reference banks	0.5		Chase Manhattan
Dai-Ichi Kangyo Bank	1/29/81	25	2 years	13.75	1/8 percent over 6-month SDR LIBOR	1		Morgan Stanley
Sumitomo Bank	1/29/81	20	3 months	14.05	The offered rate on Chemical Bank's SDR deposits (about 1/4 percent above bid rates)	1	Rollover	Chemical Bank International
Chemical Bank	6/30/80	25	3 months	11.40	Fixed	1		Chemical Bank International
Chemical Bank	6/30/80	25	6 months	11.10	Fixed	1		Chemical Bank International

[1] In addition, tap issues mostly by a group of seven banks (Barclays Bank International, Chemical Bank, Citibank, Hong Kong and Shanghai Banking Corporation, Midland Bank, National Westminster Bank, and Standard Chartered Bank) were issued for amounts of SDR 350–550 million. The individual issues were usually for SDR 500,000, with maturities of three to six months that could be rolled over.
[2] Not available.

The development of SDR-denominated current accounts opens the possibility of using commercial SDRs as a transactions medium. If this use is to develop, it will entail the development of clearing systems.

Clearing Arrangements

Financial obligations denominated in SDRs are generally established and repaid by means of a transmission or vehicle currency, usually the U.S. dollar. The introduction of SDR-denominated current accounts opens the possibility of using deposits in these accounts as a means of payment for both financial and commercial obligations, which would enhance the role of the SDR in the international financial system. Settlement of SDR-denominated obligations with private SDR deposits would generally require that the payor and payee both maintain accounts with the same bank or that their respective banks maintain SDR-denominated interbank deposits with each other (i.e., maintain the standard correspondent banking relationship). Additionally, if such settlements are to become widespread, it would be necessary to have some means of clearing and settling multilaterally the SDR claims arising among banks as a result of the movement of SDR deposits among their clients in payment of commercial and financial obligations. A scheme for using the official SDR to facilitate such settlements is outlined later on in the section entitled "Fund Influence on Use of SDR Outside the Fund." Alternatively, use could be made of clearing facilities that already exist to clear secondary market transactions in Eurobonds, or the Fund could help to develop or could provide such a facility. Participants in one of these facilities, Euroclear, can already maintain cash SDR accounts to pay for securities. Internationally active commercial banks could maintain SDR clearing accounts with one of these clearing facilities or with an international official institution such as the Bank for International Settlements or the Fund.

General Issues

Advantages of SDR as Unit of Account for Financial Obligations

The primary advantage of the SDR as a unit of account for financial obligations is the stability provided by its basket valuation. This stabilizing effect tends to make the value of, and interest rate on, obligations denominated in SDRs less vulnerable to swings in exchange and money markets than those of obligations denominated in any one currency. This feature has attractions for both borrowers and lenders of funds in international markets.[3] The unit offers a straightforward means of portfolio

---

[3]For a discussion of the SDR's advantages, see Putnam (1981).

diversification, and transactions costs are lower than those required to effect diversification into each component currency. In addition, borrowers might be able to borrow by issuing an obligation denominated partly in a currency that they would find difficult or impossible to borrow individually, especially if other investment outlets in that currency are restricted by regulations. This is, however, a drawback from the viewpoint of authorities who wish to control direct and indirect access to their currencies. Once the SDR is viewed more as a currency than as a basket of currencies, lending banks will try to balance their SDR-denominated assets with SDR-denominated liabilities, rather than covering their positions in the component currencies, and this drawback will no longer exist.

From an investor's or depositor's viewpoint, the SDR is a prudent investment, since, as a practical matter, it represents a blending of yields.[4] An SDR deposit or forward purchase may also be used as a partial hedge against commercial or financial uncertainties, particularly when the depositor does not know the currency he will need at maturity; has expenditure needs in several currencies, the amounts of which are not known in advance or can fluctuate irregularly; or has commitments in currencies pegged to the SDR. Companies with a variety of actual or potential foreign suppliers and customers and multinational corporations may well find themselves in these situations.

Pricing of SDR Issues

When the first SDR-denominated bonds were issued, the market in short-term SDR-denominated obligations was not well developed, and interest rate quotations were not readily available for other than a limited range of maturities. Consequently, it was difficult for the issuers of the bonds to determine interest rates. The rates tended to be set at a slight discount from the weighted average of the rates in the markets for instruments denominated in the component currencies and with comparable maturities.[5] More recent issues have had floating interest rates. The rates are set in three ways:

[4]As observed by Federal Reserve Board Governor Henry Wallich (1980, p. 130), "In the exchange market, any currency may be expected so to position itself that its total return, interest plus expected appreciation, is equal to that of other currencies allowing for factors of convenience and political risk. *Ex post* it will undoubtedly turn out that some currencies appreciated or depreciated in ways not expected, making total returns unequal. An investor gifted with superior foresight could take advantage of this. But the average investor or monetary authority will be better off with the lower risk of a diversified portfolio, of which the SDR claim ... [is a] prime instance."

[5]Weights were initially taken from the currency composition of the SDR valued in the spot market. The use of spot rates, however, gives an incorrect weighting pattern and an upward bias to the calculated interest rate since currencies with a low interest rate are underrepresented and vice versa. The use of forward exchange rates of the same maturity would produce the correct weights.

(1) Using rates quoted by banks for SDR deposits of a particular maturity, the number of reference banks has varied between five and eight, with a minimum of three quotations required from among the group of reference banks—a currency approach.

(2) Using the weighted average of the London interbank offered rates[6] of the SDR component currencies, generally for three-month or six-month deposits—a basket approach.

(3) Using the London interbank offered rate for U.S. dollars, adjusted for the forward premium or discount of the other SDR component currencies against the U.S. dollar for delivery in six months—a basket approach.

These approaches represent the ways in which banks and other subscribers to these issues may fund their investment by borrowing the component currencies, by borrowing SDR deposits from other banks, or by borrowing U.S. dollars and selling the component currencies forward. Borrowers in SDRs assuming floating-rate obligations have been offered spreads similar to those offered to comparable borrowers of individual currencies (Sobol (1981–82)).

SDR Exchange Rate

There are two general approaches to establishing the SDR exchange rate when a deposit is made. Banks are generally prepared to quote two sets of interest rates on SDR deposits, one for deposits constituted at the going exchange rates of the component currencies at the time the deposit is arranged, and another for deposits constituted at the official rate as established and announced by the Fund. The interest rate on the latter type of deposit is generally lower, since banks cannot deal at the middle rates, which are used to establish the official SDR rate. Also the banks may bear some exchange risk if the deposit is constituted after noon, London time, since exchange rates will have changed since the official valuation was established. On maturity, the exchange rate used is usually the official rate, because the depositor is then locked into the deposit and prefers a valuation that is fixed neutrally rather than one established by the depository bank. For bond and note issues, the official exchange rate is generally used.

The documentation associated with deposits, CDs, and other obligations usually indicates what is to happen if the Fund does not issue an official rate. However, the need for such a provision has been reduced, since the Bank of England, at the request of the Fund staff, began in August 1981 to publish the exchange rates it supplies to the Fund for calculation

---

[6]The London interbank offered rate (LIBOR)—that is, the rate at which banks in London offer Eurocurrencies in the interbank placement market.

of the official SDR/U.S. dollar rate. The official rate can be calculated by anyone as long as the London exchange market is open. Some loan documents call for repayment in the component currencies if an exchange rate for the SDR is not available for the day on which an obligation matures. This approach makes it unnecessary to establish an exchange rate. Use of the component currencies is becoming increasingly popular for the repayment of deposits on maturity; for example, a deposit of SDR 10 million would be repaid as 4.6 million deutsche mark, 7.4 million French francs, 340 million yen, 0.71 million pounds sterling, and 5.4 million U.S. dollars.

Redefinition Risk[7]

The possibility that the Fund will alter the definition of the SDR during the life of an obligation is addressed in the documentation for various SDR-denominated obligations. There are three approaches to the definition of the SDR unit for purposes of the obligation in these circumstances.

"Current" definition. The definition of the unit follows precisely the definition of the official SDR, and any changes in the latter immediately affect the value of the former. This approach has been generally used for SDR capital market issues.

"Constant" definition. It is agreed between the bank and the customer that the definition of the unit for the purpose of the obligation will remain unchanged for the life of the obligation, irrespective of any changes made by the Fund. This is the method used in time deposits and for short-term CDs, up to a normal maximum maturity of 12 months. It has also been used in one syndicated loan denominated in SDRs.

For a period after the change in valuation in January 1981, the Fund made exchange rates calculated using the former 16-currency unit available to those deposit-taking organizations that had accepted deposits based on the 16-currency valuation. The last request for this information was met in October 1981.

"Lagged current" definition. The definition of the unit follows any changes made by the Fund in the definition of the SDR, but the implementation of those changes (for the purposes of the obligation) is delayed until the start of the next interest period or comparable date. This technique is used for floating-rate certificates of deposit and most syndicated loans and, in concept, is treated like the repayment and simultaneous readvancement of the loan.

For floating-rate obligations for which the lenders are funding their investment by borrowing in the three-month or six-month Eurodeposit

---

[7]This section draws on Wragg (1981 a).

markets, the lagged current definition appears to be most suitable, since it eliminates redefinition risk for the lender while returning within a short period to the official definition.

Legal Obstacles

In a number of member countries, banks are forbidden to accept SDR-denominated deposits or to extend SDR-denominated loans even to nonresidents. This may reflect general restrictions on commercial banks' operations denominated in other than domestic currency. In other countries, loans and deposits may be allowed in selected foreign denominations, but the law or regulations have not been altered to extend this treatment to obligations that are denominated in SDRs.

III. OTHER USES OF THE SDR AS UNIT OF ACCOUNT

Use for Invoicing

What little is known to the staff about trade invoicing practices and the pricing of internationally traded goods and services indicates that the SDR is rarely used for such purposes, despite its apparent advantages. In one interesting instance, the Wm. Wrigley Jr. Co. of Chicago, Illinois, a multinational corporation, uses the SDR for intracompany pricing of the finished product. Since 1975, transit tolls payable to the Suez Canal Authority by vessels using the waterway have been denominated in SDRs. The member countries of the Organization of Petroleum Exporting Countries discussed the possibility of pricing crude oil in SDRs when they met in Gabon in 1975, but no action was taken.

The very limited use made of SDRs for pricing partially reflects the continued lack of familiarity with the SDR and its potential advantages. In addition, it has only recently become practicable to make payments in SDRs. While SDR obligations can readily be discharged in almost any currency, a wider ability to make payments in commercial SDRs would increase the attractiveness of SDR invoicing.[8]

Use by International Organizations and Conventions

A number of international organizations use the SDR as a unit of account or as the basis of a unit of account.[9] In addition, various interna-

---

[8] A full discussion of the possibilities for SDR invoicing is contained in Karlik (1982).

[9] This use is discussed further in Gold (1980, pp. 20-39) and Gold (1981, pp. 26-34 and 40-43).

tional conventions use the SDR as a standard of value in which to express monetary magnitudes, notably conventions expressing limits of liability for carriers in the international transport of goods and persons (see Appendix II). In some cases, the SDR has been adopted in these conventions to replace the Poincaré or Germinal franc, both of which are defined by reference to fixed quantities of gold. For example, the Universal Postal Union's unit of account is the gold franc, which has been declared by a legal instrument of the organization to have a specified relationship to the SDR—SDR 1 equals 3.061 gold francs. Therefore, in practice, international postal accounts are prepared in SDRs.

In a related matter, the United Nations Commission on International Trade Law and the Committee on International Monetary Law of the International Law Association have been studying the possibility of developing a maintenance-of-value clause for inclusion in international conventions. The endeavor is based, in part, on the consideration that currencies continually depreciate in terms of the goods and services that they can purchase. Being defined in terms of currencies, the SDR does not maintain its purchasing power over goods and services.

It was therefore considered that it might be technically feasible to use an international price index to adjust nominal amounts that are specified in SDRs for the loss of purchasing power. The national price indices contained in this international index would be those of the five countries whose currencies comprise the SDR, with these indices assigned weights corresponding to the currency composition of the SDR. (See United Nations (1981), Effros (1982), and von Furstenberg (1981).)

Use as Currency Peg

Fifteen member countries of the Fund peg their exchange rates to the SDR. In 1980, nine of the countries for which information is available accounted for 0.30 percent of world exports of goods and services and 0.48 percent of world imports of goods and services. A country choosing to peg its exchange rate must frame its domestic monetary policy, in the absence of exchange controls over capital movements, in the light of the monetary policy of the country to whose currency its own currency is pegged. Currencies are sometimes pegged precisely in order to foster this monetary discipline. From this point of view, the choice of the currency or unit to which to peg is heavily influenced by the domestic rates of inflation in the candidate currencies. These, in turn, reflect domestic monetary policies and are reflected in the behavior of exchange rates. The SDR averages the behavior of the five most important currencies. To the extent that the members issuing these currencies have relatively low inflation rates, the SDR is a relatively attractive standard of value to which to peg the currencies of countries not wanting to chance independent monetary policies.

IV. FUND INFLUENCE ON USE OF THE SDR OUTSIDE THE FUND

One aspect of the SDR's development and use tends to support another. Wider use of the SDR as a unit of account helps to familiarize the world with its existence. Invoicing goods and services in SDRs can be expected to increase the demand for actual payments in SDRs. Wider use of commercial SDRs for settlement of financial obligations increases the attractiveness of SDR invoicing and accounting. A more attractive and widely used official SDR stimulates the development of the commercial SDR and vice versa.

The Fund has jurisdiction over only its own, official SDR. However, the nature of that asset, especially the composition of the currency basket, importantly affects the attractiveness of commercial SDRs. In addition, the attitude of the Fund may influence policies of member countries dealing with the role of SDRs in their respective banking systems. In light of the preceding discussion of the SDR outside the Fund, this section lists a number of ways the Fund might choose to exercise that influence.

Composition of SDR Basket

The currency composition of the SDR as determined by the Fund determines the composition of the SDR unit as used outside the Fund. Moreover, the Fund is obliged to continue to exercise this influence through its responsibility to review periodically the currencies included in the SDR basket and the relative weight attached to each of them. Because member countries have large SDR-denominated creditor and debtor positions in the Fund, and because of the high voting majority needed to change the definition of the SDR, parties using or holding SDR-denominated claims can feel assured that any adjustment will be reasonable and will not favor either group. Simplification of the basket to five currencies provided an impetus for the use of the SDR to denominate financial obligations, as was explained above. The procedure of announcing well in advance the timing of revisions to the valuation basket and the principles on which they will be made enables the Fund to maintain over time the representativeness of the SDR basket without the need for unexpected changes in the currency composition or weighting pattern of the basket, thereby avoiding undesirable disruptions in the value of the SDR. The care that has been taken, when revisions have been made in the valuation basket, to ensure continuity of value under the old and new baskets at the time of the changeover has had a similar effect.

Valuation and Interest Rate

Aside from the definition of the basket, commercial SDRs take on characteristics (exchange value, interest rate, maturity, etc.) in response to market considerations that are quite independent of similar characteristics given the official SDR by the Fund. However, differences in these characteristics may affect the choices of official holders between using or holding official or commercial SDRs. To limit such differences and to promote the complementary, parallel development of official and commercial SDRs, the valuation and interest rates of the two must be related over the long run.[10]

Clearing Arrangements

The official SDR as currently constituted could be used to facilitate interbank clearings of obligations arising out of the use of SDR-denominated deposits by banks' customers to settle financial and commercial obligations. One approach would require the willingness of official institutions to accept SDR-denominated clearing accounts from commercial banks operating within their jurisdiction. With this approach, the settlement of an SDR payment between individuals using two separate banks in two separate countries would be made by reducing one bank's holdings of SDRs with its central bank, increasing the receiving bank's holdings with its own central bank, and transferring official SDRs between the two central banks on the books of the Special Drawing Rights Department.[11] As many central banks do not currently accept SDR-denominated accounts from commercial banks, some encouragement by the Fund would help such a scheme to become operational. Alternatively, an international institution such as the Bank for International Settlements, or the Fund itself, could be asked to be the agent for an international clearing system in commercial SDRs. This would involve commercial banks' opening SDR-denominated accounts with the agent. These balances could be used by the banks in settlement of debtor and creditor positions arising through the transfer among them of SDR-denominated deposits.

---

[10]A number of the possible improvements discussed in the companion paper—"Possible Further Improvements in the Existing SDR," Chapter 12 in this volume—are motivated by this consideration.

[11]This scheme is described in greater detail in Coats (1982), Callier (1983), van den Boogaerde (1983), Kenen (1983 a, 1983 b), and Coats (1983).

Disseminating SDR Information

The SDR is either unknown or imperfectly understood outside a small group in the international financial community. A lack of knowledge about the SDR and the potential benefits associated with its use are among the main reasons it is not more widely used in international transactions. Consequently, a sustained and more intensive program to better inform bankers, brokers, and international traders about the SDR may be warranted. A few articles on this subject are currently available or in preparation, but more public presentations by Fund personnel might also be helpful.

A substantial number of participants in international financial markets use the telescreen services of the major financial news organizations. Official SDR exchange rates appear on one of these screens with some delay. The Fund could subscribe as a contributor to one or more of these screen services, which would enable it to disseminate information on SDR exchange rates more widely and quickly than at present. It would also enable more newspapers to print SDR exchange rates in their financial pages.

Numerous international organizations might advantageously adopt the SDR as a unit of account, a means of settlement, and a store of value. As in private finance and commerce, the potential benefits to these organizations from using the SDR are largely unrecognized. The Fund might increase its efforts to explain these benefits to such institutions. It would help the standing of the SDR if the World Bank were to borrow, lend, and contract in SDRs.

Official Borrowing in SDRs

International organizations could significantly boost the development of the SDR by borrowing in that unit. The increase in SDR-denominated assets would expand the market's awareness of the SDR and improve the ability of banks to match SDR liabilities against true SDR assets rather than cover their exchange exposure with a currency cocktail. This would further stimulate their willingness to accept SDR deposits.

Intergovernmental loans could be denominated in SDRs. Use of the SDR would also be enhanced if monetary authorities issued liabilities denominated in SDRs rather than in their own currencies against foreign exchange when other monetary authorities borrowed foreign exchange from them for intervention or reserve diversification. In particular, denominating "swap" credits in SDRs would generally reduce the exchange risk to be shared and would facilitate more diversified holdings in foreign exchange portfolios without exerting pressure in foreign exchange markets.

Relaxation of Legal Restraints

The Fund could encourage members to relax or abolish the legal obstacles to the use of the SDR as a unit of account for financial obligations. It could at least be accorded by monetary authorities the same treatment as the most-favored foreign currency within their domains.

APPENDICES

I. Sample SDR Certificate of Deposit

(FRONT)

Certificate Number

NEGOTIABLE SDR CERTIFICATE OF DEPOSIT

XYZ BANK
LIMITED

SDR _____
Maturity Date _____ Fixed
LONDON _____ 19 ____

LONDON BRANCH
1 ABACUS STREET, EC1Z 1AB.

XYZ BANK LIMITED CERTIFIES THAT

the sum of _____ SDRs (as defined on the reverse hereof) has been deposited on terms that it is payable to Bearer at the above address on surrender through the medium of a Recognised Bank of this Certificate, on the _____ fixed together with interest at the rate of _____ percent. per annum, calculated on actual days on a 360 day year basis from the date hereof to the Maturity Date only, payable at maturity. Payment of the deposit and interest will be made in the manner stated on the reverse hereof.

This Certificate shall be governed by English Law.

For and on behalf of XYZ BANK LIMITED

_____ Authorised Signature

(REVERSE)

For the purposes of this Certificate an SDR is the aggregate of the following amounts of the following currencies (being, at the date hereof, the components of one Special Drawing Right of the International Monetary Fund):-

CURRENCY	AMOUNT
U.S. dollar	0.54
Deutsche mark	0.46
Japanese yen	34.00
French franc	0.74
Pound sterling	0.071

Payment of the deposit and interest will, save as provided below, only be made in U.S. dollars. For the purpose of calculating the amount of these payments the U.S. dollar value of an SDR shall be that fixed by the International Monetary Fund for a Special Drawing Right comprising the currencies and amounts listed above as at two business days (which shall be days upon which banks are open for business in both London and New York City) prior to the Maturity Date stated on the face hereof. If the International Monetary Fund shall not fix the U.S. dollar value of such a Special Drawing Right on such day, payment of each SDR deposited as stated on the face hereof will be made in the currencies and amounts listed above and payment of interest on each such amount will be made in such respective currencies.

All payments will be made by draft or telegraphic transfer on New York City or, in the case of a payment in any currency other than U.S. dollars, on the principal financial centre applicable to such other currency.

Source: Chemical Bank International Limited, London.

II. SDR AS UNIT OF ACCOUNT

The international organizations and international conventions that use the SDR as a unit of account or as the basis of a unit of account are listed below.

International organizations
African Development Bank
African Development Fund
Arab Monetary Fund
Asian Clearing Union
Asian Development Bank
Development Bank of the Great Lakes Countries
Economic Community of West African States
European Conference of Postal and Telecommunications Administrations
Inter-American Development Bank
International Center for Settlement of Investment Disputes

International Development Association
International Fund for Agricultural Development
International Monetary Fund and its Administered Accounts
Islamic Development Bank
Nordic Investment Bank

International conventions
Agreement on Government Procurement
Athens Convention Relating to the Carriage of Passengers and Their Luggage by Sea
International Convention on Civil Liability for Oil Pollution Damage
Convention on Civil Liability for Oil Pollution Damage Resulting from Exploration for and Exploitation of Seabed Mineral Resources
Convention on the Carriage of Goods by Sea
Convention on the Contract for the International Carriage of Goods by Road
Convention on the Contract for the International Carriage of Passengers and Luggage by Road
Convention on the Contract for the International Carriage of Passengers and Luggage by Inland Waterway
Convention on the Establishment of an International Fund for Compensation for Oil Pollution Damage
Convention on Limitation of Liability for Maritime Claims
Convention Relating to the Limitation of the Liability of Owners of Inland Navigation Vessels
Convention for Rhine Navigation
European Convention on Products Liability in Regard to Personal Injury and Death
International Telecommunications Union
Nordic agreement for short-term financial assistance
Montreal Protocols amending the Warsaw Convention of 1929 on international carriage by air, the Hague Protocol of 1955, and the Guatemala City Convention of 1971, and a fourth (new) protocol.
Universal Postal Union

The SDR is under consideration as a unit of account for the following international purposes:

Convention on International Multimodal Transport
Organization for Economic Cooperation and Development (OECD) Code of Liberalization of Capital Movements
OECD Code of Liberalization of Current Invisible Operations
International Airline Transport Association

REFERENCES

Bank of England, *Quarterly Bulletin*, Vol. 22 (March 1982), p. 47.

Callier, Philippe, "The SDR as a Means of Payment: A Comment on Coats," International Monetary Fund, *Staff Papers*, Vol. 30 (September 1983), pp. 654–55.

Coats, Warren L., Jr., "The SDR as a Means of Payment," International Monetary Fund, *Staff Papers*, Vol. 29 (September 1982), pp. 422-36.

_____, "The SDR as a Means of Payment: Reply to Comments by Callier, Kenen, and van der Boogaerde," International Monetary Fund, *Staff Papers*, Vol. 30 (September 1983), pp. 662-69.

Effros, Robert C., "Unit of Account for International Conventions is Considered by UN Commission on Trade Law," *IMF Survey*, Vol. 11 (February 8, 1982), pp. 40-41.

Godsell and Company, "Special Drawing Rights: A Presentation From Godsell & Co., Limited" (mimeographed, London, April 1981).

Gold, Joseph, *SDRs, Currencies, and Gold: Fourth Survey of New Legal Developments*, IMF Pamphlet Series, No. 33 (Washington, 1980).

_____, *SDRs, Currencies, and Gold: Fifth Survey of New Legal Developments*, IMF Pamphlet Series, No. 36 (Washington, 1981).

Karlik, John R., "Some Aspects of Using the SDR to Invoice Private International Goods and Services Transactions" (International Monetary Fund, April 23, 1982).

Kenen, Peter B. (1983 a), "The SDR as a Means of Payment: A Comment on Coats," International Monetary Fund, *Staff Papers*, Vol. 30 (September 1983), pp. 656-61.

_____ (1983 b), "Use of the SDR to Supplement or Substitute for Other Means of Finance," Chapter 7 in this volume.

Naudin, Thierry, "Le marché des certificats de dépôts en D.T.S.," *Agence Economique et Financière*, special 1981 edition (December 1981), pp. 118-20.

Putnam, Bluford H., "The SDR: A New Tool in Exposure Management," *Euromoney* (October 1981), pp. 315-17.

Sobol, Dorothy M., "The SDR in Private International Finance," Federal Reserve Bank of New York, *Quarterly Review*, Vol. 6 (Winter 1981-82), pp. 29-41.

United Nations, "A Unit of Account for International Conventions," Annex I to *Universal Unit of Account for International Conventions*, UNCITRAL Doc. A.CN.9.200 (New York, May 12, 1981), pp. 4-6.

van den Boogaerde, Pierre R., "The SDR as a Means of Payment: A Comment on Coats," International Monetary Fund, *Staff Papers*, Vol. 30 (September 1983), pp. 650-53.

von Furstenberg, George M., "Price Deflators for Special Drawing Rights (SDRs) Over the Past Decade," *Review of Public Data Use*, Vol. 9 (March 1981), pp. 1-20.

Wallich, Henry C., "International Monetary Evolution," *Aussenwirtschaft*, Vol. 35 (June 1980), pp. 126-34. Remarks presented at Columbia University, New York, February 20, 1980.

Wragg, Lawrence de V. (1981 a), "Commercial Transactions in SDRs—Some Documentation Considerations," *Business Law Review*, Vol. 2 (October 1981), pp. 315-17.

_____ (1981 b), "The SDR Revolution—Speedy and Smooth," *International Herald Tribune*, November 24, 1981, Euromarket Supplement, Part I, p. 9s.

Biographical Sketches of Participants*

Arriazu, Ricardo H. Argentina
Economic and financial consultant to several Argentine financial institutions and Professor at the Universidad de Belgrano, Buenos Aires. He has been an economic advisor to the Presidency of the Central Bank of Argentina, an Alternate Executive Director of the International Monetary Fund, a Deputy and Participant in the Interim Committee, and Professor at the Universidad Católica Argentina (Buenos Aires).

Bruno, Michael Israel
Professor of Economics at Hebrew University (Jerusalem) since 1970. He has been Joint Director of the Bank of Israel's Research Department, Visiting Professor at the Massachusetts Institute of Technology and Harvard University, and Economic Policy Advisor to the Government of Israel. Mr. Bruno is a Research Associate of the National Bureau of Economic Research, a Fellow and Member of Council of the Econometric Society, and Foreign Honorary Member of the American Academy of Arts and Sciences.

Buiter, Willem H. United Kingdom
Cassel Professor at the London School of Economics. He has been Assistant Professor of Economics and International Affairs at Princeton University, Professor of Economics at the University of Bristol, and Consultant and Visiting Scholar at the International Monetary Fund. He is an Editor of *Economic Journal*.

Claassen, Emil-Maria France
Professor of the University of Paris-Dauphine since 1973 and at the Institute Européen d'Administration des Affaires since 1981. He has been Maître de Recherche at the Centre National de la Recherche Scientifique in Paris, Privat-Dozent at the University of Cologne, and Professor at the

---

*The country appearing to the right of each participant's name is the country he resided in at the time of the Conference on International Money, Credit, and the SDR and does not necessarily indicate his citizenship.

University of Giessen. Mr. Claassen has also been a Postdoctoral Fellow at the University of Chicago and a Visiting Professor at the Universities of Kabul, McGill, Mannheim, Pittsburgh, Queen's, and South Carolina.

Cooper, Richard N. United States
Maurits C. Boas Professor of International Economics at Harvard University since 1981. He has been Under Secretary of State for Economic Affairs in the U.S. State Department and Frank Altschul Professor of International Economics and Provost at Yale University. Mr. Cooper has also been a Senior Staff Economist on the (U.S.) Council of Economic Advisers and a staff member of the National Security Council.

Corden, W. M. Australia
Professor of Economics at the Australian National University. He has been Nuffield Reader in International Economics and a Fellow of Nuffield College, Oxford University. Mr. Corden has taught at the University of California at Berkeley, the University of Minnesota, Princeton University, and various Australian universities. He has been a consultant to several international organizations and governments.

De Grauwe, Paul Belgium
Professor of Economics at the University of Louvain since 1976. He has been a Research Fellow at the Brookings Institution and an Economist at the International Monetary Fund. Mr. De Grauwe has been a Visiting Professor at the Universities of Brussels, Michigan, and Paris.

de Vries, Rimmer United States
Senior Vice President and Head of International Economics Department at Morgan Guaranty Trust Company since 1978. He is the editor of *World Financial Markets* and a member of the *Time* Board of Economists; the Advisory Committee of the Institute for International Economics; the Board of Directors of the Institute for International Development, Inc.; and the Conference Board Economic Forum.

Dornbusch, Rudiger United States
Professor at the Massachusetts Institute of Technology since 1977. He has also taught at the Universities of Chicago and Rochester. Mr. Dornbusch has been a Visiting Professor at the Fundação Getulio Vargas in Rio de Janeiro.

Eaton, Jonathan United States
Associate Professor of Economics at Yale University. He is a Research

Associate of the National Bureau of Economic Research. Mr. Eaton has been a Lecturer and Assistant Professor of Economics at Princeton University, a Visiting Associate Professor at the Graduate Institute of International Studies in Geneva, and a Visiting Fellow at the Australian National University.

Fekete, János Hungary
First Deputy President of the National Bank of Hungary. He is Deputy Chairman of the Hungarian International Bank (London); Deputy Chairman of the Central-European International Bank (Budapest); and a board member of the International Bank for Economic Cooperation (Moscow), the International Investment Bank (Moscow), the Central Wechsel- und Creditbank (Vienna), and the Hungarian Bank for Foreign Trade. Mr. Fekete is a Governor of the International Monetary Fund and a member of the Consultative Group on International Economic and Monetary Affairs (Group of Thirty) and of the International Conference of Commercial Bank Economists.

Fischer, Stanley United States
Professor of Economics at the Massachusetts Institute of Technology since 1977. He has been a postdoctoral Fellow and Assistant Professor at the University of Chicago and a Fellow of the Institute for Advanced Studies at Hebrew University (Jerusalem). Mr. Fischer has also been a Visiting Lecturer at Hebrew University and a Visiting Scholar at the Hoover Institution, Stanford University.

Frenkel, Jacob A. United States
David Rockefeller Professor of International Economics at the University of Chicago. He is a Research Associate of the National Bureau of Economic Research, an Editor of the *Journal of Political Economy*, an Associate Editor of the *Journal of Monetary Economics* and *Economics Letters*, and a Fellow of the Econometric Society. Mr. Frenkel has been a consultant to the International Monetary Fund, the World Bank, and the Bank of Israel.

Grassman, Sven Sweden
Research Fellow at the University of Stockholm since 1971. He has been Secretary of the Swedish Balance of Payments Committee and a member of the (private, Swedish) Council of Economic Advisers and the Government Council of Industrial Policy. Mr. Grassman has been a Visiting Scholar at Stanford and Princeton Universities and at the Federal Reserve Board in Washington.

Grubel, Herbert, G. Canada
Professor of Economics at Simon Fraser University (Vancouver) since 1972. He has been Assistant Professor at Stanford University and the University of Chicago and an Associate Professor at the University of Pennsylvania. Mr. Grubel has held research positions at the Australian National University; Nuffield College, Oxford University; and the U.S. Treasury. He has been Visiting Professor at the University of Nairobi and President of the North American Studies Association. Mr. Grubel is a member of the Board of Editors of the Fraser Institute (Vancouver).

Kenen, Peter B. United States
Walker Professor of Economics and International Finance and Director of International Finance Section, Princeton University since 1971. He has also taught at Columbia University, where he served as Provost and Chairman of the Economics Department. Mr. Kenen has been a consultant to the (U.S.) Council of Economic Advisers, the Bureau of the Budget, the Federal Reserve Board, the U.S. Treasury, and the United Nations. He was a Fellow of the Center for Advanced Study in the Behavioral Sciences, a Guggenheim Fellow, and a Visiting Research Professor at the University of California at Berkeley. Mr. Kenen is a member of the Council on Foreign Relations and the Consultative Group on International Economic and Monetary Affairs (Group of Thirty).

Keyzer, Marinus W. France
Principal Administrator, Capital Markets Division of the Organization for Economic Cooperation and Development since 1978. Before that, he was on the staff of the central bank of the Netherlands and worked in commercial banking as a specialist in institutional portfolio management.

Komiya, Ryutaro Japan
Professor of Economics at the University of Tokyo since 1969. He served as the University's Dean of the Economics Faculty and its Deputy President. Mr. Komiya was a Visiting Professor at Stanford University and a member of the United Nations Group of Eminent Persons to Study the Role of Multinational Corporations and Their Impact on Development and on International Relations. He was also a member of the Organization for Economic Cooperation and Development's Group of Independent Experts on Non-Inflationary Growth.

Lomax, David F. United Kingdom
Group Economic Adviser at National Westminster Bank since 1975. He formerly served in the Federal Reserve Bank of New York and in the Brit-

ish Foreign Office and Department of Economic Affairs. Mr. Lomax is a regular broadcaster and speaker.

Masera, Rainer Italy
Head of the Research Department at Banca d'Italia since 1982. He has been an Economist at the Bank for International Settlements and has taught at the Istituto Universitario di Bergamo and the University of Rome. Mr. Masera was Joint Chairman of the Monetary Policy Group of the Center for European Policy Studies (Louvain) and an alternate member of the European Economic Community Monetary Committee. He is one of the two Italian members of the Group of Ten's Group of Deputies.

Neumann, Manfred J. M. Federal Republic of Germany
Professor of Political Economy at the University of Bonn since 1981. He has been Professor of Economics at the Freie Universität Berlin and an Economist at the Deutsche Bundesbank.

Parkin, Michael Canada
Professor of Economics at the University of Western Ontario. He has been a member of the Shadow European Economic Policy Committee. Mr. Parkin has also been Visiting Professor at Brown and Osmania Universities; Visiting Scholar at the Reserve Bank of Australia; and Visiting Fellow at the Hoover Institution, Stanford University. He is Managing Editor of the *Canadian Journal of Economics*.

Purvis, Douglas D. Canada
Professor of Economics at Queen's University (Kingston, Ontario) since 1980. He has been Visiting Economist at the Reserve Bank of Australia and Consultant to the Bank of Canada. Mr. Purvis is a member of the Canadian Department of Finance's Economic Advisory Panel and Editor of the John Deutsch Round Tables on Economic Policy.

Roper, Don United States
Professor of Economics at the University of Utah. He has been an Economist with the Federal Reserve Board. Mr. Roper has also been a Visiting Professor at the Australian National University and the Institute for International Economic Studies at the University of Stockholm.

Swoboda, Alexander K. Switzerland
Professor of Economics at the Graduate Institute of International Studies in Geneva. He is also Director of the International Center for Monetary and Banking Studies at the Institute and teaches at the University of Geneva.

(continued on p. 592)

Mr. Swoboda has been a Postdoctoral Fellow in Political Economy and Visiting Assistant Professor at the University of Chicago and a Visiting Professor at Johns Hopkins University's Bologna Center, the London School of Economics, and Harvard University.

Thygesen, Niels Denmark
Professor of Economics at the University of Copenhagen since 1971. He has worked in the Danish Ministry of Economic Affairs, as Economic Adviser to the Malaysian Ministry of Finance, and as Head of the Organization for Economic Cooperation and Development's Monetary Division. Mr. Thygesen has been Adviser to the Bank of Denmark since 1972 and has served on several expert committees in the European Communities. He is a Senior Research Fellow at the Center for European Policy Studies (Louvain).

Willett, Thomas D. United States
Horton Professor of Economics at Claremont Graduate School and Claremont McKenna College (Claremont, California). At Claremont, he is also Chair of the Graduate Economics Faculty, Director of the Claremont Center for Economic Policy Studies, and a Research Associate of both the Center for the Study of Law Structures and the Keck Institute of International Strategic Studies. Mr. Willett has taught at Cornell and Harvard Universities and has been Senior Staff Economist at the (U.S.) Council of Economic Advisers and both Director of International Monetary Research and Deputy Assistant Secretary for International Research and Planning at the U.S. Treasury.

Williamson, John United States
Senior Fellow at the Institute for International Economics since 1981. He has been a Professor at Pontifícia Universidade Católica do Rio de Janeiro, Massachusetts Institute of Technology, and the Universities of Warwick and York. Mr. Williamson has also been an Advisor to the International Monetary Fund and Economic Consultant to the U.K. Treasury.

Author Index